I0132156

# Diplomatic Games

# DIPLOMATIC GAMES

SPORT, STATECRAFT, AND
INTERNATIONAL RELATIONS
SINCE 1945

EDITED BY
HEATHER L. DICHTER
AND ANDREW L. JOHNS

UNIVERSITY PRESS OF KENTUCKY

Copyright © 2014 by The University Press of Kentucky
Paperback edition 2020

Scholarly publisher for the Commonwealth,
serving Bellarmine University, Berea College, Centre College of Kentucky, Eastern
Kentucky University, The Filson Historical Society, Georgetown College,
Kentucky Historical Society, Kentucky State University, Morehead State
University, Murray State University, Northern Kentucky University, Transylvania
University, University of Kentucky, University of Louisville, and Western
Kentucky University.
All rights reserved.

*Editorial and Sales Offices:* The University Press of Kentucky
663 South Limestone Street, Lexington, Kentucky 40508-4008
www.kentuckypress.com

Library of Congress Cataloging-in-Publication Data

Diplomatic games : sport, statecraft, and international relations since 1945 / edited
by Heather L. Dichter and Andrew L. Johns.
    pages cm
  Includes bibliographical references and index.
  ISBN 978-0-8131-4564-8 (hardcover : alk. paper)—ISBN 978-0-8131-4565-5 (pdf)
  —ISBN 978-0-8131-4566-2 (epub)
  1. Sports and state. 2. Sports—International cooperation. 3. Sports—Political
aspects. 4. International relations. I. Dichter, Heather, author, editor of
compilation. II. Johns, Andrew L., 1968-  author, editor of compilation.
  GV706.35.D57 2014
  306.4'83—dc23                                    2014019785

ISBN 978-0-8131-8028-1 (pbk. : alk. paper)

This book is printed on acid-free paper meeting
the requirements of the American National Standard
for Permanence in Paper for Printed Library Materials.

∞

Manufactured in the United States of America.

Member of the Association
of University Presses

# Contents

# Introduction

## Competing in the Global Arena:
## Sport and Foreign Relations since 1945

### *Andrew L. Johns*

Serious sport has nothing to do with fair play. It is bound up with hatred, jealousy, boastfulness, disregard of all rules and sadistic pleasure in witnessing violence: in other words it is war minus the shooting.
>—George Orwell, "The Sporting Spirit"

We see, therefore, that war is not merely an act of policy but a true political instrument, a continuation of political intercourse carried on with other means.
>—Carl von Clausewitz, *On War*

In late February 2013, former NBA star Dennis Rodman visited the Democratic People's Republic of Korea (DPRK) in what several media outlets characterized as a "basketball diplomacy" mission aimed at encouraging "openness and better relations with the outside world." Rodman, whose antics both on and off the court overshadowed his prodigious skill as one of the best rebounders and defenders in NBA history, seems like an odd choice to be a diplomatic emissary—an unofficial one, to be sure—of the United States to North Korea. His unique public persona aside, his visit occurred only weeks after the Pyongyang regime conducted its latest and most powerful nuclear test, which was strongly criticized by the United States, its allies, and other world powers for defying the United

Nations' ban against the North Korean nuclear program. Making the trip even more intriguing was the fact that the US Department of State had recently warned against a humanitarian visit by former New Mexico governor Bill Richardson and Google executive chairman Eric Schmidt. But as Aidan Foster-Carter, a Korea expert at Leeds University, told the Voice of America, Rodman's visit to the rogue state could potentially pay dividends: "We're in a bad place with North Korea and the nuclear test and so on. . . . If someone tries something different, you know, outside the box, what harm can it do?"[1]

Rodman's surreal appearance courtside with the DPRK's supreme leader Kim Jong-Un is by no means the first time that sport and diplomacy have intersected. In the wake of World War I, Germany was excluded punitively from the 1920 Antwerp Olympics and the 1924 Paris Olympics.[2] Twelve years later, Jessie Owens's historic performance at the 1936 Berlin Olympics completely discredited the Nazi regime's public diplomacy efforts to showcase the superiority of their political and racial ideology to the world. The tragic attack on Israeli athletes by Palestinian terrorists at the 1972 Munich Olympics highlighted the intransigent and deadly nature of the centuries-old conflict in the Middle East.[3] And the 1980 and 1984 Summer Olympics were marred by reciprocal boycotts by the United States and the Soviet Union (and their respective allies) in the midst of the tensions of the resurgent Cold War.

But the Olympic Games are only the most obvious moments of confluence. In the 1950s, sport played a key role in the Eisenhower administration's propaganda efforts to influence international opinion of the United States "because they effortlessly stirred the interest of a wide audience."[4] During the George W. Bush administration, the US Department of State's budget for sports grants and sports programming jumped from $600,000 to over $5,000,000, with Undersecretary of State for Public Diplomacy Karen Hughes leading the effort to connect sports and US diplomatic activity.[5] And perhaps most famously, the People's Republic of China invited the US National Table Tennis team to play in an exhibition in Beijing in 1971, making them the first Americans to visit the country since 1949. Most observers agree that this "ping-pong diplomacy" was an important step on the path to the normalization of relations between the two countries nearly eight years later.[6]

Why have two seemingly disconnected paradigms like sport and for-eign relations overlapped so frequently?[7] The answer is at once compli-cated and intuitive. Sport can, in the words of the legendary broadcaster Jim McKay, capture the "thrill of victory and the agony of defeat." This is true for individuals, teams, and even countries—consider, for example, the national reaction in the United States to the disparate Olympic experi-ences of the US men's hockey team in 1980 and the US men's basketball team in 1972. Sport can be about twenty impoverished children playing soccer barefoot in the street or on a dilapidated field. It can be about pampered millionaire athletes playing in front of tens of thousands in stadiums with lavishly appointed luxury suites, not to mention millions of others watching on sixty-inch plasma screen televisions. Sport reflects common interests shared across borders and has the capacity to bring together groups otherwise divided by history, ethnicity, or politics. Sport can also transcend the playing field and influence society, culture, politics, and diplomacy. It can be a peaceful tool of goodwill or used as leverage to coerce behavior. It can exacerbate existing nationalistic tensions or be used to promote development and strengthen alliances. It can have a sig-nificant economic impact on a country or region, and it can be used as an effective weapon of propaganda. In short, sport is at once parochial and universal, unifying and dividing, and has the potential to fundamentally affect relations between individuals and nations.

As a result of its ability to cross political, cultural, social, gender, reli-gious, and economic boundaries and provide a common foundation, sport is especially suitable as a vehicle to build bridges between governments and peoples. That helps to explain why high-profile athletes such as base-ball Hall of Famer Cal Ripken, two-time Olympic medalist and five-time world champion figure skater Michelle Kwan, NBA stars Juwan Howard and Dikembe Mutombo, and WNBA all-star Nikki McCray were among those selected by US secretary of state Condoleezza Rice as "American Public Diplomatic Envoys."[8] Moreover, the competitive aspects of sport allow it to function as a benign substitute for more lethal encounters, as suggested in the Orwell and Clausewitz quotes in the epigraph. Better for the United States and Iran to compete against one another in a soccer match or wrestling meet and possibly pave the way for better relations, for example, than for their mutual enmity to prevent any meaningful diplo-matic contact and potentially devolve into a shooting war.[9] Thus sport, as historian Peter Beck notes in his seminal work on British football, "offer[s] one instrument capable of both reflecting and influencing the course of international relations."[10]

The essays in this volume focus on the nexus of sport and foreign relations from an international perspective since the end of World War II. During the years since 1945, not only did international relations become more complex as a result of forces such as decolonization and the long Soviet-American struggle of the Cold War, but sport experienced an explosive growth in both popularity and significance—political, social, cultural, economic, and diplomatic—in the global arena. As both of these trends have accelerated in the chaotic post–Cold War international environment, the intersection of sport and foreign relations has become even more pronounced; witness the Chinese government's investment in the success of the 2008 Summer Olympics in Beijing, for example.[11] This reality stands in stark contrast to the efforts of international sport leaders—who have for over a century consistently and idealistically espoused the rhetoric that sport and politics were (and should be) separate—to maintain a Chinese wall between their competitions and the vicissitudes of international relations.[12] Indeed, as Barbara Keys has noted, the postwar period has been one in which "the politicization of sport reached an apogee."[13]

Collectively the essays that follow make a compelling case for the utility of using sport as a lens to better understand foreign relations and vice versa. While scholars have begun to look at this relationship sporadically, this anthology represents one of the few attempts to systematically engage what is an emerging field of its own based on multiarchival and multinational research.[14] This nexus touches on numerous intriguing historical questions, including the political uses of sport by governments in foreign affairs; how cultural exchanges, private diplomacy, and nongovernmental organizations (NGOs) influence international relations; and how sport factors into the global economy.[15] As the authors demonstrate in the chapters that follow, sport appears in greater frequency in government documents and diplomatic correspondence in the postwar period, and scholars have increasingly recognized the importance of these relationships, particularly (although certainly not exclusively) when considering the international megaevents such as the Olympic Games or the Fédération Internationale de Football Association (FIFA) World Cup in soccer—or football to the world outside the United States.

This anthology not only addresses this relationship specifically but also engages the mechanism of public diplomacy, the role of culture in international relations, issues of nationalism and imperialism, the nexus of domestic politics and foreign policy, the woefully understudied issue of intra-alliance politics, and the individual and collective histories of the countries highlighted in the essays. The global approach taken in the volume—both in terms of countries and sports—allows the authors to better understand how and why governments intervene in, wield, and manipulate sports to their advantage, and how sport-related considerations influence the making and implementation of foreign relations. The chapters establish that, although local or specific factors have tremendous impact on the nature of the diplomacy concerned, governments typically intervene in international sport for three primary reasons: first, to maintain and strengthen alliances; second, to promote policies or political positions at home and abroad; and, third, to increase national prestige. The essays that follow demonstrate on a broad and global scale how governments use sport to achieve specific foreign policy goals.

Sport became particularly important during the Cold War as a site for direct, head-to-head competition between the two ideologically opposed camps. Both Washington and Moscow—and their allies—used sport as part of a broader propaganda offensive to certify and promote the superiority of their respective systems without the fear of a real ("hot") war or nuclear destruction.[16] For example, according to Sebastian Coe—the four-time Olympic champion runner, multiple world-record holder, and Conservative member of Parliament from 1992 to 1997—British prime minister Margaret Thatcher "never really understood sport until it migrated—and sometimes mutated—beyond the back page, or impacted on other areas of policy." Yet when sport and foreign relations intersected, she showed no reluctance to attempt to deploy sport as a weapon in her diplomatic arsenal to achieve her international goals. Thus Thatcher asked British athletes to boycott the 1980 Olympics in Moscow, and in 1982 she considered ordering UK football teams to pull out of the World Cup after Britain went to war with Argentina over the Falkland Islands.[17]

Many of the chapters in this anthology demonstrate how sport could both ease and obstruct diplomatic relations among and between the Cold

War alliances. Evelyn Mertin discusses the complex relationship between the Soviet Union and the German Democratic Republic as the two strongest sport states within the communist bloc. On the other side of the Iron Curtain, the North Atlantic Treaty Organization (NATO) developed a coordinated policy to prevent East Germany from gaining a stronger position in the international community through sporting events, particularly world championships. These endeavors were not without dissent, as Heather Dichter shows on behalf of the Norwegians in NATO. John Soares argues that states did not always provide unwavering support for fellow members of their Cold War bloc, which was especially apparent in ice hockey contests between the Soviet Union, Czechoslovakia, the United States, and Canada. Antonio Sotomayor explores the complicated politics of Puerto Rico as a commonwealth of the United States and host of the Central American and Caribbean Games. Yet the efforts by governments to secure their desired outcome within international sport were not always successful, as Nicholas Evan Sarantakes notes. When a government did not understand how international sport worked, its efforts to influence sport could be disastrous, as with the US effort to create alternative games while boycotting the Moscow Olympics in 1980. And Kevin Witherspoon demonstrates how the US-Soviet basketball rivalry during the Cold War served as "ersatz warfare" that reflected the tensions of the superpower conflict.

In addition, states created as a result of decolonization after World War II used sport as a way to gain recognition or international prominence, or they sought to use sport as a way to promote their political agendas through public diplomacy.[18] States outside of Europe and North America also attempted to use sport in their efforts to assert their prerogatives, negotiate the international environment dominated by Cold War considerations, and enhance the international standing of nonaligned and newly independent states. Cesar Torres shows how Argentina, in the first decade of the Cold War, sought to host major international sporting events to bolster its status within Latin America as well as pursue a leading role among nonaligned states in the Third World. Fan Hong and Lu Zhouxiang examine how China used several international sport opportunities to demonstrate its own strength, both in relation to the nonaligned movement and in comparison to the two superpowers. Aviston Downes looks at how cricket influenced diplomatic relationships in the Caribbean and in Africa during the international anti-apartheid campaign. And Pascal Charitas considers how decolonization in Africa resulted in a concerted effort by the French to maintain control on the continent through sport diplomacy rather than cede influence and national prestige to other international powers.

The literatures of the history of international relations and the history of sport have changed dramatically in the past three decades.[19] Rather than simply examining cables between capitals and embassies and focusing on the high-level decisions made by presidents, kings, and foreign ministers—as several critics derisively characterized the field in the early 1980s—foreign relations scholars have used a vastly expanded repertoire of methodological and thematic approaches to better grapple with the totality and complexity of interactions between countries, peoples, and cultures.[20] The intersection of sport and diplomacy exemplifies this broadened understanding of what constitutes "foreign relations," although in studies of the Cold War, "sport" and specific athletic events and endeavors have appeared only infrequently in the indexes of books by foreign relations scholars.

Sport history has experienced a similar expansion of its focus. In the introduction to a special issue of the *Journal of Contemporary History* in 2003, Jeffrey Hill wrote that within the field, "much of its emphasis has been on the politics of sport rather than the contribution of sport to wider political processes."[21] Sport historians rarely broached questions of global diplomacy despite the recognition by David Kanin and others that the "calls for the separation of sport and politics are futile" because events such as the Olympic Games "have thrived on ties to global affairs."[22] Moreover, many works on sport and politics focused largely on domestic political issues rather than considering the state's relationship with foreign powers. But as scholars have expanded their source bases beyond newspapers and archival collections from sport organizations to include deep immersion in government documents, the field has increasingly engaged and embraced the intersection of sport and foreign relations.[23]

Thus the development of the scholarship dealing with the nexus of sport and international relations remains in an embryonic stage even as the individual historiographies of sport history and foreign relations continue to expand and diversify at an almost exponential pace. While much of the scholarly focus on this relationship has appeared as specific case studies in articles, more in-depth monographic studies have helped to create a foundation for a more robust field, as noted more comprehensively in the bibliography at the end of the volume.[24] These essays, then, are designed to stimulate increased scholarly attention on issues that cross disciplinary boundaries, intervene in and challenge the assumptions of multiple historiographical discussions, and help provide a broader perspective on questions of significance in both fields.

More specifically, in historiographical terms this nexus falls squarely within the realm of the field of public diplomacy, broadly conceived, as many of the authors in this anthology demonstrate. Public diplomacy has attracted increasing interest from scholars who explore how governments influence public or elite opinion in a foreign country for the purpose of turning the foreign policy of the target country to its own advantage.[25] Public diplomacy encompasses a wide range of diplomatic activities, including propaganda, cultural exchange, and, since nations act in their self-interest, explanation of common interests. The literature on public diplomacy represents a facet of Joseph Nye's conception of soft power ("the ability to get what you want through attraction rather than coercion or payments")[26] rather than focusing on elements of hard power that have traditionally occupied historians of US foreign relations. In general, hard power refers to military and economic power, while soft power encompasses cultural activities such as sport and the arts, areas not considered in the traditional purview of the diplomatic corps.[27]

Yet different authors mean different things when referring to this type of diplomacy, which results in the existing literature on public diplomacy being somewhat uneven and sporadic. It ranges from examinations of cultural diplomacy and propaganda to specific cases studies of public diplomacy programs supported by various bureaucracies and administrations—although the field is rapidly changing as the scholarship becomes more sophisticated and nuanced.[28] Moreover, while the majority of the literature focuses on US efforts—particularly during the Cold War—public diplomacy is an international phenomenon employed by nations large and small to enhance their prestige and further their foreign policy goals. In this volume, public diplomacy plays a key role. For example, Jenifer Parks focuses on the zero-sum game of the Cold War, showing how the Soviet

Union attempted to sway nonaligned states to favor the communist bloc by providing support and training for their domestic sport programs and assistance to guarantee their participation in the 1980 Olympics. Scott Laderman uses surfing to demonstrate how the sport became not only a globalized cultural phenomenon but also was transformed into an unofficial diplomatic tool during the 1980s. And Wanda Wakefield reveals how US efforts to transform Austrian opinion during its postwar occupation involved a significant injection of Marshall Plan aid into the Austrian ski industry.

Of course, these issues and relationships are contemporary as well as historical. As we have seen recently with the controversy over gay rights at the 2014 Winter Olympic Games in Sochi, Russia, protests by international antislavery and human rights advocates against the decision to award the 2022 World Cup to Qatar, the continuing threat of terrorism at major athletic competitions worldwide, and, of course, Dennis Rodman's foray into diplomacy, sport and foreign relations remain closely connected as nations compete in the global arena.[29] Exploring the intersection of sport and foreign relations provides a unique window through which both fields can be better understood and allows scholars an opportunity to intervene meaningfully in numerous historiographical conversations. We hope that this volume spurs other scholars to take up this nexus in their scholarship, particularly as government documents from the latter portion of the twentieth century continue to become available through declassification and increasing access to international archives. As Thomas Zeiler suggests in his concluding essay, this anthology has only scratched the surface of the potential of this field. It is not intended to be comprehensive, either topically, geographically, or thematically. Indeed, much research remains to be done, not only regarding the major sporting states and dominant powers within the international system but also among the smaller states and regional powers that utilize sport to the advantage. Moreover, scholars need to engage questions dealing with issues such as the economics of professional sports, religion, and technology in the global sports arena from the perspective of foreign relations. But we believe that the essays that follow will help to expand what is a vibrant and timely literature and promote increased exploration of these important historical questions.

## Notes

1. "Basketball's Dennis Rodman Visits North Korea," Voice of America News, February 26, 2013, http://www.voanews.com/content/ex-basketball-star-dennis-rodman-arrives-in-north-korea/1610925.html, accessed March 4, 2013. Two months later, Rodman asked the North Korean leader to "do me a solid" and release Kenneth Bae, a Korean American sentenced to fifteen years of hard labor for unspecified "hostile acts" against North Korea. See "Twitter Diplomacy for Dennis Rodman," May 8, 2013, http://espn.go.com/nba/story/_/id/9253734/dennis-rodman-asks-north-korea-kim-jong-un-free-kenneth-bae-us, accessed May 10, 2013. Professor Sung-Yoon Lee of the Fletcher School of Law and Diplomacy at Tufts University, who expressed skepticism about Rodman's diplomatic efforts, conceded that while "theatrics are not equal to politics . . . theatrics are not entirely irrelevant to politics" and that if Rodman "unwittingly sows the seeds of reality in the fantastical world of the North Korean leader . . . then his latest courting of the Marshal may rightfully come to be remembered one day, indeed, as a game-changer." Quoted on the CNN website, http://www.cnn.com/2013/09/05/opinion/lee-dennis-rodman/index.html?hpt_hp_14, accessed September 5, 2013.

2. The international community imposed sanctions against the nations responsible for starting World War I. As a result, in addition to Germany (which had been slated to host the cancelled 1916 Olympics in Berlin), Austria, Hungary, Bulgaria, and Turkey were banned from competing in the 1920 Olympics. The International Olympic Committee (IOC) chose Antwerp as the host city in recognition of the suffering endured by the Belgian people during the war.

3. The terrorists explained why they chose the Munich Olympics as the stage for their attack: "We recognize that sport is the religion of the western world. . . . So we decided to use the Olympics, the most sacred ceremony of this religion, to make the world pay attention to us." Quoted in Barrie Houlihan, *Sport and International Politics* (New York: Harvester Wheatsheaf, 1994), 2.

4. Kenneth Osgood, *Total Cold War: Eisenhower's Secret Propaganda Battle at Home and Abroad* (Lawrence: University Press of Kansas, 2006), 263. Indeed, the United States Information Agency (USIA) succeeded in using sport in a variety of ways. One story described the experience of Polish refugee Jan Miecznikowski, a long-distance runner at the University of Houston "'who escaped from his Communist-dominated homeland . . . and asked for political asylum in the free world.'" Such features conveyed "targeted messages" to world audiences in support of US foreign policy goals. See Osgood, *Total Cold War,* 263–64.

5. "Sports Diplomacy and Understanding Athletic Culture," http://casnocha.com/2007/08/sports-diplomac.html, accessed December 9, 2010. The US Department of State has used sport extensively to support one of its main priorities for its public diplomacy efforts, nurturing "common interests and values between Americans and people of different countries, cultures, and faiths across the world." See

Spencer C. Cocanour, "Sports: A Tool for International Relations," thesis, Air Command and Staff College, Air University, April 2007, 4.

6. For other instances, see for example "Pakistan Prime Minister in India for Cricket Diplomacy," CNN.com, http://www.cnn.com/2011/WORLD/asiapcf/03/30/india.pakistan.cricket/index.html?hpt-Sbin, accessed April 7, 2011, and H. E. Chehabi, "Sport Diplomacy between the United States and Iran," *Diplomacy & Statecraft* 12, no. 1 (March 2001): 89–106.

7. In the US context, there is a long history of sport diplomacy. As Richard Arndt points out in his study of cultural diplomacy in the twentieth century, as early as 1888 an all-star baseball team traveled around the world demonstrating the new national pastime, with the tour memorialized in a photo of the uniformed players draped over various parts of the Sphinx in Egypt. But the use of sport as cultural diplomacy accelerated after World War II, both in the Olympics and with athletes such as Mal Whitfield, who traveled to Africa for the USIA in the 1950s. See Richard T. Arndt, *The First Resort of Kings: American Cultural Diplomacy in the Twentieth Century* (Washington, DC: Potomac Books, 2005), 402.

8. "Those who contribute to State's athletic initiatives attribute their success to the universal nature of sport. . . . 'Virtually all cultures and all citizens have an interest in and appreciation for sport. This makes it one of the best methods for exchange'—especially for diplomats operating in an age when the opinions of foreign publics are so crucial for success. Interestingly, the United States is one of only a few countries that does not have an official Minister of Sport." See USC Public Diplomacy blog, quoted in "Sports Diplomacy and Understanding Athletic Culture," http://casnocha.com/2007/08/sports-diplomac.html, accessed December 9, 2010.

9. Chehabi, "Sport Diplomacy between the United States and Iran."

10. Peter Beck, *Scoring for Britain: International Football and International Politics, 1900–1939* (London: Frank Cass, 1999), 8. One example of this influence is seen in the fact that UN Resolution 757 in 1992 included sport as a recognized element within UN sanctions policy. See Cocanour, "Sports," 20.

11. The US-Chinese rivalry continued at the 2012 London Olympics, and many observers suggested that while it was not quite the same as the Cold War, "it still serves as a political backdrop to what could become a contentious battle of superpowers in the Olympics for decades to come." Bob Young, "China Emerges as Team USA's New Olympic Rival," *Arizona Republic*, August 2, 2012. See also Fan Hong, Duncan Mackay, and Karen Christensen, *China Gold: China's Quest for Global Power and Olympic Glory* (Great Barrington, MA: Berkshire Publishing Group, 2008), and Xu Guoqi, *Olympic Dreams: China and Sports, 1895–2008* (Cambridge, MA: Harvard University Press, 2008).

12. In a speech following his election as president of the IOC in September 2013, Thomas Bach vowed to enforce the Olympic Charter and recognized that while sport cannot be a platform for politics, the IOC could not be apolitical: "We have to realize that our decisions at events like Olympics [sic] Games, they have

political implications." Quoted at GameBids.com, http://www.gamebids.com/eng/other_news/1216136767.html, accessed September 11, 2013.

13. Barbara Keys, "Sport and International Relations: A Research Guide," *SHAFR Newsletter* 32, no. 1 (March 2002), http://www.shafr.org/publications/review/march-2002, accessed August 26, 2013.

14. The question of whether "mainstream" political and social historians should engage with the history of sport is addressed in Paul Ward, "Last Man Picked: Do Mainstream Historians Need to Play with Sports Historians?," *International Journal of the History of Sport* 30, no. 1 (January 2013): 6–13. On page 11, Ward argues that sport historians "need to think about how to ensure that their books and articles directly address the needs of other historians, drawing out the wider significance of their research, keeping up the quality, and engaging fully with historians working in social, political and other forms of cultural history."

15. Keys, "Sport and International Relations." On these issues, see for example Houlihan, *Sport and International Politics*; Lincoln Allison, ed., *The Changing Politics of Sport* (Manchester: Manchester University Press, 1993); Barbara Keys, "The Internationalization of Sport, 1890–1939," in *The Cultural Turn: Essays in the History of U.S. Foreign Relations,* ed. Frank A. Ninkovich and Liping Bu (Chicago: Imprint Publications, 2001), 201–20; and Walter LaFeber, *Michael Jordan and the New Global Capitalism* (New York: Norton, 1999).

16. On the expansion of the Cold War to nontraditional areas such as science, sport, and other types of "soft power," see for example Osgood, *Total Cold War.*

17. Ian Herbert, "A Minute's Silence? Margaret Thatcher Was Not One of Us When It Came to Sport," *The Independent,* April 10, 2013, http://www.independent.co.uk/sport/football/news-and-comment/ian-herbert-a-minutes-silence-margaret-thatcher-was-not-one-of-us-when-it-came-to-sport-8566642.html, accessed April 15, 2013. Herbert's article refers to the "absence of any kind of empathy between Thatcher and the world of those in sport" but does underscore that "she used this realm when it suited her." Coe was among the British athletes who refused Thatcher's request and competed in the Moscow Games in 1980.

18. On this point, see for example Tony Smith, "New Bottles for New Wine: A Pericentric Framework for the Study of the Cold War," *Diplomatic History* 24, no. 4 (Fall 2000): 567–91. In 2011, after the creation of the country of South Sudan, Xan Rice wrote in *The Guardian:* "A new country needs many things: passports, stamps, a currency, an international dialing code, to name a few. For Republic of South Sudan, there was a further urgent priority–a football team." *The Guardian*, July 21, 2011. Indeed, the South Sudan national soccer team played its first match the weekend before the country officially became independent and joined the Confederation of African Football (CAF) and FIFA within a year.

19. A roundtable in the *Journal of American History* on the state of the field in US foreign relations history provides an excellent overview of the recent literature. See Thomas W. Zeiler, "The Diplomatic History Bandwagon: A State of the Field," *Journal of American History* 95, no. 4 (March 2009): 1053–73, and the responses in that

issue by Fredrik Logevall, "Politics and Foreign Relations," 1074–78; Mario Del Pero, "On the Limits of Thomas Zeiler's Historiographical Triumphalism," 1079–82; Jessica C. E. Gienow-Hecht, "What Bandwagon? Diplomatic History Today," 1083–86; and Kristin Hoganson, "Hop off the Bandwagon! It's a Mass Movement, Not a Parade," 1087–91. The most recent overview of the historiography of sport can be found in David L. Andrews and Ben Carrington, eds., *A Companion to Sport* (Hoboken, NJ: Wiley-Blackwell, 2013). Of particular interest to those interested in the nexus of sport and foreign relations are the chapters on "Sport and Globalization," "U.S. Imperialism, Sport, and 'The Most Famous Soldier in the War,'" and "Sport, Palestine and Israel."

20. Michael J. Hogan and Thomas G. Paterson, eds., *Explaining the History of American Foreign Relations*, 3rd ed. (New York: Cambridge University Press, forthcoming). Previous editions of the Hogan and Paterson volume appeared in 1991 and 2004.

21. Jeffrey Hill, "Introduction: Sport and Politics," *Journal of Contemporary History* 38, no. 3 (July 2003): 355.

22. David Kanin, *A Political History of the Olympic Games* (Boulder, CO: Westview, 1981), ix.

23. For early examples of this paradigm shift, see James Riordan, *Sport, Politics, and Communism* (Manchester: Manchester University Press, 1991); Pierre Arnaud and James Riordan, eds., *Sport and International Politics: The Impact of Fascism and Communism on Sport* (London: E & FN Spon, 1998); James Riordan and Arnd Krüger, *The International Politics of Sport in the 20th Century* (London: E & FN Spon, 1999); and Douglas Booth, *The Race Game: Sport and Politics in South Africa* (London: Frank Cass, 1998).

24. For examples of the literature in this emerging field, see Roger Levermore and Adrian Budd, eds., *Sport and International Relations: An Emerging Relationship* (London: Routledge, 2004); Aaron Beacom, *International Diplomacy and the Olympic Movement: The New Mediators* (New York: Palgrave Macmillan, 2012); Barbara Keys, *Globalizing Sport: National Rivalry and International Community in the 1930s* (Cambridge, MA: Harvard University Press, 2006); Sayuri Gurthrie-Shimizu, *Transpacific Field of Dreams: How Baseball Linked the United States and Japan in Peace and War* (Chapel Hill: University of North Carolina Press, 2012); Toby Rider, "The Olympic Games and the Secret Cold War: The U.S. Government and the Propaganda Campaign against Communist Sport, 1950–1960," PhD diss., University of Western Ontario, 2011; Stephen Wagg and David L. Andrews, eds., *East Plays West: Sport and the Cold War* (London: Routledge, 2006); John Gripentrog, "The Transnational Pastime: Baseball and American Perceptions of Japan in the 1930s," *Diplomatic History* 34, no. 2 (April 2010): 247–73; Laurent Dubois, *Soccer Empire: The World Cup and the Future of France* (Berkeley: University of California Press, 2010); Russ Crawford, *The Use of Sports to Promote the American Way of Life during the Cold War: Cultural Propaganda, 1945–1963* (Lewiston, NY: Edwin Mellen, 2008); and Douglas Booth, "Hitting Apartheid for Six? The Politics of the South

African Sports Boycott," *Journal of Contemporary History* 38, no. 3 (July 2003): 477–93. A special issue of *Sport in Society* in 2008 examined "Sport and Foreign Policy in a Globalizing World." The issue included articles dealing with topics such as terrorism and sport, decolonization, normalizing postwar relations with Japan, and human rights. See *Sport in Society* 11, no. 4 (2008).

25. Although the methods have grown more sophisticated with the advent of mass media technology, public diplomacy and propaganda have been a staple of international relations for centuries. During the Crusades, for example, Richard I of England plucked the eyes from his prisoners and returned them to Saladin in an effort to mold the image that Richard's enemies had of him. For an overview on how propaganda has been employed in support of foreign policy goals, see Oliver Thomson, *Easily Led: A History of Propaganda* (Stroud, Gloucestershire: Sutton, 1999).

26. Joseph S. Nye Jr., "Soft Power and American Foreign Policy," *Political Science Quarterly* 119, no. 2 (Summer 2004): 256.

27. One problem in defining public diplomacy reflects the way in which the US government views activities that fall into its scope. On this point, see James Critchlow, "Public Diplomacy during the Cold War: The Record and Its Implications," *Journal of Cold War Studies* 6, no. 1 (Winter 2004): 75–89. The nature of contemporary public diplomacy also complicates the issue, as Ron Robin argues in "Requiem for Public Diplomacy?," *American Quarterly* 57, no. 2 (June 2005): 345–53.

28. See for example Arndt, *The First Resort of Kings*; Laura A. Belmonte, *Selling the American Way: U.S. Propaganda and the Cold War* (Philadelphia: University of Pennsylvania Press, 2008); Nicholas J. Cull, *The Cold War and the United States Information Agency: American Propaganda and Public Diplomacy, 1945–1989* (New York: Cambridge University Press, 2008); Penny M. Von Eschen, *Satchmo Blows Up the World: Jazz Ambassadors Play the Cold War* (Cambridge, MA: Harvard University Press, 2006); Robert Dallek, *The American Style of Foreign Policy: Cultural Politics and Foreign Affairs* (New York: Oxford University Press, 1983); Gifford D. Malone, *Political Advocacy and Cultural Communication: Organizing the Nation's Public Diplomacy* (Lanham, MD: University Press of America, 1988); Jarol B. Manheim, *Strategic Public Diplomacy and American Foreign Policy: The Evolution of Influence* (New York: Oxford University Press, 1994); Osgood, *Total Cold War*; Kenneth A. Osgood and Brian C. Etheridge, eds., *The United States and Public Diplomacy: New Directions in Cultural and International History* (Leiden: Brill, 2010); Gregg Wolper, "Wilsonian Public Diplomacy: The Committee on Public Information in Spain," *Diplomatic History* 17, no. 1 (Winter 1993): 17–34; Wilson P. Dizard, *Inventing Public Diplomacy: The Story of the U.S. Information Agency* (Boulder, CO: Lynne Rienner, 2004); Jessica Gienow-Hecht, *Transmission Impossible: American Journalism as Cultural Diplomacy in Postwar Germany* (Baton Rouge: Louisiana State University Press, 1999); Walter Hixson, *Parting the Curtain: Propaganda, Culture, and the Cold War, 1945–1961* (New York: St. Martin's, 1997); Nancy Snow, *Propaganda, Inc.: Selling America's Culture to the World* (New York: Seven Stories, 1998);

and Hans N. Tuch, *Communicating with the World: U.S. Public Diplomacy Overseas* (New York: St. Martin's, 1990).

29. The decision to hold the 2022 World Cup in Qatar has faced widespread global criticism from the beginning, not only because of concerns over human rights and human trafficking but also because of the intense heat during the summer that would only be partially ameliorated by the state-of-the art stadiums the country plans to build (not to mention allegations of irregularities in the bidding and decision-making processes). FIFA president Sepp Blatter, while conceding that the decision might have been "a mistake" and that it was "not rational" to play soccer in Qatar in June and July, emphasized the "political and geo-political realities" that influenced the decision: "I think it is high time that Europe starts to understand that we do not rule the world any more, and that some former European imperial powers can no longer impress their will on to others in faraway places. We must accept that football has moved away from being a European and South American sport—it has become the world sport." Blatter went on to characterize the sport as a "global unifying force for the good" and asserted that the "Qatar World Cup promises to help unite an unstable region of the world by bringing hope and joy to millions who have suffered for decades." Quoted at Inside World Football, http://www.insideworldfootball.com/fifa/13216-exclusive-with-sepp-blatter-everyone-complains-about-winter-2022-but-what-about-discrimination, accessed September 10, 2013. On the geopolitical considerations and ramifications of international soccer, see for example Paul Darby, "Africa and the 'World' Cup: FIFA Politics, Eurocentrism and Resistance," *International Journal of the History of Sport* 22, no. 5 (September 2005): 883–905.

Part 1

# Alliance Politics

# 1

# "A Game of Political Ice Hockey"

## NATO Restrictions on East German Sport Travel in the Aftermath of the Berlin Wall

*Heather L. Dichter*

The creation of the North Atlantic Treaty Organization (NATO) in 1949 was designed to keep the United States involved in European affairs, both to prevent a return to the American isolationism that developed after World War I and to serve as a bulwark against the increasing Soviet influence in Europe as the Iron Curtain of the Cold War cut right through Germany. In the spring of 1954, when the Soviet Union granted sovereignty to the German Democratic Republic (GDR), the three Western wartime allies—Great Britain, France, and the United States—reaffirmed their support of the Federal Republic of Germany (FRG) as the only legitimate German state because it had the only freely elected government on German territory. The transatlantic alliance supported this position regarding West Germany's eastern neighbor, passing a resolution that NATO members "are not prepared to recognise the so-called German Democratic Republic as a sovereign state or to treat the German authorities there as a government." With the Federal Republic's accession to NATO the following year (1955), the rest of the alliance members agreed to maintain the isolation of East Germany and to exclude it from the international community.[1]

As a result the GDR sought alternative avenues with which to gain recognition. Realizing the difficulty of securing formal (de jure) recognition by states and international organizations, the East German state, with the support of its Soviet bloc allies, sought to force de facto recognition through acceptance of representations of the GDR, such as its coat of arms, flag, and trade missions. The East German regime particularly hoped that through international sport, with its frequent use of flags and anthems, it could gain de facto recognition on a large scale. The Soviet Union and the other communist bloc members frequently advocated for East German membership inside international sport federations as well as participation by separate East German teams at international sport competitions throughout the 1950s and 1960s. International sport federations, which select the host cities and venues for their sporting events, decided individually whether or not to accept East Germany as a member.

Because of the transitory nature of international sport, with world championships changing locations every year and the Olympic Games changing locations every four, NATO continually confronted the issue of East Germany's attempts to participate in international sporting events in their countries once the Federal Republic became a member in 1955. Because of NATO's support of the Federal Republic's stance regarding the GDR, the German-German relationship, as the events of the early 1960s demonstrate, cannot solely be viewed through a bilateral lens. Within NATO, West Germany frequently had to defend its policies toward its eastern neighbor to persuade its allies to uphold a similar position. Even though international sport asserted autonomy in conducting its own affairs, NATO member countries coordinated their efforts within the transatlantic organization to block the increasingly more frequent attempts by East Germany to send a national team (separate from West Germany) to international sporting events.[2]

The continued concern by NATO and the diplomatic corps regarding international sport reveals that the transatlantic alliance, although created for military purposes, quickly expanded its purview to other areas. By examining NATO's impact on the German-German sport relationship, this chapter addresses an area of NATO activity that has received almost no attention: the transatlantic alliance's concern with the media coverage and popular opinion regarding NATO's actions. Scholars have examined in detail the origins of NATO as a way of ensuring American involvement in European affairs after 1945 or, more recently, the expansion of the organization after the end of the Cold War. Because NATO was initially conceived as a military alliance, its military strategy and nuclear policies have also been extensively studied. Within a few years of the creation of NATO, the organization recognized that many aspects of politics and society impacted their military alliance. By the end of 1950, NATO had created its own Information Service and, three years later, had established a permanent Committee on Information and Cultural Relations, both of which sought to promote NATO through public diplomacy efforts within alliance members. As the Cold War was ending, historian Norman Graebner wrote that "NATO has come to embody more than military values, that it stands for political, civilizational, even spiritual values common to the parts of Europe it represents and to North America as well." Even with this realization of the expansion of what fell under the purview of NATO's functions, scholars have rarely moved past the military aspects of NATO strategy in their studies.[3]

As this chapter demonstrates, NATO and its member states were greatly concerned with what their domestic populations thought about NATO policies. When political controversy struck international sporting events held in NATO countries, the military alliance considered these issues vital to maintaining security and unity and therefore sought to influence international sport. Although NATO supported West Germany's policy of not recognizing the GDR, East German attempts to participate with its own team, flag, and anthem at athletic events in NATO countries forced member states to balance their national interests with coordinated NATO policies. States on both sides of the Iron Curtain also recognized that the popularity of international sport provided an excellent venue to persuade the public of their position within the Cold War. These issues became acute after the construction of the Berlin Wall in August 1961 forced NATO to counter East German propaganda with their own domestic media efforts aimed at swaying public opinion.

NATO unity was particularly challenged by widespread media coverage of sport on both sides of the Iron Curtain, which made dealing with East Germany a public matter and not a purely internal political issue within the transatlantic alliance. Hosting major international sporting events, including world championships, draws extensive media coverage and helps cities and countries increase their prestige. However, the efforts to maintain NATO's policy of not recognizing the GDR, including the refusal to permit East German athletes to enter their countries to compete in sporting events, often damaged a country's international prestige and caused a public outcry when the level of athletic competition was then diminished as a result of these political decisions. Spectators want to see the best athletes from across the globe, and when top competitors are barred from participating or other teams withdraw in solidarity, the public is less inclined to purchase tickets. International sport federations, attempting to prevent politics from interfering with the successful organization of their world championships, became intimately involved in world affairs. National representatives to these sport nongovernmental organizations (NGOs) from NATO states conferred with their country's foreign ministry, and at times the presidents of these international federations appealed (unsuccessfully) to heads of state to facilitate the smooth organization of their world championships.

These international sporting events therefore became key sites for NATO public diplomacy efforts. The transatlantic alliance hoped that placing blame for the political interference in sport on East Germany and the Soviet bloc would help maintain alliance policies as well as promote their position among their own populations. NATO's actions in response to the construction of the Berlin Wall forced international sport to address the German question. At the same time, the continued discussion of international sport within NATO reveals not only the broad understanding of what issues impacted the military alliance but also the complicated process of balancing national interests with policies agreed among all alliance members.

The Federal Republic attempted to thwart these East German claims through its policy of nonrecognition of East Germany, which came to be known as the Hallstein Doctrine. This policy, named for West Germany's foreign minister, Walter Hallstein, sought to prevent countries from initiating diplomatic relations with East Germany. The Bonn government believed that recognition of the GDR would signal the permanent status of a divided Germany.[4] The failure by most states and international organizations to recognize the GDR, while at the same time establishing formal relations with the Federal Republic, provided further validity to Bonn's claims regarding the lack of legitimacy of East Germany. Once

NATO accepted the Federal Republic as a member in 1955 and agreed to support the Hallstein Doctrine as its own policy, the entire transatlantic alliance was very soon confronted with the problems of the German-German relationship, including within the realm of international sport. The Italian delegation to NATO reported in May 1955 that it had denied travel visas the previous month to an East German rugby team that wanted to participate in an international tournament, because the GDR was not recognized as a sovereign state. The chairman of NATO's Committee on Information and Cultural Relations, where the Italians reported this visa refusal, noted that the Italian action was in line with NATO policy and no further discussion ensued.[5] By the end of the decade, however, the GDR and the Soviet Union took actions in an attempt to pressure the West to acknowledge the second German state, which ultimately forced the political and sport worlds to confront these issues simultaneously.

In November 1958, Soviet leader Nikita Khrushchev sent an ultimatum to the three Western powers, threatening to unilaterally sign a peace treaty with the GDR because no peace treaty with Germany had been signed in 1945. Khrushchev's ultimatum was an effort to compel the Western powers to negotiate a four-power treaty and, ideally, end West Berlin's status as a democratic outpost deep inside East Germany. West Berlin was particularly problematic for the communist state because by 1958 it was the point of exodus for more than 90 percent of all East Germans fleeing to the Federal Republic. To the Western powers, a Soviet–East German unilateral treaty would transfer to the GDR the responsibility of checking papers for Western military members traveling to and from West Berlin, thus forcing representatives of the Western states to interact in an official capacity with representatives of a state which the Western powers did not recognize. Although Khrushchev's ultimatum largely came to naught, efforts to force the West to recognize the GDR in some capacity did not end there.[6]

In its effort to assert its sovereignty and gain de facto recognition from the international community, the East German government also turned to the promotion of state symbols. As part of the tenth anniversary celebrations of the GDR in October 1959, the East German state introduced a new flag with the emblem of the worker and peasant state in the middle of the black-red-gold flag. This addition to the flag differentiated the East German flag from the plain black-red-gold flag of West Germany, which had also been the flag of the Weimar Republic (1918–1933). The Federal Republic considered the new East German flag a symbol of the division, as compared to the basic tricolor, which alluded to national unity in freedom. The West German government considered the display of the East German flag a disturbance of the constitutional peace and a breach of law and order. The Bonn government therefore banned the flying of the GDR flag anywhere in the FRG, including at sporting events.[7]

This new East German flag quickly became a problem for sport organizers in NATO countries as well as for NATO itself. National flags are an important part of international sporting events, particularly continental and world championships. Often the flags of all competing countries are hung inside an arena or flown around the top of a stadium. In addition, the flags of the top three competitors are raised while the national anthem of the winner is played during the victory ceremony. Organizers of a world championship were required to invite all members of that international sport federation—which included East Germany for those few federations that had decided by the late 1950s to recognize the GDR.

The importance that the GDR gave to its new flag and anthem became a point of contention at the 1961 Ice Hockey World Championships in Geneva, Switzerland, and prompted NATO to reevaluate its position regarding East German participation in sporting events. Although East and West Germany did not play each other in the round-robin stage, they ultimately met on the last day of the tournament to determine their places in the final standings. The West German team, however, refused to take the ice against East Germany if it had to go through the traditional postgame ceremony where the victor's flag is raised and national anthem is played. The International Ice Hockey Federation (IIHF) informed both sides that, per the standard procedure for all international ice hockey matches, both teams must pay respects to the winning side's flag and anthem at the end of the game. If West Germany disobeyed this procedure, the IIHF threatened to expel the Federal Republic. The West German ice hockey federation proposed to East German officials that an incident concerning the flags could be avoided through a renunciation of the victory ceremony. The GDR representatives rebuffed this proposal, insisting on their right to receive recognition as a victor—and a state. Rather than chance losing and be forced to recognize the East German flag and anthem, West Germany forfeited the game. The West German press reported in the sports pages that the West German sport leaders had regretted that the "sporting and fair" proposals for an alternative to the victory ceremony were not accepted and, as a result, the game was forfeited. The Federal Republic averted providing de facto recognition of East Germany's flag and anthem and also avoided violating IIHF rules as well as expulsion. The West German hockey team fell to last place, while East Germany received a 5–0 "walkover" victory and a fifth-place finish.[8]

By not playing the game against East Germany, the West German ice hockey federation directly brought the politics of the Hallstein Doctrine into international sport. Had the West German team lost and stood at attention to the East German flag and anthem—symbols that represented the separation of Germany—then West Germany would have granted implicit recognition to the regime in the east. For this reason West German sport leaders forced the ice hockey team to forfeit the game. The *Times* (London) reported that "some members of the west German team . . . were visibly upset when they heard of the decision to withdraw" and noted that the crowd booed loudly upon the announcement of the game's cancellation. The *New York Times* speculated that the West Germans "evidently figured [an East German victory] was going to happen." A major Swedish paper, *Svenska dagbladet,* reported the "flag war" on the front page alongside its coverage of the Swedish team's fourth-place finish. Taking into consideration the possibility that West Germany might not win, the West German sport officials therefore selected the option that coincided with their government's policies.[9]

Nonetheless, East Germany used this incident for propaganda purposes, attempting to demonstrate that West Germany was the culprit in bringing politics into athletics. *Neues Deutschland* reported the ice hockey incident on its front page, claiming that "the West German sports leadership has once again confirmed with its cancellation of the sports match on Sunday for all of the world that it is compliant to Bonn's politics of the Cold War." The East German paper claimed that instead of hurting the German Democratic Republic, "millions of West German sportsmen will be more isolated with the application of the Hallstein doctrine in international sport." A cartoon on the front page by Klaus Arndt showed a puck in the shape of the GDR symbol sailing past West German chancellor Konrad Adenauer as the goaltender, demonstrating an East German victory—and in this case at the expense of the Federal Republic—in the

Figure 1.1. "Das und der Tor," *Neues Deutschland*, March 14, 1961.

fight to recognition (see figure 1.1). The caption *"Das und der Tor"* plays on the two meanings of "Tor" based on the gender of the preceding article: the goal or the fool. The East German paper attempted to make Adenauer appear foolish for getting involved in sporting affairs, being scared that actual goals by the East German hockey team would translate into victory for the GDR regime's goals. By excoriating the West Germans (and drawing Adenauer into the affair) for mixing politics with sports, the East Germans hoped to improve their own international stature from the ice hockey events. As the official state newspaper, *Neues Deutschland* of course did not mention any of the East German efforts to introduce politics into sport but instead placed all of the blame on the West German government.[10]

In addition, the East Germans also attempted to demonstrate a rift among the Western allies because the US hockey team had played against—and lost to—the East German team just a few days before the West German team refused to play the East German team. These ice hockey incidents prompted further discussion among American diplomats and within NATO regarding how to deal with East German teams. The German representative to the Committee of Political Advisors advocated a strict enforcement of the guidelines previously established by NATO. He argued that the "surest way of handling [the] problem was to exclude GDR teams but that if [governments] did not find this possible then he suggested visas be issued only on condition anthem not be played, nor flag flown etc." The American diplomats concurred with their West German counterparts, considering sport the "most troublesome category" of travel attempted by East Germans. However, the State Department realized that although other NATO member states recognized this problem, "in the absence of agreed, uniform practices many members will be reluctant to expose themselves to domestic criticism by taking [a] stiff line." This ice hockey incident revealed the tensions between the government support for NATO policies and the role of public opinion, particularly when Cold War politics impacted popular sporting events.[11]

While East Germany claimed a political victory from the 1961 ice hockey championships, these gains were short-lived. By 1961 over three million East Germans had fled to West Germany, primarily via West Berlin. To stem this flow the East German regime fortified the border between the two sectors of the city with barbed wire on the night of August 12–13, 1961. The GDR leadership saw this measure as a way to secure its own borders and solidify its legitimacy among its citizens. East German athletic officials welcomed the construction of the Berlin Wall because it hindered the opportunity for athletes to defect to West Germany. With a much smaller population (seventeen million East Germans compared to more than fifty million West Germans), the GDR could not continue to afford the brain—or brawn—drain.[12]

West Germany reacted to the construction of the Wall with outrage at the physical representation of the Iron Curtain of communism, considering it a further attempt at restricting the rights and freedoms of Germans living in Berlin. Television crews filmed an angry Willy Brandt, the West Berlin mayor, at the new barbed-wire border. To the West German sport leaders, these East German actions violated the ideals of international sport. West German sport therefore responded to the Berlin Wall with a complete break in all German-German athletic interaction, declaring that the construction of the Berlin Wall "is contrary to the fundamental principles of humanity and, in our field, means a violation of all the principles of the world of sport." The ability of people, including athletes and officials, to travel freely in and to Berlin had always been an important issue for the West, which is why the Western allies had airlifted food and supplies to West Berlin multiple times a day for nearly a year in 1948–1949 when the Soviets had blocked ground and water access to West Berlin. The construction of the Wall abruptly ended this freedom of movement. In addition, the Ministry of the Interior supported this position, noting that in the aftermath of the Berlin Wall, the appearance of East German athletes inside the Federal Republic—regardless of whether they wore the East German symbol—was a public safety issue.[13]

Because the East German leaders viewed the Berlin Wall as a form of border control, they felt that the West Germans had overreacted by canceling all German-German sporting events. East German sport officials blamed the West Germans, arguing that it was the West German Olympic Committee that made the decision on August 16 to break off sport relations with East German athletes.[14] The East German sport leaders in no way equated this action or its date as being related to the construction of the Berlin Wall. This internal political event—the construction of the Wall by East Germany on East German soil—was therefore made geopolitical, with a wider impact on German-German relations, through the perceived violation of the apolitical ideals of international sport. With these August 1961 actions, the political issues that had largely been the purview of diplomats and politicians now became a major point of concern for international sport federations and the broader public. The construction of the Berlin Wall and NATO's continued nonrecognition of East Germany thus forced NATO member states to confront a vocal media and popular opinion opposed to NATO actions.

The Berlin Wall not only closed the intra-German border and ended German-German sporting events, it also solidified NATO support of

West Germany and its policies. The Western powers submitted a protest over these actions to the Soviets two days after the division of Berlin. Previous Soviet and East German restrictions on the freedom of travel between the Federal Republic and West Berlin in the fall of 1960 had prompted the three Western powers controlling the Allied Travel Office (ATO) to suspend the granting of temporary travel documents (TTDs) to East Germans except in cases of compassion, health, emigration, or visitation of relatives. Travel applications for sport, trade, professional, political, cultural, press, and tourism reasons did not receive approval. These restrictions had been lifted in March 1961, but with the construction five months later of the Berlin Wall, which completely halted movement between the two parts of the divided city, the ATO reinstated the immediate suspension of all TTDs for East Germans "except for most urgent compassionate cases." NATO was informed of these changes, which included a ban on travel by East German athletes and sport officials.

These renewed travel restrictions for East Germans soon became a major problem within NATO because two member states were hosting world championships in early 1962: the United States (ice hockey in Colorado Springs) and France (Alpine skiing in Chamonix). The international federations for both of these sports had already recognized the GDR as an independent member. Thus both France and the United States faced a possible de facto recognition of East Germany by permitting those athletes to enter their countries for the world championships, flying the East German flag, and playing its anthem if any GDR athletes won.[15]

Colorado Springs prepared to host the 1962 Ice Hockey World Championships at the renowned ice rink at the Broadmoor Resort. The US Army's Maj. Gen. Marshal S. Carter, who later became the director of the National Security Agency (1965–1969), served on the organizing committee and, in the months between the construction of the Berlin Wall and the ice hockey championships, met with Department of State officials several times to discuss the issue of East German participation. At these meetings the State Department briefed Carter on the NATO-wide travel restrictions and that, even if the current situation in Berlin changed, the State Department would not sanction entry into the United States of a "national" team purporting to represent the GDR. The organizing committee understood this position and was "counting heavily" on the ATO rejecting the East German team's application, thus relieving the organizers of responsibility for the inability of the GDR to participate in the event.[16]

In the weeks preceding the tournament, the IIHF began to fear that the United States would refuse entry to the East German team. Although two separate German teams had competed in the previous world championships (the 1961 tournament in neutral Switzerland), the last tournament held in the United States (the 1960 Winter Olympic Games in Squaw Valley) had accepted only one German team, which represented a combined Germany.[17] The East German visa issue received major press coverage in Colorado, other snowbelt states, and Canada. The *Lowell* (MA) *Sun* said that American and Soviet bloc officials were "playing a game of political ice hockey over whether an East German team can enter this country to compete in the world hockey championships." The Canadian president of the IIHF, Robert LeBel, the two American representatives, Thayer Tutt and Walter Brown, and the president of the European Ice Hockey Federation, John F. "Bunny" Ahearne, responded to the various possibilities bandied about the press. LeBel expressed surprise when the possible visa refusal arose but reassured "that the championships will be held in Colorado Springs." The IIHF leadership quickly dismissed the idea of a joint, all-German ice hockey team in 1962 because the Berlin Wall had drastically changed the German-German sport relationship. The international federation accepted the American organizers' explanation that the United States had not refused to grant visas to the East German team but, instead, the ATO had denied the travel permits. Thus the United States had not violated a 1959 IIHF decision that stated that events scheduled in countries unable to guarantee the travel of all member teams would be transferred to another country.[18]

The US State Department cited the NATO-coordinated policy for why the East German ice hockey team could not obtain visas for the IIHF World Championships. NATO countries, in support of West Germany and the Hallstein Doctrine, did not recognize East German passports, which thus necessitated the requirement for East Germans to obtain TTDs to enter NATO countries. Following several inquiries regarding the possibility of the East German hockey team participating in the world championships in Colorado Springs, the Department of State publicly issued the following statement:

It should be noted that there are two sets of procedures involved in the travel of East Germans to Western countries. Under long-established Allied regulations a resident of East Germany desiring to travel to the West must receive a temporary travel document (in lieu of a passport), issued by the tripartite Allied Travel Office in West Berlin, and a visa issued by the country to which he desires to travel. These two procedures are interrelated in the sense that if the individual applicant is not eligible for a visa, the ATO will not issue a temporary travel document. On the other hand, if the travel of certain categories of East Germans is, as a matter of ATO policy, restricted or prohibited, the question of a visa issuance does not really arise.

Under existing policy established as a result of the erection of the Communist wall in Berlin and subsequent Communist restrictions on free circulation in Berlin, it is highly questionable that temporary travel documents could be issued to an East German ice hockey team. For this reason the issue of American visas is not a controlling factor.[19]

The American organizers of the 1962 hockey championships therefore informed the public that they should not be held responsible for East Germany's inability to participate. It was, instead, a decision made by another body. Of course, they failed to mention that the other body—the ATO—included American diplomatic representation.

The players involved attempted to deflect the blame by claiming to their local media or critics a lack of responsibility on their own part. The Colorado Springs organizers, particularly in their discussions with the IIHF to prevent the event being transferred to another country, argued it was neither their fault nor the result of the United States government but instead the ATO in Germany. The State Department's press release also took that stance. The ATO, located in West Berlin, sought to quell East German criticism by displacing the decision-making capability onto NATO because the ATO would not grant a TTD if a country would not grant an entry visa. IIHF president LeBel had also said publicly that the matter was "more a NATO issue" and that the IIHF would not lodge a protest with the State Department. Within NATO, many smaller states, facing domestic pressure from their national sport federations and international federation representatives, were concerned that these decisions would impact their own ability to host upcoming sporting events or submit applications to organize for world championships. To minimize conflict and maintain NATO unity, the representatives from the three powers emphasized to the transatlantic alliance the role of the ATO in this process.[20]

East Germany and its communist allies instead blamed the United States and NATO for the visa refusal and continued to raise the issue in the press. The East Germans viewed the refusal to grant the TTDs required for their entry to NATO countries as barring GDR athletes "from their basic right to take part in free international sports exchanges." *Neues Deutschland* attempted to exploit the athletes' difficulties through a series of articles excoriating the United States and its NATO allies. Although the Soviet Union had been arguing both publicly and within the ice hockey federation for East German participation or the relocation of the championships, rumors of a Soviet and Czechoslovak withdrawal from the event began circulating by the end of January. American diplomats believed that the Soviets had to balance the "political desirability of demonstrating solidarity with [their] East German brethren" with Soviet prestige, since the Soviet team was expected to do well at the championships. The Soviet Union had, in fact, decided by early February (one month before the tournament began) to withdraw its team but planned to delay announcing this decision until closer to the event to cause increased difficulties for the Americans. A mere two and a half weeks before the world championships were to begin on March 8, the teams from the Soviet Union, Czechoslovakia, Romania, and Yugoslavia announced their withdrawal from the tournament in solidarity with the East German team.[21]

Even as the world championships began with a depleted field, the barbs from both sides of the Iron Curtain continued. At the IIHF meeting the night before the event kicked off, Colorado governor Steve McNichols told the hockey federation members: "Irrespective of political feelings, all countries should compete in an event that has the international scope of a world tournament. It is the great tradition of Americans that we enjoy the right to win and the right to lose. Apparently this is not the feeling in some other countries." The Czechoslovak delegate, Miroslav Subrt, who still attended the meeting even though his team had withdrawn, responded to McNichols's claims about the countries that chose to boycott the event. Subrt rebutted: "You have talked about competition. We have a very good team and are not afraid to compete. We did not send a team because we are supporting an IIHF member—East Germany." Subrt's comments followed a Soviet news report from three days earlier that the Czechoslovak team had traveled to Moscow for a two-game friendly series, since neither team was participating in the world championships anymore. The Czechoslovak coach had said to the press that "the tournament in Colorado Springs and Denver can in no way be regarded as a world championship since the teams of the USSR and Czechoslovakia are among the world's best." The 1962 Ice Hockey World Championships, however, continued under the auspices of the IIHF. Five teams, including East Germany, were not in Colorado Springs. The teams that did travel to the United States had to schedule replacement teams for their pretournament exhibition games, with West Germany substituting the University of Michigan for Czechoslovakia. Sweden won the title, with the Canadians taking the silver and the home team Americans placing third; West Germany placed sixth.[22]

While the sport and government officials dealt with the ice hockey world championships, ski officials also confronted a similar problem because the French town of Chamonix was hosting the 1962 world championships in Alpine skiing. Following NATO policy, the French refused to grant visas to athletes from the GDR and also placed the blame on the tripartite ATO instead of the Ministry of Foreign Affairs (Ministère des Affaires Étrangères, or MAE). Newspapers on both sides of the Iron Curtain suggested that the International Ski Federation (FIS) would cancel the Chamonix events if France denied the entry to the East German skiers. The French government faced considerable domestic pressure from French ski officials and in the press to grant visas to the East German skiers. *Le Monde* reported that the president of the French Ski Federation met with MAE officials four times to advocate for the East German skiers to receive travel permits so that the Chamonix event could continue as planned.[23]

The MAE held firm to the NATO position and refused to grant visas to the East German skiers, but it also sought support for maintaining this position. Because of the simultaneous public outcry over East German participation in the skiing and ice hockey world championships, French and American diplomats remained in close communication. The MAE was particularly concerned that the Americans would bow to political pressure and grant visas to the East German ice hockey team, which would then weaken France's ability to maintain the NATO position. The French ambassador in Washington requested help from the State Department as well as the other pertinent ambassadors stationed in the US capital. The French government requested that the Americans in particular, as well as the other NATO states, help prevent the ski championships from being transferred away from Chamonix. The foreign ministries actively sought to influence the international sport federations by speaking with their representatives. The State Department contacted the American embassy in Bern, where the FIS executive committee was meeting to make its decision regarding Chamonix, and requested that embassy officials approach the American representative, John Stanley Mullin. The State Department also recommended informing Mullin that it was "likely representatives of other NATO countries being approached similarly." Government officials hoped that if international sport also adopted the NATO position with respect to East Germany, then their attitude would be accepted more widely across their domestic populations. The West German delegation to NATO reminded its alliance members that "sporting events attracted the public notice and there was some advantage in bringing home to public opinion the facts about the nature of the DDR regime and the reasons for not letting that regime make capital out of sporting events."[24]

At the same time that the rumors surrounding a Soviet and Eastern bloc withdrawal from the ice hockey world championships appeared, the ski federations from these countries also threatened to boycott the Chamonix events over the East German travel issue. These withdrawal threats prompted the FIS to hold an emergency meeting in Bern, Switzerland. During this emergency session, the French delegate reiterated that the French Ski Federation "could not be blamed" for the situation regarding East German visas because "the decisions came from much higher places." The FIS agreed to continue its efforts to facilitate East German participation in Chamonix. In a 7–5 vote, the FIS also agreed that if no resolution could be found within forty-eight hours, the title "World Championships" would be removed from the Chamonix events but that the competition could continue under any other name. The FIS also decided that if the Chamonix events were not deemed the world championships, an Alpine world championship would not be held in any other venue or country that year.[25]

The foreign ministries recognized the widespread public interest in these sporting events, noting how closely the press reported on the decisions affecting the world championships. Some French papers hinted that the government would request from NATO an exception to the travel ban for the East German skiers to compete in Chamonix. *Le Monde* noted the government position, quoting a foreign ministry official's statement that "France is not the only country responsible for this situation because the US and Great Britain take part equally in the tripartite bureau." The paper also criticized the proposal to remove the world championships designation from the event, claiming that action would create a moral prejudice against France from the international community as well as significant financial losses for the event organizers and the Chamonix ski resort.[26] The press coverage and criticism of this decision extended beyond NATO states. The *Neue Zürcher Zeitung*, a conservative Swiss newspaper, decried the FIS for its decision, stating that the federation

> in the battle for freedom and human dignity in sports, hides behind regulations in order to evade a courageous decision; that after less than six months August 13, 1961 is already forgotten; that the "wicked" NATO authorities are attacked in the West for refusing entry to the "dear" athletes from the East, whereas it is actually those same NATO authorities which have seen to it that the Berlin wall has not long since been put up along the Atlantic and which by their firm stand constitute the sole guarantee that we are still able in the West to make any decision at all as to whether sport events are to be held.[27]

Immediately after the FIS voted to give the matter forty-eight hours to find a resolution before the event would lose its world championships designation, the *New York Times*'s foreign correspondent Robert Daley addressed the Chamonix issue in a column reiterating the *Le Monde* sentiments. Daley noted how each party blamed another group for the decisions and criticized the international federation's action as coming too late. The FIS president's telegrams to US president John F. Kennedy, French president Charles de Gaulle, and British prime minister Harold Macmillan requesting their personal intervention to resolve the problem with East German athletes' travel, Daley said, sounded more like an ultimatum. He believed it was highly unlikely any of the three men would take any action that "might appear that governments had knuckled under to a ski federation."[28]

Without any change on the part of France or NATO, the FIS announced that the Chamonix event would not hold the world championships designation. The Czechoslovak team was the first to depart France, ostensibly because of its poor showing in preliminary meets. Over the next two days the Soviet, Polish, and Yugoslavian teams all left France as well, even though they too had participated in the warm-up events at nearby French mountains. The Western press attempted to downplay these withdrawals, noting that the strong Austrian team was still entered in the competition, along with the full Canadian and US teams. Although the event went ahead as planned but without the world championships designation, Daley noted that "the spirit has gone out of the town." Chamonix, he argued, was the biggest loser in terms of ticket sales, television broadcast revenues, and tourism income.[29]

The conclusion of the ski events in Chamonix did not, however, end the issue inside the FIS. The French representative commented publicly that "it is unfair that we should suffer because of political developments. In the end France has not erected the Wall in Berlin but rather the Soviet Zone has." The close vote removing the world championships designation from Chamonix demonstrated that other members concurred. Mullin, who also served as a vice president of the FIS, believed that "the inability to obtain visas arose directly from acts taken by the east Germans themselves"—namely, the Berlin Wall. Immediately after the conclusion of the Alpine competition in Chamonix, the FIS officials departed for Zakopane, Poland, for the world championships in the Nordic events. In both Zakopane and again at its meeting in Copenhagen in June, the FIS executive debated the validity of the emergency meeting that had removed the world championships designation from Chamonix and the possibility of reinstating it. The issue was only resolved when the full FIS membership met at its May 1963 Congress. After nearly sixteen months of discussions, the communist bloc finally agreed to withdraw its opposition and the Congress restored the title "world championships" to the Chamonix event along with the gold medals for the victors. This decision is exactly what *New York Times* columnist Daley had predicted a year earlier.[30]

In both of these cases, the United States and France avoided a de facto recognition of having to deal with the passports, flag, or anthem of East Germany. Nonetheless, the difficulties encountered in organizing these world championships, combined with the significant media attention showered on these international sporting events, forced the State Department, the MAE, and their diplomatic corps to spend considerable time and effort on the issue. The American and French foreign ministries held firm on refusing East German athletes' entry into their countries so soon after the construction of the Berlin Wall. By maintaining this position, France and the United States reaffirmed their commitment to upholding NATO policy, supported their West German ally, and continued the procedures that they had themselves developed in the ATO. The two states understood that NATO unity and the perceived strength of the Western coalition both domestically and abroad depended on upholding policies to which all members had agreed. At the same time, the international federations for ice hockey and skiing became increasingly important actors within international affairs. Their decisions impacted more than just their sport as they negotiated with the diplomats from NATO member states and appealed to their government leaders. Recognizing the popularity of sport, both the sport federations and governments made public statements to the press, each hoping that the media coverage would strengthen their position and force the other side to buckle under the weight of popular opinion.

While the ice hockey and skiing federations confronted the intrusion of the Cold War on their 1962 world championships, East German travel visas (both in general and for sport) again became a contested issue inside NATO. When NATO's Committee of Political Advisors first discussed the travel ban for the East German ski and ice hockey teams in late January 1962 in the midst of the public outcry in the press, the American and French delegates presented the issue primarily for information so that member states could uphold the same official position and demonstrate to their publics a united front within NATO. The assistant secretary-general for political affairs, R. W. J. Hooper (of the United Kingdom), chaired the meeting and reaffirmed NATO's position on the matter, stating that "there was no question at this stage of relaxing the ban on the issue of TTDs to East German sportsmen." Yet, within a week—just days before the Chamonix event was about to begin—the Norwegian delegation began advocating for a relaxation on the travel ban for sport.[31] This action ignited a renewed debate within NATO regarding the ability of East German athletes to travel to NATO countries. Other member states were concerned that the impact of the NATO-wide travel ban on East German athletes would significantly hinder their own ability to host future international sporting events. The Norwegian insistence on this matter inside NATO as a result of its concern for domestic public opinion demonstrated to NATO and its member states the broad reach the issue of East German travel for sport had.

Norway led the charge among the smaller NATO states (especially the northern ones) in the effort to remove the sport category or at least to permit exceptions to the overarching ban. Because of the colder climate and specific ice or snow surfaces required, fewer countries compete at the elite level in winter sports as compared to the sports contested at the Summer Olympic Games. The smaller number of countries contributing to the pool of elite-level athletes meant that any restriction on a country from sending its winter sport athletes would have a greater impact on the caliber of competition. These factors influenced the decision of winter sport federations, such as the International Bobsled and Tobogganing Federation, to admit the FRG before many other international sport federations after World War II and contributed to the significance of the 1972 Summit Series in ice hockey between Canada and the Soviet Union.[32]

Norway, which considers itself the birthplace of skiing, attaches considerable importance to hosting skiing events.[33] The Norwegian public therefore wanted to have the best skiers in the world compete at events held in Norway, especially the Holmenkollen competition, one of the most important annual ski-jumping events. In the midst of the Chamonix and Colorado Springs discussions within NATO, the Norwegian delegation had not complained when East German athletes withdrew from the 1962 European Speed Skating Championships in Oslo after being unable to procure travel documents. However, when it became apparent that the best ski jumper in the world would not be able to participate in the Holmenkollen in March 1962, the Norwegian delegation expressed its concern. East Germany's Helmut Recknagel had won the individual large hill event at the 1960 Olympic Games at Squaw Valley (as part of an all-German Olympic team) and at the recent world championships in

Nordic skiing, placed third in the individual normal hill event at Zako-pane, and had previously won the Holmenkollen in 1957 and 1960. The Holmenkollen organizers and the general public called on the Norwegian government to enable Recknagel to enter the country so that he could again compete in 1962.[34]

The Norwegians asked West Germany to grant an exception to the travel ban for Recknagel for the Holmenkollen event. The Federal Repub-lic's permanent representative to NATO informed his Norwegian coun-terpart that a TTD could not be granted for Recknagel because doing so would both violate NATO policy and bring negative publicity inside West Germany and other NATO member states. In addition, the German representative reminded his Norwegian counterpart that the French, who had themselves faced great difficulties following the refusal of travel docu-ments for Chamonix, "would most certainly refuse a TTD to Recknagel, even if the Federal Government would agree." This message, however, did not stop the Norwegians from raising the issue in the North Atlantic Council meeting the following day, pleading that Recknagel's inability to participate at the Holmenkollen because of a "NATO ban would result in considerable loss of NATO popularity in Norway." Norway received sup-port from the other "cold countries" of Canada, Denmark, and Iceland, but the Federal Republic, France, the United States, and Great Britain held firm that no exceptions should be made for sport, nor should a relax-ation of the travel ban be considered.[35]

Public opinion and media coverage, especially inside Norway, played an important role in shaping discussions on this topic both inside NATO and among diplomats. The American representative noted that the Nor-wegians had "strong arguments for relaxation [of the] travel ban on Ger-man athletes in terms of public opinion which would be strongly adverse [*sic*] to NATO if ban maintained." The American embassy in Oslo re-ported that while the topic was met by an "emotional intensity" in Nor-way, the Norwegian government had regrettably not taken initiative and used the "Holmekollen problem to bring home once again to Norwegian public that Khruschchev [*sic*] is playing for keeps in Berlin and this means that Norway has to forego [*sic*] some pleasures. Instead [the Government of Norway] will almost certainly wait and be forced by political timid-ity to take defensive position." The Utenriksdepartement (Norwegian Foreign Ministry) knew that Recknagel evoked a strong reaction among the public, which is why it also was in frequent communication with the Norwegian Ski Federation, which worked to minimize the coverage of the East German travel ban in the press.[36] By playing both angles at the same time, the Utenriksdepartement hoped to minimize domestic criticism but also use that same public opinion to work for a travel ban exception.

The Norwegian attempt to use public opinion as a way to change NATO policy—or at least receive a special exemption from the travel ban for Recknagel in 1962—was unsuccessful. This decision did not, however, quell the debate inside NATO, which continued over the next few years. Of all the travel restrictions for East Germans, the blanket refusal for sport prompted more difficulties and discussions than any other category because of the greater public appeal of sport compared to other fields such as agriculture or science. The smaller NATO states who argued for exceptions to, or the removal of, the ban on sport from the travel restrictions feared that, following the debacles with Chamonix and Colorado Springs, international sport federations would only hold events in Soviet bloc or neutral states, thus benefitting the communist states and hurting NATO.[37] These accusations forced the four powers to work harder at maintaining the unity of NATO over the tripartite and German policies regarding travel for East Germans. These foreign ministries not only sought to convince their NATO allies of the benefits of the travel ban for East German sportsmen, but their efforts also extended to influencing their national representatives to international sport federations.[38]

In fact, the sports organizations in the Federal Republic used the same argument as NATO and the ATO for why they ended all German-German sport activity in August 1961. The West German Olympic Committee claimed that "the Soviet-occupied zone of Germany hermetically shuts off the Eastern part of Germany from the Western part and stops the free traffic of the people living in both parts of our country." The United States and the United Kingdom, two of the states running the ATO and deciding which East Germans received TTDs, frequently reminded the other NATO states that they would be willing to consider relaxing the travel restrictions in a quid pro quo situation in which the Soviets and East Germans themselves eased restrictions on West Berlin. While many of the smaller NATO states may have wanted a relaxation of the travel ban for East German athletes, they ultimately concurred in February 1962 "that such action at this time would be ill-advised, particularly in view of Soviet harassment in the air corridors to Berlin." In addition, the NATO member states recognized that, with all of the attention the media had already given to the issue of East German athletes' travel, any decision taken quietly to change NATO policy would surely be noticed by the media and publicized widely.[39]

Although representatives of international sport had long espoused the necessity of separating politics from sports, the East German travel issue not only demonstrated the close relationship between sport and politics but also that sport federations, as international NGOs, could serve as influential actors in world affairs. Because governments had to approve visas for citizens from the Soviet bloc to enter their countries, the foreign ministries of NATO member states were thus drawn into the sport debates concerning the GDR. NATO member states supported the FRG's policy of not recognizing the communist East German state. With the ATO's refusal to grant TTDs, East German skiers and hockey players were prevented from participating in world championships in France and the United States just six months after the physical division of Berlin. Refusing visas to East German athletes might have violated the principles of the Olympic movement and international sport but so too did the building of the Berlin Wall, which limited the free movement of citizens in Berlin. Thus, while many international sport leaders attempted to address only sport-related issues before the construction of the Berlin Wall, such as with the 1961 Ice Hockey World Championships, the changed geopolitical situation after August 1961 meant that sport leaders could no longer remain uninvolved when these political issues encroached on their sporting events.

The construction of the Berlin Wall forced NATO states to weigh four-power and NATO policies against their own national interests. Although East Germany itself had prevented free travel with the construction of the Wall, it attempted to gain sympathy within the international community by exploiting the refusal of the ATO and NATO states to grant travel documents to East Germans for international sport competitions. Communist bloc states had, since the Soviet Union had joined the Olympic movement in 1951, been using the head-to-head competition of international sport as propaganda for the success of their political system.[40] Thus when the GDR introduced its own flag and anthem in 1959 and demanded their use at international events for sport and otherwise, the Federal Republic's allies within NATO supported the extension of the Hallstein Doctrine to include the nonrecognition of these new symbols of the East German state. These events demonstrate how the Federal Republic's position regarding East Germany, one of the central problems during the first half of the Cold War, was influenced not only by the big three Western powers but also the entirety of the transatlantic alliance. States wanted the prestige that comes with hosting a major international sporting event, but they also recognized that they had agreed to a policy as a NATO member state.

The publicity campaigns regarding the inability of East German athletes to travel to and participate in international competitions was, to the four powers, just more propaganda attacks from the Soviet bloc because of the inability of East Germany to make gains in other areas. Nonetheless, NATO governments and foreign ministries watched public opinion and the popular media coverage of this issue. The French and Norwegians each used the opinions expressed in their domestic press to either maintain support for the travel ban, in the case of Chamonix, or receive an exemption for the Holmenkollen. NATO's continued discussion of this topic throughout the 1960s always took into consideration the press coverage and how any policy change would be viewed by the public and media. These debates inside NATO and the corresponding discussions between NATO delegations and their foreign ministries demonstrate how broadly the transatlantic alliance interpreted what constituted a threat to the organization and its unity.

As the 1960s progressed, however, more international sport federations accepted the political division of the Cold War and granted official recognition to the GDR. West Germany, the three powers, and NATO found it increasingly difficult to maintain the nonrecognition of East Germany and public support for these decisions, particularly when they impacted the ability to host international sport. In the aftermath of Chamonix and Colorado Springs, the International Weightlifting Federation transferred its 1962 World Weightlifting Championships from Hershey, Pennsylvania, to Budapest, Hungary, so that East Germany could participate.[41] While NATO and the international sport community confronted the problems surrounding East German participation, similar issues arose within international sport from the division of Korea and the China-Taiwan split. While these other political conflicts also fought over recognition, flags, and national symbols, the geographical position of China, Taiwan, and North and South Korea on the other side of the world in Asia meant that no comparisons with the East German situation were made within NATO.

Furthermore, as the State Department noted, travel restrictions pertaining to athletes from China, Taiwan, North Korea, or North Vietnam "would be based on national policies rather than NATO policies. Therefore . . . travel of athletes from these countries does not appear to be matter on which all NATO countries must necessarily agree." The NATO states considered the travel ban on East German athletes more hurtful for the Soviet bloc than for themselves because the withdrawal of communist teams only punished the well-trained elite athletes who were deprived of the opportunity to compete against the rest of the world's best—much in the way that Western and Soviet bloc athletes would feel deprived of their Olympic opportunities in 1980 and 1984, respectively, as a result of the competing boycotts of the Moscow and Los Angeles Games.[42]

As Cold War politics increasingly invaded sport, the International Olympic Committee (IOC), concerned over travel restrictions, sought guarantees from the ATO as well as the national governments for all of the cities bidding to host the 1968 Olympics. These issues only disappeared at the end of the decade with the beginning of détente and the simultaneous acceptance of the postwar status quo by the IOC when it finally granted full recognition to the GDR just days before the 1968 Summer Olympic Games in Mexico City. This closure to the nearly two-decade German problem in sport foreshadowed the political agreement between the German states. The FRG and the GDR established a bilateral relationship and finally recognized each other with the signing of the Basic Treaty in 1972.[43]

Yet, before the normalization of the German-German relationship, each new instance in the 1960s of the travel ban impacting sport and the subsequent public and media discussions on the topic prompted NATO to reopen its own debates regarding the travel restrictions for East Germans, possible relaxations or special exemptions for the travel ban, and the arguments for maintaining this policy. To NATO member states, particularly the FRG and the three powers controlling the ATO, these were not simply questions of sport but rather grave concerns over security, NATO unity, and perceived communist advantages during the Cold War. As a result, international sport became a serious concern within NATO and at some of the highest levels within foreign ministries. The communist bloc demonstrated its understanding of the importance of sport through its development of state-run athletic programs to foster elite athletes to display to the world the strength of communism, and the Western alliance equally understood the role that sport played in the Cold War by devoting valuable time and energy from the diplomatic corps toward confronting the growing position of the GDR within the international community.

## Notes

The author would like to thank the Society for Historians of Foreign Relations for providing funding for part of this research. Many archives and organizations have graciously granted me access to their files, in particular the NATO archivists in Brussels and the staff at the Rauner Library at Dartmouth College. The author also thanks Mark Rice, Katrin Urschel, and the anonymous reviewers from the University Press of Kentucky for their insightful comments.

1. C-R(54)15—Summary Record of a meeting of the Council held at Palais de Chaillot, Paris, on Tuesday, 20th April, 1954, 22 April 1954, North Atlantic Treaty Organization Archives, Brussels, Belgium (hereafter NATO), and C-M(54)37(Final)—Soviet Grant of "Full Sovereignty" to the East Zone of Germany, June 25, 1954, NATO.

2. William Glenn Gray, *Germany's Cold War: The Global Campaign to Isolate East Germany, 1949–1969* (Chapel Hill: University of North Carolina Press, 2003); Margarete Myers Feinstein, *State Symbols: The Quest for Legitimacy in the Federal Republic of Germany and the German Democratic Republic, 1949–1959* (Boston: Brill, 2001); David Childs, "The German Democratic Republic," in *Sport under Communism: The U.S.S.R., Czechoslovakia, the G.D.R., China, Cuba,* ed. James Riordan, 2nd ed., rev. (London: C. Hurst, 1981), 81; and Uta A. Balbier, *Kalter Krieg auf der Aschenbahn: Der deutsch-deutsche Sport, 1950–1972; eine politische Geschichte* (Paderborn: F. Schöning, 2007).

3. Francis H. Heller and John R. Gillingham, eds., *NATO: The Founding of the Atlantic Alliance and the Integration of Europe* (New York: St. Martin's, 1992); Gustav Schmidt, ed., *A History of NATO: The First Fifty Years,* 3 vols. (New York: Palgrave, 2001); Stephen Twigge and Alan MacMillan, "Britain, the United States, and the Development of NATO Strategy, 1950–1964," *Journal of Strategic Studies* 19, no. 2 (June 1996): 260–81; Kara Stibora Fulcher, "A Sustainable Position? The United States, the Federal Republic, and the Ossification of Allied Policy on Germany, 1958–1962," *Diplomatic History* 26, no. 2 (Spring 2002): 283–307; Sean M. Maloney, "Berlin Contingency Planning: Prelude to Flexible Response, 1958–63," *Journal of Strategic Studies* 25, no. 1 (March 2002): 99–134; Mary Ann Heiss and

S. Victor Papacosma, ed., *NATO and the Warsaw Pact: Intrabloc Conflicts* (Kent, OH: Kent State University Press, 2008); Linda Risso, "'Enlightening Public Opinion': A Study of NATO's Information Policies between 1949 and 1959 Based on Recently Declassified Documents," *Cold War History* 7, no. 1 (February 2007): 45–51; Linda Risso, "'Don't Mention the Soviets!' An Overview of the Short Films Produced by the NATO Information Service between 1949 and 1969," *Cold War History* 9, no. 4 (2009): 501–12; Linda Risso, "Propaganda on Wheels: The NATO Travelling Exhibitions in the 1950s and 1960s," *Cold War History* 11, no. 1 (2011): 9–25; and Norman A. Graebner, "Reflections at a Turning Point," in *NATO*, ed. Heller and Gillingham, 435.

4. Gray, *Germany's Cold War*, and Dennis L. Bark and David R. Gress, *A History of West Germany: Vol. 1, From Shadow to Substance, 1945–1963* (Oxford: Basil Blackwell, 1989), 374.

5. AC/52-R/33—Committee on Information and Cultural Relations Summary Record of a meeting held at the Palais de Chaillot, Paris, on Thursday, 5th May, 1955, 10 May 1955, NATO.

6. Hope Harrison, *Driving the Soviets Up the Wall: Soviet-East German Relations, 1953–1961* (Princeton, NJ: Princeton University Press, 2003), 96–116.

7. AC/119-WP(59)112—Internal and External Situation of the Soviet Occupied Zone, October 27, 1959, NATO; Feinstein, *State Symbols,* 40–51; and AC/119-WP(60)3—New Flag of the Soviet Occupied Zone of Germany, January 13, 1960, NATO.

8. "Das Ultimatum des Eishockey-Weltverbandes," *Frankfurter Allgemeine Zeitung,* March 13, 1961, 5; Horst Eckert and Ernst Martini, *90: IIHF 90th Anniversary, 1908–1998* (Zürich: IIHF, 1998), 119–20; and "Hallstein Doktrin bringt Niederlage," *Neues Deutschland,* March 13, 1961, 1. The West German hockey federation also had to pay any costs that the rink incurred for the cancellation of the game. Minutes, Emergency Meeting at the 45th Annual Congress of the IIHF, Geneva, March 1961, *LIGH/IIHF Procès Verbaux/Minutes, 1955–1963,* International Ice Hockey Federation, Zürich, Switzerland (hereafter IIHF).

9. "Politics Harass German Sport," *The Times* (London), March 15, 1961, 11; "Canada Trounces Soviet Union and Captures World Amateur Hockey Crown," *New York Times,* March 13, 1961, 39; "Västtyskar lämnade w.o. 'Flaggstrid,'" *Svenska dagbladet,* March 13, 1961, 1; Despatch 183, Paul H. Pearson, AmConsul Göteborg to Department of State, February 17, 1961, Record Group (RG) 59, Department of State Central Decimal Files (CDF) 1960–63, 800.453, Box 2239, National Archives, College Park, Maryland (hereafter NA); and Despatch 704, G. Alonzo Stanford, AmEmbassy Stockholm to Department of State, February 21, 1961, RG 59, CDF 1960–63, 800.453, Box 2239, NA.

10. "Hallstein Doktrin bringt Niederlage," *Neues Deutschland,* March 13, 1961, 1, and *Neues Deutschland,* March 14, 1961, 1.

11. Telegram 496, Lightner, Berlin to Secretary of State, March 14, 1961, RG 59, CDF 1960–63, 800.453, Box 2239, NA; Airgram POLTO G-1536, Finletter,

USRO, Paris to SecState, March 29, 1961, RG 59, CDF 1960–63, 862.181, Box 2644, NA; and Circular CG-845, Rusk, Department of State to AmEmbassy Bonn, April 4, 1961, RG 59, CDF 1960–63, 862.181, Box 2644, NA.

12. Bark and Gress, *A History of West Germany: Vol. 1,* 468.

13. Harrison, *Driving the Soviets,* 207; H. Passlack, Deutscher Fußball-Bund to FIFA, September 1, 1961, Correspondence with National Associations GER (FRG) 1955–1961, Fédération Internationale de Football Association, Zurich, Switzerland; Bark and Gress, *History of West Germany: Vol. 1,* 213–17; and Vermerk über die Besprechung mit einer Kommission der Innenminister der Länder und dem Präsidium des Deutschen Sportbundes am 1. März 1962 im Bundesministerium des Innern, March 1, 1962, B 38 / 57, Politisches Archiv des Auswärtiges Amt, Berlin, Germany (hereafter PAdAA).

14. Statement of the Presidium of the NOC of the German Democratic Republic, August 19, 1961, Republique Democratique Allemagne, Correspondance 1951–1962, International Olympic Committee Archives, Lausanne, Switzerland (hereafter IOC).

15. Harrison, *Driving the Soviets,* 207; AC/119-R(60)32—Committee of Political Advisers Meeting held on Tuesday, 13th September 1960, Action Sheet, 16 September 1960, NATO; C-M(60)92—Restrictions on Issue of Temporary Travel Documents to East German Residents, October 31, 1960, NATO; Hope Harrison, "The German Democratic Republic, the Soviet Union and the Berlin Wall Crisis," in *The Berlin Wall Crisis: Perspectives on Cold War Alliances,* ed. John P. S. Gearson and Kori Schake (New York: Palgrave Macmillan, 2002), 105; AC/119-R(61)10—Committee of Political Advisers Meeting held on March 14, 1961, Action Sheet, March 17, 1961, NATO; Telegram 192, Lightner, Berlin to Secretary of State, August 14, 1961, RG 59, CDF 1960–63, 862.181, Box 2644, NA; and C-R(61)40—Summary Record of a Restricted meeting of the Council held at the Permanent Headquarters, Paris, on Thursday, 31st August, 1961, 13 September 1961, NATO.

16. Airgram CA-684, Rusk, Department of State to USBER Berlin, December 19, 1961, RG 59, CDF 1960–63, 800.453, Box 2239, NA.

17. The Squaw Valley team was composed entirely of West German players. Rather than select the best athletes from both states for team sports on the All-German Olympic team, the East German and West German teams played against each other, with the winning team earning the right to compete at the Olympic Games. Ergänzungen zum Kommuniqué und Beschlußprotokoll, East-West NOK, November 18, 1959, Heft 208, Deutscher Olympischer Sportbund, Frankfurt, Germany.

18. "Visa Problems Plague East German Pucksters," *Lowell* (MA) *Sun,* January 11, 1962, 24; Telegram 903, Rusk, Department of State to USBER Berlin, January 11, 1962, RG 59, CDF 1960–63, 800.453, Box 2239, NA; "Official Feels Hockey Title Play Will Be in Colo. Spgs.," *Greeley* (CO) *Daily Tribune,* January 11, 1962, 27; Airgram CA-684, Rusk, Department of State to USBER Berlin, December 19, 1961, RG 59, CDF 1960–63, 800.453, Box 2239, NA; Ahearne to Deutscher Eislauf-Verband, February 3, 1962, DY 12/2051, Bundesarchiv Berlin (hereafter BArchB);

Airgram A-438, Lightner, US Mission Berlin to SecState WASH and AmEmbassy BONN, February 11, 1962, RG 59, CDF 1960–63, 800.453, Box 2239, NA; Minutes of the 46th Annual Congress of the I.I.H.F., March 7–13, 1962, *LIGH/IIHF Procès Verbaux/Minutes, 1955–1963,* IIHF; and "Situation Unsettled as Visa Problem Arises: May Hold World Hockey in Calgary or Edmonton," *Lethbridge* (AB) *Herald,* January 25, 1962, 7.

19. CG1621/12—Restriction on the Issue of TTDs—Refusal of TTDs to an East German ice hockey team which was to take part in the Colorado Spring Ice Hockey World Championship (March 8–18), FO 371/163681, National Archives of the United Kingdom, Kew, Richmond, Surrey (hereafter UKNA), and Telegram 963, Ball, Department of State to USBER Berlin, January 26, 1962, RG 59, CDF 1960–63, 800.453, Box 2239, NA.

20. Telegram 903, Rusk, Department of State to USBER Berlin, January 11, 1962, RG 59, CDF 1960–63, 800.453, Box 2239, NA; Airgram A-326, Lightner, US Mission Berlin to SecState WASH, AmEmbassy BONN, January 5, 1962, RG 59, CDF 1960–63, 800.453, Box 2239, NA; "Allies to Be Asked to Life Ban on E. German Ice Team," *Greeley* (CO) *Daily Tribune,* February 1, 1962, 10; C-R(62)10—Summary record of a meeting of the Council held at the Permanent Headquarters, Paris, on Wednesday, March 7, 1962, NATO; and Letter, AE Donald, United Kingdom Delegation to NATO to W. J. A. Wilberforce, Central Department, Foreign Office, January 31, 1962, FO 371/163681, UKNA.

21. Without the five teams from the communist bloc, the tournament only had two pools (Championship and Pool B) instead of three pools, as was the case in 1961 and 1963. "New Aspects to the Visa Problem," *Bulletin of the National Olympic Committee of the German Democratic Republic,* no. III (1965): 37, John Stanley Mullin Collection (JSM), Box 5, Folder 19, Rauner Library, Dartmouth College, Hanover, NH (hereafter RLDC); "Was wird aus der Eishockey-Weltmeisterschaft?," *Neues Deutschland,* January 26, 1962, 8; "Diskriminierung verurteilt," *Neues Deutschland,* March 11, 1962, 8; Telegram 1439, Lightner, Berlin to Secretary of State, February 5, 1962, RG 59, CDF 1960–63, 800.453, Box 2239, NA; "Plans for World Hockey Play in Springs Continue," *Greeley* (CO) *Daily Tribune,* January 30, 1962, 12; "If Germans Kept Out: Soviets, Czechs Won't Play in United States," *Lethbridge* (AB) *Herald,* January 30, 1962, 6; Heinze, Aktennotiz überein Telefongrspräch mit dem Genossen Alfred Neumann aus Moskau am 7.2.1962 um 16.45 Uhr, February 7, 1962, DY 12/2051, BArchB; Avery Brundage, "Visits Expected," June 3, 1961, Avery Brundage Collection (ABC), Box 92, University of Illinois Archives, Champaign, IL (hereafter UIA); "Revised Hockey Draw Will Omit Five Nations," *New York Times,* February 20, 1962, 42; "Eishockey wie geplant," *Frankfurter Allgemeine Zeitung,* January 31, 1962, 6; and Eckert and Martini, *90,* 121, 259.

22. "Put Politics in Background When Engaging in Sports, Steve Urges," *Greeley* (CO) *Daily Tribune,* March 8, 1962, 26; "Czech Icers in Moscow," *Greeley* (CO) *Daily Tribune,* March 5, 1962, 15; and "W. German Icers to Play Michigan," *Greeley* (CO) *Daily Tribune,* February 21, 1965.

23. Telegram 3673, Gavin, Paris to Secretary of State, January 30, 1962, RG 59, CDF 1960–63, 800.453, Box 2239, NA; "European Officials Willing to Cancel Title Skiing," *New York Times,* February 2, 1962, 34; "Keine Weltmeisterschaften!," *Neues Deutschland,* February 6, 1962, 6; Telegram 3707, Gavin, Paris to Secretary of State, February 3, 1962, RG 59, CDF 1960–63, 800.453, Box 2239, NA; and "Les Championnats du Monde de Chamonix risquent d'être annulés," *Le Monde,* January 31, 1962, 15.

24. A. E. Donald, United Kingdom Delegation to NATO, Paris, to W. J. A. Wilberforce, Foreign Office, February 2, 1962, FO 371/163681, UKNA; Telegram 3707, Gavin, Paris to Secretary of State, February 3, 1962, RG 59, CDF 1960–63, 800.453, Box 2239, NA; Telegram 310, Washington to Foreign Office, February 3, 1962, FO 371/163681, UKNA; Telegram 477, Rusk to AmEmbassy Bern, February 2, 1962, RG 59, CDF 1960–63, 800.453, Box 2239, NA; and A. E. Donald, UK Delegation to NATO, Paris, to W. J. A. Wilberforce, Foreign Office, February 7, 1962, FO 371/163681, UKNA.

25. Protocol of the Meeting of the International Ski Federation, February 4, 1962, JSM, Box 3, Folder 5, RLDC.

26. A. E. Donald, United Kingdom Delegation to NATO, Paris, to W. J. A. Wilberforce, Foreign Office, February 2, 1962, FO 371/163681, UKNA, and "Les Championnats du Monde de Chamonix risquent d'être annulés," *Le Monde,* January 31, 1962, 15. Donald only mentioned in his letter what was reported in the February 1 NATO Committee on Information and Cultural Relations meeting. He did not specifically refer to any articles in the French press.

27. Translation, "Second-Rate World Championships," attached to L. D. Battle, Memorandum for McGeorge Bundy, February 22, 1962, RG 59, CDF 1960–63, 800.453, Box 2239, NA, and "Halbwertige Weltmeisterschaften," *Neue Zürcher Zeitung,* February 7, 1962, 4.

28. Robert Daley, "Cut Off at the Impasse," *New York Times,* February 6, 1962, 54.

29. "Pas de Soviétiques a Chamonix," *Le Monde,* February 8, 1962, 8; "Chamonix Skiing Meet Loses Its World Championship Designation," *New York Times,* February 6, 1962, 54; "Soviet Union-Rumania Walkout Mars Chamonix Nontitle Skiing," *New York Times,* February 7, 1962, 61; "Austrian Skiers Hint at Boycott," *New York Times,* February 8, 1962, 52; "Ski Tourney Name Changed," *Lowell* (MA) *Sun,* February 2, 1962, 10; and Robert Daley, "Politics: A Threat to World Sports," *New York Times,* February 13, 1962, 42.

30. "Ein Sportultimatum an die freie Welt," *Frankfurter Allgemeine Zeitung,* February 6, 1962, 8; John Stanley Mullin to Merritt H. Stiles, April 24, 1962, JSM, Box 3, Folder 3, RLDC; FIS Protokoll No. 1, Meeting of the FIS Council in Zakopane, February 15, 1962, JSM, Box 3, Folder 5, RLDC; FIS Council Protokoll No. 2, Meeting of the FIS Council in Zakopane, February 15, 1962, JSM, Box 3, Folder 5, RLDC; FIS Council Meeting Zakopane 1962 No. 1, February 21, 1962, JSM, Box 3, Folder 5, RLDC; Minutes, FIS meeting, Copenhagen, Denmark, June

15, 1962, JSM, Box 3, Folder 5, RLDC; Minutes of the XXIVth International Ski Congress, Athens, May 20–24 1963, JSM, Box 3, Folder 10, RLDC; Daley, "Cut Off at the Impasse," 54; and Robert Daley, "Hope Is Revived for World Skiing," *New York Times,* February 10, 1962, 38.

31. A. E. Donald, UK Delegation to NATO, to W. J. A. Wilberforce, Foreign Office, January 31, 1962, FO 371/163681, UKNA; and A. E. Donald, UK Delegation to NATO, to W. J. A. Wilberforce, Foreign Office, February 7, 1962, FO 371/163681, UKNA.

32. Procès-Verbal, 1950 FIBT Congress, February 4, 1950, Fédération International de Bobsleigh et de Tobaganning, Milan, Italy. For the Summit Series and the role of ice hockey during the Cold War, see John Soares's contribution in this volume.

33. E. John B. Allen, *The Culture and Sport of Skiing: From Antiquity to World War II* (Amherst: University of Massachusetts Press, 2007). The popularity of skiing in Norway continues, as demonstrated by the success of the 2011 world championships in Nordic skiing held in Oslo. "Oslo Stages Unforgettable FIS Nordic World Ski Championships 2011," FIS website, March 6, 2011, http://www.fis-ski.com/uk/news/pressreleases/press-releases-2011/oslo-2011-close.html (accessed April 23, 2011).

34. Notat, Knut Hedemann, Reiserestriksjoner for Øst-Tyskland. — Deltakelse i Holmenkollrennene, March 7, 1962, 18.1/74 Öst-tyske innreisebestemmelser, Bind VII Fra 1/1.62–31/3.62, Utenriksdepartementet, Oslo, Norway (hereafter UD); Telegram 356, Wharton, Oslo to Secretary of State, March 10, 1962, RG 59, CDF 1960–63, 862B.181, Box 2673, NA; "Norway Bars Skiers from East Germany," *New York Times,* March 13, 1962, 42; and John Stanley Mullin to Merritt H. Stiles, April 24, 1962, JSM, Box 3, Folder 3, RLDC.

35. Gebhardt von Walther to Jens Boyesen, Ambassador of Norway to NATO, March 6, 1962, B 38 / 57, PAdAA; Telegram D 10043, NATO-delegasjonen i Paris to Utenriksdepartementet, March 6, 1962, 18.1/74 Öst-tyske innreisebestemmelser, Bind VII Fra 1/1.62–31/3.62, UD; Telegram POLTO CIRC 89, Finletter, Paris to Secretary of State, March 7, 1962, RG 59, CDF 1960–63, 862B.181, Box 2673, NA; Memorandum No. 84, North Atlantic Council, Restrictions on Travel by East German Sportsmen, Council Meeting, March 7, 1962, FO 371/163682, UKNA; and Notat, Knut Hedemann, Reiserestriksjoner for Øst-Tyskland—Deltakelse i Holmenkollrennene, March 7, 1962, 18.1/74 Öst-tyske innreisebestemmelser, Bind VII Fra 1/1.62–31/3.62, UD.

36. Telegram POLTO CIRC 89, Finletter, Paris to Secretary of State, March 7, 1962, RG 59, CDF 1960–63, 862B.181, Box 2673, NA; Telegram 356, Wharton, Oslo to Secretary of State, March 10, 1962, RG 59, CDF 1960–63, 862B.181, Box 2673, NA; and Notat, Knut Hedemann, Reiserestriksjoner for Øst-Tyskland—Deltakelse i Holmenkollrennene, March 7, 1962, 18.1/74 Öst-tyske innreisebestemmelser, Bind VII Fra 1/1.62–31/3.62, UD.

37. A. E. Donald, UK Delegation to NATO, Paris, to J. S. Whitehead, Foreign Office, March 1962, FO 371/163682, UKNA.

38. See, for example, State Department correspondence with John Stanley Mullin, vice president of the FIS; Foreign Office correspondence with Lord Exeter, president of the International Association of Amateur Athletics and a vice president of the IOC; and the Auswärtiges Amt with Willi Daume, president of the West German Olympic Committee and member of the IOC.

39. Nationales Olympisches Komitee für Deutschland to International Olympic Committee, October 20, 1962, ABC, Box 127, UIA; Telegram 270, Foreign Office to Moscow, February 5, 1962, FO 371/163681, UKNA; Telegram D 10017, NATO-delegasjonen i Paris to Utenriksdepartementet, February 7, 1962, 18.1/74 Öst-tyske innreisebestemmelser, Bind VII Fra 1/1.62–31/3.62, UD; AC/119-R(62)7—Action Sheet, Committee of Political Advisers Meetings held on February 13 and 14, 1962, February 15, 1962, NATO; Airgram POLTO A-913, Finletter, USRO, Paris to Sec-State Washington, February 14, 1962, RG 59, CDF 1960–63, 800.453, Box 2239, NA; AC/119-R(62)8—Action Sheet, Committee of Political Advisers Meeting held on February 20, 1962, February 22, 1962, NATO; and A. E. Donald to J. S. Whitehead, March 6, 1962, FO 371/163681, UKNA.

40. Jenifer Parks, "Verbal Gymnastics: Sports, Bureaucracy, and the Soviet Union's Entrance into the Olympic Games, 1946–1952," in *East Plays West: Sport and the Cold War*, ed. Stephen Wagg and David L. Andrews (London: Routledge, 2007), 28; and Alfred E. Senn, *Power, Politics, and the Olympic Games* (Champaign, IL: Human Kinetics, 1999), 102–4.

41. Airgram A-565, Lightner, US Mission Berlin to SecState Washington, March 29, 1962, RG 59, CDF 1960–63, 800.453, Box 2239, NA, and International Olympic Committee, request for visas for participation in sport events in NATO countries, January 1964, République Democratique Allemagne, Correspondance 1963–1971, IOC.

42. See Fan Hong and Lu Zhouxiang's chapter in this volume. The foreign ministries were in fact discussing the two-China and two-Korea problems in sport. However, these discussions remained separate among the diplomatic correspondence until later in the 1960s when NATO states had to provide government guarantees in order to bid for the 1968 Olympic Games and once maintaining the Hallstein Doctrine became increasingly tenuous. For example, see R. Cecil, "International Olympic Committee," February 10, 1965, FO 371/183165, UKNA; Telegram 1742, Ball, Department of State to Paris TOPOL, May 21, 1963, RG 59, CDF 1963, Box 3240; and Airgram A-751, McSweeney, AmEmbassy Moscow to Department of State, March 27, 1962, RG 59, Department of State, Central Decimal File, 1960–63, 862B.181, Box 2673, NA.

43. This recognition could not happen earlier because the French city of Grenoble hosted the Winter Olympics that year and the French government maintained its support of the official NATO position of not recognizing East Germany. Otto Mayer to Allied Travel Office, April 17, 1962, République Democratique Allemagne,

Correspondance 1951–1962, IOC; CG1621/39—T.T.D.s for East Germans—French proposal to use Olympic C'ttee participants' cards as travel documents to enable East Germans to compete in world championships, April 17–June 14, 1962, FO 371/163682, UKNA; Telegram 1584, Department of State to AmEmbassy Paris TOPOL, April 25, 1963, RG 59, Department of State, Central Foreign Policy File, 1963, Box 3240, NA; IOC General Session Minutes, Mexico City 1968, October 7–11, 1968, Wolf S. Lyberg, IOC General Session Minutes, Volume IV (1956–1988); Lord Killanin, *My Olympic Years* (London: Secker & Warburg, 1983), 110; and Dennis L. Bark and David R. Gress, *A History of West Germany: Vol. 2, Democracy and Its Discontents, 1963–1988* (Oxford: Basil Blackwell, 1989), 202–21.

2

# Steadfast Friendship and Brotherly Help

## The Distinctive Soviet–East German Sport Relationship within the Socialist Bloc

*Evelyn Mertin*

The bipolar power structure of the Cold War suggests clearly delineated concepts of friends and foes both within and between both blocs. This model of international politics also transferred over to the sport relationships of the involved nations, inevitably having an impact on the international sport movement. For communist propaganda planners, successful results and shining medals gained by any athlete east of the Iron Curtain contributed to the accomplishment of communist sport. The image of friendly and supportive sport relationships among communist countries was created for the public, but these concepts nonetheless remained politically induced and restrictive. By analyzing the sport relationship between the Soviet Union and East Germany—two of the most powerful sporting nations during the Cold War—this chapter examines the consequences and challenges arising from the conflict between real interests and publicly declared alliances.

The German Democratic Republic (GDR) was founded from the Soviet Occupation Zone in 1949 as a communist state in close political cooperation with the Union of Soviet Socialist Republics (USSR), and both its state and social system closely followed the Soviet example. Therefore, it is not surprising that close cooperation can also be seen in the area of sport. In order to develop physical culture and sport according to communist beliefs, officials and administrators in the Soviet Occupation Zone and later in the GDR considered the Soviet sport system as their model and profited from previous experiences from Moscow.[1] The friendship that laid the foundation for the relationship between these two countries in all areas was also the basis for their sport relationship.

Before considering the sport contacts between the GDR and the USSR, it is helpful to provide an overview of the experience and development of these sporting nations in international sport leading up to the time under consideration in this chapter, as their bilateral contacts must always be considered within the framework of each nation's achievements and desires to improve their success at the international level. After the 1917 October Revolution, physical culture and sport were not left to develop according to social influences or personal initiatives in the Soviet Union. Attempts to create autonomous sport structures or traditional sports and gymnastics movements, such as the Slavic Sokol, were prevented through the implementation of an efficient and exclusively centralized organization.[2] Existing structures were dissolved and new organizations created. In many areas where physical culture and sport had not yet been institutionalized, this process had to be initiated and developed.

The new communist system of physical culture and sport was planned as a national venture with the main goals of enhancing defense, health, and integration.[3] The young Soviet state was not (actively) part of the international Olympic movement for several reasons. Even though the International Olympic Committee (IOC) continued to recognize the National Olympic Committee (NOC) of prerevolutionary Russia and its IOC members until 1932, the USSR was not invited to any of the Olympic Games between the two world wars because it was considered part of the "so-called 'sanitary cordon,'" when a political and economic blockade covered Soviet Russia and its sporting contacts."[4] At this time, the communist state tried to establish its own international workers' sport movement in contrast to the "bourgeois" Olympic Games.[5] During the 1930s the Soviet attitude toward international sport began to change, initiated by an intensive effort to break old and set new world records.[6]

Soviet participation in the international sport movement did not occur until after the Second World War. The new situation in world politics
and growing ideological conflicts led to a change in the attitude of Soviet
leaders toward participation in international sport. By the mid- to late
1940s, the arena of international sport was no longer considered a possible threat to the Soviet system but instead seen as a platform with great
propaganda potential. Ideologists and politicians expected the successful
participation of Soviet athletes in worldwide competitions and championships to have a positive effect on the image of the Soviet Union. The intention was that achievements in elite sports would influence the sympathy
of foreign audiences toward communist society.[7] Competing successfully
in international sport was now recognized as a worthy and effective instrument of public diplomacy against the ideological opponents during
the Cold War.

Gaining positive (political) effects from international sporting success
was a strategy also applied to GDR sport. After 1945 the sport system in
the Soviet Occupation Zone and later in the GDR distanced itself from
its National Socialist past and followed the Soviet example of establishing
a new ideological reasoning with respect to sport. The following analysis
will show that while the GDR began under the auspices of the Soviet
Union, East Germany increasingly gained independence and self-confidence within the realm of sport.

The study of East German sport has often focused on the rivalry with
West Germany or, since its public disclosure, on the state-sponsored doping program.[8] Before the fall of the Iron Curtain in 1989, the sport relations between the GDR and the USSR were only sporadically mentioned.
Even in more recent academic studies these contacts remain largely inci-
dental or tangential.[9] Some of these scholars used pointed titles or subtitles
such as "From Teacher to Rival"[10] or "From Apprentice to Model Pupil
and Opponent,"[11] suggesting a change in the relationships. Although the
West German journalist and close observer of German sporting politics
Willi Knecht called the GDR's high-proficiency sport program a "Soviet
trauma" because East German athletes were increasingly exceeding Soviet achievements,[12] articles published in the GDR and the Soviet Union
also frequently assured readers of the high status of their friendly sport
relationships.[13]

Influential factors affecting the bilateral relations between these countries included the development of a high proficiency level in sport, cooperation in the field of sport scientific work and research, and the integration of communist representatives in international sport organizations. At the same time, the mutual avowal and promise of friendship and cooperation were constant factors within the bond of a so-called proletarian internationalism.[14] The overriding goal was to foster the much hoped-for superiority of communist sport. Once these publicly displayed relationships were stripped of the rhetorical assurance of friendship within the Soviet bloc, however, the sport political contacts were complex and—without a doubt—not always harmonious.

Different expectations and a variety of views of the meaning and extent of cooperation developed in the characterization of sport comparisons. The sport historian Gunter Holzweißig names three influential factors that dominated the Soviet-East German relations: the delayed dissemination of research results, the common rivalry between two leading sporting nations, and the ideological hurdles.[15] However, there is a fourth factor that needs to be considered: the constant foreign currency shortage. On one hand, this made close cooperation in training and research desirable; on the other hand, the issue of saving money served as an explanation for downsizing delegations and reducing exchange programs. This brief overview of research in bilateral relations already exemplifies the bias between the officially acclaimed friendship and the challenges of such close collaboration. The vast correspondence between leading sport administrators in the GDR and in the Soviet Union often displayed a less friendly tone than the public proclamations on the ideological rhetoric of friendship.

By examining both the official declarations of friendship between the GDR and the Soviet Union with respect to sport and the contrasting points of view expressed internally, this chapter demonstrates the ways in which sport complicated diplomatic relations among and between allied countries. Although sport was one of the most hotly contested spaces between the two Cold War camps, this does not mean that all of the countries within each camp were fully aligned on all fronts. NATO member states had their own difficulties maintaining a united front when it came to international sport during the 1960s and so did states within the communist bloc.[16] Harold E. Wilson Jr. has noted the desire by Romanian leader Nicolae Ceaușescu to demonstrate his power and autonomy within the communist bloc by sending a team to the 1984 Olympic Games in Los Angeles instead of participating in the Soviet-led boycott.[17] Unlike Ceauşescu's Romania, the GDR was in many ways often considered the model communist bloc member state. Thus the extent to which the official and private views regarding the Soviet–East German sport relationship diverged reveals a more nuanced understanding of the polarization of the Cold War, where the GDR sought to achieve success on the medal podium at the expense of West Germany, the West in general, and the Soviet Union.

## The Contractual Cornerstones

As communist countries with the sport systems directed by the state, Soviet and East German sport must be viewed within their broader bilateral relationship. The two states signed major sport friendship treaties with each other in 1966 and 1977. However, these treaties signed by the leading representatives in the sport administrations only represent the official position of the Soviet–East German relationship, preserving the political and social bonds between the two states. On their own, these treaties do not reveal the complexity of the relationship between the communist allies. In fact, these contractual agreements do not represent the results of talks, meetings, or developments specifically in the area of sport and politics. Instead, these treaties must be considered as follow-up contracts for basic state agreements.

Sports historian Holzweißig has argued that the sport relationship between the Soviet Union and the GDR can be divided in three phases: 1949–1966, 1966–1977, and post-1977.[18] The treaties of friendship signed in 1966 and 1977 each marked the beginning of a new stage and served as the foundation of the Soviet–East German sport relationship. In the first phase, from the creation of the GDR as a state in 1949 until the 1966 treaty, the Soviet Union supported the practical establishment of GDR sport as well as its content-based ideological definition.[19] The Contract about Relations between the German Democratic Republic and the Union of Socialist Soviet Republics, signed on September 20, 1950, was followed by a cultural agreement on April 25, 1956, which also established the general framework for sport relations.[20] Mission statements such as "Learning from the Soviet Union, means learning to win" or "No secrets among friends" represented the external version of these contacts.[21] With increasing success in the 1950s, GDR sport grew from its role as a penniless, inexperienced, and needy pupil toward a partnership that often revealed character traits of an "acrimonious rivalry."[22]

In 1966 the two states signed the Treaty of Friendship on the Consolidation and Deepening of the Brotherly Cooperation between the Sport Organizations of the German Democratic Republic and the Union of Sport Societies of the Union of the Socialist Soviet Republics. This treaty refers in its preamble to the Contract about Friendship, Mutual Assistance and Cooperation established on June 12, 1964.[23] With this treaty, the relationship can be considered an "equal partnership."[24] As the 1966 sport friendship treaty was being prepared, the German Gymnastics and Sport Union (DTSB) and the Ministry for Foreign Affairs (MfAA) in East Berlin emphasized that the sport contract was an elaboration and implementation of the political contract of 1964: "In order to guarantee a meaningful cooperation of sport and culture with regard to the work abroad the treaty of friendship is to be based on the cultural agreement between the USSR and the GDR of 1964."[25] The special interest shown by the MfAA originates from its efforts to support a complete accreditation of the GDR in the field of sport in order to achieve its foreign policy goals.

The new (political) alliance contract, signed by Soviet premier Leonid Brezhnev and East German leader Erich Honecker on October 7, 1975, with the title Contract about the Friendship, Cooperation and Mutual Assistance between the Soviet Union and the GDR, was intended to provide a tighter bond between both states, especially in security matters. This 1975 friendship treaty was, like its 1960s predecessor, also followed by a revised form of the sport contracts. On July 26, 1977, Manfred Ewald, president of the DTSB from 1961 to 1988 and president of the NOC of the GDR from 1973 to 1990, and Sergei Pavlov, chairperson of the Soviet sport committee from 1968 to 1983 and president of the Soviet Olympic Committee from 1977 to 1983, signed the Treaty of Further Consolidation and Deepening of Brotherly Friendship and Mutual Cooperation between the Sport Organizations of the German Democratic Republic and the Committee for Physical Culture and Sport at the Council of Ministers of the Union of Socialist Soviet Republics. The revised version of this treaty in 1977 consolidated bilateral cooperation in top-level sport and included an increase in exchange among factory and school teams. In this third phase, the GDR was officially upgraded to "the most important sport partner" of the Soviet Union.[26]

The 1977 treaty was signed during a visit by Pavlov to the Sixth Children and Youth Spartakiad and the Gymnastics and Sportfestival in Leipzig, but this meeting between the leading figures of sport administrators of these two communist brother states hardly mirrored the "good results of the mutual cooperation" mentioned in the treaty.[27] A report by the Soviet general consul in Leipzig not only mentions Ewald's criticism about the lack of preparation by the Soviet partner to comply with the agreed sport meetings and to send high-class athletes, but it also states Pavlov's criticism of the lack of willingness of the GDR to share research results in the field of sport with Soviet scientists.[28] These apparent differences between the public rhetoric of friendship and practical implementation have the typical features of communist propaganda.

A fourth phase may be added as the conflicts between the two contractual parties intensified in the mid-1980s. At the end of 1984 and beginning of 1985, the Four Year Program for Cooperation between the Sport Leaders in the USSR and the GDR for the Olympic cycle until 1988 was not renewed. Although this is not a framework treaty comparable to the friendship treaties of 1966 or 1977, the elaboration of such programs, annual calendars, and so forth can be considered the actual realization of these treaties.[29] Ewald and Marat Gramov, chairperson of the Soviet sport committee and president of the Soviet Olympic Committee from 1983 to 1990, did not sign this agreement.[30] Although this was not a basic treaty or official contract, the facts that difficulties had not been resolved and that the agreement went unsigned between the sport leaders show the extent of the discontent in the sport relationship between the two states.

The function of the sport friendship treaties and their use as propaganda—only allowing the interpretation of a continuing growth of Marxist-Leninist ideals as well as the progress in achievements of the communist society and economy—concealed the growing gap between the pretense of communist ideology and reality. Therefore, in the case of the USSR and the GDR, the *factual* sport relationship is hardly represented within the treaties of friendship. The quality and value of the cooperation depended on the particular goals and expectations. The regular and continuous organizational form of the sport relationship within Europe was determined by three elements: (a) treaties of friendship in sport common among the communist countries, (b) sophisticated forms of bilateral and multilateral cooperation, and (c) the superordinate party institutions and state offices controlling the accomplishment of sport contacts in terms of CPSU (Communist Party of the Soviet Union) expectations. Thus, the framework for sport exchanges was clearly defined within the ideologically predetermined relationship established between the two states in political, economic, and cultural areas. Within these preconditions, each delegation was eager to enforce the wishes and demands of the treaties but also preserve their own interests.

## Goals, Expectations, and Realities

Both the Soviet Union and the GDR developed expectations concerning their bilateral sport relationship that changed according to the developments within sports and within the political interests of each state. The sport contacts can be seen as a mirror of the actual relationship between the two states, while at the same time the sport relationship also depended on these political relations for its own development. In addition, a dividing line must be drawn between common and individual interests. While cooperation brought advantages to the development of the communist world of sport, the expectations of cooperation also included direct gain for each country's own development in the field of sport. Thus, while a mutually beneficial relationship was promoted publicly, at times each state's individual sport goals, especially winning Olympic medals, stood at odds with the aims of the bilateral treaties.

One common interest was to establish sport as a link between the states and especially their people to stabilize communism in society. The contractual agreements between the GDR and the USSR not only served bilateral considerations, but in addition these sport contracts were assigned a "model character for the net of bilateral treaties."[31] The Soviet Union used these treaties of friendship in sport as a basis to stabilize bilateral sport contacts in Eastern Europe and thereby contribute toward an additional safeguard of the political bloc by spreading their influence in a cultural and social area. A frequent and successful exchange of athletes was believed to have a positive effect within the states but also across the communist bloc. The much-flaunted cohesion and efficiency of the communist brotherly bond were supposedly equally demonstrated in cultural fields.

The unity shown in sports was intended to demonstrate the general superiority of communism to a worldwide audience because of the global interest in sports. Sport relations that easily demonstrated the "determined and steadfast friendship that connects our people [Soviet Union and GDR]" were useful for the propaganda department.[32] This unity could hardly be illustrated more clearly elsewhere or to more citizens in the communist bloc than in sport. Reporters therefore covered the Soviet-GDR competitions and training camps, particularly when internationally acclaimed athletes participated. These exchanges moved beyond elite-level sport and also took place at the level of school and factory teams. Visits of individual prominent athletes on special occasions were considered part of the publicly displayed mutual approval. Ewald, for example, asked the Soviet sport leaders to "delegate" the gymnast Ludmilla Turiščeva and the weight lifter Vasilij Alekseje to "express the German-Soviet friendship in a special way" at the Ninth Parliament of the Free German Youth (the communist youth movement of the GDR) on May 29, 1971.[33]

Reports written by Soviet delegates who traveled to the GDR as part of these exchanges noted the special attention given to hospitality and public reactions. Following an international table tennis tournament in 1969, the Soviet delegation stated that "the welcome of the Soviet athletes was very friendly. The competitions were well organized and were happily visited by many spectators."[34] Later that year, the Soviet delegation returning from a judo event noted that "the press addressed a lot of attention to the Soviet athletes. Coaches were interviewed before the competitions about the preparation and chances of our athletes. . . . The organizers devoted a lot of attention to our delegation."[35] The reputation and authority won and confirmed in this way played an important role for both partners. However, this pretense could also be the source of irritation if one party canceled previously arranged competitions or did not send its best athletes. The delegation of the GDR mentioned in talks with the Soviet sport committee in 1967 "that sending weak [Soviet] delegations to the GDR neither enhanced the reputation of the USSR nor supported the authority of the GDR."[36] These reports from both parties show that the two states had a mutual interest in exchanges of high-quality athletic performance and organization.

A further argument used to support the development of cooperation was the optimal use of financial resources. The Soviet delegation, for example, called for a "joint line" of action concerning sport equipment in a speech at the annual conference of communist sport leaders in Varna, Bulgaria, in December 1970. The need to act as a collective was justified because until then sport equipment had been bought abroad, requiring *Valuta* (foreign currencies) and therefore creating an immense financial burden for Eastern bloc states. A further example, also mentioned in this speech, was the shared use of high-altitude training camps. At first the Soviet delegate's comments reiterated the propaganda: collective training camps would support the feeling of internationalism, and "we [the Soviet delegation] are sure that the true friendship among the youths of our countries emerges especially during these training camps."[37] A few paragraphs later, the delegate mentioned the financial benefits gained by shared high-altitude training camps.[38] Although the Soviet Union advocated for a pooling of financial resources in sport, a cost-efficient approach toward the cooperation between the USSR and the GDR often went against each state's own interests. Nonetheless, this argument for saving costs by acting together, while not publicly proclaimed, later became less important because of the increasing sport rivalry between the GDR and Soviet Union, as will be shown later in this article.

In fact, the common goals and expectations established for the sport relationship between both communist countries hardly developed beyond the official rhetoric of friendship and the promise of united communist appearance in sport during the 1960s and 1970s. The common position publicly presented during the 1984 Olympic Games in Los Angeles and the questions surrounding the increasing professionalism and commercialism of international sports and the Olympic movement imply that, within sport, political consensus existed between the two allies. However, examining the Soviet–East German relationship at a deeper level than the public statements and propagandized friendship demonstrates that individual interests were not balanced on every issue. While the Soviet Union sought to create a counterpropaganda campaign for the Los Angeles Olympics and directed the discussions and decisions taken, the GDR played along or rather had to agree to these actions. On the other hand, the battle against the ongoing move to professionalism and commercialism was mainly an East German priority, whereas the Soviet Union took on a more open position toward this question.[39]

The Soviet Union and the GDR had common expectations concerning international relations issues as they related to sport. The Soviets not only wanted to present a unified and homogeneous appearance of the communist sport organizations but also wanted to demonstrate their leadership within the communist bloc. The recognition of the GDR under international law was clearly a major point of interest for both countries.[40] They arranged their sport politics and corresponding activities accordingly, including, as Heather Dichter has shown in chapter 1, their decisions to withdraw from sporting events in response to travel bans imposed on East German athletes. After the GDR sport federations were accepted by the respective international federations and the IOC, the venues of the Olympic Games in 1972 (Munich) and in 1980 (Moscow) became the new basis for joint actions. Now questions concerning West Berlin or the name of the "NOC for Germany" (as the West German Olympic Committee called itself) became key topics of sport political discussions and the foundation of joint expectations.

This presentation of the allegedly "common interests" reveals that in many cases the interest in successful sport achievements for each country was considered of the upmost importance. Approaches toward both reducing costs and increasing efficiency or the realization of the idea of a "steadfast friendship" could not withstand the increasingly intensifying sport rivalry between the two states. Both sport systems developed according to the Olympic motto *citius, altius, fortius* (faster, higher, stronger) and aimed for maximum success. Thus sport contacts were not limited to exchanges in the fields of science and training theories. These areas were, of course, central to the sport friendship, but the shifting focus to several other individual interests shows that the sport relationship was also accompanied by additional expectations.

In the first decades of its existence, the GDR readily accepted the support offered by the Soviets to create its sports system and to expand the network of children and youth sport schools.[41] By the middle of the 1960s, then, the GDR had developed into a sport power. Just as the GDR relied on Soviet help to gain acceptance within the international system, East German sport also needed Soviet support to achieve international recognition. Although East Germany was a full member within the communist bloc, the country was not recognized fully by all sport federations or the IOC. The GDR thus knew the Soviet Union was its strongest ally in its quest for international recognition in sport. Nonetheless, a report issued by the GDR embassy in Moscow in 1958 shows that the East Germans did not always find their issues taken as seriously as they wished by their Soviet comrades. This report criticized the Soviet lack of knowledge on the special German situation in sports: "Comrade Dr. Schuster explained . . . that leading sport officials from the socialist countries did and do not always have a decisive definition of our German policy [*unsere Deutschlandpolitik*] and therefore do not always understand the specific situation of the GDR. To a certain extent this also applies to Soviet sport officials."[42]

Although East German sport needed Soviet support for its development both domestically and internationally, this relationship also created an ambivalent situation. On the one hand, the increase in sport success was the emancipation of GDR sport, and its leaders wished to distance themselves from their Soviet partners to act without restrictions or having to share these achievements. On the other hand, the political and propaganda connections had increased from years of Soviet support as well as political realities. There was no way that sport would detract from this situation. East German sport officials used the sport relationship with the Soviet Union to actively fulfill their duties as the "smaller brother" in the communist bloc and as a junior partner to the USSR. This strategy was demonstrated in speeches by GDR delegates at conferences or meetings in which they explicitly emphasized the superiority of the communist system in the field of sport and recognized the important role which the Soviet achievements had played. Special gratitude was publicly and explicitly addressed to the comrades from the Soviet Union.[43] The dutiful deference was also shown in telegrams and congratulations for state holidays, party meetings, and special remembrance days sent by the East German sport organization to the sport committee of the Soviet Union, such as the celebratory telegram sent by the president of the GDR Olympic Committee to the Soviet Olympic Committee on the occasion of the fiftieth anniversary of the October Revolution.[44] Furthermore, the sport leaders of the GDR made efforts to support the Soviet position at communist sport meetings to ensure that it received no interference.[45]

If Soviet officials criticized a lack of cooperation among GDR sport officials, then Ewald would skillfully deflect any criticism by taking the position of the "grateful" partner in his response. He included the ideological aims and interpretation of cooperation in his arguments exploiting the propaganda rhetoric of friendship and leaving his Soviet counterpart no room for argument. An example of Ewald's strategy of gratitude and deference becomes apparent in his response to criticism expressed by his Soviet colleague Pavlov during an autumn 1969 meeting: "I devoutly believe that we . . . do not have to accuse ourselves of anything according to our cooperation with you. I have often emphasized that we have been very, very much supported by you in order to achieve our current level as we always did everything to cooperate openly and frank. I have emphasized that we shall never forget this and that we are willing to tell our Soviet comrades everything we know. We wouldn't have understood Marxism-Leninism and the current politics correctly if we thought that we, our little country, could do anything alone."[46] The Soviet Union also believed that strong GDR sport achievements, particularly over West Germany, could be effectively used in propaganda to demonstrate the apparent superiority of the communist sport system. The general results of communist countries at the Olympic Games were regularly honored during the annual conferences of communist sport leaders and were interpreted as evidence for this alleged superiority. An overview of the percentage of Olympic medals won by communist countries from the 1952 through 1972 Games was published in an information bulletin for the 1976 Montreal Olympics. In 1952, the first postwar Games with Soviet participation, communist states won 30.1 percent of all medals, and in 1972 that number had increased to a staggering 56.1 percent.[47]

The USSR, however, did not want to see its leading position in the world of sports or its status as the leading power within the communist bloc put at risk. The increasing success of GDR athletes and the concurrent increasing isolation of the East German sport system from the outside world—and at times from the Soviet Union—evoked criticism and lack of understanding with their partner to the east. In the 1960s the Soviet Union expected and demanded an equal exchange. The phrase "To learn from the Soviet Union, means to learn how to win," with which the Soviet Union had readily presented its sport system to GDR officials, was meant to be followed by equally mutual and frank cooperation. In a way, the Soviet Union believed it was time for the East Germans to "repay" for their years of education and instruction. Thus the meeting between the two sport leaders, Pavlov and Ewald, can be seen as a rare occasion in which confidential matters, expectations, and criticism were expressed. In an attempt to decrease tensions, Pavlov openly pointed at the changed situation, the increasing success of GDR athletes, and the Soviet Union's expectations of an exchange in which each party gives and takes its share.[48] He warned that the new power of the GDR sport system had to be considered in future planning so that both parties would profit from the exchange. The special interest of the Soviet Union was reflected in the expectation to reform its sport relationship to the GDR so that the one-sided giving would be replaced by a balanced form of give-and-take.

The change in GDR sport, from a little brother requiring the help of the Soviet Union to create and develop the communist structures to a powerhouse at the international level, meant that each state's individual interests and needs were drastically different than they had been in 1950. Mutual cooperation and success by both states on the playing field enabled both the Soviet Union and GDR to publicly proclaim the superiority of the communist system, as both a way of life and as an organizer of sport. East Germany relied on the support from the Soviet Union more than the help of any other country in its quest for international recognition, and the communist bloc states could save valuable funds by combining training camps. However, as the GDR became one of the Soviet Union's biggest competitors for prestigious Olympic medals, the cracks in the sport friendship started to appear, and the intense rivalry created by sport became quite apparent in the Soviet–East German relationship.

## The Organizational Structures of the Sport Friendship

The friendship treaties and expectations established by them mainly constitute the political-contractual side of the sport relationship between the USSR and the GDR. The ideological connection of both states and the acts of brotherly friendship within the communist bloc set high standards and requirements in sport. After the signing of the first treaty of friendship in sport in 1966, the practical realization of the treaty's goals had to be assured to prevent the agreement from turning into empty propaganda. Therefore, the Ständige Gemeinsame Kommission (SGK, or Permanent Joint Commission) was founded in spring 1967. The vice president or deputy chairperson of each sport organization was responsible for the implementation of the agreed-upon points of the treaty of friendship.[49] Similar commissions were also established to manage the sport relations between other communist states. These commissions worked out annual plans to manage the tasks set by each treaty in the areas of training, competitions, sport science, educational matters, leisure and recreational sport, and youth sports.[50]

At first it had been planned that the SGK would meet two or three times a year as needed.[51] After that initial year, meetings were held every year or every other year alternately in the USSR or in the GDR, although the meetings were not held with any regularity. In 1967 the SGK met three times, in 1968 only once, and the fifth meeting did not take place until September 1970.[52] While the SGK was tasked with carrying out the decisions taken at a higher level, it also had to create a network of working groups (*Arbeitsgruppen,* or AG) for specialized issues. The first four temporary AGs were established in March 1967: AG1 for Olympic preparation and acclimatization (regarding the altitude concerns about the 1968 Mexico City Olympics), AG2 for research in high-proficiency sport, AG3 for sport facilities and equipment, and AG4 for cooperation among universities and academic institutions.[53] In September 1968 the AG for medical assistance was added.

In addition to the AGs, expert groups were put together with members from sport federations or departments of the umbrella federation. Work and cooperation within the SGK and its subgroups required time to be institutionalized, although reports dating from September 1968 show that the GDR delegates were not always satisfied with the speed and process of actions.[54] The regular meetings of the SGK and their documentation in the form of internal reports and public statements may be considered a mirror of the Soviet–East German sport relations. On the one hand, communiqués were published detailing the events of the meetings, with brief overviews of the topics discussed. On the other hand, each delegation wrote detailed reports for its own sport organization, including less euphorically formulated minutes of the talks. These reports, which were not intended for public knowledge, convey a more accurate representation of the atmosphere and the quality of these meetings. The set phrase for the first few years was the description that the meeting had taken place in "an atmosphere of friendship and complete agreement."[55] The report from the sixteenth meeting of the SGK in 1979 mentioned the "open and factual, but always amicable and constructive atmosphere."[56] By 1981 the set term of "complete agreement" had been replaced by the phrase "mutual understanding."[57] The different terminology reflects the nuances within the sport relationship as it changed over the time and the increasing distance between the two partners.

Although the SGK was established as a commission to make decisions and agree upon plans, and both parties prepared meticulously for these meetings, the true power of decision remained at the highest level with the two sport leaders, Pavlov and Ewald. These two men solved problems that could not be solved at lower levels. This again meant that questions and minor details concerning such issues as training camps, exchange of athletes, or visiting delegations were discussed by the men with the most power in East German and Soviet sport even though these organizational matters had been delegated to lower committees.

An additional organizational area addressed by the SGK in the AGs and within bilateral talks at the highest level was the "reconcilement of mutual questions of interest within national and international sport movements."[58] Within this broad topic was discussion about the "current problems of the international Olympic movement." The regular and frequent contacts at the executive level and below (SGK) were used to find agreement on matters of joint interest prior to the annual conferences of the communist sport leaders. Previously determined expectations and preferences were expressed by ballot or in plenum discussion. This kind of tactical cooperation and reconcilement is explicitly mentioned in the GDR delegation's report about the annual conference in Pyongyang in 1983: "Thereupon the Polish comrades withdrew their suggestion. Our delegation did not give an opinion on this matter, as the Soviet comrades (due to an earlier ballot) did not attach great importance to it and we considered a discussion about formalities inappropriate at this point of the conference."[59]

Thus the organizational structures established between the GDR and Soviet Union were especially designed for the public staging of this sport friendship. The SGK was mainly responsible for the implementation and elaboration of annual plans and competition calendars. The multitude of commissions, task forces, and expert groups leave no doubt that the sport relationship was constantly discussed, analyzed, and evaluated by the two states. These structures demonstrate that implementation of practical sport contacts and transnational exchanges required an accordingly extensive bureaucracy.

## The Challenge of Putting Ideas into Practice

Even with a mutually beneficial sport relationship between the Soviet Union and the GDR fostered since the creation of East Germany, frustrations with the organization of the sport contacts grew on both sides. Until the sport friendship treaty of 1966 finally determined who was responsible for problems or misunderstandings, the delegations regularly contacted their embassies in order to express resentment and discontent. The establishment of the SGK and its subcommittees after the signing of the 1966 treaty did not end the conflicts concerning sport. Both Pavlov (and his successor Gramov) in the Soviet Union and Ewald in the GDR addressed the problems that arose in the bilateral sport relationship, and they also continued to involve their governments and foreign ministries in efforts to resolve these issues or repair the animosity created by sport disputes. Particularly as East Germany made the battle for athletic supremacy, which had been a two-country showdown between the Soviet Union and the United States, into a three-country contest, the mutual friendship between the communist bloc allies became increasingly strained. Sport problems frequently became a point of diplomatic discussion, and the two states did not always act as friendly to each other as the mutual treaties of friendship outlined. Instead, each state became more selfish and private with respect to sport knowledge and training, refusing to share with its communist brothers.

In contrast to the propagandized friendship within the communist bloc, Soviet relations with other states of the bloc did not always present themselves as open and flexible as one might have expected. For example, the Soviet Union remained a country with strict, bureaucratic entry regulations for citizens from allied states. These travel regulations contributed to a relatively weak sport exchange between the GDR and the Soviet Union on a medium and lower level even though a highly bureaucratic organizational structure existed specifically to arrange these contacts.[60] Structural and organizational hurdles such as applying for travel visas and entry allowances or the maintenance of a formal protocol, which was to be strictly followed, hardly left any room for spontaneous visits among friends, joint regattas, or races held at short notice or any other type of friendly international sport contacts that determine regional or even local exchanges. The centralist control, typical for the communist system, determined the character of sport relations between countries. Thus sport contacts between the Soviet Union and the GDR focused mainly at the level of elite sports and in the fields of science and sport technology. These limitations, however, did not mean that the relatively low rate of sport exchange guaranteed either excellent athletic performances or a smooth process.

An incident that took place during a friendly competition between Soviet and East German divers in Moscow in 1958 clearly shows that both parties had to get acclimated to the mutual sport friendship and its associated rites. By mistake the West German anthem was played instead of the anthem of the GDR during the opening ceremony of the event in Moscow's Luzhniki Stadium. This error not surprisingly caused quite a stir and some irritation among the delegates from the GDR. Although an apology was offered by the organizers and a "specially called" representative of the Soviet sport committee, this "embarrassing incident" turned into a topic of diplomatic talks.[61] The MfAA instructed its embassy in Moscow in the following way: "We ask you to mention the incident of playing the national anthem of the Federal Republic . . . at a suitable moment in the Third European Department. We are aware that it was not intended to play this anthem in front of our athletes, but we should not ignore this matter in silence."[62] The mix-up was not without consequences for the responsible technician: both he and the director of the natatorium were fired, and the director of the Lushniki Stadium received a formal reprimand.[63]

Such a faux pas must be regarded as a special case. However, sport officials from both parties felt discontent in the bilateral sport activities. In March 1957 a meeting between representatives of the East German embassy and the Soviet sport committee took place to discuss the sport relationship. Both parties complained about the unsatisfactory organization of sport between the two countries, but at the same time both sides expressed the desire to increase contacts. The Soviet representatives also expressed their strong dissatisfaction with the intent behind some of the exchanges, arguing that sending Soviet coaches to the GDR should not be for the purpose of coaching East German athletes but should instead be for meeting with GDR coaches to share techniques and experiences.[64] This criticism of the one-sidedness of the sport relationship was increasingly expressed and discussed in later years.

The increasing number of complaints brought forward by the head of a delegation, such as having too little milk for the entire team in a Moscow hotel or the dirty gym at a volleyball match against Dynamo Berlin, were not resolved in so-called comradely meetings between the delegation heads but rather developed into "diplomatic actions with an attached bitter aftertaste."[65] After such complaints had been forwarded by the East German embassy in Moscow to the Soviet sport committee, the attaché for culture at the Soviet embassy in Berlin expressed the complaints brought forward by the Soviet sport committee, addressing the East German DTSB. To stop this ping-pong game of complaints the East German sport federation requested that the GDR embassy reprimand any dissatisfied head of a delegation "who expressed such inane complaints." In its closing remarks, this letter emphasized the excellent relations between the Soviet Union and the GDR. The aim of this letter, to prevent any further harm and to soothe the tension that had developed, is just as obvious as the chosen tactics of the DTSB to accept its "faults" and, by doing so, once more acknowledging the oft-cited "moral superiority" of the Soviet partner.[66]

In the following years, the Soviet sport leaders would call the political powers to pressure the East German sport officials when necessary. These diplomatic contacts were purposefully used either to strengthen the leading political role of the Soviet Union or to push for achieving goals that the bilateral meetings, despite the acclaimed atmosphere of friendship and the publicly promoted mutual understanding, could not find any common agreement. In late 1979, Pavlov addressed a report to the Central Committee of the CPSU on "a few aspects about the sporting cooperation with the GDR" and explained that representatives of the DTSB had pursued a position unacceptable from a Soviet point of view concerning the questions of doping controls prior to the Olympic Games in Moscow in 1980.[67] Because Pavlov had not been able to change the position of the East German sport officials, which he considered a danger for the "socialist authority," he suggested that "the embassy of the USSR in the GDR should be asked to inform the central committee of the Socialist Unity Party of Germany about this matter."[68] By doing so, the responsible officials of the DTSB would be brought back on track. Probably the most prominent example of well-directed political pressure to ensure the solidarity of East German sport officials was the decision to boycott the

Olympic Games in Los Angeles in 1984 following the Soviet example. In his 1994 memoir, Ewald remembered that the boycott request was presented directly to him in a meeting with Honecker. Ewald, also a member of the Politburo, was told that any special or individual decision by the GDR in the question of participation would cause the Soviet Union to apply economic pressure.[69]

The Soviet–East German sport relationship changed as a result of the increasingly successful performance of GDR athletes and the corresponding increase in their sport leaders' self-confidence. These transformations were accompanied by an intensified rivalry that was addressed at the highest organizational level within sport. Until the end of the 1960s, the Soviet side had shown patience and even forbearance in the handling of expectations and considerations toward its East German partners. In 1968, however, the situation had changed within Soviet sport: the results of the Soviet team at the Summer Olympics in Mexico City had been officially announced as weak and triggered a reorganization of official structures.[70] In this context, the meeting between Pavlov and Ewald in September 1969 clearly displayed the new position taken by the Soviet Union. Pavlov addressed Ewald: "You are now a very dangerous sporting rival. Therefore, we must consider mainly our own interests [in setting up an exchange plan]. Of course we want—and I say this frankly—to see our interests fulfilled."[71] This was not the last time that this rivalry was mentioned, as it increasingly was raised in Soviet–East German sport meetings.[72]

But Pavlov's comment in which he not only calls the GDR athletes rivals but also classifies them as "very dangerous" is an unmistakable caesura. Pavlov signaled very clearly that a continuing of the sport relations under the conditions up to this point was no longer acceptable to the Soviet Union. The unusual nature of this meeting becomes obvious in the fact that—against the usual protocol—problems within the sport relationship and controversial positions were directly addressed. It seems characteristic of the centralized sport systems and the structured sport exchange that disagreements and controversial positions were raised at the highest level. Yet the mutual criticism was balanced and equally shared within this meeting. Pavlov was eager to influence the relations in such a way that a shift toward a more equal giving and sharing could be achieved. The Soviet sport leader unmistakably warned the GDR not to isolate itself in the area of sport.[73] At the same time, Ewald rejected any criticism of deficient preparedness and repeatedly emphasized the limitations of exchanges at the highest levels, particularly the difficult-to-control sharing of scientific and training practical experience among coaches.[74]

Shortly after this frank and clear discussion, a Soviet delegation visited East Germany November 20–30, 1969, to gain a comprehensive understanding of child and youth sport in the GDR and to study the principles behind East German success in order to adopt similar approaches in Soviet sport. At the end of the visit, a communiqué was published according to the traditional protocol between the two countries, expressing the official evaluation of the sporting relations. There was—of course—no sign of the discontent, mutual criticism, or allegations that had dominated the September meeting.[75] Rather, the public display once more contained glossy, content-free phrases that seemed typical of the propagandized friendship.

Even though a more open cooperation and exchange had been arranged following the critical 1969 talks, the Soviet side grew increasingly doubtful about the real willingness of their East German partners. A report issued by the Soviet delegation after visiting Kienbaum in the GDR March 18–25, 1970, documents the following: "During the complete visit not a single athlete was in Kienbaum, the GDR delegates explained [that this was the case] in order not to disturb the discussions!"[76] While the East Germans tried to broaden the arranged exchanges on a practical level between athletes and coaches, they also tried to limit the transfer of knowledge within these friendly sport exchanges. They evaded requests or concrete demands of Soviet delegates and only made visits to research institutions possible after several repeated pointed inquiries. The East Germans delayed the transmission of particular information with the comment that it was forbidden to accept offers without having the corresponding confirmation by the DTSB federations.[77] Although Pavlov had warned the East Germans not to retreat into self-isolation, GDR officials hardly changed their behavior. The phrase "no secrets among friends" used in the early sport relationship and that offered the GDR so many advantages for the development of its sport system had clearly lost its meaning.

The Soviet Union began to realize that the drawback was not limited to the bilateral relations with the GDR and started to suspect far-reaching consequences.[78] Soviet officials noticed increasing East German bilateral sport exchanges with other communist states, and they suspected the

GDR was attempting to isolate the Soviet sport movement within the communist bloc.[79] Further discontent grew when East German athletes withdrew from competitions in the Soviet Union while simultaneously increasing their sport contacts with Western countries. In 1981 a rescheduling of a track-and-field meeting in the USSR caused serious discord among Soviet officials when they discovered that East German athletes had competed against American athletes during the initially arranged period.[80] Such forms of malpractice and breach of contract were usually discussed at meetings of the SGK as well as among the sport leaders.

Soviet sport officials not only applied political pressure through the foreign ministries but also implemented their own restrictions on the East Germans when they believed the GDR's erratic behavior was endangering certain goals. Especially in the early 1970s, the Soviets were less willing to allow the East German "friends" to use special training centers in the USSR, which was a clear about-face from the 1960s. In 1970 the Soviets withdrew their offer to let the GDR use the training camp in Sachalin prior to the 1972 Winter Olympics in Sapporo. They offered the excuse of too few jumping facilities and not enough hotels.[81] In 1967 the Soviet side had provided the GDR with more training opportunities in the high-altitude training camp at Zaghkadsor after the GDR agreed to build and finance twelve bungalows there. An inquiry by the GDR as to whether its athletes could use those facilities from 1970 to 1972 went unanswered by the Soviet sport committee, which remained "undecided because of the quality of the camp and the requirements of additional lodging of foreign athletes." The cancellation in 1971 of GDR use of the Zaghkadsor training camp was finally justified by the explanation that two-thirds of the facilities were not available and that even Soviet athletes had to use training facilities abroad.[82]

Even these alleged sanctions did not affect the formal transfer of knowledge between the GDR and the USSR or shift it to a voluntary basis. After a ten-day visit to the GDR to increase their knowledge of the "scientific information in the area of sport," Soviet sport officials openly reported the sealing-off of East German sport science. In East Germany, the sport science information plan had been classified as highly confidential and only intended for internal use. It had required an immense effort and persuasion on the part of these officials to access such an information plan from the previous year.[83]

These events and reports demonstrate that the sport relationship hardly improved after the frank encounter in the late 1960s. In 1971 Pavlov attempted a new strategy by trying to publicly emphasize a "new phase within the sport relationship." He downplayed the difficulties within the exchange and maintained that the time had come for a new and better relationship and therefore required a broadening of the contacts.[84] This topic was discussed at the November 1971 meeting of the SGK. The report issued by the East German delegation includes the claims and demands expressed by the Soviet representatives. The new need to focus on the most important questions, with an appeal for "real cooperation" and the implicit need to "save financial resources and human research capacities,"[85] can be interpreted as the first effort toward making the sport exchange more directed and efficient. The result was the focus—or rather limitation—of high-level exchanges to four sports (track and field, swimming, ice skating, and skiing) and six scientific fields.[86]

Yet even this narrowing of exchanges did not guarantee smooth relations or a more balanced exchange. A meeting of the Soviet sport committee on January 29, 1983, addressed the "unsatisfying preparation" of Soviet athletes for the 1984 Winter Games in Sarajevo. The Soviet officials noted their displeasure with the East Germans' behavior, particularly the imbalanced exchange of knowledge. The Soviets questioned why Soviet athletes were not allowed to train in the GDR while East German athletes trained in Kazakhstan. The head of the sport committee did not allow the discussion to get out of hand, but the minutes recorded his comment that "the thing is, they can study and copy us better than we can [study them]."[87] The final report from the Soviet Olympic Committee president, Gramov, to the central committee of the CPSU about the results of the 1984 Olympics in Sarajevo failed to mention that the GDR won more gold medals and stood atop the (unofficial) medal count, ahead of the Soviet Union.[88] This intentional omission reveals that the Soviet sport leadership did not judge the superiority of the GDR sport system as a communist success but rather as an unwelcome shift of sport dominance within the bilateral competition.

However, it was not only the East German side that withheld information. The Soviet side did not always openly promote all decisions or activities either. The GDR felt inadequately informed about the sport relationship between the Soviet Union and the Federal Republic of Germany. This unease was apparent in the issues that the East Germans compiled in their "thesis for the summit-talk" in preparation for their meeting with Soviet sport leaders in Moscow in May 1968. The East German representatives seemed surprised by previous meetings between Pavlov and Willi Daume, president of the (West) German Sport Federation from 1950 to 1970 and president of the NOC for Germany from 1961 to 1992, which had taken place without any prior consultation with the GDR. The East German officials only discovered that the USSR and West Germany planned a joint training camp for divers by watching West German television. The East Germans felt ignored and sought to address this issue at the summit talks.[89] A further example of the Soviet double-cross was the statement to the DTSB in which the Soviet sport committee said that no negotiations with the (West) German Sport Federation would take place during the Olympic Games in Munich in 1972.[90] In fact, official talks regarding the Soviet–West German sport relationship took place during the Olympic Games between Pavlov, V. I. Koval, and West German representatives Wilhelm Kregel, Hans Gmelin, and Karl-Heinz Gieseler.[91] As this meeting was not arranged at short notice, the Soviet side must have passed false information to its East German counterparts in order to prevent any demands or criticism concerning this meeting.

The Soviet–East German sport relationship, initially viewed as a mutually beneficial friendship, transformed as the GDR became a rival for Olympic medals. Both sides became increasingly suspicious of each other, refraining from sharing knowledge and training camps and criticizing their communist brothers to their governments. Although this relationship was clearly becoming more fractured and difficult to maintain, these problems nonetheless remained hidden from public view. The two states continued to promote their treaties of sport friendship, even if the wording for some of the brotherly support was tempered in later years.

## Conclusion

The early motto "No secrets among friends" hints at the hope and expectations of the Soviet–East German friendship in sport. The description of the various facets of these sporting contacts and their development, however, has conveyed that goodwill and political alliance alone were not sufficient to guarantee smooth cooperation in the field of sport. Increasing rivalry, as well as individual national interests, prevented the maximum development of the Soviet–East German sport relationship. The attempt to structure the sport relationship primarily through elite-level sport demonstrates the failure of the publicly promoted brotherly solidarity and the unlimited exchange of knowledge and experience in the field of sport.

While secrets are not often kept among friends, individuals nonetheless must look after their own advantages and knowledge when it concerns serious rivals. The bilateral sport relationship between the GDR and Soviet Union has also shown that the changes within the relationship were caused mainly by the increasing success of the GDR in international sport, which triggered different expectations by each side of the friendship. While the GDR increasingly sought to maintain control over avoiding the transfer of sport knowledge, the Soviet side thought that East German sport development had progressed to a point where a more even balance between the two states was necessary in their relationship. Finally, the limitation of any exchange in high-proficiency sport to four selected sports was designed to ensure a high quality. Before international sport had fully accepted East Germany, the Soviets publicly proclaimed solidarity with their GDR comrades. Once the GDR received international recognition from the Olympic family, Soviet representatives in the IOC reduced their open statements on solidarity with the GDR and initiatives that supported East German interests.[92]

In summary, the quality of the sporting relationships between the Soviet Union and the GDR did not correlate with the official rhetoric of friendship. Discontent, criticisms of loyalty and obligation, and a lack of frankness and honesty could be found on both sides. The Soviet–East German relationship cannot be characterized as simply a dominant power and submissive little brother. Both sides contributed to the complicated relationship between the two biggest sport powers behind the Iron Curtain. While the implicit superiority of the big brother Soviet Union initially fostered ideas of mutual cooperation between the two states, particularly as the Soviet Union supported East Germany within the international system, the increasing success achieved by East German sport at the international level led to a growing and intense rivalry within the communist bloc. Whereas sport was often viewed during the Cold War as a way to bring athletes from both sides of the Iron Curtain together, behind that wall sport could also, at times, contribute to diplomatic flare-ups and increased tensions that undermined the publicly proclaimed steadfast friendship and brotherly help. The goals each state sought to achieve, both at home and especially at the international level, in many cases conflicted with the mutually agreed-upon goals for the two states together or the communist bloc as a whole.

## Notes

1. In a summit talk with Soviet sport leader Sergei Pavlov in 1969, East German sport leader Manfred Ewald said, "There is hardly anything we have not adapted or continued to develop taken from the Soviet Union." Protocol "Niederschrift über eine Besprechung mit Vertretern der sowjetischen Sportleitung vom 15./16.9.1969 (Moskau und Ulan Bator)," October 28, 1969, Stiftung Archiv der Parteien und Massenorganisationen der DDR, Berlin (hereafter SAPMO), DY 12/3159.

2. This movement developed at the beginning of the 1860s as an expression of the Slavic quest for independence and national autonomy.

3. James Riordan, "The USSR," in *Sport under Communism: The U.S.S.R., Czechoslovakia, The G.D.R., China, Cuba,* ed. James Riordan (Montreal: McGill-Queen's University Press, 1978), 16–19.

4. Michail Prozumenshtshikov, *Bol'shoj sport i bol'shaja politika* (Moscow: Rosspen, 2004), 168.

5. Barbara Keys, "The Dictatorship of Sport: Nationalism, Internationalism, and Mass Culture in the 1930s," PhD diss., Harvard University, 2001, 173.

6. "The [Soviet] press was . . . filled with exhortations to break records; books and pamphlets tabulating current Soviet records urged sportsmen on to new heights. Initially the chairman of the Physical Culture Council called for Soviet athletes 'to break all records set by bourgeois sportsmen . . . within two or three years.'" Ibid., 217.

7. Prozumenshtshikov, *Bol'shoj sport,* 14.

8. Uta Balbier, *Kalter Krieg auf der Aschenbahn: Der deutsch-deutsche Sport 1950–1972; Eine politische Geschichte* (Paderborn: Schöning, 2007); Martin H. Geyer, "On the Road to a German 'Postnationalism'? Athletic Competition between the Two German States in the Era of Konrad Adenauer," *German Politics and Society* 25, no. 2 (2007): 140–67; G. A. Carr, "The Involvement of Politics in the Sporting Relationships of East and West Germany, 1945–1972," *Journal of Sport History* 7, no. 1 (1980), 40–51; Steven Ungerleider, *Faust's Gold: Inside the East German Doping Machine* (New York: St. Martin's, 2001); Paul Dimeo, *A History of Drug Use in Sport 1876–1976* (London: Routledge, 2007); and Rob Beamish and Ian Ritchie, *Fastest, Highest, Strongest: A Critique of High-Performance Sport* (London: Routledge, 2006).

9. Norbert Lehmann, *Internationale Sportbeziehungen und Sportpolitik der DDR* (Münster: Lit, 1986), 522–38; Gunter Holzweißig, *Diplomatie im Trainingsanzug: Sport als politisches Instrument der DDR in den innerdeutschen und internationalen*

*Beziehungen* (Munich/Vienna: Oldenbourg, 1981), 89–96; Hans Joachim Teichler, "Vom Lehrling zum Musterschüler und Konkurrenten: Die sportpolitischen Beziehungen der DDR zur UDSSR [*sic*]," in *Proceedings of the 6th Congress of the International Society for the History of Physical Education and Sport "Sport and Politics"* (July 14–19, 1999, Budapest), ed. Katalin Szikora (Budapest: Semmelweis University, 2002), 296–303; and Willi Knecht, "DDR-Leistungssport wird zum sowjetischen Trauma," *Deutschland Archiv* 9 (1976): 945–50.

10. Holzweißig, *Diplomatie im Trainingsanzug*, 89.

11. Teichler, "Vom Lehrling," 296–303.

12. Knecht, "DDR-Leistungssport," 945–50.

13. Günther Wonneberger, *Körperkultur und Sport in der DDR: Gesellschaftswissenschaftliches Lehrmaterial* (Berlin East: Sportverlag, 1982), 138–46.

14. Shades are only traceable by analyzing the chosen set phrases within the brotherly declarations.

15. Holzweißig, *Diplomatie im Trainingsanzug*, 96.

16. See Heather Dichter's chapter in this volume.

17. Harold E. Wilson Jr., "The Golden Opportunity: Romania's Political Manipulation of the 1984 Los Angeles Olympic Games," *Olympika* 3 (1994): 83–97.

18. Lehmann, *Internationale Sportbeziehungen*, 522–38.

19. Ibid., 523–24. For further analysis of the Soviet influence on sport in the Soviet Occupation Zone, also see Walter Schulz, "Die Stellung der Kultur- und Sportpolitik im System der Auswärtigen Politik der Deutschen Demokratischen Republik und ihre Bedeutung für das Staatsbewusstsein der DDR-Bevölkerung," inaugural diss., Rheinische Friedrich-Wilhelms-Universität Bonn, 1978, 75–76.

20. Holzweißig, *Diplomatie im Trainingsanzug*, 91.

21. Lehmann, *Internationale Sportbeziehungen*, 524; Teichler, "Vom Lehrling," 297; and Schulz, *Die Stellung*, 76.

22. Holzweißig, *Diplomatie im Trainingsanzug*, 91.

23. Schulz, *Die Stellung*, 78.

24. Lehmann, *Internationale Sportbeziehungen*, 525.

25. Memorandum, International Department of the MfAA, "Vermerk über eine Beratung mit Genosse Heinze, Sekretär des DTSB, beim Bundesvorstand des DTSB in Berlin am 18. April 1966," April 18, 1966, Politisches Archiv des Auswärtigen Amts, Berlin (hereafter PA AA), MfAA B, Bd. 999/69.

26. Lehmann, *Internationale Sportbeziehungen*, 537.

27. These took place from July 11 until August 2, 1977, in the Zentralstadion in Leipzig. Contract "Vertrag über die weitere Festigung und Vertiefung . . . ," July 26, 1977, SAPMO, DY 12/6359.

28. In this context, Ewald criticized that the Soviet sport leaders sent second-rate athletes to encounters in the GDR, while they sent world-class athletes to competitions in capitalist countries. Protocol, general consulate of the USSR in Leipzig, "Bericht zum VI. Turn- und Sportfest sowie 6. Kinder- und Jugendspartakiade in

Leipzig", [July 1977], Rossiskij Gosudarstevennoj Archiv Novij Istroii, Moscow (hereafter RGANI), f. 5, op. 73, d. 303.

29. Assessment "Einschätzung des gegenwärtigen Standes unserer [DDR] Beziehungen zum Komitee für Körperkultur und Sport beim Ministerrat der UdSSR," [1969], SAPMO, DY 12/2450.

30. Memorandum "Aktennotiz über ein Gespräch zwischen den Vizepräsidenten des DTSB der DDR, Genossen Prof. Dr. Röder, und dem Stellvertreter des Vorsitzenden des Komitees für Körperkultur und Sport beim Ministerrat der UdSSR, Genossen Kolessov, am 10.5.1985 in Moskau," May 10, 1985, SAPMO, DY 12/3181.

31. Holzweißig, *Diplomatie im Trainingsanzug,* 91.

32. "Feste und unverbrüchliche Freundschaft, die unsere Völker [Sowjetunion und DDR] verbindet," taken from Assessment "Einschätzung des gegenwärtigen Standes unserer [DDR] Beziehungen zum Komitee für Körperkultur und Sport beim Ministerrat der UdSSR," [1969], SAPMO, DY 12/2450.

33. Memorandum "Aktennotiz über ein Gespräch mit dem Genossen Kowal, Leiter der Hauptabteilung für internationale Verbindungen des Komitees für Körperkultur und Sport der UdSSR, 31.3.-1.4.1971," [April 1971], SAPMO, DY 12/3181.

34. Report "Bericht über die Teilnahme sowjetischer Sportler am internationalen Tischtennis-Turnier in der DDR (Potsdam, 5.-8. Februar 1969)," [February 1969], Gosudarstvennoj Archiv Rossikoj Federazii, Moscow (hereafter GARF), f. 7576, op. 31, d. 315.

35. Report "Bericht über die Teilnahme der Sportler der UdSSR am internationalen Turnier 'Freundschaft' im Judo, 19.-21.12.1969 Berlin [Ost], DDR 1.-7.07.1969," [1969], GARF, f. 7576, op. 31, d. 315.

36. Report "Bericht über die Beratungen mit der Sportleitung der UdSSR und Tagung der Ständigen Gemeinsamen Kommission in der Zeit vom 1. bis 4. Februar 1967 in Moskau," [February 1967], SAPMO, DY 12/3180.

37. Paper "Referat des Delegationsleiters des Komitees für Körperkultur und Sport beim Ministerrat der UdSSR bei der Jahreskonferenz der Sportleitungen sozialistischer Länder in Varna 1970," [1970], GARF, f. 7576, op. 31. d. 665.

38. Ibid. These thoughts were presented in the context of calling for a better and more effective coordination of collective actions within communist sport in preparations for the Olympic Games in Munich 1972.

39. Teichler, "Vom Lehrling," 299–301.

40. On the history of the East and West German quarrel concerning the recognition and acceptance in international sports after World War II, see Tobias Blasius, *Olympische Bewegung, Kalter Krieg und Deutschlandpolitik 1949–1972* (Frankfurt a.M.: Lang, 2001), and Balbier, *Kalter Krieg.*

41. Wolfgang Buss, "(Sport)politisch-historischer Handlungsrahmen," in *Der Sport in der SBZ und frühen DDR. Genese—Strukturen—Bedingungen,* ed. Wolfgang Buss and Christian Becker (Schorndorf: Hofmann 2001), 144–45, and René Wiese, "Der Ursprung der Kinder- und Jugendsportschulen der DDR—eine so-

wjetische Geburt?," *Deutschland Archiv. Zeitschrift für das vereinigte Deutschland* 37 (2004): 3.

42. Memorandum "Vermerk über eine Besprechung Dr. Schusters mit dem Vorsitzenden des Staatlichen Komitees für Körperkultur und Sport der DDR in der Botschaft der DDR in Moskau am 22. August 1958," August 22, 1958, PA AA, MfAA A, Bd. 499.

43. Argumentationspapier des NOK der DDR zu "Themen und Problemen des Olympischen Kongresses 1973," Bundesarchiv, Berlin (hereafter BArch), DR 510/261, and Speech by Heinz Schöbel, "Festansprache Dr. Schöbels, des Präsidenten des NOK der DDR und Mitglied des IOC zur Feier des NOK der DDR aus Anlaß des 75: Geburtstages des modernen Olympismus," BArch, DR 510/74.

44. Schöbel to NOC of the USSR, November 3, 1967, BArch, DR 510/878.

45. The delegation of the GDR, for example, emphasized the status of the USSR during the annual conference of sport leaders by requesting the formulation of a basis document directed under the auspices of the Soviet delegation. Memorandum "Vorschläge von Ergänzungen in den Schlußfolgerungen der Tagung der Leiter der Sportorganisationen der sozialistischen Länder durch die Delegation der DDR, Ulan Bator 18. September 1969," [1969], SAPMO, DY 12/2450.

46. Protocol "Niederschrift über eine Besprechung mit Vertretern der sowjetischen Sportleitung vom 15./16.9.1969 (Moskau und Ulan Bator)," October 28, 1969, SAPMO, DY 12/3159.

47. "Informationsbulletin über die Teilnahme der sowjetischen Mannschaft an den XXI. Olympischen Sommerspielen 1976 in Montreal 'nach Sportarten,'" 1976, GARF, f, 7576, op. 31, d. 2708. According to this, communist countries won 30.1 percent of Olympic medals in 1952, 33.4 percent in 1956, 37.2 percent in 1960, 36.3 percent in 1964, 41.6 percent in 1968, 47.5 percent in 1972, and 56.1 percent in 1976.

48. Protocol "Niederschrift über eine Besprechung mit Vertretern der sowjetischen Sportleitung vom 15./16. 9. 1969 (Moskau und Ulan Bator)," October 28, 1969, SAPMO, DY 12/3159.

49. Memorandum "Richtlinie für die Aufgabenstellung und Arbeitsweise der Ständigen gemeinsamen Kommission auf der Grundlage des Freundschaftsvertrages zwischen den Sportleitungen der DDR und der UdSSR," January 18, 1967, PA AA, MfAA B, Bd. 999/69.

50. Wonneberger, *Körperkultur und Sport,* 141.

51. Memorandum "Richtlinie für die Aufgabenstellung und Arbeitsweise der Ständigen gemeinsamen Kommission auf der Grundlage des Freundschaftsvertrages zwischen den Sportleitungen der DDR und der UdSSR," January 18, 1967, PA AA, MfAA B, Bd. 999/69.

52. Wonneberger, *Körperkultur und Sport,* 141.

53. The task force for acclimatization was abandoned after the Olympic Games in Mexico City in 1968 as it was intended to address only the problems caused by the extreme altitude at those Olympic Games. Memorandum "Richtlinie für die

Aufgabenstellung und Arbeitsweise der Ständigen gemeinsamen Kommission auf der Grundlage des Freundschaftsvertrages zwischen den Sportleitungen der DDR und der UdSSR," January 18, 1967, PA AA, MfAA B, Bd. 999/69; "Protokoll der 4. Tagung der Ständigen Gemeinsamen Kommission der DDR und der UdSSR in Berlin [East], 3.-4.09.1968," 1968, SAPMO, DY 12/3180.

54. Memorandum "Informationsbericht über den Verlauf und die Ergebnisse der 4. Tagung der Ständigen Gemeinsamen Kommission der Sportleitungen der DDR und der UdSSR am 3. und 4.9.1968 in Berlin [East]," September 12, 1968, SAPMO, DY 12/3179.

55. Joint Communiqué "Gemeinsames Kommuniqué über die 6. Tagung der Ständigen Gemeinsamen Kommission der Sportleitungen der DDR und der UdSSR vom 10. bis 12. Februar 1971 in Berlin [East]," February 1971, SAPMO, DY 12/3180.

56. Report "Bericht über die 16. Tagung der Ständigen Gemeinsamen Kommission der Sportleitung der DDR und der UdSSR in Moskau, 2.-5.10.1979," October 1979, SAPMO, DY 12/3183.

57. "Protokoll 19. Tagung der Ständigen Gemeinsamen Kommission der Sportleitung der DDR und der UdSSR in Moskau, 3.-6.11.1981," November 1981, SAPMO, DY 12/3183.

58. "Protokoll der 8. Tagung der Ständigen Gemeinsamen Kommission der Sportleitung der DDR und der UdSSR in Berlin [East], 22.-26.05.1973," May 1973, SAPMO, DY 12/3183.

59. "Bericht der Delegation der Sportleitung der DDR über die Teilnahme an der 32. Jahreskonferenz der Sportleitungen sozialistischer Länder in Phjöngjang [sic], KDVR, 20.-26.09.1983," September 1983, SAPMO, DY 12/3164.

60. Lehmann notes that exchange in the field of sport hardly took place in the medium or lower ranks. He also suggests that there was no expansion of sporting contacts after 1977. Lehmann, *Internationale Sportbeziehungen*, 534.

61. Memorandum, Girndt (East German embassy in the USSR) to MfAA, "Betr. Länderkampf UdSSR—DDR im Turm- und Kunstspringen," Moscow, August 5, 1958, PA AA, MfAA A, Bd. 499.

62. Letter, Kundermann (MfAA) to König (Embassy of the GDR in Moscow), August 12, 1958, PA AA, MfAA A, Bd. 499.

63. Memorandum "Vermerk über eine Besprechung Dr. Schusters mit dem Vorsitzenden des Staatlichen Komitees für Körperkultur und Sport der DDR in der Botschaft der DDR in Moskau am 22. August 1958," August 22, 1958, PA AA, MfAA A, Bd. 499.

64. Letter, East German Embassy in the USSR to MfAA, "Betr.: Sportbeziehungen DDR-UdSSR," March 21, 1957, PA AA, MfAA A, Bd. 499.

65. Letter, Heil (secretary of the international department of the DTSB) to Reich (department of culture of the East German embassy in the USSR), July 18, 1963, PA AA, MfAA A, Bd. 499.

66. The first part of the letter contains a clear admission of guilt. Heil to Reich, July 18, 1963, PA AA, MfAA A, Bd. 499.

67. The GDR had made a suggestion to "elaborate on a bilateral 'secret agreement for the protection of the interests of the athletes of the USSR and GDR.' Basically the proposal amounted to concealing possible facts about the intake of pharmaceutical substances forbidden by the IOC by athletes from the USSR and the GDR, in this case when analyses were conducted in the laboratories in Kreischa (GDR) or Moscow." Memorandum by Pavlov to the Central Committee of the CPSU, "Über einige Aspekte der sportlichen Zusammenarbeit mit der DDR," November 29, 1979, RGANI, f. 5, op. 76, d. 202.

68. Ibid.

69. Manfred Ewald and Reinhold Andert, *Manfred Ewald—Ich war der Sport. Wahrheiten und Legenden aus dem Wunderland der Sieger* (Berlin: Elefanten, 1994), 174–84, quote: 182.

70. Evelyn Mertin, *Sowjetisch-deutsche Sportbeziehungen im "Kalten Krieg"* (St. Augustin: Academia Verlag, 2009), 127.

71. Protocol "Niederschrift über eine Besprechung mit Vertretern der sowjetischen Sportleitung vom 15./16.9.1969 (Moskau und Ulan Bator)," October 28, 1969, SAPMO, DY 12/3159.

72. Mertin, *Sowjetisch-deutsche Sportbeziehungen,* 136.

73. Protocol "Niederschrift über eine Besprechung mit Vertretern der sowjetischen Sportleitung vom 15./16.9.1969 (Moskau und Ulan Bator)," October 28, 1969, SAPMO, DY 12/3159.

74. This was based on Ewald's earlier point of criticism that Soviet coaches expected more information from their East German colleagues than they would hand out themselves. He limited the framework of any exchange by letting Soviet coaches receive information on methodological questions to East German coaches, but any "organizational questions about elite sport" were not to be discussed with everyone. Here they would have to pass a "higher level." Pavlov alluded to this situation by promising to tell coaches "not to show much curiosity in their questions." At the same time, he warned that the isolation of the East German research was not as defined by the communist community. Protocol "Niederschrift über eine Besprechung mit Vertretern der sowjetischen Sportleitung vom 15./16. 9. 1969 (Moskau und Ulan Bator)," October 28, 1969, SAPMO, DY 12/3159.

75. "Kommuniqué über den Freundschaftsbesuch einer Delegation des Komitees für Körperkultur und Sport beim Ministerrat der UdSSR in der Deutschen Demokratischen Republik," November 1969, SAPMO, DY 12/6359.

76. Report "Bericht des Aufenthalts einer Delegation des Komitees in der DDR (18.-25. März 1970, in Kienbaum)," March 1970, GARF, f. 7576, op. 31, d. 674.

77. Ibid.

78. Report "Bericht der Methodiker [Novikov/Butenko/Juferov] der Abteilung wissenschaftliche forschende Arbeit des Komitees" on the occasion of their visit to Kienbaum 1970, GARF, f. 7576, op. 31, d. 674.

79. Report "Bericht des Aufenthalts einer Delegation des Komitees in der DDR (18.-25. März 1970, in Kienbaum)," 1970, GARF, f. 7576, op. 31, d. 674.

80. Letter, A.N. Efimenko (head of department track and field) and N.I. Politiko (head coach) to S.P. Pavlov, November 10, 1981, GARF, f. 7576, op. 31, d. 7266.

81. Report "Bericht des Aufenthalts einer Delegation des Komitees in der DDR (18.-25. März 1970, in Kienbaum)," 1970, GARF, f. 7576, op. 31, d. 674.

82. Ibid.; Report "Bericht über die Beratungen mit der Sportleitung der UdSSR und die Tagung der Ständigen gemeinsamen Kommission in der Zeit vom 1. bis 4. Februar 1967 in Moskau," February 8, 1967, SAPMO, DY 12/3180; Memorandum "Ergebnisse der zweiseitigen Gespräche während der Jahreskonferenz der Sportleitungen sozialistischer Länder 1971," September 25–30, 1971, in Bukarest, SAPMO, DY 12/3160.

83. Report "Bericht der Reise sowjetischer Vertreter in die DDR zur Untersuchung des Zustands der wissenschaftlichen Information im Bereich des Sports (20.-30.11.1970)," 1970, GARF, f. 7576, op. 31, d. 674.

84. Protocol "Niederschrift über Gespräche zwischen Delegationen der Sportleitung der DDR und der UdSSR auf der Ebene ihrer Vorsitzenden in Moskau, 6. Mai 1971," May 6, 1971, SAPMO, DY 12/3181.

85. Report "Bericht über den Aufenthalt einer Delegation der DDR zur 7. Tagung der Ständigen Gemeinsamen Kommission der Sportleitung der DDR und der UdSSR in Moskau, 10.-13.11.1971," November 1971, SAPMO, DY 12/3180.

86. Mertin, *Sowjetisch-deutsche Sportbeziehungen,* 129–31.

87. Taken from the stenogram "Meeting with Colleagues from the Committee," January 29, 1983, GARF, f. 7576, op. 31, d. 8671.

88. Letter, Gramov to Central Committee of the CPSU, "Über die Ergebnisse der Teilnahme sowjetischer Sportler an der XIV. Olympischen Winterspielen in Sarajewo," March 13, 1984, RGANI, f. 5, op. 90, d. 144. The GDR gained the top rank in the (unofficial) medal count with nine gold, nine silver, and six bronze medals. Second place went to the USSR with "only" six gold, ten silver, and nine bronze medals, followed by the United States (four, four, none) and Finland (four, three, six). Karl Adolf Scherer, *100 Jahre Olympische Spiele: Idee, Analyse und Bilanz* (Dortmund: Harenberg 1995), 390.

89. Memorandum "Thesen für die Leitungsgespräche am 23./24. Mai 1968 in Moskau" by the department for international relations/Communist states in the DTSB, [1968], SAPMO, DY 12/3179.

90. Protocol "Niederschrift über die Gespräche zwischen den Sportleitungen der DDR und der UdSSR am 26.7.1972 in Moskau," July 1972, SAPMO, DY 12/3181.

91. Koval according to Willi Knecht, "Sportpolitische Bilanz 1972," Deutschland Archiv 5(1972)12, 1283–1284. Karl-Heinz Gieseler remarked in an interview (June 14, 2006, in Neu-Isenburg) that this meeting between Soviet and West German sport officials had been planned and was by no means held spontaneously.

92. On the Soviet–East German cooperation in Olympic questions see Mertin, *Sowjetisch-deutsche Sportbeziehungen,* 144–52.

# 3

# Welcoming the "Third World"

## Soviet Sport Diplomacy, Developing Nations, and the Olympic Games

### *Jenifer Parks*

In a 1959 article on sport exchanges titled "Za Druzhbu!" (To Friendship!), the vice president of the National Olympic Committee (NOC) of the USSR, Mikhail Pesliak, announced the first Soviet sports delegation to Africa. Ukrainian soccer players had traveled to Egypt, Sudan, and Ethiopia, becoming in Pesliak's words the "first explorers in our [Soviet] sports journey into the depths of Africa, to countries who have great sympathy for the Soviet Union."[1] From the Soviet Union's entrance into the Olympic Games in 1952, sport became a key facet of Soviet foreign relations. High-profile, international meets provided an opportunity for the Soviet Union to display the strength of its socialist system. Sport also provided a way for the Soviet Union to win friends abroad through sport aid and exchanges of expertise, equipment, and personnel. Under Joseph Stalin's leadership, most sport exchanges were between the Soviet Union and its Eastern European satellite states. After Nikita Khrushchev came to power, however, international sport relations were expanded, and the developing world became a key target of a new Soviet initiative to bring more nations into the Olympic movement. Under the leadership of Leonid Brezhnev, Moscow secured the bid to host the Olympic Games, and sport relations with the developing world became a key component in the campaign to make the 1980 Summer Olympics the biggest and the best.

In this chapter, I seek to understand the relationship between Soviet foreign policy and sport relations as they worked together to expand Soviet influence in the world and prove socialist supremacy through sport. Sport in the Soviet Union has become a fruitful area of investigation.[2] Much existing literature on the Olympic Games examines the relationship between international sport and politics, emphasizing the internal politics of the Olympic movement, as well as the use of the Olympics by state actors to promote national prestige.[3] Many Western works on Soviet participation in the Olympics have explored specific instances where Cold War rivalries played out in the international arena.[4] Recent studies have also explored the use of sport by state actors to achieve foreign policy goals.[5] Other works have acknowledged the role of athletes serving as international ambassadors of their nation through their dominance on the field as well as their image off the field.[6]

Soviet sport policy can be seen as one part of a larger arena of public diplomacy, which Geoffrey Cowan and Nicholas J. Cull define as "an international actor's attempt to advance the ends of policy by engaging with foreign publics."[7] Such engagement "became a more substantial area during the Cold War, dominated by campaigns to garner support for the delicate balance of nuclear weapons and the ideological battle for the hearts and minds of people around the world."[8] Cultural competition between the two superpowers increasingly became an "all-encompassing effort involving such things as sporting events, cultural attractions, economic activities, education, trade, diplomacy, and scientific achievement."[9] Cultural outreach helped each superpower exercise its "soft power" during the Cold War by attracting potential client states that "wanted to follow [either the United States or the USSR], admiring its values, emulating its example, and/or aspiring to its level of prosperity and openness."[10] Somewhat sooner than their American rivals, the leaders of the Communist Party of the Soviet Union (CPSU) as well as those of various state organs increasingly recognized the potential of sport competitions, exchanges, and aid programs as important avenues to win client states around the world.

As the Cold War divided the world between Western and socialist spheres, the United States and the Soviet Union competed to attract developing nations to their respective ideological and socioeconomic camps. The increasing availability of documents since the end of the Cold War has allowed scholars to analyze Soviet support for anticolonial movements as well as the role of local actors in this struggle for influence in the developing world.[11] Recent literature from the perspective of the global South (including chapters in this volume) has enhanced our understanding of how newly independent and developing nations used sport for their own ends. Scholarship on sport and colonialism has shown that colonial sport could often be the site of conflict and of challenge to the colonial authority and an important avenue for creating local, regional, and national identities outside of and counter to imperial goals.[12] Similarly recipients of development aid were not necessarily mere objects of Cold War superpower agendas. Rather, leaders of newly independent nations saw the development of culture as a way of legitimizing their rule and uniting their countries.

For example, African leaders saw the development of sport, including the building of stadiums and organization of national sports leagues, as a means to engage with the developed world on a more equal footing.[13] In addition, leaders in the developing world embraced sport to meet their own national ends and to promote their own country's image internationally and for political reasons unrelated to the Cold War rivalry between East and West.[14] Recent literature on sport in the global South has also revealed the agency of developing nations to challenge the Cold War order through athletic success in international and especially regional games as well as through boycott of international sporting contests.[15] The influence of developing nations can also be seen in attempts to promote solidarity among former colonial possessions in the transnational black power movement against racial discrimination in international sports.[16] As the Soviet Union and the United States sought to influence emerging nations in the global South, they both had to take regional concerns into account as they implemented their policies.

Sport diplomacy was a crucial part of Soviet cultural diplomacy, which according to Cull was used "to build a picture of the Soviet state as a place that valued expression, cultivated excellence, and tolerated diversity."[17] Since the picture could not obscure the reality of Soviet repression indefinitely, according to Cull, Soviet cultural diplomacy failed in the long term to convince the world of Soviet peaceful intentions. Other works have suggested that international exchange weakened domestic support for the ruling regime by opening up the Soviet Union to Western influence. Barbara Keys argues that participating in international sport opened "Soviet culture to internationalist currents often subversive of broader regime goals."[18] Similarly, Yale Richmond contends that Soviet cultural exchanges, especially with the United States, contributed significantly to the end of the Cold War and the dissolution of the Soviet Union by exposing the Soviet Union to Western ideas that highlighted its internal contradictions.[19]

As the Cold War battle focused on the developing world in the 1960s and 1970s, however, the Soviet Union was able to capitalize on anti-imperialist and anti-Western sentiments to portray itself as a loyal friend to newly independent nations. James Riordan and Victor Peppard suggest that the "ambiguity and ambivalence found in sport diplomacy may be one of its greatest strengths" because it can convey "more than one message simultaneously."[20] Soviet sport administrators massaged that ambiguity very carefully, emphasizing both the Olympic ideal of "sport for all" and the Marxist-Leninist ideology of anticolonial struggle as they promoted sport in the developing world. In this way, Soviet administrators could portray the Soviet Union as the true voice of democracy abroad, while painting their Cold War rival, the United States, as arrogant and discriminatory toward the rest of the world. The USSR used international sport as part of its strategy to sway world opinion, spearheading major expansions in membership and sport outreach to the developing world. In the short term, Soviet representatives realized Soviet propaganda and foreign policy goals in international sport by cultivating the friendly side of Soviet power, but the 1979 invasion of Afghanistan exposed the neoimperialist ambitions of the Soviet Union, demonstrating the limits of Soviet sport diplomacy during the Cold War.

## Soviet Sport Diplomacy under Stalin

In the early years of the Soviet Union, Soviet sport theorists perceived international competitive sport, including the Olympic Games, as elitist and "bourgeois." Therefore, Soviet leaders rejected the Olympic movement and formed the Red Sport International (Sportintern) to promote revolutionary class consciousness abroad through athletic meets with communist sporting organizations. While Soviet sport organizations began to pursue more mainstream sport relations in the early 1930s, progress toward joining the international sporting world was halted during the political purges of the late 1930s, when the Politburo of the Central Committee of the CPSU denied petitions to join international sport organizations, and sport officials, athletes, and trainers became victims of the Great Terror as the secret police killed, imprisoned, and exiled millions of Soviet citizens.

After the Allies' victory during World War II, Soviet leaders demonstrated more willingness to consider Soviet involvement in mainstream, international sport organizations as a way to promote Soviet prestige abroad. The postwar atmosphere in the Soviet Union was marked by optimism as a new generation of party and government cadres sought solutions to the many problems facing the USSR.[21] It was in this mood that Soviet sport officials proposed that Soviet athletes enter the Olympic movement. In December 1948 the Central Committee of the CPSU issued a resolution to "win world supremacy in major sports in the immediate future," and Soviet sports administrators began to push for Soviet athletes to compete in the Olympic Games.[22] Soviet sport officials believed that the Soviet Union should take a leadership role in international sport organizations and use positions within the International Olympic Committee (IOC) to increase the socialist presence in the Olympic movement. In requesting IOC membership, the vice chairman of the All-Union Committee on Physical Culture and Sports (Sports Committee), Petr Sobolev, suggested that Soviet representatives could also further Soviet foreign policy and attract more support for the Soviet Union by increasing peaceful relations through sport.[23]

On April 18, 1951, a joint declaration from the Central Committee and Council of Ministers authorized the Sports Committee to form an NOC.[24] Five days later, Sobolev sent a telegram to the IOC requesting recognition of the newly formed Soviet Olympic Committee.[25] Some Olympic organizers sought to bring the Soviet Union into the Games, fueled by the movement's ideals of bringing the nations of the world together in a spirit of peace and "a respect for universal fundamental ethical principles" of "friendship, solidarity and fair play."[26] Others, such as the vice president of the IOC, Avery Brundage, feared that the Soviet Union's entrance would compromise Olympic ideals of amateurism and freedom from political interference. Accepting Soviet promises to comply with IOC rules and regulations, the IOC recognized the Soviet Olympic Committee in 1951 and elected its president, Konstantin Andrianov, to join the organization. Upon entering his first IOC meeting, Andrianov assured his fellow members that he would "cooperate sincerely with the IOC for the good of the Olympic Movement in his country and for world peace."[27] The following summer, Soviet athletes made an impressive debut in their first Olympics in the Helsinki Games of 1952, coming in a close second to the United States in the medal count with seventy-one, compared to seventy-six.

Despite their successful Olympic debut, Soviet sports ties under Stalin were influenced by the emerging Cold War with the United States. Training resources were directed toward defeating the United States and, outside of the Olympic Games and world championships, sport exchanges tended to remain within the socialist bloc, serving as a tool to further consolidate the Soviet sphere of influence in Eastern Europe. Soviet actions within the IOC were also directed toward strengthening the socialist influence against a perceived Anglo-American bias, and Soviet IOC members made obtaining recognition for the separate NOCs for the German Democratic Republic (GDR) and for the People's Republic of China (PRC) key goals within the organization.[28] This bloc mentality mirrored the early days of the Cold War that increasingly divided Europe between the new superpowers.

## "Peaceful Coexistence" and Soviet Sport Diplomacy in the Developing World

After Stalin's death in 1953, Soviet foreign policy shifted from a posture of confrontation and isolation to one of increased engagement with the West, and this new atmosphere of "peaceful coexistence" ushered in an era of expanded international ties. The Khrushchev period was marked by notable successes in the superpower competition over world opinion. On October 4, 1957, Soviet scientists launched *Sputnik*, the first man-made satellite to orbit the earth, and on April 12, 1961, Yuri Gagarin became the first man in space, giving the USSR important victories in the space race and an early lead in the race to the moon. Moreover, during this period, Soviet athletes secured their status as the dominant sports power, winning the most medals at every Olympic Summer and Winter Games held between 1956 and 1964.

Khrushchev's uneven foreign policy and tendency toward brinkmanship, however, led to a number of international crises. The 1956 Hungarian Revolution left thousands dead at the hands of security forces and Soviet soldiers. Confrontation with Western powers in Berlin resulted in the construction of the Berlin Wall in 1961 to divide the city. The Cuban Missile Crisis of 1962 threatened to end in nuclear war between the superpowers, convincing Khrushchev to abandon his failed attempt at nuclear diplomacy.[29] Also, Soviet relations with the PRC soured when Chairman Mao Zedong and his colleagues felt Khrushchev had betrayed basic tenants of Marxism, embracing ideological heresy and abandoning the worldwide socialist movement by pursuing warmer ties with the United States.

Also during this period, the focus of the Cold War shifted southward. As anticolonial movements in Asia, Africa, the Middle East, and Latin America heated up, former colonies resisted European influence in those regions, and both superpowers saw an opportunity to promote their own system while undermining their Cold War opponent. Cultural diplomacy became a key avenue for both sides to increase their influence in these regions, and sport was seen as a particularly fruitful avenue for exercising "soft power" in the developing world. As Kenneth Osgood notes, "the [US] Information Agency capitalized on this natural interest in sports to spread positive messages about life in the United States."[30] Similarly Soviet officials promoted sport exchanges to demonstrate the successes of the socialist sport system and to show Soviet support for progress in newly independent nations.

From 1953 to 1964, under Khrushchev's leadership, Soviet administrators projected an image abroad in international sport circles as peace-loving sport enthusiasts looking to expand the Olympic movement throughout the world. Emphasizing the commonalities between their own goals and Olympic ideals, Soviet representatives strove to increase the socialist presence and influence in international sport organizations. Bringing more socialist members into the IOC and international federations would hopefully increase votes in favor of Soviet proposals and help guarantee Soviet candidatures for leadership positions. At the same time, Soviet allies in Eastern Europe began to resist Soviet control, and the PRC challenged Soviet leadership of the socialist world. Growing tensions and cleavages within the socialist bloc even began to play themselves out in international sports, complicating the jobs of Soviet sport administrators. Especially after the Hungarian Revolution, Soviet sport exchanges with their socialist neighbors became scenes of anti-Soviet incidents when fans attending matches in the GDR and Poland shouted epithets such as "Ivan, go home," and Bulgarian spectators threw projectiles at Soviet teams.[31] At the same time, Asian countries such as the PRC as well as Indonesia were challenging the Soviet Union for influence in the region.[32] As socialist solidarity seemed to be splintering and fracturing, Soviet sport administrators saw Africa and the Middle East as promising arenas for increasing Soviet authority through sport diplomacy. Soviet administrators maintained an outward image of socialist solidarity within international sport organizations, while at the same time shifting focus and resources to the support of newly emerging nations in the developing world.[33]

As part of their strategy, Soviet sport administrators introduced a Soviet proposal to reorganize the IOC on the model of the United Nations, guaranteeing representation on the committee to all nations from all regions of the globe, including newly independent states of Africa, Asia, and the Middle East. Securing recognition of newly independent nations in the IOC would not only build support for Soviet influence within the Olympic movement but also would help portray a positive image of the USSR among leaders and publics of the global South. In their efforts to win friends in the non-Western world, Soviet representatives capitalized on elitist and often racist assumptions of many IOC members such as Brundage (now president), who betrayed a genuine bias against expanding the movement to the developing world. At the 1955 Paris IOC meeting, he argued that the IOC needed "protection" from Olympic committees being organized by "outsiders" who had not been properly educated in Olympic ideals and "countries not experienced in Olympic affairs, such as Liberia, Rhodesia, Nicaragua, Indochina, Bolivia, and many others."[34] Before new NOCs could be recognized, Brundage advocated, "We should really, of course, send a representative of the IOC to all these countries in order to teach them the Olympic philosophy before they are recognized and someday I hope this can be done."[35] Such statements, no doubt, reinforced the perception of bias within the IOC and provided ammunition for Soviet Olympic Committee members to portray themselves as the only reliable friends of the developing world in the organization.

To Brundage and others among the old guard, the traditional selection process was crucial to the IOC's autonomy as it reinforced the sense among members that they were representatives of the Olympic movement to their countries and should not see themselves as delegates of their home nation. The selection process also ensured, in the words of Brundage, that all members "were of the same general type and they were soon welded into what has so often been called the 'Olympic Family.'"[36] Many in the IOC feared that the Soviet proposal, calling for representation from all regions of the globe, as well as international federations and all recognized NOCs, would threaten the independence and status of the organization. For these reasons, when the IOC members finally discussed the proposal at the 1961 IOC Session in Athens, it failed, with only seven votes in favor and thirty-five against.[37] Soviet administrators concluded that to insist upon their reorganization plan would antagonize "the majority of IOC members" and suggested that the Soviet Union pursue a new path of "gradual democratization of the IOC" through the active promotion of membership candidatures from socialist and developing countries.[38]

Soviet IOC members continued their push to expand the Olympic movement at the Fifty-Ninth IOC Session held in Moscow in 1962. Despite the failure of most of their proposals at the Moscow session, the Soviet representatives succeeded in getting the IOC to make expanding the Olympic movement to new states of Asia and Africa a priority. Other notable Soviet successes included the passing of the Soviet proposal to ensure geographic representation on the IOC executive board (EB) and the election of Andrianov to that board.[39] By the mid-1960s, the number of NOCs from Africa and Asia had expanded from three African and eighteen Asian in 1952 to twenty-two and twenty-six, respectively, in 1964.[40] Yet the Soviet Olympic Committee still regarded expanding IOC membership of socialist countries and "young states of Asia and Africa" as one of its chief tasks, noting that at the time there were only eight IOC members from socialist countries, five from Africa, and seven from Asia.[41] To help developing nations enter the Olympic movement, Andrianov also promoted the formation of a special commission of the IOC to provide sport aid to Africa.[42] In 1971 his Committee for International Olympic Aid was eventually combined with the International

Institute for the Development of NOCs to form the Commission for Olympic Solidarity.[43]

In addition to their support of Asian and African candidatures to the IOC, Soviet officials expanded sport diplomacy in the developing world to "strengthen the friendship and cultural cooperation of the Soviet Union with foreign countries."[44] This was to be accomplished through a wide variety of foreign sport exchanges and contacts, including participating in world championships and the Olympic Games, exchanging physical education specialists, sending Soviet sports specialists to developing countries, participating in international scientific congresses and meetings, exchanging training literature and films, lending help to foreign countries in the training of sports personnel, building sports arenas and playing fields, developing sports equipment, and, last but not least, participating in meetings of international sport organizations. Underscoring the importance of sport exchanges to Soviet foreign policy, Mikhail Pesliak, vice chairman of the Sports Committee, maintained that "the exchange of sports delegations has become one of the most important channels of international relations."[45]

As more and more nations of Asia and Africa won their independence in the 1960s and 1970s, many leaders looked toward the Soviet Union as a model for rapid industrialization and modernization and sought Soviet expertise in how to build their new nations into modern economic powers, recognized and respected internationally. Despite the IOC's insistence on sport outside politics, Soviet sport administrators exploited the political potential of sport exchanges, organizing competitions, sending coaches and trainers, offering scholarships for coaches and educators to train in the Soviet Union, and providing sport equipment and expertise in building sport facilities. Participation in the Olympic Games became an important status symbol for newly emerging nations, and many leaders sought support and material aid from the Soviet Union to build their sport systems. For example, in 1960 and 1961, 2,050 rubles' worth (approximately US$1,850) of sports inventory was sent to Togo, Sudan, and Zanzibar, including trophies, badges, footballs, basketballs, football uniforms, barbells, boxing gloves, track hammers, javelins, and discuses.[46] In a plan for cultural cooperation between the USSR and the Somalian Republic for 1963, the Soviet Sports Committee planned to send "various specialists, professors and teachers, textbooks for geography, help with hospitals, help with schools, lectures, etc." as well as doctors and translators to Somalia. They also planned to send teachers to work in a high school that had been built with help from the Soviet Union. In exchange, Somalia would send writers, musicians, journalists, linguists, students, and medics to the USSR.[47] Although the agreement did not specifically mention sports, its inclusion in the Sports Committee reports demonstrates that sport aid was part of a broader initiative of public diplomacy in the developing world.

Soviet athletes and trainers enjoyed a degree of cultural power and status, and the hosts of Soviet delegations also hoped to harness that cultural power to fulfill their own domestic and foreign policy goals. In negotiating relations with the Soviet Union, newly independent countries of Asia and Africa insisted on reciprocity. When the Libyan Olympic Committee invited the Moscow Lokomotiv soccer team for a sport festival, it included a request that the USSR invite a Libyan soccer team to the USSR in 1963 "on the same conditions."[48] In a meeting with the Soviet ambassador to Libya, the head of the Sport Festival Commission and Libyan Olympic Committee member Massoud Zentut "expressed the hope that fans of football in Libya will again see Soviet football players in their stadiums."[49] This remark implies that the popularity that Soviet athletes enjoyed in developing countries could be translated into domestic legitimacy. Soviet administrators hoped that the popularity of Soviet teams would also translate into positive feelings about the Soviet Union and its socialist system abroad. There is some evidence to suggest that this was the case, as the Sports Committee received correspondence from a young Moroccan athlete requesting information about life and sport in the USSR.[50]

Sport aid to developing nations was often couched in terms of expanding international sport and spreading the ideals of the Olympic movement, but it also formed an important part of spreading Marxist-Leninist ideology and the Soviet socialist system. In an article discussing newly independent states and the United Nations, an unknown Soviet author linked the accomplishments of the Soviet people in "building a new society" to the task of "the struggle for peace and freedom for all peoples." According to the author, the United Nations played an important role in making 1960 "the year of Africa," with special initiative shown in that organization by the Soviet Union. "Sixteen independent states appeared on the African continent in only one year. . . . These peoples more and more are beginning to discover the noble world role that lay before them; they are beginning to distinguish their true friends from their hidden enemies." The article goes on to link the struggle for independence with sport, praising the accomplishments of newly independent athletes from Africa and Asia who were "laying claims to future victory in international sport."[51] In a 1960 article in *Fizkul'tura i sport,* Sports Committee vice chairman Sobolev explained the importance of reaching out to former colonies: "It is an indisputable fact that a successful fight with colonialism and an increase in the number of independent states gave an impetus to the development of sport in the countries that were liberated from colonial oppression. . . . These newcomers perhaps will not immediately show high results, but that they will find in the Olympic Village thousands of friends, instilling in their hearts an ardent feeling of friendship, and they will return to their homeland passionate propagandists for sport—this is unquestionable."[52] While articulated in the language of Olympic ideology, by linking Olympic participation to the anticolonial struggle such reports served to project an image of the Soviet Union as friend to newly independent nations. Sobolev continued: "The African continent threw off the chains of colonial servitude, and with the tribune of the congresses was heard the voice of the messengers of young states of Africa, starting out on the path of independent development of economics, culture and sports, their voices raised for the defense of the principle of the equality of all sportsmen, without regard to differences of skin color."[53] Soviet sports officials contrasted their push to expand Olympic membership to emerging nations with the "reactionary" West, which sought to reduce the Olympic program and limit the number of athletes who could participate.[54] As Sports Committee chairman Nikolai Romanov noted, "open[ing] wide the door [of the Olympics] to the athletes of free countries of Africa" would bolster Soviet efforts to counteract the "political interests of the Americans and other imperialist circles."[55] When coupled with increasing sports aid to Africa and Asia, Soviet denouncements of Western reactionaries were designed to attract more client states in the developing world and strengthen the position of the Soviet Union in the IOC.

Racial inequality in the United States aided Soviet efforts to attract African allies. The United States Information Agency (USIA) tried to mitigate the negative impact that racial violence and discrimination had on US credibility abroad, asserting that the country was a sincere supporter of racial equality and economic prosperity for all. However, incidents of discrimination and violence continued and received worldwide attention throughout the 1950s and 1960s. It did not help that nonwhite world leaders and politicians often experienced racial discrimination firsthand when visiting the United States. According to Osgood, fourteen major instances were reported of racial discrimination against diplomats from Africa, Asia, the Caribbean, and Latin America between 1957 and 1961.[56] These incidents received outraged coverage in local presses throughout the developing world where historical memory of colonial violence and discrimination at the hands of white officials was recent and widespread.

To counter negative images, the USIA organized a campaign to stress the achievements of black Americans and included tours of black writers, musicians, entertainers, and athletes as part of their cultural diplomacy with the developing world. The USIA even planned an unprecedented exhibit acknowledging the problem of racial inequality in America while demonstrating the amount of progress that the country, and African Americans in particular, had made from the time of slavery. Criticism and pressure from southern congressmen convinced President Dwight D. Eisenhower to quash the exhibit despite the positive response from many exhibit visitors who "found 'new respect' for America" having the courage to give an honest portrayal of the country's history with race.[57] As Damion Thomas demonstrates, however, by the 1960s African tours of American black athletes were no longer having the desired effect for the US State Department. Rather than demonstrating the progress of US race relations, black athletes "were increasingly willing to stand in opposition to American policy, thus altering the political nature of their trips abroad. Coupled with the escalation of the Vietnam War, the altered political landscape after decolonization, the militancy of the Black Athletes helped severely hinder the aims of the program."[58] As Joseph S. Nye Jr. has pointed out, "if a country's culture, values, and policies are not attractive, public diplomacy that 'broadcasts' them cannot produce soft power."[59] In the battle for hearts and minds in Africa, the United States was at a distinct disadvantage because the realities of racial inequality exposed the hypocrisy of its attempted cultural exports.

## Welcoming the World to the 1980 Moscow Olympics

Khrushchev's colleagues ousted him in October 1964, and Leonid Brezhnev replaced him as general secretary of the CPSU. In the mid-1960s, after Khrushchev's disorienting domestic reforms and international nuclear brinkmanship, Brezhnev's leadership offered a degree of peace and security. The establishment of détente with the West resulted in arms control agreements, expanded trade and cultural exchange between the United States and the USSR, and the signing of the Helsinki Final Act in 1975, recognizing the postwar European boundaries and committing both countries to recognize human rights. Yet this period also saw the implementation of the Brezhnev Doctrine after the 1968 invasion of Czechoslovakia. Asserting the right to intervene wherever socialist regimes were threatened, Warsaw Pact countries used their military might to abort the Czechoslovakian reform program. At the same time, the Soviet Committee for State Security (KGB) cracked down on the growing dissident movement at home.

Although sport ties had increased under Khrushchev, it was only under Brezhnev that the Soviet Union began to pursue a bid to host the Olympic Games. After losing to Montreal as host city for the 1976 Olympics, Moscow won the bid to host the 1980 Summer Games. As the first socialist country to host the Games, the Soviet Union hoped to prove its status as a world power and vanguard of the socialist world. The Moscow organizing committee (Orgcom) needed to ensure that as many countries as possible would accept its invitation to compete in order to make the Games a propaganda success. In the lead-up to the Moscow Olympics, the international and propaganda departments of the Orgcom sent legions of representatives abroad to promote the Games and secure guarantees from NOCs that they would send their athletes to compete. The Orgcom's efforts also advanced Soviet foreign policy interests. In their decree on international relations for 1975, the Orgcom linked hosting the 1980 Olympic Games with the "program of peace" announced at the twenty-fourth congress of the CPSU in 1971 as well as the "historic decision" taken at the Conference on Security and Cooperation in Europe held in Helsinki in the summer of 1975.[60] The agreement reached at Helsinki included provisions for "sports meetings and competitions of all sorts on the basis of the established rules, regulations, and practice."[61]

The participating states agreed to expand links and contacts in a number of other areas that would be facilitated by the Moscow Games as well as the activities of the Orgcom, including tourism, international conferences and meetings of international organizations, cultural exchange, information exchange, and education.[62] However, the Orgcom presidium also used its activities to propagandize abroad "the Soviet way of life, the peace-loving foreign policy of the Soviet government, and the achievements of the Soviet people in building a communist society."[63] In this way, the Moscow Olympiad can be seen as the culmination of Soviet cultural diplomacy through sport and an opportunity to promote the achievements of the Soviet Union to a worldwide audience.

Sport diplomacy became a key component of the success of the Moscow Games as the Olympics increasingly became the scene of political dissent. Acts of protest, boycott, and even terrorism were seen by many as effective and appropriate ways to express displeasure against political conditions or to effect change, and individuals and groups found the Olympic Games and its worldwide television coverage a useful forum for spreading their message to a global audience. At the Munich Games, a terrorist attack on the Israeli team by the Palestinian group Black September, in which eleven athletes and coaches were killed, marred the festival and alerted Olympic organizers that the Games had become a serious security risk. Several African nations boycotted the Montreal Olympics to protest the system of apartheid in South Africa, creating anxiety in the Orgcom that such a boycott could happen to them too. Even before Moscow was officially elected, various groups had already begun discussing the possibility of boycotting a Moscow Olympics. The Orgcom feared possible boycotts of the Games on several different fronts related to international tensions surrounding South Africa, Israel, and the PRC. Soviet sport leaders spent three years attempting to defuse these sometimes overlapping issues and to ensure maximum participation. Their efforts largely succeeded until war in Afghanistan and a new political confrontation with the United States resulted in a US-led boycott of the Moscow Olympic Games just months before they were to begin.

While Moscow prepared to host the Olympic Games, the growing anti-apartheid movement began increasingly to express its convictions through the rejection of sport ties, putting Soviet organizers in an awkward position. In his exploration of the anti-apartheid movement in sport,

Douglas Booth analyzes the sport boycott of South Africa and "sports boycott as a strategy for political and social change."[64] Booth acknowledges the role of Eastern bloc counties in pushing the exclusion of South Africa from mainstream international sport federations and the Olympic Games, but he does not fully explore in depth how or why Soviet and East European representatives pushed the South Africa boycott. As with their other campaigns, Soviet representatives used the anti-apartheid struggle to promote Soviet public diplomacy in Africa and to ensure maximum participation by African nations in the 1980 Games. Like the "democratization" campaign earlier, the Soviet Union was in a much stronger position to win support from African nations because the antiracist message fit well within the Marxist-Leninist, anti-imperialist framework at the core of Soviet ideology.

Soviet and other socialist representatives to the IOC and international federations (IFs) had long been vocal in persuading those organizations to expel South Africa and Southern Rhodesia from their ranks. As early as 1963, Andrianov used his status as an EB member to draw the attention of the IOC to racial discrimination in South Africa.[65] Through his help, the question of barring South Africa from the 1964 Games was brought before the IOC and a strongly worded resolution was adopted warning South Africa that they would be banned from the Olympic Games unless the South African government changed the policy of racial discrimination in sport.[66] The IOC officially banned South Africa from competing in the Olympic Games in 1970, formally revoking recognition of the South African Olympic Committee.[67] Many countries, however, maintained ties and competitions with South African teams in various sports. In protest over New Zealand's competitions with South African athletes, many African countries withdrew from the 1976 Montreal Olympics. Fearing that African countries might likewise boycott the Moscow Games, the Moscow Orgcom and Soviet representatives to international sports organizations fought to prevent individual countries from continuing sports ties with racist regimes.[68]

Soviet representatives had been pushing for more participation by African, Asian, and Latin American countries in the Olympic movement since the 1950s, but the drive to get developing countries recognized by the IOC took on a renewed fervor in the lead-up to 1980. The Orgcom enlisted the help of Sports Committee personnel in establishing contacts

and negotiating sport cooperation with developing countries by providing them with methodological and material help to build their domestic
sport programs and bring them into the Olympic movement.[69] In their
campaign to guarantee African participation in the 1980 Games, the
Orgcom, the Sports Committee, and other Soviet sport organizations expended considerable resources to convince these countries to participate
and to ensure their recognition by the IOC to make it possible. By linking
participation in the Moscow Olympics to anticolonial and anti-apartheid
movements, Orgcom representatives found a receptive audience in sport
leaders from developing nations.

For example, in his meeting with the head of Yemen's Ministry of Public, Work, and Youth Affairs, IOC member and Orgcom vice president
V. G. Smirnov secured the Yemeni representative's promise to participate
in the 1980 Games as a way to "decisively battle against the remnants of
colonialism and racism in all its manifestations."[70] The minister of culture
of the Republic of Congo (Brazzaville), in his meeting with Orgcom representatives, intimated that Africans were "particularly sensitive to racial
discrimination and would respond badly to the slightest manifestation of
injustice." He expressed the hope that Moscow would be the most representative Olympic Games in history and promised that his country would
not participate in a boycott.[71] In his meetings with representatives from
Kuwait and Iraq, Orgcom vice president V. I. Koval promised Soviet help
in preparing their athletes for the Games as well as other Soviet sports
aid under the rubric of "sports cooperation."[72] This aid took the form of a
combination of money, equipment, coaches, and sports facilities, as well
as scholarships for coaches to study in the Soviet Union. By 1980 hundreds of coaches were working in over thirty developing nations, including "some forty coaches visit[ing] fifteen developing countries for seminars
and coaching schools" in 1980 alone.[73] All of these efforts required close
cooperation between the Orgcom and other departments. Along with the
Orgcom, the Sports Committee, the KGB-run Dinamo sports society,
and the Ministry of Defense sport section used their resources to send
sport equipment, inventory, and specialists to emerging nations.[74]

Even though African leaders accepted Soviet aid and agreed to compete in Moscow, many made it clear that their support of the Games
would not be allowed to undermine their commitment to the anti-apartheid struggle. In 1978 the United Nations General Assembly considered

an International Convention against Apartheid in Sport, making matters considerably more complicated for the Orgcom and the IOC. Soviet sports administrators had to find a compromise between supporting the anti-apartheid movement throughout the developing world and the interests of the IOC and IFs, which saw such a resolution as an unwelcome intrusion of political interference by the United Nations in international sports. Calling for sanctions on countries that maintained sport ties with South Africa, a UN convention, if passed, could obligate Moscow to exclude those countries from participating in the Olympic Games. This would go against the IOC Charter, which requires all recognized NOCs to be invited to the Games. Inviting those countries, however, could encourage African nations to boycott the Moscow Olympics. Fearing that a convention could threaten the success of the Games, Soviet officials urged the socialist camp to use its influence in the IOC and IFs to guarantee the exclusion of South Africa from international competitive sport.[75]

While working to bar South Africa from the Olympics, Soviet representatives also sought to convince African leaders to abandon the call for sanctions and declare their support for the Games in Moscow. The Nigerian sports leader and president of the Supreme Council on Sport in Africa, Abraham Ordia, warned that if Soviet representatives did not support the UN convention against apartheid in sport, including the proposal of sanctions, African nations "would be forced to hold their own private regional sports meets and would struggle against apartheid in sport 'by their own methods.'"[76] However, some other African leaders resented what they saw as Nigerian pretensions to power on the continent.[77] Others sympathized with the Soviet side but at the same time maintained that "African countries must use all opportunities to fight against apartheid."[78] Peter Onu, undersecretary-general of the Organization for African Unity, argued that Africans did not believe in the concept of "sport outside of politics" but saw sport as a place where they could achieve goals that they could not achieve in the political arena. However, he also believed that if the Orgcom could get the support of Ordia, "no problems with the Olympic Games in Moscow would arise."[79] The convention was not adopted before the 1980 Games, but the anti-apartheid movement shows clearly that developing nations used sport for their own national and regional interests, which did not always match the goals of their Cold War patrons.

Soviet leaders reported some success in their efforts to increase the participation of African countries in the Olympic movement, securing assurances that African countries would compete in Moscow. By February 1979, the Supreme Council of Sports in Africa had taken a unanimous resolution to support the Moscow Games, and the IOC had given temporary recognition to a number of NOCs, including those of Angola, Mauritius, Yemen, and Mozambique.[80] To guarantee a wide representation of African and other developing nations at the Moscow Games, Smirnov and Andrianov worked to get IOC funds to help pay for transportation to bring athletes from poorer countries to the Olympics. At its meeting in San Juan in June 1979, the Solidarity Commission allocated one million pounds to subsidize travel expenses for athletes coming to the 1980 Winter Olympics, to be held in Lake Placid, New York, as well as the Summer Olympics in Moscow.[81]

While Soviet representatives worked to soothe tensions and address concerns in Africa, a separate set of difficulties related to Asia and the Middle East threatened the Moscow Games. The participation of Israeli athletes posed a challenge on a number of levels. Some members of the Jewish community in the United States remained convinced that the Moscow organizers would try to exclude Israel from the Games, based on the Soviet government's generally anti-Israel foreign policy and because of its restrictions on Soviet Jewish emigration.[82] Soviet officials also feared that various circles in the West that disagreed with Soviet government treatment of Jewish dissidents posed a significant boycott threat. One such organization, the Committee for the Boycott of the Olympic Games in Moscow, actually wanted to organize a boycott of both the Moscow and Lake Placid Games because neither the United States nor the Soviet Union "respected human rights and democratic liberties" and because their rivalry "threatened peace throughout the world." Comparing both countries with Nazi Germany, the organization, formed in Paris, suggested that if the international community had boycotted the 1936 Berlin Olympics, "Hitler's barbarism and the triumph of national socialism perhaps could have been avoided."[83] For both superpowers, the Olympics were seen as a venue to increase their international prestige, but as this boycott movement demonstrates, the Games could also expose the host country to international scrutiny and criticism.

The Moscow organizers also worried that oil-rich Arab countries, which tended to be either strongly anti-Israel or closely tied to the United States or Great Britain, might also initiate a boycott either as a protest against the participation of Israel or to curry favor with the West, should the United States decide to boycott the Games in support of Israel.[84] Refusing to invite Israel would not only encourage boycotts from the West and its allies, but it would countermand the Olympic Charter and put the Soviet Union at risk of expulsion from the Olympic movement. When the Indonesian government refused visas to athletes from Israel to compete in the 1962 Asian Games in Jakarta, the IOC withdrew its backing and threatened to revoke recognition of the Indonesian Olympic Committee.[85] To counter possible threats to the Moscow Olympics, the Orgcom increased its efforts to attract such countries as Kuwait, Bahrain, Brunei, and the United Arab Emirates to the Olympic movement.[86] As with African sport leaders, Soviet representatives attempted to balance the expectations of Asian countries with IOC requirements for hosting the Olympic Games, publicizing their strict adherence to IOC rules yet addressing Asian leaders' underlying concerns in other ways while also offering sporting aid and assistance.

Despite the continuing tensions, Soviet organizers' multifaceted public diplomacy campaign bore substantial results as the Games drew nearer. In March 1979, Afghanistan's NOC confirmed to the IOC that it would send ten freestyle wrestlers and officials to the Moscow Olympics.[87] The IOC executive board gave provisional recognition to Vietnam at its meeting in Nagoya in October 1979, along with the NOCs of Angola, Laos, Mauritania, and Mozambique. The EB accorded full recognition to Bahrain at that same meeting. In November the IOC processed applications for recognition from Bangladesh, Botswana, the British Virgin Islands, Djibouti, Grenada, Qatar, São Tomé and Príncipe, Seychelles, and the Yemen Arab Republic, and DPR of Yemen. The status of the two Chinas was left to the full IOC membership through a postal vote.[88] By December 31, 1979, the NOCs of San Marino, Somalia, Monaco, Andorra, Uganda, and Honduras had confirmed their participation in the Moscow Games, although Albania and Saudi Arabia refused to participate, and the Orgcom still awaited final word from Malawi, Lesotho, Paraguay, Belize, Guatemala, and Haiti.[89] In February 1980, IOC director Monique Berlioux informed the Orgcom's chairman Ignati Novikov that the NOCs of Angola, Bangladesh, Laos, Mauritania, and Seychelles had received full recognition at the EB meeting at Lake Placid and could now be officially invited to participate in the Games.[90]

At the same time as Moscow prepared to host the Games of the XXII Olympiad, the Brezhnev leadership took an increasingly aggressive line in its Cold War foreign policy, which would help to undermine the Olympic project and contribute to the breakdown of East-West détente. Buoyed by American tentativeness following the disastrous Vietnam War and eager to maintain its status as leader of the socialist world, the USSR intervened directly or through its Cuban proxies in several wars throughout the global South.[91] After costly proxy wars in Angola and Ethiopia, a 1978 communist coup in Afghanistan brought the superpower rivalry to the Soviet Union's southern border. As an Islamist insurgency against the new regime and factionalism among Afghan communists continued to destabilize the regime on its volatile Central Asian border, the Soviet Politburo authorized Soviet military intervention to put down the insurgency and return control of the country to a reliable ally.

Outside the control of the Orgcom, the Soviet invasion of Afghanistan undermined support in the West for détente and inspired sixty nations to boycott the 1980 Summer Olympics, demonstrating the limits of sport diplomacy to ensure the success of the Games. On December 27, 1979, Soviet troops invaded Afghanistan. Eager to send a message that such aggressive action would not be tolerated, on January 14, 1980, the Jimmy Carter administration issued an ultimatum to the Soviet Union: exit Afghanistan by mid-February, or the Games will be boycotted. When Carter's threat failed to induce the Soviet leadership to abandon its mission in Afghanistan, Carter officially announced the boycott one month later. After the House of Representatives and the Senate passed a resolution not to send athletes to the Games, the United States Olympic Committee (USOC) agreed. In mid-April the USOC announced its decision to support the Carter administration's boycott, and the government warned its athletes that they could lose their passports if they traveled to the Games. Carter then began work to convince US allies to support the boycott. While Carter and other Western leaders, such as British prime minister Margaret Thatcher, saw the boycott as an opportunity to take a hard line against Soviet belligerence, Olympic supporters, athletes, coaches, and officials around the world decried the boycott as an unacceptable political interference with the Olympic Games.[92]

Despite the absence of sixty countries, Moscow still welcomed eighty nations to the Games, where 5,179 athletes competed in 203 events. Even many Western nations and US allies attended despite the boycott, among them NATO countries—Great Britain, France, Belgium, Greece, Iceland, Italy, Luxembourg, the Netherlands, Denmark, and Portugal—and countries of the British Commonwealth, including Australia and New Zealand. Some of these countries sent smaller delegations and marched under the Olympic flag instead of their national flags, but the presence of their athletes significantly reduced the impact of Carter's boycott. Furthermore, the Orgcom could boast good results for its efforts to expand international sport over the last decades, with several developing nations competing in the Olympic Games for the first time, including Angola, Vietnam, Botswana, Laos, Nicaragua, Seychelles, Mozambique, and Cyprus.

## Conclusion

The period between 1953 and 1980 could be seen as the high point of successful sport diplomacy by the Soviet Union, and during this period the USSR scored significant Olympic victories over its Cold War rival. After coming in a very close second place to the United States in 1952, the Soviet national team went on to "win" almost every Olympic Games in which it competed, until the breakup of the Soviet Union in 1991. Besides Soviet dominance in the medal count, the Soviet Union's entrance into the Olympic movement in the early 1950s changed the shape of international sport as Soviet representatives exploited anticolonial sentiments in an attempt to gain support from newly independent nations in the developing world. Through Soviet efforts, the IOC expanded dramatically, welcoming more members from socialist and developing nations into the organization, and the number of countries participating in the Olympics also increased markedly between 1952 and 1980. In the 1972 Munich Games, 121 countries competed, compared to 69 in the 1952 Helsinki Games. While the push to expand the Games was intended to win more support for the Soviet Union abroad and increase Soviet-friendly membership in the IOC, by pressing the international sports world on questions of race and decolonization, Soviet representatives helped open the way for more global representation within international sport. Furthermore, when the Games were finally held in Moscow in 1980, increased participation by developing nations helped counter the impact of the US-led boycott.

Despite the Soviets' successes in bringing newly independent countries into the Olympic Games, their invasion of Afghanistan demonstrated the limits of Soviet sport diplomacy. Not only did the invasion undermine Soviet sport administrators' efforts to ensure that the 1980 Moscow Olympics was the most widely attended, biggest, and best celebration of the Soviet Union's status as superpower and that Moscow won the hearts and minds of world opinion, but the invasion brought into stark contrast the image that Soviet diplomats tried to portray. Although the USSR attempted to justify the invasion as being an integral part of the worldwide anticolonial struggle and confirmation of Soviet support for revolution, many viewed it instead as proof that the Soviet Union was itself a colonial power with imperialist ambitions. The invasion also sparked a renewal of tension between the United States and the USSR, which along with the concomitant arms buildup overshadowed attempts at diplomacy through cultural exchange. This breakdown of Soviet-American sporting relations was especially visible in the US-led boycott of the 1980 Summer Olympics and the communist bloc boycott of the 1984 Summer Olympics in Los Angeles. Whereas Soviet sport administrators previously had occupied a key position in the USSR's international relations strategy, they now found themselves sidelined by military decisions made beyond their sphere of influence, marking an end to the golden age of Soviet sport diplomacy.

## Notes

1. *Fizkul'tura i sport* (Physical Culture and Sport), April 1959, 7.

2. See for example, Robert Edelman, *Spartak Moscow: A History of the People's Team in the Workers' State* (Ithaca, NY: Cornell University Press, 2009) and *Serious Fun: A History of Spectator Sports in the USSR* (New York: Oxford University Press, 1993); Barbara Jean Keys, *Globalizing Sport: National Rivalry and International Community in the 1930s* (Cambridge: Harvard University Press, 2006); and Mike O'Mahony, *Sport in the USSR: Physical Culture—Visual Culture* (London: Reaktion, 2006). Recent articles include Evelyn Mertin, "The Soviet Union and the Olympic Games of 1980 and 1984: Explaining the Boycotts to Their Own People," and Jenifer Parks, "Verbal Gymnastics: Sports, Bureaucracy, and the Soviet Union's Entrance into the Olympic Games, 1946–1952," in *East Plays West: Sport and the*

*Cold War,* ed. Stephen Wagg and David Andrews (London and New York: Routledge, 2006); Barbara Keys, "Soviet Sport and Transnational Mass Culture in the 1930s," *Journal of Contemporary History* 38, no. 3 (2003): 413–34; and Robert Edelman, "A Small Way of Saying 'No': Moscow Working Men, Spartak Soccer, and the Communist Party, 1900–1945," *American Historical Review* 107, no. 5 (2002): 1441–74.

3. Allen Guttmann, *The Games Must Go On: Avery Brundage and the Olympic Movement* (New York: Columbia University Press, 1984) and *The Olympics: A History of the Modern Games,* 2nd ed. (Urbana and Chicago: University of Illinois Press, 2002); Christopher Hill, *Olympic Politics* (Manchester and New York: St. Martin's, 1992); John Hoberman, *The Olympic Crisis: Sport, Politics and the Moral Order* (New Rochelle, NY: A. D. Caratzas, 1986) and *Sport and Political Ideology* (Austin: University of Texas Press, 1984); Lincoln Allison, ed., *The Global Politics of Sport: The Role of Global Institutions in Sport* (London and New York: Routledge, 2005) and *The Changing Politics of Sport* (Manchester: Manchester University Press, 1993); Thomas M. Hunt, *Drug Games: The International Olympic Committee and the Politics of Doping, 1960–2008* (Austin: University of Texas Press, 2011); Kevin B. Witherspoon, *Before the Eyes of the World: Mexico and the 1968 Olympic Games* (Dekalb: Northern Illinois University Press, 2008); and Xu Guoqi, *Olympic Dreams: China and Sports, 1895–2008* (Cambridge: Harvard University Press, 2008).

4. See Wagg and Andrews, eds., *East Plays West;* Robert E. Rinehart, "'Fists Flew and Blood Flowed': Symbolic Resistance and the International Response in Hungarian Water Polo at the Melbourne Olympics, 1956," *Journal of Sport History* 23, no. 2 (1996): 120–39; Donald E. Abelson, "Politics on Ice: The United States, the Soviet Union, and a Hockey Game in Lake Placid," *Canadian Review of American Studies* 40, no. 1 (2010), 63–94; John Soares, "Cold War, Hot Ice: International Ice Hockey, 1947–1980," *Journal of Sport History* 34, no. 2 (2007): 207–30; and Joseph M. Turrini, "'It Was Communism versus the Free World:' The USA-USSR Dual Track Meet Series and the Development of Track and Field in the United States, 1958–85," *Journal of Sport History* 28, no. 3 (2001): 427–71.

5. See, for example, Nicholas E. Sarantakes, *Dropping the Torch: Jimmy Carter, The Olympic Boycott, and the Cold War* (New York: Cambridge University Press, 2011); Derick L. Hulme, *The Political Olympics: Moscow, Afghanistan, and the 1980 U.S. Boycott* (New York: Praeger, 1990); Paul Corthorn, "The Cold War and British Debates over the Boycott of the 1980 Moscow Olympics," *Cold War History* 13, no. 1 (2013): 43–66; and Daniel James Lahey, "The Thatcher Government's Response to the Soviet Invasion of Afghanistan, 1979–1980," *Cold War History* 13, no. 1 (2013): 21–42.

6. See Victor Peppard and James Riordan, *Playing Politics: Soviet Sport Diplomacy to 1992* (Greenwich, CT: JAI Press, 1992); James Riordan, "Rewriting Soviet Sports History," *Journal of Sport History* 20, no. 3 (1993): 247–58; James Riordan, *Sport, Politics, and Communism* (Manchester and New York: Manchester University Press, 1991); and Pierre Arnaud and James Riordan, *Sport and International Politics:*

*Impact of Fascism and Communism on Sport* (London and New York: E & FN Spon, 1998).

7. Geoffrey Cowan and Nicholas J. Cull, "Preface: Public Diplomacy in a Changing World," *Annals of the American Academy of Political and Social Science* 616 (March 2008): 6. Other works on public diplomacy during the Cold War include Frederick C. Barghoorn, *The Soviet Cultural Offensive: The Role of Cultural Diplomacy in Soviet Foreign Policy* (Princeton, NJ: Princeton University Press, 1960); Wilson P. Dizard Jr., *Inventing Public Diplomacy: The Story of the U.S. Information Agency* (Boulder and London: Lynne Rienner, 2004); Kenneth Osgood, *Total Cold War: Eisenhower's Secret Propaganda Battle at Home and Abroad* (Lawrence: University Press of Kansas, 2006); and Yale Richmond, *Cultural Exchange and the Cold War: Raising the Iron Curtain* (University Park: Pennsylvania State University Press, 2003).

8. Eytan Gilboa, "Searching for a Theory of Public Diplomacy," *Annals of the American Academy of Political and Social Science* 616 (2008): 55.

9. Osgood, *Total Cold War*, 368.

10. Joseph S. Nye Jr., "Public Diplomacy and Soft Power," *Annals of the American Academy of Political and Social Science* 616 (2008): 94.

11. The most complete exploration of Cold War intervention in the developing world is Odd Arne Westad, *The Global Cold War: Third World Interventions and the Making of Our Times* (Cambridge: Cambridge University Press, 2007). For more on Soviet policies in the developing world, see Vladislav M. Zubok, *A Failed Empire: The Soviet Union in the Cold War from Stalin to Gorbachev* (Chapel Hill: University of North Carolina Press, 2007), chaps. 7 and 8; Sergey Mzov, *A Distant Front in the Cold War: The USSR in West Africa and the Congo, 1956–64* (Stanford, CA: Stanford University Press, 2010); Alessandro Iandolo, "The Rise and Fall of the 'Soviet Model of Development' in West Africa, 1957–64," *Cold War History* 12, no. 4 (2012): 683–704; and Roger E. Kanet, "The Superpower Quest for Empire: The Cold War and Soviet Support for 'Wars of National Liberation,'" *Cold War History* 6, no. 3 (2006): 331–52.

12. Laura Fair, "Kickin' It: Leisure, Politics and Football in Colonial Zanzibar, 1900s–1950s," *Africa* 67, no. 2 (1997): 224–51, and Mattia Fumanti, "Burying E.S.: Educated Elites, Subjectivity and Distinction in Rundu, Namibia," *Journal of Southern African Studies* 33 (2007): 469–83.

13. Peter Alegi, *African Soccerscapes: How a Continent Changed the World's Game* (Athens: Ohio University Press, 2010). See also Benjamin Talton, "1960s Africa in Historical Perspective: An Introduction," *Journal of Black Studies* 43 (2012): 7.

14. Witherspoon, *Eyes of the World;* Chris Bollssmann, "Mexico 1968 and South Africa 2010: Sombreros and Vuvuzelas and the Legitimisation of Global Sporting Events," *Bulletin of Latin American Research* 29 (2010): 93–106; Robert Huish, "Punching above Its Weight: Cuba's Use of Sport for South-South Cooperation," *Third World Quarterly* 32, no. 3 (2011): 417–33; and Cesar Torres, "Peronism, International Sport, and Diplomacy," chap. 5 in the present volume.

15. See Antonio Sotomayor, "The Cold War Games of a Colonial Latin American Nation: San Juan, Puerto Rico, 1966," and Fan Hong and Lu Zhouxiang, "Politics First, Competition Second: Sport and China's Foreign Diplomacy in the 1960s and 1970s," chaps. 7 and 12, respectively, in the present volume.

16. Douglas Booth, *The Race Game: Sport and Politics in South Africa* (London and Portland, OR: Frank Cass, 1998); Aviston D. Downes, "Forging Africa-Caribbean Solidarity within the Commonwealth? Sport and Diplomacy during the Antiapartheid Campaign," chap. 4 in the present volume; and Damion Thomas, "Playing the 'Race Card': US Foreign Policy and the Integration of Sports," in *East Plays West,* ed. Wagg and Andrews, 216.

17. Nicholas J. Cull, "Public Diplomacy: Taxonomies and Histories," *Annals of the American Academy of Political and Social Science* 616 (2008): 45.

18. Keys, *Globalizing Sport,* 160. See also Keys, "Soviet Sport," 416.

19. See Richmond, *Cultural Exchange.*

20. Riordan and Peppard, *Playing Politics,* 9.

21. Elena Zubkova, *Russia after the War: Hopes, Illusions, and Disappointments, 1945–1957,* trans. Hugh Ragsdale (Armonk, NY: M. E. Sharpe, 1998).

22. Riordan and Peppard, *Playing Politics,* 62. See also Arakadii Apollonov, "Stalinskaia zabota o protsvetanii fizicheskoi kul'tury v SSSR [Stalinist Concern for the Prosperity of Physical Culture in the USSR]," *Fizkul'tura i sport* (Physical Culture and Sport), December 1949, 4.

23. Short Report on the IOC, Gosudarstvennyi arkhiv Rossiiskoi Federatsii (State Archive of the Russian Federation, GARF), f. 7576, op. 2, d. 699, ll. 4–5. This report is undated, but a copy of it dated December 8, 1950, was submitted to the Central Committee on December 14, 1950; see Rossiiskii gosudarstvennyi arkhiv sotsial'noi i politicheskoi istorii (Russian State Archive of Social and Political History, RGASPI), f. 17, op. 137, d. 237, ll. 155–57.

24. Handwritten note, May 11, 1951, RGASPI, f. 17, op. 137, d. 237, l. 125, and handwritten note, April 25, 1951, RGASPI, f. 17, op. 137, d. 557, l. 20.

25. Sobolev to Edstrom, telegram, April 23, 1951, Aksel' Vartan'ian, "Sekretnyi arkhiv Akselia Vartaniana [Secret Archive of Aksel' Vartan'ian]," September 16, 2002, *Sport-ekspress,* available from http://www.sport-express.ru. See also GARF, f. 7576, op. 2, d. 667, ll. 6–7.

26. *The Olympic Charter,* Fundamental Principles, p. 9, available from http://www.olympic.org.

27. 45me Session du CIO, Vienna, May 7, 1951, Avery Brundage Collection, Record Series 26/20/37, Box 90, University of Illinois Archives, Champaign, Illinois (hereafter ABC).

28. For more on the problem of GDR recognition, see Heather L. Dichter, "'A Game of Political Ice Hockey': NATO Restrictions on East German Sport Travel in the Aftermath of the Berlin Wall," in the present volume.

29. Oleg Troyanovsky, "The Making of Soviet Foreign Policy," in *Nikita Khrushchev,* ed. William Taubman (New Haven, CT: Yale University Press, 2000), 217.

30. Osgood, *Total Cold War,* 263.

31. Report on Serious Occurrences at Sports Competitions in Socialist Countries, 1961, GARF, f. 9570, op. 1, d. 688, ll. 161–63.

32. For more on the role of the PRC and Indonesia in Asian sports, see Hong and Zhouxiang, "Politics First, Competition Second," in the present volume.

33. For more on the contradictions between official socialist solidarity and the complex reality of Eastern bloc relations, see Evelyn Mertin, "Steadfast Friendship and Brotherly Help: The Distinctive Soviet–East German Sport Relationship within the Socialist Bloc," in the present volume.

34. Minutes of the Fiftieth IOC Session, June 14–18, 1955, IOC.

35. Ibid.

36. Brundage to members of the IOC, January 30, 1954, Record Series 26/20/37, Box 70, ABC.

37. Meeting minutes of the Fifty-Eighth IOC Session, June 19–21, 1961, International Olympic Committee Archive, Lausanne, Switzerland (hereafter IOC).

38. Proposal on the Future Activities of Sports Organizations of the USSR in the IOC, GARF, f. 9570, op. 1, d. 689, l. 74. It is not clear who wrote this report or for whom, but considering the content and its location among other materials related to the Fifty-Eighth IOC Session in Athens, it is reasonable to assume that the report was written by workers in the International Sports Relations Section of the Sports Committee and that the intended audience was the Sports Committee leadership and probably the Central Committee.

39. Spravka on Participation of Soviet Sports Organizations in Work of International Sports Associations, August 20, 1962, GARF, f. 9570, op. 1, d. 827, ll. 20–26.

40. Oral Report of Central Soviet of Sports Organizations and Societies on Preparation of Soviet Athletes for XVIII Olympic Games in Tokyo, June 1964, GARF, f. 9570, op. 1, d. 254, l. 13.

41. Ibid., l. 35.

42. Report of Soviet Representatives to Meetings of the EB IOC and EB with IFs in Lausanne, June 1963, RGANI, f. 5, op. 55, d. 11, l. 167. See also Iu. Mashin to Central Committee, April 25, 1963, Ibid., l. 126.

43. "Olympic Solidarity: Creation and Development," Olympic.org: Official Website of the Olympic Movement, available from http://www.olympic.org/Documents/Reports/EN/en_report_1072.pdf.

44. Minutes of the Plenum of the Central Soviet of the Union of Sports Organizations and Societies, July 7, 1961, GARF, f. 9570, op. 1, d. 83, l. 111. In 1959 the Sports Committee was reorganized and administration of sports was placed under the Central Soviet of the Union of Sports Societies and Organizations. However, the leadership remained intact, and the Sports Committee was reconstituted in 1968. The author has continued to use the name Sports Committee to avoid confusion.

45. Ibid., l. 112. Pesliak reported that the Soviet Union hosted 67 foreign sport delegations in 1952, compared with 407 in 1960. The Soviet Union sent 399 sport delegations abroad in 1960, compared to only 44 in 1952.

46. Report of Gifts sent to Africa, 1960–61, GARF f. 9570, op. 1, d. 1673, l. 8.

47. Plan for Cultural Cooperation between the USSR and the Somalian Republic for 1963, GARF f. 9570, op. 1, d. 1097, ll. 6–8.

48. Ambassador to Libya Notes from Meeting with the chairman and secretary of the Sports Festival Commission, December 17, 1962, GARF f. 9570, op. 1, d. 1097, ll. 12–13.

49. Ibid., l. 13.

50. GARF f. 9570, op. 1, d. 1834, ll. 94–96.

51. *Fizkul'tura i sport,* January 1961, 2.

52. Ibid., August 1960, 2.

53. Ibid., December 1960, 10.

54. Ibid.

55. Spravka on Participation of Soviet Sports Organisations in work of International Sports Associations, August 20, 1962, GARF, f. 9570, op. 1, d. 827, l. 40.

56. Osgood, *Total Cold War,* 277.

57. Ibid., 285.

58. Thomas, "Playing the 'Race Card,'" 216.

59. Nye, "Public Diplomacy," 95.

60. Decree of the Presidium of the Orgcom Moscow, April 1, 1976, On the Results of Establishment of International Relations for 1975, GARF, f. 9610, op. 1, d. 36, l. 39.

61. Final Act, Conference on Security and Cooperation in Europe, Organization for Security and Cooperation in Europe, Helsinki, 1975, 41, available at http://www.osce.org/documents/mcs/1975/08/4044_en.pdf.

62. Ibid., 41–56.

63. Decree of the Presidium of the Orgcom Moscow, April 1, 1976, On the Results of International Relations for 1975, GARF, f. 9610, op. 1, d. 36, l. 39.

64. Booth, *The Race Game,* 2.

65. Report of Soviet Representatives to Meetings of the EB IOC and EB with IFs in Lausanne, June 1963, RGANI, f. 5, op. 55, d. 11, l. 168.

66. Minutes of the Sixtieth IOC Session, October 16–20, 1963, Baden-Baden, Germany, IOC.

67. Minutes of the Meeting of the Sixty-Ninth IOC Session, Amsterdam, May 12–16, 1970, IOC. The vote to expel South Africa from the Olympics was close: thirty-five in favor, twenty-eight against, and three blank ballots.

68. Minutes of the Meeting of the Joint Commission of Sports Organizations of Socialist Countries for Cooperation in Preparation and Staging of the Olympic Games, February 16, 1979, GARF, f. 9610, op. 1, d. 440, l. 30.

69. Copy of Report to Soviet of Ministers on course of preparation for 1980 OG Moscow, January 27, 1977, GARF, f. 9610, op. 1, d. 119, l. 9.

70. Notes of Meeting of V. Smirnov with the Manager of the Office of the Minister of Public, Work, and Youth Affairs, July 12, 1977, GARF, f. 9610, op. 1, d. 194, ll. 6–7.

71. Notes from Meeting with Minister of Culture, Art, and Sport of the Republic of Congo, December 8, 1977, GARF f. 9610, op. 1, d. 195, ll. 1–2.

72. Notes of Meeting of Koval and Minister of Work and Public Affairs of Kuwait, n.d. 1977, and Notes of Meeting of Koval with Minister of Youth of the Iraqi Republic, November 29, 1977, GARF f. 9610, op. 1, d. 195, ll. 7, 22–23.

73. Riordan and Peppard, *Playing Politics,* 109.

74. Decree of the Orgcom Executive Bureau and the Sports Committee Collegium, April 24, 1978, GARF, f. 9610, op. 1, d. 226, l. 6.

75. Minutes of the Meeting of the Joint Commission of Sports Organizations of Socialist Countries for Cooperation in Preparing and Staging the Olympic Games, February 26, 1979, GARF, f. 9610, op. 1, d. 440, l. 27.

76. Report of Trip to the United States of the Orgcom Delegation, June 1978, GARF, f. 9610, op. 1, d. 279, l. 32.

77. Ibid., l. 13.

78. Note of Meeting of V. I. Prokopov with Jo Jeli, member of Executive Bureau ANK South Africa, August 3, 1978, GARF, f. 9610, op. 1, d. 300, l. 11.

79. Notes of Meeting of V. Kudriavtsev with Peter Onu, undersecretary-general of Organization of African Unity, GARF, f. 9610, op. 1, d. 300, ll. 17–18.

80. Minutes of the Meeting of the Joint Commission of Sports Organizations of Socialist Countries for Cooperation in Preparation and Staging of the Olympic Games, February 26, 1979, GARF, f. 9610, op. 1, d. 440, l. 19. See also Resolution from Supreme Council of Sport in Africa, July 11, 1978, COJO of the Summer Games in Moscow 1980 Correspondence 1975–1978, IOC.

81. Lord Killanin to I. Novikov, August 21, 1979, COJO of the Summer Games in Moscow 1980 Correspondence 1979, IOC.

82. Len Alpert to Congressman Jack Kemp, September 26, 1977, NOCs USSR Correspondence 1977–79, IOC.

83. Committee for the Boycott of the Olympic Games in Moscow to M. Berlioux, September 7, 1979, COJO of the Summer Games in Moscow 1980 Correspondence 1979, IOC.

84. Report on the Work of the Delegation of Orgcom in Bangkok as Observers at VIII Asian Games, December 1978, GARF, f. 9610, op. 1, d. 301, ll. 32–33.

85. Report of the EB IOC meeting and meeting of the EB with IFs, February 7–8, 1963, RGANI, f. 5, op. 55, d. 11, l. 57.

86. Report on the Work of the Delegation of Orgcom in Bangcok as Observers at VIII Asian Games, December 1978, GARF, f. 9610, op. 1, d. 301, l. 33.

87. Democratic Republic of Afghanistan NOC to IOC, March 6, 1979, COJO of the Summer Games in Moscow 1980 Correspondence 1979, IOC.

88. M. Berlioux to I. Novikov, November 8, 1979, COJO of the Summer Games in Moscow 1980 Correspondence 1979, IOC.

89. V. Popov to M. Berlioux, telegram, December 31, 1979, COJO of the Summer Games in Moscow 1980 Correspondence 1979, IOC.

90. M. Berlioux to I. Novikov, February 16, 1980, COJO of the Summer Games in Moscow 1980 Correspondence 1980–1993, IOC.

91. Kanet, "The Superpower Quest for Empire," 337.

92. For more on the 1980 boycott movement and its effects, see Sarantakes, *Dropping the Torch;* Corthorn, "The Cold War and British Debates over the Boycott of the Olympics"; Lahey, "The Thatcher Government's Response to the Soviet Invasion of Afghanistan 1979–80"; and Hulme, *The Political Olympics.*

Part 2

# The Decolonizing World

# 4

# Forging Africa-Caribbean Solidarity within the Commonwealth?

## Sport and Diplomacy during the Anti-apartheid Campaign

*Aviston D. Downes*

The impact of the international anti-apartheid sports campaign on West Indies cricket is a theme that has attracted some attention within a celebratory nationalist framework.[1] The subject has also attracted modest attention by other historians and political scientists interested in the wider international political and diplomatic dimensions of this subject.[2] Marc Keech and Barrie Houlihan have identified sport as a potential bridge-builder between erstwhile estranged nations or, alternatively, a vehicle through which to register disapproval against a state and its governing ideology.[3] They have labeled this latter expression of sport "negative sport diplomacy." Houlihan has also argued that "international sporting contact has provided [governments] with a low-cost, but high-profile resource for publicizing their policy on international issues or towards specific states."[4]

Keech and Houlihan contend that for the major world powers, sport usually represents a relatively minor element in "a wide repertoire of military, economic and diplomatic resources to choose from."[5] As such, then, sport diplomacy is a "soft option," a tool that can be mobilized with minimal socioeconomic costs or dangerous political or diplomatic fallout. Yet they also noted that "for poorer countries negative sports diplomacy is much more likely to indicate a paucity of resources for the conduct of international relations than the careful selection of an appropriately measured response."[6]

Undoubtedly developed countries possess a wider panoply of resources with which they can bring diplomatic pressure upon adversaries. But any suggestion that sport is some low-cost disposable resource left to Third World nations for "negative" political deployment is seriously flawed reasoning. Such a hypothesis undervalues the economic as well as the politically symbolic weight of the partnerships forged among sport, music, film, and the modern media. It could be argued, for example, that the game of cricket had emerged as the richest cultural resource of the Commonwealth Caribbean by the 1960s. Although short in terms of the natural resources normally utilized to generate wealth in the industrialized North, the Caribbean's contribution and impact in the world in terms of music, culture, and sport cannot be underrated. By 1970 the region could claim the world's greatest cricket all-rounder in the person of its captain, Garfield (later Sir Garfield) Sobers. The West Indies were winners of the first two Prudential World Cup competitions in the 1970s, and the team proceeded to world dominance in the sport. The names and faces of the region's professional cricketers were and remain more recognizable than any of its captains of commerce or any of its prime ministers.

The game of cricket had for some time been a cultural arena within which social power expressed in class and racial discrimination was both perpetuated and contested. Cricket, one of the English games shorn of its pre-Victorian "impurities" by the middle of the nineteenth century, emerged as the quintessential metaphor for British civilization and its engagement with the rest of the world. Indeed, in the Caribbean context, the game became the main cultural vehicle by which colonial whites and their progeny sought to assert the retention of their identity as English gentlemen in the tropics. While such an ideology was imbibed firsthand by the sons of that mostly white, privileged middle class through a handful of elite schools consciously reorganized along the English public school model, some colonialists argued for exposing a representative minority of the struggling nonwhites to this training, with a view that the consequent creation of a black middle class would serve as a buffer and broker against social revolution. The dominant white planter-merchant class was reluctant to embrace the "civilizing mission" to the emancipated black population by enthusiastic reformist clergymen, educators, and promoters of liberal sport. Instead, exclusion, except in the most menial aspects of the game, was the lot of black working-class West Indians. The exclusionary agenda ultimately failed, however, to prevent the rise of a truly inclusive national sport by the mid-twentieth century. Indeed, the middle-class British claims that sport was the most effective instrument of imperialism seemed particularly true of the anglophone Caribbean.

Forms of popular protests punctuated the Caribbean in response to poor colonial conditions such as dilapidated housing, poor sanitation, disease, skyrocketing infant mortality, and shortened life expectancy since the nineteenth century. Although a number of the colonies were rocked by a series of labor rebellions between 1934 and 1938, decolonization in the anglophone Caribbean was generally incremental and relatively peaceful. In *Beyond a Boundary* (1963)—his seminal cricket biography and analysis of the game—Cyril Lionel Roberts James, an anticolonial intellectual from Trinidad, explains the enthusiasm for this English cultural expression in the context of exploitation and discrimination: "I haven't the slightest doubt that the clash of race, caste and class did not retard but stimulated West Indian cricket. I am equally certain that in those years social and political passions, denied normal outlets, expressed themselves so fiercely in cricket (and other games). . . . The class and racial rivalries were too intense. They could be fought out without violence or much lost except pride and honour."[7]

By the time colonial and imperial cricket contests resumed after World War II, the complexion of the game had literally changed in the Caribbean with the composition of the team a more realistic picture of Caribbean demographics. Nevertheless, having evolved into a predominantly black outfit, the regional team was still dutifully led by a white or near-white captain of dubious ability. Leadership on the field of sport, then, was surely out of step with the fresh currents of nationalism and decolonization sweeping across the anglophone Caribbean. The securing of universal adult suffrage by the early 1950s in some colonies resulted in the wholesale removal of the white planter-merchant ruling class and its replacement by black premiers, chief ministers, and cabinets of black ministers driving social transformation. The formation of the ill-fated West Indies Federation in 1958 signaled the possibility of a pan-Caribbean nationalism but collapsed in 1962, leading to insular demands for independence.

Even as the sun was setting on the British Empire in the Caribbean, in Rhodesia and South Africa the dark clouds of apartheid threatened to thwart black hopes and aspirations there. Apartheid and international opposition to it evolved alongside the ongoing project of decolonization in Africa and the Caribbean, thus providing a high-profile political issue around which to deepen nationalism at home while making newly independent states "visible" on the international stage. That the ideological and political evil of apartheid was rooted in antiblack racism would have had special resonance for both the new black African and Caribbean nations. Thus the campaign provided an opportunity for the forging of solidarity between these new black states. After all, the concept of Pan-Africanism popularized by Jamaican Marcus Garvey and expressed in the organization of the United Negro Improvement Association (UNIA) had inspired anticolonialism within Africa and its diaspora since the early 1930s.[8] The Commonwealth served to provide a forum for functional cooperation and a postimperial solidarity for Britain and her former colonies. But while there were no longer officially recognized "white self-governing" and "black crown colony" polities, racism leveled at aborigines, first peoples, blacks, and Asians found fertile ground in the "white" Commonwealth nations.

A very important continuity with the past was the celebration of unity and friendships through sport. A British official once boasted that sport "was another link in the chain of oneness and wholeheartedness which binds the sons of Great Britain with the children of the Greater Britain in that undefeated, age undaunted, whole—our British Empire."[9] Having been accorded "Test status" as a fellow member of the Imperial Cricket Council in 1928, the West Indies fully embraced that game as its arena of expressing their sociopolitical agenda. Except for South Africa itself, however, cricket did not capture the imagination of black Africans as it did for their Caribbean counterparts. Nevertheless, other sporting disciplines and competitions did provide opportunities for African-Caribbean solidarity. In 1930 the British Empire Games were launched in Hamilton, Canada, to bring Britain and her colonies closer together. Held every four years, these games (renamed the Empire and Commonwealth Games from 1954) provided an even wider playing field on which to embrace empire or reject it. Indeed, the Commonwealth Games consistently became a favorite target through which African states sought to embarrass sections of the "white Commonwealth" soft on apartheid.

This is not to suggest a united front in either the Caribbean or Africa on the political modalities of sport. Moreover, racism was not the only driving ideology confronting black African and Caribbean states and their neocolonial partners. Jenifer Parks, in her chapter in this volume, illustrates that a growing shift in Soviet policy from the late 1940s witnessed the USSR joining the International Olympic Committee (IOC) in 1951. The Soviets followed up with an assertive state-sponsored games-training program that deliberately reached out to the fledgling African and Asian states, among others. Added to these cultural and sporting propaganda programs, the Soviet Union openly condemned the racial politics of southern Africa and other Western nations. It was the USSR's representative on the IOC who was instrumental in the early 1960s in raising the question of the legitimacy of South Africa's membership in the IOC.[10] Nevertheless, the Cold War politics of this period constituted an ideological altar upon which often good sense and public morality were sacrificed.

The importance of sport policy as an instrument of international politics and diplomacy was not lost on the new African states. In giving expression to this philosophy, in 1966 the thirty-two-member Organization of African Unity (OAU) established the Supreme Council for Sport in Africa (SCSA) to formulate international sport policy for the bloc. From its inception, the SCSA intervened in international sport to bring pressure upon the racist regimes of southern Africa. In 1968 it initiated a campaign to pressure the IOC to withdraw its qualified invitation to South Africa to participate in the 1968 Mexico Olympics. The newly independent Caribbean states of Jamaica, Guyana, and Barbados supported this initiative and proceeded in December of that year to support UN Resolution 2389 (XXIII), which called upon "all States and organizations to suspend cultural, educational, sporting and other exchanges with the racist regime and with organizations or institutions in south Africa which practice *apartheid*."[11]

The independent states of the anglophone Caribbean were slow in institutionalizing sport within their international political agenda. In 1973 the Caribbean Community (CARICOM) was formed to foster regional integration, but apart from establishing a sports desk at its secretariat, no serious diplomatic role was envisaged for sport. Consequently these Caribbean states came to depend heavily from 1976 on policy positions enunciated by the nongovernmental organization West Indies Cricket Board of Control (WICBC) and of the Gleneagles Agreement of the Commonwealth from 1977.

But sport was more than a cultural practice to bear the ideological weight of nationalism. Many sportsmen, naive perhaps, envisaged their sport as an individualistic pursuit of fame and fortune in a free marketplace. At the same time cricket and other sports were being invested with a political agenda, there were signs that the growing globalized professionalization of sport could depoliticize and unhinge it from nationalism. The conservative world of cricket, for instance, was awakened in 1978 by the Australian media magnate Kerry Packer, whose "cricket circus" contracted a significant number of professional cricketers to play under floodlights in colored clothing before the glare of television cameras for unprecedented sums. Moreover, many Caribbean citizens were not convinced that the black sporting icons of the region should be placed at the front line of the battle to directly bear the burden of compliance. In short, they are professional sportsmen and not politicians.

It was against this background that in 1959, Frank Worrell, popularly perceived as heir apparent to the captaincy of the West Indies Team, was invited by the South African Cricket Board of Control (SACBOC) to bring a black West Indies team to play a similar one in South Africa. This proposed all-black encounter was consistent with the racist policy enunciated in 1956 by Dr. Theophilus E. Donges, South Africa's minister of the interior, that whites and blacks should organize their sports separately.[12]

Between 1956 and 1958, the National Non-European South African XI played nonwhite teams from Kenya and Rhodesia, and by 1959 the emergence of an exciting West Indies team could not go unnoticed. Worrell himself had become a symbol of hope, and he was persuaded that black cricket stars could inspire the downtrodden blacks in South Africa. In his letter to Dennis Brutus, executive secretary of the South Africa Sports Association (SASA), Worrell wrote that "this tour will be of inestimable benefit to the Coloured people."[13] Strong support for this view came from the journalist and social critic C. L. R. James, who had returned to Trinidad in support of Eric Williams and the People's National Movement. In his capacity as editor of that party's newspaper *Nation*, James launched a relentless campaign to have Worrell appointed as the first tenured black West Indies captain. He also encouraged Worrell and his team to tour South Africa because in his opinion the presence of outstanding black players in South Africa would be an inspiration to oppressed black South Africans and a way of exposing the irrationality of apartheid.[14] However, his friend, compatriot, and fellow nationalist, the outstanding West Indies cricketer Learie Constantine, disagreed, contending that such a tour would only legitimize apartheid. In a letter dated June 3, 1959, the SASA warned the WICBC that "the tour . . . will be a grave setback to our hopes, and may defer them indefinitely."[15]

But disagreement was also in evidence on the African end. A decade later, Basil D'Oliveira, one of the members of the nonwhite South African team wrote: "It was the non-European politicians who called for the tour to be cancelled. I feel particularly sad that they should be restricting the developments of sport because they insist on mixing it up with politics. The ways of politicians, black and white, are a mystery to me."[16] In spite of significant support from some quarters in both South Africa and the Caribbean, Worrell and the WICBC made the cautious decision to call off the tour. The contending arguments that emerged as a result of the aborted Worrell tour would persist in virtually every occasion in which a ban or boycott was contemplated. There was as strong a "keep politics out of sport" lobby as there was a side that advocated the efficacy of sporting boycotts and bans.

The ascendance of Worrell to the captaincy in 1960 was a symbolic indication that the agenda of decolonization in the Caribbean was irreversible. As James observes, "the 'Case for West Indian Self-Government' and 'It isn't cricket' had come together at last and together had won a signal victory."[17] The succession of the captaincy by Garfield Sobers from Worrell symbolized, according to James, the logical evolution of a Caribbean nationalism rooted among the broad masses. "When Sobers was appointed captain of the West Indies he was the first genuine native son to hold that position, born in the West Indies, educated in the West Indies, learning the foundations of his cricket benefit of secondary school, or

British university."[18] Sobers had emerged from very humble circumstances to become, arguably, the world's greatest cricketer, but he was very slow to grasp the national and global political significance of his captaincy.

## Garfield Sobers and the Rhodesia Affair

On Tuesday, September 8, 1970, the *Advocate News* of Barbados announced that Garfield Sobers, captain of the West Indies Cricket team, was booked to play in a weekend double-wicket competition in Rhodesia. This excursion was most inopportune because it came within a few months of an intensive protest campaign in Britain coordinated by Barbados-born Jeff Crawford to abort a proposed South African tour of England. Under the banner of "the West Indian Campaign against Apartheid Cricket," many Afro-Caribbean employees of London Transport vowed not to service trains and buses providing transportation to the cricket grounds.[19]

But Sobers's diplomatic faux pas cut even deeper because his Rhodesian escapade coincided with the Third Non-Aligned Summit Conference in Lusaka, Zambia (September 8–10, 1970). The Non-Aligned Movement had its beginnings in 1955 at the Bandung Conference and embraced independent nations committed to peaceful, nonracist, anti-colonial nationhood and a determination not to be pawns of the major world powers. By 1970 the young Commonwealth Caribbean nations (Jamaica, Trinidad and Tobago, and Guyana) were full members of that body; the exception was Barbados with observer status.[20] Cuba was then the lone nonanglophone Caribbean member. To President Forbes Burnham of Guyana, having committed his country to "the struggle in those parts of the yet politically unemancipated countries of Africa" and having offered $50,000 to aid African freedom fighters, the presence of a frolicking West Indies captain entertaining Ian Smith in Rhodesia was a profound embarrassment.[21] Similarly, Sen. Frank Walcott, general secretary of the powerful Barbados Workers Union, launched a stinging condemnation of Sobers's action while outlining the international significance of this West Indian hero. According to Walcott, "Mr Sobers is an international personality and represents the heart and soul of millions of people in the West Indies who see their symbol of pride and equality with nations in Garfield Sobers. . . . None of the Prime Ministers [of the Caribbean] represents the total emotional feelings like Gary

Sobers who is acclaimed by all West Indians as their symbol of world fame and equality."[22]

Sobers returned to Barbados on September 15, 1970, and explained to an eager press, "I thought at first it would be a good thing for me because, first of all, I am a cricketer and I personally think of cricket and not politics."[23] Although the government, opposition members of parliament, and Barbadians generally were sympathetic to their local icon, questions as to Sobers's suitability for captaincy came from other regional leaders of every political stripe. For instance, Archibald Codrington, the former mayor of Georgetown, Guyana, pointed out, "I'll let him [Sobers] know that it is politics that has made him a West Indian cricket captain."[24] President Burnham of Guyana, still smarting by the embarrassment Sobers caused him and other Caribbean delegates at the Non-Aligned Summit stated: "Indeed, it is tragic that a man so outstanding in the field of sport is not sufficiently intelligent to understand the relationship between international sport and international politics, and politics generally. He ought to remember that had it not been for politics people like him would never have been captain of West Indies team."[25]

Burnham also threatened to declare Sobers persona non grata "for his foolish and ill-advised stand" unless an apology was forthcoming. Michael Manley of Jamaica observed that Sobers "may not be welcomed anywhere by people who believe that justice is bigger than even sport."[26] A cloud enveloped the proposed Indian cricket tour of the Caribbean, as allegedly Prime Minister Indira Gandhi contemplated the withdrawal of the Indian team. Eric Williams, prime minister of Trinidad, dispatched Wes Hall, the former Barbados fast bowler, home to obtain a firsthand account from Sobers. The crisis only abated after the prime minister of Barbados, Errol Barrow, intervened and drafted a skillfully worded "apology" that Sobers signed and the Guyanese president accepted.[27]

As Andrew Johns notes in the introduction to this volume, sport has always had a political dimension, in spite of the popular rhetoric to negate such an association. That hard reality crept up even more forcibly on the Caribbean by the early 1970s with the intensification of the anti-apartheid sporting boycotts and territorial exclusion as legitimate responses to those who failed to uphold the antiracial embargo. Fortuitously, the emergence of the anti-apartheid sport campaign coincided roughly with decolonization in Africa and, from 1962, the serial attainment of political independence by a number of anglophone Caribbean territories. Thus these individual newly emerging "black" nation states found in the anti-apartheid sport campaign a voice to herald their arrival on the international stage and an even wider platform from which to address the vestiges of institutional racism that had fertilized slavery and colonization.

From their arrival into the global arena of sovereign states from the early 1960s, Caribbean nations supported the evolving international anti-apartheid campaign. In 1971 the independent Caribbean territories supported UN Special Resolution 2775D (XXVI), adopted on November 29, 1971, which called "upon individual sportsmen to refuse to participate in any sports activity in a country in which there is an official policy of racial discrimination or *apartheid* in the field of sports." In 1973, Trinidad and Tobago's representative at the UN condemned the readmission of South Africa to play in the South American Zone of the Davis Cup tennis tournament.[28] In 1974 the Guyana and Trinidad and Tobago governments refused to permit a private cricket team sponsored by the British financier Derrick Robins to play in their respective countries because he had taken a similar team to play in South Africa. However, the authorities in Barbados, St. Lucia, Dominica, St. Kitts, Montserrat, Grenada, and Antigua did not see the accommodation of the Derrick Robbins's team as problematic. Indeed, Lester Bird, member of the Antigua Labour Party and president of the Antigua Cricket Association, accepted Robins's explanation that taking multiracial teams to South Africa helped to break down apartheid.[29]

Until 1975, then, there had been no clear guidelines to determine what would constitute a violation, although Guyana decided unilaterally to ban any soul who coached or played any sport in racist southern Africa. It took the embarrassment to the Trinidad and Tobago government in 1975, occasioned by that nation's Body Building Association's decision to send a team to South Africa, to force the twin-island nation to address the problem. As Trinidad and Tobago was a Commonwealth Caribbean representative on the UN Special Committee against Apartheid, this humiliating episode catalyzed its cabinet at a meeting on November 13, 1975, to formulate a policy to withhold official and financial support from the Body Building Association as well as all organizations and individuals that insisted on sporting contact with South Africa.[30]

## The Long Hot Summer of 1976

Although these efforts to compete against South Africa caused problems, it was the "Greenidge Affair" in February 1976 that served as the final catalyst to drive Caribbean governments to craft a policy outlining their position on the treatment of teams and individuals that violated the sport ban on South Africa. Although a selected batsman for the Barbados Cricket Team, Geoffrey Greenidge had been denied entry to Guyana because in 1975 he played in Rhodesia and South Africa with an International Wanderers team. The Barbados Cricket Association (BCA) recalled its team from Guyana, resulting, for the first time, in the cancellation of an interregional match under the auspices of the WICBC.

The issue had become not simply a matter of discord within the region. The WICBC predicted a possible fiasco come 1978, when the Australians—who had in their team individuals who played in southern Africa—were due to tour the Caribbean. Consequently, the WICBC dispatched correspondence to every minister of sport to ascertain each government's policy on the divisive issue. Moreover, such a matter had evolved beyond domestic considerations; it had become a foreign policy one. As such, it was referred for the agenda of the meeting of the CARICOM Standing Committee of Ministers Responsible for Foreign Affairs, which convened in Trinidad in March 1976. No consensus was reached.

It was no secret that Barbadian cricketers constituted the majority of West Indian players prepared to defy the sports boycotts of southern Africa. Barbados therefore proceeded to set out its official stance, and at a cabinet meeting on March 25, 1976, the government adopted the following policy: "The Barbados Government's policy in respect of sportsmen who participated in sport in South Africa and other countries with racist regimes henceforth should be one of disapproval and non-support of any such Barbadian or Barbadian sporting organisation."[31]

While unsupportive of sportsmen who played in South Africa, Barbados was not prepared to ban such individuals. Frederick Smith, Barbados's minister of sport, said, "If for monetary or other reasons an individual wants to go to South Africa, we won't stop him."[32] The Barbados position was therefore similar to that enunciated by Trinidad and Tobago in 1975. Jamaica and Guyana took the toughest stand; the latter declared that it "would not accept any cricketers, Guyanese, West Indian or any other nationality who played in South Africa or Rhodesia."[33]

With these policy positions coupled with that of the fellow-membership of the International Cricket Conference (ICC), the WICBC met in May 1976 and drafted a policy that reflected, at least, the common principles that could be gleaned from Barbados, Trinidad and Tobago, Jamaica, Guyana, and the ICC. The resulting policy statement read:

> The West Indies Cricket Board of Control wishes to reiterate its total opposition to the systems of apartheid as obtain in South Africa and Rhodesia and advises that all players from Caribbean territories under its jurisdiction who play cricket or coach in South Africa or Rhodesia will not be permitted to participate in matches organized under the auspices of the Board either at home or abroad.
>
> In addition, the Board re-affirms that no official team from any country which tours South Africa or Rhodesia will be welcome in the West Indies unless and until there is complete multi-racial cricket and teams are selected solely on merit in those countries.[34]

A CARICOM heads-of-government meeting also discussed the matter. Errol Barrow, prime minister of Barbados, reiterated his cabinet's position that while his country would not support any sporting contact by its citizens with white-ruled southern Africa, "nationals of other countries would not be banned from entering into, or playing in Barbados."[35] Dr. Eric Williams, the prime minister of Trinidad, summed up his position when he said, "I do not like political interference in sport."[36] The enunciated policy of the WICBC was perhaps clearest: it would ban any recalcitrant player in any regional or international match under its auspices. Likewise it would not accept an "official" national team that had competed in white-ruled southern Africa. They, however, did not presume to ban foreign individuals who played or coached in their private capacity. Indeed, this emerged as the position of virtually all of the CARICOM states except Guyana, whose position remained to ban all teams and individuals, official or private, that played or coached in white-ruled southern Africa.

The no-banning of foreign private individuals was reiterated by Barbados to the United Nations. On the September 22, 1976, the newly elected

Barbados Labour Party government led by Tom Adams, through its UN permanent representative, Dr. Donald Blackman, unequivocally reaffirmed the policy formulated by the previous administration: "nationals of other countries who had previously played in racist countries would not, at this time, be banned from entering and playing in Barbados if their entry was sought as members of a national team of a country with which Barbados had sporting relations."[37] It did not, however, explicitly absolve Barbadian or West Indian players, and when taken together with the May 1976 WICBC statement, left the door ajar for punitive measures for local and regional defaulters. This presumably moderate position seemed rational for territories heavily dependent on tourism. Moreover, a number of West Indies cricketers played alongside and became friends of South African cricketers who, as some West Indians, were professionals of clubs in England or Australia.

## The Gleneagles Agreement and UN Declaration

Political events elsewhere in the Commonwealth contributed to the intensity of 1976. The 1974 Commonwealth Games in New Zealand were saved from a boycott led by the Supreme Council for Sport in Africa after New Zealand's Prime Minister Norman Kirk bowed to pressure to have a proposed South African rugby tour and the Federation Cup Tennis Tournament called off.[38] In late 1975, however, the National Party of Robert Muldoon was elected on a platform that promised noninterference in sport. Consequently, in early 1976, South Africa participated in the World Softball Championships in New Zealand, and a rugby tour of South Africa was also organized for 1976.

Unmoved by agitation from the various anti-apartheid campaigns, the SCSA, and personal pleas, the Muldoon government gave its blessing to the New Zealand tour of South Africa even after the Soweto uprising.[39] The Organization of African Unity (OAU), through the SCSA, called upon the International Olympic Committee to expel New Zealand from the 1976 Montreal Olympics. The IOC refused ostensibly because rugby was not an Olympic sport. As a result, all of the African countries (except Senegal and Ivory Coast) withdrew from the Games.[40] Cuba, Jamaica, Barbados, Trinidad and Tobago, and Guyana had all sent teams to Montreal, but Guyana was the only Caribbean nation to withdraw its contingent in solidarity with the African position.

This was an embarrassing blow to Canada's Prime Minister Pierre Trudeau, under whose leadership Canada had gained a favorable reputation as a bridge builder between Third World states and the developed industrialized countries. However, the withdrawal of African states from the Montreal Games raised Canada's fears that the Commonwealth Games scheduled for Edmonton in 1978 would meet a similar fate. If such a boycott were to take place, Canada's new liberal image would be tarnished, and the Commonwealth Games could be reduced to an embarrassing all-white affair. Thus Canada, with the assistance of Jamaica's Michael Manley, lobbied the (mainly black) Commonwealth states, and Trudeau himself sought the support of Britain and Australia to dissuade New Zealand from its official policy of maintaining sporting contacts with South Africa. Such efforts apparently bore no fruit, but certainly it was urgent that there be a satisfactory agreement ready for ratification by the June 1977 Commonwealth heads-of-government meeting in the United Kingdom. Commonwealth secretary-general Shridath Ramphal was identified as the principal diplomat to coordinate this effort. Ramphal met Trudeau in Ottawa in March 1977 and subsequently contacted Manley, Julius Nyerere of Tanzania, and Kenneth Kaunda of Zambia to constitute a committee to develop the draft policy.[41]

Prime Minister Manley, an avid cricket fan, had emerged by then as a respected advocate for the deployment of sport as a diplomatic weapon in the arsenal against apartheid. In late May 1976 he sent a statement to the International Seminar on the Eradication of Apartheid and in Support for Liberation in South Africa meeting in Havana, Cuba, in which he advocated, inter alia, the preparation of an International Convention on Apartheid and Sport.[42] Manley's proposal found substantial support among the African, Asian, Latin American, Caribbean, and Eastern European states within the UN, but Canada cautioned that though some Western countries might support a declaration, they were unlikely to provide similar commitment to the more punitive convention.[43] With its Resolution 31/6F passed in November 1976, the UN established the Ad Hoc Committee on the Drafting of an International Convention against Apartheid. In his *History of West Indies Cricket,* Manley notes: "In that very year [1977] Caribbean nations were pressing for wider sanctions against South Africa in sport. Indeed, with Jamaica playing a leading role, the Commonwealth heads-of-government meeting in London in the summer of 1977 had worked out guidelines for sanctions which were embodied in the Gleneagles agreement."[44]

From 1977, therefore, Commonwealth Caribbean states were on the front lines in devising anti-apartheid sport strategies within the Commonwealth as well as within the United Nations. In fact, the UN conferred its Gold Medal Award on Manley in 1978 for his outstanding role in the anti-apartheid movement.[45] At the UN, Trinidad and Tobago held membership of the Special Committee against Apartheid. In addition, Barbados and Jamaica were among the seven states added to that body in January 1977 to constitute the Ad Hoc Committee on the Drafting of an International Convention against Apartheid in Sports. In May 1977, Barbados's representative was appointed as a vice chairman and Jamaica's Lucille Mair as rapporteur.[46]

The Commonwealth heads-of-government meeting convened in London in June 1977 with the expectation that the flurry of diplomatic activity of the previous year would lift the cloud overshadowing the Edmonton Commonwealth Games. At its weekend retreat at the Gleneagles Hotel in Perthshire, Scotland, a select committee chaired by Manley and including Trudeau, Muldoon, and the leaders of Singapore, Nigeria, and Tanzania hammered out the final accord.[47] In their final communiqué from London, the Commonwealth heads of government agreed "vigorously to combat the evil of apartheid by withholding any form of support for, and by taking every practical step to discourage contact or competition by their nationals with supporting organizations, teams or sportsmen from South Africa or any other country where sports are organized on the basis of race, colour or ethnic origin."[48] Meanwhile, the UN Ad Hoc Committee had set about its work convening its first meetings in May 1977. It established a working group that included Canada and Barbados, was chaired by Mair, and was charged with the responsibility of drafting an international declaration against apartheid in sport. The group held twelve meetings in the space of three months and submitted its draft declaration to the Ad Hoc Committee on August 10, 1977. The declaration was transmitted to the UN General Assembly on November 10, 1977.[49]

When the International Declaration against Apartheid in Sports came before the UN General Assembly (as UN Resolution 32/105 M) on December 14, 1977, it was supported by 125 nations; none opposed. However, while Australia and Canada were the "white" Commonwealth nations that supported the declaration, New Zealand and Britain were among the fourteen states that abstained.[50] In the majority of its eighteen articles, states were being called upon to be more active in the sporting isolation of South Africa. Some states were clearly concerned about the import of Article 11 of that declaration, in which states were thereby agreeing to support the preparation of a convention against apartheid in sport. UN declarations often "indicate that the parties do not intend to create binding obligations but merely want to declare certain aspirations."[51] However, Britain and New Zealand were not even prepared to endorse this UN declaration, which they saw as the thin edge of the convention wedge. Given their abstention, their own half-hearted commitment to the Gleneagles Accord of the Commonwealth was not surprising.

Until 1979 when the UN General Assembly reaffirmed its position on apartheid in sports, Britain and New Zealand remained among the abstainers.[52] Since 1971 Britain had consistently contended before the UN that inasmuch as it abhorred apartheid, as a government it could not interfere in the policies adopted by nongovernmental sport organizations.[53] Interestingly, that noble position did not constrain Prime Minister Margaret Thatcher and her Conservative government from pressuring British athletes to join the call by US president Jimmy Carter for a boycott of the 1980 Moscow Olympic Games because of the Soviet invasion of Afghanistan in December 1979.[54] To her minister of sport, she wrote: "In an ideal world, I would share entirely the philosophy of the Olympic movement that sport should be divorced from politics. Sadly, however, this is no longer a realistic view."[55] But hers was a politics of ideological convenience; no effort had been expended to dissuade the British Lions rugby team from touring South Africa that year. Such hypocrisy incensed the African and Caribbean representatives on the Commonwealth Games Federation, who insisted on the discussion of the matter at their meeting in July 1980.[56]

Clearly neither the Commonwealth's Gleneagles Accord nor the UN Declaration against Apartheid in Sports offered any lasting solution and were furthermore rendered ineffective among the Commonwealth nations owing to the recalcitrance of Britain and New Zealand. Basically these agreements were not vested with any legal obligation, nor could they stipulate any sanction for their abrogation. Predictably, then, another "crisis" erupted within the Caribbean in 1981 on the occasion of an

English cricket tour of the region. This centered on England's late inclusion of Robin Jackman, who was summarily deported from Guyana after President Burnham was briefed about Jackman's playing and coaching stints in South Africa. The entire English team left Guyana for Barbados after an assurance by Prime Minister Tom Adams that they could stay in Barbados, but whether Jackman could play necessitated a CARICOM decision.[57]

That decision came in the early hours of Wednesday, March 4, 1981, following a meeting convened by the foreign minister of Barbados, Henry Forde, and attended by ministers or other high-ranking government officials of sport or foreign affairs from Jamaica, Antigua, and Montserrat. In their statement, they noted that the Gleneagles Agreement did not address the issue of sanctions against sportsmen who played or coached in South Africa in their private, individual capacity. Moreover, this "third party principle" was still the subject of prolonged debate within the United Nations. Under such circumstances, then, the tour could continue unhindered, but it was acknowledged that the governments of CARICOM would have to consult again on the matter and pursue the strengthening of the agreement at the forthcoming Commonwealth heads-of-government meeting.[58]

Once again, it was Guyana whose inflexible position disrupted international cricket in the region. There was a view that Guyana's position was motivated by the state socialism in which the Burnham regime nationalized the sugar and bauxite industries. But this seems rather speculative. Manley too had flirted with his brand of socialism in Jamaica but did not renege on the principles common to the 1978 WICBC statement and the Gleneagles Accord. Cold War politics did shape approaches to the anti-apartheid movement. In the Caribbean, however, governments were motivated by a straightforward assault on the antiblack racism officially espoused in southern Africa but also evident and widespread in Europe. In any case, by then the Burnham regime was widely recognized (though never openly articulated within CARICOM leadership circles) to be illegitimate by virtue of rigged elections, discriminatory against Indo-Guyanese, and even murderous. Some cynics therefore viewed Burnham's actions as a mere smoke screen behind which to hide these many infelicities. Indeed, Cameron Tudor, a former Barbados foreign minister, openly questioned the Guyanese president's moral authority and unilateral high-handedness. He said, "We are all opposed to the South African regime, but some of us cannot easily perceive the distinction between the death of Steve Biko in police custody and the death of Walter Rodney under police surveillance [in Guyana]."[59]

If Guyana demonstrated an ultrasensitivity to playing sport in racist South Africa, New Zealand's approach was cavalier and disrespectful. The New Zealand government permitted South Africa's all-white Springbok national rugby team to tour that country in 1981, an action that led many African leaders to threaten a boycott of the Brisbane Commonwealth Games, scheduled for 1982. Edward Seaga and Maurice Bishop, the prime ministers of Jamaica and Grenada, respectively, raised the matter at the Commonwealth heads-of-government meeting that was convened in Melbourne between September 30 and October 7, 1981. The Commonwealth reaffirmed its commitment to the Gleneagles Accord but acknowledged its obvious deficiencies. In fact, Seaga urged fellow heads to pursue the speedy conclusion of the UN's convention against apartheid in sport.[60] The Commonwealth Games Federation adopted a code of conduct in October 1982 that was intended to shore up the Gleneagles Accord by setting out clear procedures to deal with breaches and also to empower the federation to exclude any country in violation. Britain and New Zealand abstained from the vote.

## West Indies Rebel Cricket Tours of 1983–1984

"The failure of Caricom Member States, to date," observed K. O. Hall, A. Thomas, and J. Farier in 1978, "to develop harmonious and co-ordinated postures and actions on the question of combating apartheid in sports could possibly have its impact first of all on individual players or athletes." They also contended that professional West Indian cricketers were virtually entirely dependent on foreign contracts because no significant professional league existed in the Caribbean and the region's governments failed to invest in these sportsmen. This meant then "for the individual cricketer, there could be a pretty wide gap between earning a livelihood and adhering to a political line where offsetting income benefits are not attached as incentives to following the political line."[61]

The fulfillment of this warning came in 1983 when news broke that a number of West Indies "rebel cricketers" had abandoned principle and as "honorary Whites" were off to play in South Africa for unprecedented sums of "blood money." Cricket commentator and writer Tony Cozier noted that the region was deeply divided over this "rebellion," which surprisingly received widespread sympathy. This was "a development which shocked those who believed opposition to apartheid and South Africa should have been a fundamental principle to all West Indians."[62] A poll published by Jamaica's *Daily Gleaner* of August 5, 1983, revealed that 68 percent of the respondents supported the tour. Cozier noted: "The West Indian people appeared confused on the issue and baffled by the inconsistencies which they saw. Nor were they persuaded by the strong condemnatory language of the militants who spoke out stridently against Rowe's rebels. What they needed—indeed, what the players needed—were explanations as why South Africa was considered beyond the pale by the vast majority of the nations of the world and why it was necessary to keep it isolated under its present system."[63] This was a sad commentary on the level of popular political consciousness that Trevor Marshall has attributed to the reliance on news filtered through the biased Western media.[64] But the problem was deeper than that. Secretary-General Ramphal had warned governments that South Africa was planning to break out of the stranglehold of isolation by financing rebel tours. He advocated that governments and sporting authorities would have to share the responsibility in sensitizing their people and sportsmen to South Africa's deception.[65]

But while Caribbean leaders spoke in international forums in fulsome terms about their countries' abhorrence of apartheid, their governments did little to educate and rally the general populace on the issue. In Barbados, for example, it was primarily the Southern Africa Liberation Committee (SALC), in concert with leading trade unions such as the Barbados Union of Teachers (BUT), the National Union of Public Workers (NUPW), and the West Indies Group of University Teachers (WIGUT); religious bodies such as the Caribbean Conference of Churches (CCC) and the Roman Catholic and Spiritual Baptist Churches; and the Movement for National Liberation (MONALI) that spearheaded popular anti-apartheid education on that island.[66]

Desmond Davies contends that for South Africa, this was "the most important coup . . . since the country went into cricket oblivion in 1970 when it was suspended by the International Cricket Conference (ICC)."[67] South Africa struck successfully at the Achilles' heel of West Indies financial vulnerability. West Indian professional cricketers had very little hope of a secure financial future commensurate with their popular standing as ambassadors of Caribbean nationhood on the world's stage. Cricket star Alvin Kallicharran informed Dr. Ali Bacher, chief recruiter for the South African Cricket Union (SACU), that "the West Indian cricketers had no financial security."[68] Financial vulnerability was also compounded by the injudicious WICBC practice of unceremoniously discarding former cricket stars during the perceived evening of their careers. This emboldened some of the rebels to sacrifice principle on the altar of financial self-interest. Caribbean governments expected their players to abide by principle alone, apparently oblivious to the fact that by the 1980s the South African regime was not only prepared to pay its way out of sporting isolation but to use sport as a weapon of counterinsurgency. One South African official is quoted as stating in the early 1980s, "We must not relegate sport to an insignificant component of our international counter-offensive."[69]

In 1979, following a fact-finding mission to South Africa, the "white" members of the ICC were inclined to readmit that apartheid state were it not for the strident opposition of the "black" nations.[70] Furthermore, with the admission of another "black" country—Sri Lanka—to full membership in 1981, South Africa's fate was sealed. As Adrian Guelke suggests, South Africa had "hoped for a split in world cricket on racial lines that would permit the return of South Africa to international competition, at least with the 'White' states."[71] The three white members of the ICC were thereafter outnumbered by the four black members.[72] South Africa's response, then, was to organize "rebel tours" as a malicious retaliatory strategy to create confusion in international cricket.

The English rebel tour of South Africa in 1982 was lukewarm; the Sri Lankan rebel tour that followed was so poor that an estimated 600,000R was lost on it. Nevertheless, South Africa's Income Tax Act allowed companies such as the SA Breweries, which sponsored these types of tours, to recoup its investments in the form of tax incentives and double deductions.[73] In respect of the West Indian rebel tour, Dr. Gerrit Viljoen, South Africa's minister of sport, stated, "In view of the tremendous benefit of the West Indian tour to sport in South Africa, my department would be willing, in the event of a shortfall in the financing of the tour, to consider sympathetically an eventual request from the S.A.C.U. for financial support to maintain their effort for the promotion of cricket."[74] Later

Viljoen informed fellow parliamentarians of the significance of securing a West Indies team. He said: "The government profoundly appreciated the exceptional initiative displayed by the cricket chiefs in achieving the breakthrough. The tour struck an important blow not only in the sporting field but also in general against the concentrated efforts to isolate South Africa."[75]

All Caribbean governments opposed the 1983–1984 rebel tours, but the liberation movements in Africa raised serious doubts about the solidarity of their brothers across the Atlantic. Desmond Davies wrote that officials of SACU exhibited the West Indian "rebels" before the press in Johannesburg reminiscent "of the days of slavery when the traders would proudly show off their prized slaves at an auction."[76] Similarly, the *Sowetan* of January 14, 1983, carried a statement from the Azanian People's Organization that said the West Indians had "soiled themselves by flirting with racism, white domination and black dispossession. . . . The tour is an extreme affront to the overwhelming majority of blacks in this country who are subjected to the worst system of exploitation and oppression."[77]

The WICBC belatedly formulated a plan for consideration by CARICOM that would have resulted in some kind of retainer contracts to be offered to about twenty players over a three-year period.[78] Those players who had defied the Caribbean's position on isolating the racist regimes of southern Africa received a lifetime ban by the WICBC, which CARICOM approved. In contrast, England's Test and County Cricket Board (TCCB) imposed a ban of three years on the English rebels, apparently to placate India and Pakistan, which vowed not to tour England unless its rebel cricketers were punished.[79] By April 1985 Graham Gooch, John Emburey, Peter Willey, and Les Taylor (members of England's "Dirty Dozen") were again eligible for selection to the English team set to tour the West Indies in 1986. Once more, the WICBC found it necessary to seek a policy directive from CARICOM in respect to visiting teams that included players who previously played in South Africa. Such a directive was especially important given the embarrassing contrasting fate of the West Indian rebels and those readmitted to England's team. A Report of a Working Group recommended a consultative intergovernmental mechanism for the harmonization of CARICOM action on apartheid in sport.[80]

The declaration adopted by the Second International Conference on Sports Boycott against South Africa held in Paris in May 1985 singled out the Guyana government for special praise for its policy and urged the other Caribbean governments to deny entry to any cricketer on the proposed English touring team "who has participated in cricketing activities in South Africa."[81] However, at the Eleventh Meeting of the Standing Committee of CARICOM Foreign Ministers held in St. Kitts in May 1985, they decided that the already tough lifetime ban of the WICBC and the principles of the Gleneagles Agreement would continue to be the guiding policy.[82] This meant that each country and its sporting bodies would continue to pursue their own remedy and retribution upon their own nationals who violated the Gleneagles Agreement.

This commitment to Gleneagles was endorsed by the CARICOM heads of government at their sixth meeting in Barbados July 1–4, 1985.[83] The leaders "agreed that with particular reference to the forthcoming tour of the region by an MCC cricket team, persons currently in breach of the Gleneagles Agreement as well as expressing an intent to violate it through sporting contacts with South Africa, were wholly unacceptable as visiting players."[84] This statement was an obvious response to a comment that Graham Gooch had allegedly made in a radio interview, that he was unrepentant about playing in South Africa and would do so again. Alan Rae, president of the WICBC, requested the TCCB to investigate the veracity of the allegation and sought Ramphal's aid to mediate. Gooch's subsequent "explanation" was dismissed as "feeble" by Roderick Rainford, secretary-general of CARICOM, while Lester Bird, deputy prime minister and minister of foreign affairs of Antigua, sought clarification from Gooch through Antigua's high commissioner in London. Gooch's explanation was accepted, and Bird stated that the "the way is clear for his visit to my country." However, Bird subsequently castigated those on the English team who had visited South Africa and vowed not to attend any of the matches scheduled for Antigua. Reuben Harris, Antigua's sport minister, publicly rebuked Bird and queried: "Why now the inconsistency? Why confuse the public? . . . Our posture has to be guided and controlled by good principle, to say the least. Therefore, Mr. Bird's statement was unfortunate, inconsistent, embarrassing, untimely and undermining."[85] Bird responded that as a private citizen, he was entitled to his views notwithstanding the official decision. His example was followed by Prime Minister George Chambers of Trinidad and Tobago, Errol Mahabir (his external minister), and President Ellis Clarke, who all stated their intention to boycott the cricket.[86]

The tour nonetheless proceeded with few hitches in spite of organized antitour campaigns, especially in Trinidad. Harris was indeed right in his concern for the lack of consistency and the creation of confusion. The Gleneagles Agreement was all well and good, but the uncomfortable question would not go away: How could one grant absolution to white rebel players who had served a three-year ban while there was no respite available to black West Indies rebels serving a lifetime ban? This cast doubts about the region's commitment to persons of poor, black, working-class origin. Indeed, Beckles has argued that by the 1980s, many black working-class West Indians had jettisoned the nationalist project as once expressed in a strong anti-apartheid stance because they felt that nationalism had not adequately addressed their socioeconomic marginality.[87]

The English cricket tour was not alone in attracting controversy in 1986, for within five months there was another impasse, this time involving the English team for the Commonwealth Games, scheduled to commence on July 24, 1986, in Edinburgh. On this occasion, the contentious issue was the inclusion of the South African–born athletes Zola Budd (long-distance running) and Annette Crowley (swimming) on the English squads against a background of the stubborn policy of the Thatcher administration to reject the imposition of economic sanctions on South Africa. Budd had represented England at the 1984 Los Angeles Olympics after securing British citizenship on April 6, 1984, a mere twelve days after her application on the claim that her grandfather was born in London. While these two athletes attracted much attention from anti-apartheid campaigners in Britain, it was not until 1986 that the African nations of the Commonwealth made a determination to withdraw from the Edinburgh Commonwealth Games on account of Crawley and Budd's inclusion.

But the raison d'être for the boycott went deeper than that. African and Caribbean states had had enough of the stubborn refusal of a Thatcher-led Conservative government to agree to economic sanctions against South Africa in solidarity with the rest of the Commonwealth. There was therefore a growing sentiment that the time had come to send a strong signal to Thatcher's regime, which continued to snub the many voices calling for enhanced sanctions on South Africa while at the same time proceeded with indecent haste to confer British citizenship on two South African athletes. Surely it was time to expose the racial sham within the

Commonwealth grouping itself. Thatcher had already emerged as a pariah a year before at the 1985 Commonwealth Heads of Government meeting in Nassau, Bahamas, because of her stance on sanctions against South Africa. On that occasion a bristling Thatcher stood her ground against those whom she later described as a "gang of bullies," and the drafting committee sweated to produce a final Commonwealth communiqué that would have been acceptable to her.[88]

As usual, it was the African nations that led the threat to the Commonwealth Games. Following the announcements by Nigeria, Ghana, Uganda, and Kenya of their nonparticipation in the games, heads of missions in London representing Jamaica, Trinidad, Barbados, Bahamas, Antigua, Guyana, and the OECS met on July 11, 1986, and after some consultation with the exiled South Africa Non-Racial Olympic Committee (SAN-ROC), agreed to advise their governments to suspend any action until the black front-line states of southern Africa met in a week's time.[89] But before then, a number of developments occurred in quick succession. By July 14, an Associated Press report stated that the Commonwealth Games Federation had disqualified Budd and Crowley from the games. Prematurely, the following day, July 15, 1986, the *Barbados Advocate* reported, "Bajans heading for Edinburgh," and that Barbadian Austin Sealy would be contesting the post of treasurer. But two days later, Michael Manley urged Caribbean governments to join the Africans in boycotting the games. Manley, who had defended the English cricket tour months earlier, argued that what was at stake on this occasion was Britain's failure to join the rest of the Commonwealth in tightening the sanctions against South Africa. As he saw it, "clearly, the situation has moved beyond the Gleneagles Agreement."[90]

Uncertainty concerning the position of a number of Caribbean states still existed. One week before the Commonwealth Games commenced, the foreign ministers of Barbados, Trinidad, and Guyana conferred by telephone, and the Barbados cabinet met to review the earlier decision to support the games. The Workers' Party of Barbados, headed by Dr. George Belle, issued a press release calling on the Barbados government to advise the country's athletes to boycott the games in response to Thatcher's intransigence.[91] On July 20, 1986, Don Norville, a sport journalist and the recently appointed press secretary to Prime Minister Barrow, issued a statement to the effect that a decision was made to withdraw from the games. Norville spoke, however, not as representative of the Barbados government but as public relations officer of the Barbados Olympic Association (BOA). Sen. Sir James Cameron Tudor, once again foreign affairs minister of the reelected Democratic Labour Party government, endorsed the BOA's decision.[92]

The convolution of Barbados's drawn-out decision-making process on this matter reveals the persistent undying ideology that sport should not be politicized. Thus the government of Barbados walked away with "clean hands," having emphasized that the decision was entirely that of the Barbados Olympic Association. Nevertheless, support for the boycott of sport in a country "soft" on apartheid was a significant development beyond the accustomed stance of seeking refuge in the Gleneagles Agreement. The Commonwealth Caribbean governments therefore stood shoulder to shoulder with their African counterparts to signal to Thatcher their disgust at her wrongheaded policy toward South Africa by boycotting the Commonwealth Games under British patronage. It seemed a fitting rebuff not only to the host nation, Great Britain, but also to the other "white" Commonwealth nations that, one year before, had demonstrated their unwillingness to endorse the International Convention against Apartheid in Sport. On December 10, 1985, the UN General Assembly finally adopted the International Convention against Apartheid in Sport (Resolution 40/64G) on which the Ad Hoc Committee had labored for so long. The Convention was adopted by 125 states; none voted against it, but all of the four white Commonwealth governments—Australia, Canada, New Zealand, and the United Kingdom—were among the 24 that abstained.[93]

The Commonwealth Games ostensibly symbolized the harmony among these diverse post–British Empire nations that, after securing independence, remained in the Commonwealth with Her Majesty the Queen as head of state. It was a perfect arena for the former British colonies to send a strong political message by their absence from the games. It also suggested that African and Caribbean leaders had come to some acknowledgment that sport was an effective weapon that could be mobilized not only against individuals or teams but also against powerful industrialized countries that continued to give comfort to South Africa.

## Sport and the Dismantling of Apartheid

But while Caribbean governments were finding new courage in the anti-apartheid sport campaign, political developments within South Africa were evolving at a greater pace than was being publicly acknowledged or reported. From 1985, significant sectors within South Africa, including sport administrators, began to consult and negotiate with the African National Congress (ANC).[94] Although the Pan-African Congress (PAC) supported the position of the South African Council on Sport (SACOS) in remaining adamant that nonracialism and equality of sports access should be preconditions for the lifting of the sport boycott, the ANC had moved to a more gradualist position where it was prepared to make concessions in the sport campaign as the carrot for more fundamental social changes within South Africa.[95] The ANC itself was unbanned in 1990, and Dr. Ali Bacher and SACU agreed to the cessation of cricket "rebel tours."[96] Indeed, Steve Tshwete of the ANC chaired the special meeting in June 1991 at which a new nonracial governing body for cricket in South Africa, the United Cricket Board of South Africa (UCBSA), was formed.[97]

Pressure was also coming from some international sport associations for South Africa's readmission to international competition. For instance, both the International Amateur Athletics Federation and the IOC unilaterally accepted South Africa's application for readmission to membership in July 1991. Nelson Mandela wrote to the ICC to indicate that South Africa's participation in the Cricket World Cup "will enhance the process of unity in sport as well as the spirit of national reconciliation."[98] Mandela also personally telephoned Manley in Jamaica to lobby the West Indies to support South Africa's readmission to the ICC.[99] If this was indeed the case, the WICBC and its representative on the ICC, Sir Clyde Walcott, seemed to be unaware, as the West Indies were the only ICC members to abstain from approving the UCBSA's application for South Africa's readmission and participation in the Cricket World Cup scheduled for 1992.[100] The Commonwealth Heads of Government summit in Harare in October 1991 had also expressed the hope that the ICC would readmit South Africa.[101]

There was a view in some Caribbean circles that international sporting bodies were rushing indecorously to welcome back the prodigal South Africa, but Mandela and the ANC embraced sport as a diplomatic tool in its negotiations with the National Party. As Douglas Booth and John Nauright have argued, the ANC wished to allay the fears of whites in a "new South Africa" under black majority rule.[102] The inaugural cricket test between the West Indies and South Africa was played in Barbados in April 1992, but the match, according to Hilary Beckles, was heavily boycotted as a belated anti-apartheid response.[103] West Indians elsewhere, however, did not share this interpretation, and it was widely believed that Barbadians boycotted the game because Anderson Cummins, one of their local cricketers, was not selected for the team. In the World Cup in 1992, South Africa beat the West Indies, and Richie Richardson, the captain of the latter team, is reported to have said, "It's just another match!" In contrast, when South Africa defeated Australia, South African president F. W. de Klerk sent a message to the South African captain, Keppler Wessels, that read, "Your victory is a victory for all of us over years of isolation and rejection."[104]

## Conclusion

The international anti-apartheid sport campaign did provide a high-profile foreign policy issue around which the new black African and Caribbean states could foster a sense of national unity and identity. International cricket provided the Caribbean with many testing cases out of which the WICBC and subsequently CARICOM were forced to attempt some harmonization of response. Nevertheless, the Caribbean seemed uneasy and tentative in so many of such cases, with Guyana pursuing its own maverick path. Indeed, it was a sad commentary that at the peak of the campaign, West Indies cricket became the prize victim of South Africa's counteroffensive while, according to Cozier, the people of the region remained divided and confused. On the other hand, the African states, through the Organization of African Unity, seemed to have been more successful in mobilizing anti-apartheid sport boycotts with the Montreal Olympics and the Edinburgh Commonwealth Games as their most spectacular successes. CARICOM lacked an institutional arrangement like the Supreme Council for Sport in Africa (SCSA) that could forge policy and procedures for regional sport.

Nevertheless, the Commonwealth Caribbean did contribute significantly to the international anti-apartheid sport campaign with its diplomats playing central roles in drafting the UN declaration and subsequent convention against apartheid and sport. Within the Commonwealth, Michael Manley and Shridath Ramphal were key figures in brokering the Gleneagles Agreement. In addition, the efforts of the Caribbean representatives on the Commonwealth Games Foundation contributed to achieving a Code of Conduct in 1982. The 1986 boycott of the Commonwealth Games in Edinburgh represented a high point in the anti-apartheid sport campaign, representing the highest degree of solidarity between the African and Caribbean states.

## Notes

1. See, for example, Hilary Beckles, *The Development of West Indies Cricket: Vol. 1, The Age of Nationalism* (Kingston: University of the West Indies Press, 1998), ch.7.

2. See K. O. Hall, A. Thomas, and J. Farier, "The Anti-Apartheid Campaign in the Caribbean: The Case of Sport," *Caribbean Journal of African Studies* 1, no. 1 (1978): 43–74; Anthony Payne, "The International Politics of the Gleneagles Agreement," *The Round Table* 320 (1991): 418–19; and Aviston Downes, "Sport and International Diplomacy: The Case of the Commonwealth Caribbean and the Anti-Apartheid Campaign, 1959–1992," *The Sports Historian* 22, no. 2 (November 2002): 23–45.

3. Marc Keech and Barrie Houlihan, "Sport and the End of Apartheid," *Round Table* 349 (1999): 109.

4. Barrie Houlihan, *Sport and International Politics* (New York: Harvester Wheatsheaf, 1994), 9–10.

5. Keech and Houlihan, "Sport and the End of Apartheid," 110.

6. Ibid.

7. C. L. R. James, *Beyond a Boundary* (London: Stanley Paul, 1963), 72.

8. See Nigel Bolland, *On the March: Labour Rebellions in the British Caribbean, 1934–39* (Kingston: Ian Randle, 1995).

9. Sir Cavendish Boyle welcoming a West Indies cricket team to England in 1906. Cited in Aviston Downes, "Flannelled Fools? Cricket and the Political Economy of the British West Indies c. 1895–1906," *International Journal of the History of Sport* 17, no. 4 (December 2000): 75.

10. See Jenifer Parks's chapter in this volume.

11. Downes, "Sport and International Diplomacy," 25.

12. Christopher Merrett, "'In Nothing Else Are the Deprivers So Deprived': South African Sport, Apartheid and Foreign Relations, 1945–71," *International Journal of the History of Sport* 13, no. 2 (August 1996): 148.

13. Cited in ibid.

14. James, *Beyond a Boundary,* 228–29, and Anna Grimshaw and C. L. R. James, *Cricket* (London: Allison & Busby, 1986), 88–90.

15. Cited in Merrett, "'In Nothing Else Are the Deprivers So Deprived,'" 148–49.

16. Basil D'Oliveira, *The D'Oliveira Affair* (London: Collins, 1969), 38.

17. James, *Beyond a Boundary,* 233.

18. Grimshaw and James, *Cricket,* 226.

19. "Sobers to Play in Rhodesia," *Advocate News,* September 8, 1970, 12; "Springboks Unwelcome in England," *Southern Africa* 3, no. 4 (April 1970): 13–14; and Peter Hain, *Don't Play with Apartheid: The Background to the Stop the Seventy Tour Campaign* (London: Allen & Unwin, 1971), 175.

20. See "Lusaka, Declarations, 1970," September 10, 1970, James Martin Center for Nonproliferation Studies, http://cns.miis.edu/nam/documents/Official_Document/3rd_Summit_FD_Lusaka_Declaration_1970.pdf (accessed September 15, 2013).

21. Quoted in Georges A. Fauriol, *Foreign Policy Behaviour of Caribbean States: Guyana, Haiti, and Jamaica* (Lanham, MD: University Press of America, 1984), 90. For details of Burnham's itinerary, see *Guyana Journal* 1, no. 5 (December 1971): 41–56.

22. "W.I. Cricket Skipper Flies In," *Advocate News,* September, 16, 1970, 16.

23. "Politics Made Sobers West Indies Captain: Guyanese Ex-Mayor," *Advocate-News,* September 29, 1970, 12.

24. Ibid.

25. "Burnham: Sobers Must Apologize," *Sunday Advocate,* October 11, 1970, 1.

26. "'Gary May Not Be Welcomed Anywhere,'" *Advocate News,* October 15, 1970, 16.

27. See Garfield Sobers, with Brian Scovell, *Sobers: Twenty Years at the Top* (London: Macmillan, 1988), 160–65.

28. United Nations Centre against *Apartheid,* "Actions Taken by Governments Concerning Sporting Contacts with South Africa," *Notes and Documents*, no. 3/76 (January 1976): 22.

29. Tony Cozier, "The South African Connection," *Benson & Hedges West Indies Cricket Annual* (1986): 16.

30. United Nations Centre against *Apartheid,* "Actions Taken by Governments Concerning Sporting Contacts with South Africa," *Notes and Documents* no. 3/76 (January 1976): 23.

31. "Statement Made by the Minister of External Affairs, Mr. Henry deB. Forde in Commemoration of Human Rights Day, December 10, 1978," in the Ministry of Foreign Affairs (Barbados), *Barbados Bulletin* 5, no. 15 (October–March 1979): 57.

32. Quoted in Tony Cozier, "West Indian Contretemps," in *Cricket in Isolation: The Politics of Race and Cricket in South Africa,* ed. André Odendaal (Cape Town: The Editor, 1977), 187.

33. Tony Cozier, "Guyana Bars Anyone Who Has Played Sport in South Africa: Another Political Threat to Cricket," *West Indies Cricket Annual* (1976): 13.

34. Quoted in Jeff Stollmeyer, *Everything under the Sun: My Life in West Indies Cricket* (London: Stanley Paul, 1983), 199.

35. Quoted in "Statement Made by the Minister of External Affairs," 57.

36. Cozier, "Guyana Bars Anyone Who Has Played Sport in South Africa," 13.

37. "Statement Made by the Minister of External Affairs," 57–58.

38. Richard E. Lapchick and United Nations Centre against *Apartheid,* "Apart-

heid Sport and South Africa's Foreign Policy: 1976," *Notes and Documents* SEM/6 (1976): 4–5.

39. Ibid., 5–6, and Payne, "The International Politics of the Gleneagles Agreement," 418–19.

40. See *Keesing's Contemporary Archives* (October 1976), 28004, and Bruce Kidd, "The Campaign against Sport in South Africa," *International Journal* 43, no. 4 (Autumn 1988): 655.

41. Kidd, "The Campaign," 655, and Donald Macintosh and Michael Hawes, *Sport and Canadian Diplomacy* (Montreal: McGill-Queen's University Press, 1994), 74–89.

42. United Nations Centre against *Apartheid,* "International Seminar on the Eradication of Apartheid and in Support for Liberation in South Africa," *Notes and Documents* SEM/1 (June 1976): 24–25.

43. Donald Macintosh, Donna Greenhorn, and David Black, "Canadian Diplomacy and the 1978 Edmonton Commonwealth Games," *Journal of Sport History* 19, no. 1 (Spring 1992): 52.

44. Michael Manley, *History of West Indies Cricket* (London: André Deutsch, 1995), 258.

45. *Caricom Perspective* 67 (June 1997): 33.

46. "Report of the *Ad Hoc* Committee on the Drafting of an International Convention against Apartheid in Sports," November 10, 1977, Official Document System of the United Nations (UN) A/32/36, http://documents-dds-ny.un.org/doc/UNDOC/GEN/N77/231/04/pdf/N7723104.pdf?OpenElement (accessed January 4, 2012).

47. Payne, "The International Politics of the Gleneagles Agreement," 420.

48. "Commonwealth Statement on Apartheid in Sport," in *Commonwealth Heads of Government Meeting: Minutes of Sessions and Memoranda* (London, June 8–15, 1977), Annex to Final Communiqué, 212–13.

49. "Report of the *Ad Hoc* Committee on the Drafting of an International Convention against Apartheid in Sports," November 10, 1977, UN A/32/36, http://documents-dds-ny.un.org/doc/UNDOC/GEN/N77/231/04/pdf/N7723104.pdf?OpenElement (accessed January 4, 2012).

50. United Nations Centre against *Apartheid,* "Resolutions on Apartheid Adopted by the United Nations General Assembly in 1977," *Notes and Documents*, no. 2/78 (February 1978): 44.

51. "Definition of Key Terms Used in the UN Treaty Collection," http://treaties.un.org/pages/Overview.aspx?path=overview/definition/page1_en.xml (accessed January 4, 2012).

52. United Nations Centre against *Apartheid,* "Resolutions on Apartheid Adopted by the United Nations General Assembly in 1978/1979," *Notes and Documents*, no. 10/79 (May 1979): 33, 44.

53. See United Nations Centre against *Apartheid,* "Actions Taken by Governments Concerning Sporting Contacts with South Africa," *Notes and Documents*, no. 3/76 (January 1976): 25.

54. See Nicholas Evan Sarantakes's chapter in this volume, which details Carter's efforts to launch an alternative to the Olympics.

55. Margaret Thatcher to Denis Flowers, January 22, 1981. Reproduced and posted online at http://politics.guardian.co.uk/foi/images/0,,1717021,00.html (accessed January 4, 2012).

56. Payne, "The International Politics of the Gleneagles Agreement," 423.

57. See Clyde Walcott with Brian Scovell, *Sixty Years on the Back Foot: The Cricketing Life of Sir Clyde Walcott* (London: Victor Gollancz, 1988), 155–56.

58. "Statement That Saved the Tour," *Advocate News,* March 5, 1981, 14.

59. "Tudor: 'No Need for Meeting,'" *Advocate News,* March 3, 1981, 1.

60. See *Commonwealth Heads of Government Meeting: Minutes of Sessions and Memoranda,* Melbourne, September 30 to October 7, 1981, 148–49, 150–54.

61. Hall, Thomas, and Farier, "The Anti-Apartheid Campaign," 61.

62. Tony Cozier, "South African Tour Controversy," *Benson & Hedges West Indies Cricket Annual* (1983): 11.

63. Ibid., 11–12.

64. Trevor Marshall, "The Anti-Apartheid Campaign in the Caribbean," in *The African-Caribbean Connection: Historical and Cultural Perspectives,* ed. Alan Cobley and Alvin Thompson (Bridgetown: University of the West Indies, Department of History/NCF, 1990), 102.

65. Shridath Ramphal, "A Healing Touch," introduction to the 1983 Report of the Commonwealth Secretary-General (London: Commonwealth Secretariat, 1983), 16.

66. See Norman Faria, *Sports and Apartheid: Caribbean Sports People and the Boycott of South Africa* (St. Michael, Barbados: SALC, 1983).

67. Desmond Davies, "Apartheid's Wrong, but the Money's Right," *Africa Now,* February 1983, 54–55.

68. Quoted in Mihir Bose, *Sporting Colours: Sport and Politics in South Africa* (London: Robson Books, 1994), 136.

69. Cited in Sam Ramsamy, *Apartheid: The Real Hurdle, Sport in South Africa and the International Boycott* (London: International Defence and Aid Fund for Southern Africa, 1982), 63.

70. Adrian Guelke, "The Politicisation of South African Sport," in *The Politics of Sport,* ed. Lincoln Allison (Manchester: Manchester University Press, 1986), 139.

71. See Adrian Guelke, "Sport and the End of Apartheid," in *The Changing Politics of Sport,* ed. Lincoln Allison (Manchester: Manchester University Press, 1993), 157. See also Mike Proctor, *South Africa: The Years of Isolation and the Return to International Cricket* (Harpenden, Herts.: Queen Anne Press, 1994), 80.

72. Proctor, *South Africa,* 80.

73. Bose, *Sporting Colours,* 134.

74. Cited in Davies, "Apartheid's Wrong," 55, and "This Is Not Just Cricket," *Azanian Frontline* (April 1983): 8.

75. Quoted in Douglas Booth, *The Race Game: Sport and Politics in South Africa* (London: Frank Cass, 1998), 145.

76. Desmond Davies, "Apartheid's Wrong," 54.

77. "West Indian Cricketers Arrive," *Sowetan,* January 14, 1983, 3.

78. Cozier, "South African Tour Controversy," 12.

79. Ramsamy, *Apartheid: The Real Hurdle,* 65. For the case of India, see Mihir Bose, *A History of Indian Cricket* (London: Andre Deutsch, 1990), 321.

80. See *Caricom Perspective* (1984), 5.

81. United Nations Centre Against *Apartheid,* "Declarations of Conferences and Seminars Organized or Co-sponsored by the UN Special Committee against Apartheid: 1981–1985," *Notes and Documents,* Special Issue (March 1986): 104. See also declaration adopted by the Second International Conference on Sports Boycott against South Africa, contained in UN A/40/343—S/17224, http://documents-dds-ny.un.org/doc/UNDOC/GEN/N85/157/06/pdf/N8515706.pdf?OpenElement (accessed January 4, 2012).

82. *Caricom Perspective* 31 (May–June 1985): 30.

83. United Nations Centre against *Apartheid, News Digest* 4, no. 85 (September/October, 1985): 9.

84. Quoted in Cozier, "The South African Connection," 16.

85. "Bird's Stand Is Slapped," *Barbados Advocate,* February 1, 1986, 1.

86. "Rae Pours Oil on Cricket's Troubled Waters," *Advocate,* February 13, 1986, 1.

87. Beckles, *Development of West Indies Cricket: Vol. 1,* 169.

88. For Thatcher's account of that Commonwealth Heads of Government meeting, see Margaret Thatcher, *The Downing Street Years* (London: HarperCollins, 1993), 516–19.

89. "Diplomats: Hold the Decision on the Games," *Sunday Advocate,* July 13, 1986, 17.

90. "Manley: Solidarity with Africa First," *Advocate,* July 17, 1986, 11.

91. "Barbados Games Team 'on Hold,'" *Advocate,* July 18, 1986, 1.

92. "Bajans Boycott Games/Government Backs BOA," *Sunday Advocate,* July 20, 1986, 1. For a good summary of the events surrounding the Games, see *Keesing's Contemporary Archives,* vol. 37 (September 1986), 34650.

93. United Nations Centre Against *Apartheid,* "Resolutions on Apartheid Adopted by the United Nations General Assembly in 1985," *Notes and Documents,* no. 1/86 (January 1986): 20–29. Abstaining were Australia, Austria, Belgium, Canada, Denmark, Finland, France, Federal Republic of Germany, Greece, Iceland, Ireland, Italy, Japan, Luxemburg, Malawi, the Netherlands, New Zealand, Norway, Portugal, Solomon Islands, Spain, Sweden, the United Kingdom, and the United States.

94. See Guelke, "Sport and the End of Apartheid."

95. See Marc Keech, "At the Centre of the Web: The Role of Sam Ramsamy in South Africa's Readmission to International Sport," *Culture, Sport, Society* 3, no. 3 (2000): 41–62.

96. See United Nations Centre Against *Apartheid,* "Register of Sports Contacts with South Africa, 1 Jan.–31 Dec. 1990," *Notes and Documents,* no. 11/91 (May 1991): 3.

97. See *United Cricket Board of South Africa Inaugural Report*, and Douglas Booth, "Accommodating Race to Play the Game: South Africa's Readmission to International Sport," *Sporting Traditions* 8, no. 2 (1992): 190.

98. Quoted in Booth, "Accommodating Race," 197.

99. Douglas Booth, "United Sport: An Alternative Hegemony in South Africa," *International Journal of the History of Sport* 12, no. 3 (1995): 112, and Booth, *The Race Game,* 192.

100. See Walcott with Scovell, *Sixty Years on the Back Foot,* 158; Proctor, *South Africa,* 125; and Booth, *The Race Game,* 191.

101. Communiqué in *Commonwealth Heads of Government Meeting: Minutes of Sessions and Memoranda* (Harare, October 16–22, 1991), 182. See also UN DPSCA/CAA 21/91, "Commonwealth Communique on South Africa" (October, 1991), 4.

102. Booth, "United Sport," 112; Booth, *The Race Game,* 192; and John Nauright, *Sport, Cultures and Identities in South Africa* (London: Leicester University Press, 1997), 154.

103. Beckles, *Development of West Indies Cricket: Vol. 1,* 166–68.

104. See Booth, *The Race Game,* 191.

# 5

# Peronism, International Sport, and Diplomacy

*Cesar R. Torres*

On June 4, 1943, a nationalist coup d'état overthrew the weak and corrupt government of Ramón Castillo, ending the decade of oligarchic rule that had begun with the first coup d'état in the history of Argentina in 1930. Then Col. Juan Domingo Perón became a prominent official in the new military government while rallying strong support from labor leaders and the working class. In early October 1945, the army, pressured by political parties and public opinion to hold free elections and distrustful of Perón's political rise, forced him to resign. Days later, on October 17, 1945, with Perón in prison, thousands of workers gathered in downtown Buenos Aires demanding his release. The military government complied; Perón was released and became a candidate in the presidential elections, which shortly after were announced for February 1946. Backed by the unions and the working class, among other groups, Perón won the elections with 52.40 percent of the votes, 9.89 percent more than his closest rival. At the end of his first six-year term in office, his electoral performance was even stronger. Perón was reelected in 1951 by a margin of more than 30 percent, with 62.49 percent of the votes. In spite of the popular support, Perón would not be able to finish his second term in office, as his government was overthrown by another coup d'état in September 1955.[1]

Whether Perón's decade as president is favorably evaluated or not, it certainly represents a dramatic turning point in Argentine politics. Perón and Peronism, as the movement that supported his regime came to be known, cut across every aspect of Argentine life, public and private. As Matthew B. Karush and Oscar Chamosa have pointed out, Perón "transformed Argentina's economy, its social structure, and its political culture in ways that continue to shape Argentine reality."[2] From the beginning, Perón presented himself as someone charting not only a new course for his country but one that broke off from its past. His nationalist and populist regime was thus articulated as "a New Argentina based on social justice, political sovereignty, and economic independence."[3] These three principles constituted the core of the "Peronist Doctrine," which aspired to provide happiness to the masses. Indeed, Perón's Argentina marked, in part, a departure from the past because the organized working class became a new political and social actor. This, according to Mariano Ben Plotkin, represented a subversion of "the accepted system of social classification existing in Argentina."[4] In Peronist Argentina, the working class was empowered and earned political citizenship. During the Peronist decade, the working class became a key factor in the political process and also the recipient of material benefits through innovative social legislation and of a whole array of social services and programs.

Sport figured prominently among the innovative social policies of Perón. The Peronist state guaranteed the masses broad access to sport. Similarly it gave unprecedented support to elite sport.[5] Perón was clearly aware that sport was a versatile tool that could be use domestically and internationally to advance political and diplomatic goals. He saw athletes as ambassadors that could project his New Argentina overseas and the hosting of international sporting events as an exceptional stage from which to do so. Prior to Peronism, Argentine sport had been largely organized and controlled by civil society; during the regime, however, it became encouraged, directed, and supported by the state. The importance that Perón placed on participation in mass sport as well as on achievements in elite sport, both at home and abroad, with returns expected from such participation and achievements, represented an unknown strategy in Argentina. Raanan Rein has aptly observed that "no Argentine government prior to Perón . . . invested as much effort and as many resources in both the development and encouragement of sport and in the effort to earn political dividends from this policy."[6] This chapter examines the ways by which

Peronism used different forms of involvement in international sport as a diplomatic tool to promote its leader's avowed New Argentina. Specifically, the Argentine Olympic excursions under Peronism, its quest for the 1956 Olympics, and the regime's organization of the 1950 Men's World Basketball Championships and the 1951 Pan-American Games will be explored as representative cases of the Peronist international sport agenda. To properly analyze these events, it is first necessary to briefly review Peronism's understanding of sport and its relation to the cultural dimension of the movement as well as its foreign policy.

## Peronist Sport

Perón was not the first Argentine president to use sport to advance political agendas, but he was the first to use it—and his critics would argue abuse it—extensively by making it a prominent subject of concern for the state. It could be argued that Perón conceived of sport as a social technology capable of being adapted to serve different purposes. Mark Dyreson has proposed that "technologies are not just machines and 'made' things—inanimate objects. Technologies are also organizations of human energy designed for problem solving."[7] He has further maintained that "some cultures have considered sport to *be* a social technology designed to reconfigure social patterns."[8] As a social technology, sport constitutes a powerful force to shape and reshape modern cultures. Although it seems that Perón never explicitly articulated a vision of sport as a social technology, his policies and commentaries on the matter implicitly reflect this vision. As will be seen, his support for sport was meant as a source for political symbolism and socialization as well as the transmission of desired moral values—all of which was tied to the building, strengthening, and diffusion of Perón's New Argentina. In the following passage, Perón not only expounds the instrumental power of sport and how profoundly it could affect the country but also assigns the state a vital role in its organization: "For me, sport has a much greater significance than has been assigned to it in our country until now. I believe that sport is a creative activity that completes and reaffirms the soul of the peoples. Without sport the peoples never have a perfected soul like we aspire for the Argentine country."[9]

The task Perón projected for sport was evidently quite ambitious. For him, sport had a tremendous capacity to influence the "soul" of a people and presumably to unify it. But the influential power of sport was not something that could be simply bequeathed to the Argentine people; rather, it was required that Argentines actively engage in sport. Thus, Perón contended three years into his first term in office that

> a distinction must be made between "spectator sports" and sports as an activity. The former postulates 10 playing and 300,000 watching, whereas the ideal would be 300,000 playing and 10 watching.
>
> The real benefit of sports lies in practising them, although spectator sports are also necessary, because they educate, create a [sporting] ambience or climate, and encourage participation.
>
> I want my country to be a nation of athletes, with educated minds and strengthened bodies. . . . We're on our way—getting there will depend on the Argentines and on the public authorities' support and promotion by all possible means.[10]

In 1955 Perón insisted that in the short run Argentina should be a country of five million athletes while clarifying that the goal was to have twenty million athletes.[11] What Perón wanted was an athlete in every Argentine. To that effect his government implemented a number of policies to encourage and support sport participation across Argentina that largely expanded opportunities to access it. For example, numerous sport organizations were aided by the state, and sport facilities were built all across the country. In addition, Peronism established an organization of high school students that featured sport participation at the center of its activities. However, the better-known initiative was probably the sport championships organized by the Fundación Eva Perón (Eva Perón Foundation), led by the president's wife, who, as is well known, had a conspicuous role in Peronism. The first sporting event organized by the Fundación Eva Perón was a soccer championship in 1948 that included more than 11,000 boys. Two years later, the number of boys participating in this championship grew to more than 100,000. In the following years, more sports were added to the program, and girls were admitted in some of them. In 1954 there were more than 215,000 children competing in ten sports. The year before, a number of championships for youth had also been created. While the championships for youth were named after the president, the ones for children were named after his wife. Participants received medical examinations, the clothing necessary to compete, and transportation. Although it was the Fundación Eva Perón that formally organized and administered both sets of championships, the state provided financial support for them. Not coincidentally, Ramón Cereijo served simultaneously as the regime's finance minister, as general manager of the Fundación Eva Perón, and as president of the organizing committee of the championships.[12]

If the Peronist state expanded the opportunities for the masses to participate in sport, it also provided extensively for elite sport. In order to oversee this expression of national sport, Perón secured ways to control it. Thus he appointed political cronies in sport federations and organizations. Notably among these institutions was the Confederación Argentina de Deportes–Comité Olímpico Argentino (Argentine Confederation of Sports–Argentine Olympic Committee), simply known by the combined Spanish acronym CADCOA.[13] From 1948 to 1955, Rodolfo G. Valenzuela, president of the Supreme Court and a devoted Peronist, served as its president. Nothing being left to chance, in 1951 a modification to CADCOA's bylaws allowed the Argentine president to appoint the institution's leader.[14] To cement the relationship between the regime and elite sport, Perón and his wife were appointed CADCOA's honorary presidents. From CADCOA, the regime was able to exert considerable influence on elite sport. Consequently the regime sponsored a variety of competitions, national and international in scope, as well as the preparation of athletes to compete both in Argentina and abroad. In regard to the latter, among the better-known are race car driver Juan Manuel Fangio and boxer Pascual Pérez, who became world champions under the aegis of Perón. In regard to the former, among the better-known are the 1950 Men's Basketball World Championship and the 1951 Pan-American Games, which were both the first event of their kind. The list of athletes sponsored by and competitions organized under the auspices of Peronism is, of course, much longer. Underlying that when it came to elite sport he had also made a break from the past, Perón recognized in the old Buenos Aires clubs "the extraordinary merit of having done by themselves what the state should have done for Argentine sport."[15] With his policies, it was the state that provided such sustenance.

The democratization of sport in Peronist Argentina was a manifestation of the regime's nationalist and populist tendencies and at the same time a calculated political investment. Both mass and elite sport were part of a political culture that created myths and symbols to generate consensus around the New Argentina. Mariano Ben Plotkin has argued that "at the center of this symbolic production was the glorification of the Peronist state and of Perón and Eva."[16] The sporting events either organized or sponsored by the regime showcased the Peronist imagery and liturgy. In addition, both Perón and Eva reinforced the regime's efforts at political socialization by attending innumerable sporting events and by welcoming the loyalty and admiration professed by many of the athletes benefited by the Peronist policies. Likewise they praised loyal athletes and offered them different presents and rewards. All these actions portrayed Perón and Eva as benefactors of the Argentine people. It is no coincidence that Perón became known, and celebrated, not only as *el primer trabajador* (the first worker) but also as *el primer deportista* (the first sportsman). It is no coincidence either that the slogan *Perón apoya el deporte* (Perón supports sport) was seen in many sporting events. According to Raanan Rein, the "gospel of Peronist sports, like the mobilization of the entire education system, was perceived as one of the more effective means to achieve that goal [national unity] and shape 'the New Argentine' in 'the New Argentina.'"[17]

*Mundo Infantil,* a Peronist weekly for children, made clear in one of its first issues that sport was a preferred means to pursue national unity: "The Campeonato Evita will make the dream of teachers and governments come true: it will unite Argentine youth over and beyond local loyalties, and even beyond provincial limits; because the voice of sports is stentorian, and powerful, and it invigorates the young like an electrical charge. Under its spell, all will feel equal, all will think the same way."[18]

To think the same way meant embracing the New Argentina. Perón believed that sport could transmit, affirm, and exemplify the moral values of his political project. He claimed, "I have always thought of a people of sportsmen because when you have that, you have a people of noble men and . . . of a profound moral sense of life."[19] Moreover, for Perón, Argentine sportsmen were "constructing the New Argentina we yearned for, an Argentina of healthy men, sturdy men, and strong men; because only healthy, tough peoples make great nations."[20] Vigor, health, and strength demanded hard work and dedication, the same values he demanded not just from athletes but from all Argentines, especially workers. Indeed, one of Perón's goals was to create better and disciplined workers. In addition, for Peronism, sport had the "potential for inspiring fraternity, co-opera-tion, social solidarity, national identity, discipline and loyalty," which were also important components of the morality of the New Argentines in the New Argentina.[21] Noticeably, while Peronism encouraged participation in both mass and elite sport, such participation remained largely voluntary.

In short, for Perón sport was a tool with an enormous capacity to as-sist in building the New Argentina. Addressing the crowd at the closing ceremony of the 1951 Pan-American Games, Perón declared that sport was "a school of healthy men, healthy of body and mind, of good men that fight for the greatness of the country without thinking of any other goal than this greatness itself." In the same address, he pronounced that "the only glory to which we aspire is to forge a just, free, and sovereign Argentina."[22] At the same time, this conceptualization of sport led Perón to use it to advertise the goals as well as the progress of the regime, domes-tically and internationally—that is, during the Peronist decade, sport also became a significant tool of cultural diplomacy. Before exploring such use, it is important to briefly appraise Perón's foreign policy.

## Peronist Foreign Policy

To understand Perón's foreign policy it is most useful to keep in mind the international context at the time he rose to power and the history of the troubled relationship between Argentina and the United States. To the ir-ritation of the United States, Argentina maintained a policy of neutrality during World War II. Although the leaders of the 1943 coup d'état sought to improve relations with the United States, the latter would only ac-cept that Argentina immediately break diplomatic relations with the Axis. Argentina complied in January 1944 and, after further pressure by the United States, declared war on the Axis in March of the following year. It was then that the United States finally recognized the Argentine military government. In spite of the concessions, anti-Argentine sentiments were still strong in certain circles within the US Department of State that con-sidered Argentina to have been pro-Axis since the beginning of the war. Spruille Braden, a hard-liner who served as ambassador of the United States to Argentina in 1945, insisted on disparaging Argentina, and espe-cially Perón, as pro-Axis. Braden first favored those Argentines opposing the military government and then actively antagonized the candidacy of

Perón to the presidency. As assistant secretary of state for inter-American affairs, Braden released on the eve of the February 1946 elections a document that, by supposedly revealing Argentine ties to the Axis during the war, was meant to undercut Perón's candidacy. Perón responded by denouncing Braden's strategy as interventionist propaganda and coining the slogan "Braden or Perón." The anti-imperialist antinomy, which "practically [eliminated] Perón's opponents from the headlines,"[23] only added to the masses' attraction to the future president's proposed program.[24]

After Perón took office, the US distrust and opposition to him continued as much as his political discourse kept emphasizing anti-imperialism. These tensions were played out in a world deeply divided by the Cold War, a conflict that pitted the United States against the Soviet Union, the two superpowers that emerged after World War II. In this divided world, Perón tried to steer an intermediate course between the two countries and their respective allies. This course was expressed in a doctrine Perón labeled *la tercera posición* (the third position).[25] The third position was a planned distancing from the East and the West, from capitalism and communism, that represented in foreign policy the Peronist principle of political sovereignty. For Perón it was a superior standpoint "because it harnessed the dynamic potential of capitalism for the good of all members of society . . . and, at the same time, it avoided the repressive and sectarian aspects of communism."[26] In 1948 he thus articulated his foreign policy: "Argentina is friendly towards all the countries of the world, does not favour hegemonies whether of the right or the left, because her international course of conduct is well defined. Its roots are found in history, but its trend is new. To its impartial consideration of present world problems is added the energy born of the principles it upholds. Our international rules are dictated by these principles, not by temporary advantages."[27]

The third position was a way to situate Argentina in the post–World War II international context and also an attempt to advance an independent foreign policy. One of Perón's goals was to create more space to maneuver and therefore to have better negotiation tools in his relations with the United States, the Soviet Union, and their respective allies. Strengthening ties with countries outside the Western Hemisphere was hoped to counterbalance the importance of the relationship with the United States. As Alberto Conil Paz and Gustavo Ferrari argued in the mid-1960s, the Peronist's third position aimed "to contain Washington's pressure or that of the inter-American system by gaining support from extrahemispheric countries. This support could be sought either in the traditional links with England or in the relations of the new Communist bloc."[28] Writing more than thirty years later, Andrés Cisneros and Carlos Escudé agreed with this vision and argued that the third position implied a rejection of the extreme positions represented by the United States and the Soviet Union while formulating an alternative that was neither capitalist nor communist.[29] This was encapsulated in the slogan *ni yanquis ni marxistas, peronistas* (neither Yankees nor Marxists, Peronists), created by some regime's supporters after Perón was ousted in 1955, which represented the third position as much as Peronist Argentina.

Perón restored diplomatic relations with the Soviet Union immediately after taking office, a gesture that indicated his intended independent foreign policy. Soon the country engaged in commercial trade with the Soviets. In the following years, the Peronist government signed commercial agreements with Bulgaria, Czechoslovakia, Poland, and Romania. At the same time, Perón strengthened the commercial ties with Western Europe, for example with Belgium, France, Italy, West Germany, and Spain. Perhaps it was Perón's support of Francisco Franco's Spanish regime that best exemplified his independence from both the Western and Eastern blocs. All of this happened while Argentina not only maintained but also tried to improve its economic and diplomatic ties with Great Britain and the United States. In the latter case, the Argentine efforts were for the most part unsuccessful or at best moderately advantageous. In many respects, the United States "continued to be disposed to make Argentina pay for its neutrality during the war."[30]

Throughout his decade in power, Perón persisted with his anti-US imperialism rhetoric, but he did not take any position negative to the United States, and both sides took certain steps at cooperation. Early on in his presidency, Perón declared that "Argentina is part of the American continent and inevitably will join the United States and the other nations of the American continent in any future conflict."[31] Indeed, another aspect of the Peronist foreign policy, compatible with its third position, was the strengthening of Pan-Americanism. For Perón, "the international doctrine of the Argentine Republic is characterized . . . [by] a deep aspiration towards continental unity."[32] Furthermore, making reference to the Inter-American Conference for the Maintenance of Continental Security and Peace held in Rio de Janeiro in 1947, he wrote that "the pacifist and creative policy we uphold will obtain the effective contribution of our country—with all its energy—to the programme the Continent is carrying out by the strong bonds of solidarity and in keeping with the ideal of democracy."[33]

Pressured by Perón, the National Congress approved in 1946 the Act of Chapultepec, which had been signed the year before at the Inter-American Conference on Problems of War and Peace held in Mexico City. The Act of Chapultepec endorsed regional security and called for collective measures in case of an attack on a signatory state by an extracontinental power. In 1947 Argentina embraced the Inter-American Treaty of Reciprocal Assistance signed earlier that year in Rio de Janeiro, which the National Congress approved in 1950. At the core of the Rio Treaty, as it is also known, is the idea that aggression against a signatory country is tantamount to an aggression against all signatory countries. In 1948 Argentina took part in the IX Inter-American Conference held in Bogotá in which the Organization of American States was created. In these forums, Argentina often challenged, largely unsuccessfully, the hemispheric leadership of the United States. For instance, the conference at which the Rio Treaty was signed was postponed twice in part because of the tension between Argentina and the United States.[34] As Harold F. Peterson has argued, "while satisfying Washington's hopes for restoration of the hemispheric front, the Argentines resourcefully found issues with which to confront the United States and to seek support from the Latin American republics."[35] To solidify its position in inter-American affairs, Perón not only engaged in multilateral regional efforts but also signed bilateral agreements with several Latin American countries, including Bolivia, Brazil, Chile, Colombia, Nicaragua, and Paraguay. The third position was amenable to Pan-Americanism, and Perón advanced it seeking influence in the Western Hemisphere.

## Peronism and Sport Diplomacy

Ezequiel Navarra, a talented billiards player, provided a glimpse of the role Perón assigned to sport in the world of diplomacy. Navarra, who in 1951 beat the accomplished U.S. player William F. Hoppe in a much-publicized exhibition organized by Perón in Buenos Aires, recalled, "Do you know what Perón told me once? That athletes are the best ambassadors the country has."[36] Perón understood that not only could athletes disseminate a positive representation of his New Argentina abroad but also that hosting international sporting events offered a unique platform to accomplish such a goal. Thus, given his unprecedented support for sport, Perón actively engaged it as a form of cultural diplomacy. Nicholas J. Cull has defined cultural diplomacy as an element of public diplomacy by which actors "attempt to manage the international environment through making its cultural resources and achievements known overseas and/or facilitating cultural transmission abroad."[37] Similarly, for Geoffrey A. Pigman, cultural diplomacy "is primarily about how governments use the culture of their nation-state or place to communicate to others about themselves."[38] Perón thought sport was a cultural expression highly adaptable to promoting his political project on the global stage. In other words, he recognized that, as a social technology, sport was also an instrument of diplomacy, "an unmistakable prism through which nation-states project their image to the world and their own people."[39] Below follows a number of the most prominent instances in which sport was used by his regime to communicate the content and accomplishments of the New Argentina. These Peronist efforts demonstrate that the regime aligned sport with its foreign policy goals.

The 1948 and 1952 Olympic excursions were perceived by Peronism as unique platforms to advertise the New Argentina. By September 1945, CADCOA announced that it had received news that the Olympic Games would be resumed in 1948. Although the host of the event was still unknown, CADCOA celebrated the news and promised that it would work to send representatives in all sports.[40] When the International Olympic Committee (IOC) confirmed in September 1946 the postal vote that had already awarded the 1948 Olympics to London, Perón had been in office for only a few short months.[41] CADCOA carried on with its Olympic preparation while Perón promised Juan Carlos Palacios, its president since 1938, financial support for the team that would travel to London.[42] In September 1947 Palacios resigned from CADCOA. Whether he was pressured to do so is open to speculation. Later that month, however, Carlos Aloé, a representative of Perón, clarified in a CADCOA meeting that the rumors saying that the president favored some officials to lead the institution were baseless.[43] Aloé said that Perón believed that it was the athletes who should elect their leaders. In the same meeting, Ramón Cereijo the regime's finance minister, renewed Perón's promise of financial support for the Olympic team "so that Argentine athletes can demonstrate the fighting spirit and the standing they had in the international order."[44]

By the time of the 1948 London Olympics, the president of CAD-COA was Ricardo Sánchez de Bustamante, who had served as vice president until Palacios's resignation. In his farewell to the Argentine delegation, Perón reiterated his support and let the athletes know, if only obliquely, their role in cultural diplomacy and their overall responsibility. He told them, "As long as I am in the government, I will sponsor any delegation, because I know full well the benefits to the country when they are properly carried out."[45] Even *El Gráfico,* a sport magazine established in 1919 that did not advocate Peronism, wrote with a spirit of cultural diplomacy that the Argentine delegation would try "to broadcast to the world the quality of our sport and of our champions."[46] Argentina sent 242 athletes to London, the country's largest Olympic delegation ever. Ten women made the delegation, a far cry from the Berlin Olympics twelve years earlier when the first—and only—female Argentine Olympian competed. The delegation was the largest among the Latin American contingents. Argentine athletes garnered seven medals in London—three gold, three silver, and one bronze—which was the same total as achieved at the 1928 Amsterdam Olympics but won while competing against a smaller number of countries. These two Olympics still represent the most successful performances of Argentine athletes at a single edition of the Games. In addition, in London fourteen athletes finished between fourth and sixth place in their events.[47] Upon the return of the athletes to Argentina, a tribute to the delegation, and to Perón and his wife, was held at the Club Atlético River Plate's stadium. In his address, Perón "drew a parallel between the athletes' achievements and the Peronist enterprise": "Let this be our tribute to the glories of sports, to the champions, to all the athletes who are constructing the New Argentina we yearned for."[48]

Even those who did not have much sympathy for Perón agreed that the country's athletes could disseminate a positive image of Argentina abroad. Félix D. Frascara wrote in *El Gráfico* of Delfo Cabrera's gold medal in the marathon that the whole stadium applauded him as well as the Argentine flag and anthem. Moreover, Frascara contended, making reference to the

Argentine flag's colors, that Cabrera "placed in the grey sky of London the light blue and white of the authentic Argentine sky."[49]

Loyal Peronist Rodolfo G. Valenzuela had been in charge of CAD-COA for almost four years when it was time to send the Argentine delegation to the 1952 Helsinki Olympics. The economy was not as propitious in 1952 as it had been in 1948, and consequently the Olympic delegation was smaller. Only athletes thought to have a good chance at succeeding in competition were chosen for the Olympic team. However, as in 1948, the 1952 delegation was supposed to embody and publicize the achievements of the New Argentina. Before the athletes embarked for Helsinki, loyal Peronist Aloé penned in *Mundo Deportivo* (a sport magazine created by the regime in 1949 to compete with *El Gráfico*) that "the New Argentina has conquered a prominent place in sport in the continent and the world; therefore its representatives not only awaken a favorable expectation and the world wants to know exactly what Perón's generation produces. . . . Consequently, our representatives make the strictest commitment with themselves and with their fellow citizens when they are chosen and accept such a responsibility before the nation."[50]

In June, Perón himself went to the port to bid farewell to the Argentine delegation. Damián Cané, writing for *Mundo Deportivo,* gave expression to Perón's idea of sport as a tool of cultural diplomacy. He wrote that the Argentine athletes were going with "a great deal of faith and steely optimism, eager to show the world the physical and spiritual health of this New Argentina."[51] A month later, the same magazine ventured in relation to the approaching Olympic Games that the summary of the event "will say that Perón's Argentina was present" and that "once again, the magnitude of its concept of peace and confraternity constituted the best example of a brotherly and friendly people to the whole world."[52] This time the delegation had 126 athletes, including eight women. It was again the largest Latin American delegation. The Argentine athletes garnered five medals: one gold, two silver, and two bronze. The single gold medal would shine for a long time, as Argentina did not win another until the 2004 Athens Olympics. In addition to the medals, in Helsinki fifteen athletes finished between fourth and sixth place in their events.[53] Whatever the evaluation of the athletic performance, once back in Argentina, Domingo Peluffo, *chef de mission* of the delegation, put a positive spin on the second Peronist Olympic excursion, declaring that the Argentine athletes had amply fulfilled Perón's diplomatic goal. Peluffo said that for the president the main purpose of the country's sport delegations was to make friends. For him, the Argentine athletes returned from Helsinki leaving behind "a profound legacy of friendship . . . and the understanding and admiration for our country today."[54]

In addition to sending delegations to the Olympic Games, Perón was also seduced by the advertising possibilities of hosting the event.[55] Although Argentine politicians and sport officials had long aspired to organize the Olympic Games in Buenos Aires, it was under Peronism that the country mounted its first full bid for the international sport festival. According to Argentine Olympic records, it was a Peronist official who instructed CADCOA to communicate to the IOC that Buenos Aires wished to host the 1956 Olympics. Late in January 1948, CADCOA sent two communications to the IOC announcing its ambition. Before the end of the month, Sánchez de Bustamante wrote to Sigfrid Edstrøm, then the IOC president, a long letter detailing the rationale for Buenos Aires's bid. For CADCOA's president, Buenos Aires deserved to host the 1956 Olympics because of Argentina's long and distinguished involvement in the Olympic movement, the widespread practice and sound organization of sport in the country, and the support that the government bestowed to sport, which was "a transcendental achievement of unquestionable benefit."[56] Furthermore, the government had pledged all necessary support for the event, including the construction of the required venues. Sánchez de Bustamante also emphasized that CADCOA's request was just because the Olympic Games had never been celebrated in South America. Therefore, hosting the event in Buenos Aires would fulfill not only a national but also a South American ambition. If the IOC voted for Buenos Aires, he argued, the decision would "SATISFY THE LEGITIMATE ASPIRATIONS OF THE GOVERNMENT OF HIS EXCELLENCY THE PRESIDENT JUAN D. PERÓN AND THAT OF THE ATHLETES OF THE CONTINENT [capitalization in original]."[57]

Although Horacio Bustos Morón and Ricardo C. Aldao, the two Argentine IOC members, expressed some misgivings about the ways of Peronism in sport, they were on board with the bid. In a letter to their IOC colleagues, they affirmed, "We have every reason to expect that the Argentine Government would grant the necessary support to permit the Organizing Committee of the XVI OLYMPIAD to successfully carry out its work."[58] The CADCOA admitted that Perón explicitly wished to organize the Olympic Games in Buenos Aires. Perón expressed his personal support in a lavish book about Argentina produced for the IOC that served as a sort of "formal invitation to celebrate the Olympic Games of 1956 in this city [Buenos Aires]."[59] A month before the April 1949 IOC session that would select the city for the 1956 Olympics, Valenzuela, then the new president of CADCOA, renewed the Buenos Aires effort by writing to the IOC. He insisted on the merits of the candidacy and stressed what the New Argentina offered the world: "The National Government will be the first and most enthusiastic supporter of the fulfillment of same [all material needs of the Olympic Games], because it does not omit any effort to make the Argentine Republic the great Country our ancestors dreamt of. Every action tends to perfect the conditions of life and to stimulate the activity of the country in all aspects. The government favours this purpose because it fully knows its value and the honour for the Argentine to act as host for the Olympic Games."[60]

The Argentine delegation to the IOC session made its final pitch to convince the IOC that Buenos Aires was the best city for the 1956 Olympics. Its efforts fell one vote short. In the closest election ever, Melbourne beat Buenos Aires in the fourth round by a vote of 21–20. The Argentines turned the close defeat into a victory. The CADCOA proclaimed that the result "comforts the spirit and satisfies the highest Argentine desires, for all that it means for our Nation and Argentine sports."[61] Encouraged by the result, Argentine authorities rapidly decided to bid for other Olympic events. In the 1950 IOC session, Buenos Aires was listed as a candidate for the 1960 Olympics and for the IOC's 1951 session. While the IOC chose Vienna for the latter, the bid for the former was obviously abandoned as Buenos Aires did not appear as a candidate when the IOC chose the city to host the 1960 Olympics in June 1955. In spite of these developments, *Mundo Deportivo* argued in 1950 that if Helsinki were unable to carry on with the organization of the 1952 Olympics due to the political and economic difficulties in Finland, Buenos Aires would be able to take on that responsibility thanks to the support that Perón would give to such enterprise.[62] Unfortunately, the persisting Peronist Olympic hope that "THE ARGENTINE GOVERNMENT AND ITS PEOPLE WILL RECEIVE WITH A TIGHT, LOYAL AND FRATERNAL EMBRACE ALL THE ATHLETES OF THE WORLD WHO COME TO OUR COUNTRY [capitalization in original]" would not be materialized.[63] Yet the bid and its rhetoric undoubtedly represented a concerted attempt to situate and advertise Argentina on the global stage.

The interest of Peronism in hosting international sporting events extended beyond the Olympic Games. For instance, while the 1948 Olympics were taking place in London, Argentine sport officials not only promoted the candidacy of Buenos Aires for the 1956 Olympics but also labored to secure other such events for the Argentine capital. The Fédération Internationale de Basketball (FIBA) decided at its congress in London to organize a men's world championship every four years between Olympic Games and also granted Buenos Aires the right to host to the first Men's Basketball World Championship. Argentina was in an advantageous position: it was a founding member of FIBA in 1932 and had a strong national team. Perhaps more important, in consonance with its campaign to host the 1956 Olympics, the Peronist government promised FIBA that it would provide sustenance for the championship, which was scheduled for October 22 to November 3, 1950.[64] Argentine sport officials had a little more than two years to prove that they could successfully organize an event of such magnitude. Even though a grand stadium for twenty-five thousand spectators was designed, it was never built.[65] However, Perón subsidized the championship, which enrolled ten teams from the Americas, Europe, and Africa.[66]

The unfolding and result of the first Men's Basketball World Championship played to the hand on Perón. The championship was decided in the last game of the tournament between Argentina and the United States, which were both undefeated. Argentina won by a score of 64–50. More than twenty-one thousand spectators wildly celebrated the Argentine victory. The political significance of the victory was not lost: the Argentines had beaten the North Americans at their game. It mattered little that the United States team primarily comprised players from the Denver Chevrolets, a corporate team, with some additional players from the Phillips 66ers, another corporate team, and the University of Oklahoma. The game was played on the night of November 3, which became known as *la noche de las antorchas* (the night of the torches) in reference to the crowds that paraded in downtown Buenos Aires celebrating the basketball success and improvising torches with newspapers.[67] *Mundo Deportivo* exuded nationalistic pride in the world champions, stating that "Argentine sport feels proud and flattered. Its sons, true 'sportsmen,' true gentlemen of sport, have demonstrated that they are worthy of this strong, prudent and powerful New Argentina."[68] For the magazine, the international success of Argentine athletes was the product of the country's social and political achievements.[69] That Perón intentionally used sport as a tool of cultural diplomacy is supported in his comment to Ricardo González, captain of the Argentine team: "What you have just done for Argentina is better than the work of one hundred ambassadors."[70]

The inaugural Pan-American Games, organized by Peronism the year after the first Men's Basketball World Championship, constituted another chance for the regime to showcase the New Argentina.[71] Although suggestions to organize Pan-American Games go back to the 1910s, the prospect of a hemispheric sporting event modeled after the Olympic Games became a distinct possibility during the 1930s. The spirit of cooperation created by the "Good Neighbor Policy" fostered by the United States for dealing with Latin America, which renounced military intervention and attempted to create an inter-American system of defense, certainly encouraged such a prospect. The cancellation of the 1940 Olympics due to World War II gave the Pan-American Games the impetus needed for their materialization. By the late 1930s, several countries had proposed cities to host a hemispheric sport festival to compensate for the temporary loss of the Olympic Games. Hemispheric sport officials met in Buenos Aires in August 1940 and conceived a more ambitious plan. They decided to establish an inter-American sport bureaucracy and to organize Pan-American Games quadrennially on a rotational basis, starting in Buenos Aires in late 1942. However, the extension of the war to the Western Hemisphere and the diplomatic tension between Argentina and the United States led in June 1942 to the postponement of the inaugural Pan-American Games. The event was subsequently postponed in 1943 and 1944. In 1945, though, certain that there would be Olympic Games in 1948, CADCOA proposed 1950 for the event. Two years later, it proposed that the Second Pan-American Sport Congress be held in London in 1948 during the Olympic Games. When the congress met, Perón had been in office for over two years. His regime keenly embraced the congress's decision to ratify Buenos Aires as the host of the inaugural Pan-American Games, which were set for February 25 to March 8, 1951. Perón who, along with his wife, was appointed an honorary president of the organizing committee, wanted the hemispheric sport festival "to serve as international proof of the regime's success" and promised CADCOA all assistance needed because "these things have to be done properly or not at all. . . . In short, I want to leave the impression that we are not counting costs."[72] For *Mundo Deportivo,* what was at stake in the organization of the event was the prestige of the New Argentina.[73]

The opening ceremony was held in the Club Atlético racing club's spanking new stadium, officially named Estadio Presidente Juan Domingo Perón. In his speech, Valenzuela declared that during the 1951 Pan-American Games, "the new Argentina . . . united with its fraternal countries, will sing its noble ideals."[74] Days earlier Perón had welcomed the foreign delegations at the Pan-American Village, saying that he was bringing "to all the brothers of America" the greetings of the Argentine people and of his country. He added that Argentina "offers this, its humble home, but it does it with the heart of a brother and of a friend. All of you should feel at home."[75] The event exuded the rhetoric of both Peronism and Pan-Americanism. It was the New Argentina that hosted the entire Western Hemisphere. This was made explicit by *Mundo Argentino,* which a few months before the event wrote that it was the youth of the New Argentina who were getting ready to receive the youth of the Americas.[76] Continental sport officials thanked Perón and his wife for their valuable provision to the inaugural Pan-American Games, without which such a demonstration of continental fraternity would not have been possible.[77] During the closing ceremony, Avery Brundage, a future IOC president who at the time was the leader of the Pan-American Sport Committee, remarked upon the role of Perón and his wife and exulted that the Pan-American Games had conquered the obstacles that divide nations.[78] After Brundage's speech, Perón declared that "the only glory we aspire to is to make a just, free and sovereign Argentina."[79] It was clear that sport and large international sporting events were, for him, means to accomplish and publicize such glory.

Even if claims of glory were hyperbolic, Argentine athletes were certainly quite successful at the 1951 Pan-American Games. The Peronist government had given them all the necessary support for proper training. Perón paid them a visit in their training camp before competition started, to encourage and wish them the success that "would be guaranteed by exertion, faith, and determination."[80] Argentine athletes did not disappoint, dominating the medal count with a total of 154 (68 gold, 47 silver, and 39 bronze), way ahead of the United States, which was second with 98 (46 gold, 33 silver, and 19 bronze).[81] Many of these athletes dedicated their triumphs to Perón, who enthusiastically showed gratitude to the athletes and congratulated them on their accomplishments.[82] In a banquet Perón hosted in the presidential residence for the Argentine athletes a few days after the closing ceremony, Valenzuela stated that "I know that in your heart . . . there is an intense love for this New Argentina of Perón and Evita." In turn Perón complimented the athletes, saying that "in these games, we have seen a new sporting spirit emerging for the first time."[83] The event was perhaps Peronist sport's finest hour, and it came in the middle of the regime's decade in power. Even *La Nación,* a newspaper opposed to Perón, agreed that the event was very well organized and that it left an advantageous image of the country.[84] *El Gráfico* concurred.[85] Expectedly, *Mundo Deportivo* argued that the New Argentina had welcomed the continent and that its people "was always caring; its hand that of a friend."[86] Even more, because of the success of the New Argentina, from now on "everybody will want to beat an Argentine, because with that their prestige is enhanced and their glory will be greater."[87] Thus, for this magazine, Argentina not only was an excellent host of the event but also projected its image to both the hemisphere and the entire world.

In addition to the cases summarized above, there were other international sporting events organized in Argentina during the Peronist decade that served as global platforms to advertise the regime as well as numerous athletes that served as its ambassadors. The list is quite extensive, and space only allows me to briefly mention some of them. Among the most illustrious athletes sponsored by Perón was aforementioned race car driver Juan Manuel Fangio. Fangio started his career in Formula One in 1950. Between 1950 and 1955, he won the category's world championship three times and was second twice. He also won in 1956 and 1957, but Perón had already been ousted. Other race car drivers sponsored by the regime included the brothers Oscar and Juan Gálvez and José Froilán González. According to the latter, those who raced abroad were named "labor delegates" of the government.[88] Boxers Pascual Pérez, who won a gold medal in the 1948 London Olympics and six years later won the first world championship for Argentina, and José María Gatica also enjoyed the support of Perón. The careers of swimmers Severo Alfredo Yantorno and Antonio Abertondo were funded by the Peronist state as well. The support extended to other athletes traveling to compete in regional and world tournaments. Similarly Perón funded the organization of several such tournaments in Argentina. Among these tournaments were the 1949 World Shooting Championship and the South American championships of different sports. Likewise, from 1953 to 1955, the Peronist state underwrote the organization in Buenos Aires of a Formula One Grand Prix, which took place on a track built by the regime. Another example was the international cycling competition known as the Vuelta al Centro de la Nueva Argentina (Tour of the Center of the New Argentina). For Perón's supporters, Argentina was at the center of the sporting world during his decade in power, and thanks to his benevolence Argentine athletes were able to tell "the fans of all latitudes that our youth has the physical and moral power to attempt any feat."[89] The sporting accomplishments made possible were "an example for the rest of the world."[90] Clearly Peronist sport saw sending athletes to international competitions and hosting such competitions as an attractive diplomatic resource to globally spread its image.

The following two examples summarize the Peronist view of sport as a form of cultural diplomacy. Before competition started at the inaugural Pan-American Games organized in Buenos Aires in 1951 with the full support of the state, Perón sent a letter to all the athletes in the country's delegation stating that they were "the synthesis of a whole people" and requesting that they "keep in mind also that with the Argentine prestige we defend the common honor that is our sacred legacy."[91] Two weeks later, Eva told the visiting delegations during the closing ceremony that "when you arrived at this warm home of everybody, we jubilantly said 'Welcome.' And now with the sadness of those who see good friends depart we say 'until you give us the next opportunity to welcome you again in the New Argentina of Perón.'"[92]

Eva's mention of friendship is telling, as Perón emphasized that one of the goals of his diplomatic efforts through sport was to build closer relationships with other countries. As shown above, athletes representing the New Argentina in international competitions were reminded that one of their goals was to make friends. This was consistent with the Peronist regime's third position in foreign affairs, which stated that the country "is friendly towards all the countries of the world [and] does not favour hegemonies whether of the right or the left."[93] Unlike the Soviet Union or the United States in the context of the Cold War, Perón did not seem to have approached international sport as a way to prove the superiority of his politics; rather, he seemed to have wanted that the New Argentina be fully recognized in the international system and acknowledged for its successes. For instance, the anti-US rhetoric of his regime did not for the most part extend to international sport. Consider *Mundo Deportivo*'s reception of the US delegation to the 1951 Pan-American Games. For the Peronist magazine, it was "brilliant" and "one of the most eagerly awaited."[94] Moreover, the talent of the US athletes "brought a vast and enthusiastic public to [the airport in] Ezeiza."[95] None of this meant that beating the United States, as happened in the final of the 1950 Men's Basketball World Championship and in the medal count of the inaugural Pan-American Games, was not noted and celebrated. All the more, in the eyes of Peronism, the prestige of the US athletes gave such victories an even more prestigious aura. These as much as all international sport victories "were presented as a collective victory for all of Argentine society, transcending the divisions of social class, origin, place of residence and political affiliation."[96]

While Peronist authorities and sport administrators from the Americas, including Brundage, emphasized the friendly ties and the spirit of inter-American cooperation forged on the sport fields of the 1951 Pan-American Games, reporters from the United States criticized the regime. Milton Bracker, writing for the *New York Times,* agreed that Perón conceived the event as an opportunity for cultural diplomacy but criticized him for doing so. In an article subtitled "Pan-American Games Serving as Platform to Extol New Argentina and Regime," Bracker wrote that "the Argentine regime is making hay out of the" occasion.[97] *Newsweek* also censured the regime along the same lines and diminished the event to a "neighborhood affair."[98] The *New York Times*'s Arthur Daley went even further, drawing an unwanted if not exaggerated comparison. Daley compared Perón's political use of the Pan-American Games to Adolf Hitler's misappropriation of the 1936 Berlin Olympics: "It is unfortunate . . . that the first Pan-American Games had to encounter the same political hobgoblins that haunted the 1936 Olympic Games at Berlin. Today we have Perón. A decade and a half ago it was Hitler."[99] Even more, Daley contended that the Argentine president was worse: "Hitler was much more circumspect."[100] In the weeks following the closing ceremony of the event, *Time* published several articles criticizing the ways of the Peronist regime and portraying its leaders unfavorably.[101]

The negative image of Perón projected by these mainstream media outlets in the United States echoed the prevailing attitude within the US government. Edward G. Miller Jr., assistant secretary of state for inter-American affairs, attended the 1951 Pan-American Games as a guest of the organizing committee. During his visit, Miller met with Perón, his wife, and other Argentine dignitaries. None of this helped change the mind of Miller, for whom the regime "has been creating its own bad public opinion not only in Washington but in the United States as a whole."[102] According to a journalistic story, when Miller boarded the plane back to the United States, "he looked 'grim, discouraged, and not a little disgusted'" because of the status of the relationship between his country and Argentina.[103]

If Perón's cultural policy through sport did not enjoy much acceptance, if any, in the United States, it fared better in other parts of the world. *El Mundo Deportivo,* a Spanish sport magazine, presented quite a different image of the New Argentina than the one advanced by the mainstream U.S. media. Diego Alcazar wrote numerous articles from Buenos Aires for the magazine. Not only did he not find any troubling political use of the 1951 Pan-American Games, but he thought that those sporting days were "memorable."[104] Indeed, Alcazar commented that he could not have dreamt those days.[105] He also stressed the quality of the organization as well as the public fervor at the competitions. In addition, Alcazar approvingly informed his readers that it was thanks to Perón that "the difficult mission to organize what we could call the Olympic Games of the Americas" was possible.[106] Another instance of a positive image of the New Argentina prompted by the Games was provided by Carlos H. Malespin, an aide of the president of Nicaragua who traveled to Buenos Aires with his country's delegation. Malespin declared that the Nicaraguan delegation was treated with cordiality and highlighted the work done by the Peróns and CADCOA, "which does so much for bringing together the countries of the Americas."[107]

Brazilian newspapers from São Paulo appeared to have preferred a strict informative narrative regarding the 1951 Pan-American Games. The commentaries and opinions rarely delved into the political, social, or economic aspects of, and evoked by, the event. For instance, *A Folha da Manhã* reported that the Argentine public attended the Games' competitions in great numbers and demonstrated both emotion and enthusiasm.[108] However, despite the fact that the newspaper informed its readers daily of the results of the competitions, it did not give much attention to Perón or any other dimension of the games than what transpired on the playing fields.[109] The exception was an occurrence after the boxing match between Argentine Francisco Núñez and Brazilian Pedro Galasso. Apparently Galasso was the clear winner, but the judges favored the local boxer. According to *A Folha da Manhã,* once the match was over, Perón left his seat of honor in the stands to congratulate Galasso for his courage, which portrayed the Argentine president as fair minded.[110] Similar to the overall tone of *A Folha da Manhã,* when reporting about the Games' opening ceremony *O Estado de São Paulo* was neither favorable nor unfavorable to the Peronist regime.[111] Much like the previous two newspapers, *A Folha da Noite* kept a similar tone. It regularly published news of the games, but the focus was exclusively on the contests and their results.[112]

The 1951 Pan-American Games did not encourage the projection of the positive image of the New Argentina desired by the Peronist regime in Brazilian newspapers from São Paulo, but in other countries the event did not attract any attention at all. For example, the *Times* of London did not publish any news related to the event even though the newspaper had a correspondent in Buenos Aires. Likewise the event was not covered by the French newspaper *Le Monde.* The absence of any coverage of the event, though, did not mean that Argentina was absent from the pages of these European newspapers during the duration of the competitions. One issue that was not lost in both the *Times* and *Le Monde* was the ongoing feud between the Buenos Aires daily *La Prensa* and the Peronist regime.[113] Other matters were covered as well, but the deeds of the Pan-American athletes did not merit any reference.[114]

Admittedly, these are a few examples of the manner in which Perón's efforts to use sport as a tool of diplomacy were received in some countries. However, if they are indicative of the foreign response to Perón's cultural diplomacy through sport, these examples speak to the efficacy of such efforts. They suggest that the foreign response was complex, far from linear, and that the Peronist state's goals in this regard enjoyed, to put it mildly, varying degrees of success. That is to say, the images of the New Argentina projected through the hosting of international sporting events and through the country's athletes competing in those events were in many cases not the desired ones and appealed to different foreign governments and publics to varying extents in media outlets.

## Conclusion

Félix D. Frascara, a critic of Perón's sport policies, wrote a few years after the coup d'état that ousted the president from power that from 1946 to 1955 a deal was struck in Argentine sport: "Perón gave everything to sport and sport gave everything to Perón."[115] Even if an exaggeration, Frascara's attempt at summarizing the sport policies of the Peronist state reveals their importance. Perón amply provided for mass and elite sport, expecting that such ample provision would result in political dividends. Critics objected to the Peronist state's systematic and generous intervention in sport. For them it simply amounted to political propaganda and demagoguery. By contrast, defenders pointed out that it was one of the regime's innovations and that it democratized access to the practice of sport. Obviously, as seen throughout this chapter, there was a political message in the official largesse bestowed to sport, from political symbolism and socialization to the transmission of desired moral values to the advertisement of the New Argentina. Whether Perón's sport policies are seen as political indoctrination or as efforts to democratize the practice of sport for the masses, it is uncontroversial that Perón recognized and used sport as a powerful social technology to shape and reshape his political project. Sport was a significant component of the larger Peronist cultural policy, which was related to the regime's symbolic production, and intersected with other components of this policy in complex ways. Frascara's attempted summary demonstrates Perón's vision of sport, both at the mass and elite levels.

In addition to "giving everything to sport" for what is known today as "nation building" (that is, the domestic use of sport to develop a sense of national identity and belonging as well as a source of symbolic unity to coalesce a polity), Perón "gave everything to sport" also to project on the global stage a positive image of his New Argentina—what is known today as a form of cultural diplomacy. Paraphrasing liberally from Richard Mandell's writing on the Soviet perception of participation in international sport, Perón learned that his compatriots cannot cheer industrial growth or the amelioration of workers' living standards in stadiums and that there are no international festivals to showcase these or other national accomplishments.[116] In other words, the Peronist state comprehended the powerful symbolism and high visibility of international sport, especially in light of its competitive character, and invested profusely in it. In doing so, it fully included sponsoring, bidding, participating, and hosting large international sporting events to the repertoire of available diplomatic instruments. Thus the athletes of the New Argentina were conceived as effective ambassadors, capable of multiplying, or even surpassing, the efforts of traditional diplomacy. Similarly, hosting large international sporting events was conceived as a platform to welcome the world to the New Argentina and to showcase it to the world.

In light of the manifold, and uneven, foreign response to the regime's efforts in international sport, it could be maintained—paraphrasing Frascara (even agreeing that his saying is revelatory but had a tint of exaggeration)—that although "Perón gave everything to cultural diplomacy through sport," it is doubtful whether "cultural diplomacy through sport gave everything to Perón." Assessing the success of cultural diplomacy is always a difficult task, and more research would hopefully complement the understanding of the manner in which the message that the Peronist state tried to convey through international sport was received and construed on the global stage. Regardless of the success of his policies, though, it is clear that while approaching sport as a social technology, Perón used it as an instrument of diplomacy and believed that athletes could play ambassadorial roles, as much as that he conceived the hosting of international sporting events as exceptional platforms to plant his New Argentina in the world and advertise globally its achievements.

## Notes

1. There is a massive body of literature on Perón and his decade in power. Mariano Ben Plotkin has included an introductory and useful selected bibliography at the end of his book *Mañana es San Perón: A Cultural History of Perón's Argentina,* trans. Keith Zahniser (Wilmington, DE: SR Books, 2003). Comprehensive surveys of the body of literature on Perón and his regime include Emilio de Ípola, "Ruptura y continuidad: Claves parciales para un balance de las interpretaciones del peronismo," *Desarrollo Económico* 29, no. 115 (1989): 331–59, as well as Cristián Buchrucker, "Interpretations of Peronism: Old Frameworks and New Perspectives," and Mariano

Ben Plotkin, "The Changing Perception of Peronism: A Review Essay," both in *Peronism and Argentina,* ed. James Brennan (Wilmington, DE: Scholarly Resources, 1998). Unless otherwise noted, this chapter's basic narrative of the Peronist decade is based on the following sources: Plotkin, *Mañana es San Perón,* 214–319, and Luis Alberto Romero, *A History of Argentina in the Twentieth Century,* trans. James P. Brennan (University Park: Pennsylvania State University Press, 2002), 91–130. For the results of the elections, see Ministerio del Interior, *Historia Electoral Argentina (1912–2007)* (Buenos Aires: n.p., 2008), 91–104, http://www.mininterior.gov.ar/asuntos_politicos_y_alectorales/dinap/publicaciones/HistoriaElectoralArgentina .pdf (accessed March 1, 2012).

2. Matthew B. Karush and Oscar Chamosa, "Introduction," in *The New Cultural History of Peronism: Power and Identity in Mid-Twentieth-Century Argentina,* ed. Matthew B. Karush and Oscar Chamosa (Durham, NC, and London: Duke University Press, 2011), 2.

3. David Rock, *Argentina, 1516–1987: From Spanish Colonization to Alfonsín* (Berkeley: University of California Press, 1987), 262.

4. Mariano Ben Plotkin, "Final Reflections," in *The New Cultural History of Peronism,* ed. Karush and Chamosa, 274.

5. In this chapter, elite sport is contrasted to mass sport and refers to those practices and policies focusing on high-level athletic performance. It does not refer to upper-class sport.

6. Raanan Rein, "'*El Primer Deportista*': The Political Use and Abuse of Sport in Peronist Argentina," *International Journal of the History of Sport* 15, no. 2 (1998): 55.

7. Mark Dyreson, *Making the American Team: Sport, Culture, and the Olympic Experience* (Urbana and Chicago: University of Illinois Press, 1998), 3.

8. Ibid.

9. "Celebróse el éxito de nuestro país en los Juegos Deportivos," *La Nación* (Buenos Aires) (hereafter *La Nación*), March 11, 1951, 7.

10. Quoted in Rein, "'*El Primer Deportista,*'" 55.

11. Juan D. Perón, "Hacia la formación de un pueblo espiritual y físicamente sano," *Perón vence al tiempo,* circa 1955, http://www.peronvencealtiempo.com.ar/textos-de-peron/hacia-la-formacion-de-un-pueblo-espiritual-y-fisicamente-sano (accessed March 1, 2012). Since according to the 1947 national census Argentina's population was almost sixteen million, Perón was probably projecting that in 1955 there would be four million more Argentines. Argentina reached twenty million inhabitants in 1960. See Sebastián Galiani and Pablo Gerchunoff, "The Labor Market," in *A New Economic History of Argentina,* ed. Gerardo della Paolera and Alan M. Taylor (Cambridge: Cambridge University Press, 2003), 143.

12. See Plotkin, *Mañana es San Perón,* 181–86, for a detailed account of the sport championships organized by the Fundación Eva Perón. Descriptions of Perón's sport policies are found in Pablo Alabarces, *Fútbol y patria: El fútbol y las narrativas de la nación en Argentina* (Buenos Aires: Prometeo, 2002), 65–82; Santiago Senén González, "Perón y el deporte," *Todo es Historia* 345 (1996): 8–20; Ezequiel Fernán-

dez Moores, *Breve historia del deporte argentino* (Buenos Aires: Editorial El Ateneo, 2010), 137–61; Rein, *"El Primer Deportista'"*; and Ariel Scher, Guillermo Blanco, and Jorge Búsico, *Deporte nacional: Dos siglos de historia* (Buenos Aires: Emecé, 2010), 281–336. Unless otherwise noted, this chapter's basic narrative of Peronist sport is based on these sources. Joaquín Lupiano Cano, "Las políticas deportivas durante la primera presidencia de Juan Domingo Perón (1946–1952)" (bachelor's thesis, Universidad Nacional de Luján, 2003), has useful information regarding the sport policies of Perón's first term in office.

13. The Confederación Argentina de Deportes and the Comité Olímpico Argentino were unified in 1927. For details about the historical development of Olympism in Argentina, see Cesar R. Torres, "Tribulations and Achievements: The Early History of Olympism in Argentina," *International Journal of the History of Sport* 18, no. 3 (2001): 59–92, and Cesar R. Torres, "The Latin American 'Olympic Explosion' of the 1920s: Causes and Consequences," *International Journal of the History of Sport* 23, no. 7 (2006): 1088–111.

14. Confederación Argentina de Deportes-Comité Olímpico Argentino, September 3, 1956, Argentine, Correspondance, 1907–1965, International Olympic Committee Archives, Lausanne, Switzerland (hereafter IOCA).

15. Quoted in Scher, Blanco, and Búsico, *Deporte nacional,* 282.

16. Plotkin, "Final Reflections," 278.

17. Rein, *"El Primer Deportista,'"* 57. On the cultural policies implemented by Peronism to generate support for the regime, see, for example, Marcela Gené, *Un mundo feliz: Imágenes de los trabajadores en el primer peronismo, 1946–1955* (Buenos Aires: Fondo de Cultura Economica, 2005), and Plotkin, *Mañana es San Perón.*

18. Plotkin, *Mañana es San Perón,* 184.

19. Juan D. Perón, *Obras completas,* 24 vols. (Buenos Aires: Proyecto Hernandarias, 1984), 14, 495.

20. Quoted in Rein, *"El Primer Deportista,'"* 69.

21. Ibid., 58.

22. "Clausuráronse ayer los Juegos Panamericanos," *La Nación,* March 10, 1951, 1.

23. Deborah L. Norden and Roberto Russell, *The United States and Argentina: Changing Relations in a Changing World* (New York and London: Routledge, 2002), 20.

24. The following are among the most important studies of the relations between Argentina and the United States and the main sources on this subject of this chapter. Carlos Escudé, *Gran Bretaña, Estados Unidos y la declinación argentina, 1942–1949* (Buenos Aires: Editorial de Belgrano, 1983); Ronald C. Newton, *The "Nazi Menace" in Argentina, 1931–1947* (Stanford, CA: Stanford University Press, 1992); Harold F. Peterson, *Argentina and the United States, 1810–1960* (Albany: State University of New York, 1964); Mario Rapoport, *Gran Bretaña, Estados Unidos y las clases dirigentes argentinas: 1940–1945* (Buenos Aires: Editorial de Belgrano, 1980); Mario Rapoport and Claudio Spiguel, *Estados Unidos y el Peronismo: La política norteamericana en la Argentina: 1949–1955* (Buenos Aires: Grupo Editor Latinoamericano,

1994); and Joseph Tulchin, *Argentina and the United States: A Conflicted Relationship* (Boston: Twayne, 1990). In their *Historia general de las relaciones exteriores de la República Argentina,* 16 vols. (Buenos Aires: Grupo Editor Latinoamericano, 1999), Andrés Cisneros and Carlos Escudé provide a comprehensive overview of Argentina's foreign policy history.

25. The third position is discussed in most of the sources listed in the previous endnote.

26. Glenn J. Dorn, "'Bradenism' and Beyond: Argentine Anti-Americanism, 1945–1953," in *Anti-Americanism in Latin America and the Caribbean,* ed. Alan McPherson (New York: Berghahn Books, 2006), 67.

27. Juan D. Perón, *The Argentine International Policy* (Buenos Aires: n.p., 1948), 4.

28. Alberto Conil Paz and Gustavo Ferrari, *Argentina's Foreign Policy, 1930–1962,* trans. John J. Kennedy (Notre Dame, IN, and London: University of Notre Dame Press, 1966), 137.

29. Cisneros and Escudé, *Historia general,* 11, 16.

30. Romero, *A History of Argentina,* 99.

31. Quoted in Conil Paz and Ferrari, *Argentina's Foreign Policy,* 141.

32. Perón, *Argentine International Policy,* 3.

33. Ibid., 13.

34. See Josef L. Kunz, "The Inter-American Treaty of Reciprocal Assistance," *American Journal of International Law* 42, no. 1 (1948): 111–20.

35. Peterson, *Argentina and the United States, 1810–1960,* 471.

36. Quoted in Scher, Blanco, and Búsico, *Deporte nacional,* 284. See also "Adiós a un símbolo del billar genial: Enrique Navarra," *Clarín* (Buenos Aires), June 10, 2009, http://edant.clarin.com/diario/2009/06/10/deportes/d-01936295.htm (accessed March 1, 2012), and Juan Rodolfo Rosemberg, "Navarra: Un apellido famoso en el mundo del billar," *El Mundo Deportivo* (Barcelona) (hereafter *El Mundo Deportivo*), June 6, 1968, 16.

37. Nicholas J. Cull, "Public Diplomacy: Taxonomies and Histories," *Annals of the American Academy of Political and Social Science* 616 (2008): 33. See the papers in this issue of the *Annals* for theoretical analyses and case studies of public diplomacy. *Inventing Public Diplomacy: The Story of the U.S. Information Agency* (Boulder, CO, and London: Lynne Rienner, 2004), by Wilson P. Dizard Jr., and *Searching for a Cultural Diplomacy* (New York: Berghahn Books, 2010), edited by Jessica C. E. Gienow-Hecht and Mark C. Donfried, are fine accounts of efforts at public diplomacy by different countries.

38. Geoffrey A. Pigman, *Contemporary Diplomacy: Representation and Communication in a Globalized World* (Cambridge and Malden, MA: Polity, 2010), 180.

39. Victor D. Cha, *Beyond the Final Score: The Politics of Sport in Asia* (New York: Columbia University Press, 2009), 2.

40. Confederación Argentina de Deportes-Comité Olímpico Argentino, *Memoria y balance general-inventario: Periodo: 1 de octubre de 1944 al 30 de septiembre de 1945* (Buenos Aires: n.p., 1945), 21–22.

41. Wolf Lyberg, *Fabulous 100 Years of the IOC: Facts, Figures—and Much, Much More* (Lausanne: International Olympic Committee, 1996), 256.

42. Palacios had also served as president of the CADCOA in 1927–1928 and 1932–1933.

43. Aloé would later serve the Peronist regime as administrative subsecretary to the president's office (1948–1952) and as governor of the Province of Buenos Aires (1952–1955). See Rein, "*El Primer Deportista*,'" 60, and Rodolfo Rodríguez, *Carlos Vicente Aloé: Subordinacíon y valor* (La Plata: Asociación Amigos del Archivo Histórico, 2007).

44. Confederación Argentina de Deportes-Comité Olímpico Argentino, *Memoria y balance general-inventario: XXVI aniversario; Ejercicio, 1 de octubre de 1946 al 30 de septiembre de 1947* (Buenos Aires: n.p., 1947), 8–9.

45. Quoted in Roberto Di Giano and Marcelo Massarino, "El peronismo y los deportes profesionales" in *El pensamiento alternativo en la Argentina del siglo XX,* 2 vols., ed. Hugo E. Biagini and Arturo A. Roig (Buenos Aires: Biblos, 2006), 2, 458.

46. "¡Ar-gen-tin-a!," *El Gráfico* (Buenos Aires) (hereafter *El Gráfico*), June 25, 1948, 28.

47. For details of the Argentine delegation and its performance, see *The Official Report of the Organising Committee for the XIV Olympiad* (London: Organising Committee for the XIV Olympiad, 1948). See also Comité Olímpico Argentino, *Olimpismo: Historia y Proyección* (Buenos Aires: Servicios Informativos Parlamentarios Argentinos, [1997]). The official report of the Games states that 242 badges were issued to Argentine athletes (p. 542). However, in its "analysis of competitors," it lists 202 Argentine athletes (p. 546). Even if there were only 202 Argentine athletes in London, it still is the largest delegation the country has ever sent to the Olympic Games, and it was the largest Latin American delegation in those Games. The sports for the medals were boxing (two gold and bronze), shooting (silver), track and field (gold and silver), and yachting (silver).

48. Quoted in Rein, "*El Primer Deportista*,'" 69.

49. Félix D. Frascara, "¡Y cantamos el himno!," *El Gráfico,* August 25, 1948, 30.

50. "Nuestra concurrencia a Helsinski," *El Gráfico,* April 24, 1952, 26.

51. Damián Cané, "Viaja el primer contingente de atletas olímpicos," *Mundo Deportivo* (Buenos Aires) (hereafter *Mundo Deportivo*), June 19, 1952, 22.

52. "Presencia de la Nueva Argentina en los XV° Juegos Olímpicos," *Mundo Deportivo,* July 17, 1952, 53.

53. For details of the Argentine delegation and its performance, see *The Official Report of the Organising Committee for the Games of the XV Olympiad. Helsinki 1952* (Porvoo and Helsinki: Organising Committee for the XV Olympiad, Helsinki 1952, 1955). See also Comité Olímpico Argentino, *Olimpismo: Historia y Proyección.* The latter lists 134 Argentine athletes instead of the 126 listed in the former's "analysis of competitors." The sports for the medals were boxing (silver and bronze), rowing (gold), track and field (silver), and weightlifting (bronze).

54. "Están de nuevo en la patria los atletas olímpicos," *Mundo Deportivo,* November 9, 1952, 22.

55. The material on the bid for the 1956 Olympics is, in part, based on Cesar R. Torres, "Stymied Expectations: Buenos Aires' Persistent Efforts to Host Olympic Games," *Olympika: The International Journal of Olympic Studies* 16 (2007): 43–75.

56. Ricardo S. de Bustamante and Emilio S. Delpech to Sigfrid Edstrøm, January 31, 1948, JO Ete 1956, Correspondance Generale, 1947–1949, IOCA.

57. Ibid. See also Confederación Argentina de Deportes-Comité Olímpico Argentino, *Memoria y balance general-inventario: XXVII aniversario; Ejercicio, 1 de octubre de 1947 al 30 de septiembre de 1948* (Buenos Aires: n.p., 1948), 28.

58. Ricardo C. Aldao and Horacio Bustos Morón to Sigfrid Edstrøm, June 28, 1948, JO Ete 1956, Correspondance Generale, 1947–1949, IOCA.

59. *Ciudad de Buenos Aires: República Argentina* (Buenos Aires: n.p., 1956), n.p.

60. Rodolfo G. Valenzuela and Santos Vicente Rossi to International Olympic Committee, March 5, 1949, JO Ete 1956, Correspondance Generale, 1947–1949, IOCA.

61. Confederación Argentina de Deportes-Comité Olímpico Argentino, *Memoria: Balance general y cuenta de gastos y recursos; XXVIII ejercicio, 1 de octubre de 1948 al 30 de septiembre de 1949* (Buenos Aires: n.p., 1949), 24.

62. Damián Cané, "¿Y si Finlandia no organiza las olimpíadas?," *Mundo Deportivo,* January 19, 1950, 26.

63. Ricardo S. de Bustamante and Emilio S. Delpech to Sigfrid Edstrøm, January 31, 1948, JO Ete 1956, Correspondance Generale, 1947–1949, IOCA.

64. See Scher, Blanco, and Búsico, *Deporte nacional,* 292–93.

65. Héctor Villita, "Un gran estadio para el básquet," *Mundo Deportivo,* May 18, 1950, 38–39.

66. "Viejo amigo del básquet, Perón alentó la hazaña," *Mundo Deportivo,* November 9, 1950, 76.

67. See Scher, Blanco, and Búsico, *Deporte nacional,* 292–96, and Fernández Moores, *Breve historia del deporte argentino,* 140–43.

68. Carlos Aloé, "Campeones Mundiales de Básquetbol," *Mundo Deportivo,* November 9, 1950, 26.

69. Ibid.

70. Quoted in Fernández Moores, *Breve historia del deporte argentino,* 145.

71. This material on the 1951 Pan-American Games is, in part, based on Cesar R. Torres, "The Limits of Pan-Americanism: The Case of the Failed 1942 Pan-American Games," *International Journal of the History of Sport* 28, no. 17 (2011): 2547–74.

72. Quoted in Rein, "'*El Primer Deportista,*'" 69.

73. Carlos Aloé, "Perspectivas para el Panamericano," *Mundo Deportivo,* October 12, 1950, 26.

74. "Se inauguraron anoche los Juegos Panamericanos," *La Nación,* February 26, 1951, 7.

75. "Efectuó una visita a la Villa Panamericana el primer magistrado," *La Nación,* February 24, 1951, 3.

76. Carlos Aloé, "El deporte como vínculo internacional," *Mundo Deportivo,* November 23, 1950, 26.

77. See, for example, "Homenaje del Congreso Panamericano al general Perón y su esposa," *La Nación,* February 26, 1951, 7; "Agradecimiento al jefe del Estado y a su esposa," *La Nación,* February 27, 1951, 3; and "Regresó la delegación de Nicaragua," *La Nación,* March 7, 1951, 3.

78. "Clausuráronse ayer los Juegos Panamericanos," *La Nación,* March 10, 1951, 1. This Pan-American Sport Committee would later become the Pan-American Sport Organization.

79. Ibid.

80. Rein, "'*El Primer Deportista,*'" 70.

81. Ernesto Rodríguez, *Libro I de los juegos panamericanos, 1951 a 2011* (Buenos Aires: Alarco Ediciones, 2011), 17. See also Steven Olderr, *The Pan American Games: A Statistical History, 1951–1999* (Jefferson, NC: McFarland, 2003), 335. These sources slightly differ with regard to the numbers of medals garnered by these countries. The difference is that for Olderr, Argentina garnered 37 bronze medals, and the United States garnered 47 gold medals, which bring their totals to 152 and 99 medals, respectively. Whatever the precise number, it is clear that Argentina dominated the medal count.

82. See, for example, "El general Perón y su esposa felicitaron a campeones," *La Nación,* March 8, 1951, 3.

83. "Celebróse el éxito de nuestro país en los Juegos Deportivos," *La Nación,* March 11, 1951, 7.

84. "Los juegos dejaron un saldo favorable," *La Nación,* March 10, 1951, 3.

85. See *El Gráfico,* March 2, 1951, 1, 4–7, and 34–35, and March 16, 1951, 4–5.

86. Carlos Aloé, "Juventud de América," *Mundo Deportivo,* March 8, 1951, 26.

87. Carlos Aloé, "La defensa del título," *Mundo Deportivo,* March 29, 1951, 26.

88. Quoted in Fernández Moores, *Breve historia del deporte argentino,* 159.

89. "Argentina deportiva ante el mundo," *Mundo Deportivo,* December 27, 1951, 10.

90. Ibid.

91. The letter was published in *Mundo Deportivo,* February 15, 1951, 65.

92. "María Eva Duarte de Perón," *Mundo Deportivo,* March 15, 1951, 6.

93. Perón, *The Argentine International Policy,* 4.

94. "Estados Unidos," *Mundo Deportivo,* March 15, 1951, 62.

95. Ibid.

96. Rein, "'*El Primer Deportista,*'" 68.

97. Milton Bracker "Peróns Make Hay on Olympic Meet," *New York Times,* February 24, 1951, 6.

98. "Neighbors at Play," *Newsweek,* March 19, 1951, 88.

99. Arthur Daley, "At Home and Abroad," *New York Times,* February 27, 1951, 44.

100. Ibid.

101. See, for example, "Argentina: Murder at La Prensa," *Time,* March 12, 1951, 40–41, and "Argentina: Capitalism Is Unconstitutional," *Time,* March 26, 1951, 40.

102. Virginia Lee Warren, "U.S. Aide at Games Chides Argentines," *New York Times,* March 5, 1951, 14.

103. "Argentina: La Prensa Muddle," *Newsweek,* March 19, 1951, 48.

104. Diego Alcazar, "Se clausuraron solemnemente los I Juegos Panamericanos," *El Mundo Deportivo,* March 21, 1951, 4. See also, for example, his articles "Vispera de inauguración de los Juegos Panamericanos" and "Los Juegos Panamericanos" published on February 28, 1951, 1, and March 14, 1951, 2, respectively.

105. Diego Alcazar, "Se clausuraron solemnemente los I Juegos Panamericanos," 4.

106. Diego Alcazar, "Alas a Buenos Aires," February 21, 1951, 1.

107. "Regresó la delegación de Nicaragua," *La Nación,* March 7, 1951, 3.

108. "Estreou vencendo em Buenos Aires o conjunto cestobolistico brasileiro," *A Folha da Manhã* (São Paulo) (hereafter *A Folha da Manhã*), March 1, 1951, second section, 5.

109. See *A Folha da Manhã* during the period of the Games.

110. "Outro titulo de campeão conquistou Okamato nos Jogos Pan-Americanos," *A Folha da Manhã,* March 6, 1951, second section, 8.

111. "Os primeiros jogos esportivos pan-americanos de Buenos Aires," *O Estado de São Paulo* (São Paulo), February 25, 1951, 8.

112. See *A Folha da Noite* during the period of the Games.

113. On the feud between *La Prensa* and the Peronist regime, and more generally its mass media policies, see James Cane, *The Fourth Enemy: Journalism and Power in the Making of Peronist Argentina, 1930–1955* (University Park: Pennsylvania State University Press, 2011), and Pablo Sirven, *Perón y los medios de comunicación (1943–1955)* (Buenos Aires: Centro Editor de América Latina, 1984).

114. See the *Times* (London) and *Le Monde* (Paris) during the period of the Games. As indicated by one reviewer, the lack of media coverage in Great Britain might have reflected the isolationism of its sport at the time.

115. Félix D. Frascara, "Deportes" in *Argentina, 1930–1960,* ed. Jorge A. Paita (Buenos Aires: Sur, 1961), 380.

116. Richard Mandell, "The Invention of the Sports Record," *Stadion* 2, no. 2 (1976): 262.

# 6

# A More Flexible Domination

## Franco-African Sport Diplomacy during Decolonization, 1945–1966

### *Pascal Charitas*

> Modern sport is connected to a world network of interdependencies
> which is characterized by an imbalance of the relations of power.
> —Joseph Maguire, quoted by Fabien Ohl in *Sociologie du sport*

The global upheaval caused by World War II called into question the continuation of colonial domination. Indeed, the progressive liberation of populations oppressed by colonialism and the resulting advent of the Third World were supported by the two superpowers of the Cold War, the United States and the Soviet Union. At both the Yalta Conference in February 1945 and the Potsdam Conference in July 1945, the victorious powers reorganized the frontiers of Europe and provided for democratic elections in the liberated countries. The creation of the United Nations (UN) in June 1945 in San Francisco—which represented the realization of the Allies' vision for the postwar world as originally announced in the Atlantic Charter on January 1, 1942—continued this trend and challenged the geographic and political boundaries of the colonial empires, specifically by calling for the liberation of their colonized lands. The seismic geopolitical changes brought on by the forces of decolonization would not only transform global relationships but would also fundamentally affect international sport. As newly independent African states joined the Olympic movement as full members, the need to reconcile the Olympic values of humanism and universalism with the conservative positions of its Western members, themselves influenced by the two Cold War blocs, became a significant diplomatic issue between these states and their former colonial masters.

Pierre Milza writes that although the colonial powers endeavored to limit the scope of the Atlantic Charter, it soon became a universal cause and fed the calls for internationalization of the colonial territories under the UN's control.[1] At the same time, according to John Darwin, the two biggest colonial empires, the French and the British, were entering their respective "second colonial occupation" and "fourth colonial occupation" phases.[2] In the French empire, the Brazzaville Conference (1944), followed by the États Généraux de la Colonisation (1945), rejected any idea of independence for France's colonies. Yet the internationalization of the colonial problem forced the empires to implement practical measures to develop their colonies through economic and social-assistance programs based on the capitalist model and UN principles. This path may in fact have represented a strategic response by the empires, as Marc Michel argues, because a geopolitical positioning of black Africa between the communist and Western blocs began to take shape at the Manchester Pan-African Congress in October 1945.[3]

The hardening of the Cold War after 1947 amounted to a bipolar world in which the belligerent parties avoided direct confrontation through the escalating arms race and nuclear threats, competing economic and social-development programs, and technological competition such as with the conquest of space. In this context, the occupation of Germany by the four powers ended in the creation of spheres of influence that were supported economically and ideologically by the two biggest powers—under the Marshall Plan by the United States and under the Cominform and the Zhdanov Doctrine by the USSR.[4] It was in this broader perspective that President Harry S. Truman announced in March 1947 that his country would provide aid to all countries where liberty was encouraged, while the Soviet Union affirmed its anti-imperialist position and support for colonized peoples. Ultimately the UN contributed to the expansion of the two US and Soviet areas of influence, both of which gradually took over the European colonial empires and promoted awareness of an "African issue" during the Cold War.

During this first phase of the new international order, according to the British scholar David Spurr, colonial empires were forced to respond to the growing US and Soviet influence among the local elites in their African—and also their Asian and Pacific—possessions. Beginning in 1947 the internationalization of the colonial problem became a strategic issue in foreign policy as a way of imposing a model of political, economic, or social development.[5] According to John Bale and Mike Cronin, sport should be considered an integral part of this new paradigm, both to understand the decolonization process and the diplomacy that followed: "Sports were a part of the colonizing process, and have remained in most colonized countries following independence. Given the presence of neocolonial relationships, however, there is clearly no unambiguous division between colonialism and postcolonialism, and it can be argued that postcolonialism is something that has yet to be achieved, that is, indeed, a scenario for the future. Indeed, the international governing bodies of sports are often still intent on a colonizing mission."[6]

The new international order thus incorporated the ongoing decolonization of both the British and the French colonies, especially following the Bandung Conference of nonaligned nations in April 1955. The United States and the Soviet Union supported anticolonial movements in Africa, which not only thwarted the plans of France and Great Britain to maintain their control over their colonies but also energized nationalist demands that the process move more rapidly and completely. Given these mutually reinforcing trends, how was France to maintain its grip on colonies that were increasingly being seduced by progressive movements, in spite of the presumed nonalignment of these territories, which were still under its domination?

Confronted with this unprecedented situation, France and other colonial powers sought to identify alternative forms of power: a more "flexible" domination based on strategies of influence, development assistance, humanitarian actions, and commercial agreements. Joseph S. Nye Jr. conceptualized these ideas in the notion of "soft power": influences and sponsorships, not orders and constraints, would henceforth define the new configurations of relationships between the powers and their colonies at the dawn of the decolonization period.[7] The waning influence of the colonial powers, especially the French, thus negatively impacted their ability to guide the behavior of their "partner" nations or at least to ensure their preponderance in the joint decision-making process. One way that the French were able to retain a semblance of influence with their former colonies was through sport, particularly allied with, as Pierre Milza, Philippe Tétart, and François Jéquier have described, the "power of the Olympic rings."[8] Sport, particularly in the African context, provides what Pierre Renouvin and Jean-Baptiste Duroselle term the "cultural action" of states' cultural diplomacy and the "cultural transfers" that Michel Espagne and Michael Werner advocate as an important area of study.[9]

As a result, during this period of decolonization both French and African sport leaders, in cooperation with politicians and diplomats on both sides, developed large international sporting events modeled on the Olympic Games. The various iterations of the games (such as the Community Games [Jeux de la Communauté] and the Friendship Games [Jeux de l'Amitié]) that developed in francophone Africa ultimately led to the present-day All-Africa Games. Yet, unlike other continental games within the Olympic movement, the origins of the All-Africa Games are inextricably tied to France's changing domestic and foreign politics in the postwar period as its African territories sought their independence. The sport and Olympic relationships in French Africa after 1945 functioned as part of

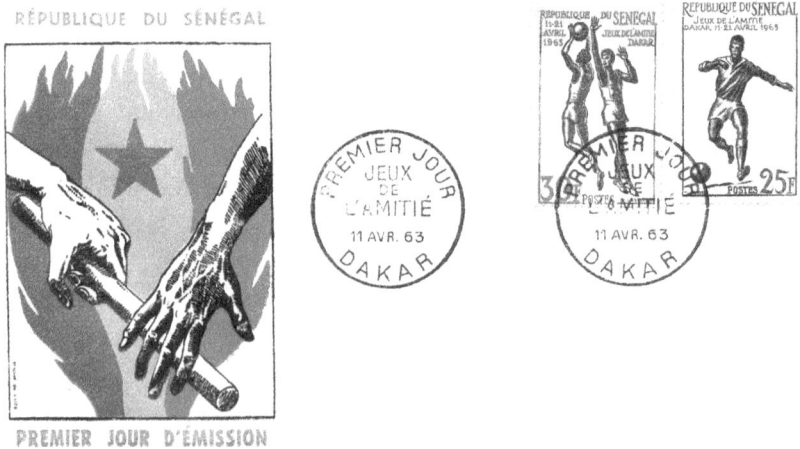

Figure 6.1. First-day issue stamps from Senegal celebrating the 1963 Friendship Games.

the cultural and public diplomacy efforts that sought to preserve strategically the French influence on one hand and, on the other, were used by the new African government and sport leaders to accelerate the visibility of the new African countries within the international community.[10]

## French Colonial Sport Policy in Black Africa

Beginning in 1946 the new French Union (Union Française) formed the cornerstone of French diplomacy. Not wanting to give full power to the colonies, yet recognizing the need to acknowledge the legitimacy of the native-born politicized elites, France introduced a dual electoral system comprising both subjects and citizens of the empire, thereby preserving the authority of metropolitan France. This entity was intended to build Franco-African unity based on recognition of the citizenship of certain subjects of the empire in 1947 in order to form a French-speaking international bloc. For France this change was a matter of strengthening its position within an international system that would now be dominated by Cold War considerations, with the Americans (and British) leading the Western powers that had emerged victorious in World War II.

In this way the associative issues of sport were developed, especially in the French colonies and territories of francophone black Africa (French West Africa and French Equatorial Africa) and became available to the empire's subjects, who were now citizens.[11] In response to the actions undertaken by the British in Africa (autonomy, the Commonwealth, and citizenship), the French territories in Africa also moved toward sporting emancipation beginning in November 1948 and aimed to create an African Olympic Committee (AOC). These actions were orchestrated by Marcel Duresse, a delegate to the National Sports Committee (CNS) and member of the French Olympic Committee (COF), who was nominated to the High Council of French West Africa to contribute to the preparation of African athletes for the upcoming 1952 Olympic Games in Helsinki.[12] Duresse was sent on a mission to Dakar, Senegal, by the CNS and the COF to set up the AOC and to assemble the appropriate material and budgetary conditions for conducting a more rational selection of athletes from francophone Africa. (Duresse had previously, in 1937–1938, taken part in the mission by the French Athletic Association [FFA] and the French sport newspaper *L'Auto* to seek out black athletes in Senegal and the Sudan.)[13] His 1948 report cited a 50 percent participation rate by athletes of color in the contingents from the United States and Great Britain at the London Olympic Games: "Public opinion as well as the sporting and journalistic world etc. have been following the performances recorded by African athletes: Siki, Diouf, and Papa Gallo to name only the best known. Since these athletes have shown themselves to be of international class without receiving special training and encouragement at the outset, it is evident that in certain sports, as has often been demonstrated, Africa is a breeding ground for champions, but they would have to be identified, trained, instilled with our methods, and given optimum opportunities."[14]

However, Duresse's report was critical of the unsatisfactory performance of the Federal Sports Committee (CFS), the structure that managed sport in French West Africa and was based in Dakar. He also emphasized the inadequacy of the financial credits provided, raising questions about the effectiveness of the colonial administration, which had dismissed this project after refusing to recruit an inspector to be responsible for it.[15] Although rule 39 of the Olympic Charter had since 1949 permitted the creation of autonomous Olympic committees overseas and was applied elsewhere around the world, it had not been applied in French territories. Sport in both French West Africa and French Equatorial Africa was copied from the metropolitan French sport system, with a CFS modeled on the CNS.[16] These organizations, controlled by the colonial administration, then received subsidies from the African sport leagues that were affiliated with the metropolitan French sport federations, both via the National Education Ministry (MEN) and the French Overseas Ministry (FOM), either for their regular business operations or by way of exception for sporting events and the establishment of sport infrastructures. In 1951 the CNS envisaged the emancipation of the French Union, but the French diplomatic service wanted to retain the utilitarian concept of the empire. In addition, the French Foreign Ministry agreed with the French members of the International Olympic Committee (IOC) that they should prevent any emancipation of sport in Africa before political independence was granted. Moreover, the pressure exerted by the IOC on the COF to separate itself from the CNS and maintain its political independence further contributed to the political and administrative problems that faced sport in the Fourth Republic.[17]

The African Olympic Committee project was an idea formed from previous experiences that had attempted to garner the greatest outcomes for the French African colonies. In 1937–1938 there was the above-mentioned FFA/*L'Auto* mission. In 1942 the Vichy regime organized the Quinzaine Impériale, a week of sport featuring African athletes. After World War II, the Félix Éboué Committee was created to honor the first black African to answer Gen. Charles de Gaulle's call for resistance against Nazism. To celebrate Éboué's role in the liberation of France, the African political elites comprised by the committee sought to use sport and to create African Games as instruments of African emancipation. These early efforts did not yield much success, but these ideas were slowly integrated into the colonial metropolitan state, which seized on the question at hand by selecting and integrating the elite African athletes into the metropole's sports through a pre-Olympic Games of the French Union. Several times between 1948 and 1957, the African deputies and French seated in the same political arenas of the French National Assembly and the French Union proposed and discussed this idea of a pre-Olympics to select the best African athletes to benefit the metropole's sport. This last project finally gave birth to the Community Games, and once the francophone colonies gained independence, it was renamed the Friendship Games.

As a result, the national political context regarding colonial matters and the international situation account for the impossibility of this project being recognized by the Olympic family, which feared a recrudescence of regional games established by Third World countries and competing with the Olympic Games. In the francophone colonial space, regional events such as the Mediterranean Games—vestiges of the IOC's African Games of 1929—enabled the native populations to express themselves in sport under the control of the home countries and to develop modern sport in Africa.[18] The same idea of an African Games was discussed in France between 1947 and 1957 by both the *élites évoluées*—the educated indigenous elites from the colonies who participated in the decolonization struggles and later the new postindependent African governments— and the metropolitan French political parties ensconced in the "colonial lobby" within the FOM and the MEN for Youth and Sports. The colonial lobby did not support the idea of a continental games, believing that if the African territories competed in a continental competition—and particularly against a metropolitan team—it would imply that each territory could have its own flag and anthem, thereby challenging the power of the French metropole.[19]

These French endeavors in Africa to select African athletes were not aimed at an Olympic emancipation of the colonized territories but instead were designed only to include elite-level athletes on a metropolitan French team. Selected players sometimes competed under the French flag between 1952 and 1960 (including Thiam Papa Gallo, Habib Thiam, Ibrahima Sall, Malick M'Baye, Souleymane Diallo, Mahamat Idriss, Marc Rabemila, Lamine Diack, and Abou Seye) and trained at the National Sport Institute (INS) in Vincennes, on the outskirts of Paris.[20] However, neither a colonial team was formed nor were intercolonial matches organized as a championship before the African independence movement. To the French sport leaders and politicians, the only goal of a diverse French team was to demonstrate on the international sporting stage that it was taking its many indigenous peoples into consideration, just as Great Britain and the United States did with their racial minorities. In this context, the incorporation of former British colonies into the Olympic movement became an area of competition and control within the IOC, with an active role played by the British Foreign Office.

Owing to the international context and the characteristics of the British colonial and imperial system, the first attempt to integrate African colonies into the IOC occurred in the British Empire. Great Britain gained a head start by hosting the 1948 Olympics in London. The choice of the British capital to host the Games was both a symbol recognizing its long resistance to the Nazi aggressors and a contribution to the ongoing postwar economic renewal, involving the reconstruction of the country and of Europe. In addition, holding the Olympics in a Western country historically linked to the United States reconstituted the Olympic Games in the context of the Cold War and promoted the development of sport according to the capitalist model, in contrast to the Soviet *Spartakiads* and their antibourgeois and anti-Olympic ideology.[21]

The number of African National Olympic Committees (NOCs) recognized by the IOC increased significantly between 1950 and 1962, even though these countries were neither politically independent nor possessed seats in the United Nations.[22] Thus the British and French colonial regimes (as well as Italy except in the case of Ethiopia) tried to act as mediators in the formation of the NOCs instituted under their guardianship.

By 1954, IOC president Avery Brundage expressed a concern with the growing divisions within the organization: "It was only after World War II that, regarding members of the IOC, reference was made to a 'European bloc,' a 'Latin bloc,' a 'Western-Hemisphere bloc,' a 'British Empire bloc' and so on. There can be no doubt that in our time all this has taken on very disturbing proportions, but the mere fact that these blocs were mentioned indicates that something is amiss. There should be no blocs or nationalisms in the International Olympic Committee."[23]

The challenge therefore was to prevent the formation of an anticolonial bloc within the IOC favoring Soviet ideology. Politically the USSR had quickly recognized the new governments in Morocco and Tunisia (1956), supported Ghana as a model for achieving independence (1957), and provided political and economic options for Sékou Touré's Guinea (1958).[24]

In 1951 the French IOC members Armand Massard and François Piétri were forced to take notice of British actions regarding the Olympic recognition issue, when the NOC from the British colony of Nigeria sought recognition in order to participate in the 1952 Summer Olympic Games in Helsinki. The French members saw this action as a dangerous precedent for its francophone black African colonies because France was still wedded to the myth of the French Union and had not initiated any decolonization processes. With this position, Massard and Piétri's attitude reflected France's national and international colonial policy as much as the conservatism of the IOC.[25] Only after 1959, as the francophone black African colonies were granted independence, did these new countries seek to join the Olympic movement and be internationally recognized through participation in the Olympic Games.

## The Friendship Games as Postcolonial French Sport Diplomacy

The decolonization process in francophone Africa began in 1956 with the application of the Loi-Cadre, a reform measure that granted greater autonomy to French possessions and colonies in Africa. This legal and institutional development was then amplified by de Gaulle's accession to power as head of the Fifth Republic in 1958. The new French constitution created the Franco-African Community. This francophone geopolitical space, modeled on the Commonwealth, gave the status of republics to the colonies, which would henceforth be linked to metropolitan France in a partnership structure.[26] French sport overseas was thus a matter of applying the revised French colonial policy in the service of the Olympic emancipation of its colonies on the international sporting scene. France had to respond to the influences of Anglo-American and Soviet imperialisms during the Cold War and also to anticolonial and nationalist movements.

To implement this "sports decolonization," the French government created the High Commission for Youth and Sport (HCJS), with Maurice Herzog—the first man to summit Annapurna—at its head from 1958 to 1966; accelerated the French decolonization process; and promoted the recognition of NOCs in francophone black Africa. France thus instrumentalized sport via the HCJS, which implemented a reform of the metropole's sporting institutions between 1958 and 1960 before undertaking any action on sport in the wider French Africa. As part of this evolution, a pivotal decision was made in 1959 to merge the existing Inter-States Schools Games with the Games of the French Union into the Community Games or Friendship Games (1960–1963), so as to create NOCs in the former French African colonies and thereby enable the emergence of a francophone space within the Olympic movement. In addition, the French political institutions, in connection with the member states of the Franco-African Community, evolved with the replacement of the FOM by the Ministry for Cooperation, a process cemented by agreements of cooperation and French-African partnerships.

Thus the executive board of the Franco-African Community discussed a bill and credits so that the Community Games reflected the support of African sport with respect to its structuring, its autonomy, and its independence, while at the same time the board also pursued French influence through other means. These games brought up a fundamental question. Since 1945 the colonial and French territory sport leagues under French colonial direction had been affiliated with the sport federations of the metropole. This relationship no longer existed once African independence was proclaimed. Yet the creation of African sport federations did not necessarily mean a rejection of the links to French sport federations. In fact, the majority of the newly created African federations remained affiliated with French sport, which allowed them to speed up efforts to reach international sport standards. The affiliation also facilitated the integration with the Olympic movement—which set the qualifying standards for international events—and culminated with participation in the Olympic Games. This patronage created two blocs of member states divided between the support for membership based on freedom and autonomy on the one hand and membership via the continuation of the delegation of power as established in 1945 on the other, reflecting the political positions during the independence process presented by federalists and confederalists. France maintained the link with its former colonies by helping with the process of internationalization of African sport by the membership in the international sport federations to avoid any Cold War influence in the Third World from the East-West ideological opposition.

The creation of the Community Games can therefore be considered as a form of "sport decolonization" because Africans began the process of asserting their leadership in the organization of international sporting events. Three days before the first Community Games in Tananarive, Madagascar (held April 13–19, 1960, at the Stadium of Mahamasina), the country proclaimed its independence through its president Philibert Tsiranana. Madagascar joined fifteen other countries from French-speaking Africa in celebrating 1960 as the year of the "sun of the independences."[27] The French organizers specifically chose Madagascar as the site of these first games because President Tsiranana supported the regime of the Franco-African Community. The Malagasy leader had also welcomed de Gaulle in 1958 at the time of the referendum from which de Gaulle's position of refereeing between the theses federalists and confederalists allowed him to protect the symbol of the French-African friendship.[28]

The games began with a message to the athletes from de Gaulle because France was considered the main organizer. The French state was represented in Tananarive by the high commissioner for youth and sport, Maurice Herzog. Immediately after the Community Games ended, Herzog said:

> One of the main conclusions that we can pull these first Community Games . . . is their importance for the future of sports. Thanks to these Games, we shall have from now on the possibility of canvassing among the youth of the diverse states of the Community. In these athletes of the Community, we can discover during the next years, I am sure, world-class elements. I would like to underline the excellent state of mind which reigned in Tananarive, as

well on the track as in stands. During these Games, I attended real demonstrations of fraternization between black and European.[29]

The games were organized according to international sport standards and modeled on the Olympic Games. At both the opening and closing ceremonies, the flags of the newly independent former colonies were raised for the first time to the sound of their respective national anthems. The athletes' oath was taken by the Malagasy triple-jumper Marc Rabemila, who had been selected to compete for France at the 1960 Olympics in Rome (and competed for Madagascar in 1964) and also studied at the Graduate School of Sports and Physical Education. A strong delegation of French sport federations, diplomats, politicians, and journalists (including seventeen members of the French media) was present along with the African and Malagasy political and sport delegations. However, the French sport delegation that participated in these games was smaller because of the absence of the sportsmen who had been selected for the Olympic Games in Rome. Except for some incidents in boxing where the new feelings of African nationalism reared their head, the games were considered a success. French companies supported construction of the sport infrastructures, and the French government provided both personnel and material support in the form of sending trainers for the African sport federations to prepare for the event and of paying for the African sport delegations' air travel to Madagascar.

Organizing the Community Games was, however, contingent on the financial support from France. The Ministry for Cooperation, led by Jean Foyer, delayed the granting of credits and the provision of some of the technical support to organize the second edition of the games. Even with the political disagreements in France over the funding of sport in Africa, the Community Games nonetheless gained the support of the Ivory Coast president, Félix Houphouët-Boigny. A former supporter of the French Union, Houphouët-Boigny expanded the games in Abidjan, where they were renamed the Friendship Games and were held December 24–31, 1961.[30] The French presence in the organization of the Friendship Games was strengthened by the participation of de Gaulle's "Mister Africa," Jacques Foccart, in the opening ceremony.[31] For the 1961 Games in Abidjan, French delegates of the HCJS and the Ministry for Cooperation continued to hold all of the key positions in the organization of the games, which once again required funding to build the sport infra-structure (swimming pool, stadiums, sports fields, and gymnasiums) that would be used for the games.[32] Furthermore, these organizational efforts accelerated the contact of the French sport federations with the various administrative levels of the African and Malagasy ministries of youth and sport and ministries of education. As during the previous games, only a few disruptive incidents happened, this time in handball (the French box-ing team was not sent).

Events that occurred between 1960 and 1962 in France, Africa, and the IOC were decisive for the continuation of the Friendship Games. The year 1960 was undoubtedly the annus mirabilis of Africa in international sport at the Olympic Games in Rome, with the participation of twelve Af-rican delegations out of eighty-three countries represented, highlighted by memorable performances by African athletes such as the Ethiopian Abebe Bikila in the marathon.[33] Yet in April 1960—before the Rome Games—IOC president Brundage wrote to IOC chancellor Otto Mayer because he was concerned about the impact of colonial independence in Africa on the Olympic movement, particularly when the problem of apartheid in South Africa reached into the sporting world.[34] African sport leaders had used the first Community Games as the opportunity to organize the first Con-ference of Sports Ministers in July 1960 (which was repeated at the 1963 games in Dakar) to discuss the continuation of these games, sport prob-lems, and exchanges between the African, Malagasy and French youths in particular for a coordinated training policy for African sport executives.[35] An African bloc constituted by francophone African groups formed in Brazzaville and then met an anglophone group from Monrovia, Liberia, at the Conference of Non-Aligned States in Belgrade in 1961.[36] Brundage in particular feared that, like the UN, the IOC would be exploited on the issue of racial discrimination.

Also contributing to the evolving situation was the fact that the French-African Community disappeared, leaving African states indepen-dent yet still bound by agreements of cooperation with France. At the same time these countries faced competing Soviet and American influ-ences as well as divisions among the African states. The Pan-African group (supported by the anglophone African countries) wished to break with the intervention of the former colonial guardianships, while those partisans of an inter-African agreement sought to maintain relations of international

cooperation. French power in the pursuit of its interests and the continuation of its civilizing mission—an aspect of which sport and its African
process of internationalization established—appeared endangered.

It was with these efforts to maintain control that the French members
of the IOC and the French HCJS proposed the International Olympic
Aid Commission (IOAC) in 1961 to accelerate the Olympic recognition
of the African states by supporting the creation of National Olympic
Committees. French IOC member Count Jean de Beaumont traveled to
Africa in 1962 to spread the Olympic ideals and promote the constitution
of African NOCs.[37] The IOAC was an instrument of geopolitical strategy
because it was established jointly by the French member Beaumont and
the Soviet members in the IOC, who hoped thereby to exert their progressive influence in Africa. The IOAC also received the support of the United
States Olympic Committee.

The commission allowed France to ensure the "Olympic emancipation" of the francophone former African colonies through the creation of
NOCs, while at the same time preventing the Anglo-American-dominated
IOC from having to see new NOCs linking up with a communist ideology. Favorable conditions were in place to create NOCs in francophone
Africa and to expedite their incorporation into the IOC. Thus, even before
many of France's former African colonies obtained political independence,
they had established their own NOCs; only once autonomy from imperial tutelage was secured were they provisionally recognized by the IOC.
This process was followed by most of France's former African colonies:
Morocco, Senegal, Ivory Coast (Côte d'Ivoire), Mali, Dahomey, the Central African Republic, Madagascar, Chad, Gabon, Guinea-Conakry, the
Democratic Republic of Congo, Congo-Brazzaville, Mauritania, Algeria,
Togo, Cameroon, Niger, and Upper Volta (now Burkina Faso). Nonetheless, all of these steps took place with the support and discreet control
of the French influence, based on partnerships established by a policy of
Franco-African cooperation at the highest level of the French state.[38]

The organization of the Friendship Games in Dakar in 1963 also
helped complete the process of supporting African sport in its integration with the international sport community. Furthermore, the delay of
one year in holding the games was also understandable because Senegal
underwent a political crisis, and the country's president, Léopold Séhar
Senghor, used the opportunity of the third edition of the Friendship

**Table 6.1.** Recognition of the First Nineteen Former French Colonies to Achieve Independence

|  | NOC formation | IOC recognition | State independence | UN recognition |
|---|---|---|---|---|
| Tunisia | 1957 | 1957 | 1957 | 1956 |
| Morocco | 1959 | 1959 | 1956 | 1956 |
| Senegal | 1961 | 1963 | 1960 | 1960 |
| Côte d'Ivoire | 1962 | 1963 | 1960 | 1960 |
| Mali | 1962 | 1963 | 1960 | 1960 |
| Dahomey | 1962 | 1962 | 1960 | 1960 |
| Mauritania | 1962 | 1979 | 1960 | 1960 |
| Algeria | 1963 | 1964 | 1962 | 1962 |
| Madagascar | 1963 | 1964 | 1960 | 1960 |
| Chad | 1963 | 1964 | 1960 | 1960 |
| Togo | 1963 | 1965 | 1960 | 1960 |
| Cameroon | 1963 | 1963 | 1960 | 1960 |
| Congo-Léopoldville | 1963 | 1968 | 1960 | 1960 |
| Niger | 1964 | 1964 | 1960 | 1960 |
| Congo-Brazzaville | 1964 | 1964 | 1960 | 1960 |
| Guinea-Conakry | 1964 | 1965 | 1958 | 1958 |
| Central African Republic | 1964 | 1965 | 1960 | 1960 |
| Upper Volta | 1965 | 1972 | 1960 | 1960 |
| Gabon | 1965 | 1968 | 1960 | 1960 |

Games to strengthen his power within Senegal and his position in the inter-African group with regard to France.[39] Although the games were still organized by French political delegates and technical advisers, they increasingly worked with African political and sporting elites for the organization of the event. The games in Dakar had the largest number of participants because they not only included Arab- and English-speaking African countries but also female athletes were allowed to participate for the first time. These changes increased the continental and international scope of the games tremendously in comparison to the initial Friendship Games and marked their zenith.

**Table 6.2.** The French and African Delegations in the Games of the Community, the Friendship Games, and the African Games (1960–1965)

| Franco-African Sport Games | 1st Community Games (Madagascar) | 2nd Friendship Games (Ivory Coast) | 3rd Friendship Games (Senegal) | First African Games (Congo-Brazzaville) |
|---|---|---|---|---|
| Total of delegations | 19 | 22 | 30 | 29 |
| Total of athletes | 750 | 1,100 | 2,500 | 2,500 |
| Total of French athletes | 90 | 93 | 131 | 0 |
| Total of sports | 8 | 9 | 9 | 10 |
| Events contested | 38 | 39 | 48 | 52 |
| Percentage of victories won by French athletes | 74% | 69% | 50% | 0% (did not participate) |

The third edition in Dakar also marked the end of the Friendship Games. Herzog announced the French withdrawal from involvement in future iterations. He and the French members of the IOC met with IOC president Brundage, who had come to attend the Friendship Games in Dakar in 1963. The politics behind the organization of the Friendship Games ultimately put an end to French participation for several reasons. First, the IOC recognized the francophone African NOCs thanks to the help of France. Second, the French sport and technical support, combined with the bilateral exchanges of cooperation with each African state, gradually enabled African sport and political executives to assume control. The legal and political collapse of the French-African Community—influenced by the international machinations of the Cold War, Third World tendencies, and Pan-Africanism—contributed to the end of the Community Games serving as a catalyst for African brotherhood and French-African friendship.

## The First African Games as Regional Games: The Pursuit of French Influence by Other Means

The decrease of French influence in the Friendship Games (especially in 1963) was noted by Lucien Paye, the French ambassador to Senegal. Paye reported the negative elements of the Friendship Games: lack of organization, xenophobia from the Arabs simultaneously against blacks and the French, coolness of the relations between Tunisians and Egyptians and between Tunisians and Algerians, and the absence of contacts between French-speaking and English-speaking Africans.[40] Paye commented to Maurice Couve de Murville, the French foreign affairs minister: "France will remain involved, it will not hold back its technical or financial efforts, and it will help the young States of Africa to reach the highest international level. It can only wish, indeed, that this role of organizer, and, in reality project manager, which it assumed until now, will transform into a discreet, but effective action, made by advice and emulation."[41] The decision regarding French nonparticipation in the next African Games reflected the new political line within French diplomacy toward Africa: an emphasis on cultural diplomacy in the form of shadows behind the African executives.

Even though Maurice Herzog had proclaimed in Dakar that France would no longer participate in the Friendship Games, the high commissioner revived the idea to organize African Games. The very name of the competition evoked the absence of French sport representation. Nonetheless, for the next African Games, planned for 1965 in Congo-Brazzaville, France maintained a presence through its cooperation and technical support. The organizing committee for the Friendship Games was then transformed into a new organizing committee for the first African Games with the replacement of the French technical executives by African sport leaders. The IOC, with the support of its French members, then recognized the African Games as regional games, similar to the Pan-American Games and the Asian Games.

In addition, African nations increasingly participated in the Olympic movement, particularly with the failure of holding the 1963 IOC session in Nairobi, Kenya, the acceleration of recognizing the African NOCs,

Figure 6.2. First-day issue stamps from the Congo celebrating the First African Games in 1965.

**Table 6.3.** African Territories and Nations Participating in the Community Games (1960), Friendship Games (1961 and 1963), and African Games (1965)

| 1st Community Games (Madagascar) | 2nd Friendship Games (Ivory Coast) | 3rd Friendship Games (Senegal) | First African Games (Congo-Brazzaville) |
|---|---|---|---|
| Cameroon | Cameroon | Algeria | Algeria |
| Central African Republic | Central African Republic | Cameroon | Cameroon |
| Chad | Chad | Central African Republic | Central African Republic |
| Congo-Brazzaville | Comoros | Chad | Chad |
| Dahomey | Congo-Brazzaville | Comoros | Congo-Brazzaville |
| France | Dahomey | Congo-Brazzaville | Congo-Léopoldville |
| French Coast of Somalia | France | Congo-Léopoldville | Dahomey |
| French Guyana | French Coast of Somalia | Dahomey | Ethiopia |
| Gabon | French Guyana | France | French Equatorial Guinea |
| Guadeloupe | French Polynesia | French Coast of Somalia | Gabon |
| Ivory Coast | Gabon | French Equatorial Guinea | Gambia |
| Madagascar | Guadeloupe | French Guyana | Ghana |
| Mali | Madagascar | French Polynesia | Ivory Coast |
| Martinique | Martinique | Gabon | Kenya |
| Mauritania | Mauritania | Gambia | Liberia |
| New Caledonia | New Caledonia | Ghana | Madagascar |
| Niger | Niger | Guadeloupe | Malawi |
| Réunion | Réunion | Ivory Coast | Mali |
| Upper Volta | Senegal | Liberia | Niger |
| | St. Pierre and Miquelon | Madagascar | Nigeria |
| | Upper Volta | Martinique | Senegal |
| | Wallis and Futuna | Mauritania | Sierra Leone |
| | | New Caledonia | Tanzania |
| | | Niger | Uganda |
| | | Nigeria | Togo |
| | | Réunion | Tunisia |
| | | Senegal | United Arab Republic |
| | | Sierra Leone | Upper Volta |
| | | Tunisia | Zambia |
| | | United Arab Republic | |
| | | Upper Volta | |

their integration in the next Olympic Games (Tokyo 1964), and the recognition of the first African Games in 1965 in Congo-Brazzaville. The
IOC continued to fear the Soviet political instrumentalization of Olympic support to the African countries, although the question of aid to the
African NOCs was supplanted by the apartheid issue. The 1963 IOC
session was the first IOC meeting scheduled in sub-Saharan Africa. (The
only previous session that had been scheduled on the African continent
was the 1938 meeting, which took place in Cairo, Egypt.) However, Kenya refused to grant visas to athletes from South Africa, Angola, and Mozambique. In the summer of 1963, the IOC moved its meeting to Baden-
Baden, West Germany, which had the effect of reducing the African
delegations because of the geographical distance.

In this atmosphere France continued to promote the African Games.
This decision reflects a new political line within French diplomacy in Africa, which was inspired by the publication in 1963 of the reports from
the secretary of commerce and trade, Jean-Marcel Jeanneney, titled "The
Politics of the Cooperation with Developing Countries, and from Léon
Pignon, who defined cooperation as "an operation, a work of concert,
an overall of efforts."[42] These reports justified a policy of cooperation for
several reasons: the duty of solidarity toward less-developed countries, the
necessity of spreading French culture and tradition, and the possibility
of obtaining (in exchange for certain assistance) indirect economic advantages and cultural enrichment. This report influenced French foreign
policy in Africa because it indicated that if public aid in the development
of France in Africa was necessary, it was a project that benefitted the African states as well as France. France's African policy, which had essentially
been a bilateral relationship, now evolved toward multilateralism, which
increasingly exposed France to competition on the continent. In reality,
this tendency consisted in delegating, little by little, part of the duties
of the Ministry for Cooperation to the Foreign Ministry, without really
transferring the jurisdiction of African politics to the Quai d'Orsay. Until
1999 these two ministries coexisted, highlighting the importance of Franco-African political relations as well as Africa's particular and privileged
status in French foreign affairs during the second half of the twentieth
century.[43]

Although France officially withdrew from participating in the African
Games, it nevertheless remained present in the event. Exchanges of tech-

nical assistance provided sport advisers, coaches, and physical education teachers from France, and financial support also materialized in the form of travel on Air France for the African sports grant holders, the preparation of the athletes, and the construction of a stadium and a swimming pool in Brazzaville. The meeting of the Technical Committee for the First African Games was held in Brazzaville February 24–29, 1964, under the aegis of the secretary-general of the First African Games situated at the Sports Center of Bancongo (Congo-Brazzaville). This meeting provided the opportunity to make the link with the aborted First African Games wanted by Pierre de Coubertin during the colonial period (in 1923) and to reaffirm for the Congolese political leaders the geopolitical upheavals in Africa. During the previous year (1963), Congo-Brazzaville had experienced a coup d'état and saw a revolutionary Marxist government led by Alphonse Massemba-Débat come to power in opposition to the politics of his predecessor, Abbot Fulbert Youlou. The new political line of the country under Massemba-Débat was dictated by a link with the sympathetic communist countries while the regime sought to gain popular support. The creation of both the National Movement of the Revolution and its youth wing in the year before the African Games contributed to the spread of these politics across the country during a climate of civil war.[44] At this Technical Committee meeting, Col. Marceau Crespin (an HCJS sport administrator) and Inspector Principal Jean Sagui (Ministry for Cooperation) represented France alongside the representatives of the African delegations. Herzog wanted to reaffirm the presence of France at a time when the country's status at the international level had been weakened by the loss of Algeria (confirmed in the 1962 Evian Agreements).

The recognition of the First African Games in Congo-Brazzaville as regional games in the Olympic movement assumes a greater political importance because of the other sporting events promoted for the newly decolonized world in the early 1960s. The same year that Brundage attended the Friendship Games, the Games of the Newly Emerging Forces (GANEFO) were held in Djakarta, Indonesia, in 1963 with fifty-one countries from Africa, Asia, Europe, and Latin America.[45] In 1965 the First African Games competed with the Fourth Pan Arab Games, held in Cairo, and the second edition of GANEFO, which took place in two phases in Pyongyang, North Korea (August 1–11, 1965), and Phnom Penh, Cambodia (December 25–26, 1965). The Phnom Penh event was called "First Asian GANEFO" to emphasize the Asian influence on the nonaligned movement. The IOC opposed these games and their clear political agenda, which was in contrast to the Friendship Games in Dakar.

The choice of Congo-Brazzaville as the site for these games of Western influence, however, was not an obvious choice. Because Congo-Brazzaville was in a pro-Soviet revolutionary enclave, the IOC did not want the influences from communism or GANEFO, which was based on the doctrine of the Conference of the Non-Aligned Movement in Bandung in 1955 and reaffirmed in Belgrade in 1961. Therefore, the IOC did not recognize these African Games as a regional event at first, only formally providing official recognition on April 11, 1965, one week before the games began. The reluctance expressed from the anglophone block, led by the British IOC member Lord Exeter (who also served as the president of the International Amateur Athletic Federation, or IAAF), stemmed from concerns that the decision to exclude apartheid South Africa did not represent the sentiment of the entire continent. This fight to expel South Africa was brought about and won by the Congolese sport leader Jean-Claude Ganga, who also served as the secretary-general of the organizing committee for the First African Games and the secretary-general of the Supreme Council for Sport in Africa. He was the spokesperson for progressive African elites who denounced apartheid.[46]

Ultimately Brundage provided Olympic recognition to the African Games to ensure an alliance with the African and nonaligned progressive movements and thus diminish the influence of the Soviet Union and its satellites.[47] Brundage's presence at the 1963 Friendship Games, organized under the aegis of France, demonstrated that they had received Olympic support. Brundage recognized the importance of the earlier games, the Community Games and then the Friendship Games, noting that thanks to them, "Africa made a commitment to the Olympic way."[48] The opening ceremony of the First African Games symbolized the unity and the success of African sport in front of a crowd of sixteen thousand spectators and sports delegations from twenty-seven countries. Morocco and Mauritania did not participate because of their preparations for the Fourth Pan-Arab Games the same year, and the strongest delegation was from the United Arab Republic with 170 athletes and coaches, followed by the teams from Senegal, Ivory Coast, and Algeria. The presence of Brundage representing the IOC and Colonel Crespin representing the French state demonstrated the geopolitical and postcolonial stakes inherent to the realization of the African Games. The temporary recognition of the African NOCs (until they met the regular terms of conditions of membership in multiple international federations) was a means for the Olympic movement to attempt to avoid the Soviet, anticolonial, and Pan-African influences. IOC support for the African Games enabled the creation of a department for the organization of the First African Games within the Supreme Council for Sport in Africa.

Within the organization of the African Games, the French also had to contend with Indonesia's influence from GANEFO, the anticolonial feelings continually espoused by the Arab states, and the communist coup d'état in Congo-Brazzaville. Yet the African Games remained well within the sphere of French influence in Africa as a result of the work of the High Commission (and later State Secretariat) for Youth and Sport.[49] The diverse French ministries that acted in a concerted effort ensured the success of the transition from direct French influence to the form of support provided to the first African Games. In addition, with more of the African continent represented in the IOC and now organized regionally, many Africans believed they also needed a governmental authority to propagate and defend Pan-Africanism, particularly the struggle against apartheid and the developmental aid for African sport. The organizing committee for the first African Games became in turn the emanation of a new intergovernmental Pan-African organization in 1966 called the Supreme Council for Sport in Africa, which was connected to the Organization of African Unity (OAU), the political institution established in 1963.[50] This organization then continued the postcolonial fight against apartheid in South Africa and Rhodesia within the IOC and also maintained the

Figure 6.3. 1966 Congo-Brazzaville stamp: "Sport unites peoples."

ideological aid for the development of African sport. Thus these games in Brazzaville prevented African sport from succumbing to the Arabic-speaking and Soviet spheres of influence. At the same time, the reactivation of the links with the African heads of state (the former French ministers of state before the colonial independences)—rather than the African ministers—underlines the durability of the colonial networks.[51]

## Conclusion

The entry of African states into the IOC was a process intricately intertwined with the global forces that dominated international affairs after 1945. The paradigm shift that occurred with the rise of the Cold War and the advent of decolonization forced the British and French to recalculate their relationships with their former colonies, and nowhere was this more pronounced than in sport, where membership in the IOC became the ultimate symbolic step of independence. The colonial policy adopted by the French in Africa of indirect control through soft power accelerated the internationalization of African sport by energizing its development. This, in turn, placed geopolitical constraints on the road to independence, which created leverage for the francophone colonies.[52] The impact of British decolonization could be seen at the Olympic Games from 1948 to 1960 through the participation of independent delegations from former British colonies Egypt, South Africa, Nigeria, Kenya, Uganda, Liberia, Ghana, Sudan, and Zimbabwe. On the other hand, the francophone African colonies were incorporated into the French national team, such as the Senegalese sprinter Abdou Seye, who won the bronze medal in the 200-meter race at the Rome Olympics and who had received direct financial support from the French government. Eventually, however, the decolonized states of anglophone Africa were joined by the newly independent francophone African states after a strategic reversal of French colonial policy. Nevertheless, the modes of administration and management in the former British colonies differed significantly from those of French colonial policy.

In addition, the strong presence of colonial administrators, who held a monopoly of power in the French empire, delayed the implementation of the Africanization of the managerial caste in the governing of the colonies. This in turn placed limits on the pace of French abandonment of its colonial policies.[53] The haste of French decolonization is explained by the approach of the two superpowers in the Cold War in the Third World. Their influence with the anticolonial and independence movements raised fears of a return to a French "African preserve" such as at Bandung in 1955, along with the continuing counterpoint of competition with British influence for the leadership of Europe. Thus, rather than definitively losing all control and influence over its empire, the French state—for a brief historic moment—accelerated the decolonization process among these African elites in order to become the favored partner of its former African colonies and sought to pursue the colonial project in other ways. From this point forward, this colonial reshaping consisted of simultaneously supporting the political independence of the African countries, with as a consequence the blessing of the UN and finally the recognition by the IOC of the NOCs from francophone black Africa. Furthermore, the total number of recognized NOCs and participating athletes between the London Olympics (1948) and the Tokyo Games (1964) almost doubled from fifty-nine NOCs and 4,092 athletes in London to ninety-three NOCs and 5,140 athletes in Tokyo as a result of the inclusion of new NOCs from both French- and English-speaking Africa.

Finally, within the Olympic movement, although the British delegates to the international federations were urging them to pressure the IOC to recognize African NOCs following the self-government model of the Commonwealth Games, France was delaying this process in its own colonial territories. The autonomy in the French colonies was still limited within a stillborn Franco-African Community, which ultimately selected the Community Games as the indispensable moment for their "Olympic emancipation." Thus, between 1959 and 1965, the intersection of two processes for the internationalization of African sport also coincided with the twin phases of Franco-Olympic and Franco-British cooperation.[54] This phase represents the moment when the colonies of these two empires were most likely to be influenced by the Soviet Union, then engaging in propaganda to recover the nonaligned nations of the Third World with GANEFO (1963) and the future African Games (1965).

Although these events also fostered competition between the British and the French over Olympic recognition of African NOCs, the anglophone and francophone African elites now had ideologies for the development of Olympic sport and for the struggle against apartheid. These new

African sport leaders could thus promote their African sporting policy at the international level via the Supreme Council for Sport in Africa. This sport diplomacy between French and African elites was possible not only because of the past colonization and the cultural links preserved but also because the African executives used sport—and emulating their former colonizers in doing so—to promote their own interests.[55] As Allen Guttmann has noted,

> The desire of the colonized peoples to compete in the same sports of the colonizing populations represents an important, and largely overlooked, factor in the spread of modern sports. It represented a means for the "deprived" to appropriate an important cultural element of the "well-to-do" that the "well-to-do" had refused to extend. Some say that emulation is nothing more than the expression of a "guilty conscience" and the proof that the colonial powers colonized everything politically, economically, and even the spirit of those colonized, but this idea is completely and empirically false. Such an assertion of "false consciousness" makes men and women who adopted the modern sports beings divested of judgment and free will.[56]

The transformation of French sport policy since 1945 through the process of African decolonization corresponded to a change in the position of France within international relations. Postcolonial sport—expressed through the examples of the Community Games, the Friendship Games, and the First African Games—is a clear example of cultural diplomacy because the form of French control over these newly independent countries was not political or military but instead was cultural and economic, with the most important goal being the dissemination of ideals, values, and thought patterns.[57] These newly independent countries demonstrated their acceptance of these French ideas not only by their participation in international sporting events but also by promoting these same values in their own right. In 1966, for example, Congo-Brazzaville issued a stamp with athletes from multiple sport and ethnic backgrounds standing above the world, with the phrase "Sport unites people."

Maurice Herzog revealed the complex nature of using sport within cultural diplomacy in the postcolonial era: "If sports are a reflection of culture, it is also natural that people choose among them, those sports that best suit their own characteristics, and that the control of one country over another is accompanied with the diffusion of its cultures, that of sports. . . . In the former French colonies one practiced mainly football, in India cricket and hockey, but nothing says that these sports will remain if the cultural influence of France and England disappear."[58] With this sentiment Herzog also provided legitimacy to the idea that French cultural influence could be maintained in Africa by sport.

## Notes

1. Pierre Milza, *Les relations internationales de 1945 à 1973* (Paris: Hachette, 1996), 18.

2. John Darwin, "Was There a Fourth British Empire?," in *The British Empire in the 1950s: Retreat or Revival?,* ed. Lynn Martin (Basingstoke: Palgrave, 2006).

3. Marc Michel, *Décolonisations et émergence du tiers monde* (Paris: Hachette, 2005), 195.

4. Têtêvi G. Tété-Adjalogo, *La question du Plan Marshall et l'Afrique* (Paris: L'Harmattan, 1989).

5. Gérard Chaliand, *L'enjeu africain, stratégies des puissances* (Paris: Seuil, 1980), 15; André Fontaine, *La Guerre froide, 1917–1991* (Paris: La Martinière, 2006); François Durpaire, *Les États-Unis ont-ils décolonisé l'Afrique noire francophone?* (Paris: L'Harmattan, Études africaines, 2005), 30; Peter Duignan and L. H. Gann, *The United States and Africa: A History* (New York: Cambridge University Press, 1987); William F. Jasper, *Global Tyranny . . . Step by Step: The United Nations and the Emerging New World Order* (Appleton, WI: Western Islands, 1992); David Ryan and Victor Pungong, eds*., The United States and Decolonization: Power and Freedom* (Basingstoke: MacMillan, 2000); Pierre-Michel Durand, "Alliance objective, Méfiances réciproques: Les États-Unis, la France et l'Afrique noire dans les années soixante," PhD diss., University of Paris III–Sorbonne Nouvelle, 2003); Sekola Mosamete, *L'Afrique et la perestroïka: L'évolution de la pensée soviétique sous Gorbatchev* (Paris: L'Harmattan, 2007), 31; David Spurr, *The Rhetoric of Empire* (Durham, NC: Duke University Press, 1993); William Roger Louis, *Imperialism at Bay: The United States and the Decolonization of the British Empire 1941–1945* (New York: Oxford University Press, 1977); Denise Bouche, "L'ouverture de l'Afrique occidentale au monde extérieur: La fin de l'Empire et l'échec de l'Union française," *Relations internationales* 34 (Summer 1983): 173–85; John Kent, *The Internationalization of Colonialism: Britain, France and Black Africa, 1939–1956* (Oxford: Clarendon Press, 1992); Christopher Clapham, *Africa and the International System: The Politics of State Survival* (New York: Cambridge University Press, 1996); and Zaki Laïdi, *L'URSS vue du Tiers-Monde* (Paris: Karthala, 1984).

6. John Bale and Mike Cronin, "Introduction: Sport and Postcolonialism," in *Sport and Postcolonialism,* ed. John Bale and Mike Cronin (Oxford: Berg, Global Sport Cultures, 2003), 3.

7. Joseph S. Nye Jr., *Soft Power: The Means to Success in World Politics* (New York: PublicAffairs, 2004).

8. Raymond Aron, *Paix et guerre entre les nations* (París: Calmann-Lévy, 1962), and Pierre Milza, Philippe Tétart, and François Jéquier, eds., *Le pouvoir des anneaux* (Paris: Vuibert, 2004).

9. Pierre Renouvin and Jean-Baptiste Duroselle, *Introduction à l'histoire des relations internationales,* 4th ed. (Paris: Armand Colin, 1991); Michel Espagne*, Les transferts culturels franco-allemands* (Paris: PUF, 1999); James N. Rosenau, *Turbulence in World Politics: A Theory of Change and Continuity* (Princeton, NJ: Princeton University Press, 1990); Jean-Claude Allain, Pierre Guillen, Georges-Henri Soutou, Laurent Theis, and Maurice Vaïsse, *Histoire de la diplomatie française: Tome 2, de 1815 à nos jours* (Paris: Librairie Académique Perrin, 2007); and Jean-Baptiste Duroselle, "Opinion, attitude, mentalité, mythe, idéologie: Essai de clarification," *Relations internationales* 2 (November 1974): 9.

10. Nicolas Ragaru and Pierre Conesa, "Les stratégies d'influence en affaires étrangères: Notion insaisissable ou absence de volonté?," *Revue Internationale et Stratégique* 52 (2003): 83–88; Nicolas Tenzer, "Constituer des réseaux d'influence: Acteurs et vecteurs de décision en affaires étrangères; Organiser l'influence, Une stratégie intellectuelle de la France," *Revue Internationale et Stratégique* 52 (2003): 89–96; Georges Ayache, "Puissance et influence dans le cadre des relations internationales post-Guerre froide: Le cas de la France," *Annuaire français de relations internationales* 7 (2006): 384–98; André Lewin, "Les Africains à l'ONU," *Relations internationales* 128, no. 4 (2006): 55–78; and Ernest Guy Sanga, *Diplomatie et diplomate: L'Afrique et le système des relations internationales* (Paris: L'Harmattan, 2010).

11. Bernadette Deville-Danthu, *Le Sport en noir et blanc: Du sport colonial au sport africain dans les anciens territoires français d'Afrique occidentale (1920–1965)* (Paris: L'Harmattan, 1997), 349.

12. Marcel Duresse was also president of the Amicale des Parisiens, founding president of the Salle Duresse and the Dakar Stadium, and the former director of the Dakar Municipal Sports Park. He described himself as the first professor of physical education in Dakar, founding secretary-general of Art et Sport d'Afrique (African Sport and Art), the organizer of every sporting and artistic event that took place in Dakar from 1939 to 1945, and secretary of the Fédération des Amicales de France.

13. Regarding this mission, see Stanislas Frenkiel and David-Claude Kémo-Keimbou, "La mission FFA/L'Auto: 'Pourquoi négliger nos noirs d'Afrique?' (December 3, 1937–January 15, 1938)," *Modern & Contemporary France* 18 (February 2010): 33–50.

14. Marcel Duresse to Robert Delmas, November 23, 1948, President of the Per-

manent Commission of the High Council of French West Africa, African Olympic Committee, Cote AOF 2953, National Archives, Dakar, Senegal.

15. Robert Delmas, President of the Permanent Commission of the High Council of French West Africa to the Governor-General and High-Commissioner of French West Africa General-Directorate of Finance, January 13, 1949, President of the Permanent Commission of the High Council of French West Africa, African Olympic Committee, Cote AOF 2953, National Archives, Dakar, Senegal.

16. Marianne Amar, "Une affaire d'Etat? L'olympisme français face aux pouvoirs publics au tournant des années cinquante (1948–1952)," in *Le pouvoir des anneaux,* ed. Pierre Milza, Philippe Tétart, and François Jéquier (Paris: Vuibert, 2004), 216, and Souaïbou Gouda, "États, sports et politiques en Afrique noire francophone: Cas du Bénin, du Congo, du Niger, et du Sénégal," PhD diss., University of Grenoble 1, 1997. See also the chapter in this present volume by Antonio Sotomayor.

17. A. Massard to O. Mayer, February 3, 1953, Correspondence of Member Armand Massard, 1953–1959, International Olympic Committee Archives, Lausanne, Switzerland (hereafter IOC). After Massard informed Otto Mayer, the chancellor of the IOC, about this project, Mayer then asked him to remove any Olympic connotation from it.

18. Mansour S. Al-Tauqi, "Solidarité Olympique: Ordre global et diffusion du sport moderne entre 1961 et 1980," PhD diss., Loughborough University, 2003, 91. The 1950s coincided with a number of the regional games that took place every four years: Mediterranean Games (Egypt, 1951), Pan-Asian Games (New Delhi, 1951), Pan-American Games (Buenos Aires, 1951), and the Pan-Arab Games (Egypt, 1953). Dikaia Chatziefstathiou, "The Changing Nature of the Ideology of Olympism in the Modern Olympic Era," PhD diss., University of Loughborough, 2005; Dikaia Chatziefstathiou, *The Diffusion of Olympic Sport through Regional Games: A Comparison of the Pre- and Post- Second War Contexts* (Lausanne: IOC-OSC Research Grant, 2008); and Dikaia Chatziefstathiou, "Cultural Imperialism and the Diffusion of Olympic Sport in Africa: A Comparison of Pre- and Post- Second World War Contexts," in *Olympic Studies Reader,* ed. H. Ren and L. Dacosta (Barcelona: Centre d'Estudis Olímpics, 2008), 111–28.

19. Yet at the Brazzaville Conference, de Gaulle had transferred power within each African territory from the "colonial lobby" to the *élites évoluées* as a way to appear as though France was following the lead of Great Britain by giving more autonomy to each territory while at the same time appeasing calls from within the United Nations to emancipate the colonized peoples.

20. This French sport institution was created in 1945 and still exists today, but after its 1975 merger with Graduate School of Sports and Physical Education (ENSEP), it has been known as the National Institute for Sport and Physical Education (INSEP).

21. Lord Aberdare to Foreign Office, May 30, 1945, Foreign Office (FO) 370/1150, National Archives of the United Kingdom, Kew, Richmond, Surrey (hereafter UKNA); Lord Aberdare to Foreign Office, May 11, 1945, FO 370/1150,

UKNA; Bob Philips, *The 1948 Olympics: How London Rescued the Games* (London: Sports Books, 2007); Janie Hampton, *The Austerity Olympics: When the Games Came to London in 1948* (London: Aurum Press, 2008), 400; and James Riordan, *Sport soviétique* (Paris: Vigot, 1980), 103–4.

22. Pascal Charitas, "Anglophone Africa in the Olympic Movement: The Confirmation of a British Wager? (1948–1962)," *African Research and Documentation* 116 (2011): 35–52.

23. Circular letter from A. Brundage to members of the IOC, January 1954, *Bulletin of the IOC* 47 (August/September 1954): 10–13.

24. Viktor Kalu Eke, "Soviet-African Relations: A Critique of the Moving Forces," in *The Soviet Union in World Politics: The Global Significance of the USSR and Issues in Soviet-African Relations*, ed. Viktor Kalu Eke (Nigeria: Fourth Dimension, 1988), 89–110.

25. Jean-Pierre Augustin and Pascal Gillon, *L'Olympisme: Bilan et enjeux géopolitique* (Paris: Armand Colin, 2004).

26. Nicolas Bancel, Pascal Blanchard, and Françoise Vergès, *La République coloniale* (Paris: Collection Pluriel, Hachette Littératures, 2006).

27. Ahmadou Kourouma, *Les soleils des indépendances* (Paris: Seuil, Fiction, Poetry and Drama, 1995).

28. The confederalist African leaders (such as Houphoët-Boigny) wanted a Franco-African Community of African republics with the principle of equality between the countries of the francophone area in Africa. The federalists (such as Leopold Sedar Senghor, first president of Senegal) wanted a type of "French Commonwealth," with two large African federations associated to France. André Saura, *Philibert Tsiranana (T1): Premier président de la République de Madagascar (1910–1978)* (Paris: L'Harmattan, 2006), 83.

29. Press release, "De retour à Paris, M. Herzog tire les conclusions des Jeux de la Communauté," *Abidjan-Matin,* April 23, 1960, no. 2633, MFILMGRFOL6649 (2539–2639), 5, French National Library, Paris.

30. Pierre Nandjui, *Félix Houphouët-Boigny: L'homme de la France en Afrique* (Paris: L'Harmattan, 1995), and Frédéric Grah Mel, *Félix Houphouët-Boigny: Biographie* (Paris: Cerap, Maisonneuve & Larose, 2003).

31. Jacques Foccart (1913–1997) served from 1960 to 1974 as the French chief of staff for African and Madagascar matters and was also the cofounder of the Gaullist Service d'Action Civique, which specialized in covert operations in Africa. Indeed, Foccart was considered to be the instigator of several coups d'état in Africa during the 1960s. In addition, he was a central figure in the creation of Françafrique, a concept originally conceived as the positive relationship between France and Africa. See Pierre Kipré, "Le témoignage de Jacques Foccart," Les Cahiers du Centre de Recherches Historiques, 30/2002, http://ccrh.revues.org/452 DOI: 10.4000/ccrh.452 (accessed July 15, 2013).

32. The stadium built in 1963 in Dakar by France is called Stade de l'Amitié and continues to be used today.

33. David Maraniss, *Rome 1960: The Olympics That Changed the World* (New York: Simon & Schuster, 2008).

34. A. Brundage to O. Mayer, April 15, 1960, Correspondence 1960–1961, A. Brundage Collection, notice: 0061526, IOC. See also the chapters in this present volume by Aviston Downes and Scott Laderman.

35. Those conferences continue today and also include francophone countries outside of France's former African colonies. One conference is for education (Conference of Ministers of National Education) and the other is for youth and sport (Conference of Youth and Sports Ministers).

36. André Urban, *Etats-Unis, Tiers-Monde et crises internationales (1953–1960)* (Paris: L'Harmattan, 2005), and Philippe Braillard, *Mythe et réalité du non alignement* (Paris: PUF, 1992).

37. Count Jean Bonnin de la Bonninière de Beaumont (1904–2002) was an aristocrat and a powerful company director. He moved freely in political and economic circles. As a financier at the Rivaud Bank, he administered and owned farmlands and mines (which today constitute the Bolloré Group) in Africa, Asia, and Indonesia. Count de Beaumont was elected to the IOC's executive board, ultimately serving as a vice president from 1970 to 1974. His presidential aspirations were not achieved, but he also served as the chairman of the IOC's Finance Commission from 1972 to 1988. He was also the president of the Association of European NOCs from 1969 to 1975. At the national level, he served as the president of the French Olympic Committee from 1967 to 1971.

38. Pascal Charitas and Yann Drouet, "La Commission d'Aide Internationale Olympique (CAIO): Nécessité d'un nouveau médiateur entre la France et l'Afrique noire? (1960–1963)," *Stadion* 33, no. 2 (2008): 207–28; agenda for meetings of the USOC, October 16, 1962, and February 12, 1963, Avery Brundage Collection, box 238, IOC; Pascal Charitas and David-Claude Kemo-Keimbou, "The United States of America and the Francophone African Countries at the International Olympic Committee (IOC): Sports Aid, a Barometer of American Imperialism? (1952–1963)," *Journal of Sport History* 40, no. 1 (2013): 69–91; Pascal Charitas, "La Commission d'Aide Internationale Olympique (CAIO): Un instrument de propagande soviétique? (1951–1962)," *Sport History Review* 40 (2009): 143–66; and Pascal Charitas, "L'Afrique au mouvement olympique: Enjeux, stratégies et influences de la France dans l'internationalisation du sport africain (1944–1966)," PhD diss., University of Paris–South, 2010.

39. Christian Roche, *Léopold Sédar Senghor: Le président humaniste* (Toulouse: Privat, 2006).

40. Abidjan Ambassade, April 26, 1963, "Les Jeux de l'Amitié de Dakar," Box 23, 1961–1970, Secret, Center of the Diplomatic Archives of Nantes.

41. Lucien Paye (ambassador of France in Dakar) to Maurice Couve de Murville (MFA, director for cultural and technical affairs), May 20, 1963, Ambassade Dakar, Box 323, Diplomatic Archives Center, Ministry of Foreign Affairs, Paris (hereafter DAC).

42. Jean-Marcel Jeanneney, *Rapport sur la politique de coopération avec les pays en voie de développement* (Paris: La Documentation Française, 1963).

43. Jean-Marc Châtaignier, "Principes et réalités de la politique africaine de la France," *Afrique contemporaine* 220, no. 4 (2006): 247–61.

44. Rémy Bazenguissa-Ganga, *Les voies du politique au Congo* (Paris: Karthala, 1997).

45. Rusli Lutan and Fan Hong, "The Politicization of Sport: GANEFO—A Case Study," *Sport in Society* 8, no. 3 (2005): 425–39. See also Fan Hong and Lu Zhouxiang's chapter in the present volume.

46. Ganga was a union activist, primary school teacher, and the first person to present youth questions to the Congolese Ministry. He was also the first Congolese person to obtain an inspector's diploma for youth and sport and served as the national director of the youth and sport program. He then became the first secretary of the Superior Council for Sport in Africa (SCSA) in 1966. Ganga was assisted by the inspector principal for youth and sport, Gérard Dorman, in the organization of the African Games.

47. A. D. Touny to J.-C. Ganga, August 38, 1964, correspondence relative to the Games of Central Africa (regional games), Press Articles 1963–1966, IOC.

48. Press release, *L'Equipe,* April 16, 1963, the National Olympic Committee for French Sport, Paris.

49. The French High Commission for Youth and Sport became the State Secretariat for Youth and Sport in 1963.

50. Luc Sindjoun, *Sociologie des relations internationales africaines* (Paris: Karthala, 2003). The SCSA was dissolved in 2013.

51. Note of the secretary-general of the Franco-African Community to the president of the republic, "Réunion du jeudi 22 avril relative aux Jeux de Brazzaville et à l'éventuelle conférence des Ministres des Sports," April 22, 1965, Brazzaville Games, J. Foccart, box AG5/FPU/2117, DAC.

52. Charles-Robert Ageron and Marc Michel, *L'ère des décolonisations,* Actes du Colloque d'Aix-en-Provence, CNRS (Paris: Karthala, 1995).

53. Nicolas Bancel, "Entre acculturation et révolution: Mouvements de jeunesse et sports dans l'évolution politique et institutionnelle de l'AOF (1945–1962)," PhD diss., University of Paris I–Sorbonne, 1999.

54. Pascal Charitas, "Les conditions d'émergence du développement sportif olympique: Comparaison entre la France et le Royaume-Uni (1944–1966)," postgraduate fellowship report, OSC-IOC, Lausanne, 2009.

55. René Girard, *Le bouc-émissaire* (Paris: Le Livre de Poche, 1986).

56. Allen Guttmann, "La diffusion des sports: Un impérialisme culturel?," in *L'Empire des sports: Une histoire de la mondialisation culturelle,* ed. Pierre Singaravélou and Julien Sorez (Paris: Belin, Collection Histoire & Société, 2010), 17.

57. Robert Frank, "Introduction," *Relations internationales* 115 (Autumn 2003): 322; Johan Galtung, "A Structural Theory of Imperialism," in *Perspectives on World Politics,* ed. Richard Little and Michael Smith (New York: Routledge, 1991); and

Allen Guttmann, *Games and Empire: Sport and Cultural Imperialism* (New York: Columbia University Press, 1994).

58. Maurice Herzog, "Les valeurs culturelles du sport en Occident," Correspondence IOAC-HCYS, 1962–1963, IOC.

Part 3

# East-West Rivalries

# 7

# The Cold War Games of a Colonial Latin American Nation

## San Juan, Puerto Rico, 1966

### *Antonio Sotomayor*

As an "unincorporated territory" of the United States yet as part of Latin America and the Caribbean, Puerto Rico presents multiple problems for academic study in areas that include nationalism, colonial/postcolonial studies, democracy/imperialism, and, of course, the politics of Olympism. Puerto Rico's balancing act of belonging to, but not being part of, both the United States and Latin America permeates the often conflictive politics of the region. Yet Puerto Rico, like the Caribbean in general—except Cuba—has been kept at the fringes of world political attention and hence also from significant academic study. This chapter will demonstrate the pivotal role Puerto Ricans played during a crucial time in Cold War history, during the 1966 edition of the oldest regional games sponsored by the International Olympic Committee (IOC)—the Central American and Caribbean Games.

In this way, for Puerto Ricans these games were vital not only to their efforts of political modernization but also to their hopes of keeping alive their Olympic persona and to their agency in dealing with Caribbean Cold War diplomacy. Moreover, the source of the conflicts in hosting the games, and the negotiations to solve them, show that although such international competition is seen as apolitical, they were a very political affair. The sport leaders involved in the matter—whether from Puerto Rico, Cuba, the United States, or the IOC—all took positions and acted within the urgency of Cold War politics.

As part of the Caribbean, Puerto Rico evidences some of the issues the "global South" faces in international sport. Puerto Rican Olympism arose from the colonial and postcolonial structures imposed by the North Atlantic powers, as seen in the anti-apartheid campaign and the solidarity movement between Africa and the English Caribbean presented by Aviston Downes in chapter 4. Nonetheless, just as sport was used by Juan Perón to showcase a "New Argentina," as Cesar Torres discussed in chapter 5, the Tenth Central American and Caribbean Games (X CACG) of 1966 in San Juan, Puerto Rico, became for Puerto Ricans the event to showcase the vitality of their new political system.

Contrary to the anti-imperialist critique of the United States by Perón, for Puerto Ricans the idea was to showcase the commonwealth under the sponsorship of Washington. Furthermore, hosting these games was also the best indicator that Puerto Ricans were a legitimate nation-member of an international sporting community. Indeed, Puerto Rico in 1966 was a stable and a vital member of Central American and Caribbean Olympism, having participated in all editions of the Central American and Caribbean Games since the second in 1930. The Puerto Rican participation in Caribbean Olympism left no doubt that this was a nation with a solid regional athletic tradition, having participated and consistently finished in the top four of the medal count since 1930.[1] Now, by being hosts of the games, Puerto Ricans opened their doors to their regional neighbors in order to show their national vitality, athletic strength, and cultural uniqueness.

After the creation of the Commonwealth of Puerto Rico in 1952 and continuing participation in the Pan-American Games (PAG) and Summer Olympic Games—Puerto Ricans had been participating in the PAG since 1955 and the Olympics since 1948—there was no doubt that Puerto Rico was a nation, at least culturally.[2] Granted, as John MacAloon states in his study of the colonial politics present in the 1979 PAG in San Juan, this nationhood was only internationally visible and applicable in sport, but it was a nation nonetheless.[3] In this regard, Félix Huertas González is correct in affirming that although Puerto Rico is not an independent nation-state, it has, as a result of the growing popularity and precedence given to Olympic competition worldwide, a presence that for many equals the status of nationhood.[4] While this nonsovereign nationhood might seem contradictory to some, it also occurs in the French and English Caribbean.[5]

However, the X CACG became not only a showcase of Puerto Rico's nationhood but also, unwillingly, of its inherent colonial status. Faced with internationally active, communist Cuba and the uncertainty of its participation at the games, the process by which the Cubans were excluded and included shows that the games were as much a window through which to see colonial and regional politics and can be called colonial Olympism. Colonial Olympism, in this regard, could constitute a new way of seeing the particular ways in which the Olympic movement developed in areas of the world that were, and/or are, affected by colonial/imperial structures. The tension of transporting the Cuban delegation to Puerto Rican territory and the subsequent moments of hostility channeled Cold War conflicts. Joaquín Martínez-Rousset has documented the connection of politics to Puerto Rican Olympism, showing how Puerto Rico's first National Olympic Committee (NOC) in 1933 was a branch of the government.[6] In the case of the 1966 X CACG, the dilemma of banning or inviting the Cubans reflected Cold War principles, forcing another conflictive situation of East versus West and bringing once again an air of hostility to the Caribbean. Tension from the Cuban Missile Crisis in 1962 still lingered in the minds, policies, and actions of the different parties involved.[7]

The conflicts surrounding these games were not limited to the bureaucracy of the government. There were many "incidents" on the ground involving athletes, spectators, the citizenry, and political groups. The pressure to defect constituted a premier tool against the Cuban delegation and by extension against the Cuban government. In the end these games demonstrated as well that while all parties involved tried to keep Olympism and politics separate, it ultimately proved an impossible task. The defense of Olympism became a political game, in which Puerto Ricans, Americans, Cubans, the IOC, and the Soviet bloc were directly involved.

The island of Puerto Rico, highly regarded for its strategic position in the Atlantic, has been called the "world's oldest colony" for a reason.[8] After four centuries of Spanish colonialism, in 1898 Puerto Rico was ceded as "war booty" to the United States as a result of the Spanish-American War. Puerto Ricans were made US citizens in 1917 just prior to the American entry into World War I, yet this citizenship lacked full parity with mainland US citizens. Puerto Ricans could not vote for president, send a full delegation to Congress to represent their interests, or be fully protected by the Bill of Rights in the US Constitution. As defined in the Insular Cases heard by the US Supreme Court in the early 1900s, Puerto Rico officially "belongs to, but is not part of, the United States."[9] For this reason, it has been argued that US citizenship was granted to Puerto Ricans not only to recruit soldiers for World War I but to secure a hegemonic hold.[10] This hegemonic relationship has been studied in regard to sport and recreation. Roberta Park has shown how sport and recreation culture, policies, and infrastructure were part of a militaristic and Americanization agenda used by Washington to secure a "benevolent" presence on the island.[11]

Even though Puerto Rico was excluded from being part of the United States, it was also prohibited from engaging in international trade or implement local tariffs.[12] Indeed, being "unincorporated" meant that Congress officially closed the door for eventual US statehood. Despite the opposition of the Puerto Rican Nationalist Party—including a revolt for independence on October 30, 1950—the Commonwealth of Puerto Rico was established in 1952.[13] The creation of the commonwealth, as Law 600 passed by Congress, followed a post–World War II decolonization trend. Yet this legal change in status mainly allowed Puerto Ricans to administer their own territory, leaving the legal parameters mentioned above unchanged.[14] Thus after 1952, Puerto Rico became a sort of mirage of an autonomous political entity. Despite this lack of political sovereignty and democratic arrangement, during the early Cold War years Puerto Rico was regarded as a showcase of democracy and capitalism,[15] mainly in comparison to the unstable republics of Latin America and the Caribbean that were plagued by dictatorships or authoritarian regimes.[16]

## Negotiating Sport and Politics

The X CACG of 1966 in San Juan is noteworthy because a national delegation was denied invitation for political reasons. This occurred when the Puerto Rican authorities denied visas to the Cuban delegation, alleging that its presence alongside approximately twenty thousand very vocal Cuban exiles in Puerto Rico constituted a threat to the stability and security of the island. Nonetheless, such denial of visas was not the first time communist Cuba was denied visas to an athletic event in the area. There had been a movement to deny visas to the Cuban delegation for the IX CACG of 1962 in Kingston, Jamaica.[17] Moreover, Cuban athletes were denied visas to the IOC-sponsored XVI World Cup of Baseball in Colombia in 1965.[18] They were also denied visas by the Guatemalan government for the soccer finals of the IOC-sponsored Confederation of North, Central American and Caribbean Association Football (CONCACAF) in 1965, and as a result of this they were denied visas for the regional soccer competitions in Curaçao. Nonetheless, the Puerto Rican case was particularly unique in that this was a US "territory" that had received many Cuban exiles and denied visas to communist Cuba, in turn a declared ally of the Soviet Union.

The development of Puerto Rican sport and Olympism had been primarily a result of the efforts of Julio Enrique Monagas. An athlete as a young student in the southern town of Ponce in the 1910s, Monagas by the early 1940s had become a close ally of the Popular Democratic Party (Partido Popular Democrático, or PPD), which headed the establishment of the commonwealth in 1952. He served as commissioner of the government-created sport institutions since 1941 and headed the Olympic Committee of Puerto Rico (COPR) since its creation in 1948. Thanks to his charismatic, populist, and dynamic sport leadership both locally and internationally, he quickly became a recognized leader in hemispheric Olympism from the 1940s through the early 1960s. For his involvement in the Olympic movement, Monagas was awarded the Olympic Order (silver) by the IOC on April 5, 1984. At that time Monagas was only the second person in the Americas to receive the award, the first one being Peter Ueberroth (gold) from the United States.

Monagas was elected president of the newly established Central American and Caribbean Sport Organization (CACSO) in a meeting held in Mexico City, February 8–10, 1960. This organization, whose creation dates back to May 13, 1959, in a meeting of NOC leaders in Kingston, was part of a larger plan of the IOC to organize Olympism in the Americas. It was considered by IOC member José de Jesús Clark Flores, from Mexico, to be the first step toward better world Olympic organization.[19]

Therefore, for Monagas the X CACG in his home country could have been the final test that would place him as a hero among Olympic leaders.

The decision to host the X CACG in San Juan was a result of much internal government discussion but also at the international level. Monagas, as president of CACSO, was able to make use of a petition by other NOCs that had declared Puerto Rico to be the ideal place to host the X CACG on account of its successful athletic history but also as a result of its strategic geographical location and tourist attractions.[20] These same regional sport leaders had expressed wanting to come to the island even if it meant running competitions in the streets or swimming events in the ocean.[21] For Puerto Ricans, the crux of the matter was that it was imperative to host the games in order to prove to the countries of the area, and the IOC, that Puerto Rico's political modernization as a commonwealth had been successful. It was, indeed, a matter of political legitimation. By hosting these games, Puerto Ricans could now say that they had "progressed" enough to be an Olympic host to other nations. Their new political status, as an *estado libre asociado*—literally in English "free associated state," yet the official version is "commonwealth"—of the United States, provided the political stature to claim true sporting autonomy and athletic diplomacy.

It is important to recognize that all groups involved in the politics within these games claimed to be protecting the Olympic ideal from political intervention. Yet, by doing this, all involved actually took very political stances that mirrored Cold War and regional political conflicts. In early 1964, Monagas asked Roberto Sánchez Vilella whether Puerto Rican authorities planned to ask the US Department of State to issue visas for the Cuban delegation.[22] Sánchez Vilella, who this same year was elected the second governor of the commonwealth, after Luis Muñoz Marín's unmatched sixteen-year incumbency, wrote to Muñoz Marín regarding the Cubans' visas. In his letter Sánchez Vilella aligned himself with an important segment of the island's population, led by Cuban refugees who wished Cuba to be banned from the games.[23] He wrote: "This Government decidedly opposes that a Cuban team come to Puerto Rico to participate in said games as long as the present Cuban regime governs that island. We do not think that their presence can be of any service but, to the contrary, it will create a difficult and intolerable situation in the country."[24]

His main reason for this ban was that there were in the island some

"18,000 Cuban refugees" who had escaped the "totalitarian and Communist regime" of Fidel Castro. Because of this, he thought it would be almost impossible to prevent "clashes" between the exiles and Castro's athletes due to "the demonstrated aggressive attitude in Jamaica as well as in Brazil and other places of the hemisphere where they have participated."[25] Yet, while these reasons were in relation to an internal conflict between two groups of Cubans in Puerto Rico, Sánchez Vilella also mentioned direct affronts by the Cuban government toward Puerto Rico. He cited the expressions of Ramón Calcinas of Cuba's United Party of the Socialist Revolution of Cuba (Partido Unido de la Revolición Socialista de Cuba, or PURSC): "Puerto Rico will be free by the fight of their people and the solidarity of all countries of this continent and of the world. . . . Puerto Rico will be free like South Vietnam will be, who is fighting against North American imperialism, just like Angola and Venezuela."[26]

Their conclusions were based on the report of a commission that studied the case and stated that Castro's government since 1959 had "developed, sponsored, and directed" an interventionist policy throughout the continent to establish "Communist regimes." Although making no direct reference to the missile crisis just two years before, the commonwealth government viewed the expressions by Calcinas as "acts of political aggression," as were other acts such as calling the Puerto Rican governor a "satrap" and "traitor"[27] and expressing his support for a "war of national liberation" in Puerto Rico.

The sentiment by the Puerto Rican government has to be viewed in light of its strong alliance and territorial status in relation to the United States, hence its inherent ideological influence to the Right and capitalism. In 1948 the local legislature adopted a McCarthyist-inspired law, commonly known as the Gag Law (Law No. 53, 1948–1957).[28] Modeled after the Smith Act, the Gag Law made illegal the open discussion and display of symbols related to Puerto Rican independence. The nationalists who remained active after the repression of the 1950s were often labeled communists, regardless of their ideological orientation, and were further persecuted by both local and federal authorities.[29] In 1987 the Federal Bureau of Investigation confirmed having kept files (known as *carpetas*) for thirty years on thousands of individuals for supposedly engaging in proindependence activities, evidencing in turn systematic harassment and surveillance of its own citizenry.

These accusations by Calcinas were most despised by the commonwealth leaders who were trying to present their new political status as a political formula of decolonization. Having a Cuban delegation in Puerto Rico attacking their autonomy went against the very athletic diplomatic mission of presenting a decolonized Puerto Rican Olympic delegation. Simply said, Puerto Rico's presence as a sporting nation represented the commonwealth's autonomy to the world. Having this autonomy mocked and attacked by communist Cubans was considered by the commonwealth government to be a political affront.

However, the intention of using sport to show a sovereign Puerto Rico under the auspices of the United States went beyond Cuba and was immersed in a world divided by East and West. The communist powers had made their position clear regarding Puerto Rico. At the 1960 United Nations assembly, Soviet premier Nikita Khrushchev had exhorted the body to place Puerto Rico in the list of colonies still to be freed.[30] Plus, according to Victor Riesel, a small contingent of Puerto Rican communists had traveled to Beijing, where it was received by a cheering crowd while the radio called for Puerto Rican "freedom from American Imperialism."[31] He continued, saying that there were Chinese communist agents recruiting in Puerto Rico, pointing as well to a Puerto Rican clandestine communist force of four to five hundred in the mountains of El Yunke, trained in Cuba and ready to start a communist revolution.

With all of this in mind, Sánchez Vilella thought it was better not to have any sort of relation with the Cubans, "not even in the field of sports."[32] He did acknowledge that the United States had revised its policy and now accepted the Soviet Union and other communist countries in Olympic Games, but the Puerto Rican case was different. According to him the Soviet Union had abandoned its support of other "wars of national liberation" and instead assumed a policy of political coexistence, something very different from the Cuban case. As a result, the commonwealth government's decision was "definite," as it vowed to "actively combat any measure before the United States government intended to allow the entry of the Cuban delegation to Puerto Rico."[33] Regardless that Washington maintained sovereignty over borders, customs, and immigration in Puerto Rico, commonwealth leaders were willing to defend their alleged sovereignty against US authority. Given the consistent support and consent to US rule in Puerto Rico, this expression by the secretary of state was particularly extraordinary. The Cubans had touched a very sensitive political nerve by accusing Puerto Ricans of being colonials. It was even more threatening because it came from a communist, former Caribbean "brotherly" country and because the games were in Puerto Rico. More than an attack on all the work of gaining international credibility by the COPR, it was an attack on the very nature of the "compact of association" with the United States.

When the news got out in early 1965 that the commonwealth government, now led by Roberto Sánchez Vilella, would oppose the granting of visas to the Cubans, it became the talk of the country, being covered as well in the press in New York and later in Chicago and Los Angeles.[34] Joaquín Martínez Rousset in his newspaper column "Desde el Dugout" pointed to the Olympic-political dilemma by indicating that Avery Brundage, as president of the IOC, could take away Puerto Rico's seat due to the interference of politics in Olympic competition. In his observation, Martínez Rousset was right: according to Olympic rules there cannot be political interference in Olympic tournaments, an issue well known by the COPR since the internal conflicts of the 1950s.[35]

By early 1965 Monagas had written to Brundage, communicating to him the commonwealth's position with regard to Cuba and the volatile situation of the Cuban exiles on the island. To this Martínez Rousset wondered, "What will happen if Cuba sends some two hundred athletes to the X Games and here they confront some 20,000 countrymen exiled and willing to send them to the firing squad?"[36] While Martínez Rousset acknowledged Brundage's earlier resolution of taking away the site of the World Championship of Basketball from Manila for the Philippine government's rejection of visas for some communist countries, he argued that in Manila there were not twenty thousand exiles from those countries. The X CACG in San Juan was a "government against government problem" from an "anticommunist" government against one "painted red."[37] He finished, affirming that "it is possible that this is the most explosive situation that the IOC has ever been stumbled within all of its history."[38]

Again, while there is no direct reference to the Cuban Missile Crisis in Martínez Rousset's article, there was an interesting use of Cold War warfare language: "firing squad," "explosive," "anticommunist," "painted red." It was, as a matter of fact, a highly problematic issue with the IOC, which attempted to uphold a strong stance against political intervention during Brundage's presidency.[39] Yet the Puerto Rican case was special, and this is precisely what Monagas told Brundage in a private cable. Although internally the commonwealth's government, if needed, was willing to go against the United States, Monagas publicly presented it as if Puerto Rico was just following US mandates when he stated that since Washington had no diplomatic relations with Cuba, the commonwealth would not intervene. Plus, Monagas continued to say, the presence of twenty thousand Cuban exiles "can be the cause of a tragedy in an activity that is supposed to foster goodwill amongst the different countries of the world."[40] The new Puerto Rican secretary of state, Dr. Carlos Lastra, indicated to the press that his government maintained its decision not to ask for the visas for the Cubans and that its decision was "in harmony" with the US Department of State.[41] As we will see later, this latter statement was not necessarily true. Moreover, the Puerto Rican authorities used their colonial relationship to appear innocent in relation to the Cubans' visas, thereby making the United States the ultimate culprit.

After Monagas called Brundage to inquire of the IOC's position, Brundage acknowledged the complexity of the problem and stated that he would need to further study the circumstances.[42] The situation was definitely complicated, because if Puerto Rico lost the privilege to host the games as a result of political interference, the alternative site options were equally problematic. One was Guatemala, yet it admitted not having the funds or infrastructure to host the games, while also declaring that it would deny visas to the Cubans. The other options were Colombia and El Salvador, which had also broken diplomatic relations with Cuba.

Brundage stood his ground and told the international press that the IOC "strongly opposed political interference in sport" and that if Puerto Rico failed to invite all nation-members of the Olympic movement in the area, it risked losing the opportunity in the future to host Olympic Games. For Monagas, the COPR was innocent of involving politics and sport, maintaining that the COPR had not been intervening with commonwealth authorities regarding the visas.[43] According to him, the decision to deny the visas was "entirely governmental" and was not related to the COPR whatsoever.

News of the problem of the Cuban visas and the X CACG began to spread throughout the Olympic world. The Central American and the Caribbean nations were expectedly attentive to the situation, and even in

Colombia there were rumors that Puerto Rico had relinquished hosting the games.[44] Coverage of the conflict reached Santa Barbara, California, Brundage's winter residence, where a newspaper reported on February 24, 1965, that the IOC president opposed the decision to ban Cubans from the games but indicated that the matter was in the hands of CACSO.[45] Nonetheless, Brundage also stated that the topic would be brought up in the next IOC meeting in Madrid. To some extent, it can be said that Brundage was hoping that CACSO would follow the IOC's nonpolitical interference and argue for the visas to be issued. The problem had definitely reached European Olympic circles when Juan Cepero from *El Mundo,* the principal newspaper in the island, reported on February 25 that Monagas had called D. T. Pain, the secretary-treasurer of the International Amateur Athletics Federation (IAAF), in London to explain the situation. Pain promised to study the case and help to resolve the issue.[46]

## An Olympic Resolution of Cold War Hostility

In the meantime, the leaders of CACSO meeting in Caracas, Venezuela, produced an unprecedented decision called the Caracas Resolution. Brundage's hopes to see CACSO oppose political intervention in Olympism vanished when CACSO, presided over by Monagas, officially passed this resolution banning the Cuban delegation from the X CACG in San Juan.[47] Citing "security concerns," CACSO also indicated that its resolution upheld the IOC's nondiscrimination statute based on race, religion, or politics. Moreover, the alternative host countries—Colombia, Guatemala, and El Salvador—indicated that physically they could not host the games and that they could not guarantee that their governments would grant the Cubans visas on account of international agreements signed in their membership of the Organization of American States.[48]

The Caracas Resolution was signed by Monagas as president of CACSO (Puerto Rico); Dr. Anibal Illueca Sibauste, vice president (Panama); José Beracasa, treasurer (Venezuela); Manuel de J. Rivas Rodríguez (El Salvador); Víctor Luque Salanueva (Mexico); and George Abrahams (Jamaica). Also present at the meeting were Gen. José de J. Clark Flores (Mexico), honorary president of CACSO and member of the IOC's Executive Board, and Dr. Julio Bustamante (Mexico), IOC member. Though the meeting resulted in the signing of the resolution, it was not without conflict. As it happened, it was a political showdown that demonstrated Monagas's weight in international sport and the politics of athletic diplomacy.

An anonymous letter sent to Brundage marked "<u>CONFIDENTIAL</u>" confirms the domestic political bias of Monagas in the matter of the Cubans' visas in an effort to "strengthening his political position with the new Commonwealth in power in Puerto Rico."[49] The author, who remains unidentified, concluded that the executive committee of CACSO (with the exception of Luque Salanueva) came ready to exclude Cuba from the games, a meeting that he rather called "the hold-up of Caracas." The sporting political pieces were well played, because regardless of the invitation of the Latin American members of the IOC, only Bustamante and Clark showed up, having no voting leverage in the final decision. As the resolution was discussed, members of the executive committee (Monagas, Illueca Sibauste, and Julio Illescas Rojas from Guatamala) complained that the IOC was too old and archaic to reach a decision on the Cuban case before the games began.

Things then got more personal, and verbal affronts even targeted Brundage. As a result of the escalating instability, the anonymous author suggested that Monagas "abandon this stupid farce" as it would get him and the Puerto Rican delegation into trouble and could even result in the withdrawal of IOC recognition to the X CACG and a ban on hosting the Olympic Games. As a matter of fact, he suggested that since there was so much discontent toward the IOC and Brundage, why not disassociate completely from the Olympic movement and carry out the games without IOC recognition? Such a suggestion resulted in more discussion and loud words. In the end, the resolution passed, and the meeting was adjourned.

Suffice it to say, the Caracas Resolution was a political struggle not only involving Cold War ideologies but also the position of Puerto Rico as a leading "country" in regional politics. Monagas, by setting the tone and content of the resolution to ban communist Cuba from the games, made the commonwealth's policy in regard to communism and set the parameters of how the games, and the region's politics for that matter, would play out. It also left clear that CACSO under Monagas's leadership was willing to go against the "old and archaic" IOC in a position relatively similar to Sánchez Vilella's willingness to go against the Department of State.

The news of the CACSO resolution reached Brundage shortly after it was made public in March 1965. As indicated in the confidential letter above, General Clark was strongly opposed to the Caracas Resolution and as a result asked Brundage and the IOC to cancel his earlier petition for IOC sponsorship of the games.[50] After a meeting of the IOC's executive board on April 12, 1965, in Lausanne, Brundage agreed with General Clark and communicated to CACSO that it needed to apply for IOC recognition of the games. This recognition was contingent upon the organizing committee inviting all regional members of the IOC to the X CACG, including Cuba, citing that the IOC had "an inflexible policy against political interference in sport, for any reason whatsoever." The meeting in Lausanne included all international amateur sport federations, which approved this policy "unanimously." Finally Brundage, regretting the situation in Puerto Rico, thought that Puerto Ricans had no excuse because the same situation regarding Cuba's participation at the CACG occurred in Jamaica in 1962.[51]

However, although the situation in Jamaica had presented the same groups involved in the conflict—that is Puerto Ricans, Cuban athletes, and some Cuban exiles—the situation was hardly the same.[52] First, regardless of whether the presence of the twenty thousand exiles in Puerto Rico was used as the rationale to ban the Cuban delegation from the games, the Cuban presence was a real threat and with the incidents in Kingston so recent, security was a practical concern for the organizing committee. Although it is true that thousands of anti-Castro Cubans had immigrated to Jamaica since the end of the Cuban Revolution in 1959, their situation was considered temporary, as Jamaica was seen as a springboard for eventual refugee status in the United States. For example, by January 1962 some 10,000 Cuban exiles had gone to Jamaica, yet 9,670 had received US visas.[53] Second, although being also heavily influenced by US Caribbean policy, Jamaica was nonetheless an independent and sovereign nation, with control over its ports, customs, and visas.[54] Puerto Rico was totally dependent on the United States regarding who could enter the island. Third, Puerto Rico, as an unincorporated territory of the United States, had to follow US policy on foreign relations, and at that time Washington had broken diplomatic relations with Cuba. Indeed, the United States had just come out of a real war scenario involving Soviet nuclear missiles in Cuba. Thus a potentially violent incident involving revolutionary Cuban athletes in a US territory with American citizens and thousands of ardent Cuban exiles was a recipe for disaster and could renew the real threat of war.

General Clark, although being isolated from the Caracas meeting, still intended to work toward including Cuba in the X CACG. He met with Monagas in late July 1965 and talked over the phone with Germán Rieckehoff Sampayo of the organizing committee to help resolve the situation. His greatest wish was that CACSO would "find its way" and not lose its "permanent recognition" within the IOC.[55] Rieckehoff Sampayo, who became another preeminent figure of Puerto Rican Olympism, became a sport leader through his work with the early stages of the local top-level basketball league, presiding over it from 1942 to 1944. From 1947 to 1949 Rieckehoff Sampayo worked at the College of Agriculture and Mechanical Arts (Colegio de Agricultura y Artas Mecánicas) in Mayagüez in the development of sport facilities, while in 1963 he founded the Equestrian Federation of Puerto Rico, which marked as well his full and official introduction into the COPR. Later in 1977, Rieckehoff Sampayo became Puerto Rico's first IOC member, and in 1980 the IOC decorated him with the Olympic Order medal.

At stake was not only the X CACG but also the very existence of CACSO and Central American and Caribbean Olympism. It seems that after the ultimatum by the IOC and President Brundage, CACSO (led by Monagas), COPR (now under the brief presidency of Francisco Bueso), and the organizing committee led by Emilio Huyke reevaluated their position and now were open to the invitation of all IOC members of the area to the games, including Cuba.[56] With this change in position, it was a matter of dealing with Puerto Rican and US authorities to issue the Cubans visas. This proved to be difficult, since the Puerto Rican government was still upholding its position of banning Cuba from the games. At least this is what can be inferred by Dr. Lastra's comments in the newspapers when he said, "We will neither help them [the organizing committee] get the visas for the Cuban players nor will we oppose the granting of such visas."[57] With broken diplomatic relations between the United States and Cuba, this might have meant that the commonwealth government was relying on a refusal of the United States to grant the visas.

What happened next is very important to understanding the politics of the CACG, how it began to resolve this problem, and the implications for international politics, including Puerto Rican colonialism. It was an outside element, once again, that interceded in Puerto Rican Olympism because Brundage, in conversation with C. Allan Steward, director of the Office of Caribbean Affairs in the Bureau of Inter-American Affairs, managed to get the Department of State to issue visas to the Cuban delegation. In fact, on December 5, 1965, Secretary of State Dean Rusk sent a cable to Felicio Torregrosa, technical director for the organizing committee, indicating that the Cubans' visas would be processed.[58] In this sense, Brundage as president of the IOC, committed the exact same error he had been decrying throughout his presidency: political interference. By assuring the Cuban visas from the State Department, he had actually interfered in a political matter to safeguard the participation of the Cuban delegation at the X CACG. Moreover, he and Steward had overridden and totally disregarded the policy of the Commonwealth of Puerto Rico of not issuing visas, an act that exposed their inherent colonial status. It became evident that Puerto Rico, although claiming sporting and even political autonomy, had to some extent failed to have fully achieved either of the two. It is exactly this colonial dynamic that separated the Puerto Rican situation from the Jamaican one and is what made, and still makes, Puerto Rico unique within Latin American politics and international sports.

With this move, the IOC was again unmasked as a political actor in the CACG and in Olympism in general. This politico-Olympic relation was certainly known back then as well. It was actually acknowledged by Steward when he stated that "it would be very bad policy for the Government to refuse visas simply because they are Cubans, because then it would prevent any U.S. city from being considered for the Olympic Games."[59] That is, Steward knew the importance of athletic diplomacy in international competition, and he was not willing to risk it because of stubborn colonial subjects. Moreover, he understood the significance of having recognition and support of the IOC if, and when, the United States wanted to host Olympic Games in the future. Even though the United States was immersed in the Cold War, it was more important to play by the rules of the IOC if it wanted to win the war on the athletic field.

It was only after Brundage himself guaranteed the visas that he finally gave IOC's patronage to the X CACG in San Juan.[60] Nonetheless, to safeguard the legitimacy of CACSO, as General Clark had requested, he later communicated to Torregrosa and the organizing committee that they needed final official recognition from CACSO.[61] But just because Brundage had obtained confirmation that the State Department would issue visas, it did not mean that the Puerto Rican government would accept it. As stated before, they were willing to confront any move by the United States to allow the entry of the Cubans into Puerto Rican territory. This is exactly what Clark noted in the Mérida meeting of December 7 and 8. At the meeting he could not get assurance from the COPR that the Puerto Rican government would accept the visas if granted.[62] In fact, he was totally opposed to the manner in which Brundage obtained the visas. Declaring that Washington was working against IOC regulations, he indicated that it was a matter of the Puerto Rican government to affirm "its acceptance to the Cuban participation."[63] Based on this, Clark gave another ultimatum to the Puerto Rican government that included a deadline of 1:00 p.m. on December 17, 1965, to "guarantee that the athletes, officials, and technicians in general [read Cuba] will be accepted." Said certification, he continued, should be addressed to CACSO with copies to IOC officials and to IOC members in Latin America. Moreover, if such certification failed to be clear and to the satisfaction of CACSO, Puerto Rico then forfeited its rights to be the site of the X CACG.[64] Once again, the ball was back in Puerto Rico's court.

If all of this was not enough, tensions kept escalating when the Soviets got involved in the matter in favor of their Cuban allies. The games were getting closer, and on December 31, 1965, Brundage replied to a letter sent by Konstantin Andrianov of the Soviet Olympic Committee saying that for the last several months he and General Clark had been "devoted to defending the right of your Cuban friends (although many claim they are not following Olympic regulations) to participate in the Central American Games, which are scheduled for Puerto Rico next year." At the end of the letter, Brundage rhetorically wondered, "When are we going to be able to concentrate on sport and not be bothered with these unsolvable political problems that do not concern us?"[65]

Not only were the Soviets paying more attention as the games drew closer, but also locally another group of Puerto Ricans entered the conflict, not against the Cuban delegation but in their favor. This group, called the Movement for Independence (Movimiento Pro Independencia, or MPI), had been founded in 1959 in Mayagüez under the leadership of Juan Mari

Bras and gathered discontented members from the Independent Puerto Rican Party (Partido Independentista Puertorriqueño), as well as from the Nationalist Party (Partido Nacionalista). The MPI's members had declared themselves to be sympathizers of the Cuban Revolution and, adopting the Cubans' methods of popular mobilization under anti-imperialist ideology, claimed the independence of Puerto Rico and expressed their solidarity with, and active support for, the Cuban delegation in Puerto Rico, vowing to protect it.[66] An MPI "manifesto" was published in the Cuban newspaper *Granma* on March 24, 1966: "The Cuban athletes will not be alone. There will be the Puerto Rican sportsmen and *independentistas* to stop the provocation plans against Cuba that Yankee imperialism intends to pursue and to answer, along with the Cuban athletes if they are forced to do it as well, said provocations in the necessary manner. The people of Puerto Rico, certainly will not permit that those worms and lackeys usurp their representation or moreover hurt our prestige and national dignity."[67] With this in mind, Monagas was visibly worried about the involvement of the MPI during the games, which according to him had set up an "embassy" in Cuba, and he even worried about possible student reinforcements brought from the Dominican Republic.[68] Moreover, Monagas thought that if Brundage were present during the games, hopefully a reign of peace, or at least composure, would be achieved. Yet Brundage declined the invitation because he needed to be present at the opening ceremony of a new museum in San Francisco that would hold his collection of Oriental art.[69]

## The Games in San Juan: A Theater of Olympism and Animosity

With the Cubans' visas approved, it appeared as though the games would be held without problems. The Puerto Rican government, although originally opposed to receiving the Cuban delegation even if the United States issued the visas, seemed now to follow US mandates and allowed the entry of Cuban athletes, thus exhibiting colonial status. This change in attitude by the Puerto Ricans was apparently a result of Reickehoff Sampayo's negotiations with local authorities.[70] Thus the threat of a Puerto Rican–US conflict was quickly subdued. Because the United States and Cuba had broken diplomatic relations, the travel plan consisted of Cubans, once having their visas, traveling to a third country, such as Mexico or Jamaica, and from there taking a commercial plane to San Juan.[71]

However, for the Cubans the extra step in travel entailed an "act of aggression" by the United States because they believed they should enter Puerto Rico without any impediment. Castro expressed his opinion as well that the whole deal was a "stupid, cynical blackmail."[72] The Cuban press also covered the problems of the visas, stating they only wanted to have relations directly with the COPR. Nonetheless, they understood that this was impossible because Puerto Rico was an *estado libre asociado* and that "the associated impedes them from being free."[73] In the end, the Cubans' visas were later taken from Mexico City, where they were issued, to Havana.[74]

The Cuban Olympic Committee (COC) had already been notified by Brundage of the problems pertaining to its alleged political interference in sport.[75] In its defense, COC president Manuel González Guerra wrote a seven-page letter dated March 30, 1966, indicating that their government did not interfere in Olympism and that they respected and strictly followed IOC rules.[76] He went on to identify that other countries had gotten away with the violation of nonreligious or political discrimination in the Olympics. For example, the Jamaican Olympic authorities had a Christian priest bless the 1962 games and "spoke of God, spoke of politics, of democracy" in their opening ceremony. Moreover, he wondered why there was no action taken against counterrevolutionaries when they "attack" the Cubans with propaganda. He believed that there was a real "threat of attack" in Puerto Rico not only from their "enemies" but also from Monagas and even the mayor of San Juan, a claim to which the IOC did not seem to give relevance. Yet the most recent form of aggression for him was that according to the United States, without IOC objection, Cubans needed to go to Mexico or Jamaica to obtain their visas, even though the Swiss embassy in Havana usually was in charge of US matters.[77]

The IOC, in its executive board meeting in Rome in April 1966, gave final recognition to the X CACG to be held in Puerto Rico, which for them was "an independent state under the protection of the United States with whom it had a custom union."[78] The unilateral and external approval of the Cubans' visas by both the United States and the IOC was silenced or unacknowledged in the official minutes. This colonial condition of Puerto Rico, even at the IOC level, was the price Puerto Ricans paid in order to be recognized as a legitimate nation, a member of the Olympic world.

For months in 1966 no one knew how the Cuban delegation would make its way, if at all, to Puerto Rico. These were moments of immense tension due to the unpredictability of the Cuban delegation and the meanings of a communist delegation in US territory at the height of the Cold War. Finally, and without the knowledge of the organizing committee or any other Puerto Rican authorities, the Cuban merchant vessel *Cerro Pelado* appeared four miles outside San Juan, at the edge of international waters, on June 10, 1966, just one day prior to the opening ceremonies. Since Puerto Rican ports were—and still are—controlled by the United States, and with the Americans not allowing Cuban vessels to enter US territory, the Cuban ship positioned at international waters so close to the United States meant trouble. This audacious, provocative, and risky move by the Cubans placed an immediate alert to all parties involved, including COPR and the organizing committee, the Puerto Rican and US governments, the IOC, and different NOCs from the Soviet bloc. It was another crisis at sea, involving East versus West, without nuclear missiles yet fertile for conflict.

Actually the leaders of the Cuban delegation had already contacted their Russian allies on June 8, 1966, saying that their "participation ed [sic] Puerto Rico under threat as the USA authorities not permitting Cuban team aircraft landing."[79] It also seems that the Cubans had contacted their allies in the island, the MPI, and informed them of their decision to travel by ship, because on June 10 a boat carrying Juan Mari Brás, Norman Pietri, and Ángel Silén went to receive the *Cerro Pelado* in open waters.[80] Mari Bras, Pietri, and Silén were not directly connected to sport, the government or the organizing committee but were known proindependence Puerto Rican leaders, sympathetic to the Cuban Revolution, and vocal about their defiance of US imperialism. In effect, it looked like the Cubans were lining up their "chess pieces" just in case they needed protection. When local authorities were informed that the Cuban vessel was just outside the international water-border, threatening a political disaster, they once more contacted emerging Puerto Rican Olympic leader Rieckehoff Sampayo to intervene between the Puerto Rican government and the Cuban leaders.

Rieckehoff Sampayo, along with other Puerto Rican authorities that included Secretary of State Lastra and Puerto Rican athletic legend Eugenio Guerra, boarded the US Coast Guard ship *Peacock,* under a downpour and great pressure from the public and press, to meet the *Cerro Pelado*. As they approached the Cuban ship, and in a moment of Caribbean and Latin American brotherhood, the Cubans cheered the Puerto Rican delegation while also playing through the speakers of the ship songs of Puerto Rican singer and Latin American sensation Tito Lara.[81] Once they reached the Cuban ship—considered Cuban territory—it took the Puerto Rican delegation, with passports in hand and on rough Atlantic waters, over an hour to board it. The Puerto Ricans were received by Capt. Cornelio Pino Izquierdo, while Rieckehoff Sampayo discussed the situation with Minister of Education José Llanusa, González Guerra, and others.[82]

The instructions given to Rieckehoff Sampayo by Gov. Sánchez Vilella were to allow the Cubans to enter the island with their visas but to not allow the ship to cross into US waters. After both sides discussed these terms for over an hour, Rieckehoff Sampayo, who had graduated from the University of Puerto Rico Law School in 1952, proposed an idea to try to dissuade them from bringing the ship into San Juan harbor. His theory was bold, as he confronted the Cuban Revolution with the exiles in Puerto Rico: "This vessel is property of the Cuban government that was seized from the property of many Cubans who currently live in Puerto Rico, without proper law procedure. If this vessel enters Puerto Rican waters and, under the Laws of Admiralty, a Cuban initiates action against the Cuban government, this ship gets detained in assurance statement and many years will pass in which it will stay in Puerto Rico under arrest."[83]

Reacting to this "theory" by Rieckehoff Sampayo, the Cubans stopped negotiations and "scribbled something to the telegraphist." During this recess in the negotiations, the Puerto Ricans were served with coffee and Cuban tobaccos. Meanwhile, it is probable that the Cubans took this opportunity to raise their complaint to their Soviet bloc allies because Brundage received emergency telegrams from the leaders of the Hungarian, Bulgarian, Romanian, and Soviet Olympic Committees. Andrianov, president of the Soviet Olympic Committee, cabled Brundage, "Ask urgent IOC official assistance for Cuban teams enter Puerto Rico."[84] The Cubans, as during the missile crisis four years before, were fully backed by their communist allies.

Nevertheless, this stressful moment was dissipated when, after some minutes, the telegraphist returned with a piece of paper for Llanusa. After reading it the Cuban delegation said, "We are ready to get off and leave the ship here."[85] It is uncertain what that piece of paper said, and it is uncertain what influence Brundage might have played in all of this, but at the end of this tense moment of sport diplomacy, the Cubans decided to leave the ship in international waters and transport the delegation to land by other means. We do have the following statement from the vice president of the COC Armando Riva Patterson from that afternoon: "The Cuban Olympic Committee considers it a great victory for sports and the Olympic movement the entrance of the Cuban delegation in San Juan Puerto Rico. . . . Once again the ever so clear ideas of the renewer of the Olympic Games Baron Pierre de Coubertin have triumphed and have put in evidence all those who really intend in a permanent manner to mix politics with sports. . . . We expect great success from these games that constitute part of the history of the nations located in Central America and the Caribe."[86] In this way, while claiming sport victory, the Cuban delegation washed its hands of political intervention by announcing its peaceful attendance at the games. By doing this, its members thought they were protecting Olympism by overcoming political obstacles. Nonetheless, they knew that real political tension on the island still persisted, warning the Puerto Rican authorities and the members of the IOC that "different groups of Cuban exiles resident . . . have proclaimed their purpose to attack our delegation."[87]

The actual transportation of the delegates began at 5:00 a.m. the next day, June 11, the day of the opening ceremonies. Dramatically and under great public pressure, several private boats went to the *Cerro Pelado* to pick up the athletes, an ordeal that lasted more than four hours. After going through customs and immigration, they were taken by bus to the opening ceremony. The fact that the Cubans were able to land peacefully on the island was not the end of the confrontations but just the beginning of the conflicts on land.

The reception of the Cubans in San Juan was full of different reactions. Some reporters indicated that the Cuban athletes were very cordial and talkative yet would not speak about politics.[88] The only Cuban representative who expressed his political dissatisfaction at the games was Llanusa, who, as soon as setting foot on one of the local boats on its way to port, accused the United States of "interfer[ring], obstruct[ing] and delay[ing]" Cuba's participation at the games.[89] Throughout the bus trip to the opening ceremonies at Hiram Bithorn Stadium, the delegation was received with crowds alongside the road by two groups: the first showing signs of support—led by the MPI—that read "Fatherland or Death, We Will Win" and "Greetings Cuban Athletes,"[90] and other groups showing hostility—led by the Cuban exiles—with signs that read, for example, "Russians Go Home." It is interesting to see the clear Cold War political alignment of these groups when the MPI used the Cuban revolutionary slogan, and the Cuban exiles wrote their sign in English referring to the Cubans as Russians.

Regardless of this political friction, the opening ceremony was realized without any major problems at 3:00 p.m. before a crowd of 19,262 spectators.[91] The official fanfare of the games was composed by Puerto Rican music idol Rafael Hernández. The opening of the games included the hoisting of the flags of the CACG, the IOC, and the city of San Juan. A chorus of a hundred voices sang the official hymns of the games, including the popular song "En Mi Viejo San Juan," to which the crowd also sang along.[92] The CACG symbolic torch, known as Fuego Azteca, reached the stadium after arriving from Mexico on June 1 and was run across the island.[93]

Despite this air of national and regional confraternity, and despite the fact that these games are known today for being peaceful and uneventful, there were moments of friction between Cuban athletes, Cuban exiles, anti- and pro-Castro Puerto Ricans. One of the most covered incidents, the one that produced the most drama, was the only known voluntary defection by a Cuban athlete at these games. Juan Pablo Vega Romero, a wrestler, defected at midnight on Sunday, June 12, not only because he was against Castro's communism[94] but because according to him there was no racial equality in Cuba.[95] Quickly after defecting from the Olympic Village, Vega Romero was taken to the US Immigration Services district offices, where he also declared wanting to be taken to the United States. Since Puerto Rico is a US territory, there is no legal difference in refugee status between the two places in cases of defection.

There was another incident with a "defector." Initially, it started as a rumor when it was reported that an athlete by the nickname "Chiqui" was trying to defect and reunite with her exiled parents who lived in Puerto Rico.[96] The reporter assured that she was being held prisoner and isolated in the Olympic Village. However, this version was later rebuked by Llanusa, who declared that the athlete, María Cristina González, was actually "rescued from unknown individuals" in a car who had tried to kidnap her.[97] She was later taken to the *Cerro Pelado* "for her safety." These rumors of defection were constant, as Llanusa dismissed the alleged seventeen defections of female athletes who tried to jump off of a Puerto Rican bus to ask for asylum.[98]

Encouragement to defect can be said to have been a systematic project to attack Castro's communist government during the games in San Juan. There was even a Puerto Rican governmental plan in place—involving the local police, the Immigration Service, and the State Department—before the games started in case of Cuban athlete defectors.[99] There was a lot of pressure from the Puerto Rican public, the media, and Cuban exiles on Cuban athletes to defect. As a matter of fact, the majority of the Cuban delegation received some sort of monetary offer to defect and make declarations against Castro's regime.[100] According to COC president González Guerra, the radio station WIAC transmitted the show of Torres Velázquez, who exhorted Cuban athletes under "provocative and offensive" expressions to defect, giving phone numbers to individuals who would give food and shelter to up to twenty-five athletes for up to thirty days. The initiative was called "Operation Jump to the Side of Freedom."[101] Moreover, according to González Guerra, the tone of the radio program offended Cuban women by calling their men "sons of blank."[102] Yet insults of "communists" were of no offense to them.

It is difficult to ascertain how many Cuban athletes were tempted to defect in San Juan, since there was absolutely no conversation about it among them due to fear of the Cuban secret police, which had allegedly infiltrated the delegation.[103] But the pressure to defect was even exerted by Puerto Rican police at the Olympic Village, who constantly invited the Cubans to "begin their flight to freedom."[104] Leaflets, handouts, and newspapers were taken to the village inviting the Cuban athletes to defect. Even priests approached some delegates persuading them to leave communist Cuba and stay in Puerto Rico, while at some games the loudspeakers announced—apparently false statements—that more Cuban athletes kept defecting. As if that was not enough, even during a bus trip from the Olympic Village to the Olympic pool there was pressure to defect. The bus driver made unplanned stops at the sport facilities of the University of Puerto Rico and later at a private house on Ponce de León Avenue that had a sign reading "Refugio" (Shelter). The bus driver then opened the door of the bus and asked the passengers, "Doesn't anybody get off here?"[105]

Invitation and pressure to defect were not the only "acts of aggression" against the Cuban delegation in Puerto Rico. There were also physically violent moments. For example, one member, Luis de Cárdenas, was attacked by a "paid agent." When the police came, they actually held De Cárdenas so that the "paid agent" could keep hitting him.[106] Moreover, during a basketball practice of the Cuban team at a private high school, Colegio Espíritu Santo, a group of *contrarrevolucionarios* provoked and attacked them, "forcing" the Cubans to fight back. At the end of the incident, a local policeman confirmed that the attack was provoked by "Cuban exiles."[107] Furthermore, the MPI upheld its sworn defense of the Cuban athletes when at a soccer match in the Baldrich neighborhood they got involved in a shoving match with a group of Cuban exiles.[108] On top of that, and more seriously, a car pulled into the Olympic Village, and two passengers "threatened" some Cuban delegates, who, reacting to the threat, made one of the aggressors drop a pistol.[109]

This gun incident was not the only one involving firearms. José Llanusa indicated that on two occasions four individuals attempted to murder him. In the first attempt, the individuals were driving an Impala and held a rifle; in the second, the same individuals, now driving a Comet, possessed handguns.[110] Reacting to these murder attempts, Llanusa denounced them as "exclusively guided by the Central Intelligence Agency of the United States." Additionally, he said that the Cuban exiles "were not directly responsible," implying that these individuals were more like puppets of the CIA who got paid to do their work.[111] But Llanusa stated that it was the constant provocations to defect—more than violent attacks—that constituted a "psychological war" against the Cuban delegation.[112]

## Conclusion

The violence and hostility at the X CACG of 1966 in San Juan, more than reflecting Cold War tensions, was a real measure of East-versus-West competition. Cuba and Puerto Rico embodied Cold War rivalries between the Soviet bloc and the United States in the athletic field and in the streets of San Juan. Indeed, the incidents outlined above tell the story of how

Puerto Rico was the site of another major war-threatening moment in twentieth-century Caribbean and Central American history.

Moreover, a deeper issue for Latin American history is that these games proved the colonial condition of Puerto Rico. Puerto Ricans, while being the protagonists and hosts of the games, became de facto subalterns to the State Department and even the IOC due to the imposed granting of the visas to the Cubans. While the Puerto Ricans' intention was to prove to their Latin American and Caribbean neighbors that they were in fact autonomous enough to host these games, what actually became evident was that their alleged political modernization came with a costly prize: continued colonialism. The imposition of the visas against the wishes of the Puerto Rican authorities demonstrated that in Puerto Rico the ultimate control over its governance lay outside the island.

The MPI was clear about Puerto Rican colonialism, and that is why it was so active during these games and overall throughout these years. On the other hand, a growing sector of the pro-US-statehood *estadista* movement also noticed this blatant political subjugation and actively attacked the commonwealth. Puerto Rican senator Arturo Ortiz Toro openly declared that "Fidel Castro has ridiculed the Commonwealth government" at the X CACG. He went on to specify his point: "The ridicule of the Puerto Rican people consists in that making claims of sovereignty, invites the Cuban athletes with great fanfare, and when they get to barely 3 miles from our beaches, a simple order by a subaltern employee of the Coast Guard stops the Cuban vessel outside our shores. This is evidence that there is no Puerto Rican sovereignty."[113]

This *estadista* movement was well known for being anti-Castro and anticommunist, in addition to anticolonialist. While there are other countries in Latin America and the Caribbean that had similar opposition to Castro's regime and that followed the broken diplomatic policies of the United States with Cuba, the fact is that Puerto Rico is the only "country" to which the United States could do this legally, unilaterally, and without questions. Nonetheless, this colonial condition of Puerto Ricans did not impede them from participating in the global context during the Cold War, characterized as it was by subtle, yet volatile events.

Although the story of Central American and Caribbean Olympism has not received deserved attention in both historical scholarship and studies of contemporary politics, it is hoped that this chapter sheds light on the real and compelling drama this region has faced. The Tenth Central American and Caribbean Games in San Juan were a premier example of Latin America and Caribbean Olympism that showed pressing and high-stakes diplomacy. Although Avery Brundage had to deal with more prominent issues during his IOC presidency, his many diplomatic maneuvers at this time show that he did pay enough attention to the Central American and Caribbean area.

Finally, when the games were over, Puerto Rico had finished in the third position overall, behind Mexico and Cuba—although they actually won more total medals than Cuba, they had fewer gold medals. This proved without a question that the Puerto Rican nation was still strong, competitive, and powerful in Latin American and Caribbean sport. Although this nationhood was colonial and subordinated, it was, nevertheless, real for many. The X CACG legitimized to Puerto Ricans the "progress" of Puerto Rican Olympism. All the obstacles to make Puerto Rico visible among the nations of the world had been conquered. From this moment on, amid persisting colonialism and Cold War conflicts, there was no looking back. Puerto Rican Olympism had been officially consolidated.

## Notes

The author wishes to thank the following individuals for their comments and suggestions at different stages in the production of this chapter: Dain Borges, Emilio Kourí, Agnes Lugo-Ortiz, Nicole Ream-Sotomayor, the members of the Latin American History Workshop at the University of Chicago, Andrew Johns, Heather Dichter, William Beezley, Brenda Elsey, and the anonymous reviewers for this anthology. Thanks also to the staff at the following archives: the University Archives of the University of Illinois at Urbana-Champaign; Archivo Fundación Luis Muñoz Marín in San Juan; Archivo General de Puerto Rico in San Juan; the National Archives and Records Administration in Washington, DC; and the Colección Puertorriqueña at the University of Puerto Rico at Río Piedras. This chapter was written with the financial support of a Mellon Foundation/Social Science Division dissertation fellowship at the University of Chicago.

1. For a documented summary of Puerto Rico's performance at the Central American and Caribbean Games since 1930, see Carlos Uriarte González, *80 años de acción y pasión: Puerto Rico en los Juegos Centroamericanos y del Caribe, 1930 al 2010* (San Juan: Nomos Impresores, 2009).

2. John Hutchinson, "Cultural Nationalism and Moral Regeneration," in *Na-*

*tionalism*, ed. John Hutchinson and Anthony Smith (Oxford: Oxford University Press, 1994), 122–31, and Partha Chatterjee, *The Nation and Its Fragments: Colonial and Postcolonial Histories* (Princeton, NJ: Princeton University Press, 1993).

3. John MacAloon, "La pitada Olímpica," in *Text, Play, and Story: The Construction and Reconstruction of Self and Society*, ed. Edward M. Bruner (Washington, DC: American Ethnological Society, 1984).

4. Félix R. Huertas González, *Deporte e identidad: Puerto Rico y su presencia deportiva internacional (1930–1950)* (San Juan: Terranova Editores, 2006).

5. This is best analyzed and shown in Laurent DuBois, *Soccer Empire: The World Cup and the Future of France* (Berkeley: University of California Press, 2010), 50.

6. R.C. No. 8, "Resolución conjunta para crear el Comité Olípico de Puerto Rico," in *50 años de Olimpismo*, ed. Joaquín Martínez-Rousset (San Juan: Editorial Edil., 2003), 73–75.

7. For a discussion of the Cuban Missile Crisis, see Aleksandr Fursenki and Timothy Neftali, *One Hell of a Gamble: Khrushchev, Castro, and Kennedy, 1958–1964: The Secret History of the Cuban Missile Crisis* (New York: Norton, 1998), and Don Munton and David A. Welch, *The Cuban Missile Crisis: A Concise History* (New York: Oxford University Press, 2007).

8. See José Trías Monge, *Puerto Rico: The Trials of the Oldest Colony in the World* (New Haven, CT: Yale University Press, 1997).

9. See Brooke Thomas, "A Constitution Led by the Flag," in *Foreign in a Domestic Sense: Puerto Rico, American Expansion, and the Constitution*, ed. Christina Duffy Burnett and Burke Marshall (Durham, NC: Duke University Press, 2001), 82–103.

10. See Efrén Rivera Ramos, *The Legal Construction of Identity: The Judicial and Social Legacy of American Colonialism in Puerto Rico* (Washington, DC: American Psychological Association, 2002).

11. Roberta J. Park, "'Forget about That Pile of Papers': Second World War Sport, Recreation and the Military on the Island of Puerto Rico," *International Journal of the History of Sport* 20, no. 1 (March 2003): 50–64, and Roberta J. Park, "From *la Bomba* to *Béisbol:* Sport and the Americanisation of Puerto Rico, 1898–1950," *International Journal of the History of Sport* 28, no. 17 (December 2011): 2575–93.

12. See James Dietz, *The Economic History of Puerto Rico: Institutional Change and Capitalist Development* (Princeton, NJ: Princeton University Press, 1986), 86–99.

13. See Miñi Seijo Bruno, *La insurrección nacionalista en Puerto Rico, 1950* (San Juan: Editorial Edil, 1997).

14. See Trías Monge, *Puerto Rico*, 107–18, and Juan R. Torruella, "One Hundred Years of Solitude: Puerto Rico's American Century," in *Foreign in a Domestic Sense: Puerto Rico, American Expansion, and the Constitution*, ed. Christina Duffy Burnett and Burke Marshall (Durham, NC: Duke University Press, 2001), 241–50.

15. William L. Ryan, "Puerto Rico, Once Poor, Is Prospering: Called Showcase of the Caribbean," *Chicago Daily Tribune,* October 14, 1962, A1. See also Dietz, *Economic History*, 240–310.

16. See Cesar J. Ayala and Rafael Bernabe, *Puerto Rico in the American Century: A History since 1898* (Chapel Hill: University of North Carolina Press, 2007), 202.

17. Jaime Plenn, "Surge movimiento para eliminar a Cuba," *El Mundo,* May 10, 1962, 37. According to Plenn, IOC member José de Jesús Clark Flores intended to travel to Jamaica for a meeting with the organizing committee but could not ensure that this topic would be covered. Plenn also stated that the recent visit by Brundage to Mexico was related to the Cuban situation but did not expand on it. Nevertheless, Plenn reported that Mexican sport leaders were confident that if such an exclusion were stated, Mexico would oppose it. He ended the article saying that former Cuban Olympic Committee members then in exile declared that the exclusion would not be based on political ideology but solely on the organization of the Cuban Olympic Committee, which was denounced as being an "organism of the Cuban state." I have not found more information on the matter. Only further research would provide more insight to fully understand the political and ideological reasons behind it and its connections to Latin American and Caribbean politics.

18. Jess Losada, "Caso de Cuba ante los Juegos Centroamericanos y del Caribe," *Boletín Deportivo, Unión Deportiva Cuba Libre* 2, no. 3 (April 1965): 1, 6, Section VI, Senator by Accumulation, Series 17, Miscellaneous Archive, Folder 273.3, Tenth CACG, Administration of Parks and Recreation, Archivo Fundación Luis Muñoz Marín, San Juan, Puerto Rico (hereafter AFLMM).

19. Letter to Avery Brundage, February 10, 1960, Avery Brundage Collection, Series No. 26/20/37, Box 199, University of Illinois Archives, Urbana, IL (hereafter UIA).

20. Antonio Cañas, "Juegos Deportivos Centroamericanos y del Caribe," Section VI, Senator by Accumulation, Series 17, Miscellaneous Archive, Folder 273.3, Tenth CACG, Administration of Parks and Recreation, AFLMM.

21. Memoria X Juegos Centroamericanos y del Caribe, 11–25 de junio de 1966, Section VI, Senator by Accumulation, Series 17, Miscellaneous Archive, Folder 273.3, Tenth CACG, Administration of Parks and Recreation, AFLMM.

22. For a biography of Roberto Sánchez Vilella, see Celina Romany Siaca, *La verdadera historia de Roberto Sánchez Vilella* (San Juan: Ediciones Puerto, 2011).

23. I refer here to a significant group of Cuban exiles in Puerto Rico who were not only openly anti-Castro and anticommunist but violently active after 1967. Certainly not all Cuban exiles in Puerto Rico were violent anticommunists, but those who were had the backing of the Puerto Rican government. See José M. Atiles Osoria, "Pro-State Violence in Puerto Rico: Cuban and Puerto Rican Right-Wing Terrorism from the 1960s to the 1990s," *Socialism and Democracy* 26, no. 1 (March 2012): 127–42.

24. "Este Gobierno se opone decididamente a que venga un equipo cubano a Puerto Rico a participar en dichos juegos mientras el presente régimen cubano gobierne en aquella isla. No creemos que su presencia pueda servir propósito alguno sino que, por el contrario, tendría a crear una situación difícil e intolerable en el país." Draft of "Letter to the Governor" by Roberto Sánchez Vilella to Julio E. Mona-

gas, Delegación cubana a Juegos Centroamericanos—1966, April 17, 1964, Sección VI, Section VI, Senator by Accumulation, Series 17, Miscellaneous Archive, Folder 273.3, Tenth CACG, Administration of Parks and Recreation, AFLMM.

25. Ibid.

26. "Puerto Rico será libre por la lucha de su pueblo y la solidaridad de todos los pueblos de este continente y del mundo. . . . Puerto Rico será libre como lo será Vietman del Sur, que está luchando contra el imperialismo norteamericano, y como lo serán Angola y Venezuela." As cited in letter from Sánchez Vilella to the governor, ibid.

27. *"Sátrapa":* a subordinate official. *Traidorzuelo*: a sort of insignificant traitor.

28. See Ayala and Bernabe, *Puerto Rico*, 160, 167.

29. Ibid., 227.

30. "Puerto Rico Ignored Nikita's Colonial Tag," *Chicago Daily Tribune,* September 25, 1960, 6.

31. Victor Riesel, "Pekin's Agents in Puerto Rico," *Los Angeles Times,* April 8, 1964, A5.

32. Draft of "Letter to the Governor" by Roberto Sánchez Vilella to Julio E. Monagas, Delegación cubana a Juegos Centroamericanos—1966, April 17, 1964, Sección VI, Section VI, Senator by Accumulation, Series 17, Miscellaneous Archive, Folder 273.3, Tenth CACG, Administration of Parks and Recreation, AFLMM.

33. Ibid., 2–3.

34. "Olympic Recognition of Cuba Clouds Puerto Rican Games," *New York Times,* August 29, 1965, S4.

35. Rule 25 of the Olympic Charter basically states that there must be no political interference or discrimination by any NOC or at any Olympic competition. For a detailed chronology of events of this controversy in the case of Puerto Rico, see letter to the IOC, September 22, 1956, Avery Brundage Collection, Series No. 26/20/37, Box 146, UIA.

36. Joaquín Martínez Rousset, "Visas para los cubanos," *El Mundo,* February 22, 1965, 17.

37. Phrased *"problema de gobierno a gobierno"* and *"pintado de rojo"* in ibid.

38. Ibid.

39. See Allen Guttmann, *The Games Must Go On: Avery Brundage and the Olympic Movement* (New York: Columbia University Press, 1984).

40. As quoted in Juan Cepero, "El problema de P.R. es muy complicado: Brundage," *El Mundo,* February 24, 1965, 13.

41. R. Santiago Sosa, "Secretario de Estado de PR Dr. Lastra reafirma decisión de no pedir visas para cubanos," *El Mundo,* February 25, 1965, 41.

42. Ibid.

43. Juan Cepero, "Declara don Julio Enrique Monagas 'Puerto Rico no le ha ofrecido a nadie la sede de los X Juegos,'" *El Mundo,* February 22, 1965, 17.

44. Joaquín Martínez Rousset, "Este cohete no llegó a la luna," *El Mundo,* February 24, 1965, 13.

45. "Brundage Is Critical of Excluding Cuba Athletes," *Santa Barbara News-Press,* February 24, 1965, E-5.

46. Juan Cepero, "Sec General de FAIA promete ayudar a resolver caso de PR y los X Juegos," *El Mundo,* February 26, 1965, 41.

47. "Caracas Resolution," Caracas, March 16, 1965, Avery Brundage Collection, Series No. 26/20/37, Box 199, UIA.

48. Letter to Mr. Avery Brundage, March 30, 1965, Avery Brundage Collection, Series No. 26/20/37, Box 199, UIA.

49. Confidential letter to Avery Brundage, n.d., Avery Brundage Collection, Series No. 26/20/37, Box 199, UIA.

50. Letter addressed to ODECABE, COPUR, and Comité Organizador de los X Juegos Centroamericanos y del Caribe, n.d., Avery Brundage Collection, Series No. 26/20/37, Box 199, UIA.

51. Letter to Mr. A. Illueca Sibauste, April 15, 1965, Avery Brundage Collection, Series No. 26/20/37, Box 199, UIA.

52. The CACG in Kingston was also the scenario for conflict between Puerto Ricans and Cubans reflecting Cold War and Caribbean politics. For example, a fight broke out in a Cuba versus Puerto Rico baseball game on August 14, 1962, at Sabina Park, after the three groups (Puerto Ricans, Cuban athletes, and Cuban exiles) exchanged politically charged insults. Needless to say, the events at Kingston constituted a charged and direct preamble to the heated situation in San Juan four years later. For more on the Kingston Games of 1962, see chapter 9 in Antonio Sotomayor, "Playing the Nation in a Colonial Island: Sport, Culture, and Politics in Puerto Rico," PhD diss., University of Chicago, 2012.

53. Jamaica Cabinet Submission (JCS), "Entry of Cubans into Jamaica," January 10, 1962, cited in Jana K. Lipman, "Between Guantánamo and Montego Bay: Cuba, Jamaica, Migration and the Cold War, 1959–1962," *Immigrants and Minorities* 21, no. 3 (November 2002): 37.

54. Ibid., 32–33.

55. Letter to Avery Brundage, September 5, 1965, Avery Brundage Collection, Series No. 26/20/37, Box 199, UIA.

56. Letter to Ing. José de J. Clark Flores, November 17, 1965, Avery Brundage Collection, Series No. 26/20/37, Box 199. UIA. See also Informe semanal No. 41, October 5–13, 1965, Administración de Parques y Recreos Públicos, Fondo Oficina del Gobernador, Serie Informes Semanales de los Jefes de Agencias de Gobierno al Gobernador de Puerto Rico, 1965–1968, Archivo General de Puerto Rico. It seems also probable that Rieckehoff Sampayo had a role in making Puerto Rican Olympic and sport institutions change their policy regarding the Cubans' visas. See Raúl Mayo Santana, *El juguete sagrado: Germán Rieckehoff Sampayo* (San Juan: Editorial Plaza Mayor, 2000).

57. Juan Manuel Ocasio, "Lastra: Hands Off Policy for Cubans," *San Juan Star,* November 11, 1965.

58. Cable to Mr. Torregrosa, December 5, 1965, Avery Brundage Collection, Series No. 26/20/37, Box 199, UIA.

59. As presented in Memorandum, December 11, 1965, Avery Brundage Collection, Series No. 26/20/37, Box 199, UIA.

60. Letter to Felicio Torregrosa, December 13, 1965, Avery Brundage Collection, Series No. 26/20/37, Box 199, UIA.

61. Cable to Felicio Torregrosa, December 15, 1965, Avery Brundage Collection, Series No. 26/20/37, Box 199, UIA, and then later in an official letter, January 5, 1966, Avery Brundage Collection, Series No. 26/20/37, Box 199, UIA.

62. Letter to Avery Brundage, December 15, 1965, Avery Brundage Collection, Series No. 26/20/37, Box 199, UIA.

63. Ibid.

64. Ibid.

65. Letter to Mr. K. Andrianov, Comité Olympique d'U.R.S.S. Skatertnyj 4, Moscow, Avery Brundage Collection, Series No. 26/20/37, Box 199, UIA.

66. See Ayala and Bernabe, *Puerto Rico,* 226–29.

67. This letter was actually written by Narciso Gabell Martínez, mission chief of the MPI in Cuba, for *Granma.* "Los atletas cubanos no estarán solos: Denuncia el MPI las maniobras del imperialismo contra Cuba en los Juegos Centroamericanos," *Granma,* March 24, 1966, Avery Brundage Collection, Series No. 26/20/37, Box 85, UIA.

68. Letter to Avery Brundage, February 22, 1966, Avery Brundage Collection, Series No. 26/20/37, Box 199, UIA.

69. Letter to Monagas, March 21, 1966, Avery Brundage Collection, Series No. 26/20/37, Box 199, UIA.

70. See Mayo Santana, *El juguete sagrado,* 180–81.

71. "Cuba Accuses U.S. of Attempt at Blackmail," *Chicago Daily Tribune,* June 30, 1966, B10.

72. Ibid.; Morris W. Rosenberg, "'Threats' at the Games Here," *San Juan Star,* July 1, 1966, 1, 14; and "Cuba Rejects U.S. Visa Plan for Games in Puerto Rico," *New York Times,* April 23, 1966, 23.

73. "Lo asociado le impide ser libre . . . ," "Temas del día," Cuban newspaper clipping found in Avery Brundage Collection, Series No. 26/20/37, Box 85, UIA.

74. Personal report by Avery Brundage, June 30, 1966, Avery Brundage Collection, Series No. 26/20/37, Box 199, UIA.

75. The alleged political interference was a "so-called 'Olympic Oath' and the hymn of the 1st National Sport Games" and other politically oriented statements made by some sports leaders as published in *Granma,* October 21, 1965. Letter to Comité Olímpico Cubano, February 16, 1966, Avery Brundage Collection, Series No. 26/20/37, Box 85, UIA.

76. Letter to Avery Brundage, March 30, 1966, Avery Brundage Collection, Series No. 26/20/37, Box 199, UIA.

77. Ibid.

78. Meeting of the Executive Board of the IOC, April 21–24, 1966, Avery Brundage Collection, Series No. 26/20/37, Box 84, UIA.

79. Cable to Avery Brundage from Moscou URSSGOVT, Avery Brundage Collection, Series No. 26/20/37, Box 199, UIA.

80. Ramón Rodríquez, "Revelan Yate MPI salió tras cubanos," *El Mundo,* June 10, 1966, Avery Brundage Collection, Series No. 26/20/37, Box 199, UIA.

81. Rafael López Sosa, "Acusa a E.U. de interferir con cubanos," *El Mundo,* June 13, 1966.

82. See transcription of interview with Rieckehoff Sampayo in Mayo Santana, *El juguete sagrado,* 176–80.

83. "Este barco es propiedad del gobierno de Cuba, el cual se ha incautado de la propiedad de muchos de los cubanos que viven en Puerto Rico, sin el debido procedimiento de ley. Si este barco entra a las aguas de Puerto Rico y, bajo la ley de almirantazgo, un cubano inicia una acción contra el gobierno de Cuba, este barco queda arrestado en aseguramiento de sentencia y van a pasar muchos años en que el mismo va a estar en Puerto Rico bajo arresto." As quoted in Mayo Santana, *El juguete sagrado,* 179.

84. Cable sent to Avery Brundage from Moscou, Avery Brundage Collection, Series No. 26/20/37, Box 199, UIA.

85. "Estamos listos para bajar y dejamos el barco aquí." As quoted by Rieckehoff Sampayo in his interview with Mayo Santana. Mayo Santana, *El juguete sagrado,* 179.

86. Cable to Avery Brundage, June 10, 1966, Avery Brundage Collection, Series No. 26/20/37, Box 199, UIA.

87. Ibid.

88. Rafael López Rosas, "Acusa a E.U. de interferir con cubanos," *El Mundo,* June 13, 1966.

89. "Interferir, entorpecer y retrasar," ibid.

90. "Leading the Chant," *San Juan Star*, June 1966. Courtesy Carlos Uriarte González.

91. The only political "incident" at the opening ceremonies consisted of the Dominican Republic flag being hoisted only halfway by their NOC president, in protest of the presence of the international peacekeeping forces in the Dominican Republic.

92. For a complete overview of the X CACG, including scores, teams, sports, and other statistical information, see Uriarte González, *80 años de acción,* 111–37.

93. Memoria X Juegos Centroamericanos y del Caribe, June 11–25, 1966, Section VI, Senator by Accumulation, Series 17, Miscelaneous Archive, Folder 273.3, Tenth CACG, Administration of Parks and Recreation, AFLMM.

94. Rafael Collazo, "Atleta cubano pide asilo politica P.R.," *El Día,* June 14, 1966, Avery Brundage Collection, Series No. 26/20/37, Box 199, UIA.

95. "Alega régimen Castro puso ELA en ridículo," *El Mundo,* June 22, 1966, 19, Avery Brundage Collection, Series No. 26/20/37, Box 199, UIA.

96. Guillermo Hernández, "Creen que está incomunicada atleta cubana quiere quedarse en P.R.," *El Imparcial,* June 22, 1966, Avery Brundage Collection, Series No. 26/20/37, Box 199, UIA.

97. Salvador Guzmán, "Llanuza dice frustra 2 atentados a su vida," *El Imparcial,* June 24, 1966, 3, Avery Brundage Collection, Series No. 26/20/37, Box 199, UIA.

98. Ibid.

99. Letter from Dr. Carlos Lastra to Salvador Rodríguez Aponte, Police Superintendent, June 3, 1966, Office of the Governor Collection, Weekly Reports of the Chiefs of Agencies of the Government to the Governor of Puerto Rico, General Archive of Puerto Rico.

100. This is according to the COC's president Manuel González Guerra, which José de J. Clark certified as true and accurate. See letter from Manuel González Guerra to Emilio Huyke, June 14, 1966, Avery Brundage Collection, Series No. 26/20/37, Box 199, UIA.

101. "Operación Salto a la Verja de la Libertad."

102. "Hijos de tal cosa." Letter from Manuel González Guerra to Emilio Huyke, June 14, 1966, Avery Brundage Collection, Series No. 26/20/37, Box 199, UIA.

103. This is according to defector Juan Pablo Vega in an interview after his defection. See Ismael Fernández, "Revelan hay agentes secretos delegación cubana," *El Día,* June 14, 1966, Avery Brundage Collection, Series No. 26/20/37, Box 199, UIA.

104. Letter from Manuel González Guerra to Emilio Huyke, June 14, 1966, Avery Brundage Collection, Series No. 26/20/37, Box 199, UIA.

105. Ibid.

106. Ibid.

107. Ibid.

108. Miranda Antonio, "Alega el MPI tergiversó incidente," *El Mundo,* June 21, 1966, 15, Avery Brundage Collection, Series No. 26/20/37, Box 199, UIA.

109. Letter from Manuel González Guerra to Emilio Huyke, June 14, 1966, 3, Avery Brundage Collection, Series No. 26/20/37, Box 199, UIA.

110. Salvador Guzmán, "Llanuza dice frustra 2 atentados a su vida," *El Imparcial,* June 24, 1966, 5, Avery Brundage Collection, Series No. 26/20/37, Box 199, UIA.

111. Ibid.

112. Ibid.

113. "Senador Ortiz Toro alega régimen Castro puso ELA en ridículo," *El Mundo,* June 22, 1966, 19, Avery Brundage Collection, Series No. 26/20/37, Box 199, UIA.

# 8

# "Our Way of Life against Theirs"

## Ice Hockey and the Cold War

### *John Soares*

By March 1968, Canadians were sick of losing international hockey competitions to the Soviet Union. Hockey was their national game; even the Russians recognized Canada as "the homeland of hockey."[1] But the USSR had started a streak of world championships in 1963 that was unmatched since the International Ice Hockey Federation (IIHF) began holding annual tournaments in 1930.[2] Olympic hockey doubled as the world tournament in Olympic years, and the Soviet gold medal in the Winter Games at Grenoble the previous month had increased its streak to five straight world titles.[3] Not only were the Canadians losing to the Soviets—even Czechoslovakia had started finishing ahead of Canada regularly. To combat the damage this losing was doing to Canada's image abroad, Ambassador Robert A. D. Ford wrote from Moscow to urge Ottawa to encourage a visit to the USSR by a National Hockey League (NHL) team. Not only was the NHL North America's top professional league—its players were almost all Canadians. In some stretches during the 1960s, there was only one non-Canadian playing in the entire league.[4]

Ford knew NHL players were far superior to the Canadian amateurs who were losing international competitions to the Soviets. His memo to the foreign ministry argued that "even one exhibition match by a good

Canadian pro hockey team here would do more for Canadian prestige in this country than all the rest of our 'cultural' efforts put together." Among that year's programs was a trip to Moscow by the Royal Winnipeg Ballet; Ford warned that "bringing ballet to the Bolshoi [Theater] will be . . . at best ineffective, at worst embarrassing." Subsidizing an NHL team's trip to Moscow "would be infinitely more worthwhile." An NHL team's visit, Ford wrote, "would create more interest than anything since the Battle of Stalingrad."[5]

Ford's comments reveal hockey's significance to Cold War politics and propaganda. Not only did Canada's hockey performance affect its prestige in the USSR, Ottawa's embassy in Prague reported that "hockey is the most potent single factor with the widest and most immediate impact on our relations with Czechoslovakia."[6] In fact, Canadian diplomats worried about the impact of hockey on their country's image in much of Europe, writing to Ottawa to express their concerns about popular reaction to Canadian teams touring the USSR, Czechoslovakia, Sweden, Finland, and West Germany. Ford's hope that a "good Canadian pro hockey team" would visit the USSR alluded to another Canadian concern: even though the overwhelming majority of NHL players were Canadian, most NHL teams were located in the United States. Expansion starting in the late 1960s placed an even larger percentage of league clubs there.[7] Ottawa's diplomats feared that Canadian players representing US cities would promote "a North American continental image" among Europeans, rather than recognition of Canadian distinctiveness.[8]

Scholars such as Walter Hixson, Gregory Mitrovich, Kenneth Osgood, and Scott Lucas have described the aggressive use of propaganda and psychological warfare in US efforts to defeat the Soviets and the Eastern bloc.[9] David Caute, Penny Von Eschen, and others have written about the importance the Americans and Soviets attached to cultural rivalry in such fields as music and dance.[10] In this "unconventional" Cold War, sports in general and hockey in particular were part of the effort to generate favorable attention in other nations. The United States, Canada, and Britain tried to create positive publicity through broadcast networks such as Voice of America, the BBC's Overseas Service, and Canadian Broadcasting's International Service. These platforms circumvented state- and party-controlled Eastern bloc media—and "Moscow spent huge sums on jamming radio signals" to counter them[11]—but a hockey team could generate positive publicity even through adversaries' normal media channels. This was true both for communist bloc coverage of teams from NATO countries and Western media treatment of Warsaw Pact athletes. Television broadcasts, for example, would display the skill of Canadian players to Soviet viewers and of Soviet players to North American audiences. Soviet sportswriters often contrasted the high culture of Soviet players with the thuggery of their capitalist rivals, and Soviet media coverage of an international tournament sometimes simply evaporated when the Soviets were losing.[12] Still, the outstanding talents of Canadian players were often evident even in coverage by Soviet newspapers such as *Pravda, Izvestia,* and *Sovietsky Sport.* And the skill of Soviets led to flattering copy in newspapers such as the *New York Times* and Toronto's *Globe and Mail.*

Sports were so important that Western diplomats worried about international competitions and communist regimes devoting lavish resources to them. Sport permitted a nation to win propaganda victories without triggering military countermeasures or crackdowns on dissidents in opposing countries; sports victories did not encourage the "false expectations that produced fruitless uprisings and loss of life," which Hixson called "the central contradiction of psychological warfare."[13] Competitive sport permitted a society's representatives to charm and dazzle adversaries, much like musicians and artists did, but it also brought more direct comparison with more objective measures than other forms of cultural competition. Reasonable listeners might dispute the relative merits of jazz, ballet, Copland, and Shostakovich, but it was easy to tell which side won a hockey game.

Because hockey was so important to Canada and Czechoslovakia, its study helps us move beyond the East-West bipolarity in understanding the Cold War.[14] Canada was a NATO ally of the United States and Britain, and Ottawa valued its connections to Washington and London. It coordinated its radio propaganda with American and British efforts to project favorable images of democratic capitalist life to all of Europe— pro-Western, neutral, and communist-controlled.[15] Still, Ottawa wanted to be recognized as an independent force in world affairs. Hockey was one endeavor in which Canada could be the world's best and in the process distinguish itself from its British and especially its American allies. To promote Canada's image, Ambassador Ford argued it was "absolutely essential" that the first NHL team to visit the USSR be "clearly identified as Canadian."[16]

For Czechoslovakia, the desire to maintain independence from its superpower ally was even more pronounced. And sport was important to Prague, which used it for explicit propaganda purposes. During the 1960s and 1970s, the Czechoslovak Olympic Committee published a magazine—in English, French, German, and Spanish—celebrating its athletes.[17] *Czechoslovak Sport* had subscription agents in nineteen countries in Europe, Africa, Asia, and the Americas.[18] Soccer might have been the most popular spectator sport in the country, and the Czechoslovak national soccer team had some great moments in international competitions, but Czechoslovak national hockey teams were frequent medalists at world competitions, regularly contended for top honors, and often beat the world's best. The Soviet streak of consecutive world championships in progress when Ford was writing in 1968 continued until Czechoslovakia took the title in 1972; by 1976–77 some observers thought the Czechoslovaks were on the verge of surpassing the USSR as the world's top amateur hockey nation. Under the circumstances, the sport had a powerful cultural importance in Czechoslovakia, especially as a form of defiance after the 1968 Soviet-led invasion.

While Canada and Czechoslovakia used hockey to demonstrate their independence from their respective superpower allies, the Soviets used their dominance of IIHF events for their own propaganda purposes. This, of course, was the Kremlin's intention with its sports program: Joseph Stalin had refused even to permit Soviet entry into international competitions without a *guarantee* of victory from Soviet sport officials.[19] Soviet officials demonstrated the importance they attached to sport by devoting substantial resources to the pursuit of gold medals—and by boasting that these victories proved the superiority of their system. The army and secret police clubs were essential components of the national hockey program, further demonstrating the program's importance to the regime. In Ford's estimation, "international sport in the USSR [was] at least ninety per cent political."[20]

While the Canadians, Soviets, and Czechoslovaks all staked claims to world hockey dominance, the less successful Americans nonetheless were frequent Olympic medalists. Few in the United States boasted that hockey ever proved the superiority of the American way of life, but like their Canadian counterparts US diplomats took seriously the attitudes of spectators from the host countries at international hockey games. They saw political significance, for example, in such things as Czechoslovak fans cheering for the Americans when they played the USSR in Prague in the 1959 world tournament.[21] During the 1963 world championships, John F. Kennedy provided more compelling evidence of the attention hockey received at the highest levels. After seeing a newspaper report about the US team's 17–2 loss to Sweden, he called aide David Hackett about the tournament. Kennedy grumbled, "Christ, who are we sending over there, girls?" He instructed Hackett to find out more about who was responsible for this "disgrace," telling Hackett that "we shouldn't send a team unless we can send a good one."[22] Hackett responded—the very next day—with a memo informing Kennedy that the Amateur Hockey Association (AHA) of the United States would be better organized and have a more talented, better coached team for the 1964 Olympics, where the US squad "will be a good team and will be representative of this country."[23]

The involvement of Canada, the USSR, Czechoslovakia, and the United States at the highest levels of international hockey contributed to the sport's unique position in the cultural Cold War. It was a team game, played in Europe, North America, and Japan, in which individual skill could be decisive. It was popular in geopolitically important nations, and it appeared to be a test of different social systems that resonated with fans in those countries—a major segment of those populations. Heightening hockey's political relevance were the close parallels between national hockey programs and their nation-states, with state-directed programs in communist nations battling privately run programs from capitalist democracies. In the American and Canadian programs, there were no central direction and little government involvement, and various private organizations often worked at cross-purposes while trying to develop national teams. This contrasted sharply with the situation in the USSR, where Soviet coaches consciously promoted a distinctively communist style of play in a centralized program that enjoyed unprecedented Olympic and world championship success.

Hockey was a particularly useful form of Cold War propaganda because it could be touted as a fair, objective measure of different societies' ability to develop talent. People on both sides of the Iron Curtain treated fan reactions during the Cold War as a useful insight into the genuine popular mood among residents of other nations. And because of what hockey tells us about rivalries within blocs, it is a useful reminder that there was much more to the Cold War than just the rivalry between the United States and Soviet Union.

## Hockey's Geopolitical Resonance

During the Cold War, hockey was played in the nations that were most important in the rivalry between communism and capitalist democracy. All but one of the Warsaw Pact members, all European neutrals, and almost all NATO democracies participated in at least one Olympic hockey tournament (see table 8.1).[24] When Ottawa wanted diplomatic support for the Canadian Amateur Hockey Association (CAHA) campaign to change IIHF eligibility rules, it sent cables to its diplomats in fifteen European countries, plus the United States, Japan, and Australia.[25] Sixteen European countries were on Ottawa's distribution list when highlight films from the NHL's Stanley Cup playoffs were available to embassies.[26]

Canada dominated world competition in its national game from its inception at the 1920 Olympics through 1952. In these years Canadian teams won six of seven Olympic gold medals and fifteen of eighteen world titles.[27] Even though the USSR won the world title at its first tournament appearance in 1954 and claimed gold at its Olympic debut in 1956, Canada remained the most dominant power through the early 1960s with world titles in 1955, 1958, 1959, and 1961. But after Sweden, the 1957 champion, won another title in 1962, the Soviets launched their era of domination. From 1963 through 1990, the Soviets won twenty of twenty-five world tournaments and six of seven Olympic gold medals.

Czechoslovakia emerged as the Soviets' stiffest competition in these years. It broke the USSR's string of titles in 1972. In 1976 and 1977 it became the only nation other than Canada or the USSR to win consecutive world championships. The Czechoslovaks added another title in 1985. The United States was not often considered a major hockey power during these years, and its teams rarely finished in the top three at world championships, but Americans had a long tradition of medaling in Olympic hockey. In fact, while the 1950s are thought of as years that began with Canadian domination and ended with the USSR taking over, at the 1952, 1956, and 1960 Olympics the United States won the most impressive collection of medals and had the best record in head-to-head meetings among these three nations (see table 8.2). American teams medaled at five

**Table 8.1.** Olympic Ice Hockey Finishes, 1948–1988

| Country | 1948 | 1952 | 1956 | 1960 | 1964 | 1968 | 1972 | 1976 | 1980 | 1984 | 1988 |
|---|---|---|---|---|---|---|---|---|---|---|---|
| Australia | — | — | — | 9 | — | — | — | — | — | — | — |
| Austria | 7 | — | 10 | — | 13 | 13 | — | 8 | — | * | 9 |
| Bulgaria | — | — | — | — | — | — | — | 12 | — | — | — |
| Canada | *1* | *1* | *3* | *2* | 4 | *3* | — | — | 6 | 4 | 4 |
| Czechoslovakia | *2* | 4 | 5 | 4 | *3* | *2* | *3* | *2* | 5 | *2* | 6 |
| Finland | — | 7 | — | 7 | 6 | 5 | 5 | 4 | 4 | 6 | *2* |
| France | — | — | — | — | — | 14 | — | — | — | — | 11 |
| Germany, East | — | — | — | — | — | 8 | — | — | — | — | — |
| Germany, West | — | 8 | 6 | 6 | 7 | 7 | 7 | *3* | 10 | 5 | 5 |
| Great Britain | 5 | — | — | — | — | — | — | — | — | — | — |
| Hungary | — | — | — | — | 16 | — | — | — | — | — | — |
| Italy | 8 | — | 7 | — | 15 | — | — | — | — | * | — |
| Japan | — | — | — | 8 | 11 | 10 | 9 | 9 | 12 | — | — |
| Netherlands | — | — | — | — | — | — | — | — | 8 | — | — |
| Norway | — | 9 | — | — | 10 | 11 | 8 | — | 11 | * | 12 |
| Poland | 6 | 6 | 8 | — | 9 | — | 6 | 6 | 7 | 8 | 10 |
| Romania | — | — | — | — | 12 | 12 | — | 7 | 9 | — | — |
| Sweden | 4 | *3* | 4 | 5 | *2* | 4 | 4 | — | *3* | *3* | *3* |
| Switzerland | *3* | 5 | 9 | — | 8 | — | 10 | 11 | — | — | 8 |
| United States | ** | *2* | *2* | *1* | 5 | 6 | *2* | 5 | *1* | 7 | 7 |
| USSR | — | — | *1* | *3* | *1* | *1* | *1* | *1* | *2* | *1* | *1* |
| Yugoslavia | — | — | — | — | 14 | 9 | 11 | 10 | — | * | — |

Medal-winning finshed are bolded and italicized.
* At Sarajevo in 1984 four teams did not qualify for the final or the consolation pool and received no final ranking despite competing.
** The United States finished fourth in 1948, but it was considered an unofficial participant because of a dispute between the AAU and AHA.
*Source:* Dan Diamond, ed. *Total Hockey*, 2nd ed., and offical Olympic reports.

of eight Winter Olympics from 1952 through 1980, including gold medals in 1960 and 1980.[28]

Canada's association with hockey meant the sport was central to that nation's prestige and public image in much of Europe. Hockey was only one facet of Canada's Cold War cultural diplomacy, as demonstrated in prior references to CBC's International Service and the Royal Winnipeg

**Table 8.2.** United States, Canada, and the Soviet Union in the Olympics, 1952–1960

RESULTS
1952
Oslo, Norway
      Canada 3, USA 3 (tie)
          Gold: Canada
          Silver: USA

1956
Cortina d'Ampezzo, Italy
      USA 4, Canada 1
      USSR 4, USA 0
      USSR 2, Canada 0
          Gold: USSR
          Silver: USA
          Bronze: Canada
1960
Squaw Valley, California, USA
      USA 2, Canada 1
      USA 3, USSR 2
      Canada 8, USSR 5
          Gold: USA
          Silver: Canada
          Bronze: USSR

STANDINGS IN HEAD-TO-HEAD MEETINGS IN THESE OLYMPIADS

| Country | GP | W | L | T | Pts. | Winning % |
|---|---|---|---|---|---|---|
| USA | 5 | 3 | 1 | 1 | 7 | .700 |
| USSR | 4 | 2 | 2 | 0 | 4 | .500 |
| Canada | 5 | 1 | 3 | 1 | 3 | .300 |

HOCKEY MEDAL COUNT IN THESE OLYMPIADS

| Country | Gold | Silver | Bronze |
|---|---|---|---|
| USA | 1 | 2 | 0 |
| Canada | 1 | 1 | 1 |
| USSR | 1 | 0 | 1 |

*Source:* Offical Olympic reports.

Ballet's tour of the USSR. Still, most of Ottawa's cultural concerns centered on "protecting [Canada] against the enormous degree of penetration of its society by American culture." In policy terms, this was an essentially domestic issue.[29] Moreover, Canadian officials understood that whatever their efforts at cultural diplomacy, few events generated as much publicity for Canada as a visit by a Canadian team, even if it was not the nation's representative at a world or Olympic tournament. In the USSR, games with Canadian teams were seen as a test of communism and capitalism; even though Soviet citizens knew about professional hockey, Ford reported that "the great majority of Russians are under the impression that the Canadian teams which come here are Canada's best."[30] Thus Soviet victories were seen in the USSR as triumphs over Canada's top players and teams, even when this was far from true.

Hockey had ramifications for Soviet perceptions of Canada, but Canadian diplomats stationed in Czechoslovakia also found "hockey fans throughout this country . . . eagerly turn every conversation with a Canadian into a hockey discussion."[31] They warned of the "political consequences" of any "defeat of Canada by a Russian team at Canada's national sport."[32] Demonstrating the link in the popular mind between Canada and hockey, an official in the Czechoslovak city of Brno told a Canadian diplomat that youngsters on their way to hockey practice "do not say they are going to the hockey rink but rather they are 'going to Canada.'"[33] During the late 1960s, ambassadors in a number of European countries, including the USSR, Sweden, Czechoslovakia, West Germany, and Finland, flooded Ottawa with correspondence lamenting the poor performance, and sometimes worse behavior, by touring Canadian hockey teams.[34]

As West Germany's inclusion on this list suggests, hockey was important to Canada's image even in countries that were not Olympic powers in the sport. More than a decade of experience in West Germany taught a Canadian diplomat that "there is almost no Canadian activity which attracts more publicity here."[35] Finland had never medaled at an Olympic or world tournament when the embassy in Helsinki reported that the 967 column inches local media devoted to just two games by a visiting Canadian hockey club in January 1968 was "more than the total press coverage Canada received during the months of October, November, and December 1967."[36] Poland often competed in the world tournament's B pool, where it was not even eligible for the world championship, but a leading Polish sports newspaper claimed that Poles paid "careful" attention to the NHL and its stars, "and the dream of every Polish boy is to be a Maurice Richard, Gordie Howe, Bobby Hull, or Stan Mikita."[37] NHL highlight films were popular even in nations that were not hockey powers, such as Belgium, Denmark, Italy, the Netherlands, and Yugoslavia.[38] In Japan too hockey was important to Canada's image, especially in connection with the 1972 Winter Olympics in Sapporo. Canada by that time had withdrawn from IIHF competitions—including the Olympics—for reasons discussed below, but Japanese organizers understood the financial importance of attendance at hockey games and Canada's box office appeal. Japanese organizers' effort to arrange for a Canadian team at Sapporo received serious attention in both foreign ministries.[39]

## Amateurism, Professionals and Propaganda

Not only did Canada lose international hockey dominance to the USSR as the 1960s progressed, but the growing strength of Czechoslovakia and Sweden made it increasingly difficult for Canada even to medal in world and Olympic events. Canadian frustration mounted, especially because eligibility rules mocked any notion of fairness in sports. The IIHF required that all players in world or Olympic tournaments be amateurs, but neither it nor the IOC applied a consistent standard of amateurism. Canada was the only hockey nation open about its top players' professionalism, and it suffered against nations able to use their best players.[40]

The "shamateurism" of communist bloc athletes is a well-known topic in sport history.[41] In the example of Soviet hockey, players trained full-time, eleven months a year, and received salaries and perks among the most generous in the communist world.[42] Elite athletes moved to the front of long lines for cars and the most desirable housing. They had opportunities for foreign travel rarely enjoyed by Soviet citizens. And with foreign travel came opportunities to profit from smuggled black-market goods and currency manipulation; athletes rarely had to worry about close scrutiny from customs and immigration officials—especially those who played regularly for the Central Army or Dinamo (secret police) clubs. While these athletes were nominally army officers or graduate students or employed in some trade, they trained full-time in their sport. As former Soviet national team captain Boris Mikhailov remembered, "I went from a private to lieutenant colonel but didn't do any army stuff."[43] Although its athletes trained full-time in their sports and were compensated as if among the elite in their society, the Soviet government claimed they were all amateurs.

Soviets often complained bitterly when critics pointed out that their approach to amateurism was a sham, but in private they sometimes conceded their athletes were not really amateurs.[44] One Soviet sports official in 1967 even admitted that a hockey game between the USSR and an NHL club—unlike one with Canadian amateurs—would be "a fair game between professionals."[45] And Soviet citizens at the time understood the professionalism of their nation's athletes. As early as 1950, the Soviet satirical magazine *Krokodil* lampooned this aspect of Soviet sport with a cartoon that showed an office where each employee's nameplate had two titles: a job title and a soccer position. Only one bona fide worker was in the office; through the window his "colleagues" were visible—out on the soccer pitch.[46] A *Krokodil* article in April 1952 complained that the best soccer players were being transferred to the clubs of the army, air force and secret police.[47] In 1969 *Pravda* even published a letter from workers on a collective farm (*kolkhoz*) complaining that their soccer team consisted of players who did no work at the farm but "receive[d] their salaries exactly on time."[48] The same professionalism and influence of clubs connected to state security organs that was part of Soviet soccer was present in other sports, including hockey.

The Soviets had great success manipulating rules of amateurism, but this practice was not limited to communist regimes. Sweden and Finland used company teams to pass off their best hockey players as amateurs. At the height of the crisis over amateurism at world hockey championships, IOC president Avery Brundage agreed that it "seem[ed] ridiculous" for the IIHF to permit the Soviets, Czechoslovaks, Swedes to participate while excluding the Canadians.[49] The other nations could use their best hockey players in world and Olympic tournaments, but Hockey Canada president Charles Hay estimated in 1970 that Canada had so many professionals ineligible that it competed at amateur events with a team no better than its thirty-first best.[50]

Unhappiness over this motivated Canada's campaign starting in the late 1960s to change IIHF rules. Canadian hockey officials wanted IIHF to conduct "open" competitions in which each nation could use its best players, pro or amateur.[51] In the summer of 1969 the IIHF reached the so-called Crans agreement permitting Canada to play nine minor leaguers at the 1970 world tournament.[52] But the deal came apart two months before the tournament. The Europeans, encouraged in the fear by IOC officials, worried their players would be ineligible for the 1972 Olympics if they competed against professionals at a world tournament.[53] The Europeans therefore reneged on the Crans agreement. In response, Canada withdrew from IIHF competitions and vowed not to return until it could use professionals.[54] This finally happened in 1977. In the interim, though, after considerable diplomatic wrangling and some international rules changes, the Canadians arranged competitions in which their professionals met the best Soviets (and Czechoslovaks and Swedes).

These competitions began with the 1972 Summit Series, eight games matching NHL all-stars against the Soviet national team. They continued in such events as the eight-game Canada-USSR series in 1974,[55] the 1975–1976 "Super Series" in which two Soviet elite league clubs played NHL teams in North America, the 1979 Challenge Cup matching the NHL all-stars and the Soviet national team, and the Canada Cup tournaments, which gave the very best hockey-playing countries in the world the chance to use their very best players regardless of where or in what league they played and whether they were amateur or professional.[56] Canada Cup tournaments were held in 1976, 1981, 1984, 1987, and 1991.

While Canada's professionals fared much better than its amateurs against the Soviets, the USSR nonetheless performed well against Canada's best. The Soviets actually outscored the Canadians in the 1972 Summit Series even though Canada won, 4–3–1. The Soviets won the 1974 Canada-USSR series, won most of the games in the 1975–1976 Super Series, humiliated the NHL all-stars in the deciding game of the 1979 Challenge Cup, won the Canada Cup in 1981, and lost only in 1987 after a heroic rally by the Canadians.

And, win or lose, regardless of opponent, the Soviets used hockey to good propaganda effect. As Ford wrote about competitions with Canadian amateurs, "when the Russians win easily the comment inevitably in the press, on TV, by spectators is that once again they have proved the superiority of the communist system over free enterprise."[57] Ford observed that "the sight of tired and sometimes disorganized Canadians trailing the Russian players lends itself rather effectively to this sort of propaganda."[58] Although the Soviets lost the Summit Series, Canada only prevailed after winning the last three games, each in Moscow and each by a one-goal margin. That the series was so close, Soviet writers explained, had "destroyed" the "myth of Canadian pros' invincibility." But more important, the Soviets claimed the Canadians had won only because they played dirty. The Soviet press denounced the Canadians for "'Foul play,' 'Hooliganism' and 'Unethical playing.'"[59] Soviet press coverage emphasized that the Canadians were "professionals," a term viewed with distaste; these professionals, many of whom had not finished high school, were compared unfavorably to the USSR's educated, cultured, amateur "sportsmen."[60] They suggested professional hockey encouraged a "brutal and dirty way of playing."[61] Professionals were driven "to win at all costs." Toiling in a capitalist system driven by the need for profits, they might even "deliberately initiate fights in order to entertain their spectators."[62]

Russians too young to read would have understood the Soviet magazine *Krokodil*'s cartoons denigrating hockey professionals. One showed a professional hockey player with a boxing glove attached to the butt end of his stick. Another series of cartoons started with the professionals' team bus arriving for a game, the second frame showed the bus being painted with a red cross logo to indicate it was being turned into an ambulance, and the final frame showed a number of injured, bandaged players climbing aboard after the game.[63]

The Soviet press not only lamented the ills of professionalism, it also gave great attention to any Canadian conduct it found objectionable—and ignored similar conduct by Soviet players. For example, the only photograph that accompanied *Izvestia* coverage of the dramatic final game of the Summit Series showed Canadian J. P. Parise threatening a referee with his stick—an incident that happened very early in the game and earned Parise an ejection.[64] Soviet coverage of the 1974 Canada-USSR series exaggerated the number of Russian players who were injured and attributed all real and imagined injuries to the Canadians' dirty play. In that 1974 series, Soviet media coverage treated Gordie Howe's gracious refusal to blame the Soviets for his injured knee as objective evidence of the Russians' fair play. Perhaps their most ridiculous claim revolved around the mask of Canadian goaltender Gerry Cheevers. Cheevers decorated his plastic facemask with painted stitches to mark the places where he would have been cut had he not worn it. The Soviets claimed the fact that Cheevers had added no stitches to his mask during the series proved that the Soviets played cleanly, when it only proved that nothing had hit his mask—not even pucks or inadvertent sticks from his own teammates.[65]

Perhaps the most entertaining single example of Soviet propaganda came in reaction to the Central Army's loss to the Philadelphia Flyers in the final game of the 1975–1976 Super Series. This was a much-anticipated matchup of the defending Stanley Cup champions, then in their heyday as the intimidating "Broad Street Bullies," and the defending Soviet elite league champions. The Flyers' physical play caused so much controversy that the Red Army club withdrew from the ice and threatened to quit the game during the first period. Eventually the Soviets returned and were defeated, 4–1.[66] A subsequent cartoon in the communist youth league newspaper—accompanying a story emphasizing the Soviet club's victory in the Super Series—depicted the Flyers as giant, cudgel-wielding monsters.[67]

Soviet media coverage emphasized the thuggish villainy of the Canadian hockey players. Admittedly, the Canadians often played a rougher and more violent game. But the Soviets committed their own illegalities, preferring sneaky, hidden cheap shots to the more overt physical confrontation of the Canadians. The Soviets were rarely, if ever, the innocent victims portrayed in Soviet media. In fact, the Soviet hockey press explained as uniquely Canadian—or capitalist—villainy even things done by Soviet players in their own elite league matches. In a disgruntled message to Ottawa in November 1974, the Canadian embassy complained about an illustrative incident. During a game between the Central Army and the Soviet Wings, an Army player responded to a penalty call by threatening the referee with his stick. The embassy reported that the official was afraid; he did not see this as mere theatricality but a real threat of violence. The episode, however, "received no publicity in the Soviet press."[68] Yet it was virtually identical to Parise's outburst in the final game of the Summit Series and far worse than the Canadian conduct that had drawn such bitter criticism during the 1974 Canada-USSR series.

## Middle Powers off the Ice—Superpowers On

For the Soviets, hockey was a simple matter of celebrating their own triumphs and denouncing capitalist villainy. For Czechoslovakia the sport was more complicated. Hockey served the regime's propaganda needs in various ways. For example, after one victory over Canadian professionals, the Czechoslovak coach claimed that the game "demonstrated the superiority of the Marxist-Leninist approach to Socialist hockey over the Canadian rough style of play."[69] Czechoslovak authorities even used Soviet hockey victories as proof of communism's superiority. Despite the enmity created by the Soviet invasion, *Czechoslovak Sport* featured the

Soviet hockey team prominently in its preview of the 1972 Winter Olympics, singling out Soviet hockey for special notice in its celebration of the "Medals Won by Countries of the Socialist Camp at the Winter Games since 1948."[70]

Prague's propaganda use of Soviet hockey success was best exemplified by a Czechoslovak-produced film about the Soviets' victorious debut at the 1954 world tournament. The Canadian embassy considered the movie "a masterpiece of propaganda," particularly effective because it "never seemed to be trying to make propaganda." The film showed the Canadians as confident "world-beaters," "mobbed" by Czechoslovak fans, stars with menial helpers looking after their equipment. In contrast, the humble Soviets, shown taking care of their own gear, easily outmatched the overconfident Canadians when they finally met on the ice. Despite the effectiveness of the propaganda, the Canadian observer figured that "the inferior position relegated to the Czechoslovak team in the film must have been galling to many in the audience." The observer even noted that some Czechoslovak fans were unusually "excited" during scenes showing Canadians delivering hard body-checks to Russians—likely not the reaction intended by the regime.[71]

As the reaction to the body-checks suggests, Prague risked attaching too much propaganda importance to Soviet hockey success. On at least two occasions in the 1950s, Western embassies reported rumors—apparently widely believed in Czechoslovakia—that Czechoslovakia's hockey team had lost its world tournament game to the USSR deliberately.[72] On an even larger scale, Czechoslovak fans believed that the 1950 arrest of as many as eleven national team members had been an act of deliberate sabotage by the regime, which damaged Czechoslovak hockey to make it easier for the USSR to win medals when it began competing in IIHF events.[73] In fact, that purge badly damaged Europe's strongest team. Before the arrests, Czechoslovakia had won the first world title after World War II, in 1947; finished second to Canada in 1948; and in 1949 become the first continental European nation to win a world championship at which Canada had competed. Following the purge, the Czechoslovaks did not return to their prior position in world hockey until the late 1960s.

Once Soviet tanks rolled into Czechoslovakia in August 1968, there was little chance any Czechoslovak team would stand accused of deliberately losing to the Soviets. Hockey, though, still caused problems for Prague. As is discussed in more detail below in the section "The Complexity of Intra-Alliance Relations and the Importance of Fans," Czechoslovak fans celebrated their hockey victories over the USSR at the 1969 world champions with such fervor that the Soviets used the episode to help hardliners install a new, more pliant leadership in Prague. In addition, the Czechoslovak government complained publicly about its own fans' behavior at a game with the USSR in the 1970 world tournament in Stockholm, although it claimed the misbehaving fans "obviously . . . included people who have left our fatherland."[74] Czechoslovak players openly displayed hostility to the USSR during their Olympic meeting with the USSR at Sapporo in 1972. Although the two teams were known for their speed and finesse, one veteran of twenty years in the NHL and the WHA[75] who saw the game said, "I've never seen a hockey game more brutal than that. The Czech goalie must have broken five sticks over Russian players."[76] Late in the game, with Czechoslovakia hopelessly behind, star Vaclav Nedomansky deliberately fired a puck at the Soviet team bench.[77]

Nedomansky caused even more headaches for Prague two years later when he defected to play professionally in the WHA. *Sports Illustrated* considered him "the most famous Communist-bloc athlete to defect to the West since 1956."[78] Defectors ordinarily received little attention in the Eastern bloc media, but not long after Nedomansky's defection the Czechoslovak national team played an exhibition against Team Canada in 1974. The absence of such a big star demanded explanation, so Prague went on the offensive. It publicly announced the defection, denouncing "the despicable practices of the Canadian hockey profiteers" and lamenting that Nedomansky "preferred the lure of quick gain and succumbed to the hockey capitalists."[79]

Nedomansky was not only one of the highest-profile defectors to the West, he also was one of the few hockey players who left a communist hockey power for North America. Not a single Soviet hockey player defected to the West before 1989, which was the same season Kremlin authorities started to permit select Soviet players to join NHL teams.[80] Czechoslovak players came with some greater frequency but still not in large numbers: when Mikal Pivonka joined the Washington Capitals before the 1986 season, he was the seventeenth Czechoslovak player to leave for the NHL.[81] Complicating the situation with Czechoslovak hockey players was the fact that not all who came to North America defected: Prague would permit players to join North American pro teams when they were over thirty and less useful to the national squad. This started with Jaroslav Jirik in 1969–1970.[82] Other aging Czechoslovak stars also played in the NHL or WHA, with Prague's approval, while some of their younger countrymen decided not to wait until they were old enough to leave with government approval.[83]

Unlike Czechoslovakia, Canada did not have to worry about defectors. But it did have to worry both about results on the ice and the conduct of its players. Canadian rules permitted much more body-checking than international rules (before a major change in 1969 brought IIHF rules into line with Canada's). Even in international games Canadians often played a much rougher and more physical style than the Europeans. As a result, "there [was] a tendency on the part of European players (and spectators) to interpret the Canadian type of play as deliberately dirty and unsportsmanlike."[84] Canadian diplomats expended considerable effort in the 1950s and 1960s to educate European audiences about the Canadian style of play; this included screenings of NHL highlight films. They wanted Europeans to understand Canadians always played tough and physical, even—especially—against each other.

Yet it was not just the Canadians' physical play that offended Europeans. Canadians, in general, tended to be more emotional and demonstrative on ice and more willing to argue with referees. Many Canadian clubs traveled abroad, even after the establishment of the national team; many players on these squads seemed not to understand the potential diplomatic significance of their actions on and off the ice, despite efforts by the foreign ministry to provide briefings for teams traveling overseas. For example, in one case in Sweden a Canadian player "renewed a fight in the penalty box," was ejected from the game, then "started to attack the public with his stick" until police got involved.[85] In another instance, the conduct of a touring Canadian team from Drummondville so angered German hosts that the local sports press nicknamed the team the "Drummond Villains."[86] As has been mentioned previously, foreign ministry files contain numerous telegrams and letters from embassies documenting the damage done to Canada's prestige and reputation by the antics of touring hockey teams.

Despite these problems, hockey sometimes brought beneficial publicity for Canada—even when the Canadians lost. The 1976 *Izvestia* tournament in Moscow demonstrated the positive and negative ways hockey could affect public perceptions of Canada. The WHA's Winnipeg Jets became the first professional team to represent Canada at that prestigious tournament. The Jets were led by aging superstar Bobby Hull and by emerging Swedish star Anders Hedberg. Hedberg was one of the first Swedish players to enjoy success in a North American professional league and one of eight Swedes on the Jets roster.[87] Winnipeg finished a disappointing fourth-place in the five-team field, losing to Czechoslovakia and the USSR, tying Sweden, and defeating only Finland. According to the Soviet press, the Jets' losses to the USSR and Czechoslovakia proved Canadian professionals could not keep up with communist programs, even after pilfering players from other nations.[88] The Soviet press also mocked Winnipeg for that dependence on foreign players, noting the "paradoxical" Jets-Sweden matchup in which "Swedes played against Swedes."[89]

Despite all this, though, Hull's appearance in Moscow was a goodwill triumph. He was already well known to Soviet hockey fans. His book, *Hockey Is My Game* (originally published in 1967), had been translated into Russian.[90] Postcards with his picture sold at hockey arena kiosks alongside those of Soviet stars.[91] *Sovetskii Sport* published a very favorable portrait of Hull in connection with the *Izvestia* tournament. It mentioned his three NHL scoring championships, his long stardom with the Chicago Black Hawks, and his legendary 120-mile-per-hour slap shot—helpfully translated for Soviet readers into the more impressive sounding 200 kilometers per hour. The article also noted the Canadian press's praise for the thirty-seven-year-old Hull's play in the previous September's Canada Cup.[92]

While in Moscow the Winnipeg star gave a press conference attended by fifty Soviet journalists; he praised the achievements of Soviet hockey and even said he was thinking about leaving his son in Moscow to learn from Soviet coaches.[93] *Izvestia* published a translated transcript of his remarks.[94] The Jets were so well received that an Air Canada official with long experience arranging sports tours to Moscow reported the Jets' send-off was the only time he had ever seen Soviet officials smiling at a tour group—an indication of the genuine goodwill that a sports tour could produce.[95]

## Hockey Replicates Communist Centralization—
## and Democratic Openness

As the Winnipeg Jets' performance in the *Izvestia* tournament showed, sport was a form of publicity and propaganda that could work to the advantage of any participating country—not just the victors. Yet it often served the USSR's purposes. The Soviets won a lot, and propagandists could properly claim their victories were a genuine achievement for the communists. While in fields such as ballet, classical music, and physics the Soviets built on established Russian traditions, in hockey the communists had started a new program in a new endeavor. The Russian Empire had not competed in IIHF hockey; Russians had played a ball hockey game on a larger ice surface but did not start playing "puck hockey" until the communist period.[96] More important, communist ideology was crucial to the program's success.

The man who emerged as the program's chief architect was a communist true-believer who considered the hockey program the practical application of communist ideology.[97] Anatoli Tarasov coached Moscow's Central Army Club, which served as the nucleus of the national team in addition to being a perennial power in the Soviet elite league. The training regimen for the national team included communist indoctrination. Players were encouraged to join party organizations such as the communist youth group *Komsomol*. Tarasov recognized that the Soviets lagged behind the Canadians in the development of individual skills and tried to neutralize this advantage by playing *kollektivnii khokkei* (collective hockey). Soviet *khokkeisti* were reminded that failure to work for the collective good was, in Tarasov's words, "a violation of one of the main principles of communist morals."[98] The Soviet national team's style, according to a Canadian government report, was "characterized by team play, discipline, precision-passing, superb conditioning, the masterful execution of fundamentals of skating, puck and body control, and an emphasis on clean body contact."[99] The emphasis on passing and team play, in contrast to the Canadian cultivation of individual skills, sharpened the differences in hockey between the capitalists and communists.

While the Central Army was a perennial power in the Soviet elite league and the nucleus of the national team, the secret police club in Moscow (Dinamo) was usually the elite league's second strongest; it also was an important contributor to the national team. The national team sometimes drew players from the Leningrad army club. Among teams not affiliated with the army or secret police, the perennially strong Spartak club was coached by Tarasov's national team colleague Arkady Chernyashev. Another frequent power in the Soviet elite league was an aviation trade union club, Wings of the Soviet (Krylia Sovetov).[100] Except for the Leningrad Army, all of these teams were based in Moscow. National team coaches could observe players in person and make informed selections for the national team.[101] The concentration of national team players on a handful of elite league clubs enabled many players to spend the entire year playing (and practicing) with their national team line-mates. And Soviet hockey officials structured the elite league schedule to ensure that the national team had ample time to prepare as a unit for Olympic and world tournaments—and later on, meetings with Canadian professionals. Tarasov took players from other clubs' development systems before they reached the elite league but generally left them with their clubs once they had reached the elite league. After Viktor Tikhonov took charge of the Central Army and the national team in 1977, he routinely took players for the Central Army who had broken into the league with other clubs.[102] At that point, almost all of the national team players were together year-round.

Soviet sports clubs had youth hockey programs as well, enabling boys as young as ten to learn the sport and the style elite Soviet coaches would demand. The Soviets claimed broad-based participation made their sports programs so successful, but young Soviet players had virtually no chance of making it to an elite league club unless they came up through one of the clubs' developmental programs. There were opportunities for community-based recreational hockey for ordinary Russians but nothing that offered a realistic chance of leading to a spot on the national team.[103]

Just as the Soviets could credibly claim that their hockey program was a communist success, a dispassionate observer could point out that Canada's struggles—and the US decline after 1980—were capitalist failings. In both nations, private organizations were responsible for the national hockey program. And in both countries these organizations and the individuals running them often pursued contradictory aims. For example, geographic squabbles were a more routine part of US hockey. Easterners, centered around Boston, and westerners, mostly from Minnesota and Michigan's Upper Peninsula, had disagreements, especially over the selection of the US Olympic team. Separate tryout camps were held for eastern and western players, and the makeup of Olympic rosters could be influenced by politics and a desire for sectional balance.

Examples of private entities in democracies working at cross-purposes could be found throughout the Cold War. The most outlandish occurred at the St. Moritz Winter Games in 1948, when the AHA and the Amateur Athletic Union (AAU) both sent hockey teams that purported to be *the* US Olympic team. The resulting crisis nearly caused cancellation of the hockey competition.[104] Professional clubs were private entities that lured the best American players away from amateur ranks—and Olympic eligibility. For example, in 1979 Joe Mullen was arguably the best American amateur, but a family emergency led him to sign a professional contract that summer, rendering him ineligible for the 1980 Olympics.[105] In the spring of 1983, Americans Brian Lawton and Tom Barrasso were two of the top five picks in the NHL entry draft, but both signed pro contracts that summer rather than play for the United States at the 1984 Olympics.[106] Even players who remained amateurs might not play in the Olympics. In the summer of 1971, US coach Murray Williamson missed a flight to Moscow—to visit and learn from Tarasov—because of a meeting with Boston College all-American Tom Mellor. Williamson wanted to see Mellor because the star's college coach "had advised him to stay in school" rather than play for the 1972 Olympic team.[107] Williamson ultimately convinced Mellor to represent his country. But as an American coach, he did not have his Soviet colleagues' inducements to ensure the nation's best players were on the Olympic roster—he could only hope to persuade some free young (amateur) men to follow him.

Canadian hockey faced similar problems and divisions. Through 1963 CAHA fielded no true national team. Instead it would select a "senior amateur" team of players over age twenty who were not playing professional hockey and add some players to strengthen the entry. Teams such as the Winnipeg Falcons, Kitchener-Waterloo Dutchmen, East York Lyndhursts, Penticton Vees, and Trail Smoke Eaters would appear as "Canada" at Olympic or world tournaments. The defending Allan Cup winners, as champions of Canadian senior amateur hockey, were usually selected, but for years any top Canadian senior amateur team could dominate the international competition. Success, though, became much harder to attain once the Soviets arrived. Starting with the 1963–1964 season, Canada developed a national team program, inspired and directed by a onetime NHL prospect who had become a Catholic priest, Father David Bauer.[108]

Father Bauer's aim was to build a team of amateur players who would study at a Canadian university while practicing and playing together.[109] He hoped his players would compete successfully and, win or lose, impress the international hockey community with their gentlemanly conduct. This latter point was particularly important given Canada's long history of sending teams abroad that antagonized the Europeans. In the pre–national team era, Canadian clubs had toured Europe often wearing uniforms that identified them as "Canada," but this practice continued even after the Canadian national team was in operation. These teams often lost and played badly, and embassies in various European countries sent back "strenuous representations" complaining about "fourth-rate hockey teams damaging the Canadian image during visits to Europe."[110] Canadian diplomats wanted Ottawa to convince the CAHA to take steps to stop these embarrassments. Canada's ambassador in Sweden grew so unhappy over the damage visiting Canadian teams were doing to his nation's image that he informed Ottawa he would not host an official embassy reception for any Canadian hockey team playing in the 1967 Ahearne Cup competition other than the national team, in "an attempt to reduce the inescapable association" of Canada with an inferior visiting club.[111]

While Canadian diplomats in Europe were increasingly frustrated by the foreign policy damage done by their nation's touring hockey players, the foreign ministry in Ottawa was divided on what to do about Canadian teams touring Europe. Officials in the Information Division believed hockey was so important to Canadian prestige that the foreign ministry had to take a more active role. Their colleagues in the European Division recognized that a free society could not simply restrict its people's lawful right to travel, no matter how much they embarrassed their country, and viewed overseas hockey tours as a "private enterprise" matter beyond their authority.[112]

Club teams continued to cause problems, but the behavior of the national team helped Canada's image abroad.[113] Correspondence from embassies about the national team often praised the players' conduct and compared them very favorably to other Canadian clubs touring Europe. But the squad Canadians called the "Nats" could not return Canada to the top of world hockey. The Russians, Czechoslovaks, and Swedes simply were too good for Canadian amateurs. It did not help that NHL owners preferred to keep their own top prospects in their organization, either with minor league or junior teams. The junior clubs, composed of amateur players under twenty, did not want to lose their best players and box office attractions.[114] But the NHL teams could have treated the Nats as a flag-draped, talent-development program: if the Montreal Canadiens and Toronto Maple Leafs each gave a number of top prospects to the Nats, Canada would have fielded a much stronger national team. In fact, NHL and junior clubs were reluctant to lend their top prospects even on a short-term basis. The Nats were denied when they sought the loan of Montreal Junior Canadiens star (and future Hall of Famer) Yvan Cournoyer "for a couple of weeks" in a bid to add some offensive punch for the 1964 Olympics.[115]

NHL owners had a plausible hockey justification for refusing to let their best prospects join the Nats. IIHF competitions used a larger ice surface and were less physical than the NHL; players who trained for world and Olympic tournaments would have to adjust when they moved to pro hockey. But there was more. Since the Nats attended university while training, they would arrive in the professional ranks older, better educated, and with other career options. They could be expected to demand higher salaries and be less accepting of traditional-style NHL management than younger, less-educated players who came through the junior ranks. In any event, with Canada's withdrawal from IIHF competitions in 1970, there was no point to continuing a national team. Canadian hockey leaders focused on arranging competition involving their professionals.

Yet even when Canada achieved diplomatic and sporting success, its hockey still illustrated the problems of a free, open society in competition with a totalitarian regime. The selection of "Team Canada" for the 1972 Summit Series produced major controversy. One of Canada's most concerted efforts to deal with the Soviet challenge had been the establishment of Hockey Canada. This organization had representation from pro, junior, and college hockey as well as the Canadian government. Among its purposes was "to support, operate, manage and develop a national hockey team or teams to represent Canada internationally."[116] In ordinary circumstances this caused confusion and overlap with the CAHA. More problematic was the preparation for the Summit Series. Hockey Canada needed the cooperation of NHL owners, who were unhappy over the establishment of the rival WHA. NHL owners would only agree to let their players represent Canada if the roster of Team Canada was restricted to NHL players. Several players who belonged on a team of Canada's very best had signed with the WHA and were thus excluded, among them Bobby Hull.[117]

NHL president Clarence Campbell justified the exclusion of Hull and other WHA players from Team Canada by saying that "there is no reason why we should put on parade the showpiece of the other side. You don't show off the competition's best product."[118] Canadians who thought the "other side" and the "competition" were based in Moscow found this decision outrageous. Toronto's *Globe and Mail* sarcastically complained about "the depths of [Hull's] perfidy" in failing to do "the loyal Canadian thing" and sign a contract with an NHL club in Chicago or some other American city. "Instead, in dark treason, he signed with the Winnipeg Jets of the newly formed World Hockey Association" and got himself disqualified.[119] Dick Beddoes, a legendary *Globe and Mail* columnist, bitterly referred to the squad throughout the series as "Team U.S. NHL."[120] This was common practice too in Hull's new home city of Winnipeg.[121] Beddoes complained that Hull had been "blackballed by the U.S. imperialists manipulating Hockey Canada" and argued that "Team U.S. NHL is proof, if additional proof is needed, that professional hockey is controlled by willful, self-enlightened operators in the United States."[122]

Beddoes and the *Globe and Mail* editorial board were not alone in expressing such sentiments. Across the country, Canadians clamored for Hull's inclusion on Team Canada and complained about the role of American interests in selecting Canada's hockey team. Because the cabinet-level Department of National Health and Welfare had representation in Hockey Canada, letters poured into offices on Parliament Hill from upset fans. Writers denounced the decision to exclude Hull as "very petty," "ridiculous," "ludicrous," "despicable," "very unpatriotic," and a "farce."[123] One nodded to the Mafia don in *The Godfather* by complaining that "the National Hockey League is . . . using the Don Corleone approach" in the Hull matter.[124] Expressing a common theme, one writer asked, "Is there no Canadian group or institution which can stand against American domination? Have we so little discretion in the planning of our own affairs that we must defer at every turn to the dictates of U.S. financial interests?"[125]

Even Prime Minister Pierre Trudeau sent a telegram imploring Hockey Canada to include Hull in the series—to no effect.[126] Despite its representation on the Hockey Canada board, Ottawa was powerless to influence player selection for Team Canada. This was a further illustration of the challenges facing a free society with limited government: Ottawa could not prevent amateur hockey teams from damaging the country's international reputation, and it could not influence the country's roster for the biggest series in the history of international hockey.

The openness of Canadian society curbed enthusiasm for copying too much of the Soviet hockey model. The Canadian government periodically commissioned reports to study Canada's international hockey performance and examine ways that it might improve.[127] But Canadians responding to the Soviet hockey challenge showed a concern similar to Americans' regarding other sports and worried that they could not readily embrace a sport program that replicated features of a totalitarian society.[128]

An additional factor curbing Canadian enthusiasm for copying the Soviet approach to hockey was a popular, persistent Canadian belief that fairer competition would produce more favorable results for Canada. Before the Summit Series, the Canadian expectation was that Canada's best would beat the USSR's best. The Soviets played the Canadians close in the Summit Series, but that had not been the strongest possible Canadian team: Bobby Orr, the greatest hockey player in the world, had missed the series because of injury, and Hull had been kept out by the small-minded exclusion of WHA players. Furthermore, because the Canadian team in the Summit Series was an all-star team assembled hastily during the NHL's preseason, some Canadians believed a midseason meeting of league teams would showcase Canadian strength. The 1975–1976 Super Series then demonstrated that Soviet elite league clubs could succeed against NHL teams, posting a record of 5–2–1. But the top NHL teams showed their league's strength: the 1975 Stanley Cup champion Philadelphia Flyers and runner-up Buffalo Sabres both easily beat their Soviet elite league opponents; the Montreal Canadiens, who would win the Cup in 1976, tied their game with the Central Army.[129] Even more important, the first Canada Cup—the tournament involving the best players from the best nations, regardless of amateur or professional status or where or in what league they played—was a triumph for Canada.

There were, naturally, some North American coaches who took the

Soviet approach seriously, but it took the emergence of the Wayne Gretz-ky–led Edmonton Oilers, who dominated the NHL in the 1980s, to win greater acceptance of Soviet-influenced styles of play. The WHA's Win-nipeg Jets of the 1970s, with a number of Swedes on their roster, had suc-cess playing a European-influenced style of play, which Edmonton's coach Glen Sather adapted in building his Oilers' dynasty.[130] Gretzky was able to put a distinctively Canadian stamp on a style of play that contained much of the creativity, puck possession, and precision passing that had long been a hallmark of the Soviets.[131]

## The Complexity of Intra-Alliance Relations and the Importance of Fans

Canadian resentment of the role played by American interests in the Hull matter was part of a broader concern about the growing US influence in Canada. At the time, books with titles such as *Close the 49th Parallel* called for Canada to assert greater control over its economy and resources and reduce the US role.[132] As part of this trend, Canadian hockey fans—that is, most of the population—believed that NHL expansion into American markets was hurting Canada's national game by diluting the quality of play and distorting the sport to sell it to people who knew nothing about it. The league and club owners seemed to value American money over the integrity of Canada's national game.

The NHL's apparent disregard for its Canadian fan base was most vividly demonstrated in the cancellation of *Hockey Night in Canada* in May 1968. This weekly television show, which had originated before tele-vision as a radio program, was a Saturday night ritual for Canadians and one of the few unifying forces in the vast, bilingual nation. During the 1968 Stanley Cup finals, the NHL was whipsawed by its commitments to deliver both a Saturday night game to CBC and a Sunday afternoon game to the American network CBS. The league would not schedule two games so close together, and it decided to accommodate its US network. Because of this decision, the authors of *The Death of Hockey* complained that "for the first time in 37 years, Saturday night was *not* hockey night in Canada [emphasis in original]."[133]

Yet this Canadian resentment of the United States was dwarfed by the hostility in the Soviet-Czechoslovak relationship. Canadians lamented US involvement in Vietnam, the American role in the Canadian economy, and declining Canadian sovereignty in the era of the North Atlantic Treaty Organization and the North American Aerospace Defense Command, but Canadians lived in a free, open, democratic, politically pluralist society in which they had substantial say over their government and the policies it pursued. After a short-lived effort at self-government with substantial communist participation, Czechoslovakia was reduced to a single-party dictatorship in February 1948. What the West denounced as the "Czechoslovakia coup," the Prague regime celebrated as "Victorious February."[134] Hockey, though, offered a number of indicators that many Czechoslovaks shared the Western view. Because it is hard to penetrate genuine public opinion in closed societies, embassy observers looked for a variety of ways to understand what the Czechoslovak people were thinking. And a sport of such importance in the country was one means of doing so.

Czechoslovak hockey fans manifested their unhappiness in many ways. As was mentioned previously, some Czechoslovaks thought Prague was too proud of Soviet hockey successes. They also were unhappy with ticket distribution for hockey games with touring Canadian teams. Instead of making tickets available to hockey fans, the authorities "carefully selected" ticket recipients "to guard against the danger of the crowd manifesting its opposition to the [communist] government."[135] This was a serious concern, as Canadian observers in the 1950s noticed that the "usual hockey crowd [was] strongly pro-Western and incidents" often occurred at hockey games. One night a crowd "chanted for 15 minutes the name of their favourite player," a national team "captain, who was at that time forbidden to play because his brother had asked for asylum in Sweden, and who had himself been sentenced to five years in prison for an attempt to escape."[136]

Imprisoned players were also an issue at a nonleague game between clubs from Prague and Brno in March 1955 that advertised popular resentment of the government. The hockey players arrested in the 1950 purge of the national team were being released, and two of them, Vaclav Rozinak and Augustin Bubnik, were scheduled to play.[137] For a nonleague game, around two thousand spectators would be expected, but seven thousand showed up to see Rozinak and Bubnik. This turnout caused officials to panic; they decided not to let the former prisoners play. This triggered a forty-five-minute riot in which spectators threw sandwiches and thermos bottles and chanted protests against the government and its leaders. Officials then revised their decision: Rozinak and Bubnik still would not play, but fans who came to see them could get a refund of their admission fee. Fans promptly stormed the ticket offices, overwhelming staff who did not have the change needed to pay the refunds. The crowd was so agitated that police called to keep order fled. Canadian officials in Prague received an anonymous description of these events they regarded as so credible and important that they sent a complete translation to Ottawa.[138]

Worries about crowd behavior apparently motivated Czechoslovak authorities planning an exhibition game with Team Canada following the 1972 Summit Series. After the Canadians reached an agreement to play Czechoslovakia's national team in Prague, the Czechoslovak federation unilaterally announced that the game would be played in Pilsen instead.[139] The federation claimed a socialist youth festival was already scheduled for the Prague arena,[140] but in Ottawa it seemed "absurd to claim that the change of venue from Prague to Pilsen . . . has been proposed for any reasons other than political, i.e., to avoid any possibility of a demonstration in the Czechoslovak capital which might be construed as inimical to the interests of the [Czechoslovak] regime and/or the Soviet Union."[141]

US embassy observers similarly found clues to Czechoslovak popular opinion in hockey. They were convinced that spectators at the 1959 world tournament games in Prague "took the opportunity presented by international competition to display basic political likes and dislikes." The American officials considered "the most notable aspect of the tournament . . . the coolness with which crowds treated the Soviet team." Significantly too, Czechoslovak fans were pro-American in every tournament game except the USA-Czechoslovakia game, even cheering for the Americans against the USSR. And the US embassy observer found local fans with whom he spoke "unanimous in their pleasure over the pro-American, anti-Soviet reactions of the crowd."[142]

Gauging popular opinion in a communist regime was, of course, difficult. It was possible that those who spoke with American (and Canadian) embassy officials were unrepresentative of the population, Czechoslovaks whose self-selection for sympathies to the West might have skewed Canadian and US embassy officials' perceptions of the Czechoslovak public. Still, the evidence available suggests hostility to the communist regime was common among hockey fans. The delight of Czechoslovak fans at scenes of Canadians viciously body-checking Soviet players in the documentary about Soviet hockey success in 1954, reported incidents of political misbehavior at hockey games, government efforts to restrict tickets for hockey games with Canada to the politically reliable, and the behavior of Czechoslovak fans at the 1970 world championships—even Prague's effort to move the exhibition game with Team Canada 1972 to Pilsen to avoid political embarrassment—all suggest that the hostility embassy observers reported was genuine.

Hockey's most important demonstration of Czechoslovak hostility to the USSR came during the 1969 world championships, the first held after the August 1968 invasion. The IIHF initially scheduled the 1969 world championships for Prague to commemorate the sixtieth anniversary of hockey in Czechoslovakia. But in September 1968, Prague announced that it could not host the tournament because of "technical, economic and organizational conditions." The US "embassy thought real concern was for prospective crowd behavior at Czechoslovakia-USSR matches."[143] When the tournament was played in Stockholm, it had serious political repercussions. Czechoslovakia defeated the USSR twice in the course of the tournament. After the first victory, Kenneth Skoug Jr. of the US embassy reported a "modest demonstration" in Wenceslas Square that led to some arrests and otherwise might have gone unnoticed had newspapers not publicized it "and, most unusually in a Communist country, revealed a few statements of the culprits, such as 'No tanks were there so they lost.' In standard Communist practice, assertions by defendants would be published only if abject confessions of guilt."[144] The apparent reason for the regime's willingness to publicize these comments became clear when the Czechoslovaks defeated the Soviets a second time, on March 28. Crowds in Czechoslovakia celebrated the victory; some chanted "Russians go home!" or "Today Tarasov, tomorrow Brezhnev."[145] One of the slogans was "Czechoslovakia 4–Occupation forces 3!"[146] US diplomat Skoug reported that he "had never seen Czechs so happy. Clearly, the city had not experienced such joy since the defeat of the Nazis in 1945."[147]

This second game had a political impact that stemmed from an attack on the Aeroflot and Intourist offices in Prague. This episode happened during the postgame celebrations, and it helped to finally topple Aleksandr Dubček, the reformist Czechoslovak leader. Dubček reported that "a team of police agents under cover as city workers"—he identified their supervisor as "the Czech minister of the interior, Josef Groesser, a Soviet agent"—"had unloaded a heap of paving stones in front of the offices."[148] Skoug pointed out that there had been little vandalism directed against the Soviets during and after the invasion. Following the second hockey game, though, he "saw burly men, none of whom looked the least bit like students, unhurriedly and dispassionately hurling large paving stones through the windows of . . . Aeroflot. No police appeared until the store windows had been completely shattered. They took no apparent action."[149] And "although Groesser said the initiators of the 'vandalism' would be discovered and brought to justice, this never happened, and his promised report was never published." Despite all of this, "a number of journalists and historians, none of whom witnessed the event, reported having heard eyewitness accounts of provocation but were reluctant to endorse it."[150] *Pravda,* which blamed a different group of provocateurs, was likely accurate when it wrote that "the provocations that took place in Prague"[151] had been "planned in advance and had far-reaching political objectives."[152]

The political outcome of the riot in Prague was that Czechoslovak hard-liners had a pretext to bring a final end to Dubček's tenure in office. The Kremlin provided an elaborate explanation of the riots. It claimed that the repeal of Prague Spring reforms after the Soviet invasion had been "favorably received by the working class, the toilers in agriculture and the majority of the working people." Despite the purported popularity of the post–August 1968 repeal of reforms, though, "forces hostile to socialism" and "right-wing revisionist and counterrevolutionary elements" were "fanning a nationalistic psychosis."[153] They were "whipping up anti-Sovietism"[154] and encouraging events of "a clearly terroristic and counterrevolutionary character."[155] Interestingly, among the evidence of this purported counterrevolutionary Czechoslovak activity were the uniforms of the Czechoslovak hockey team: "For the first time in recent years," they "did not show the name of their socialist homeland. Only the seal depicting a lion remained." The Soviets also complained about the "poorly disguised gesture made by Czechoslovak television, which organized a long period of 'interference' on the screen when the Soviet national anthem was played after the USSR team's victory over the Canadians."[156]

Demonstrating the zeal with which the Soviets made their case for intervention in Czechoslovakia, in one diplomatic conversation a Soviet official spun out what his American counterpart considered "a bizarre fantasy" of events in 1968—that a "subversive anti-Party 'group'" had been "consciously stirring up trouble" in Czechoslovakia and was planning to take over the Communist Party at an upcoming Party Congress "and to withdraw from the Warsaw Pact." Acting "in cahoots with agents of" West Germany, these renegade Czechoslovaks were even planning for "the eventual formation of a 'third force' alliance in Central Europe, independent of both the USSR and the U.S."[157] This Soviet position—that counterrevolutionaries were running wild in Czechoslovakia and being encouraged by West German and other Western agents—justified the August 1968 invasion and in April 1969 demanded a change in leadership in Prague. Dubček, who had remained in power following the invasion but with many limitations, was finally removed after the hockey riots.

After this crackdown, future hockey games between Czechoslovakia and the USSR were even more passionate. The regime in Prague wanted to see players and fans behave responsibly, but Czechoslovak players and fans mostly wanted to defeat the Russians. This was evident in such previously discussed events as the Czechoslovak fans' behavior at the 1970 world championships and the brutality of the Czechoslovak players in their 1972 Olympic meeting with the Soviets.

Significantly, unhappiness over the Soviet invasion was not limited to the Czechoslovaks. Stockholm took its neutrality seriously, and the Swedish hockey federation often voted with the USSR at IIHF meetings, but ordinary Swedish hockey fans responded sharply to the invasion. Swedish hockey officials cut off hockey ties with the USSR—at least for a short period—to protest the invasion, triggering "bitter criticism" in the Russian newspaper *Sovietsky Sport*.[158] As Sweden hosted the 1969 world tournament, most of the fans in attendance at games were Swedes; they cheered overwhelmingly for Czechoslovkia. During the first USSR-Czechoslovakia contest, a crowd of seven thousand chanted, "Dubček! Dubček!" at the end of the game.[159] During the second game, "more than 10,000 pro-Czech Swedish fans put on another ear-splitting performance." Fans waved signs that read, "Your tanks can't help you here."[160]

The Swedes were not alone. The Canadian embassy reported after the 1971 world championships in Bern that continuing Swiss anger over the Soviet invasion of Czechoslovakia affected their treatment of the Soviet hockey team. "The atmosphere in neutral Switzerland," the embassy reported, "at least at the level of the ordinary Swiss spectator, was openly anti-Soviet." It described a "shameful scene" during the contest between the United States and the USSR. The Swiss fans booed and whistled at the Soviets "throughout the entire game." After the Soviets won, the teams lined up for the customary salute of the victor's flag and the playing of its national anthem, during which "the whistling and booing reached such a piercing intensity that the unfortunately very long Russian national anthem, played at full strength on the loud speakers, could not be heard. The Russian players stood on the ice, looking around in bewilderment at this expression of open dislike on the part of the Swiss crowd."[161]

Sport, then, demonstrated hostility to the Soviets among its allies and neutrals, in circumstances in which politics often encouraged people to conceal their true feelings. But the Soviets also used feedback from sporting events in assessing popular attitudes in the West. Despite the hostility of Western governments, the Soviets and their allies took comfort that real popular opinion, and genuine friendship for communist nations, was revealed by the fans and journalists who praised the superior skills of Soviet hockey players or denounced the thuggery of their Canadian rivals. For example, the Czechoslovak media quoted a Swedish newspaper praising Soviet hockey and denigrating the Canadians after the USSR's triumphant debut at the 1954 world championships.[162] *Komsomol'skaya Pravda* quoted a Finnish newspaper's observation that the Soviets had demolished the "myth" of Canadian hockey professionals' superiority in the Summit Series.[163] Canadian criticisms of Team Canada 1972 that appeared in the *Ottawa Journal, Montreal Star,* and *Toronto Star* were quoted with evident pleasure by the official Soviet news agency TASS and the newspaper *Sovietskaya Rossia.*[164]

On both sides of the Iron Curtain, then—and in neutral nations—hockey fans and journalists provided information that contradicted the official line. But this similarity conceals more than it reveals. Westerners were freer and given more latitude to criticize their own society, its representatives, and its government. Canadian anti-Americanism was more openly expressed than Czechoslovak anti-Sovietism. And, in the end, its consequences could be dealt with more easily by the governments involved, in ways that would maintain popular support for their regime and its alliance connections.

## Conclusion

Canadian star Phil Esposito said that hockey during the Summit Series "was not a game anymore, it was war . . . our way of life against theirs."[165] Often it seemed that the Soviets were winning that war. Although the USSR lost the Summit Series, it regularly beat Canadian professionals, and it dominated Olympic and world tournaments. The facts that its program began during the Soviet regime and that its leaders developed a distinctly communist style of play further strengthened their claims that hockey demonstrated the superiority of communism in generating progress and developing human potential. Even Moscow's friends in Prague sometimes touted Soviet hockey success as evidence of communism's superiority.

Yet not all Czechoslovaks agreed. Many of them saw hockey as a means to assert their nation's distinctiveness and independence. A lot of Czechoslovak hockey fans were happy to see anybody beat the Soviets—even the Canadians, who were the very epitome of capitalist hockey—and they would cheer for the Americans in games against the USSR. In general, the capitalist democracies were far less successful in hockey than the USSR and Czechoslovakia. Yet the source of hockey problems in Canada and the United States was the very openness of the capitalist democracies that so many people—on both sides of the Iron Curtain—found appealing.

In the end, hockey was a source of bragging when teams won and a source of complaints when they lost. But while the Soviets were often successful in hockey matchups against Canada, and the Canadian diplomats were often driven to frustration over their inability to control Canada's image in Europe, in the end Canada's freedom looked more appealing to more people than did the Soviets' hockey dominance. The actual results of hockey competitions did not give us a lot of clues about the final outcome of the Cold War, but the response of many people who cared about those competitions did.

## Notes

The author wishes to acknowledge research support from Fulbright Canada, the University of Notre Dame, and the Institute for Scholarship in the Liberals Arts (ISLA) at Notre Dame, which helped make this article possible. He would like to thank the anonymous outside readers and students in his seminar on the Cold

War at Notre Dame in the fall of 2012 for their comments. He also would like to acknowledge the research assistance provided by Jack Healy and the encouragement and assistance received from Heather Dichter, Randall Germain, Jim Hershberg, Andy Holman, Linda Przybyszewski, Leo Ribuffo, Sayuri Guthrie-Shimizu, Jeremi Suri, and Chris Young.

1. Soviet coach Anatoli Tarasov, quoted in MOSCO to EXTER, no. 2764, December 16, 1968, Record Group (RG) 25, External Affairs, vol. 10527, file 55–26-HOCKEY, part 7, file title Cultural affairs—Sports competition—Hockey, Library and Archives Canada, Ottawa, Canada (hereafter LAC).

2. Canada won the first six world tournaments ever held, claiming the top prize at the Olympics in 1920, 1924, and 1928, then winning world tournaments in 1930 and 1931 before claiming the 1932 Olympic gold medal.

3. This held until 1972 and 1976, when the IIHF held separate Olympic and world tournaments. For the remainder of the Cold War, the IIHF hosted only Olympic tournaments in Olympic years; the Olympic champion was *not* recognized as the world champion, and there was no separate world tournament in 1980, 1984, and 1988.

4. "Williams Only U.S. Citizen in Ranks of NHL," *Boston Globe,* January 28, 1962, C56; John Powers, "Made in USA: Americans Growing, Thriving in NHL," *Boston Globe,* October 3, 1980, 53; and Ray Fitzgerald, "Williams Was One of a Kind," *Boston Globe,* July 14, 1981, 45.

5. Canadian Embassy, Moscow to Under-Secretary of State for External Affairs, no. 222, March 4, 1968, RG 25, vol. 10527, file 55–26-HOCKEY, part 6, file title Cultural affairs—Sports competition—Hockey, LAC.

6. Canadian Embassy, Prague, to Under-Secretary of State for External Affairs, no. 66, February 11, 1966, RG 25, vol. 10527, file 55–26-HOCKEY, part 2.1, file title Cultural affairs—Sports competition—Hockey, LAC.

7. Two of the so-called Original Six teams in operation from 1942–1943 through 1966–1967 were based in Canada (Montreal and Toronto); other clubs were based in US cities (Boston, Chicago, Detroit, and New York). In the expansion of the late 1960s and early 1970s, the league added only one Canadian city and eleven US cities.

8. Appendix C: Report by the Embassy in Prague on the visit of the Cincinnati Stingers to Czechoslovakia—September 22, 1977, attached to "Hockey and Canada's Image Abroad," brief submitted by the Department of External Affairs to the Parliamentary Committee on International Hockey, Senator S. L. Buckwold, Chairman (unsigned, undated), RG 29, National Health and Welfare, vol. 2077, file Hearings of Committee on International Hockey, LAC.

9. Walter Hixson, *Parting the Curtain: Propaganda, Culture and the Cold War, 1945–1961* (New York: St. Martin's Griffin, 1998); Gregory Mitrovich, *Undermining the Kremlin: America's Strategy to Subvert the Soviet Bloc, 1947–1956* (Ithaca, NY: Cornell University Press, 2000); Kenneth Osgood, *Total Cold War: Eisenhower's Secret Propaganda Battle at Home and Abroad* (Lawrence: University Press of

Kansas, 2006); and Scott Lucas, *Freedom's War: The American Crusade against the Soviet Union* (New York: New York University Press, 1999).

10. David Caute, *The Dancer Defects: The Struggle for Cultural Supremacy during the Cold War* (Oxford: Oxford University Press, 2005), and Penny M. Von Eschen, *Satchmo Blows Up the World: Jazz Ambassadors Play the Cold War* (Cambridge: Harvard University Press, 2006).

11. Michael Cotey Morgan, "The Seventies and the Rebirth of Human Rights," *The Shock of the Global: The 1970s in Perspective,* ed. Niall Ferguson, Charles S. Maier, Erez Manela, and Daniel J. Sargent (Cambridge, MA: Belknap, 2010), 242.

12. For example, the Canadian embassy in Moscow reported that during the 1971 *Izvestia* tournament, which the Soviets won despite an opening-game defeat, "many [Soviet] newspapers suddenly stopped reporting on the tournament when it appeared the Soviet team had lost its chance to finish first." Canadian Embassy Moscow to Under-Secretary of State for External Affairs, January 6, 1972, RG 25, vol. 10920, file 55–26-HOCKEY-1-USSR, part 1, file title Cultural affairs—Sports competition—Hockey—Between Canada and other countries—Union of Soviet Socialist Republics, LAC.

13. Hixson, *Parting the Curtain,* 77.

14. This point was made by Sayuri Guthrie-Shimizu in commenting on the author's presentation at a panel at the American Historical Association conference in January 2010.

15. Bernard J. Hibbitts, "The CBC International Service as a Psychological Instrument of Canadian Foreign Policy in the Cold War, 1948–1963," MA thesis, Carleton University, 1981, and "Canadian Broadcasting Corporation International Service," *External Affairs* 18 (1966): 133–36.

16. Canadian Embassy, Moscow to Under-Secretary of State for External Affairs, No. 222, March 4, 1968.

17. *Czechoslovak Sport* 13, no. 1 (1966): inside front cover.

18. The countries where *Czechoslovak Sport* had subscription agents included Australia, Austria, Belgium, Canada, Cuba, the United States, France, Finland, Ghana, Great Britain, the Netherlands, India, Italy, Morocco, East Germany, West Germany, Sweden, Switzerland, and Tunisia. *Czechoslovak Sport* 12, no. 1 (1965): inside front cover.

19. Jim Riordan, "The Rise and Fall of Soviet Olympic Champions," *Olympika: The International Journal of Olympic Studies* 2 (1993): 25–44, and Jenifer Parks, "Verbal Gymnastics: Sports, Bureaucracy, and the Soviet Union's Entrance into the Olympic Games, 1946–1952," in *East Plays West: Sport and the Cold War,* ed. Stephen Wagg and David L. Andrews (London: Routledge, 2007), 27–44.

20. The Canadian Ambassador, Moscow to the Secretary of State for External Affairs, no. 404, April 29, 1965, RG 25, vol. 10527, file 55–26-HOCKEY, part 1.2, file title Cultural affairs—Sports competition—Hockey, LAC.

21. Foreign Service Despatch no. 479 from AmEmbassy, Prague to Department of State, April 3, 1959, Record Group (RG) 59, Records of the Department of State,

1955–1959 Central Decimal file, box 4062, file 800.453/4–359, National Archives, College Park, MD (hereafter NA).

22. "U.S. Hockey Team Loss to Sweden," March 13, 1963, Telephone Recordings Dictation Belt 15A.2, JFKPOF-TPH-15A, John F. Kennedy Library, Boston, MA (hereafter JFKL), http://www.jfklibrary.org/Asset-Viewer/Archives/JFKPOF-TPH-15A-2.aspx (accessed November 27, 2012).

23. Memorandum, David L. Hackett to the President of the United States, March 14, 1963, folder Justice: 1/63–3/63, box 80, President's Office File, JFKL.

24. The following nations competed in Olympic hockey tournaments between 1948 and 1988 (inclusive): Australia, Austria, Bulgaria, Canada, Czechoslovakia, Finland, France, the German Democratic Republic, the German Federal Republic, Hungary, Japan, Italy, Netherlands, Norway, Poland, Romania, the Soviet Union, Sweden, Switzerland, the United Kingdom, the United States, and Yugoslavia. Among NATO democracies, only Belgium (which had a tradition of hockey in the 1910s and 1920s), Denmark, Iceland, and Luxembourg never played Olympic hockey during the Cold War.

25. See, for example, Under-Secretary of State for External Affairs to the Posts Listed Below, July 16, 1969, no. J-(M)-1929, RG 29, vol. 2176, file 215–5–9, part 1, file title Fitness and Amateur Sports—Hockey Canada—Telex Messages From External Affairs, LAC.

26. Memorandum from J. A. McCordick for the Under-Secretary of State for External Affairs, No. J-(Multi)-746, March 29, 1966, RG 25, vol. 10527, file 55–26-HOCKEY, part 2.2, file title Cultural affairs—Sports competition—Hockey, LAC, and Under-Secretary of State for External Affairs, No. J-(Multi)-368, February 7, 1968, RG 25, vol. 10527, file 55–26-HOCKEY, part 6, LAC.

27. Canada finished second in each of the competitions at which it did not claim the top prize. Source: "IIHF World Championships," International Ice Hockey Federation, http://www.iihf.com/iihf-home/history/all-medallists/men.html (accessed November 30, 2012), and "Olympic Ice Hockey Tournaments, Men," International Ice Hockey Federation, http://www.iihf.com/iihf-home/history/all-medallists/olympics/men.html accessed November 30, 2012.

28. US hockey teams won silver medals in 1952, 1956, and 1972. In addition, the US team tied for third place in 1976 but missed a bronze medal on the tie-breakers (see Bernard Kirsch, "W. German Squad Dashes U.S. Hopes," *New York Times,* February 15, 1976, S1). Before World War II, US teams had won silver medals in 1920, 1924, and 1932, and bronze in 1936.

29. Louis Bélanger, "Redefining Cultural Diplomacy: Cultural Security and Foreign Policy in Canada," *Political Psychology* 20 (1999): 681.

30. The Canadian Ambassador, Moscow, to the Secretary of State for External Affairs, no. 404, April 29, 1965, RG 25, vol. 10527, file 55–26-HOCKEY, part 1.2, file title Cultural affairs—Sports competition—Hockey, LAC.

31. Canadian Embassy, Prague, to Under-Secretary of State for External Affairs, no. 66, February 11, 1966, RG 25, vol. 10527, file 55–26-HOCKEY, part 2.1, file title Cultural affairs—Sports competition—Hockey, LAC.

32. Quote from Desptach no. 169, March 7, 1954, from the Chargé d'Affaires a.i., Prague, to Under-Secretary of State for External Affairs, RG 25, vol. 8203, file 8137-D-40, part 1.1, file title World Hockey Championships—Canadian Participation, LAC.

33. Canadian Embassy, Prague, to the Under-Secretary of State for External Affairs, no. 66, February 11, 1966, RG 25, vol. 10527, file 55–26-HOCKEY, part 2.1, file title Cultural affairs—Sports competition—Hockey, LAC.

34. Part 4 of 55–26-HOCKEY in External Affairs' volume 10527 contains a number of lamentations from European posts. See RG 25, vol. 10527, file 55–26-HOCKEY, part 4, file title Cultural affairs—Sports competition—Hockey, LAC.

35. Canadian Embassy, Bonn, to Under-Secretary of State for External Affairs, no. 66, January 20, 1965, RG 25, vol. 10526, file 55–26-HOCKEY, part 1.1, file title Cultural affairs—Sports competitions—Hockey, LAC.

36. Canadian Embassy, Helsinki, to Under-Secretary of State for External Affairs, no. 29, January 31, 1968, RG 25, vol. 10527, file 55–26-HOCKEY, part 6, LAC.

37. Witold Domanski, "Press Report from Poland," *Przeglad Sportowy,* n.d., in RG 25, vol. 10527, file 55–26-HOCKEY, part 2.2, LAC.

38. Canadian Embassy, Copenhagen, to Under-Secretary of State for External Affairs, no. 142, April 18, 1967, RG 25, vol. 10527, file 55–26-HOCKEY, part 3, file title Cultural affairs—Sports competition—Hockey, LAC; Canadian Embassy, Brussels, to Under-Secretary of State for External Affairs, no. 393, June 20, 1967; Canadian Embassy, Rome, to Under-Secretary of State for External Affairs of State, no. 1121, July 10, 1967; Canadian Embassy, Belgrade to Under-Secretary of State for External Affairs, no. 362, July 6, 1967; and Canadian Embassy, The Hague, to Under-Secretary of State for External Affairs, no. 218, June 22, 1967; RG 25, vol. 10527, file 55–26-HOCKEY, part 4, LAC.

39. See, for example, Tokyo to OTT EXT, no. 921, June 1, 1971; H. O. Moran to A. E. Ritchie, June 18, 1971; L. E. Lefaive to L. A. D. Stephens, June 24, 1971; Canadian Ambassador, Tokyo, to Under-Secretary of State for External Affairs, no. 432, August 12, 1971, RG 25, vol. 10920, file 55–26-HOCKEY, part 15, file title Cultural affairs—Sports competition—Hockey, LAC; and Mitchell Sharp to John Munro, September 24, 1971, RG 25, vol. 10920, file 55–26-HOCKEY, part 16, file title Cultural affairs—Sports competition—Hockey, LAC.

40. Americans too were open about the professionalism of their hockey players in the NHL and minor leagues. But so few Americans claimed these positions before expansion began in 1967–1968 that it had little impact on US Olympic hockey teams before the 1970s.

41. For some examples of discussions of the subject, see Allen Guttmann, "The Cold War and the Olympics," *International Journal* 43 (1988): 554–68; Jim Riordan, "Playing to New Rules: Soviet Sport and Perestrokia," *Soviet Studies* 42 (1990): 133–45; Riordan, "Rise and Fall of Soviet Olympic Champions"; Alfred Erich

Senn, *Power, Politics and the Olympic Games* (Champaign, IL: Human Kinetics, 1999), esp. 83–95; and Robert Edelman, *Serious Fun: A History of Spectator Sports in the USSR* (New York: Oxford University Press, 1993), 217–19.

42. This description of the Soviet sports program is based on a reading of Anatoli Tarasov, *Road to Olympus* (Toronto: Pocket Books, 1972); James Riordan, "Soviet Sport and Soviet Foreign Policy," *Soviet Studies* 26 (1974): 322–43; James Riordan, *Sport and Soviet Society: Development of Sport and Physical Education in Russia and the USSR* (Cambridge: Cambridge University Press, 1977); Yuri Brokhin, *The Big Red Machine: The Rise and Fall of Soviet Olympic Champions* (New York: Random House, 1978); Robert F. Baumann, "The Central Army Sports Club (TsSKA): Forging a Military Tradition in Soviet Ice Hockey," *Journal of Sport History* 15 (1988): 151–66; Jim Riordan, "The Role of Sport in Soviet Foreign Policy," *International Journal* 43 (1988): 569–95; Riordan, "Playing to New Rules"; and Riordan, "Rise and Fall of Soviet Olympic Champions."

43. *Do You Believe in Miracles? The Story of the 1980 U.S. Hockey Team,* prod. Brian Hyland, HBO Home Video, 2001.

44. For an example of a defense of the Soviets' amateur purity, see "USSR Hockey Coach Responds to Criticism," *Washington Post,* February 11, 1972, D4.

45. From MCOW to EXTER, no. 4204, December 8, 1967, RG 25, vol. 10527, file 55–26-HOCKEY, part 5, file title Cultural affairs—Sports competition—Hockey, LAC.

46. "Bolel'shchiki," *Krokodil,* May 10, 1950, 13. This cartoon appeared, with English caption, in "Reds Hope to Rule Sports Too," *U.S. News & World Report,* August 20, 1954, 36. Copy found in Avery Brundage Collection (ABC), Record Series 26/20/37, box 245, folder Avery Brundage Book—Russia Sports Book 1954, University of Illinois Archives, University of Illinois Library, Urbana, IL (hereafter UIA).

47. Foreign Service Despatch no. 745, Moscow to the Department of State, May 10, 1952, RG 59, Department of State Decimal File 1950–1954, box 5166, file 861.453/5–1052, NA. The article is "Vesennie Proischestviya," *Krokodil,* April 30, 1952, 12.

48. Quoted in Airgram A-1344, AmEmbassy MOSCOW to Department of State, November 1, 1969, RG 59, Central Foreign Policy Files, 1967–1969, box 334, file CUL 15 USSR 1/1/67, NA. The ambassador's conclusion was that "*Pravda's* purpose in publishing this letter does not seem to be to challenge this system but to point out that the job of supporting athletes should not be allowed to become too much of a burden for individual enterprises."

49. Avery Brundage to Severin Lovenskiold, April 2, 1970, ABC, box 216, folder Ice Hockey 1970–72, UIA. It bears mentioning that Brundage, a purist on amateurism, believed "it is impossible to keep as highly commercialized a sport as ice hockey . . . amateur at an international level. It is time we faced this situation," by which he meant end Olympic hockey (and preferably the Winter Games too). Quoted in Avery Brundage to James Worrall, January 28, 1970, ABC, box 119, folder Canada—1970 World Ice Hockey Championships, UIA.

50. "Address by Charles Hay, President, Hockey Canada to the Calgary Chamber of Commerce, March 4, 1970," ABC, box 119, folder Canada—1970 World Ice Hockey Championships, UIA.

51. Canada's proposals fit in with a contemporary trend in which other sports that previously limited their most prestigious competitions to amateurs began permitting professionals. The best example of this is tennis. In 1968 the French championships (renamed the French Open) and Wimbledon were opened to professionals.

52. Crans, Switzerland, was the location of the IIHF meeting where this agreement was reached.

53. See Bulgarian Ice Hockey Federation, Dansk Ishockey Union, et al., to IOC, November 3, 1969, and Telegram, Avery Brundage to Russian Olympic Committee, December 8, 1969, both in ABC, box 119, file Canada NOC/Canadian Olympic Association 1968–69, UIA.

54. Donald Macintosh and Donna Greenhorn, "Hockey Diplomacy and Canadian Foreign Policy," *Journal of Canadian Studies* 28 (1993): 101–5.

55. The 1974 Canada-USSR series matched the Soviet national team against all-stars from the World Hockey Association.

56. Team Canada in 1972 was limited to NHL players, and in 1974 the Canada squad was limited to WHA players. In the Canada Cup, the Canadian team drew players from both North American pro leagues. Sweden used players from the NHL and WHA along with those still playing in Europe; so did Finland.

57. MOSCO to EXTER, no. 2697, December 9, 1968, RG 25, vol. 10527, file 55–26-HOCKEY, part 7, LAC.

58. Canadian Ambassador, Moscow, to the Secretary of State for External Affairs, no. 404, April 29, 1965, RG 25, vol. 10527, file 55–26-HOCKEY, part 1.2, LAC.

59. Quoted in "Hooliganism," *Winnipeg Free Press,* September 29, 1972, 1.

60. Ibid.

61. Anatoli Tarasov, quoted from his article in *Sovetskii Sport,* September 4, 1971, translation attached to Canadian Embassy, Moscow, to Under-Secretary of State for External Affairs, no. 687, October 14, 1971, RG 25, vol. 10920, file 55–26-HOCKEY, part 16, LAC.

62. "Razvye eto khokkei? Polemicheskie zametki," *Komsomol'skaya Pravda,* January 13, 1970, translation attached to Canadian Embassy, Moscow, to Under-Secretary of State for External Affairs, no. 101, January 30, 1970, RG 29, vol. 2176, file 215–5–9, part 1, LAC.

63. *Krokodil,* October 1972, 13.

64. B. Fedosov, "Posle Voc'mogo Khokkeynogo Raunda," *Izvestia,* September 30, 1972, 6.

65. MOSCO to EXTOTT, no. 2072, October 9, 1974, RG 25, vol. 10922, file 55–26-HOCKEY-1-USSR, part 11, file title Cultural affairs—Sports competition—Hockey—Between Canada and other countries—Union of Soviet Socialist Republics, LAC.

66. John Soares, "Cold War, Hot Ice: International Ice Hockey, 1947–1980," *Journal of Sport History* 34 (2007): 215–16.

67. "Schyot Tret'ei Serii—Pobednii!," *Komsomol'skaya Pravda,* January 13, 1976, 4.

68. Canadian Embassy, Moscow, to Under-Secretary of State, no. 835, November 27, 1974, RG 25, vol. 10922, file 55–26-HOCKEY-1-USSR, part 11, LAC.

69. The coach's remarks were summarized, not quoted, in Appendix C: Report by the Embassy in Prague on the visit of the Cincinnati Stingers to Czechoslovakia—September 22, 1977, "Hockey and Canada's Image Abroad," brief submitted by the Department of External Affairs to the Parliamentary Committee on International Hockey, Senator S. L. Buckwold, Chairman (unsigned, undated), RG 29, National Health and Welfare, vol. 2077, file: Hearings of Committee on International Hockey, LAC.

70. "Survey of Medals Won by Countries of the Socialist Camp at the Winter Games since 1948," *Czechoslovak Sport* 19, no. 3 (1971): 8–9.

71. Memorandum, attached to Numbered Letter no. 193, from The Canadian Legation, Prague, to Under-Secretary of State for External Affairs, March 24, 1954, RG 25, vol. 8203, file 8137-D-40, part 1.1, LAC.

72. Translation of anonymous letter attached to Numbered Letter no. 145, Canadian Legation, Prague, to Under-Secretary of State for External Affairs, Ottawa, March 3, 1955, RG 25, vol. 8203, file 8137-D-40, part 1.2, LAC, and Foreign Service Despatch no. 479 from AmEmbassy, Prague, to Department of State, April 3, 1959, RG 59, Records of the Department of State, 1955–1959 Central Decimal file, box 4062, file 800.453/4–359, NA.

73. There is disagreement over whether ten or eleven players were arrested. See Frantisek Bouc, "Once Were Champions," *Prague Post,* January 30, 2002, and "Worst Wrong Done to Czechoslovak Hockey Fifty Years Ago," Czech News Agency, March 10, 2000.

74. "USSR-CSSR Hockey Game," Prague Domestic Service, March 19, 1970, published in *Foreign Broadcast Information Service Daily Report,* FBIS-FRB-70–055, March 20, 1970, under heading "Incidents of Anti-Sovietism Reported, Czechoslovakia," D4.

75. The World Hockey Association (WHA) was a rival to the NHL that existed from 1972–1973 until four surviving teams merged into the NHL in 1979–1980.

76. 1972 US Olympic team member Mark Howe, quoted in Kevin Allen, *USA Hockey: A Celebration of a Great Tradition* (Chicago: Triumph Books, 1997), 68.

77. "USA Pulls a Surprise," in *1972 United States Olympic Book* (New York: United States Olympic Committee, 1972), 260, and Allen, *USA Hockey,* 68.

78. Mark Mulvoy, "Check and Double-Czech," *Sports Illustrated,* July 29, 1974, 52. In 1956, of course, a number of Hungarian Olympians defected during the Melbourne Olympics.

79. "Press Reports on Defection of Two Hockey Stars," October 22, 1974, published in *Foreign Broadcast Information Service Daily Report,* Eastern Europe, FBIS-EEU-74–205, October 22, 1974, D5.

80. The first Soviet player to defect was Aleksandr Mogilny. For Soviet reaction, which likened the team that signed Mogilny to "a horse thief," see "Reaction to Hockey Player Mogilny's Defection," May 6, 1989, published in *Foreign Broadcast Information Service Daily Report,* Soviet Union, FBIS-SOV-89–088, May 9, 1989, 13.

81. John Feinstein, "As Hockey-Playing Czech, Pivonka Broke No New Ground with Departure," *Washington Post,* July 26, 1986, B6.

82. "Blues Acquire Player from Czechoslovakia," *Chicago Tribune,* September 12, 1969, C4; Jeff Z. Klein, "Jaroslav Jirik, 71, Czech Hockey Star," *New York Times,* July 12, 2011; and Dan Diamond, ed., *Total Hockey: The Official Encyclopedia of the National Hockey League,* 2nd ed. (New York: Total Sports, 2000), 1226.

83. Feinstein, "As Hockey-Playing Czech," and Bill Brubaker and Robert Fachet, "NHL Teams Go Underground to Get Czechs," *Washington Post,* July 27, 1986, C1, C5.

84. Memorandum from European Division to Under-Secretary of State for External Affairs, February 1, 1955, RG 25, vol. 8203, file 8137-D-40, part 1.1, LAC.

85. Despatch no. 92, Canadian Minister, Stockholm, to Under-Secretary of State for External Affairs, March 10, 1954, RG 25, vol. 8203, file 8137-D-40, part 1.1, LAC.

86. BONN to EXTER, no. 57, January 16, 1968, RG 25, vol. 10527, file 55–26-HOCKEY, part 6, LAC.

87. Prior to 1972 only a couple of Swedish players had played at the top level of professional hockey in North America. Five Swedes came to North American starting in 1973–1974; Hedberg was among the seven who joined the WHA or NHL in 1974–1975, with Swedes continuing to come in increasing numbers after that. *Svenska Spelare Utomlands,* October 3, 2007 (document in possession of author).

88. "Soviet Newspaper Not Impressed," *Winnipeg Free Press,* December 20, 1976, 51.

89. "Kanada—4, Shvetsia—4," *Sovetskii Sport,* December 18, 1976, 3.

90. Canadian Embassy, Moscow to Under-Secretary of State for External Affairs, No. 787, December 13, 1971. The popularity of Hull's book led one Foreign Ministry official to joke, "Maybe we should cancel the Stratford Theatre tour and hire a ghostwriter for [Boston Bruins superstar] Bobby Orr as a substitute program." FAI to FAP, December 23, 1971. Both in RG 25, vol. 10920, file 55–26-HOCKEY, part 16, LAC.

91. Robin Herman, "Hull, though Ailing, Is Favorite at Soviet Tourney," *New York Times,* December 18, 1976, 14.

92. P. Katin, "Edin vo mnogikh litsakh," *Sovetskii Sport,* December 16, 1976, 3.

93. Reyn Davis, "Even in Russia, a Hull of a Time," *Winnipeg Free Press,* December 16, 1976, 65, and "Bobbi Khall: Rad, Chto Snova v Moskvye," *Izvestia,* December 17, 1976, 6.

94. "Bobbi Khall: Rad, Chto Snova v Moskvye," *Izvestia,* December 17, 1976, 6.

95. Reyn Davis, "Daley Saves Day for Jets," *Winnipeg Free Press,* December 22, 1976, 37.

96. For more on the origins of Soviet hockey, see Edelman, *Serious Fun,* esp. 110–17.

97. Titles crucial to the author's understanding of the Soviet hockey program include Baumann, "The Central Army Sports Club"; Tarasov, *Road to Olympus;* and Edelman, *Serious Fun.*

98. Tarasov, *Road to Olympus,* 46.

99. "Interim Report on Minor Amateur Hockey in Canada," RG 29, vol. 2076, file Interim and Status Reports, LAC.

100. From 1955 through 1982, the Central Army was the Soviet champion twenty-two times, with five second-place finishes and one third-place finish. In that same period, Dinamo Moscow claimed eleven second-place finishes and twelve third-place finishes. Spartak Moscow won four Soviet championships and posted seven second-place finishes and six third-place finishes. Kryla Sovetov won two elite league championships and had four second-place finishes and four third-place finishes. "Laureaty Sovetskogo Khokkeya" in V. D. Sysoev, *Igraet TsSKA* (Moscow: Voenizdat, 1982), 162–63.

101. This point was made by Robert Edelman in discussions at various conferences on sport history.

102. Baumann, "The Central Army Sports Club," 160.

103. "Interim Report on Minor Amateur Hockey in Canada," RG 29, vol. 2076, file Interim and Status Reports, LAC.

104. See Gordon MacDonald, "'A Colossal Embroglio': Control of Amateur Ice Hockey in the United States and the 1948 Winter Olympic Games," *Olympika: The International Journal of Olympic Studies* 7 (1998): 43–60, and John Soares, "'Very Correct Adversaries': The Cold War on Ice from 1947 to the Squaw Valley Olympics," *International Journal of the History of Sport* 30, no. 13 (2013): 1536–53.

105. Dave Anderson, "West 49th's Hockey Landmark," *New York Times,* April 13, 1995, B11. In the course of his pro career, Joe Mullen scored more than five hundred career goals, and he topped fifty goals in a single season—both marks that place him among the greatest to ever play the game. No player from the US team at Lake Placid scored as many goals in a single NHL season or for his career.

106. Lawton, the first American ever selected with the number-one overall pick, signed with the Minnesota North Stars. Barraso signed with the Buffalo Sabres. Lawrie Mifflin, "U.S. Squad Emphasizes Youth," *New York Times,* July 5, 1983, B13, and Lawrie Mifflin, "U.S. Olympic Hockey Team Faces a Tough Task," *New York Times,* September 18, 1983, S12.

107. Tom Caraccioli and Jerry Caraccioli, *Striking Silver: The Untold Story of America's Forgotten Hockey Team* (Champaign, IL: Sports Publishing, 2006), 36.

108. Morris Mott, "The Canadian National Team, 1963 to 1970," in *Total Hockey: The Official Encyclopedia of the National Hockey League,* ed. Dan Diamond (New York: Total Sports, 1998): 434–38.

109. For more on the national team, see Mott, "The Canadian National Team,"

and Brian Conacher, *Hockey in Canada: The Way It Is!* (Toronto: Gateway Press, 1970).

110. Canadian Embassy, Prague to Under-Secretary of State for External Affairs, no. 459, September 29, 1967, RG 25, vol. 10527, file 55–26-HOCKEY, part 4, LAC.

111. Canadian Embassy, Stockholm to Under-Secretary of State for External Affairs, no. 219, June 26, 1967, RG 25, vol. 10527, file 55–26-HOCKEY, part 4, LAC.

112. For a good example of constraints on official Ottawa, see Information Division to European Division, April 22, 1968. Insight into the divisions within Ottawa is found in the response, European Division to Information Division, April 26, 1968. Robert A. D. Ford gives a complete statement of the importance of hockey to Canada's prestige in Canadian Embassy, Moscow to Under-Secretary of State for External Affairs, no. 222, March 4, 1968. All in RG 25, vol. 10527, file 55–26-HOCKEY, part 6, LAC.

113. MOSCO to EXTER, no. 1911, September 10, 1968, RG 25 vol. 10527, file 55–26-HOCKEY, part 7, LAC.

114. *Report of the Task Force on Sports for Canadians* (Ottawa: Queen's Printer, 1969), 30.

115. Conacher, *Hockey in Canada,* 33.

116. "Government Policy Re Hockey Canada," n.d., MG 28 I 263, vol. 18, file 300–6–1 Future Role of Hockey Canada 1969–1974, LAC.

117. Roy MacSkimming, *Cold War: The Amazing Canada-Soviet Hockey Series of 1972* (Vancouver: Greystone Books, 2012), 15–19.

118. Quoted in Dan Proudfoot, "Bobby Hull Won't Play for Canada, Says Campbell," *Globe and Mail* (Toronto), July 24, 1972, S2.

119. "Canada Will Hold the Coats," *Globe and Mail* (Toronto), July 14, 1972, editorial page.

120. "By Dick Beddoes," *Globe and Mail* (Toronto), August 10, 1972, 36.

121. Jay Scherer, Gregory H. Duquette and Daniel S. Mason, "The Cold War and the (Re)articulation of Canadian National Identity: The 1972 Canada-USSR Series," in *East Plays West,* ed. Wagg and Andrews, 176.

122. "By Dick Beddoes," *Globe and Mail* (Toronto), August 10, 1972, 36.

123. Joan and Lloyd Penner to C. Campbell, July 18, 1972; Len Donald to Hockey Canada, July 1972; F. Kennedy to Hockey Canada, July 17, 1972; George Kropinski to Hockey Canada, July 18, 1972; Linda Keckalo to Sirs, July 14, 1972; and P. G. Casola to Hockey Canada, July 29, 1972. All in Hockey Canada files, MG 28 I 263, vol. 5, file 300–16 Hockey Canada Office files—General Complaints—Team Canada & Bobby Hull, LAC.

124. Wm. Ropeham to Hockey Canada, July 18, 1972, in Hockey Canada files, MG 28 I 263, vol. 5, file 300–16, LAC.

125. Brian R. Cauthery and family to the National Hockey League Players Association, July 15, 1972, Hockey Canada files, MG 28 I 263, vol. 5, file 300–16, LAC.

126. Telegram, Pierre Elliott Trudeau to Charles Hay, July 14, 1972, Hockey Canada files, MG 28 I 263, vol. 5, file 300–16, LAC.

127. See, for example, "Hockey and Canada's Image Abroad," brief submitted by the Department of External Affairs to the Parliamentary Committee on International Hockey, Senator S. L. Buckwold, Chairman (unsigned, undated), RG 29, National Health and Welfare, vol. 2077, file Hearings of Committee on International Hockey, LAC, and *Report of the Task Force on Sports for Canadians.* Although it dealt with other sports and with fitness more generally, the Task Force on Sports for Canadians (commissioned by the new Trudeau administration) was chiefly concerned with improving Canada's performance in world and Olympic hockey.

128. For more on Americans' concerns about the Soviet model, see Jeffrey Montez de Oca, "The 'Muscle Gap': Physical Education and U.S. Fears of a Depleted Masculinity, 1954–1963," in *East Plays West,* ed. Wagg and Andrews, 123–48.

129. The score of the Montreal–Central Army game was 3–3. Buffalo thrashed the Wings, 12–6. For more on the Super Series, especially the Montreal–Central Army game, see Todd Denault, *The Greatest Game: The Montreal Canadiens, the Red Army and the Night That Saved Hockey* (Toronto: McClelland & Stewart, 2011).

130. For more on the Jets' influence in Europeanizing North American pro hockey and serving as a model for Sather's Oilers, see John Soares, "East Beats West: Ice Hockey and the Cold War," in *Sport and the Transformation of Modern Europe: States, Media and Markets, 1950–2010,* ed. Alan Tomlinson, Christopher Young, and Richard Holt (London: Routledge, 2011), 45.

131. This argument is made in greater detail by Ken Dryden, the former all-American from Cornell University who earned a law degree from McGill University while starring for the NHL's Montreal Canadiens. After winning six Stanley Cups in eight seasons with Montreal and playing for Team Canada in the 1972 Summit Series, Dryden went on to a career in public service in Canada. See Ken Dryden, *The Game,* 20th anniversary ed. (Toronto: Wiley, 2005), 289–92.

132. Ian Lumsden, ed., *Close the 49th Parallel, Etc.: The Americanization of Canada* (Toronto: University of Toronto Press, 1975).

133. Bruce Kidd and John Macfarlane, *The Death of Hockey* (Toronto: New Press, 1972), 31.

134. See, for example, "Prague Rally," Prague Domestic Service, February 24, 1970, published in *Foreign Broadcasting Information Service Daily Report,* FBIS-FRB, 70–058, February 25, 1970, under the heading "Festivities Mark February Victory, People's Militia, Czechoslovakia," D8.

135. Numbered Letter no. 145, Canadian Legation, Prague, to Under-Secretary of State for External Affairs, March 3, 1955, RG 25, Volume 8203, file 8137-D-40, part 1.2, LAC.

136. Chargé d'Affaires a.i., Canadian Legation, Prague to the Secretary of State for External Affairs, February 23, 1955, RG 25, vol. 8203, file 8137-D-40, part 1.1, LAC.

137. According to a letter dated March 3, which the Canadian legation in Prague passed on to Ottawa, the two players named "Rosinak" and "Bubnik" were members of the 1947 world championship team who had been released from prison two

months earlier. Because the players arrested in 1950 were released from prison in 1955, and Augustin Bubnik and Vaclav Rozinak were among them, the author has concluded that these were the players whose scheduled presence contributed to the large fan turnout and subsequent riot. See translation attached to Numbered Letter no. 145, Canadian Legation, Prague, to Under-Secretary of State for External Affairs, March 3, 1955, RG 25, vol. 8203, file 8137-D-40, part 1.2, LAC, and "Worst Wrong Done to Czechoslovak Hockey Fifty Years Ago," Czech News Agency, March 10, 2000.

138. Translation attached to Numbered Letter no. 145, Canadian Legation, Prague, to Under-Secretary of State for External Affairs, March 3, 1955, RG 25, vol. 8203, file 8137-D-40, part 1.2, LAC.

139. Prague to EXTOTT, no. 708, August 16, 1972, RG 25, vol. 10920, file 55–26-HOCKEY-1-CZECH, part 1, file title Cultural affairs—Sports competition—Hockey—Between Canada and other countries—Czechoslovakia, LAC.

140. Prague to EXTOTT, no. 713, August 16, 1972, RG 25, vol. 10920, file 55–26-HOCKEY-1-CZECH, part 1, LAC.

141. Redraft Memorandum, GEA to GEP, August 17, 1972, RG 25, vol. 10920, file 55–26-HOCKEY-1-CZECH, part 1, LAC.

142. Foreign Service Despatch no. 479 from AmEmbassy, Prague to Department of State, April 3, 1959, RG 59, Records of the Department of State, 1955–1959 Central Decimal file, box 4062, file 800.453/4–359, NA.

143. Kenneth N. Skoug Jr., *Lost Fight for Freedom, 1967–1969: An American Embassy Perspective* (Westport, CT: Praeger, 1999), 227.

144. Ibid., 228.

145. Alvin Shuster, "Aeroflot Office Burned in Prague," *New York Times,* March 29, 1969, 5.

146. Quoted in Dino Numerato, "Between Small Everyday Practices and Glorious Symbolic Acts: Sport-Based Resistance against the Communist Regime in Czechoslovakia," *Sport in Society: Cultures, Commerce, Media, Politics* 13, no. 1 (2010): 112.

147. Skoug, *Czechoslovakia's Lost Fight for Freedom,* 229.

148. Alexander Dubček, *Hope Dies Last: The Autobiography of Alexander Dubcek,* ed. and trans. Jiri Hochman (New York: Kodansha International, 1993), 236–37.

149. Skoug, *Czechoslovakia's Lost Fight for Freedom,* 229.

150. Ibid., 230. Skoug gives more detail in note 19 on page 240.

151. "Hockey and Nationalistic Frenzy," *Pravda,* March 31, 1969, 5; translation in "After the Hockey Match," *Current Digest of the Soviet Press* 21, no. 13 (April 16, 1969): 19.

152. "In a Frenzy," *Komsomolskaya Pravda,* April 1, 1969, 4; translation in "Steps Are Taken to Curb Czechoslovak News Media," *Current Digest of the Soviet Press* 21, no. 14 (April 23, 1969): 6.

153. "Hockey and Nationalistic Frenzy." 18–19.

154. "Meeting of the Presidium of the CCP Central Committee," *Pravda,* April 4, 1969, 4; translation in "Steps Are Taken to Curb Czechoslovak News Media," 5.

155. "Session of the Presidium of the SCP Central Committee," *Pravda,* April 10, 1969, 4; translation in *Current Digest of the Soviet Press* 21, no. 15 (April 30, 1969): 18.

156. "In a Frenzy," 6.

157. Memorandum of Conversation, September 5, 1968, Boris N. Sedov, 2nd Secretary, Soviet Embassy, and Raymond Garthoff, U.S. NATO/TDY/Dept., National Security File, Files of Spurgeon Keeny, box 3, Lyndon B. Johnson Presidential Library, Austin, TX.

158. Canadian Embassy, Moscow to Under-Secretary, no. 1088, December 18 1968, RG 25, vol. 10527, 55–26-HOCKEY, part 7, LAC.

159. "Czechs Win Hate Match, Refuse to Shake with Russian Losers," *Globe and Mail* (Toronto), March 22, 1969, 1.

160. "Czechs Near World Title with 4–3 Win over Russia," *Globe and Mail* (Toronto), March 29, 1969, 1.

161. Canadian Embassy, Berne, to Under-Secretary of State for External Affairs, May 3, 1971, RG 25, vol. 10920, file 55–26-HOCKEY, part 15, LAC.

162. Numbered Letter no. 193, Canadian Legation, Prague, to Under-Secretary of State for External Affairs, March 24, 1954, RG 25, vol. 8203, file 8137-D-40, part 1.1, LAC.

163. Translation attached to Canadian Embassy, Moscow to Under-Secretary of State for External Affairs, September 7, 1972, no. 575, RG 25, vol. 10921, file 55–26-HOCKEY-1-USSR, part 4, file title Cultural Affairs—Sports competition—Hockey—Between Canada and other countries—Union of Soviet Socialist Republics, LAC.

164. Canadian Embassy, Moscow, to Under-Secretary of State for External Affairs, no. 607, September 28, 1972, RG 25, vol. 10921, file 55–26-HOCKEY-1-USSR, part 4.1, file title Cultural Affairs—Sports competition—Hockey—Between Canada and other countries—Union of Soviet Socialist Republics, LAC.

165. Quoted in David Tucker, untitled news report, United Press International, September 28, 1982.

# 9

# "Fuzz Kids" and "Musclemen"

## The US-Soviet Basketball Rivalry, 1958–1975

### *Kevin B. Witherspoon*

The 1972 Olympic basketball gold-medal game is widely considered one of the most memorable—and from the American perspective, notorious—sporting events ever played. The American team, undefeated in Olympic play up to that point and heavily favored in the game, lost to the Soviets, 51–50. Of course, the one-point defeat is only a small part of the story, as it came after an extremely controversial sequence of events in which the final three seconds were played three times, with the Soviets scoring the winning basket only on their third try. Players and coaches from the US team were so angered at the result that they declined to accept the silver medals, which still remain unclaimed in a vault at the International Olympic Committee (IOC) headquarters in Switzerland more than forty years later. The Americans were convinced that they had been cheated and deserved the gold medals, not silver—a perception that still lingers today.[1]

The outcome of that single game, and its incredible final moments, has attracted much attention from historians. While no consensus has been reached on a number of key points—how unjust were the officiating decisions; to what extent were American players and coaches responsible for their own defeat; should the players, even in the midst of protest and controversy, have accepted the silver medals—historians and media members studying the event have remained firmly focused on the game itself. What they have largely ignored is the fact that the 1972 Olympic game is only one in a series of many clashes between the two teams that both reflected and helped to shape the national mood in that era. Those historians who have discussed the broader changes to "Team USA" have done so primarily to explain the 1972 defeat.[2]

This chapter intends to examine the evolution of the American international team in the years leading to, and following, the 1972 Olympics. Its primary focus will not be the 1972 team itself, which as noted has received much attention from historians, but rather an array of other international contests, particularly the annual exchanges between the US and Soviet teams, which began in 1958. The outcome of such contests and other international games provided ample evidence that American supremacy in the sport was eroding and that the 1972 Olympic final should not have come as a surprise. These games, more than simply reflecting victories and defeats for the two nations, offer historians an opportunity to consider diplomacy between the nations as a whole.

A growing number of historians have taken to studying the cultural aspect of the Cold War, as the superpowers struggled to achieve not only military or tactical superiority but also to win allies at the periphery of the Cold War through the arts, music and radio, literature and magazines, student exchanges, and many other elements of culture.[3] A small but growing number of historians have considered the role of sport in this "cultural Cold War," as both powers implemented athletes as diplomats and "cold warriors."[4] The basketball rivalry of this era provides an opportunity to consider the impact of sport diplomacy in a number of ways. First, why was the world treated to such an intense series of games in the midst of détente, a period of supposed goodwill between the powers? Similarly, how sincere were the sides in engaging in these athletic "goodwill" exchanges? Were they genuinely friendly games, or were they "ersatz warfare," as at least one historian has described them?[5] Finally, these games reflected not only an American interest in winning the games but also in defending American masculinity. Particularly when facing the Soviets, whose teams were always experienced and tended to be built around strong, tough, big men, the Americans more and more suffered due to the youth of its team, which was replaced on a nearly annual basis. Only after the humiliation of the 1972 final, when the "boyishness" of the American team was identified as a contributing factor in the defeat, did organizers of the sport set out to repopulate the team with bigger, stronger, and tougher players. In the years after 1972, the Americans determined not only to beat the Soviets and avenge their loss but to physically beat them into submission. The games became not only a matter of national pride but also a defense of American masculinity.

## A Rivalry Born: US-Soviet Basketball, 1958–1971

In 1958 a team of American basketball players drawn from the leading Amateur Athletic Union (AAU) teams toured the Soviet Union and played a series of six games against top Soviet teams in Moscow, Tbilisi, and Leningrad. Soviet spectators, driven by curiosity and swelled with national pride, provided a raucous environment at each of the games, especially the first two in Moscow. Even the fourth game, played on an outdoor court following a two-hour rainstorm in Tblisi against the Azerbaijani team, drew an enthusiastic sell-out crowd. That first year, the US team swept all six games, despite two close games against the Soviet national team in Moscow and an especially close call in the fifth game against a team from Leningrad.[6] The basketball exchanges became an annual event, usually with a favorable result for the Americans.

These games were played under the auspices of the Cultural Exchange Agreement between the two nations that led to exchanges across an array of cultural activities, from student exchange programs to visits by writers, musicians, dancers, scholars, and various exhibitions.[7] Throughout the 1960s and much of the 1970s, the United States and the Soviet Union also "exchanged" athletes on a regular basis, at times sending half a dozen teams or more across the Iron Curtain annually. Many such exchanges drew little publicity, as when wrestlers, tennis players, or little-known college squads toured the Soviet Union. Other visits attracted considerable media attention, as when American swimmers, gymnasts, and track stars traveled abroad.[8] Without question, the events that created the biggest stir were the famous dual track meets, which also began in 1958 and continued into the mid-1970s. These track meets became front-page news in the late 1950s and early 1960s, as events pitting the top athletes in the world became mano-a-mano battles for world supremacy. The decathlon contests pitting the American star Rafer Johnson against the Soviet champion Vasily Kusnetsov were especially gripping.[9] The basketball exchanges occupied a relatively low rung on the popularity ladder, especially in the United States, where the games were often held in modest gymnasiums and field houses on campuses across the country. They attracted some popular and media interest but nothing approaching the media bonanza that surrounded the dual track meets.

Basketball may seem an odd sport for this sort of exhibition—it is, after all, a purely American game and one in which the Americans had utterly dominated international play up to that point. But in fact the Soviets embraced the opportunity to contest this sport. Such ambitions to achieve success in an "American" sport are in keeping with Soviet notions of the importance of sport and the symbolic significance of athletic success. Driving a state-directed sports apparatus of massive proportions, the Soviet leadership by the late 1950s directly equated athletic victories with political and ideological strength. Victories in the international arena demonstrated the superiority of the Soviet system. As one Soviet official explained, victory in athletics "provides irrefutable proof of the superiority of socialist culture over the moribund culture of capitalist states."[10] Thus, defeating a recognized global power such as the United States in any sport symbolized a broader social victory for the Soviets. Defeating the Americans in their "own" sport, basketball, was the ultimate representation of Soviet organizational, physical, and mental acumen.[11]

With that in mind, Soviet sports officials placed an emphasis on fortifying their basketball program. While the Soviet national team was not created until 1947, in a very short time and with the full backing of the government-driven sports machine, they developed a team that was highly successful in international competition. Drawing players from the full breadth of the Soviet Union, they found athletes with the skills necessary to forge a formidable team.[12] From the Baltic states Latvia and Lithuania came players known for their skill, discipline, and knowledge of the game.[13] From Russia, and particularly Moscow, came players renowned for their fitness, strength, courage, and will. And from Georgia came players recognized for their quickness and improvisational skills, coupled with an admitted disdain for playing defense.[14]

Together, players from all three regions united to create very good teams, even early in Soviet international play. In fact, the Soviets won the European championship in their first significant international contest and made the gold-medal game in their first Olympics, 1952 in Helsinki, which they lost to the Americans. From that point forward, the US-Soviet rivalry played out with some regularity on the basketball court, most often in the championship game of some international tournament or during their annual basketball exchanges. And while the Americans continued to win those head-to-head matchups, the margins of victory steadily decreased, until for the first time the Soviets defeated the Americans at the 1959 world championships in Santiago, Chile—and in convincing fashion, 62–37. An American magazine account the following year recalled: "The U.S. team lost to the Soviet team—still a believe-it-or-not incident—and became immediately the butt of jokes. . . . According to the *New York Times* sports columnist Arthur Daley, 'it was a propaganda defeat of the first magnitude.'"[15]

Having broken through with their first significant victory, the Soviets continued to chip away at American dominance in the sport. In 1960 a Soviet team toured the United States, winning four out of six games against local amateur teams. In their first victory on American soil, the Soviets defeated the Akron Goodyear Wingfoots—hardly top American talent. They followed that victory with a thrilling 96–93 overtime victory over the Denver D-C Truckers, AAU national champions that year. Such victories provided fodder for the Soviet propaganda machine, while the Americans dismissed them as meaningless exhibition games. American spokesmen praised the improving Soviet team but at the same time longed for greater support for the American effort and for better players on the court.[16]

In 1961 an American team toured the Soviet Union, winning all eight games on the trip. The fact that politics was not absent from these exchanges was made clear by the three-day delay in launching the trip, as the US embassy in Moscow was besieged following the Bay of Pigs incident in Cuba. Perhaps sport helped calm the situation, as the trip proceeded without further incident, and Soviet crowds again turned out in great numbers to watch the games. Despite their winless record in the series, the Soviets came away from the games having lost several close decisions and also having learned much from watching the Americans, facts noted by American trip organizers.[17] In 1962 the Soviets returned to the United States, winning just two out of six games. As the annual exchanges mounted, a pattern developed: American organizers were forced to put subpar teams on the court, for a variety of reasons, and the nation at large paid little attention to the results of the games. Attendance for the games on American soil was mediocre and robust for those in the Soviet Union. Americans understood that the teams representing the "United States" in such games were second- and third-rate amateur teams, a far cry from top professional teams. It became commonplace for the Americans to fall back on excuses in explaining the losses: it was impossible to muster top players for such games; American players tended to suffer under international rules (which differed slightly from those in the United States); the Soviet players were "professionals" and held an overwhelming advantage over the American "amateurs"; and the games were friendly exhibitions, of no consequence. For the Soviets, however, a victory under any circumstances bolstered their national reputation, and they consistently sent members of their national team—the best the Soviet Union had to offer—for what the Americans considered meaningless games.[18] As Marquette University coach Al McGuire said of a later tour, "the propaganda value to the Russians . . . is tremendous. If we lose, the rest of the world won't know who was or who wasn't on our team, all they'll know is that the Russians beat us."[19]

While both sides spoke favorably of the public-relations benefits of the tours, a handful of incidents in the 1960s anticipated the bitterness of the games of the early 1970s. In 1964 an American team toured the Soviet Union in April and May, managing to win only three games while losing five. The American press, amateur sports groups, and the athletes themselves voiced frustration and concern in the wake of these defeats. AAU vice president Clifford Buck credited an improved, and experienced, Soviet team with the wins, noting that "the Soviet Unions' National team is composed of largely the same personnel as was used in the 1960 Rome Olympics."[20] Other Americans were more deeply concerned with the defeats, such as Harvard University coach Floyd Wilson, who expressed his frustration: "When are we going to realize that we should never send anything less than our best to compete against the Russians? The damage the U.S. image abroad suffers every time one of our teams is defeated by a Soviet team is staggering. . . . Whether we Americans like it or not, the people over there consider any sporting event between the U.S. and Russia to be a struggle between the two nations themselves. . . . No matter what, we should never send a team there on a competitive basis unless it can be done to our advantage."[21] The Soviets, in order to preserve the momentum generated by such victories, canceled a scheduled tour by National Basketball Association (NBA) players the next month, who instead romped through twenty-one games in Yugoslavia and Poland, winning all by at least twenty points. The Soviets declined to play them, fearing not only defeat but perhaps lopsided defeat. Two years later, the Soviets added to American frustration by abruptly canceling the scheduled annual contest in protest against American involvement in Vietnam.[22] Finally, at the 1967 world championships, the United States beat the Soviets 59–58 in a controversial early-round game eerily similar to the 1972 Olympic final. With about ninety seconds to go and the score tied, a chaotic sequence occurred. Seemingly in the same instant, American player Jay Miller attempted to get off a shot, the shot-clock buzzer sounded, and the referee whistled a foul against the Soviet center. The officials conferred and incorrectly awarded the Soviets two free throws. The Americans walked off the court. After about five minutes, the call was reversed, and the Americans were given two shots for the foul. The Soviets were incensed and, after the loss, threatened to withdraw from the tournament. The incident only subsided days later, after the Soviets overcame that loss to win the gold medal, defeating Yugoslavia while the Americans lost to both Yugoslavia and Brazil. Nonetheless, the controversial game remained lodged in the minds of Soviet players and administrators, and "avenging" that loss became a common talking point in years following when the two teams met.[23]

Even as tensions between the two sides mounted with each passing game, the Soviets studied and mimicked their American competitors, soaking in every bit of information they could in an effort to match the Americans at their own game. Soviet journalist Anatoly Pinchuk described the extent of their interest, explaining that coaches and players studied every detail in magazine articles about the Harlem Globetrotters, Pete Maravich, Lew Alcindor, and Bill Walton, lessons written by Bill Russell and Bob Cousy, volumes written and shared by American coaches, and especially videotapes of Jerry West.[24] Despite arguments to the contrary from American star Jerry Lucas, who asserted in 1962 that the Soviet "improvement has been negligible," in fact the Soviets did improve.[25] While they would never exude the natural talents and fluid grace that defined the best American players, they did evolve beyond the huge but clumsy players common on the earliest Soviet teams.[26] By the late 1960s, Soviet teams were generally sound with the ball, employed efficient ball movement, shot the ball well, and—Lucas's criticism notwithstanding—were sprinkled with players who, while not flashy, were quick and versatile. No one would claim that the Soviet players could match the top talent in the NBA, but the Americans could no longer simply paste together a squad of leading amateurs and expect victory. The gap had indeed closed.

## American Disappointment: 1971–1972

And then came the Soviet team's tour of the United States in 1971, which played out in an atmosphere of growing malaise. Frustration with the Vietnam War was peaking, the economy was beginning to flounder, and the positive vibrations of the 1960s were becoming a distant memory. In the midst of this difficult time, the Soviets sent a team that included six players from their 1968 Olympic team and nine expected to play in the 1972 Olympics. They matched up against American teams usually consisting of top local AAU talent, with the occasional college player thrown in. And while everyone professed to have a good time during this tour, and the Soviet players took in movies, listened to Elvis, and bought blue jeans and records, the Soviet team also went on an unexpected winning streak. When the Soviets had won six straight games, the Americans brought in several top players, including Artis Gilmore, for the seventh game in Indianapolis. They lost that one too. Then, before the eighth game, the Americans sent the Soviets on a roundabout ten-hour trip to their destination, Albuquerque, New Mexico, after which they were forced to sit through a press conference before being taken to their hotel. The Americans also brought in three professional players from the American Basketball Association (ABA), but they lost again, by a score of 91–67. It was not until the ninth and final game of the tour, after thoroughly gorging themselves on American food and exhausting themselves with all manner of American entertainment, that the Soviets lost a game, 94–91, to a team of Utah all-stars.[27] The whippings of that 1971 tour served as a wake-up call for the Americans and proved that the Soviet team could no longer be readily beaten by just an average American amateur team. The next meeting between the two was that infamous final game at the 1972 Munich Olympics.

Both the Americans and the Soviets arrived at the final game in Munich having gone undefeated in eight games, most by wide margins. For the United States, the toughest challenges had come from Brazil and Spain. The US team trailed for much of the game against Brazil, before ultimately prevailing 61–54, and a solid Spanish squad tested the Americans before falling 72–56. The Soviets were tested as well, especially in a rollicking 100–87 victory over Puerto Rico and a hard-fought 67–61 win over Cuba in the semifinal game.[28] For both teams, perhaps the greatest challenge was overcoming the emotional blow dealt to the Olympics five days prior to the gold-medal game, when eleven members of the Israeli team were killed during the infamous raid by Palestinian terrorists. Many wondered whether the Games should resume after the tragedy, and several American players expressed doubts about playing the final game.[29] IOC president Avery Brundage and Olympic organizers, however, decreed that "the Games must go on," and thus the teams met in the gold-medal game.[30]

What followed was one of the most notorious defeats in American sports history. In truth, the Americans played sluggishly and trailed the Soviets throughout the game. The American team came to life in the final minutes, rallied late from a ten-point deficit, and in the final minute had a chance to win. The Americans cut the lead to one point with thirty-eight seconds to go. The Soviets attempted to protect their lead, but on the next trip down the court their center, Alexander Belov, inexplicably attempted a shot and then threw a wild pass off the rebound, which wound up in the hands of American guard Doug Collins. Collins controlled the ball, drove to the other end, and as he went up for the go-ahead layup was fouled hard, undercut by Soviet player Zurab Sakandelidze. Collins crashed to the floor. He was unconscious for a few seconds but recovered and coolly made both free throws to put the Americans ahead, 50–49, with three seconds on the clock.

And then the world witnessed the controversial finish. The Soviets inbounded the ball and ran two seconds off the clock, their offense in disarray. But with Soviet coaches and players crowding the officiating table, the referee ordered play stopped. Officials conferred, along with the secretary-general of FIBA (the International Basketball Federation), R. William Jones of Great Britain, who—against international basketball rules—had come down from the stands to intervene. Breaking from the huddle, the officials ruled that the Soviets had attempted to call a time-out before Collins's second free throw, meaning they should have had time to set a play before inbounding the ball. The referee then returned the ball to the Soviets, who inbounded the ball again, this time launching an errant pass the length of the court. The horn sounded, apparently ending the game. The Americans celebrated. But the officials conferred again, ruling that the game clock had not been reset to three seconds, so they played it one more time. This time, the Soviets were able to score by making a length-of-the-court pass and lay-up. Even that finish was controversial, as Belov, who received the pass, bumped an American defender in order to get at the ball. No foul was called, the basket counted, and the Soviets won, 51–50.[31]

The aftermath of the game witnessed a combination of shock, anger, and dismay in the United States. Brundage was swamped with letters of complaint and protest, most from Americans and many from children, including one who lamented: "The Olympic basketball game that was on last night was not very fair because the judge or official turned the clock back three seconds after the Americans had already beat the Russians. Will you reschedule the game because it really wasn't fair to the Americans?"[32]

The Americans lodged a formal complaint with the Olympic Jury of Appeals, a five-man committee. Members voted along Cold War party lines (the Italian and Puerto Rican members supported the American grievance, while the Cuban, Polish, and Hungarian members voted to uphold the outcome), the claim was denied, and the final score was allowed to stand. There were many questions about those final moments, some of which are disputed to this day. Most hinge on poor governance of the game by the referees: the Soviets had attempted to call a time-out too late, and once the ball was in Collins's hands at the free-throw line, no stoppage should have been allowed; after the first Soviet attempt in the final moments, Jones approached the scorer's table and ordered that three seconds be put back on the clock, an unprecedented breach of the rules governing such situations; on the final inbound, the referee appeared to instruct American player Tom McMillen to back away from the end line, allowing the Soviet player to throw his pass without obstruction; the Soviet player inbounding the ball appeared to step on the line as he threw; and Belov appeared to push an American player while catching the pass prior to the final basket, which should have been called a foul. Such points, while controversial and in some cases still unresolved, are outside the scope of this paper and have been thoroughly hashed out elsewhere.[33]

Other complaints, involving the administration of the American team and, especially, the selection of the team, are more relevant to this discussion. Those observers who are willing to concede that the Americans were at least partially responsible for their own defeat are quick to question the coaching decisions of Coach Henry "Hank" Iba. Indeed, Iba had come out of retirement to coach the team, and some argued that the game had passed him by. Rather than play to the strength of his team and run an up-tempo, fluid offense, Iba insisted on a methodical, slow, half-court offense, in which players passed the ball many times prior to taking a shot. While that method had been effective in the games leading up to the final (and, it might be added, in the two previous Olympics in which Iba-coached teams won the gold medal), it seemed to stifle the team in the final game, especially in the first half. The Americans were hesitant with their passes, virtually never went for quick baskets, and committed several turnovers early. The Soviets seized momentum and held a lead of between five and ten points for most of the game.[34]

A related issue was the roster itself. While better than the weak amateur teams that had faced the Soviets during the disastrous 1971 tour, it was weaker than American Olympic teams of the past. Up to that point, the United States had been able to win Olympic gold by assembling a squad of top collegiate players, overcoming relatively easily the absence of any players who missed the Games. In 1968 a team described by one writer as "ragamuffins, leftovers, and rag-tags," a team with "no stars," won the gold medal with relative ease.[35] But as international competition—and especially the Soviet team—improved, the American team did not, and in 1972 the absence of several key players clearly hurt the team's chances. The most significant absentee was Bill Walton, star center for the University of California, Los Angeles (UCLA) Bruins and one of the greatest collegiate players of all time. Whether he skipped the games as a conscientious objector (he protested American action in Vietnam) or because of a previous sour experience playing for a US national team (which was his own explanation) or because of injury (as John Wooden, his coach at UCLA, explained), Walton opted not to play for the 1972 team. There were other important absences as well. Swen Nater, Walton's backup at UCLA and himself a skilled center, abandoned the team after losing twenty pounds in the bootcamp-style training camp. A host of other top players did not play for the US team because they were moving on to professional basketball in the ABA, which would make them ineligible for the Olympics. These included Julius Erving, Bob McAdoo, and George McGinnis.[36] And finally, some top college players could not play for Team USA because the National Collegiate Athletic Association (NCAA) did not sanction the team and would declare them ineligible. Such players included Len Elmore and David Thompson. It is hard not to believe that the Americans would have prevailed in Munich had these players—or any one of them—played for the team.[37]

## American Redemption: 1973 and Beyond

The dispiriting defeats in the 1971 series and the humiliation in Munich invigorated the US basketball program with a new sense of urgency. No longer were these games mere exhibitions for the Americans—they had become a matter of American pride and patriotism. In addition, basketball was no longer merely a sideshow in the realm of international athletics. The AAU had long emphasized other sports, most notably track and field, as preeminent in the Cold War sporting rivalry. Swimming, boxing, and even wrestling were also celebrated. Such individual sports narrowed the rivalry into riveting one-on-one duels, crowning a clear victor in absolute fashion. Since 1958—the same year that the basketball exchanges began—the annual track-and-field dual meet had drawn far more attention than any of the basketball games.[38] But suddenly, in the aftermath of Munich, basketball moved to the forefront of the Cold War, and American victory became essential.

The Americans had to wait nine months for an opportunity to avenge the loss. In May 1973 the Soviets returned to the United States for a six-game series, with largely the same team that had prevailed in Munich. The quality of the American team was vastly superior to the 1971 squad and compared favorably with the Olympic team. It included Doug Collins, Bobby Jones, Tom Henderson, and Jim Brewer, who were on that 1972 Olympic team and were eager for revenge. Officials from the AAU and the NCAA—under much public pressure and at the urging of Congress—put aside long-standing differences and cooperated in assembling the strongest squad possible to face the Soviets.[39] Perhaps surprisingly, Bill

Walton had helped forge the compromise by the two organizations so he could play for the US team.[40] Former Boston Celtics star Bob Cousy was brought in to coach. Other top American players included Swen Nater and Providence University star Ernie DiGregorio. It was described in the press—and by former Olympic coach Pete Newell—as the best US team since the 1960 Olympic team, which included such players as Jerry West, Oscar Robertson, Walt Bellamy, and Jerry Lucas.[41]

Enthusiasm for the games in the United States, unlike previous exhibition games against the Soviets, soared, as the opportunity to avenge the defeat in Munich provided an enticing story line. Popular interest in the games was demonstrated by the fact that tickets for the first game sold out weeks in advance, that the series was covered in many national magazines and prominent newspapers, and that the sell-out crowds at the games were passionate and loud. The theme of redemption played prominently in the press, as *Newsweek* magazine dubbed the series "an affair of honor."[42] Echoing this theme, the lead story in the game-one program announced it with the opening sentence, "Was it a fluke when the Soviet Union beat the United States in basketball at the Olympic finals in Munich last year?"[43] *Sports Illustrated* described the pressure on the US team, writing that they had "so much to lose . . . proving that while basketball was born here, it certainly wasn't going to die here. Not just yet. . . . The Americans embraced the series as if it were a chance to avenge Sputnik, the grain deal . . . as well as that embarrassing loss in Munich."[44] For their part, the Soviets were confident, even smug. At one preliminary press conference, when asked about Walton, the Soviet coach, Vladimir Kondrashin, asked, "Is he white or black?" as if he had never heard of the all-world star.[45]

The first game was played in Los Angeles in an electric atmosphere. Any expectation that the hype and excitement surrounding the event would lead to friendly pleasantries on the court was quickly shattered by the rough play. Coach Cousy described the action after the game, saying, "It's mayhem out there, especially under the basket. The international game is very, very physical inside. We just couldn't get the ball inside to Walton. He must have been knocked down four or five times." He underscored the point, adding, "We've got to be more physical."[46] Cousy's impressions were certainly borne out on the trainer's table and in the locker room, which was described as a field hospital, with virtually every player bumped and bruised and several bandaged. "Pound for pound," said Tom

Henderson, "they'll beat you to death." Most damaging, Walton injured his left knee during the game and did not return for the rest of the series.[47] Despite the physical beating, the US team prevailed, 83–65.

In game two in San Diego, the Soviets "manhandled" the Americans, winning 78–76, as the action grew even rougher than the first game.[48] American forward Ron Behagen was ejected from the game for swinging elbows. Bobby Jones led the US team in rebounding despite "being bent and mashed into Silly Putty by the brawny Russians."[49] In that same game, Jones took a charge from Ivan Dvorni, one of the toughest Soviet players. "I saw him coming," said Jones, "and you can't imagine the things that went through my mind. At U.N.C. I would have stood there because we always take charges. Then I thought, 'He's 6'10" and 240.' And then at the last moment, I thought, 'I'm going to do it for my country.' That was the most terrifying moment I've had in my life."[50] During the game Cousy complained so bitterly of bad calls that he was given a technical foul. Afterward, accusations of dirty play came from both sides. Swen Nater was the target of the most pointed criticism from the Soviet coach Kondrashin, who said, "Nater goes out with his elbows and is not a sportsman. . . . [He] is a dirty player, a very dirty player."[51]

The game-two beating convinced Cousy and his staff that they had to bring in even tougher players to survive the rest of the series. "We know what we're up against now," he said. "Our players realize that the games are won inside. We just have to be as physical as they are."[52] Cousy called upon some of the most notoriously rough players in college basketball to join the squad for game three in Albuquerque, including the University of Maryland's Len Elmore, Indiana University's Steve Downing, and Providence's Marvin "Bad News" Barnes. Barnes had been one of the last players cut at the Olympic tryouts, so he was offered redemption of a different sort. "They told me at the Olympic tryouts that I played too rough," he said, "but now they want me because I do play rough."[53] Before game three, Cousy handed over the pregame speech to one of his assistants, Buster Sheary, former coach at the College of the Holy Cross. Sheary, sixty-four years old, got down on his knees and gave an emotional speech, invoking references to God and country. Cousy left the room nearly in tears. The United States held the Soviets without a field goal for the first three and a half minutes and went on to win 83–67.[54]

The series only got tougher in the final games. The United States won the fourth game, in Indianapolis, but the rough play continued, as there were eighty-eight fouls, leading to six foul-outs for the Soviets and four for the Americans.[55] The fifth game, in New York, evoked memories of 1972. The game was officiated by Renato Righetto of Brazil, who had also called (and many feel blown) the game in Munich. Near the end of this game in New York, he called a charging foul against a Soviet player with his team ahead 73–69 and under a minute remaining. When the US team managed to tie the game at 73 at the end of regulation time, the Soviet coach nearly pulled his team from the game. But the Soviets stayed, finished the game, and lost 89–80. To some, it felt like a "Munich Rerun" in reverse. Alexander Belov, who had scored the winning basket in Munich, even commented after the game, "It looks as if the Americans and the referees got their revenge for Munich."[56] The game was also just as violent as the other games in the series, with eight players fouling out and many players sporting "black and blue marks and scars on their knees" in the aftermath.[57] With the victory in game five, the United States held an insurmountable 4–1 advantage in the series, and along with it "some measure of revenge for the disputed 51–50 loss to Russia in the Olympic final at Munich last year," as one writer described it.[58] While the Soviet players downplayed any such connection, a number of American players and staff expressed pleasure in the series victory.

The last game of the series, played in Baltimore, was the roughest of all. The referees called seventy-five fouls, and six Soviets and three Americans fouled out in what the *New York Times* described as a "rough and tumble finale."[59] Belov fouled out on a play in which he was hit in the face by Nater and left with his hands covered in blood. American players, nursing their wounds after the game, complained about both the tight officiating that interrupted the flow of play and the rough tactics of the Soviets. Elmore said, "They haven't mastered all the mechanics of the game, but they make up for it by punching and grabbing stuff."[60] The Soviets won the game 72–64.

The Americans were proud of their accomplishment in winning four out of six games against a formidable opponent and achieving a measure of redemption for the defeat in Munich. Coach Cousy articulated the deeper significance of the contest, saying, "Despite all the moaning, there's an inherent patriotism in all of us. This was one of the motivating factors in my accepting the job. I thought I'd get a kick out of representing my country against the first team ever to beat us in Olympic competition. This was a chance for us to get even. It may sound corny at this stage, but it was an important consideration."[61] The celebration was muted, however, by the realization that the Americans could no longer beat the Soviets with anything less than an excellent team. Cousy reflected on the new state of affairs in international basketball: "We have to send our best players to the Olympic Games, and we have to resolve the battle between the AAU and the NCAA. We're not going to beat them if we don't send our best players. . . . Any team we send to the Olympics must have muscle. The Russians are capable of beating any amateur or college team in the United States under international rules."[62]

Despite the claim that victory in the 1973 series secured revenge for the defeat in Munich, in fact the feud between the squads continued to play out on the court for months, and even years, after the series concluded. Only a few days after that brutal sixth game, the Soviet team played a final game on its US tour, against the AAU champions, the Lexington Marathon Oilers, on their home court in Lexington, Kentucky. Despite the late addition of several top college players to the Oilers, the Soviets still unleashed some of their frustrations on the undermanned squad, winning easily 109–87. Ken Davis, a veteran of the US 1972 Olympic squad, played for the American team in Lexington, losing again to his bitter rivals. Even as the US team celebrated a victory in the overall series, Davis noted, "There may be a day when the U.S. can't compete internationally unless some changes are made in the way we approach the competition."[63]

It was not until a few months later, at the 1973 World University Games, that both players and the media declared that the Americans fully exacted their revenge for the 1972 Olympic debacle. The games were played in Moscow before a "whistling, hooting" crowd of twelve thousand fans, and the Soviets were heavy favorites, with six players from their 1972 Olympic team. The Americans had only one. The American team was also younger than the one the Soviets played in the United States and included fewer stars. But led by North Carolina State University's David Thompson, Quinn Buckner of Indiana, and Marvin Barnes, the Americans won a surprising 75–67 victory over the Soviets in the championship game, securing a record of 19–0 for the tournament and, for the moment, reasserting American international dominance.[64] After that victory, many articles in the American press emphasized the element of revenge, as one

Figure 9.1. Lakeland College coach and Team USA manager Duane Woltzen cuts down the net after the US victory in the gold-medal basketball game at the 1973 University Games in Moscow. (Photo by Glenn Sondby; University of Arkansas Archives)

that read, "The American basketball victory restored the prestige that was lost in last summer's 51–50 loss to the Russians at Munich." Tom Burleson, the only US team member who had played in Munich, said, "I'm glad I was able to have a part in this. . . . Beating the Russians has been burning inside me for a long time. I'm only sorry the other eleven at Munich couldn't be here with us."[65] As if to symbolically bury the hatchet, the howling mob of Soviet fans eventually took to cheering the Americans in their resounding victory.

Further humbling the Soviet team was a scandal that broke shortly after those games and after the Soviets surprisingly lost to Spain at the European basketball championships that October. The scandal originated in reports of players smuggling various goods back from their trip to the United States. A Soviet sports editor wrote, "The national team returned home burdened not with a heap of victories, but with a heap of unprecedented customs violations."[66] A related, and even more damning, development was that the Soviet players had become "soft" after their exposure to the West, expecting to be pampered and coddled like Western athletes were. Simply put, they were more difficult to control than they had been prior to their travels abroad. The editor noted that after so much time on the road, "there was practically no time for indoctrination work with the team, even for ordinary training."[67] As Americans worried that the Soviet team now matched them on the court, Soviet administrators bemoaned the fact that the players also mimicked the Western stars in their off-court behavior.[68] Neither side, it seemed, was happy with the situation.

The teams continued to clash occasionally throughout the 1970s, with sporadic instances of violence and/or controversy. At the 1974 world championships in San Juan, Puerto Rico, the Soviets prevailed in the championship game, 105–94. For them, the game restored some of the prestige the team had lost in the scandals of the previous year. For the Americans, it seemed once again to send the message that only a team of the best players would be good enough to beat the Soviets from that point forward. The US team was not without talent and included players such as Quinn Buckner, John Lucas, and Luther "Ticky" Burden of the University of Utah, all of whom fought passionately to win. They earned the admiration of the Yugoslavian players, one of whom commented: "The U.S. team, they finally seem like fighting for country. Always before they seem like playing for Gulf Oil or somebody."[69] Despite the best efforts of these very good players, the Soviet team was simply better.

The following year, the Soviets returned to the United States for another tour, playing fourteen games against a number of strong college teams and top amateur clubs. The Soviet team, which included several "giants" over seven feet tall, won half of the games and generally enjoyed themselves on the visit. Still, the games were not without controversy. In the second game, at Indiana University, Soviet coach Kondrashin was so incensed with a foul call that he pulled his players from the floor, resulting in a five-minute delay. They returned and completed the game, losing 94–78. Several games later, after the Soviets had beaten respectable teams from Syracuse University and the University of Richmond, Dean Smith, the coach at the University of North Carolina, was determined to stop the losing streak. Smith was slated to coach the US squad at the 1976 Olympics and did not want to concede another victory to the Soviets. In a hard-fought game, UNC prevailed 82–78 but only after Coach Kondrashin threatened to pull his team from the floor after a series of questionable calls.[70] The series set the stage for the Montreal Olympics of 1976, where everyone hoped to see what was promising to be an epic rematch of the 1972 final. Alas, the Soviets failed to make the gold-medal game in those Olympics, losing to Yugoslavia in the semifinals. The world would have to wait until 1988 for the Americans and Soviets to meet again in the Olympics.[71]

## Settling the Score: Basketball as Diplomacy

The US-Soviet basketball rivalry offers an opportunity to add depth and nuance to a consideration of great-power diplomacy during these years of the Cold War. First, it is interesting that these intense clashes on the basketball court occurred at the same time that the broader diplomacy between the two sides was moving toward détente. While recent studies suggest that the good feelings between the United States and the Soviet Union in the period of détente have been overstated, there was at least an ebb in the nuclear tension between the two sides, and the fear of nuclear annihilation reached one of its lowest points of the Cold War.[72]

In the midst of this period, the two sides met in the most hotly contested basketball games of the entire Cold War, and the bad blood flowed freely between players, coaches, fans, and media on both sides. At the same time, Bobby Fischer and Boris Spassky clashed in their epic chess championship series, which was a source of drama and tension between the two powers through much of late 1971 and early 1972. At the risk of extrapolating too much meaning from sporting events at times considered trivial, we might infer from such episodes that the period of détente did not lessen by much—if at all—the tensions between the two powers. If there was an era of good feelings between the two, it did not take much for those feelings to turn bad. A chess match, a basketball game, a tour of players from the other side quickly brought to the surface the feelings of fear, suspicion, and even hatred that characterized the Cold War.[73]

Put another way, according to historian Daniel Johnson in his book, *White King and Red Queen,* détente provided a brief period in which the fear of nuclear annihilation receded just enough that other events took on heightened attention. He was writing about Fischer-Spassky, but the thought applies as well to basketball in the early 1970s. While prior to this we may have been too consumed with Cold War fears to care much about basketball, as the grander political clash seemed to ease somewhat, such things as chess matches and basketball games returned to prominence.[74]

The basketball series of this era also suggest that sports are influenced by an internal diplomacy that may well trump the external forces at work. Players, fiercely competitive and driven by their own desire to succeed as individuals and as a team, get caught up in the heat of the moment. They fight back when attacked. They struggle against long odds and work to overcome seemingly insurmountable obstacles. The improved Soviet team of the late 1960s now posed a legitimate threat to American supremacy on the court. So when the American team was battered by the Soviet squad in the 1971 tour and then cheated out of the gold medal at the 1972 Olympics, the players on the US team in 1973 responded fiercely, regardless of how profoundly the spirit of détente may have permeated the rest of society.

As just one example, Mike Bantom, an American from the 1972 team, faced his old nemesis when he played against the Soviets in Italy twelve years later. The Soviets started to play roughly, and Bantom found himself playing like a man possessed. He forgot all about scoring baskets and playing good basketball, and just started elbowing and kneeing opposing players at every opportunity. The Soviet coach, still Vladimir Kondrashin, approached Bantom at halftime and asked, "Why are you doing this?" Bantom replied, "I know who you are and I know what you're doing. You, more than anybody, should know why I hate you sons of bitches."[75] So, perhaps the internal politics of a team or an event trump the greater international politics of an era. Perhaps the players involved in the 1973 exchange were more concerned about avenging the 1972 loss and beating their Soviet rivals than in honoring the spirit of détente that seemed to be prevailing in international affairs.

There were still other factors at work that may have heightened the importance of these basketball games. Concerns on the home front left Americans in need of a victory. In a period when the nation was being pulled apart by a host of divisive issues—from the end of the Vietnam War to the Watergate scandal to the oil crisis and declining economy to the struggles of all manner of social movements—the national basketball team taking down its fiercest rival gave the nation something to cheer about. In a small way, these games helped to unify a country badly in need of such unifying forces.

Another analytical approach is to consider these contests in relation to the "muscle gap," which essentially refers to a concern that the Soviets had an advantage in physical strength and, by extension, virility. Taken to the extreme, the muscle gap pointed to the feminization of the American male, in contrast to the rugged, virile Soviet. Jeffrey Montez de Oca has discussed this phenomenon in an earlier period of the Cold War, but the basketball clashes of the early 1970s provide an interesting case study.[76]

In articles describing the two teams throughout this period, constant reference is made to the fact that the Soviets were tougher and more physical in their play. They are less graceful and athletic but win by pummeling their opponents into submission and utilizing fouls strategically. The American players are frequently referred to as "kids" or "boys," and other descriptions include phrases such "Fuzz Kids,"[77] "gangly," and possessing "rhythm and fluidity."[78] In contrast, the Soviet players are usually described as men, virtually every article emphasizes their size and strength, and other descriptions include "brawnier," brutish," and "muscleman."[79] It is impossible to miss the suggestion that the Soviet players were bigger and stronger when reading descriptions such as "the muscular Russians . . . moved the ball well and crashed the boards with the vigor of the Minnesota Vikings' front four."[80]

Such statements are a subconscious expression of the muscle gap, with its concerns about the virility and strength of American men. Basketball games between the United States and the Soviet Union became not only a test of international power or even athletic superiority but a test of manhood. Can we overcome the muscular brutes from the other side? Or have we become weak and soft? The muscle gap was played out in one mini-drama that was central to these events, at the end of the 1972 gold-medal game. The Americans in general were knocked around by the Soviets in that game, but in the final seconds it was Doug Collins, rail-thin and boyish in appearance, who was hammered to the ground by one of the Soviet players on his way to the hoop—the American boy clocked by the Russian man. That Collins was able to recover from the blow and make the free throws is not only a testament to his basketball skill but his manhood. In the end, though, it was the Russian strongman Belov, by elbowing aside two American players to catch the pass, who scored the winning basket. In that game, anyway, brawn prevailed.

It was important in the 1973 series, then, that the United States not only beat the Soviets but do so in a rough, physical way. Coach Cousy did not discourage his players from playing rough; in fact, his comments from this period often include compliments of his players who had fouled out or delivered a hard foul. In defense of his oft-criticized center Nater, Cousy said, "I wish he could play 40 per cent more aggressively, and if that means 40 per cent dirtier, that's all right with me."[81] He recruited to the team several players known for their toughness and encouraged his current players to get tougher. This was not only a basketball series and a Cold War clash—it was a rite of passage for these young men.

## Conclusion

The US-Soviet basketball rivalry of this era illustrates the complexities of great-power diplomacy during the Cold War. As with other sporting clashes, the games offered a venue where tensions between the two sides could play out—if not entirely without violence, at least without putting the fate of the planet at risk. Unlike other cultural endeavors, such as musical or ballet performances, literature, or works of art, basketball games ended with a clear winner and a clear loser. And while the Soviet Union, with its tightly controlled government-sport network, made greater propaganda value of its victories, both sides equated victory on the court with broader social and cultural superiority. Considering the violence and intensity of this rivalry in the early years of the 1970s, it is impossible to accept that the sport exchanges were conducted purely in the interest of "goodwill." For both sides, games against their bitter rival took on added significance, especially when the attention of the nation was heightened. Marquette coach Al McGuire voiced the concerns of many in 1973 when he said, "When the Russians come over here for a basketball tour in a couple months, they'll be here to bury us. And they might. Because the way it is now, our best college players won't be on the team. . . . You'd think something like this would be bigger than the feud [between the AAU and the NCAA], that it would mean so much that they'd stand up together for the country."[82]

Nonetheless, the contests did offer both sides a glimpse into the human qualities of their rivals, removing a layer of secrecy and fear that, throughout the Cold War, made the other side seem monolithic and terrifying. As athletes locked in fierce competition learned, those on the other side of the diplomatic divide were human too. Athletes on both sides seemed to have respect for the others, and most of their comments to the press—and even in memoirs—indicate that there was a sincere undercurrent of goodwill within the games. Cousy, for all his complaining during the heat of battle, expressed a degree of admiration for the Soviets when the 1973 series was completed. And athletes on both sides spoke highly of their opponents on the other side—when they were not complaining about vicious play and cheap shots. Even the "robotic" Soviets showed at times that they were not humorless, as when Ivan Edeshko told a reporter, "The people in America same as Russia. Same!" Then, he added with a wink, "Especially the girls."[83] Players, coaches, and event organizers all felt pulled in both directions, by a profound desire to beat their rival, while at the same time developing a begrudging respect for their opponent. As Soviet long jumper Igor Ter-Ovanesyan explained during one of the dual track meets, "We found ourselves equally able to be ferocious on the running track and friendly in everyday life."[84] The media also conveyed this dichotomy of emotions, at times embracing moments of goodwill and friendship between the two sides and at other times stoking the people's desire to crush its rivals, sometimes in the same article. Unlikely as it might have seemed, in sport—unlike in nuclear diplomacy or traditional warfare—one could be *both* bitter rivals and friends at the same time. A Soviet Olympic basketball official summarized this duality, when he said, "We like to beat America, but only because America is very strong—and we want to be stronger."[85]

After the 1972 Olympic final, the Americans and the Soviets did not meet again in an Olympic basketball game until 1988. In 1976 the Soviets did not make it to the gold-medal game, won by the Americans, and the 1980 and 1984 Games were spoiled by the "dueling boycotts." When they did play again in 1988, the Soviet team—again experienced, well-rounded, and tough—defeated an inferior American squad of leading collegiate players, driving home once and for all the need for the United States to put its best players on the court. It did just that, with the famous "Dream Team" at the 1992 Olympics in Barcelona. One can scarcely imagine a period of greater change than the one between the 1988 and 1992 Olympics, as the fall of the Soviet Union meant that the "Unified Team" of 1992 was a shell of the former Soviet teams and in fact was inferior to the teams from several of the former Soviet republics. The Lithuanian contingent, always a key component of Soviet success, played independently for the first time and won the bronze medal.[86] Meantime, the Dream Team, populated by many of the top professional players of all time, destroyed all opponents in its path, making a mockery of the entire tournament. Its absolute dominance proved what many Americans had been saying for decades, that no international team stood a chance against a squad of the best American professional players. But, with the Cold War over and once-great rivals vanquished, the victory in Barcelona stands merely as an epitaph for the always intriguing US-Soviet basketball rivalry.[87]

## Notes

1. Gary Smith, "A Few Pieces of Silver," *Sports Illustrated,* June 15, 1992, 64–77.

2. The best historical treatment of that infamous game are in Carson Cunningham, *American Hoops: U.S. Men's Olympic Basketball from Berlin to Beijing* (Lincoln: University of Nebraska Press, 2009), 202–32, and Christopher Clark Elzey, "Munich 1972: Sport, Politics, and Tragedy," PhD diss., Purdue University, 2004, 254–93. Both studies consider the game in its full context and review all aspects of the controversy. And while both mention some of the recent defeats and struggles of the US national team, neither fully ties together the games prior to, and following, 1972. Gary Smith of *Sports Illustrated* interviewed all of the American players and many other actors in his fine article "A Few Pieces of Silver." A more detailed, if less even-handed study of the 1972 contest is Mike Brewster and Taps Gallagher, *Stolen Glory: The U.S., the Soviet Union, and the Olympic Basketball Game That Never Ended* (Los Angeles: G.M. Books, 2012). For the Soviet perspective, see Anatoly Pinchuk, "From Helsinki to Munich," in *USSR-USA Sports Encounters,* ed. Victor Kuznetsov and Mikhail Lukashev (Moscow: Progress Publishers, 1977), 101–20. A number

of documentaries examine the game. The one offering the most thorough analysis of US international basketball in general is from referee Artenik Arabadjian in *:03 from Gold,* directed by George Roy (HBO Sports and Black Canyon Productions, 2002). Others include Dave Revsine, *ESPN Classic Big Ticket: 1972 Olympic Basketball* (ESPN Classic, 2004), http://www.youtube.com/watch?v=NuBm0PRt23I (accessed August 3, 2013), and Chris Fowler, *ESPN SportsCentury: Three Seconds of Chaos* (ESPN Classic, 2002), http://www.youtube.com/watch?v=60IMdwuLe_o (accessed August 3, 2013).

3. Among such studies of the "Cultural Cold War" are Laura A. Belmonte, *Selling the American Way: U.S. Propaganda and the Cold War* (Philadelphia: University of Pennsylvania Press, 2008); Walter L. Hixson, *Parting the Curtain: Propaganda, Culture, and the Cold War* (New York: St. Martin's, 1997); Helen Laville and Hugh Wilford, eds., *The U.S. Government, Citizen Groups and the Cold War: The State-Private Network* (New York: Routledge, 2006); Scott Lucas, *Freedom's War: The American Crusade against the Soviet Union* (New York: New York University Press, 1999); Frances Stoner Saunders, *Who Paid the Piper? The CIA and the Cultural Cold War* (London: Granta Books, 1999); and Kenneth Osgood, *Total Cold War: Eisenhower's Secret Propaganda Battle at Home and Abroad* (Lawrence: University Press of Kansas, 2006).

4. Among such studies of sport and the Cultural Cold War are Barbara Keys, "The Early Cold War Olympics, 1952–1960: Political, Economic and Human Rights Dimensions," in *The Palgrave Handbook of Olympic Studies,* ed. Helen Lenskyi and Stephen Wagg (Houndsmills, UK: Palgrave Macmillan, 2012); Alfred Erich Senn, *Power, Politics and the Olympic Games* (Champaign, IL: Human Kinetics, 1999); Stephen Wagg and David L. Andrews, eds., *East Plays West: Sport and the Cold War* (New York: Routledge, 2007); Damion L. Thomas, *Globetrotting: African American Athletes and Cold War Politics* (Urbana: University of Illinois Press, 2012); John Soares, "Cold War, Hot Ice: International Ice Hockey, 1947–1980," *Journal of Sport History* 34, no. 2 (2007): 207–30; Thomas M. Hunt, "American Sport Policy and the Cultural Cold War: The Lyndon B. Johnson Presidential Years," *Journal of Sport History* 33, no. 3 (2006): 273–97; Toby C. Rider, "The Olympic Games and the Secret Cold War: The U.S. Government and the Propaganda Campaign against Communist Sport, 1950–1960," PhD diss., University of Western Ontario, 2011; and Jenifer Parks, "Red Sport, Red Tape: The Olympic Games, the Soviet Sports Bureaucracy, and the Cold War, 1952–1980," PhD diss., University of North Carolina–Chapel Hill, 2009.

5. See, among others, Bart Buckel, "Nationalism, Mass Politics, and Sport: Cold War Case Studies at Seven Degrees," master's thesis, Naval Postgraduate School, 2008, and Kurt Edward Kemper, *College Football and American Culture in the Cold War Era* (Urbana: University of Illinois Press, 2009).

6. G. Russell Lyons, "United States Team Scores Success in Basketball Tour of Russia," in *Official A.A.U. Basketball Guide, 1958–59* (Indianapolis, IN: AAU 1959); 1959 Amateur Athletic Union Men's Basketball Committee Report, Avery

Brundage Collection (hereafter ABC), Folder AAU Basketball, Box 8, University of Illinois Archives, Urbana, IL (hereafter UIA). The AAU Basketball publication in this and subsequent references can be found at the Amateur Athletic Union Headquarters in Orlando, FL.

7. Information regarding the origins and organization of these exchanges may be found in the Bureau of Educational and Cultural Affairs Historic Collection, University of Arkansas Special Collections, Fayetteville, AR.

8. Ibid. See, for example, Vladimir Khotinsky, "U.S. Gymnasts in Riga," *Soviet Life,* January 1972, 60, and Alexei Srebnitsky, "Richmond Track and Field Meet: The First U.S.-U.S.S.R. Indoor Match," *Soviet Life,* August 1972, 61.

9. Robert M. Turrini, "It Was Communism vs. the Free World: The USA-USSR Dual Track Meets and the Development of Track and Field in the United States, 1958–1985," *Journal of Sport History* 28, no. 3 (2001): 427–71, and David Maraniss, *Rome 1960: The Olympics That Changed the World* (New York: Simon & Schuster, 2008), 1–23.

10. As quoted in James Riordan, "The Impact of Communism on Sport," in *The International Politics of Sport in the Twentieth Century,* ed. James Riordan and Arnd Kruger (New York: Taylor and Francis, 1999), 57.

11. Among many studies of Soviet sport are Baruch Hazan, *Olympic Sports and Propaganda Games: Moscow 1980* (New Brunswick, NJ: Transaction, 1982); Jim Riordan, "Elite Sport Policy in East and West," in *The Politics of Sport,* ed. Lincoln Allison (Manchester: Manchester University Press, 1987): 67–89; James Riordan, "Soviet Sport and Soviet Foreign Policy," *Soviet Studies* 26, no. 3 (July 1974): 322–43; James Riordan, *Sport in Soviet Society* (Cambridge: Cambridge University Press, 1977); James Riordan, *Soviet Sport: Background to the Olympics* (New York: New York University Press, 1980); Victor Peppard and James Riordan, *Playing Politics: Soviet Sport Diplomacy to 1992* (Greenwich, CT: JAI Press, 1993); Robert Edelman, *Serious Fun: A History of Spectator Sports in the USSR* (New York: Oxford University Press, 1993); and Henry W. Morton, *Soviet Sport: Mirror of Soviet Society* (New York: Collier, 1963).

12. Edelman, *Serious Fun,* 144–46.

13. Ironically, the development of the Lithuanian basketball program had been aided a great deal by American Lithuanians, who often traveled back to their homeland to assist the team and even to play for the Lithuanian national team during its foundational period of the 1930s. Alfred Erich Senn, "American Lithuanians and the Politics of Basketball in Lithuania, 1935–1939," *Journal of Baltic Studies* 19, no. 2 (1988): 146–56.

14. Pinchuk, "Helsinki to Munich," 105–6.

15. John J. Karch, "How the Soviet Union Exploits Sports," *American Legion Magazine,* February 1962, 47, and Thomas, *Globetrotting,* 75–79.

16. James Banks, "Visit of U.S.S.R. Teams to U.S.," *Official A.A.U. Basketball Guide, 1960–61* (Indianapolis, IN: AAU, 1961).

17. Clifford Buck and Lyle M. Foster, "The Russians Lost and Learned," *Official A.A.U. Basketball Guide, 1961–62* (Indianapolis, IN: AAU, 1962).

18. M. K. "Bill" Summers, "World Tournament: 1963," *Official A.A.U. Basketball Guide, 1963–64* (Indianapolis, IN: AAU, 1964).

19. Dave Anderson, "Al McGuire: 'Stand Up Together,'" *New York Times,* February 24, 1973, 19.

20. Clifford H. Buck, "A.A.U. Team Tours Abroad," *Official A.A.U. Basketball Guide, 1964–65* (Indianapolis, IN: AAU, 1965), 16.

21. *Amateur Athlete,* June 1964, 6. The challenges confronted by American basketball officials in this regard are similar to those confronted by Canadian hockey officials, who in similar fashion frequently sent "amateur" teams to play against Soviet "professional" teams during this same period. Canadian officials expressed similar frustration at being hamstrung by the international rules of amateurism, which forced the Canadians to put inferior teams on the ice to defend their national sport. See John Soares's chapter in the present volume.

22. Dave Gregg, "International Tour of U.S. National Basketball Team," *Official A.A.U. Basketball Guide, 1966–67* (Indianapolis, IN: AAU, 1967), 17.

23. Barnard L. Collier, "Soviet Quintet Protests Victory of U.S. in '59–'58 Tourney Game," *New York Times,* June 6, 1967, 54. See also articles in the *New York Times* as follows: June 8, 1967, 63; June 9, 1967, 56; June 10, 1967, 36; June 11, 1967, 10; and June 12, 1967, 60.

24. Pinchuk, "From Helsinki to Munich," 101–6.

25. Jerry Lucas, "The Basketball Gap Isn't Closing," *Sports Illustrated,* November 19, 1962, 77.

26. Among them the seven-foot-three giant Yan Kruminsh, who during the 1959 Soviet tour of the United States, was jeered for missing shots two feet from the basket. "The 7-Foot-3 Russian," *Newsweek,* December 7, 1959, 100.

27. Jerry Kirshenbaum, "The Russians, Thanks Be, Are Leaving," *Sports Illustrated,* June 7, 1971, 76–81. See also *New York Times* articles: "Soviet Five to Tour U.S.," May 2, 1971, 17; "Protests, U.S. Quintet Fail to Deter Soviet," May 22, 1971, 23; and "Utah Five Edges Soviet," May 30, 1971, 3.

28. Marsha Smelkinson, "The 1972 Olympic Basketball Story, or Will We Ever Really Know What Happened?," *A.A.U. News: 1972 Basketball Story,* located in LA 84 Foundation archives, Los Angeles, CA, and Cunningham, *American Hoops,* 217–20.

29. Brewster and Gallagher, *Stolen Glory,* 116–25, and *ESPN Classic Big Ticket: 1972 Olympic Basketball.*

30. See Allen Guttmann, *The Games Must Go On: Avery Brundage and the Olympic Movement* (New York: Columbia University Press, 1984).

31. Cunningham, *American Hoops,* 221–28; Elzey, *Munich 1972,* 270–76; and Smelkinson, "1972 Olympic Basketball Story." See "USOC Appeal to the IOC Executive Board on the Final 1972 Olympic Basketball Game," in ABC, Folder "Games of the XXth Olympiad, Munich, Germany, 1972 USA-USSR Basketball," Box 185, UIA.

32. See letters in ABC, Folder "Games of the XXth Olympiad, Munich, Germany, 1972 USA-USSR Basketball," Box 185, UIA.

33. See footnote 2 for such sources.

34. Ibid.

35. Dave Gregg, "USA 'No Stars' Win Olympic Championship," *1969–70 Official A.A.U. Basketball Guide* (Indianapolis, IN, 1970), 10.

36. Arthur Daley, "The Protection of a Perfect Record," *New York Times,* June 13, 1972, 55.

37. Elzey, "Munich 1972," 255–60, and Cunningham, *American Hoops,* 207–8.

38. Turrini, "Communism vs. the Free World."

39. Neil Amdur, "Congress Warns 2 Sports Groups," *New York Times,* March 6, 1973, 53; "N.C.A.A. and A.A.U. Attempt Accord," *New York Times,* April 3, 1973, 54; Gordon S. White Jr., "A.A.U. Asks Use of College Stars," *New York Times,* April 4, 1973, 48; and Gordon S. White Jr., "N.C.A.A. Dragging Out Approval of A.A.U.'s Basketball Bid," *New York Times,* April 5, 1973, 64.

40. "People in Sports: Walton's Plea," *New York Times,* March 27, 1973, 59.

41. "May Be Best U.S. Team Since 1960—Newell," *USA vs. USSR Basketball, Sunday, April 29, 1973, The Forum Inglewood,* official game program, author's copy, 15.

42. "Remember Munich," *Newsweek,* May 7, 1973, 67, and "Soviet Olympic Champion Five Is Set for U.S. Tour in Spring," *New York Times,* February 14, 1973, 30.

43. "The Russians Are Coming, the Russians Are Coming—They've Arrived," *USA vs. USSR Basketball, Sunday, April 29, 1973, The Forum Inglewood,* official game program, 12.

44. Barry McDermott, "It Was a New Game All Down the Line," *Sports Illustrated,* May 14, 1973, 28.

45. "Remember Munich," *Newsweek,* May 7, 1973, 67.

46. "Walton Injures Knee, but U.S. Wins Easily," *Basketball Bulletin,* July 1973, 46. Copies of *Basketball Bulletin* in this and subsequent references can be found at the LA 84 Foundation Archives, Los Angeles, CA.

47. "Mayhem from Moscow," *Newsweek,* May 14, 1973, 129–30, and "U.S. Five Defeats Russians, 83–65," *New York Times,* April 30, 1973, 39.

48. "U.S. Loses, 78–76, to Soviets Five," *New York Times,* May 1, 1973, 36.

49. McDermott, "New Game," 29.

50. Ibid.

51. "U.S.-Soviet Series Begins to Heat Up," *New York Times,* May 2, 1973, 95.

52. "Rough Play Cited by National Fives," *Basketball Bulletin,* July 1973, 46.

53. Dave Anderson, "Agent 00$ and the American Way," *New York Times,* May 5, 1973, 29.

54. "Behagen Aids U.S. in 83–67 Triumph," *New York Times,* May 3, 1973, 55, and McDermott, "New Game," 34.

55. "U.S. Turns Back Soviet Five, 83–75," *New York Times,* May 1973, V-5.

56. "Like Munich Rerun, Only Different—U.S. Wins in Overtime," *New York*

*Times,* undated clipping, LA 84 Foundation archives, USA vs. USSR Basketball, 1973.

57. Sam Goldaper, "U.S. Five Defeats Soviet, 89-to-80," *New York Times,* May 8, 1973, 49.

58. "Crowd Inspired U.S. Stars to Clinch Series," *Basketball Bulletin,* July 1973, 47.

59. "Soviet Quintet Downs U.S., 72–64," *New York Times,* May 10, 1973, 63.

60. William Gildea, "Soviets Finally Use Fast Break," *Basketball Bulletin,* July 1973, 49.

61. "Soviet Cagers' Devotion Impressed Unpaid Cousy," *Basketball Bulletin,* July 1973, 51.

62. "Russians Invent New Way to Play," *New York Times,* May 11, 1973, 35.

63. Dave Long, "Area Olympian Awaits Second Russian Game," *Basketball Bulletin,* July 1973, 49; "Russian Stars Defeat U.S. AAU Champs, 109–87," *Basketball Bulletin,* July 1973, 48; and "Soviet Five Buries A.A.U. Best, 109–87," *New York Times,* May 12, 1973, 23.

64. "USA World University Games Basketball Totals, 19–0," *Basketball Bulletin,* September 1973, 17.

65. "U.S. Basketball Team Has Revenge," *Basketball Bulletin,* September 1973, 9.

66. Hedrick Smith, "Olympic Champions Assailed as Prima Donnas and Smugglers," *New York Times,* October 25, 1973, 61.

67. Ibid., and Neil Amdur, "Increase in Tours by Russian Teams Tied to Commercialism," *New York Times,* October 25, 1973, 61.

68. Robert Edelman notes similar actions by Soviet soccer players on foreign tours in *Spartak Moscow: A History of the People's Team in the Workers' State* (Ithaca, NY: Cornell University Press, 2009), 299–300.

69. Curry Kirkpatrick, "Judged in the World's Court," *Sports Illustrated,* July 22, 1974, 23.

70. Joe Jares, "Their Goal Is Gold in '76," *Sports Illustrated,* November 24, 1975, 24.

71. Cunningham, *American Hoops,* 249.

72. Among many studies of détente are John L. Gaddis, *The Cold War: A New History* (New York: Penguin, 2006); Richard Pipes, *U.S.-Soviet Relations in the Era of Détente* (Boulder, CO: Westview, 1981); Richard Stevenson, *The Rise and Fall of Détente* (Urbana: University of Illinois Press, 1985); and Jeremi Suri, *Henry Kissinger and the American Century* (Cambridge, MA: Belknap Press, 2009). See also Chris Elzey, "Cold War on the Court: The 1973 American-Soviet Basketball Series," *North American Society for Sport History Proceedings and Newsletter* (2000): 17–18. LA 84 Foundation, http://library.la84.org/SportsLibrary/NASSH_Proceedings/NP2000/NP2000o.pdf (accessed June 10, 2012).

73. David Edmonds and John Eidinow, *Bobby Fischer Goes to War: How a Lone American Star Defeated the Soviet Chess Machine* (New York: HarperCollins, 2004).

74. Daniel Johnson, *White King and Red Queen: How the Cold War Was Fought on the Chessboard* (New York: Houghton Mifflin, 2008).

75. Smith, "A Few Pieces of Silver," 70.

76. Jeffrey Montez de Oca, "The 'Muscle Gap': Physical Education and U.S. Fears of a Depleted Masculinity, 1954–1963," in *East Plays West,* ed. Wagg and Andrews, 123–48.

77. "U.S. Basketball Team Has Revenge," *Basketball Bulletin*, Sept. 1973, 9.

78. See, for instance, Sam Goldaper, "Lists Vary as Russians Shop Here," *Basketball Bulletin,* July 1973, 45, and Goldaper, "U.S. Five Defeats Soviet, 89-to-80."

79. See, for instance, "U.S.-Soviet Series Begins to Heat Up"; "Russians Invent New Way to Play"; and "Soviet Union's Five Wins Tour Opener."

80. George Solomon, "Russians Win Series Finale," *Basketball Bulletin,* July 1973, 50.

81. "Mayhem from Moscow," 130.

82. Anderson, "Al McGuire."

83. McDermott, "New Game," 35.

84. Igor Ter-Ovanesyan, "A Soviet Champion Tells His Own Story," *Sports Illustrated,* August 6, 1962, 16.

85. Will Grimsley, "Russian Goal—to Beat America," *Chicago Daily News,* August 17, 1960, 50.

86. Alfred Erich Senn, "Perestroika and Lithuanian Basketball," *Journal of Sport History* 17, no. 1 (1990): 56–61.

87. Cunningham, *American Hoops,* 288–349.

# 10

# The White House Games

## The Carter Administration's Efforts to Establish an Alternative to the Olympics

### *Nicholas Evan Sarantakes*

The Greeks of antiquity invented both international relations and international sport. Despite this shared origin, scholars have rarely studied sport
and international affairs in conjunction with one another. The modern
Olympics are a natural venue for scholars of international affairs interested in sport. Founded—or, more accurately, "reestablished"—in the
nineteenth century, the Olympic movement has proven quite resilient,
having survived two world wars and the Cold War. Many politicians of
extremely different political tints have attempted to bend the movement
to their needs and interests, none more so than Jimmy Carter. In 1980 the
United States initiated what for a brief time became the biggest challenge
ever to the very existence of the modern Olympics when Carter proposed
a boycott of the Moscow Summer Games. There was no comparison between the power of the US government and the International Olympic
Committee (IOC) in 1980, and yet the American effort failed. Why?

The answer is rather simple. Carter displayed poor judgment at the
strategic level. Opinions of the day depicting him as weak and indecisive
were—to be direct—wrong. As president, Carter showed resolution and

determination, but he was far too willing to immerse himself in the details of a problem, which produced a rigidity in policy that was counterproductive to his own goals and interests. A perfect example of this tendency was the effort of his administration to create a set of counter-Olympics to those held in Moscow.

This account will also explore the nature of the relationship between the Olympics and world affairs. In many ways Thucydides, with his account of the twenty-seven-year-long Peloponnesian War, is considered the founding father of both international relations and history. Robert Gilpin of Princeton University paid enormous tribute to the Athenian in his book *War and Change in World Politics:* "In honesty, one must inquire whether or not twentieth-century students of international relations know anything that Thucydides and his fifth-century compatriots did not know about the behavior of states."[1] Indeed, one of the major tenants of Thucydides's work is an examination of the factors motivating state behavior. He famously argues that for any state, motivating factors come down to "fear, honor, and interest."[2]

While Thucydides is—as Gilpin argues—very good at offering insights into the working of the international politics, his account is hardly the last word. Moreover, there are also problems with Thucydides's assessment of international relations. The three motivations he suggests are never going to be equal in strength, and he offers little guidance on which is more important and why. He also ignores the power of ideas—be they in the form of religion or ideology—and the importance of values, mainly in the form of culture. It is clear from his account that public opinion in Athens shaped the policies of that city-state, and the power of ideas, which is a major commodity of modern media, has only grown in importance since that time.

The boycott has been the subject of several specialized studies. A number focus primarily on the American perspective, with specific attention paid to the internal deliberations of the Carter administration.[3] The international implications of the boycott have also been examined by both sport historians and scholars of foreign relations.[4] This chapter builds on the existing historiography and uses international sport—a cultural phenomenon with which Thucydides would have been familiar—to provide some important correctives and insights into understanding world affairs. To be more specific in this context, an examination of a small episode in the 1980 Olympic boycott and the effort to establish a set of alternative athletic contests to the Olympics helps show the interaction of power with ideas and culture in world affairs.

When the Soviet Union invaded Afghanistan in December 1979, Carter and his subordinates feared that this operation would destabilize US-Soviet relations. This initiative, they believed, demanded a US response, which raised the obvious question: What could the United States hope to do about the Soviet intervention? The National Security Council met on the second day of the new year to consider a series of potential responses. The State Department prepared a special paper for this meeting, listing the available options. The president littered the margins of this paper with observations and opinions on most of the suggested courses of action. When it came to the Olympics, the discussion exaggerated the importance of the United States or any other nation to the status of the Games: "US withdrawal from Summer Olympics in Moscow would be serious blow to Soviet international prestige." The paper also noted that the Olympics option had limited utility and cut both ways: "Refusal to participate in the summer games would be too delayed a response, and would hurt American athletes far more than it would affect Soviet policies or actions." What is most interesting about this section is that Carter passed over it without written comment.[5]

Carter's diary shows that he had seen in that paper what he wanted to see about an Olympic boycott, but it also indicates that he was alert to the clear limits of this option: "The Olympics issue would cause me the most trouble and be the most severe blow to the Soviet Union. Only if many nations act in concert would it to be a good idea." In the weeks to come, however, Carter and his administration would move forward with the boycott while ignoring that important qualification about the significance of securing international cooperation and support.[6]

## Domestic Political Considerations

The Carter administration tried initially to keep its options open on the Olympic question, but the news media intervened and became the decisive factor in bringing about the boycott. "Oddly enough," White House Counsel Lloyd Cutler recalled, "the first recommendations that we should not go to Moscow came from the Americans reporters who had spent time in the Soviet Union."[7] On January 10, Robert G. Kaiser, the former Moscow correspondent for the *Washington Post,* wrote in an editorial for his paper: "There should be no underestimating the significance the Soviets themselves put on their selection. They have been treating this Olympiad as one of the great events of their modern history." The Summer Games gave Western nations leverage over the Soviet Union that they had never enjoyed before. "The idea that an Olympiad could collapse because of international disapproval of actions by the Soviet government would certainly sink in." He believed the results would be powerful: "An effective boycott of the Games this summer would be a tremendous blow to Soviet prestige; but perhaps more significant, the collapse of this Olympiad would send a genuine shock through Soviet society." Kaiser even argued that "these Olympics could cause the first serious challenge to the legitimacy of Soviet power in many years." National Security Advisor Zbigniew Brzezinski liked Kaiser's arguments and made sure that Carter saw the column.[8]

Carter decided that the United States would boycott the Moscow Games and took the message to the American people on January 20, appearing on the Sunday morning television talk show *Meet the Press.* After the appropriate introductions, moderator Bill Monroe of NBC News asked if the United States would boycott the Olympics. "Neither I nor the American people would support the sending of an American team to Moscow with Soviet invasion troops in Afghanistan," the president replied. "I have sent a message today to the United States Olympic Committee spelling out my own position, that unless the Soviets withdraw their troops within a month from Afghanistan that the Olympic games be moved from Moscow to an alternative site, or multiple sites, or postponed or cancelled."[9]

Four days before making that statement, Carter had assigned Lloyd Cutler with the job of "pulling together the Government's position on the Olympics." A rising star within the Carter administration, Cutler was one of the few "Washington insiders" with direct access to the president. A sixty-two-year-old lawyer, Cutler had been an influential figure in Democratic circles for years and had ended up on the Nixon administration's infamous enemies list. He joined the Carter administration in 1979 as White House counsel and was instrumental in helping Carter find a way out of the Soviet brigade fiasco.[10] What made Cutler influential was not his courtly style or measured speech but his willingness to do exactly as the president wished.[11] Throughout the Olympic boycott, Cutler doggedly did as Carter instructed and often invoked these desires as reasons enough to pursue various options even when these actions blurred the focus of US strategy and policy. The effort to establish a counter-Olympics is a prime example. At the same time, he also showed a marked unwillingness to disagree with Carter, give him contrary advice, or report bad news. As far as Cutler was concerned, his job was policy implementation rather than formulation.[12] Cutler's deputy, Joe Onek, did much of the day-to-day work on the boycott.[13]

Carter made his boycott decision without meeting or talking with—even by phone—any official of the IOC or the US Olympic Committee (USOC). The president and his lieutenants cared little about these institutions, but they understood domestic American politics well enough. To make a long story short, they had to do something, and the boycott played well with the public. Three major national polls conducted in mid-January found significant majorities in favor of the boycott. An ABC–Louis Harris study reported that 55 percent of the American people supported a boycott, with another 39 percent in opposition and the remaining 6 percent being uncertain. A Gallup poll conducted a few days later produced similar results: 56 percent in support, 34 opposed, and 10 undecided. An NBC poll that started its survey the day the Gallup poll ended suggested that the division was tighter, with proponents of the boycott at 49 percent, those opposing at 41 percent, and the undecided at 10 percent.[14]

The fluidity of these numbers became apparent rather quickly, however. Public support for the boycott began to fade almost immediately once the 1980 Winter Olympics started in February at Lake Placid, New York. Sports columnist Ken Denlinger of the *Washington Post* argued that this change took place even before the start of the opening ceremonies. The boycott had been "a miscalculation of American passion for Olympic sport." Denlinger explained, "Americans are wildly apathetic about the Olympic sports, until a month or so before they take place."[15]

Yet despite the shift in public opinion, Carter refused to reconsider his position. On February 19, at the annual meeting of the American Legion, he said the Soviet invasion of Afghanistan had "altered the careful balance of forces in a vital and a volatile area of the world." He characterized the response of his administration as strong and that included the boycott of the Moscow Olympics: "That deadline is tomorrow, and it will not be changed." As a *Washington Post* reporter covering the speech noted, this statement drew "strong applause" from an otherwise silent crowd. To add strength to this message, Carter, relying on Cutler's advice, ordered the US Army to cut all ties to the USOC in support of efforts to prepare for Moscow.[16]

As if there was any doubt about the president's meaning, the White House staff reinforced his message. Cutler appeared on the NBC's *Today* show the morning of February 20. There was no chance, he said, that US athletes would compete in Moscow. He also predicted that thirty to forty nations would take part in the boycott. The White House press office also released a statement, noting that "Soviet forces have not even begun to withdraw from Afghanistan." As a result, the president's "decision remains unchanged."[17]

Newspaper editorial coverage in response to the announcement of this diplomatic ultimatum was unambiguous and strong. "The U.S. Olympic Committee can't have it both ways. Either it stands with the President or with the Kremlin," declared the editors of the *Philadelphia Inquirer.* One of Carter's hometown papers, the *Atlanta Constitution,* praised his actions: "Setting a deadline on Afghanistan was the right decision and following through was the proper course to take. Let the world know Uncle Sam's word is his bond." The *Commercial Appeal* of Memphis declared, "The boycott will work, regardless of how many countries join in." This editorial also added, "The boycott can be a symbol of U.S. determination."[18]

While editorial support was strong initially, national opinion toward the boycott began to shift and became even more qualified as the Winter Olympics continued. Americans started to realize that there was a moral and ethical basis for participating in the Summer Games. The magic of the Winter Olympics was one thing; the stunning success of the US hockey team was something else altogether. Marshall Brement of the National Security Council realized the "miracle on ice" had changed public sentiment. "The Olympic situation seems to be disintegrating," he warned Brzezinski. "If we are not careful, our magnificent hockey win may fuel domestic sentiment against the boycott." A week later a headline for an article in the *New York Times* declared: "THE OLYMPIC BOYCOTT, NOW LAGGING, STILL FACES HURDLES: THE CARTER ADMINISTRATION MAY AT LEAST GET A GOLD MEDAL FOR TRYING."[19]

Brzezinski claims that he saw that public sentiment had turned against the boycott and recommended to the president that the administration give up on the effort. In his memoirs, the national security advisor writes: "By late February it became clear to me that [Cutler's] efforts were getting nowhere and that at best we would obtain only a partial boycott by other states of the Moscow Olympics. I briefed the President on February 22, and soon thereafter we dropped our effort to organize an alternative event, concentrating on making certain that in addition to the United States some other key countries refrained from participating." While this account sounds reasonable, Brzezinski is quite wrong; the administration and Carter were still committed to the idea of alternative Games well past that date.[20]

A public opinion poll that the USOC commissioned showed that while the public continued to support a boycott, the trends in public sentiment were reversing. The Roper Organization conducted this survey during the first week of March. In response to the question "Now that the Winter Olympic Games are over, would you say they made you feel more proud of our country, or less proud, or didn't they affect your feelings one way or the other?" Seventy-five percent said, "More proud." When asked if the United States should boycott Moscow in wake of what happened at Lake Placid, 58 percent still favored the boycott. A survey from Gallup conducted at roughly the same time found that 63 percent of the public supported a boycott. Another question the Roper pollsters asked showed that the support for the boycott was hollow. When asked if it was "proper" to use the Olympics for political purposes regardless of what might have been done in the past, 67 percent said it was wrong. When asked if the United States should send a team to Moscow if the Soviets withdrew even though it would be after Carter's February 20 deadline, 63 percent of the public said the Americans should be present. Foreign Service officer William J. Dyess studied these figures and noted in a report that ended up on Carter's desk, "It seems there is sizable and strong support, at the present, for reconsidering the U.S. position, 'if the Russians should pull out of Afghanistan before the games take place.'"[21]

The Soviets were coming to similarly dismissive views about the boycott. Boris Ponomarev, Central Committee secretary for international relations of the Communist Party of the Soviet Union, met with his Bulgarian, Czechoslovakian, East German, Hungarian, and Polish counterparts on February 26, telling them that Carter's efforts to use the boycott against international socialism had failed. The boycott crisis was far from over, but the Games would go on as scheduled regardless of US policy. It was also in the political interests of the Soviet Union to have as many athletes from as many countries take part in the Olympics.[22]

Carter made a direct effort to bolster the fading support for his policy. At a press conference held just after the Winter Olympics ended, he explained, "I do believe that the overwhelming support that I've so far seen in America will not wane for our refusal to go to the Olympics in Moscow."[23] The president's confidence in the boycott notwithstanding, there were members of the White House staff who worried about the Winter Olympics' impact on public opinion. Two staff members working for Cutler in the boycott effort advised him that the administration should hold a briefing for the summer Olympians "to counter the post–Lake Placid erosion of support which has begun."[24]

## In the Land of the Blind

Cutler and Onek paid little attention to the loss of support for the boycott domestically, much less critical sentiment abroad. The main focus of the administration in early March was organizing the alternative Olympics. "The primary purpose for holding alternative international games is to increase the number of major nations which decide not to send teams to Moscow this summer," Cutler and Onek informed the Special Coordination Committee, a subcommittee of the National Security Council that Brzezinski chaired. Yet there was another reason for arranging these athletic events as well: "A secondary purpose is to alleviate the disappointment of athletes who might otherwise be deprived of a major world class competition this summer."[25] In a memo he sent directly to the president, Cutler stated, "Other governments believe their NOC's [National Olympic Committees] and athletes would prefer a set of international world class competitions to replace the Olympics." Next to this sentence, Carter wrote: "So would I."[26]

This sentiment was significant in the administration's calculations. Carter and his lieutenants understood that the athletes would suffer. Onek observed years later:

Obviously for many of the athletes it was an extraordinary—all were disappointed. For some it is a bigger thing than others, obviously. Although I must say I began to feel less sorry for the athletes the more I met them only because they had their whole lives had such charmed lives. I met with the volleyball team. Very nice women, and they said something like, "Oh, we are so disappointed because we wanted to play"—I can't even remember— "we wanted to play the Chinese again. And we played them in Japan and we played them in China and we really wanted to meet them in Moscow" or whatever. Okay, I haven't been to Japan. In other words, these were people who were leading very full and happy lives as athletes and they weren't exactly the under privileged of the world.[27]

There was popular support for the counter-Olympics. "There can—and should—be summer alternatives," an editorial in the *Washington Post* declared. "That calls for serious planning now." Carter understood this fact. At a press conference that predated the editorial, he stated, "I am going to pursue aggressively—already am—the holding of international, quality, alternate games." He added, "I believe the Americans will support this alternative effort. I do not believe, under any circumstances, that Americans would support our going to the Moscow Olympics this summer."[28]

Cutler knew he had to deliver on Carter's public statements. In many internal meetings, he invoked the president's name and authority to win arguments and overcome opposition. The summary of one of these sessions reads: "Mr. Cutler said it is necessary to take some action. Time is running out, and unless we are prepared to show determination, there is a high risk that this issue, where the President's prestige is so heavily committed, will fall apart."[29] The result of this presidential push was a rigidity in policy that ran almost 180 degrees counter to the public image of the administration. This inflexibility worried Al McDonald, deputy White House chief of staff. He believed "that organizing alternate games is going to be a difficult dealt to pull off at best" and feared that "it could prove to be an embarrassment to the President." He suggested "the more general his statements on specifics the better while reaffirming his commitment to do his best for the athletes."[30]

Carter ignored this advice at his own peril. "I told Cutler the alternate games would fail because they require the sanction of the international federations," Peter Ueberroth, the president of the Los Angeles Olympic organizing committee, wrote in his memoirs. "It was clear he and his associates didn't know a thing about international amateur sports." Ueberroth got even angrier after he attended a White House meeting on setting up alternative Games in March. At the meeting, a list of nations that the United States was asking for support was distributed. "South Africa stood out like a beacon. Damn it, I thought, Carter, Cutler, and the rest of them didn't have a clue." The reason Ueberroth was angry: the IOC had banned South Africa from participating in the Olympics since 1964 for that nation's racial policies of apartheid. Bob Berenson, a member of White House domestic policy staff, was candid about their shortcomings: "Look, we don't have anyone in the White House who works on sports. When all this started, I was the only one there who even knew anyone on the US Olympic Committee. We were listing countries who would boycott that didn't even have Olympic teams. We've learned an awful lot lately."[31]

Even if the Carter White House could have overcome the administrative issues involving the international federations (IFs), logistics posed another huge problem. Cities need six to eight years to prepare for the Olympics for a reason. Few municipalities have a mass transit system or police force capable of handling the influx of people normally associated with the Olympics. Nor could any urban area produce fifty or sixty thousand empty hotels rooms needed to house the competitors, officials, media, and fans in the time available. "It's more complicated than organizing a burlap-bag foot race for a Sunday picnic," one coach told the *Christian Science Monitor*.[32]

These difficulties became apparent to some within the administration even before the Lake Placid Games ended. Few countries responded to a White House invitation to attend a meeting to begin planning for a new set of competitions. The Canadians in their response stated that using Montreal, host of the debt-ridden 1976 Summer Games, was not a possibility. Marshall Brement told Cutler he was "uneasy and considerably less optimistic about our prospects." There was no chance of putting together any competition at the same time of the Moscow Olympics. While Brement conceded that the chances of organizing some event that would take place after Moscow were better, "the odds of achieving this are nevertheless still quite slim." His advice to Cutler was blunt: "If we are not willing to go all out on this, the chances of failure are large, and we would probably be better off dropping the idea of alternate games altogether and concentrating only on an Olympic embargo." This recommendation was sound, but with the president personally committed to the idea, Cutler knew he had to move forward in this area.[33]

Others were worried as well that the administration was squandering precious resources in trying to establish an alternative set of games. Nelson Ledsky, head of the State Department task force on the boycott, warned Vance in early March, "The starch seems to be slowly going out of our boycott effort." Numerous foreign governments were facing difficulties in getting their NOCs to honor the boycott: "The fact that many states and national Olympic committees (including the USOC) are waiting as long as possible before accepting or declining their invitation to Moscow in the hope of a change in the situation in Afghanistan has prevented us from developing a bandwagon of support especially in Africa and Latin America."[34] The fact that the Soviet Union had an established sport diplomacy program in these regions (which Jenifer Parks discusses in another chapter of the present volume) was something that Carter administration officials knew little about.

Cutler, though, had already begun work on establishing the alternative Games, despite the fact that he knew nothing about the role that international athletic federations played. In early February, Michael Scott, an attorney with the legal firm Squire, Sanders & Dempsey, met with Onek, an old acquaintance, and they discussed the role of the federations. Scott was counsel to the National Collegiate Athletic Association and knew something about sport administration. At Onek's request, he investigated the role of the federations. A week later, he wrote Onek, and his news was not particularly good: "An effort to hold an event 'competitive' with the summer Olympic Games will encounter substantial difficulties, particularly with reference to the asserted 'jurisdiction' of the various IFs. That jurisdiction, however, rests exclusively upon an international network of de facto consensual arrangements among private parties, and can be effectively exercised only by means of threats of disqualification to athletes who participate in events not approved within the framework of this private network." There was hope but only if the administration wanted and was prepared to challenge the various federations. "The essential issue posed for proponents of 'competitive' games is whether they are prepared directly to confront this IOC-based international cartel, and to encourage participating athletes to do so as well." After getting this letter, Onek and Berenson made some phone calls to several US national sport federations and discovered Scott was right.[35]

Cutler quickly adapted to this information. He arranged a meeting with Thomas Keller, the president of the Fédération Internationale des Sociétés d'Aviron (International Federation of Rowing Associations). Cutler was slowly learning that individual nongovernmental organizations supervised the play of specific sports. Since they were international in nature, they could—and often did—ignore the interest, policies, and even laws of a number of nations. They had to heed only those states in which they were based or in which they wanted to hold a contest. Keller, a Swiss chemical engineer, was particularly influential among the people who regulated international sport. In addition to his work with the rowing federation, he was also president of the Association Générale des Fédérations Internationales de Sports, an organization of all international sport federations, even those not associated with the Olympics. The problem was that Cutler and Onek knew little of Keller's personal history. He had been a rower in the 1950s but never got to compete in the Olympics because the Swiss Olympic Association decided to boycott the 1956 Olympics in Melbourne, Australia, in protest over the Soviet Union's invasion of Hungary.[36]

In the discussion that followed, Keller appeared more knowledgeable about domestic American politics and US foreign policy than his hosts were about international sport. Cutler and Onek told Keller that they had assurances from the governments of most Western European nations that they would boycott the Moscow Olympics, and they said that the IOC would end up canceling the Games. The US government wanted the IFs to authorize a two-week event in August open to all athletes regardless of nationality, including the Soviets. Cutler told him that the Soviet Union was unacceptable to serve as an Olympic host because it had invaded another country. The US position had historical precedent, he explained. During the Olympic Games of antiquity, the city-state of Elis could not wage war during the event.[37] (Cutler's example was both weak—in American politics ten years ago is ancient history—and wrong—there never was any "Olympic truce" in the Greece of old.)

Keller was loyal to the Olympic movement. According to the sanitized language of the memorandum documenting this meeting, he told the Americans that their proposal "would be a knife in the back of the IOC." He said it was one thing for an individual federation to sponsor events following the conclusion of the Olympiad, but it was another thing entirely for them to band together and stage what amounted to a set of counter-Olympics. When Onek argued that the US government wanted to provide a venue for athletes to compete at the highest level, Keller dismissed the idea. Athletes who competed at Moscow were unlikely to appear at another event a few weeks later. There was only so long they could stay in peak physical condition, and medalists were unlikely to risk the stature of their Olympic achievement at some ad hoc contest. He also added that sport was a poor tool for use in diplomacy. Onek and Ledsky quickly disagreed, telling him that the Games were extremely important to the Soviets. According to the minutes, "Mr. Keller again regretted the American decision, but said he understood that the train had left the station and that it was now too late to change the American position." And on that note, this highly unproductive meeting came to an end.[38]

The White House counsel and his staff were soon privately admitting what they had denied in public a few weeks before—organizing another set of competitions would be difficult. "Alternative games are impractical unless the planning begins now and firm commitments are made within a month," Cutler and Onek informed the Special Coordination Committee. "There is no single site other than the Soviet Union which can host all the Olympic events in 1980."[39] The problem was with Carter. When Cutler informed him that it was "impracticable" to hold a series of contests in one site but that it would be possible to hold the events at different locations around the world, the president noted on the margin: "good." According to the record of the March 6 meeting of the Special Coordination Committee, Cutler told the group that the administration "should know by the end of March whether the alternative games are a realistic prospect." Carter, though, had already decided. When he saw that line, he underlined it and wrote in the margin: "They *must* [be] held."[40]

Cutler was not one to deny the obvious even if the president insisted on an unworkable policy. Organizing an alternative to Moscow faced a number of problems: "Foremost is the persisting opposition of the international federations." Cutler, however, was more than willing to put his own spin on events. According to him, several factors explained the refusal of these organizations to cooperate. "The federations are entrenched, ably led, Soviet-infiltrated and totally unsympathetic to the boycott." Still, he had to deliver. Carter wanted an alternative Olympics. Cutler's solution: use US antitrust laws against the collusion of the federations and the IOC.[41]

Sitting back in Dublin, the Baron Killanin of Galway, the IOC president, watched the White House effort without much concern. The Carter administration was "doomed to failure." According to Lord Killanin, "what they did not understand was that without the cooperation of the international federations no such competition would be possible. The IFs agree, for their own benefit as much as for that of the Olympic movement, not to hold major competitions just before or during the period of the Games."[42] The White House had no intention of consulting Killanin on their efforts, but there were a number of commentators in American media outlets, large and small, who knew this endeavor would fail. Harrison Dillard, who won four gold medals at the 1948 and 1952 Olympics in various sprinting and hurdling events, denounced the idea early on. "Staging the various events in different cities is not only impractical but totally foreign to the Olympic concept," he explained in a *Cleveland Press* editorial. The idea of putting on alternate games subsidized by the United States is simply ridiculous on the face of it."[43]

Others agreed. "Excuse me, Mr. President, but your latest plan for an alternative Olympics—or whatever you choose to call it—is a bad one," Ken Denlinger declared in the *Washington Post.* The "semi-Olympics" would undermine the boycott. Even though they were open to all, it was unlikely that the Soviet Union and other Eastern European nations would participate, and they were major powers in almost all of the twenty-one Olympic summer sports. He also wondered who would pay for this gathering. "The bottom line here, it seems, is that there is no happy alternative for an Olympic experience, no reality that will replace shattered dreams." In a *Los Angeles Times* guest editorial, sociologist Harry Edwards of the University of California at Berkeley noted that the logistical, economic, and political requirements of hosting an Olympics-like event made such an event almost impossible to organize. The alternative Games proposal "portends some problems of a size matched only by the naiveté exhibited by the Carter Administration in its approach to the issue." This proposal also suggested both incompetence and weakness: "Is the White House serious in asking the American public to accept the notion that this nation's foreign policy has been reduced to employing a boycott of a sports event as the principal non-military response to what Carter has called the 'greatest threat to world peace and security since World War II'? If so, we should be debating questions of considerably greater gravity than whether this country should participate in the 1980 Summer Games." The boycott was bad policy, Edwards declared, but Carter had put his personal credibility on the line. "The President appears to have painted himself into a corner and then set the wall behind him on fire."[44]

Serious efforts at implementing the alternative Games started only in the middle of March. Australian minister of home affairs Robert Ellicott met with Undersecretary of State for Political Affairs David Newsom and informed the US government that if the alternative Games were ever going to happen, they needed to have some agreed-upon plans in place by the end of March. "I agree," Carter noted in the margin of the memo informing him of this meeting.[45] Despite this careful warning, the president neither gave this policy more resources nor found a way to retreat from its implementation. He maintained his course.

The administration slowly came to realize that it needed someone with the appropriate expertise to administer this effort. "Promotion of alternative games is not a job for amateurs, even high-ranking public officials," Cutler and Onek explained. They had four people in mind: Ueberroth; Petr Spurney, executive director of the Lake Placid Olympics organizing committee; Steven Ross, chief executive officer of Warner Communications and principal shareholder of the New York Cosmos soccer team; and television producer David Wolper, who was the head of the television committee for the 1984 Los Angeles Summer Olympics. Spurney met with Onek, who found he was willing to help, but Spurney still had work to do wrapping things up with Lake Placid and would not be available until mid-April. Ueberroth and Wolper agreed to attend a White House meeting on the alternative Games. "I offered my assistance in making the best of a bad situation," Ueberroth noted. Wolper agreed to help because of his concerns about the welfare of athletes.[46]

Information about Wolper's involvement got back to Killanin, and he decided to take action. He wrote Robert Kane, the president of the USOC and told him that his organization and the Los Angeles Olympic Committee needed to steer clear of any involvement with the Carter administration's effort: "It has been rumoured that certain persons connected with the Games in Los Angeles are assisting the White House Staff in regard to 'their' games. This of course could jeopardise the Olympic Games in Los Angeles." The Irishman was worried that the Carter administration in its ignorance of international sport regulations and policies would get the USOC suspended. Kane got the message. "The so called Alternative Games are the mechanism of the White House," he told Killanin. "We have not associated with them at all. In fact, the very name is abhorrent to us and we've said so." He closed, telling Killanin that he still held out hope that the United States might attend the Moscow Games.[47]

Ueberroth was also worried. Uncertainty about Moscow was making its way to Los Angeles and slowing down progress on 1984. He told the *Los Angeles Times,* "We have no involvement in such proposed games and believe they are counterproductive for our mutual objectives." Still, another month would pass before he got Killanin to issue a press release that reassured the Californians that the IOC would take no action to strip them of the Games.[48]

Efforts to organize a set of counter-Games died with a whimper in Geneva, Switzerland. In mid-March, Cutler, Wolper, and other US officials traveled to Europe for a planning meeting for the alternative Games. Lord Killanin called the gathering "a Gilbert and Sullivan style meeting." Only twelve nations of the twenty-five invited sent representatives to the meetings held at the British consulate general. Very little was decided. The group selected no name for this competition, a site, or an organizer. Douglas Hurd, secretary of state at the British Foreign Office, made it clear that none of the governments involved was going to get into the business of organizing sporting events. At a press conference that followed, Hurd and Cutler stressed the positive and argued that they had made significant progress. "What we have to do now, as a result of these meetings, is to get in touch with the various sporting organisations some national, some international," Hurd explained. British reporters tended to ask questions of Hurd, while Americans focused on Cutler. The White House lawyer went out of his way to explain that the Games they were planning were benign in intent: "They would pose no threat to the future of the unitary Olympic movement." Hurd made this same point. Of course, what none of the reporters or Hurd knew was that Cutler was still arguing that the

US government should use antitrust laws against the IOC and the athletic federations. When a *New York Times* reporter asked what would happen if the Soviets changed their policy in Afghanistan, he got two different responses that show how differently the allies viewed the issue. "Then that would be a completely new suggestion," Hurd replied. Cutler, on the other hand, was stringent in his response. The United States would "not send a team under any circumstances."[49]

Europe showed little interest in these proposed Games. The Soviets made it clear that they had no interest in participating in any alternative contests. Interviewed on French radio, Vladimir Popov, first deputy chairman of the Moscow Olympic organizing committee, said, "You see, quite naturally we reject this meeting because it contradicts the regulations and rules of international athletic federations. This is nothing but an additional act in the show some are attempting to set up around the Olympic games in Moscow, a show rooted in speculative political theories."[50]

## Defeat

Time is in many ways the most precious commodity mankind has. Once it is lost, there is no way to make good its loss. Such was very much the case in the 1980 Olympic boycott. While the US government diverted precious time and energy trying to create these alternative Games, support for the boycott faded in Western Europe. Although Prime Minister Margret Thatcher's government backed the American initiative, the Labour Party and the British Olympic Association (BOA) were of different minds. Denis Howell, a member of Parliament who had served as the minister of sport in the cabinet of Harold Wilson, circulated a memo that indicated that the position of the government "is not shared by HM opposition." Thatcher had been in office for just under a year, and the Labour Party, smarting over its defeat, was looking for a fight. This development was significantly different from the generally bipartisan support that the boycott enjoyed in the United States. What took place in Britain was a major political confrontation. "We decided that every statement of Government had to be contested in Parliament and in the media," Howell explained.[51] Neither Carter nor anyone else in his administration did anything to support Thatcher in this crucial period.

Politics often makes for strange alliances. Even though he was a citizen of the Republic of Ireland, Killanin could speak in the House of Lords, but he thought that using his peerage to speak out against the boycott was inappropriate. The result of Killanin's reluctance was that the Marquess of Exeter became the primary defender of the Moscow Olympics among the lords. A member of the IOC, including decades on its executive committee and as a vice president, Lord Exeter had earlier in his life competed in three Olympics, winning gold in the hurdles at the 1928 Amsterdam Games and silver in the same event four years later in Los Angeles. After his athletic career came to an end, Exeter was the chair of the organizing committee for the 1948 London Olympics and served as president of the International Amateur Athletics Federation for several decades. "Transferring the Games elsewhere at such short notice is quite impractical," he told the other peers.[52]

Lord Exeter opposed the boycott on principle and provoked a debate within the chamber on the Olympics. "International sport is the one great worldwide, generally accepted movement bringing the young together in friendship and understanding and it would be a tragedy to do something which would damage it," he said. An undersecretary in Thatcher's cabinet, the Baron Bellwin of the city of Leeds, responded, "To carry on as if nothing had happened would be to acquiesce and contribute to a massive propaganda success for Russia." He added that it might be difficult to move the Games from Moscow but "impossible it is not."[53]

Bernard Levin, a columnist for the *Times* of London, dismissed Exeter's arguments as "foolish and empty." In a two-part essay that appeared in his paper on back-to-back days, he noted that under the Olympic charter the Soviet Union never should have been awarded the Games in the first place. "The *whole* of the Soviet Union's participation in the Games and more particular her holding of them in Moscow is designed with a view to political profit." Aiming his wrath directly at Lords Exeter and Killanin, and Sir Denis Follows, chairman of the BOA, he said the Olympic movement gave the three a deluded sense of their own self-importance, which allowed them to make the absurd argument that politics was not a factor in Moscow's role as host: "How can such men live in a moral miasma of this kind and still swear—nay, believe—that the air is sweet? There is only one way, and it is by no means original, nor are they the only men who follow it. They accept in their honest, gullible good will, any lie the Soviet authorities tell them, however transparent, preposterous or disgusting, instead of ruthlessly seeing the turn in their own hearts."[54] Howell challenged these views on the pages of the *Daily Telegraph*. "It is absurd to suggest that participation in this summer's Olympics is an endorsement of Russian policy as it is to suggest that our presence at Lake Placid automatically endorses American policy," he argued.[55]

Levin's arguments carried little weight with the BOA. On March 4, the organization approved a simple resolution: "The National Olympic Committee confirms that it is its present intention to send a British team to the Olympic Games. However it will defer its reply to the invitation to participate until its next meeting on 25th March." The association had delayed before taking this vote in an effort to coordinate their response with other European committees. The organization also waited to act out of respect for actions that Thatcher said were under way to persuade the Soviets to leave Afghanistan.[56]

Parliament was in the process of debating a boycott and that discussion continued in one form or another until the start of the Summer Games in Moscow, but the critical moment came two weeks later while Cutler was in Switzerland. The House of Commons spent seven hours on March 17 debating British participation in the Olympics. The Lord Privy Seal, Sir Ian Gilmour, introduced the following resolution: "That this House condemns the Soviet invasion of Afghanistan and believes that Great Britain should not take part in the Olympic Games in Moscow." It was one of the most extensive debates Parliament had ever had on a sport-related topic. The Speaker of the House remarked at the start of the debate that he had indications that fifty members wanted to discuss the issue at hand. Allowing that many to speak was "quite impossible" but just barely. Forty-nine individuals addressed the Commons that evening.[57]

Gilmour started with a long speech in support of the boycott that was interrupted several times. His reasoning was similar to that one could find in the Carter White House at the time: "There is no question but that for the Soviet Union, holding the Olympic Games [in] Moscow is of supreme importance. It sees the Games as a propaganda exercise from which it hopes to derive very great advantage. Conversely, a decision by several Western countries to absent themselves from the Games will have a powerful impact upon the Soviet population at large." Numerous speakers favoring the same position followed.[58]

As the debate rolled past 7:00 p.m., Labour came to dominate the comments, as the Conservatives had at the beginning. Ron Brown of Edinburgh Leith claimed, "It is quite clear that the Prime Minister is using Afghanistan to divert attention from the record unemployment and rampant inflation in this country." Toward the end, Howell spoke: "If country after country decides that the only way to confront evil is to destroy the good contained in the Olympic Games and international sport, that is a prescription for the end of international sport as we know it." The debate came to an end at 10:14 p.m. The House divided 315–147, approving the resolution.[59]

Although the House of Commons had endorsed the boycott, it was a less than impressive victory. With public opinion polls in the Great Britain showing the public opposed, many MPs skipped the vote. "It is impossible to pretend that the Commons vote on British participation in the Olympics was the decisive, clear-cut, moral pronouncement which ideally it should have been," the *Daily Telegraph* declared in an editorial.[60]

Cutler stopped in England just after this vote on his way back from the futile meeting in Geneva. He arrived looking for foreign support for the alternative Games. Instead, he found a situation that was much more fluid than he expected. The boycott was in serious trouble in the United Kingdom. Although Thatcher's government staunchly supported this effort, she was unwilling to use any authoritarian or legal mechanisms against the Olympians such as the seizure of passports. As a result, Cutler had to lobby for the basic idea of a boycott, which was something he was not entirely prepared to do. He arranged to meet with Follows at the Bath Club in London. Once the meeting began, he quickly realized the basic idea of a boycott was in danger. Sir Denis made it clear to Cutler that his organization would have nothing to do with the boycott. Cutler also met with Dennis Howell at the US embassy. The American began by reviewing the situation, predicting that over a hundred countries would boycott, and saying that President Carter wanted to give the athletes a chance to compete since they had invested so much in their training. "Within minutes it was obvious that Cutler knew little about sport and less about international sport," Howell noted. The Englishman explained that planning for the alternative Games was a waste of time and effort. Nothing would compensate the athletes for the loss of the Olympics. Cutler did not understand or chose not to understand what Howell was attempting to explain. "It was as though he believed the Olympic Games was a commodity to be bought and sold on the money markets of the world," Howell later said. He then tried to explain that the Olympics were an international movement and had to transcend the foreign policy of any one nation, even that of the Soviet Union.[61]

Cutler had been out-argued, so he tried another approach. He asked what would trouble Howell—a Soviet invasion of Austria? Yugoslavia? When would he favor calling off the Games? "I want to discover your breaking point," he asked, pointedly. Howell had been elected to the Birmingham City Council when he was seventeen and had been a member of Parliament for over twenty years; he knew how to argue and refused to respond to Cutler's questions. He told the American lawyer that they were hypothetical as far as the 1980 Olympics went. When the conversation ended, Cutler admitted he had never encountered the arguments that Howell had made. As he was leaving, Cutler made a clumsy effort to impress Howell with his authority. He said he would later be meeting with the president of the United States and asked if the British politician had any message for him. Howell replied, "This country is governed by Magna Carta not Jimmy Carter."[62]

Cutler's meetings in London had gone poorly. He knew the situation in the United Kingdom was grave, and he reported as much when he returned to Washington: "We are in serious danger of losing the British." The Carter administration had squandered precious time trying to organize an alternative Olympics. The ramifications of this misuse of time were immense. If the United Kingdom attended, so might many of the nations on the continent. "Other West European Governments and NOCs may say that this makes an effective boycott impossible, and make this an excuse for going to Moscow themselves," Cutler said. However, he excelled at covering his own mistakes. In his memo, he made no mention of his meeting with Howell and dismissed Follows. "Sir Dennis is a living Colonel Blimp," he stated. "He is a pure Olympian who puts aside all responsibilities as a citizen of the West in favor of sports as the last hope of world peace." In small signs of his own cultural ignorance, Cutler misspelled Follows's name, gave incorrect information about his professional background, and called the British Olympic Association the "British Olympic Committee."[63]

Although Cutler could hide or minimize his mistakes within the administration, it was obvious to outside observers that the meeting in

Switzerland had been a disaster. In the *Los Angeles Times,* Kenneth Reich, a political reporter, wrote that the Olympians were "fighting back effectively against the boycott drive." Reich referred to a number of unnamed sources from the White House and the State Department who had been trying to build support abroad who admitted that things were going poorly: "Some believe the White House is being outmaneuvered."[64]

Indeed, things only got worse for Carter. Despite Thatcher's strong support for the boycott and alternative Games, she left the final decision on these matters to the BOA. "We have the highest admiration for the Olympic ideals," the prime minister informed Follows after the vote in the House of Commons. "It is not we who are perverting that idea; rather, it is the Soviet Union which is making cynical use of the idealism of sportsmen to try to convince the world that its invasion of Afghanistan is a little local matter of no importance." The Soviet Union was a threat, and it was the duty of all British subjects to oppose its evil. "Free countries must bring home as dramatically as possible that this sort of action cannot be taken with impunity," she said.[65] Follows offered no encouragement in his response. He said he would make sure all BOA members saw her letter before they voted. The association, though, had no interest in Carter's alternative to Moscow that Thatcher was backing: "We exist solely for the purpose of organising and co-ordinating the United Kingdom's participation in the Olympic Games."[66]

On March 25 the BOA ignored the vote in Parliament and the position of Thatcher's government and accepted the Soviet invitation to the Moscow Games. When the BOA made its decision public, its reasoning was straightforward. "The British Olympic Association, which exists to organise and co-ordinate British participation in the Olympic Games, has agreed to accept forthwith to send a team to Moscow this summer," declared a statement the organization released. Fifteen of the nineteen British national sport-governing bodies supported this decision. In making this decision, the association had rejected the request of the Thatcher government that it wait until May. "The BOA has not come to this decision lightly," its press statement said. "It has given careful and we hope proper attention to the views expressed in Parliament as it has taken note of the responses of the public and aspirations of the competitors."[67]

Baron Noel-Baker of the city of Derby, a silver medalist at the 1920 Antwerp Olympics and recipient of the Nobel Peace Prize in 1959, explained why the Olympians had decided to go to Moscow. The Games, he argued, "have given the whole world a vision of all-embracing international friendship and co-operation, which was in sharp contrast to the folly and wastes of the arms race of war. . . . The Games in Moscow will serve the short-time and long-time cause of peace."[68]

The vote in London was worse than Cutler could have imagined. Despite its international nature, the Olympic movement was primarily a European phenomenon. The Games, modern and ancient, had started in Europe. At that point in time only one Asian nation, Japan, had ever hosted the Olympics. The Games had never been held in South America or Africa. Five of the six IOC presidents had been Europeans. The United States was the only major Olympic power located outside of Europe. As a result, it was clear to many observers—but not the Carter administration—that Europe would determine the fate of the boycott. The coordinated move on the part of the NOCs of France, Spain, and Italy was a development of exceptional importance. These three organizations, following developments in the United Kingdom closely, voted to go to Moscow the same day the British made their decision. The actions in these countries failed to garner as much attention in the United States or in the White House as the decision in London, but Carter and his lieutenants had suffered another significant defeat.[69]

The Europeans knew what had happened. At the next scheduled meeting of the IOC's executive board, the members had a lengthy discussion and analysis of the boycott. Col. Raoul Mollet, president of Belgium's Olympic committee, praised Follows and his national committee. Their stand against the British government had had an enormous ripple effect throughout the continent.[70]

The Olympians had defeated the Carter administration, and the Americans knew it. "The federations do not now share our concept of international sports festival," Berenson informed Cutler and Ledsky. "Almost all raise very practical concerns." One of the biggest problems was scheduling issues. A number of sports already had planned events during the time the White House staff wanted to hold the event, nor did most want to take part in competitions that would involve the federations of other sports.[71] Work would continue on the alternative, semi-, or counter-Olympics well into May, but after March the effort was pro forma while the administration refocused on its efforts to implement the boycott. A track-and-field event eventually took place in Philadelphia, but it hardly compared to the gathering in the Soviet Union.

## Conclusion

The alternative Olympic Games might seem like a minor episode in the Cold War and Carter's administration, but it is nonetheless important for a number of reasons. First, it shows that culture matters in world affairs as do ideas. The leaders of the Olympic movement were too attached to their creed to give up on it when their national governments decided it was in the interest of their nations to do so. As a result, it would seem that Thucydides's famous description of international relations as being a function of power—fear, honor, interest—is a bit too narrow.

With that point made, a second issue needs to be discussed: not all motivating factors are equal. A number of US allies supported the Carter administration in its efforts to establish alternative Games, but these commitments to alliance solidarity were rather weak. Soviet actions in Southwest Asia were not the cause of much concern in Western Europe, which was the heart and soul of the Olympic movement. Although the IOC has little power compared to that of a nation-state, much less one that is a major world power, the nature of its structure and the commitment of Olympians to the ideology and culture of their movement was something that governments around the globe saw little need or inclination to challenge. Culture and power collided in this affair, and while fear, honor, and interest had more sway, they were hardly absolute.

Finally, while power is a crucial commodity in the affairs of nations, outcomes often are not simply a function of who is stronger or weaker in certain resources. The skills and abilities of national leadership are extremely important in determining the final results. This fact becomes abundantly clear in examining the Carter record. The president was never good at choosing between alternatives. His "hands-on" leadership style squandered valuable energy—and more important, time—in a futile effort that was doomed even before it began. While the administration had attempted to set up some sort of alternative to Moscow, it was unable to concentrate its energies on the boycott itself. It had done little to pressure the European NOCs or the national governments of their allies while it attempted to organize alternative Games. As a result, Carter suffered a huge reversal, as Western Europe decided to attend the Olympics, which was crucial to the overall failure of the boycott.

## Notes

The author thanks Michael Creswell, Galen Perras, and Sarandis "Randy" Papado-poulos for their assistance.

1. Robert Gilpin, *War and Change in World Politics* (New York: Cambridge University Press, 1981), 227–28.

2. Robert B. Strassler, ed., *The Landmark Thucydides: A Comprehensive Guide to the Peloponnesian War* (New York: Simon & Schuster, 1996), 43.

3. For example, David B. Kanin argues that the boycott was a "qualified success" because it "robbed from Moscow the sense of international legitimacy that the Games normally provide the Olympic host." David B. Kanin, *A Political History of the Olympic Games* (Boulder, CO: Westview, 1981), 108, 145. Martin Barry Vinokur makes a similar argument about the boycott being important as a mechanism for public relations in *More Than a Game: Sports and Politics* (New York: Greenwood, 1988), 116. Derick L. Hulme Jr. was the first scholar to focus on the boycott itself and bases his study on contemporary American press accounts, public documents, and the memoirs of key individuals in the campaign. Although more critical of the Carter administration than Kanin, Hulme ultimately comes to a similar assessment, calling the boycott "only partially successful." He believes that the boycott was a safe form of protest against the invasion of Afghanistan that posed little risk to the United States. See Hulme, *The Political Olympics: Moscow, Afghanistan, and the 1980 U.S. Boycott* (New York: Praeger, 1990), x, 9, 17–18, 128. Stephen R. Wenn and Jeffrey P. Wenn examine an attention-getting episode when the Carter administration enlisted the aid of Muhammad Ali. They believe Ali's mission was far more successful than is commonly thought. See Wenn and Wenn, "Muhammad Ali and the Convergence of Olympic Sport and U.S. Diplomacy in 1980: A Reassessment from Behind the Scenes at the U.S. State Department," *Olympika: The International Journal of Olympic Studies* 2 (1993): 45–66. Tom Caraccioli and Jerry Caraccioli's *Boycott: Stolen Dreams of the 1980 Moscow Olympic Games* (Washington, DC: New Chapter Press, 2008) is a collection of oral histories of American Olympic athletes and the impact—usually negative—that the boycott had on their careers. The most extensive and wide-ranging study is Nicholas Evan Sarantakes, *Dropping the Torch: Jimmy Carter, the Olympic Boycott and the Cold War* (New York: Cambridge University Press, 2011), which despite its title is international in focus and looks at the boycott as part of the Cold War.

4. Willi Knecht offers a German perspective that focuses on domestic politics in *Der Boykott* (Cologne: Verlag Wissenschaft und Politik, 1980). Sandra L. Kereliuk offers a preliminary account of the Canadian debate on the Olympics in "The Canadian Boycott of the 1980 Moscow Olympic Games," in *Sport and Politics,* ed.

Gerald Redmond (Champaign, IL: Human Kinetics, 1986). For a more extensive study, see the fifth chapter of Donald Macintosh and Michael Hawes with contributions from Donna Greenhorn and David Black, *Sport and Canadian Diplomacy* (Montreal: McGill-Queen's University Press, 1994), 90–107. Lisa Forrest offers a hybrid history/memoir of the boycott debate in Australia, which was politics in its most vicious and nasty form, in *Boycott: Australia's Controversial Road to the 1980 Moscow Olympics* (Sydney: ABC Books, 2008). In a detailed examination of the boycott in the United Kingdom, Kevin Jefferys argues Margaret Thatcher's approach to the boycott was a middling one that alienated sports officials without using enough persuasion or coercion. See Jefferys, "Britain and the Boycott of the 1980 Moscow Olympics," *Sport in History* 32, no. 2 (September 2012): 279–301. Paul Corthon, on the other hand, believes that the Thatcher cabinet lost control of the terms of the debate as it turned into a discussion of state power, human rights, and détente. See Corthon, "The Cold War and British Debates over the Boycott of the 1980 Moscow Olympics," *Cold War History* 13, no. 1 (2013): 43–66. Daniel James Lahey notes that Thatcher offered fierce support for the boycott but was much more tepid in her support of economic sanctions against the Soviet Union for its invasion of Afghanistan. See Lahey, "The Thatcher Government's Response to the Soviet Invasion of Afghanistan, 1979–1980," *Cold War History* 13, no. 1 (2013): 21–42. Flavio de Almedia Lico and Katia Rubio examine Brazil's opposition to the boycott despite the strong influence the United States had at the time on that nation's economy in "The Brazilian Position Considering the Boycott of the 1980 Moscow Olympic Games," in *Olympia als Bildungsidee: Beiträge zur Olympischen Geschichte und Pädogogik*, ed. Annette R. Hofmann and Michael Krüger (Wiesbaden: Springer Fachmedian Wiesbaden, 2013), 113–31.

5. Carter's handwritten comments are on Brzezinski to the President, January 3, 1980, folder Southwest Asia/Persian Gulf-Afghanistan [12/26/79–1/4/80], box 17, Geographic File, Papers of Zbigniew Brzezinski, Donated Historical Collections, Jimmy Carter Library, Atlanta, Georgia (hereafter cited as JCL).

6. Jimmy Carter, *White House Diary* (New York: Farrar, Strauss and Giroux, 2010), 387. Carter's diary, however, must be used with caution. He has played fast and loose with its construction. There are very different versions of this passage in the published version of his diary and his memoirs. Compare the passage that appears in this study to the version in his memoirs: "We had a long discussion about the 1980 Olympics. We will make a statement saying that this issue is in doubt, but not make a decision yet about whether to participate. This one would cause me the most trouble, and also would be the most severe blow to the Soviet Union. Only if many nations act in concert would I consider it to be a good idea." Jimmy Carter, *Keeping Faith: Memoirs of a President* (New York: Bantam Books, 1982), 474.

7. Lloyd Cutler Exit Interview Oral History, March 2, 1981, 6, Brzezinski to the President, no date, folder Olympics 6/79–2/80, box 48, Subject Files, National Security Advisor Files, Staff Office Files, Jimmy Carter Presidential Materials, JCL.

8. Brzezinski to the President, n.d., folder Olympics 6/79–2/80, box 48, Sub-

ject Files, National Security Advisor Files, Staff Office Files, Jimmy Carter Presidential Materials, JCL.

9. "Interview of the President on Meet the Press," January 20, 1980, folder Olympics 6/79–2/80, box 80, Subject Files, National Security Advisor Files, Staff Office Files, Jimmy Carter Presidential Materials, JCL.

10. The Soviet brigade fiasco was a political firestorm that US senators manufactured out of ignorance over a Soviet army unit that had been stationed in Cuba since 1960. The unit remained on the island as part of the agreement that ended the 1962 Cuban Missile Crisis.

11. McDonald to Cutler, January 16, 1980, folder Olympics—Memos, 1–2/80, box 102, Lloyd Cutler Files, Counsel's Office Files, Staff Office Files; Notes, January 16, 1980, folder #21, box 12, Steno Pad Chronology File, Papers of Alonzo L. McDonald, Donated Historical Collections; and Daily Diary, January 16, 1980, folder 1/16/80, box PD-70, President's Daily Diary, Staff Office Files, Jimmy Carter Presidential Materials, JCL.

12. Carter to Powell, January 17, 1980, folder Olympics—Memos/Correspondence to President 1–2/80, box 103, Lloyd Cutler Files, Counsel's Office Files, Staff Office Files, Jimmy Carter Presidential Materials, JCL.

13. Joe Onek Oral History by the author, June 22, 2007.

14. ABC News–Harris Survey, January 22, 1980, folder Olympics—Publications and Pamphlets, 1–4/80, box 104, Lloyd Cutler Files, Counsel's Office Files, Staff Office Files, Jimmy Carter Presidential Materials, and Hodding Carter to The Secretary, January 29, 1980, folder RE 15 1/1/80–3/31/80, box RE2, Sports-Recreation Files, Subject Files, White House Central Files, JCL.

15. *Washington Post,* February 14, 1980.

16. "American Legion: Remarks at the Legion's Annual Conference," February 19, 1980, *Public Papers of the President: Jimmy Carter, 1980* (Washington, DC: Government Printing Office, 1981), 346 (hereafter *Public Papers*); *The Washington Post,* February 20, 1980; and Cutler Memorandum for the SCC, February 20, 1980, and Brzezinski to Secretary of Defense, February 22, 1980, folder Olympics, 6/79–2/80, box 48, Subject Files, National Security Advisor Files, Staff Office Files, Jimmy Carter Presidential Materials, JCL.

17. The White House News Summary, February 21, 1980, JCL; "1980 Summer Olympics: White House Statement on U.S. Withdrawal from the Games to Be Held in Moscow," February 20, 1980, *Public Papers,* 356–57.

18. *Philadelphia Inquirer,* February 20, 1980; *Atlanta Constitution,* February 21, 1980, and *Commercial Appeal,* February 22, 1980.

19. *New York Times,* March 2, 1980; Brement to Brzezinski, February 25, 1980, folder Olympics, 6/79–2/80, box 48, Subject Files, National Security Advisor Files, Staff Office Files, Jimmy Carter Presidential Materials, JCL.

20. Zbigniew Brzezinski, *Power and Principle: Memoirs of the National Security Advisor, 1977–1981* (New York: Farrar, Straus, Giroux, 1983), 434.

21. Dyess to Deputy Secretary, March 21, 1980, attached to Cutler to Carter,

March 24, 1980, folder Olympics—Memos/Correspondence to President, 3/80, box 103, Lloyd Cutler Files, Counsel's Office Files, Staff Office Files, Jimmy Carter Presidential Materials, JCL.

22. "Report on the Meeting of the Foreign Secretaries of the Closely Cooperating Socialist Countries in Moscow on 26 February 1980," February 29, 1980, *Cold War International History Project Bulletin* 14/15 (Winter 2003–Spring 2004): 213.

23. "Interview with the President," February 25, 1980, *Public Papers,* 388.

24. Berenson and Jenkins to Cutler, February 27, 1980, folder Olympics—Memos, 1–2/80, box 102, Lloyd Cutler Files, Counsel's Office Files, Staff Office Files, Jimmy Carter Presidential Materials, JCL.

25. Cutler and Onek to Special Coordination Committee, February 25, 1980, folder Olympics—Memos/Correspondence to President 1–2/80, box 103, Lloyd Cutler Files, Counsel's Office Files, Staff Office Files, Jimmy Carter Presidential Materials, JCL.

26. *Washington Post,* March 8, 1980; "Interview with the President," February 25, 1980, *Public Papers,* 388; and Cutler to the President, February 18, 1980, folder Olympics—Memos/Correspondence to President 1–2/80, box 103, Lloyd Cutler Files, Counsel's Office Files, Staff Office Files, Jimmy Carter Presidential Materials, JCL.

27. Joe Onek Oral History with the author, June 22, 2007.

28. *Washington Post,* March 8, 1980; "Interview with the President," February 25, 1980, *Public Papers,* 388; and Cutler to the President, February 18, 1980, folder Olympics—Memos/Correspondence to President 1–2/80, box 103, Lloyd Cutler Files, Counsel's Office Files, Staff Office Files, Jimmy Carter Presidential Materials, JCL.

29. Lloyd Cutler Exit Interview Oral History, March 2, 1981, 8; Cutler to McIntyre, folder Olympics—Alternative Games 1–7/80, box 101; McDonald to Cutler, March 21, 1980, folder Olympic—Memos, 3–4/80, box 103, Lloyd Cutler Files, Counsel's Office Files, Staff Office Files, Jimmy Carter Presidential Materials; and Special Coordination Committee Meeting, March 20, 1980, folder Meetings—SCC 291 3/20/80, box 32, Brzezinski Donated Material, JCL.

30. Lloyd Cutler Exit Interview Oral History, March 2, 1981, 8; Cutler to McIntyre, folder Olympics—Alternative Games 1–7/80, box 101; McDonald to Cutler, March 21, 1980, folder Olympic—Memos, 3–4/80, box 103, Lloyd Cutler Files, Counsel's Office Files, Staff Office Files, Jimmy Carter Presidential Materials; and Special Coordination Committee Meeting, March 20, 1980, folder Meetings—SCC 291 3/20/80, box 32, Brzezinski Donated Material, JCL.

31. In his memoirs, Ueberroth says it was April, but internal evidence shows that it was actually March. He and his ghostwriters made a number of small factual errors of this type. Peter Ueberroth with Richard Levin and Amy Quinn, *Made in America: His Own Story* (New York: Morrow, 1985), 79–80, and Hulme, *Political Olympics,* 108.

32. *Christian Science Monitor,* February 21, 1980.

33. Brement to Cutler, February 13, 1980, folder Olympics, 6/79–2/80, box 48, Subject Files, National Security Advisor Files, Staff Office Files, Jimmy Carter Presidential Materials, JCL.

34. Ledsky to Secretary of State, March 8, attached to Brement to Brzezinski and Aaron, March 10, 1980, folder Olympics, 3/80, box 49, Subject Files, National Security Advisor Files, Staff Office Files, Jimmy Carter Presidential Materials, JCL.

35. Scott to Onek, February 13, 1980, and Berenson and Onek to Cutler, February 15, 1980, folder Olympics—Alternative Games 1–7/80, box 101, Lloyd Cutler Files, Counsel's Office Files, Staff Office Files, Jimmy Carter Presidential Materials, JCL.

36. Memorandum of Conversation, February 26, 1980, folder Olympics—Memos, 1–2/80, box 102, Lloyd Cutler Files, Counsel's Office Files, Staff Office Files, Jimmy Carter Presidential Materials, JCL.

37. Ibid.

38. Ibid.

39. Cutler and Onek to Special Coordination Committee, February 25, 1980, folder Olympics—Memos/Correspondence to President 1–2/80, box 103, Lloyd Cutler Files, Counsel's Office Files, Staff Office Files, Jimmy Carter Presidential Materials, JCL.

40. Cutler to the President, February 18, 1980, folder Olympics—Memos/Correspondence to President, 1–2/80, box 103, Lloyd Cutler Files, Counsel's Office Files, Staff Office Files, Jimmy Carter Presidential Materials; emphasis in the original notation on Special Coordination Committee, March 6, 1980, folder Meetings SCC 284 3/6/80, box 32, Papers of Zbigniew Brzezinski, Donated Historical Collections, JCL.

41. Memorandum from Cutler, March 20, 1980, folder Olympics, 3/80, box 49, Subject Files, National Security Advisor Files, Staff Office Files, Jimmy Carter Presidential Materials, JCL.

42. Killanin, *My Olympic Years,* 192.

43. *Cleveland Press,* January 18, 1980.

44. *Washington Post,* March 9, 1980, and *Los Angeles Times,* March 9, 1980.

45. Vance to Carter, March 10, 1980, folder State Department Evening Reports, 2/80, box 40, Plains File, Jimmy Carter Presidential Materials, JCL.

46. Ueberroth with Levin and Quinn, *Made in America,* 80; Onek, Memorandum for the File, March 12, 1980, folder Olympics—Alternative Games 1–7/80, box 101; and Cutler and Onek to Special Coordination Committee, February 25, 1980, folder Olympics—Memos/Correspondence to President 1–2/80, box 103, Lloyd Cutler Files, Counsel's Office Files, Staff Office Files, Jimmy Carter Presidential Materials, JCL.

47. Killanin to Kane, March 5, 1980, and Kane to Killanin, March 20, 1980, folder 824, box 52a, Papers of Robert Kane, US Olympic Committee Library and Archives, US Olympic Committee Training Center, Colorado Springs, CO.

48. Ueberroth with Levin and Quinn, *Made in America,* 81–82, and *Los Angeles Times,* March 19, 1980.

49. Killanin, *My Olympic Years,* 192; *Tribune de Geneve,* March 18, 1980; *La Suisse,* March 18, 1980; *The Guardian,* March 19, 1980; *Times* (London), March 19, 1980; *New York Times,* March 19, 1980; and Hurd and Cutler Press Conference Transcript in U.S. Mission Geneva to the Secretary of State, March 18, 1980, folder Olympics, 3/80, box 49, Subject Files, National Security Advisor Files, Staff Office Files, Jimmy Carter Presidential Materials, JCL.

50. Hazan, *Olympic Sports and Propaganda Games,* 149.

51. Aaron Beacom, "A Changing Discourse? British Diplomacy and the Olympic Movement," in *Sport and International Relations: An Emerging Relationship,* ed. Roger Levermore and Adrian Budd (London: Routledge, 2004), 102, and Denis Howell, *Made in Birmingham: The Memoirs of Denis Howell* (London: Queen Anne Press, 1990), 292, 296–97.

52. House of Lords, *The Parliamentary Debates (Hansard),* 5th series, vol. 404 (London: Her Majesty's Stationery Office, 1980), 981.

53. *Daily Telegraph,* February 1, 1980.

54. *Times* (London), February 6 and 7, 1980.

55. *Daily Telegraph,* February 20, 1980.

56. Follows to Thatcher, March 7, 1980, Moscow Olympic Files, British Olympic Association Archives, London (hereafter BOA). The research for this chapter took place before a 2007 flood that destroyed much of the BOA's archives. As a result, researchers using this material in the future will probably find this collection organized in different fashion than the citations here indicate.

57. House of Commons, *Parliamentary Debates (Hansard),* 5th series, vol. 981 (London: Her Majesty's Stationery Office, 1980) 31–168.

58. Ibid.

59. Ibid.

60. *Daily Telegraph,* March 19, 1980.

61. The Howell-Cutler meeting has grown more dramatic and more confrontational with its retelling. The source for this rendering is Howell's fairly reserved account: Howell, *Made in Birmingham,* 303–4; see also Neil Macfarlane with Michael Herd, *Sport and Politics: A World Divided* (London: Willow Books, 1986), 225–26.

62. Howell, *Made in Birmingham,* 303–4, and Macfarlane with Herd, *Sport and Politics,* 225–26.

63. Memorandum from Cutler, March 20, 1980, folder Olympics, 3/80, box 49, Subject Files, National Security Advisor Files, Staff Office Files, Jimmy Carter Presidential Materials, JCL.

64. *Los Angeles Times,* March 21, 1980.

65. Thatcher to Follows, March 19, 1980, Moscow Olympic Files, BOA.

66. Ibid.

67. BOA Press Statement, March 25, 1980, Moscow Olympic Files, BOA.

68. James Riordan, "Great Britain and the 1980 Olympics: A Victory for Olympism," in *Sport and International Understanding,* ed. Maaret Ilmarinen (New York: Springer-Verlag, 1984), 142.

69. *Financial Times,* March 19, 1980, and Kanin, *Political History of the Olympic Games,* 136. The representatives of fifteen national committees had met in Brussels on March 22 and declared that they would all vote to send teams to Moscow. Press Release by Western European NOCs, March 22, 1980, Annex 10 to Minutes of the Meeting of the IOC Executive Board, April 21, 22, 23, 1980, 52, 53, International Olympic Committee Archives, Lausanne, Switzerland (hereafter IOC).

70. Minutes of the Meeting of the Executive Board, April 21, 22, and 23, 1980, 11–14, IOC.

71. Hulme, *Political Olympics,* 30, and Berenson to Cutler and Ledsky, March 27, 1980, folder Olympics [Working File] 2–3/80, box 105, Lloyd Cutler Files, Counsel's Office Files, Staff Office Files, Jimmy Carter Presidential Materials, JCL.

# 4

# Sport as Public Diplomacy

# 11

# Reclaiming the Slopes

## Sport and Tourism in Postwar Austria

*Wanda Ellen Wakefield*

Although the task of fighting and defeating the war machines of Nazi Germany and the Japanese Empire was daunting for the United States, the struggle to ensure postwar peace and prosperity proved to be a significant challenge as well. When the war ended, both Germany and Japan lay in ruins, and much of the rest of Europe had been devastated by long years of combat. Although US authorities might have wished to quickly end the occupations of the conquered countries and bring the troops back home (something that the soldiers and sailors themselves certainly desired), postwar exigencies required a commitment to an extended American presence. Europeans and Asians would not be allowed to starve while the United States had the means to feed them. Nor would their economies be allowed to founder while Washington had the ability to invest in their recovery. In addition, the United States would not sit idly by and allow the expansion of communist influence in Western Europe while it had the ability to demonstrate the benefits of capitalism and democracy. Soldiers, sailors, civilian administrators, and representatives of nongovernmental organizations from the United States therefore became key actors in the postwar recovery and symbols of American resolve. One site for this work was Austria, which, like Germany, was divided among the four victorious

powers (United States, Soviet Union, Great Britain, and France) and occupied from 1945 to 1955.

Sport historian Rudolph Mullner has recently argued that in many
ways skiing was already established as a national sport in Austria before
World War II. After the war, the restoration of Austria's ski tourism industry was crucial to the improvement of the postwar economy but also
to the development of a national identity replete with optimism about
the future. Therefore, the reporting in newspapers and on radio during
the late 1940s and 1950s about Austria's ski heroes offered hope where
previously there had been none. Then, when Anton Sailer swept the gold
medals at the 1956 Winter Olympic Games in Cortina d'Ampezzo, Italy,
he became the representative of a new forward-thinking Austria ready
to show the world its finest qualities.[1] Yet none of this would have been
possible absent the work of American occupation authorities who realized
the importance of ski tourism to the Austrian economy and the Austrian
people.

When American troops arrived in Austria at the end of World War
II, they found an enormous task ahead of them. In May 1945 they encountered tens of thousands of displaced persons who needed care immediately. They also discovered Nazi troops who needed to be disarmed
and repatriated. Most important for the future of that Alpine country,
soldiers from the US Army's Forty-Second Infantry Division and their
comrades faced the enormous challenge of feeding and housing not only
themselves but also the Austrian people. In the short run, food and housing received the most attention, but as the emergent situation stabilized,
American troops—along with their British and French counterparts—
began the long project of rebuilding the Austrian economy and integrating it into the emerging Western economic system. By 1948 the Marshall
Plan would provide funds to the Austrian government to accelerate that
process. Initially, however, the effort to restore and rebuild the country fell
to the military forces that had originally been tasked with occupying the
defeated country. But as the historian James Jay Carafano suggests, the
Americans who undertook their postwar work in Austria in 1945 did so
with little direct guidance from Washington.[2]

There has been considerable attention paid recently to the problem of
displaced persons in the wake of World War II.[3] They included refugees
from the Red Army and communism; concentration camp survivors and

slave laborers from the Balkans, France, and other German-occupied territories who had been forced to work for the Nazi war machine; and thousands of ordinary citizens affected by the fighting. The displaced persons in the American zone of occupation became the responsibility of the military governments until they figured out where to go now that they were free to make their own decisions. The commander of the Forty-Second Infantry Division, Maj. Gen. Harry J. Collins, reported after the winter of 1945–1946 that the United States had established 121 large camps offering food and shelter for displaced persons during those cold months.[4]

Much less attention has been paid to the men, women, and children of Austria who had survived the war and found themselves in a very peculiar position. Were they citizens of the enemy (Adolf Hitler was born in Austria), given the incorporation of Austria into greater Germany following the *Anschluss* in 1938? Were they citizens of a liberated state? Or were they people who had fallen between the cracks in terms of postwar planning? Moreover, with their country divided for administrative purposes among the four Allied powers, had they lost the ability to freely move from one zone of occupation to another? Given that they would soon have a new government approved by the Allies after a November 1945 election, would they rapidly see the end of occupation or would it continue for many years? Whatever the answers to those questions, American soldiers and their commanders realized that the road to recovery would be long and fraught with peril. Yet they also realized that the key to Austrian economic and social recovery and political rehabilitation would lie first in ensuring adequate food and shelter, then in rebuilding infrastructure—especially for transportation and education—and finally with the restoration of businesses and industries—particularly those that would bring in foreign currency, such as tourism.

From 1945 until the end of 1947, the responsibility for restoring the Austrian economy and infrastructure was primarily in the hands of the military governments in the French, British, and American zones; the commanders in the Soviet zone had a distinctly different mandate and purpose. In the American zone, soldiers contributed to this process by sharing food from their mess halls with Austrian children. For those children they also provided entertainment and sport facilities. They rebuilt schools and vetted teachers to be sure they were free from Nazi influence. US commanders also worked with local authorities to make local hotels fit for habitation in the hope that empty hotel space would begin enticing international visitors to the country. In 1948 the Marshall Plan provided money for further improvements in infrastructure such as airports and a new road from Italy to Austria. Marshall Plan funds were also used to reestablish the Salzburg Music Festival and to promote the festival and Austrian ski resorts in the United States. An examination of the evidence clearly demonstrates that ski and music festival tourism were understood by the Austrian government as it applied for Marshall Plan assistance to be key to ensuring that the country would be able to obtain the necessary hard currency to complete its postwar recovery. In addition, the US efforts during this period should be understood as a critical element of its broader public diplomacy efforts in the postwar period to not only rebuild and rehabilitate Austria but also to further its broader European foreign policy goals.

## Immediate Stabilization

As the immediate challenge facing the US military was to feed and house the occupation forces, the soldiers seized surviving hotels, hostels, and private houses to provide needed billeting space. Recognizing that this might lead to civilian discontent, commanders understood that they would need to create programs and policies that would assure the Austrian people of their good intentions and determination to see that the Austrians were returned to their homes and businesses as soon as possible. Because the goal of the US occupying forces was to eventually restore full sovereignty, American soldiers became public diplomats, whether they wished to or not, as they took control over the administration of the Salzburg and Upper Austria lands to which they had been assigned. As public diplomats, they had, in the words of Andrew Johns in the introduction to this volume, the responsibility to explain the "common interests" shared by Austrians and Americans.

Although much of western Austria had not faced the same degree of devastation as Germany had during the fighting at the end of the war, thousands of houses and hotels had been demolished along with roads, bridges, and communication lines, all of which would need to be restored in order to begin the process of reconciliation and economic recovery. Thus, long before the idea of significant American aid for European recovery had been conceived by US Army general and future secretary of state George C. Marshall, troops of the Forty-Second Infantry Division and other US military outfits found themselves directly and specifically tasked with helping their former enemies survive the immediate postwar years. As the Moscow Declaration of 1943 had deemed Austria to have a peculiar status as both an enemy and a country to be liberated from Nazi rule, the soldiers who first encountered the Austrian people had to decide on their own how best to handle the enormous responsibilities that had fallen into their laps with German surrender, responsibilities that demanded they exhibit a friendly and helpful attitude whenever they dealt with civilians.[5]

Decades later the men of the Forty-Second Infantry Division had a chance to sit back and reflect on their time in Austria. Many of those former soldiers eventually answered surveys conducted by the United States Army Heritage and Education Center (USAHEC) at Carlisle Barracks, Pennsylvania, detailing their prewar, wartime, and postwar experiences. They also contributed letters exchanged between themselves and their families written while they were in Austria. These contemporary documents and the responses to later surveys provide significant insight into the challenges they faced and how they dealt with the frustrations involved in transitioning from a combat force to an occupying force with a very different mission.[6]

The first project was to care for the children. When Gen. Mark Clark arrived in Vienna to take up his post as high commissioner for Austria, he realized that tens of thousands of young people were at risk of starvation. He therefore immediately ordered troop messes in the American zone to provide up to four hundred calories of food daily to needy children.[7] In his recollections, T5 Robert J. Calhoun of the Forty-Second recalled that his unit mess fed the young people without complaint when they saw the pitiful condition of so many of the Austrians and displaced persons they encountered. According to S.Sgt. Russell G. Jeske, they just "felt sorry for [all] of them."[8] Although many of Calhoun's colleagues later complained about the burdens they faced while caring for *adult* displaced persons, they did appreciate the need to see that *children* be cared for. Calhoun himself clearly understood that not only were he and his colleagues dealing with the immediate situation but also recalled that he and his colleagues were determined to create a contrast between their area in

Linz and the circumstances on the other side of the Danube where the "Russians treated civilians terribly" in their zone.[9] Calhoun remembered hoping that these efforts by the Americans to help care for the children of Austria would lead to more friendly relations between the United States and Austria in the future.

During his 1972 debriefing conversations, General Clark made it clear that in his mind feeding the people was part of his responsibility and that the fact that the United States had the wherewithal to do so gave him an upper hand in dealing with the Soviets, who, Clark believed, would have been perfectly content to keep the people of Vienna starving while they systematically looted the city. Therefore, Clark not only ordered feeding programs for the American zone but also made sure that the French had sufficient food to take care of the people in the Tyrol, which had become part of the French zone of occupation at the end of the war.[10] Despite his best efforts in this regard, however, Clark recalled that he had to struggle with a lack of resources, a fact that he pointed out to President Harry Truman when the president criticized Clark and Gen. Dwight D. Eisenhower in Germany for their alleged failure to do all that they could for displaced persons and children.[11]

The danger to children from unexploded ordnance and unsecured weapons was also on the minds of American troops during the summer of 1945. Thomas Stewart Brush of the Forty-Second remarked in a letter home that a young child had recently been seriously injured after an explosive he was playing with detonated.[12] Brush was unsure whether the young boy ultimately survived his injuries but was able to report that other people injured in the explosion were treated and released by American authorities. Obviously, for the Americans it was important to see to children's safety if they wanted to ensure the support of the local population. Therefore, the job of clearing explosives and confiscating guns became an urgent matter immediately after the war as well.

The US Military Government (USMG) also began planning for the reopening of schools in the fall of 1945. Acting on the advice of the *Military Government Handbook, Austria,* prepared by the staff of British field marshal Sir Harold Alexander in April 1945, American troops began the systematic reorganization of education in Austria, first by shutting down the so-called Nazi schools and youth organizations that had been proponents of Nazi ideology throughout the country. Those groups providing for the "recreational, physical or moral welfare of youth" would only be allowed to continue their work after obtaining military permission.[13] Similarly, Directive 23 of the Allied Control Commission for Germany ordered the shutdown of Nazi-influenced international and national sports organizations.[14] As in Germany, Austrian teachers would only be allowed back in classrooms after renouncing any Nazi sympathies.

The USMG also encouraged the work of nongovernmental organizations such as the Red Cross and the American Friends Service Committee, which began providing food and entertainment for the Austrian children as soon as hostilities ceased. Because of this focus on education, during the entire period from 1945 through 1949 both Clark and Lt. Gen. Geoffrey Keyes, Clark's successor as high commissioner, provided constant updates to Washington on the progress being made toward denazification and the reopening of public schools throughout the country. Indeed, Clark emphasized that as early as the fall of 1945, British, French, and American troops had rebuilt enough schools to provide classroom space for approximately 50 percent of elementary-age students in Austria.[15]

To further provide for the needs of Austria's children, the Americans and French established a variety of summer camps for local youth later during the occupation period. In his July 1948 report, Keyes remarked that his forces provided tents and food for those camps on an ongoing basis. By 1949 American efforts on behalf of Austrian children included the construction of a playground in Voecklabruck, a youth center in Marchtrenck, and bleachers for a sports field in Linz—all with the goal of providing activity for children during the summer months.[16] In cooperation with the Ministry of Education and the Austrian Olympic Committee, American soldiers also provided instruction in basketball and volleyball to approximately a thousand young people during the summer of 1949 and sponsored a Golden Gloves boxing tournament for five hundred boys in Linz.[17]

The French went even further by establishing winter camps at three Tyrolean mountain resorts for young people from Sweden, Italy, France, Switzerland, Great Britain, Belgium, and the Netherlands along with their Austrian counterparts.[18] There the youth could ski and sled and—most important from the perspective of the occupying forces—learn to respect one another. Eventually, of course, occupation authorities hoped that many of those young people would return to the Tyrol as tourists, bringing with them much-needed foreign currency. To further emphasize the need to attract tourist dollars, General Keyes mentioned with approval the fact that newsreel footage of Queen Juliana of the Netherlands arriving in the Tyrol for recreation in February 1949 was widely distributed within twenty-four hours of her visit.[19] He hoped that newsreel images of this kind would help persuade outsiders that Austria was finally returning to normal.

## Restoration of Tourism

In 1973 General Clark remarked that, in his view, the United States had made a major mistake in accepting postwar governance over the Salzburg and Upper Austria provinces. Whether it would have been possible for the US Army to occupy other regions in Austria—given its forces' immediate postwar location in the Salzburg area—Clark obviously regretted that "the United States was perfectly happy to get the ski area and Chamois hunting and fishing [areas]" rather than the industrial regions of eastern Austria and viewed American actions in that regard as an unwarranted appeasement of the communists.[20] On the other hand, within a few months of the occupation, military and civilian advisors had concluded that one essential key to Austria's postwar recovery lay in the revival of tourism—and that tourism would by necessity have to start in the areas occupied by the Americans and French where skiing, hunting, and fishing were likely to bring in international visitors with money to spend. Moreover, American commanders encouraged the reestablishment of the famous Salzburg Music Festival, as they believed that tourists would surely be drawn back to Austria for the music. Before tourism could begin again, however, a number of issues needed to be resolved.

One issue facing occupation authorities was the disentanglement of Austrian tourism resources from the practices and procedures put in place by the Germans following the *Anschluss*. Although the USMG reported to Washington in October 1946 that Nazis and Nazi supporters were not in charge of the tourism industry from 1938 through 1944, a substantial amount of evidence suggested that, as part of the larger project of denazification, hotel owners and their staffs had to be subject to significant review.[21] Furthermore, most hotel spaces had been seized for use by the occupying armies. As Brush wrote home, even though he was billeted in a hotel that had been "much damaged in the war," he was for the first time since Paris sleeping on sheets, a luxury that he much appreciated.[22] Despite the need for occupation billets and denazification, members of General Clark's staff supported an early plan by the Austrian government to rehabilitate three hundred tourist hotels, which required a $10 million investment in 1947–1948.[23]

The new Austrian government, elected in November 1945, quickly established a Chamber of Tourist Traffic under the Ministry of Trade and Reconstruction to facilitate the return of international visitors to the country. Although the war had devastated the tourist resorts and entertainment centers that needed to be rebuilt, the chamber also had to re-establish prewar connections with international travel agencies and trade representatives before opening the country to foreign guests.[24] Authorities, therefore, eagerly welcomed a representative from the Atlantic Lloyd Traveling Agency early in 1947, who was in the country to assess the level of accommodations that would be available to tourists from the United States. Travelers would likely need to rely on civilian transportation, so one major American goal was to open Austrian airspace to domestic and international airlines as soon as possible. Although the Soviets consistently opposed the restoration of civilian air service to Austria, American authorities apparently told the Lloyd representative that they would allow at least four Pan American Airways clippers to land in Salzburg as soon as there was enough interest among tourists to warrant those flights.[25] The airport reopened in 1949 for a three-month-long "test" of its ability to support civilian aviation.[26] Furthermore, despite ongoing vociferous complaints by Soviet representatives, at Allied meetings the Americans continued to push for access to the Vienna airport for Pan Am, Air France, KLM, SAS, and British European Airways.[27]

Another problem hindering the rapid redevelopment of the tourism industry was the need to ensure that outsiders had the appropriate passports and visas. The question of who should have the responsibility for issuing tourist visas—the Austrian government or the occupation authorities—bedeviled discussions at most meetings of the four powers. The United States supported the right of the Austrian government to control its borders as early as 1947 and continued to insist that the Austrians be allowed to do so despite objections from the Soviet Union.

The first break in the impasse over visas occurred in October 1947 when the decision was reached to allow foreigners with valid passports and Austrian visas (issued not by the government but by the occupying authorities) to travel across zonal boundaries without additional permission from the military governors of those zones. Shortly thereafter the Austrian Federal Railroad and Bus System reported that it had had to add more buses on important routes due to a significant increase in "holiday traffic"—some of which was from international visitors.[28] By December 1948 Austria was issuing its own visas, and in 1949 an agreement approved by the United States (although not necessarily embraced by the Soviets) allowed Austrians and Italians to cross their mutual border without first acquiring any visa.[29] Since a significant amount of tourist dollars would eventually come from Italian visitors, this enhanced ability to travel freely was most helpful for the recovery of the Austrian economy. Nevertheless, despite all of these agreements, the Soviets continued to harass outsiders and frustrate the British, French, and American authorities by requiring further identification for individuals entering the Soviet zone around Vienna.[30]

American soldiers living in and around Salzburg recognized the possibility for future tourism in the region. In their recollections, many emphasized the sheer beauty of the area, while lamenting the fact that they were stuck there in the army. Brush wrote home in September 1945 that he realized that despite his anger over the points system (which determined discharge dates for American troops) and the likelihood that he would still be in Austria the following year, he "should remember that many tourists and émigrés paid vast sums before the war—and will again—just to come here where I am. That is undeniably true: I might pay them myself for the privilege. But no one in his right mind would pay a plug nickel to come here under the Army."[31] Similarly, T5 Calhoun wrote his parents after arriving in the Tyrol that it "would cost a young fortune to see all the places and beautiful sights we are seeing."[32] Calhoun also told his parents that despite their advice, he was not planning on learning to ski while in Austria, although he often went rowing on Lake Schliersee.[33] However, Pfc. Samuel A. Jones did take advantage of his time in Austria to clear his mind of images from the liberation of Dachau, and he later remembered how much he appreciated being able to spend several three-day weekends skiing in the beautiful mountains.[34]

By 1947 continuing improvements in the American zone made visits by international tourists possible. Substantial amounts of building materials were now available, with the majority going to private construction projects. Furthermore, the Austrian government was able to arrange for the "the transport, reception of, and accommodation of a limited number of foreign tourists" during the winter of 1946–1947.[35] The 1947 Vienna Spring Fair entertained approximately five thousand foreign guests when it opened on March 23.[36] Because of the rugged winter, however, Washington was advised that although the US forces had 150 tons of bituminous material in their zone, they would still need at least 6,000 additional tons to repair and patch roads that had been damaged by the heavy snow before the summer camping and travel season began.[37] Eventually much of the cost for American activities in the Salzburg and Upper Austria provinces was covered by the Marshall Plan—and the use of those funds was added to the monthly reports from American commanders. For example, commanders reported in the spring of 1949 that the money to bring in much-needed shoes and clothing for the Austria people would be covered by the European Recovery Program (ERP) in the future.[38]

## The Marshall Plan Provides Financial Support for Austrian Reconstruction

In the sixty-plus years since the Marshall Plan was first proposed, scholars have established a clear narrative of the program's purposes, occasional failures, and obvious successes. As they have shown, by 1947 the efforts by the United States and its allies to provide aid to a prostrate Europe had failed to establish a new stability on the continent. Italy and France seemed on the verge of electing communist governments. Britain's austerity program had left its citizens at a poverty level not appreciably different than what they had experienced during the worst days of World War II.[39] And Germany and Austria, still occupied by the Allies, were suffering from the destruction of their infrastructure, inability to gain international credit, and ongoing questions about the ultimate status of their states after the occupations finally ended.

Therefore, the United States, as the only major industrialized nation to survive World War II with its manufacturing capacity intact and with its midwestern farmers eager to sell their produce, became the primary global source for capital, food, and heavy machinery. The United States also helped create a structure that ultimately allowed the Europeans themselves to determine the shape of their recovery. At Harvard University's commencement in June 1947, Secretary of State Marshall proposed the program, which would eventually carry his name, that would facilitate exchanges among the Allies to create a comprehensive system for European recovery. Yet, in none of these discussions, nor in the vast majority of the English-language monographs published since 1950 discussing the Marshall Plan, was the matter of restoring the Austrian ski industry specifically addressed, despite the clear understanding of American military commanders from 1945 through 1947 that the restoration of tourism would be an important part of their mandate.[40]

By the beginning of 1947 the United States government was very concerned by the slow pace of European recovery. Even though the American high commissioner in Austria was able to point to certain successes— such as the restoration of train service and the reopening of a nitrogen fertilizer plant—much still needed to be done. As Undersecretary of State Dean Acheson remarked that spring, he feared that in the absence of food and fuel imported from America the Europeans faced the serious prospect of anarchy as their frustrations grew and their needs remained unmet.[41] Given that danger, Acheson concluded that American national interests demanded that the United States needed to help in the relief and reconstruction of as much of Europe as possible. In an extensive discussion of how that recovery should be organized, the US Department of State agreed that even the defeated, occupied, and divided German state would need ongoing aid because before the war it had been a crucial component of the European economy. The State Department also believed such aid might tie at least the western part of Germany into the Western capitalist economic system.[42] The memorandum stressed the danger that European states and the European people might embrace communism if economic conditions did not improve, which would also threaten "the values of individual responsibility and political restraint which had become traditional on the Continent." Meanwhile Marshall continued to emphasize that eventual European recovery would depend not on the United States but, ultimately, on the Europeans themselves.[43]

The State Department memorandum focused on three areas crucial for the redevelopment of Europe. One was in agriculture, where farmers both inside and outside of Austria urgently needed new implements, fertilizer, and laborers. Another was in transportation, as not only were many roads and bridges destroyed during the war not yet repaired, but railroad rolling stock was still in very limited supply (particularly given the Soviet "reparations" program, which confiscated material from its occupation zones in Austria and Germany). Finally, the State Department concluded that for full recovery to succeed, the European states would have to reach agreements about rates of currency exchange and the reduction of tariffs. As the memorandum made clear, the United States would extend aid only where a country's needs could not be met otherwise and that such aid must be concentrated for maximum effect. Special consideration would also be given to recovery plans involving multiple nations (as with the resolution of the coal situation in the Benelux countries, which established the precursor to today's European Union).

Although the majority of these postwar discussions were directed at the situation in the Allied nations, especially France and West Germany, relatively little consideration was given to the needs of Austria and during the initial phases of ERP planning. Nevertheless, the Austrian government elected in November 1945 under the leadership of Karl Renner was entitled to submit aid requests just like any other state—with the obvious exception of those lands within the Soviet sphere of authority, which reflected Moscow's refusal to accept Western aid for reconstruction in its zones of occupation and for the restoration of infrastructure in its Eastern European satellites. Since the Soviet influence and communist ideology had been soundly defeated in that first postwar election—the Austrian Communist Party received the support of only 6 percent of the country's eligible voters—the US commitment to the reconstruction of this "liberated" Austria came to be seen as both a moral and practical obligation. This was certainly the view of General Clark, who was determined to continue to limit communist influence in the country.[44]

One early focus for American occupation troops and, eventually, ERP planners was the revival of the Salzburg Music Festival. The reestablishment of this historic music program would not only entertain the approximately fifteen thousand US troops in the region, it would also provide entertainment and a morale boost for the local population and would eventually bring foreign visitors back to Salzburg. In order to create additional ways for people to enjoy their limited leisure time, members of the Women's Army Corps (the women's branch of the US Army) arrived in Austria shortly after the occupation began and started to reopen movie houses (showing only those films approved by the Information Services Branch of the Armed Forces, of course) and libraries.[45] Meanwhile, local Austrian hoteliers quickly began planning for their own futures, even as their hotels were occupied by displaced persons and soldiers, as they hoped to reopen as soon as possible to international visitors. In Zell am See, civilian workers during the summer of 1945 managed to clear the approach to a local ski area and begin repairs to the ski lift. Their work was apparently rewarded that winter as many American soldiers took advantage of the opportunity to learn to ski or to enhance their skills with the assistance of Austrian ski instructors. (Indeed, World War II proved crucial to the development of an Alpine ski industry in the United States as soldiers who had trained with the Tenth Mountain Division at Camp Hale in Colorado returned home to establish the new resorts of Aspen and Vail.)

Frustrated with the points system, American soldiers needed appropriate entertainment. Designed to further an understanding of Austria and the role that the troops were playing in its postwar development, efforts to reestablish Austria's ski resorts meshed well with programs encouraging them to participate in training exercises and educational opportunities.[46] As James Jay Carafano noted in his study of the Austrian occupation, American troops took many photographs memorializing their time in the country. Those photographs emphasized "skiing, swimming, playing baseball, and sightseeing rather than ruined cities."[47] Whether those American troops (who learned to ski while in Austria) would spend money to come back and see the country again as tourists was ultimately less important than their time already spent encouraging the rapid development of sports venues, which promoted ongoing international tourism.

Between 1947 and 1952, the Austrian government asked for and received several million dollars in Marshall Plan aid. At first, these funds were used to purchase foodstuffs to meet the nutritional needs of the Austrian people. Although food aid had been initially distributed by the US Army in its own occupation zone and by the French in theirs, even after Austrian rations reached the goal of fifteen hundred calories per day established by General Clark, the American military government was wary about passing that responsibility for feeding the people on to civilian authorities. They feared that the Soviets would keep local officials from distributing food aid equitably (or at all) in their occupation zone. After 1947 Marshall Plan money was also used to finance big industrial projects such as a mountain dam to provide hydroelectric power to the people of Austria and Czechoslovakia (thus meeting the cross-border, multinational assistance mandate favored by the State Department).

As for the use of Marshall Plan assistance to re-create the Austrian tourist industry as a means to ensure the country's eventual economic independence and self-sufficiency, in 1949 Theodore G. Pozzy, the chief of the Economic Cooperation Administration's Paris tourism office, argued that the Austrian government should definitely invest some of its aid in tourist facilities. He explained that his office had been trying to encourage Americans to visit the continent but that the infrastructure for tourism needed to be redeveloped before people would be interested in visiting Austria, where more than a quarter of prewar hotel rooms were still in disarray, or other war-torn parts of Europe.[48] At the same time, Clyde N. King, the head of the Marshall Plan program in Austria, supported Pozzy's idea and called for a substantial investment in tourist amenities.[49] The key for both Pozzy and King was their understanding that if international tourists were to spend their money in Austria, the country would be able to avoid a negative balance of payments with the rest of the world.

Obviously, music and skiing drew visitors to Austria—and had done so for decades. Significant Alpine tourism began in the late nineteenth century as British travelers, especially, began to spend winter months in the Swiss resorts of St. Moritz, Klosters, and Davos. While in the Swiss mountains, they experimented with sledding, notably the famous sled races from Davos to Klosters that established luge as a new sporting tradition.[50] They also took advantage of new technologies such as the early ski lifts that enabled interested individuals to ski at higher altitudes and down more rugged slopes than ever before. This interest in visiting the high mountains of Europe extended to Austria as well, where by the beginning of the twentieth century German and British tourists began visiting Kitzbuhel and other Austrian resorts to hike during the summer and ski during the winter.[51]

After World War I, that ski tourism tradition continued. In the much smaller postwar Austrian state, entrepreneurs also began luring visitors to Salzburg where an annual music festival honoring Mozart was reestablished in 1920.[52] Almost immediately the Salzburg region began to benefit from the large number of European and American visitors who came to hear the music—and often to attend the Oberammergau Passion Play in the years it was staged across the border in Bavaria. Money spent during each year's festival season would be among the most important sources of revenue for the Austrian government until 1938 when many of the festival's most important players, such as Arturo Toscanini, fled Austria after the German takeover.[53] After numerous cancelations from visitors from Britain and the United States, the festival became essentially a pro-Nazi cultural exhibition endorsed and controlled by the German leadership.

As for Alpine and Nordic skiing, the Lower Austria Ski Club had been founded in 1892. Then, in 1902, the Kitzbuhel Winter Sports Association was established, and its members began preparing their Alpine valley to welcome the world by building a ski-jump facility and grooming trails around the resort for local and international athletes. British tourists first took advantage of these new facilities when the Ski Club of Great Britain held Nordic and Alpine races at Kitzbuhel. After World War I, Kitzbuhel hosted the inaugural Hahnenkamm downhill race in 1923 and built its first ski lift in 1926.[54] Shortly thereafter the first Kandahar ski competitions were held at St. Anton. Combining revenue from ski tourism and the Salzburg Festival (as well as visits to Vienna), Austria earned approximately $34 million in foreign exchange during 1937, which represented 15 percent of the country's total income.

In the immediate aftermath of World War II, the prospect of restoring Austria's tourism industry seemed bleak. Aside from the large number of hotels (25 percent) and hotel furnishings (80 percent) destroyed during the war, Allied forces had commandeered most of the remaining hotel space to house themselves and displaced persons. Indeed, efforts to hold a new Salzburg Festival in 1947 were thwarted by the Allied refusal to free up rooms for visitors. As a US Army spokesman stated, although "American policy has been to aid the Salzburg Festival," General Collins would not evict displaced persons in order to house tourists from Britain and elsewhere.[55] Furthermore, American authorities were at the time unwilling to provide additional food rations to meet the needs of outsiders. Therefore, as a practical matter, the *New York Times* advised its readers in April 1947 that Austria was simply in no shape to receive visitors.[56]

By the end of 1947, however, things had changed. Reporting for the *New York Times,* travel writer Diana Rice announced that as of December 15, 1947, fifty of the leading Austrian hotels—including those at St. Anton and Kitzbuhel—were ready to welcome tourists. New ski lifts were already in operation. The Allies had also ensured that approved tourist hotels were "well stocked with food."[57] Kitzbuhel's tourism officials had also begun a program to train local boys as skiers and ski guides to help ensure that visitors would have a fun and safe time on the slopes. Thanks to these efforts, according to Rice, approximately $250,000 was spent by foreign tourists in Austria during the winter of 1947–1948.

Two years later, after local efforts to bring visitors back to the nation had begun to bear fruit, Theodore Pozzy called for even more investment in Austria's tourism industry. Acknowledging the industry's importance to Austria's overall economic revival, Pozzy encouraged the government to apply for Marshall Plan money in 1949 to pay for advertising in American newspapers and magazines to lure more visitors from the United States. The following year Austria used ERP funds for the further development of infrastructure such as roads, bridges, and railroads and also used "loans or grants for tourism, agriculture, forestry, and housing," according to John MacCormac of the *New York Times*.[58] A mere five years after that, visitors to Austria were spending upward of $70 million annually to listen to music, hike in the mountains, eat in Vienna, and ski down the mountain slopes at St. Anton, Kitzbuhel, and other resorts.[59] The number of these international visitors continued to climb, especially after the withdrawal of occupation forces pursuant to the State Treaty of 1955 (which guaranteed Austria's neutrality) freed up more hotel beds throughout the nation.[60]

Although the number of tourists and the amount of money they spent each year increased, for Austria the opportunity to host the Winter Olympic Games meant the chance to demonstrate on a larger stage that they were open for business. Immediately after the successful conclusion of the 1956 Winter Olympic Games held at Cortina d'Ampezzo on the other side of the Brenner Pass, entrepreneurs in Innsbruck—which had been part of the French zone at the end of World War II—began planning to make a bid to host the Games in 1964. They understood that hosting the Olympics would allow for further investment in local infrastructure in and around Innsbruck and, hopefully, throughout the rest of Austria, encouraging more visits by international travelers. They also hoped that by becoming an Olympic city they could contribute to the ongoing revival of the Austrian economy. As the Innsbruck organizing committee went about its work on sports venues, more and more athletically inclined tourists were being drawn to the region. As *Sports Illustrated* writer Paul Ress concluded shortly before the 1964 Games began, thanks to Austrian Toni Sailer's successes at Cortina d'Ampezzo and the estimated $20 million dollars in Marshall Plan aid spent by the Austrian government, thousands of tourists were traveling to Austria—rather than Switzerland—for their (less expensive) winter ski adventures.[61]

The Austrians succeeded in their bid to host the Winter Olympic Games at Innsbruck, and the country looked much different than it had in the immediate aftermath of World War II. Certainly Olympic visitors in 1964 did not face the calorie restrictions that were common in Austria immediately after the war. Yet, although there were no more displaced persons, and Allied troops had left the country, organizers still worried that they would be unable to house all of the people arriving for the Games. Nevertheless, the postwar building boom in Austria meant that there were more than six thousand hotel beds in the city itself by the end of 1963. In addition, accommodations for at least three thousand were available at Seefeld, the venue for Nordic events, and fifteen hundred beds were available in area pensions. Organizers also established bus service to and from Innsbruck for people who found hotel rooms in St. Anton and Kitzbuhel.[62]

Thus the long-awaited and eagerly anticipated international tourists came to Innsbruck in 1964 for the Olympics, found food and accommodation, and returned home with stories about the beauties of Austria— just as the men of the Forty-Second Infantry Division had done during and after the occupation that began in 1945. By the end of the twentieth century, Austria would be referred to as the "Disneyland of Europe," as millions of visitors traveled to the country annually to enjoy the nation's food, terrain, and music. Indeed, the number of tourists who would travel annually to Austria continued to rise from fifty million in 1950, to fifty-nine million in 1970 and ninety-five million in 1990. As Generals Clark and Keyes and Secretary Marshall had hoped and planned for five decades earlier using US public diplomacy, Austria—a nation broken economically and socially by the *Anschluss* and World War II—successfully used American resources invested after the war to restore and rebuild, thereby becoming a stable member of the world community and one of the leading tourist destinations in Europe.

# Notes

I would like to thank Heather Dichter and Andrew Johns as well as my anonymous readers for their careful attention to this manuscript. Their help was invaluable. I would also like to thank Darleen Farley, an ace copy editor, for finding the typos that all of the rest of us missed. Finally, this is for my wife, Pam, who has stuck with me through thick and thin over these decades.

1. See Rudolph Mullner, "The Importance of Skiing in Austria," *International Journal of the History of Sport* 30, no. 6 (2013): 659–73.

2. James Jay Carafano, "The Occupation of Germany, Austria, Trieste, Japan, Okinawa and Korea," in *Companion to American Military History,* vol. 2, ed. James C. Bradford (Malden, MA: Wiley-Blackwell, 2010), 564–71.

3. Ben Shephard, *The Long Road Home: The Aftermath of the Second World War* (New York: Knopf, 2010); Anna Marta Holian, *Between National Socialism and Soviet Communism: Displaced Persons in Postwar Germany* (Ann Arbor: University of Michigan Press, 2011); Mark Wyman, *DPs: Europe's Displaced Persons, 1945–1951* (Ithaca, NY: Cornell University Press, 1998); Gerald Leonard Cohen, *In War's Wake: Europe's Displaced Persons in the Postwar Order* (New York: Oxford University Press, 2012); G. Daniel Cohen, "Between Relief and Politics: Refugee Humanitarianism in Occupied Germany, 1945–1946," *Journal of Contemporary History* 43, no. 3 (2008): 437–49; and Adam R. Seipp, "Refugee Town: Germans, Americans, and the Uprooted in Rural West Germany, 1945–52," *Journal of Contemporary History* 44, no. 4 (2009): 675–95.

4. Harry J. Collins, *Year of Progress: Commanding General Reviews 42nd's Occupation Job in Austria* (Vienna: Headquarters, US Forces in Austria, 1946).

5. For Austria's peculiar status, see Peter Thaler, *The Ambivalence of Identity: The Austrian Experience of Nation-Building in a Modern Society* (West Lafayette, IN: Purdue University Press, 2001), and James Jay Carafano, *Waltzing into the Cold War: The Struggle for Occupied Austria* (College Station: Texas A&M University Press, 2002).

6. Historians in recent years have recognized the problems with oral history and other memoirs because memories have been demonstrated to change over time and telling. Regarding some of the problems with oral history and ways in which to use it, see Lynn Abrams, *Oral History Theory* (New York: Routledge, 2010), and Robert Perks and Alistair Thompson, eds., *The Oral History Reader* (New York: Routledge, 2006). The most famous collection of memories from World War II is Studs Turkel, *The Good War: An Oral History of World War II* (New York: New Press, 1997).

7. Mark Clark, *Senior Officers Debriefing Program: Conversations with Lt. Colonel Forest S. Rittgers, Jr., 27 October 1972* (Carlisle Barracks, PA: Military History Institute, 1972), 29.

8. Russell G. Jeske, World War II Veteran Survey Collection (WWIIVSC), Forty-Second Infantry Division, box 1, US Army Heritage and Education Center, Carlisle, Pennsylvania (hereafter USAHEC).

9. Robert J. Calhoun, WWIIVSC, Forty-Second Infantry Division, box 1 USAHEC.

10. Clark, *Senior Officers Debriefing Program*, 10. The original wartime plans for the occupation of Austria did not include a zone of occupation for France. Tony Sharp, *The Wartime Alliance and the Zonal Division of Germany* (Oxford: Clarendon, 1975), and Alice Hills, *Britain and the Occupation of Austria, 1943–45* (Basingstoke: St. Martin's, 2000).

11. Clark, *Senior Officers Debriefing Program*, 28–29.

12. Thomas Stewart Brush, July 19, 1945, WWIIVSC, Forty-Second Infantry Division, box 1, USAHEC.

13. *Military Government Handbook, Austria, April 15* (Vienna: B. Spies, 1945–1955), 4, 12–13.

14. Heather Dichter, "'Strict Measures Must Be Taken': Wartime Planning and the Allied Control of Sport in Occupied Germany," *Stadion* 34, no. 2 (2008): 193–217.

15. U.S. Allied Commission for Austria, *The Rehabilitation of Austria, 1945–1947*, vol. 3 (Vienna: Headquarters, US Forces in Austria, 1945–1947), 92.

16. *Report of the United States High Commissioner, Civil Affairs, #33 July, 1948* (Vienna: Headquarters, US Forces in Austria, 1948). Bleachers are raised seating for sports venues.

17. *Report of the United States High Commissioner, Civil Affairs, #47 September, 1949* (Vienna: Headquarters, US Forces in Austria, 1949), 41.

18. Ibid., 20, and *Report of the United States High Commissioner, Civil Affairs, #39 January, 1949* (Vienna: Headquarters, US Forces in Austria, 1949), 39.

19. *Report of the United States High Commission, Civil Affairs, #42 April, 1949* (Vienna: Headquarters, US Forces in Austria, 1949), 42.

20. Clark, *Senior Officers Debriefing Program*, 3, 7. For the division of Austria, see Sharp, *Wartime Alliance*.

21. *Military Government Austria, October 21, 1946*, vol. 2 (Vienna: Headquarters, US Forces in Austria, 1946), 15.

22. Thomas Stewart Brush letter, March 12, 1946, WWIIVSC, Forty-Second Infantry Division, box 1, USAHEC.

23. *Military Government Austria, 1 October 1946*, vol. 1 (Vienna: Headquarters, US Forces in Austria, 1946), 98. Given the date of Clark's report, it is likely that these plans had been made by the Austrian government before the announcement of aid through the Marshall Plan.

24. *Military Government Austria, 21 October 1946*, vol. 2 (Vienna: Headquarters, US Forces in Austria, 1946), 15. See also *Civil Affairs Austria, July, 1948, #33* (Vienna: Headquarters, US Forces in Austria, 1948), 43, for a list of those individuals who had been declared acceptable after analysis of their Nazi ties.

25. *Military Government Austria, #17, March 1947* (Vienna: Headquarters, US Forces in Austria, 1947), 92.

26. *Civil Affairs Austria, July 1949, #45* (Vienna: Headquarters, US Forces in Austria, 1949) 43.

27. *Civil Affairs Austria, August, 1949, #46* (Vienna: Headquarters, US Forces in Austria, 1949) 20, 44, and *Civil Affairs Austria, December 1948, #38* (Vienna: Headquarters, US Forces in Austria, 1948), 43.

28. *Civil Affairs Austria, July, 1948, #33* (Vienna: Headquarters, US Forces in Austria, 1948), 121.

29. *Civil Affairs Austria, April, 1949, #42* (Vienna: Headquarters, US Forces in Austria, 1949).

30. "The Situation in Austria," *Intelligence Review* 112 (April 15, 1948): 42–46.

31. Thomas Stewart Brush letter, September 23, 1945, WWIIVSC, Forty-Second Infantry Division, box 1, USAHEC.

32. Robert J. Calhoun letter, May 13, 1945, WWIIVSC, Forty-Second Infantry Division, box 1, USAHEC.

33. Robert J. Calhoun letter, July 6, 1945, WWIIVSC, Forty-Second Infantry Division, box 1, USAHEC, and Robert J. Calhoun letter, October 10, 1945, WWIIVSC, Forty-Second Infantry Division, box 1, USAHEC.

34. Samuel A. Jones, WWIIVSC, Forty-Second Infantry Division, box 1, USAHEC.

35. *Military Government Austria, Report of the U.S. High Commissioner, #18, April, 1947* (Vienna: Headquarters, US Forces in Austria, 1947), 141, 95. Nitrogen plants had been a particular focus of Allied bombing campaigns as the fertilizer they produced was also a critical component of bombs.

36. *Military Government Austria, #17, March, 1947* (Vienna: Headquarters, US Forces in Austria, 1947), 92.

37. Ibid., 186.

38. *Civil Affairs Austria, #42, April 1949* (Vienna: Headquarters, US Forces in Austria, 1948–1949), 98.

39. Growing up in Brighton, England, during and after the War, Sheila Baker remembered her first encounter with a "Marshall Plan banana." Because she had never seen one before, she decided to eat the entire thing, skin and all. Conversation with Sheila Baker, Buffalo, New York, March 1995. For information about aspects of the postwar economic situation in Europe and the beginnings of the European Community, see Barry Eichengreen, *The European Economy Since 1945: Coordinated Capitalism and Beyond* (Princeton, NJ: Princeton University Press, 2006), and John Gillingham, *Coal, Steel and the Rebirth of Europe, 1945–1955: The Germans and French from the Ruhr Conflict to the Economic Community* (Cambridge: Cambridge University Press, 2005).

40. See, for example, *Fifteen Years of Activity of the Economic Commission for Europe, 1947–1962* (New York: United Nations, 1964), which details the various committees and reports generated by the commission during those years. See also Günter Bischof, Anton Pelinka, and Dieter Stiefel, eds., *The Marshall Plan in Austria* (New Brunswick, NJ: Transaction, 2000); Michael Hogan, *The Marshall Plan: America, Britain and the Reconstruction of Western Europe, 1947–1952* (New York: Cambridge University Press, 1987); Brian Angus McKenzie, *Remaking France: Americaniza-*

*tion, Public Diplomacy, and the Marshall Plan* (New York: Berghahn Books, 2005); Charles S. Maier and Günter Bischof, eds., *The Marshall Plan and Germany: West German Development within the Framework of the European Recovery Program* (New York: Berg, 1991); and Reinhold Wagnleitner, *Coca-colonization and the Cold War: The Cultural Mission of the United States in Austria after the Second World War,* trans. Diana M. Wolf (Chapel Hill: University of North Carolina Press, 1994).

41. Dean Acheson, "The Requirements of Reconstruction," *Department of State Bulletin* 16, no. 411 (May 8, 1947): 991–94, Harry S. Truman Library, Independence Missouri (HSTL), Marshall Plan Research Online File, http://www.trumanlibrary.org/whistlestop/study_collections/marshall/large/documents/pdfs/8-8.pdf#zoom=100 (accessed September 5, 2013).

42. Clark Clifford, "Certain Aspects of the Economic Recovery Problem," ca. July 1947, HSTL, Marshall Plan Research Online File, http://www.trumanlibrary.org/whistlestop/study_collections/marshall/large/documents/pdfs/6–1.pdf#zoom=100 (accessed September 5, 2013).

43. George C. Marshall, "European Initiative Essential to Economic Recovery," *State Department Bulletin* 16, no. 415 (June 5, 1947): 1159–60, HSTL, Marshall Plan Research Online File, http://www.trumanlibrary.org/whistlestop/study_collections/marshall/large/documents/pdfs/8–7.pdf #zoom=100 (accessed September 5, 2013).

44. Milton Colvin, "Principal Issues in the U.S. Occupation of Austria, 1945–1948," in *U.S. Occupation in Europe after World War II,* ed. Hans Schmitt (Lawrence: Regents Press of Kansas, 1978), 108. See also Clark, *Senior Officers Debriefing Program.*

45. Donald R. Whitnah and Florentine E. Whitnah, *Salzburg under Siege: U.S. Occupation, 1945–1955* (New York: Greenwood, 1991), 17.

46. Soldiers from the Forty-Second Infantry Division also studied academic subjects at their "Rainbow University." For a combat history of the division during World War II, see Hugh C. Daly, *42nd "Rainbow" Infantry Division: A Combat History of World War II* (Baton Rouge, LA: Army and Navy Publishing Company, 1946). See also diverse soldier memoirs from the Forty-Second Infantry Division in the World War II Veteran Surveys Collection at the USAHEC.

47. Carafano, *Waltzing into the Cold War.*

48. "Intensive Tourism Advised in Austria," *New York Times,* February 19, 1949, 6.

49. "Progress Reported in Austrian Economy," *New York Times,* February 5, 1949, 5.

50. Susan Barton, *Healthy Living in the Alps: The Origins of Winter Tourism in Switzerland, 1860–1914* (Manchester: Manchester University Press, 2008). For the history of the International Luge Federation, established by Austria's Bert Isatisch, see www.fil-luge.org.

51. Arnold Lunn, *Memory to Memory* (London: Hollis & Carter, 1956), and E. John B. Allen, *The Culture and Sport of Skiing: From Antiquity to World War II* (Amherst: University of Massachusetts Press, 2007). For a discussion of the develop-

ment of Alpine and Nordic skiing from the point of view of the sport's international governing body, see the International Ski Federation, www.fis-ski.com.

52. Michael P. Steinberg, *The Meaning of the Salzburg Festival: Austria as Theater and Ideology, 1890–1938* (Ithaca, NY: Cornell University Press, 1990), and Stephen Gallup, *A History of the Salzburg Festival* (London: Weidenfield & Nicolson, 1987).

53. For the 1937 festival, see Herbert F. Peyser, "Salzburg Festival Closes Tomorrow," *New York Times,* August 30, 1937, 25, detailing the various questions as to whether the festival would be able to continue given increasing international tensions. For the 1938 festival, see "Salzburg Festival—1938 Edition," *New York Times,* September 25, 1938, 161, describing the "Nazification" of Salzburg.

54. Robert Daley, "Home Town Put Sailer on Skis and He Put Town on Map," *New York Times,* January 24, 1960, S5. For more on Sailer's successes at the 1956 Olympic Winter Games at Cortina d'Ampezzo, see "Beau of Cortina," *Sports Illustrated,* February 13, 1955.

55. Albion Ross, "Austria Urges U.S. to Oust Displaced Persons at Spa," *New York Times,* May 17, 1947, 4. Collins also refused to force the approximately fourteen hundred Jewish refugees living in eight hotels at Bad Gastein to leave their accommodations. See also "Room Need a Threat to Salzburg Festival," *New York Times,* July 14, 1947, 24.

56. "Tourists to Europe," *New York Times,* April 13, 1947, 110.

57. Diana Rice, "The Field of Travel," *New York Times,* December 7, 1947, 344.

58. John MacCormac, "Austria Still Dependent on Marshall Aid Despite Long Strides Toward Recovery in '50," *New York Times,* January 2, 1951, S9.

59. John MacCormac, "Austria Is Ruling Economy at Last," *New York Times,* January 4, 1956, 60.

60. For more on the financial obligations to which Austria committed to ensure Soviet support for the 1955 State Treaty, see Brenden M. Jones, "Austria Becomes Free—at a Price," *New York Times,* May 22, 1956, 17.

61. For more on Sailer's three gold medals at Cortina, see Anton Sailer, http://www.olympic.org/anton-sailer. See also Paul Ress, "A Fight for Life by the Home Team," *Sports Illustrated,* January 27, 1964.

62. Robert Daley, "Slushy Innsbruck Waits in Vain for Winter to Join the Olympics," *New York Times,* February 6, 1964, 21; Fred R. Smith, "The Winter Olympics," *Sports Illustrated,* August 12, 1965; and Roy Terrell, "Olympic Winter in the Tyrol," *Sports Illustrated,* November 11, 1963.

# 12

# Politics First, Competition Second

## Sport and China's Foreign Diplomacy in the 1960s and 1970s

### *Fan Hong and Lu Zhouxiang*

Sport is not only a major form of human interaction but also one of the central ways in which a society reflects its ideology and identity, as well as its place in international politics and relations. This is particularly true in China, where sport has played an important role in the country's political and diplomatic strategy since the early twentieth century. Sport was seen by politicians as one of the most suitable vehicles for political diplomacy. It helped, for instance, to strengthen relationships with nations of the Non-Aligned Movement (NAM) and to establish the leadership of the People's Republic of China (PRC) in the Third World. It also enabled China to both oppose Western imperialists and to make approaches to those same diplomatic antagonists through a medium that benefitted from an apolitical image. Sport served China's political and diplomatic goals.

This chapter focuses on Chinese foreign policy toward and involvement with the NAM and its relationship with and policy toward the two superpowers, the United States and the Soviet Union, during the Cold War. It will also examine some major sporting events—such as the

Fourth Asian Games in 1962, the Games of the Newly Emerging Forces (GANEFO) in 1964, the Asian-African Table Tennis Friendship Invitational Tournament in 1971, and the Asian-African–Latin American Table Tennis Friendship Invitational Tournaments held between 1973 and 1980—and their influence on these relationships. Moreover, the chapter analyzes the combination of internal and external factors that shaped Chinese foreign policy and Chinese sport in the 1960s and 1970s and argues that, from the very beginning, sport was used to serve the PRC's foreign policy, which focused on uniting the newly independent countries in Asia, Africa, and Latin America to compete against the United States and the Soviet Union. This policy helped China to establish its position as a leading power in the Third World and played a significant part in changing the political landscape of the world. In the 1970s, following changes to China's foreign policy, sport was used by Beijing to reengage with Western countries—most significantly the United States—and to rebuild China's image and influence in the Third World. Several international sporting events held during this period played pivotal diplomatic roles in bringing China to the center stage of world politics.

## Chinese Foreign Policy toward the NAM in the 1960s and 1970s

After World War II, the awakening of nationalism that occurred within the colonies of Western imperial powers in Asia, Africa, and Latin America gave birth to many independent nation-states. Indeed, fifty nations claimed independence in the 1940s and 1950s.[1] These new countries were nationalistic and competitive, and their independence that resulted from the wave of postwar decolonization turned a new page in world politics and fundamentally altered the paradigm of international relations.

The PRC was a member of the socialist camp, and therefore Chinese foreign policy in the 1950s concentrated primarily on strengthening the country's relationship with the Soviet Union. Yet it also focused on supporting liberation movements in Asia, Africa, and Latin America. Beijing began to forge relationships with newly independent countries that had historical backgrounds similar to China's and soon established foreign relations with some of the leading Third World countries in Asia, including India (1950), Vietnam (1950), and Indonesia (1951). The key milestone in the relationship between China and the newly independent countries in the Third World came in April 1955 when the Asian-African Conference was held in Bandung, Indonesia. The objective of the conference was to unite the newly independent countries in Asia and Africa to resist Western colonial and imperialist powers and to pursue a more independent course of action in regional and global politics.[2] The countries represented at the Bandung Conference were aggregately referred to as the Newly Emerging Forces. Through its participation at the Bandung conference, the PRC established a close relationship with the Newly Emerging Forces, especially Indonesia.[3]

Following the Bandung Conference, the first conference of the heads of state of nonaligned countries was held in Belgrade in September 1961. It consolidated the unity of the Newly Emerging Forces and led to the establishment of the NAM in 1961. The aim of the NAM was to unite all the developing countries in Asia, Africa, and Latin America and to assert their equal rights with the world superpowers, particularly in respect to their national and regional interests. This goal coincided with one of the central objectives of Chinese foreign policy, which was to "fight against imperialism and colonialism."[4] Due to the Sino-Soviet alliance, China could not be considered a nonaligned state, but it joined the NAM as one of the organization's seventeen observers.

By 1961, however, the Sino-Soviet relationship had begun to fracture. As the fissures between the communist allies widened, China's departure from the Soviet and Eastern European camp motivated Beijing to seek the support of the nonaligned, emerging states and to strive to create a new world structure in which China would play a key role. Consequently, in the 1960s and 1970s, China started providing significant amounts of aid to some of the Newly Emerging Forces. Beijing hoped that a combination of aid and trade would help China build friendly relations with these countries and therefore increase its geopolitical influence in Asia, Africa, and Latin America.

## China and the Fourth Asian Games (1962)

In addition to foreign aid and commercial relations with these developing countries, sport became another significant means for China to increase its influence among the NAM member states. Soon after the establishment of the NAM, sport became a battlefield for international politics between the Eastern socialist bloc, the Western capitalist bloc, and the Newly Emerging Forces—the Third World countries in Asia, Africa, and Latin America. The political strife in sport began in 1962 when the Fourth Asian Games took place in Indonesia. The Asian Games had started in 1951 under the leadership of the Asian Games Federation (AGF) and were acknowledged by the International Olympic Committee (IOC). The Fourth Asian Games were due to be held in Indonesia in 1962. At the time, President Sukarno had just established himself as one of "The Initiative of Five" of the NAM.[5] He looked on the games as a means of strengthening his own position among the Newly Emerging Forces that were "struggling against capitalism and trying to create a new world order." The PRC was a useful ally in this endeavor and was therefore invited to join the Asian Games in Jakarta. The PRC also tried to use this opportunity to establish its position as a leader of the Newly Emerging Forces.[6]

However, there was a major obstacle to the PRC's participation: the PRC was not a member of the AGF, but the Republic of China (ROC) was. The Chinese Communist Party (CCP) had defeated the Nationalist Party (KMT) in the Chinese Civil War and established the PRC in October 1949. The KMT and its government retreated to Taiwan in April 1949 and remained there as the ROC, also called Taiwan. Taiwan was a founding member of the AGF and had represented China in the first three Asian Games in 1951, 1954, and 1958.[7] Therefore, the Indonesian embassy in Beijing informed the PRC's government at the end of 1961 that Jakarta would have to invite Taiwan to participate in the Fourth Asian Games. The Chinese Sports Ministry suggested four possible alternative solutions for Indonesia:

1. Invite the PRC instead of Taiwan to represent China
2. Invite neither Taiwan nor the PRC
3. Invite Taiwan but not recognize it as a country and, therefore, not raise its national flag at the games
4. Invite Taiwan and acknowledge Taiwan as a country[8]

The second solution was seen as the most feasible option, and the Chinese Sports Ministry in Beijing and the PRC embassy in Jakarta hoped to convince Indonesia to adopt it. Chinese premier Zhou Enlai and foreign minister Chen Yi both wrote to President Sukarno to try to persuade him to exclude Taiwan from the games.

On March 1, 1962, however, the Jakarta organizing committee sent an invitation letter to Ho Geng-sheng, who was a board member of the AGF and the representative of Taiwan, and invited him to attend a preparatory meeting for the Fourth Asian Games in Jakarta in April 1962. Predictably Beijing was not happy with this news. Although the PRC was not a member of the AGF, it had diplomatic relations with Indonesia. On May 31, the Chinese embassy in Jakarta sent a memo to the Indonesian government, stating: "The Chinese government sincerely hopes that the Asian Games held by Indonesia will be a great success. But the Chinese government cannot ignore those imperialists and their followers who want to use the Asian Games to create 'two Chinas.' These activities will not only harm the friendship between the PRC and Indonesia, but also harm Indonesia's fight against imperialism."9

At the same time—and following separate protests from some Arab countries on the issue of Zionism, which ran counter to the ethos of the NAM—Indonesia decided not to allow Taiwan or Israel to attend the games and refused to issue visas to athletes from those two countries.10

This political action by Indonesia enraged the IOC and the international federations (IFs) for weightlifting and athletics. They warned Jakarta that the Fourth Asian Games would face sanction and would no longer be recognized by the IOC since it would not tolerate a sporting event tainted by politics.11 Taiwan also protested against Jakarta's decision. Yan Zhengxing, head of the Taiwan Asian Games delegation, stated publicly, "I sincerely urge all the athletes and sports organisations to uphold justice, disqualify Indonesia as the host of the Fourth Asian Games and refuse to acknowledge the Games."12

Jakarta disregarded the warnings of the IOC and the two IFs. On August 24, 1962, the foreign minister of Indonesia formally announced that Taiwan and Israel would be expelled from the Fourth Asian Games. The IOC and the IFs immediately stated that they would not recognize the games, since they had become a political sporting event. Nevertheless, with strong support from the NAM member states, the Fourth Asian Games went ahead and took place from August 24 to September 4, 1962, with 1,460 athletes from sixteen countries competing. Indonesian athletes performed well and won forty-eight medals, including twenty-one golds.

Although the PRC could not participate because it was not a member of the AGF, diplomats from Beijing had successfully persuaded the organizers to excluded Taiwan from the games. In so doing, Beijing had demonstrated its significant political and diplomatic influence over Indonesia and other NAM nation-states.

## China and the Games of the Newly Emerging Forces

After the Fourth Asian Games, the IOC decided on February 7, 1963, to suspend the membership of the Indonesian Olympic Committee for an indeterminate period of time for not having protested against its government's discriminatory action against Taiwan and Israel. The IOC stated, "The IOC and the IFs are completely opposed to any interference in sport on political, racial or religious grounds, and particularly any which prevents the unhindered passage of competitions and officials between their member countries."[13] Two days later the Indonesian Sports Ministry responded with a strongly worded statement that included a proposal for a new world games: "The exclusion of Indonesia from the Olympic Games will not harm Indonesia. On the contrary, Indonesia will now have the freedom to organise a new Games without the participation of imperialists and colonialists. The new Games is GANEFO—the Games of the Newly Emerging Forces—Asia, Africa, Latin America and the socialist countries. . . . It is time for the new emerging countries to have a revolution to destroy the spirit and structure of the international sports movement, which is controlled by imperialists and colonialists."[14] Three days later, on February 12, China declared its support for the proposal and sent a congratulatory telegram to the Indonesian Olympic Committee. The Arab League, which had appreciated Jakarta's decision to exclude Israel from the games, also asked its member states to support Indonesia and protest against the IOC.[15]

On February 13, 1963, President Sukarno formally announced that Indonesia would host GANEFO in opposition to the IOC. He even compared the significance of GANEFO to the Indonesian independence movement against Dutch colonists between 1945 and 1949. Sukarno stated that, in Indonesia, sport would be used to further the country's political aims, namely world friendship and peace. For Sukarno and the PRC, the Olympic Games were nothing but a tool of the old established forces that were engaged in discriminatory actions against Asian, African, and Latin American nations. Now these tyrannized nations were going to use GANEFO as a tool to assess their own prerogatives and demonstrate their independence.

It is important to realize that Jakarta and Beijing had begun to prepare for GANEFO long before the IOC suspended Indonesia's membership. Prior to the Fourth Asian Games, the Chinese government had gathered experts from the foreign and sport ministries to analyze the feasibility of organizing an alternative sport competition. Following careful study, these experts indicated that after World War II, the colonized and semi-colonized countries in Asia, Africa, and Latin America had become independent but that the imperialist countries that dominated the IOC still denied them equal rights and status in international sport affairs.[16] The new games, therefore, would attract those newly independent countries. At the same time, GANEFO could provide a unique stage for the PRC to demonstrate its power and influence over those countries. After the Fourth Asian Games, a Chinese sporting delegation visited Indonesia on November 22, 1962, to exchange views on GANEFO. The PRC agreed to use its influence to persuade other Asian and African countries to join the games. In addition, a special research department was set up to advise Indonesia on GANEFO.[17]

Liu Shaoqi, chairman of the PRC, visited Indonesia in April 1963 and signed a joint declaration with Sukarno that criticized the IOC and reaffirmed China's support for GANEFO: "The Chinese government condemns the IOC's arbitrary decision to exclude Indonesia from the Olympic Games. The Chinese government strongly supports the GANEFO proposed by President Sukarno and will make every effort to contribute to GANEFO."[18] Although China was still suffering under the economic crisis brought about by the Great Leap Forward, the Chinese government helped to build new stadiums in Jakarta and donated sports facilities and equipment for GANEFO.[19] It was also reported that the PRC had agreed to give the Indonesians an $18 million donation for the games and to pay the transportation costs for all the delegations at GANEFO.[20]

A preparatory conference for GANEFO was held in Jakarta in April 1963, with the PRC, Cambodia, Guinea, Indonesia, Iraq, Mali, Pakistan, North Vietnam, the United Arab Republic (UAR/Egypt), and the Soviet Union in attendance. In addition, Ceylon (renamed Sri Lanka in 1972) and Yugoslavia sent observers. The assembled countries agreed on the aim of GANEFO: "The Games was [sic] to be based on the spirit of the 1955 Bandung Conference and the Olympic ideals, and was to promote the development of sport in new emerging nations and to cement friendly relations among them."[21] At the conference, an organizing committee for the games was established. Indonesia was elected the chair country, while China, the United Arab Republic, and the Soviet Union became the chair countries for Asia, Africa, and Europe, respectively. The conference declared that GANEFO would be held every four years in Third World countries. The first games would take place in Jakarta in November 1963. All the Newly Emerging Forces would be invited to join GANEFO.

Although the IOC and many IFs—including the Fédération Internationale de Football Association (FIFA), the Fédération Internationale de Natation (FINA, for swimming), the International Amateur Athletics Federation (IAAF, later the International Association of Athletics Federations), and the International Weightlifting Federation (IWF)—warned their members in June 1963 not to send teams to GANEFO, forty-eight countries from Africa, Asia, Europe, and Latin America participated in the games, which were opened on November 10, 1963. The games lasted for twelve days, and 2,404 athletes competed in twenty events. The badminton men's single final, between China and Indonesia, became a game of diplomatic importance. The Chinese player kept gaining the advantage and was on the verge of defeating the Indonesian player. Taking into consideration both Sino-Indonesian relations and the booming nationalism in Indonesia at the time, Marshal He Long, Chinese vice premier and minister of sport, instructed the Chinese player to lose to his opponent, and so the Indonesian player took the gold medal.[22]

By the time of the first GANEFO, the Sino-Soviet split had already occurred, severing the unity of the communist camp and creating three world power blocs: the United States and Western Europe, the Soviet Union and Eastern Europe, and the PRC. Both the Soviet Union and the PRC were eager to gain the support of the nonaligned emerging states. In pursuit of that goal, the Soviet Union provided some financial support to and participated in GANEFO in November 1963. In order not to jeopardize its stature in the Olympic movement, however, the Soviet Union did not send its first-class, Olympic-seeded athletes to the games.[23] In contrast, the PRC sent its 229 best athletes to Jakarta. It also provided strong political, financial, and organizational support to GANEFO and was instrumental in ensuring the success of the games.

After the games, Chairman Liu and Premier Zhou sent a congratulatory telegram to President Sukarno. It praised GANEFO as "a great victory of the newly emerging countries against imperialism and new colonialism's control over international sport."[24] In China GANEFO was interpreted as a successful diplomatic mission that had helped China consolidate its relationships with many Third World countries. When the Chinese delegation returned to Beijing, it was received by top Communist Party leaders, including Deng Xiaoping, Peng Zhen, and He Long.[25]

GANEFO was also praised by many Third World countries. It was seen as a significant propaganda victory over the Western powers. Camara Mamadi, the head of the Guinean delegation, commented, "The development of sports and relationships based on friendship and solidarity among the New Emerging Forces has contributed, in our opinion, to the quest for world peace; similarly, GANEFO has made a positive contribution to the struggle against colonialism and imperialism."[26] Kim Ki Soo, head of the North Korean delegation, stated, "All of the imperialists and the old forces have failed in their intrigues to prevent the peoples of the New Emerging Forces from attending these friendly games. . . . The delegation of the Democratic People's Republic of Korea calls for the development of an independent sports movement for the peoples of the New Emerging Forces, completely free from imperialism and colonialism and from the influence of the old forces of all hues."[27]

GANEFO had posed a real threat to the IOC, challenging its hegemony in the Third World. During the games, a council consisting of thirty-six member countries was established. It proposed that GANEFO continental committees be established in Asia, Africa, Europe, America, and Australasia, and that each member country have its own national GANEFO committee.[28] The intention was to create a new order in world sport. Avery Brundage, the president of the IOC, voiced his fear of such a development in a letter to the Marquess of Exeter, the president of the International Amateur Athletics Federation. With regard to the African Games proposed by some African countries, he wrote:

> If we want to hold the Olympic world together we must not let these 37 countries be led into the GANEFO camp, which may

easily happen. Peking, China is very active now in Africa, and Congo Brazzaville has recently received from it a $20,000,000 loan. The Egyptians are organising the second GANEFO Games in Cairo in 1967 . . . the Indonesian Embassy in Switzerland is inviting the National Federations and the Swiss NOC [National Olympic Committee] to the reception on the anniversary of the First GANEFO Games. This is probably also taking place in other places. The Arab countries and a few others are sympathetic. . . . We . . . will probably drive them all into the receptive arms of the GANEFO crowd if we are not most careful.[29]

Thus the GANEFO movement intended to divide and fragment the Olympic movement, to emphasize the political realities of the new world structure, and to fan the political ambitions of the new and nonaligned states, especially Indonesia. In addition, GANEFO provided an ideal stage upon which the PRC could project its image, extend its influence, and unite with the countries of the Third World. Furthermore, it enabled Beijing to compete with the other two power blocs—the Soviet Union and Eastern Europe, and the United States and Western Europe. Its geopolitical significance was equivalent to or even greater than that of the 1955 Bandung Conference. Through the successes achieved at the games, both in terms of sport and diplomacy, the PRC established its leadership among the Newly Emerging Forces and greatly reinforced its power and status in international politics.[30]

After the first GANEFO, Beijing took a leading position in organizing the subsequent games and seized the opportunity to expand its influence in Asia, Africa, and Latin America through sport. The Second GANEFO was scheduled to take place in 1967 in Cairo, the capital of the UAR, with Beijing as an alternative site. However, the UAR requested that Beijing donate a stadium for the second games. The request was discussed in Jakarta in May 1965 in a meeting between the secretary-general of the Chinese Sports Ministry, Huang Zhong, and representatives from the UAR at the tenth anniversary of the 1955 Bandung Conference. They failed to reach an agreement.[31] The donation that Cairo had requested was equal in value to the Algiers Conference Complex that China had donated for the Second Asian-African Conference, due to be held in Algeria in 1965.[32] Zhou discussed the issue with UAR representatives at the

Asian-African leaders' summit, which was held in Cairo in June 1965. Both parties agreed to move the Second GANEFO to Beijing. Soon after the agreement, the Capital Indoor Stadium was built in Beijing in preparation for the games.[33]

In order to reinforce its influence in Asia, the PRC developed a plan to host an Asian version of GANEFO. In September 1965, the second session of the GANEFO council was held in Beijing, with thirty-nine delegations in attendance. A GANEFO Asian committee was formed. Beijing played a major role in its formation, and a Chinese official became the chairman of its executive committee. The proposal for an Asian GANEFO to take place in Cambodia in 1966 was approved. It was designed to compete against the IOC-backed Asian Games, which would also take place in 1966.

The aim of the Asian GANEFO was to reinforce China's leadership in the Third World and to challenge the United States and the other Western powers. Therefore, the games were underwritten to a large degree by the PRC. In line with the infrastructural focus of China's other diplomatic projects—for example, the Algiers Conference Complex built for the 1965 Second Asian-African Conference and the TAZARA Railway Project for Tanzania and Zambia—the Chinese government helped to build a fifty-thousand-seat stadium as well as other sport facilities in Phnom Penh, the capital of Cambodia, and agreed to train three hundred referees for the games in just five months. With the support of Norodom Sihanouk, the Cambodian leader, the games were held from November 25 to December 6, 1966—almost overlapping with the Fifth Asian Games, which took place in Bangkok on December 9–20 and from which the PRC had been excluded and in which Taiwan was included. More than 2,000 athletes from seventeen countries and regions participated in the Asian GANEFO. Chinese athletes competed in eighteen sporting events, won 133 gold medals, and broke two world records. At the same time, about 1,945 athletes from eighteen countries and regions, most of which had close relationships with the West, took part in the Fifth Asian Games in Bangkok.[34]

Despite the success of the Asian GANEFO, GANEFO was approaching its end. In West Asia, the UAR was unable to host the games as planned due to financial problems. In Southeast Asia, Indonesia—one of the leading members of GANEFO—turned its back on China after

Sukarno's regime was overthrown by General Suharto, who was backed by the United States.[35] The coup turned the nucleus of the NAM and China's key ally into a pro-American state. In Northeast Asia, China, the major sponsor and initiator of the games, was entering the turmoil of the Cultural Revolution and did not have the time or energy required to maintain them. The Second GANEFO, which was scheduled to be held in Beijing in 1967, quietly disappeared. Although GANEFO was a short-lived event, it was regarded by PRC leaders as one of the most successful diplomatic missions of the 1960s because it had helped the newly established communist state to win support from, and build up its position in, the Third World.

### Ping-Pong Diplomacy: The Old and New Stories (1971–1980)

The world changed rapidly in the second half of the 1960s, and China, preoccupied with its Cultural Revolution, struggled to adjust to a more complicated model of international politics.[36] Sino-Soviet relations almost ceased to exist. The ideological and political split between the two socialist countries escalated into a series of border conflicts in early 1969.[37] Faced with threats from the Soviet Union, the PRC leadership felt an urgent need to prioritize national security and began to change its views on the relationships between China, the Soviet Union, and the United States. The central government's think tank suggested that China's foreign strategy should take advantage of the conflict between Washington and Moscow to seek a new and cooperative Sino-American relationship.[38] The new policy also focused on resuming and consolidating friendly relations with African, Asian, and Latin American countries in an effort to undo the damage caused by the Cultural Revolution.

An opportunity to put this new foreign relations strategy into action came at the Thirty-First World Table Tennis Championships in Nagoya, Japan, in February 1971. Although Sihanouk, now exiled, had asked Beijing to boycott the championships because the recently established Khmer Republic was sending a team to represent Cambodia,[39] Zhou decided that he wanted to send the Chinese national team to Japan. However, he would need approval from Mao Zedong. In his briefing with Mao on March 14, 1971, he explained the political and diplomatic importance of the sporting event:

In order to win support from the Japanese people, we accepted the invitation from our Japanese friends earlier this year and decided to send a team to the 31st World Table Tennis Championships. . . . It is a good opportunity for us to protest against the Japanese right wing and to develop the Sino-Japanese friendship.

We are about to send our officials to Japan. The King of Cambodia has requested that we boycott the Khmer Republic's team. We agreed to his request and have promised to unite with North Korea to boycott the Khmer Republic's team. We have also decided to boycott the South Vietnamese team and to seek Arab Union and Syrian advice before confronting the Israeli team. . . . Our policy is friendship first, competition second. Politics is the most important thing. . . . Please advise if we should send the team to Japan and if we should be prepared for any kind of danger.[40]

Mao approved Zhou's proposal and instructed, "Our team should go, even if there is danger of death."[41] For the PRC leadership, sending the Chinese team to Japan was an important diplomatic move. The objective was to reopen China to the world. Mao read all the reports on the movements of the Chinese team in Japan. He explained it to his comrades: "This [sending the team to Japan] is very important. After the reconnaissance, we must act with initiative. We should take the opportunity to let them see whether China is still an iron block [that refuses to open its door to the world]."[42]

Thus the famous "ping-pong diplomacy" that marked the beginning of a thaw in Sino-American relations had its origins in the communication between Chinese and American athletes during and after the championships. The diplomatic door between Beijing and Washington had been opened unexpectedly by table tennis and would lead to a watershed moment in international relations. On July 11, 1971, Henry Kissinger, President Richard Nixon's national security advisor, traveled secretly to the PRC to meet with Zhou and discuss a potential summit. On February 21, 1972, Nixon and Mao held their historic meeting in Beijing. Seven days later, the two leaders issued a joint communiqué that marked a major shift in the foreign policy of both countries and subsequently changed the direction of world politics.

While the ping-pong diplomacy heralded in a new era in Sino-American relations, China also took the opportunity to renew its relationships with its old friends in the Third World—relations that had been suspended for more than five years by the Cultural Revolution. The PRC's objective was to unite the Third World countries to resist the superpowers and to strengthen China's position in international politics. Chinese table tennis teams were sent out to visit foreign countries and served as ambassadors for the PRC. After their visits to several Asian and African countries—including North Korea, Nepal, the UAR, and the Republic of Mauritius—a joint announcement was issued in Nagoya on April 8, 1971, that "the Asian-African Table Tennis Friendship Invitational Tournament will be held in Beijing in the near future. The goal is to consolidate the friendship between the peoples of Asia and Africa."[43]

In August 1971 the organizing committee for the Asian-African Table Tennis Friendship Invitational Tournament was established in Beijing, and the tournament was held in Beijing on November 3–14, 1971.[44] Fifty-one countries took part in the tournament, which was also attended by representatives from the International Table Tennis Federation and the Supreme Council for Sports in Africa. The participating countries, most of which were undeveloped countries in Africa and Southeast Asia, hoped to use this sport tournament like GANEFO to cement friendly political and economic relations. The tournament was not only a sporting but also a diplomatic event. It received the highest levels of attention and publicity in China. On November 1, 1971, a national banquet was held by Vice Premier Li Xiannian to welcome all the participants. Two days later, Li and Marshal Ye Jianying attended the opening ceremony. On November 14, 1971, Premier Zhou attended the closing ceremony. Zhou and other CCP leaders received all the athletes and representatives the following day.[45] The event was one of the PRC's biggest engagements with the Third World countries since the Cultural Revolution had begun in 1966.

During the tournament, the representatives of the participating countries met and agreed that Latin America would join the next one. Thus a new Asian-African–Latin American Table Tennis Friendship Invitational Tournament would be held in the near future. Chile, China, Ecuador, Egypt, Japan, Mauritius, Nepal, Nigeria, North Korea, and Tanzania were elected as the board members of the new tournament's preparatory committee.[46] Its first meeting was held in Beijing on November 14, 1971, and a liaison office was established in Beijing. The organizing committee for the tournament was established in Beijing on May 15, 1973.[47]

The First Asian-African–Latin American Table Tennis Friendship Invitational Tournament was held in Beijing from August 25 to September 6, 1973, as planned.[48] More than eleven hundred athletes and representatives from eighty-six countries took part.[49] At the reception in the Great Hall of the People, Premier Zhou and other CCP leaders received all the participants, making it an important political and diplomatic event. The political significance of the tournament was also reflected in the list of VIPs who attended the opening ceremony on August 25. Nearly all the top CCP leaders—including Zhou, Mao's successor Hua Guofeng, Mao's wife Jiang Qing, Vice Premier Deng Xiaoping, Vice Chairman of the CCP Wang Hongwen, Marshal Zhu De, Marshal Ye Jianying, Marshal Xu Xiangqian, and Marshal Nie Rongzhen—appeared at the festivities. Members of the Standing Committee of the Politburo of the CCP Central Committee—including Zhang Chunqiao, Yao Wenyuan, and Dong Biwu—were also present.[50] The Nigerian representative's speech at the opening ceremony highlighted the clear diplomatic mission of the tournament: "This Invitational Tournament is an important landmark in history. It will consolidate the friendship between the peoples of Asia, Africa, and Latin America, build solidarity between Third World countries and facilitate co-operation. I sincerely hope the flame that we lit in Asia today will travel to Africa and Latin America. Our slogan is 'friendship first, competition second.' Long live the friendship between the peoples of Asia, Africa, and South America!"[51]

Like the 1971 Asian-African Table Tennis Friendship Invitational Tournament, the 1973 tournament was a propaganda sporting event. The Chinese media paid special attention, and its opening ceremony became the headline for all the major newspapers in China, including the *People's Daily* and the *Guangming Daily*.[52] In the following days, the Xinhua News Agency and all the newspapers and radio and television stations in China covered the event in detail, including the matches and the athletes' cultural and social visits to the Great Wall, the Forbidden City, local communities, schools, and factories.[53] A song called "Ping Pong Brings Friendship" became popular in China during the period, and the tournament's slogan, "Our Friends all over the World," was also widely used.

A meeting was held during the tournament to discuss its future development. It reemphasized that the aim of the event was to "promote the friendship between the peoples and athletes of Asia, Africa, and Latin America through table tennis." The minutes of the meeting concluded: "Asian, African, and Latin American countries have similar historical backgrounds and are facing the same struggle for survival [against imperialist and colonial powers]. We are all aware of the importance of solidarity and co-operation. Sport will increase the solidarity between the peoples of Asia, Africa, and Latin America. Athletes should take this opportunity to contribute to the friendship and solidarity between Asia, Africa, and Latin America." The representatives also agreed that the next tournament would take place in Nigeria in 1975.[54]

Two years later, the Second Asian-African–Latin American Table Tennis Friendship Invitational Tournament took place in Nigeria's capital city Abuja on July 13–26, 1975, with representatives from seventy Third World countries. For the Chinese, the trip to Africa was half sport and half politics. Chinese athletes and coaches had two missions: to win gold medals and, at the same time, to consolidate China's diplomatic relations with African and South American countries. The Chinese team won the gold medals for the men's team, women's team, men's singles, and women's singles events. All the members of the Chinese team, including twelve athletes, two coaches, and three officials, were received by Gen. Yakubu Gowon, head of the Federal Military Government of Nigeria. After the tournament, the team paid a diplomatic visit to Senegal from July 28 to August 5 and played several friendly matches there.[55]

Latin America was the next stop for the Asian-African–Latin American Table Tennis Friendship Invitational Tournament. The third tournament took place in Mexico on October 12–27, 1976.[56] Forty-five countries took part in the sixteen-day event.[57] After the tournament kicked off, a news report in China's *PLA Daily* highlighted its political and diplomatic significance: "This Tournament is another achievement in the Third World countries' struggle against imperialism, colonialism, and hegemony. . . . Three years after the first Invitational Tournament, which was held in Beijing in 1973, it is evident that the flowers of friendship bloom in Asia, Africa, and Latin America."[58] The tournament returned to Asia in 1980 when it was hosted by Japan. It took place in Tokyo on September 2–7, 1980. Some 223 athletes from thirty-three countries competed in seven events. Afterward, September

8–19, the Chinese team toured Japan, playing friendly matches with local teams.[59]

By hosting and participating in the Asian Table Tennis Friendship Invitational Tournament in 1971 and taking part in the four Asian-African–Latin American Table Tennis Friendship Invitational Tournaments held between 1973 and 1980, China consolidated its relationship with many Third World countries and gained benefits both in sport and international politics. With strong support from these allies, Beijing began a campaign to regain its seats in the AGF and then the IOC and, finally, successfully claimed its position as the representative of China in the Asian and international sport worlds.[60]

At a governing council meeting of the AGF in Bangkok on September 18, 1973, the Iranian and Japanese representatives introduced a draft resolution titled "The All-China Sports Federation (of the PRC) Should Represent China at the AGF." It argued that the AGF could not represent the whole of Asia without the inclusion of the PRC. It proposed expelling Taiwan and including the PRC in the AGF and at the Asian Games. The proposal was supported by Pakistan and Afghanistan and was approved at the meeting by a vote of 5–0. Two months later, the PRC became a member of the AGF Asian Olympic Sports Committee by a vote of 38–13 at a special session in Iran on November 16, 1973.[61]

The IFs followed in the footsteps of the AGF. Between May and October 1974, the PRC replaced Taiwan to become the sole representative of China in the International Weightlifting Federation (May 1), the International Federation of Associated Wrestling Styles ( May 3), the International Fencing Federation (May 16), the International Basketball Federation (July 11), the International Gymnastics Federation (July 20), the World Badminton Federation (August 31), and the International Volleyball Federation (October 9). At the same time, the PRC renewed its membership in FIFA (June 11), the IAAF (August 30), FINA (September 14), the International Shooting Sport Federation (September 18), and the International Cycling Union (August 11).

Regaining IOC membership was the PRC's ultimate goal. It would symbolize China's sporting and political position in the world. A majority of Third World countries strongly supported China's attempts to return to the IOC given all its efforts over the previous thirty years, especially the last three years prior to the PRC's acceptance by the IFs. At the IOC session held in Varna, Bulgaria, in October 1973, a Zambian representative urged the IOC to acknowledge the PRC as the representative of China. The "two Chinas issue" was discussed again at the Eighteenth IOC Executive Board Meeting held in Rome on May 13–17, 1975. The majority of the representatives welcomed the proposal to allow the PRC to become the IOC member for China.[62] A few days later, at the IOC Annual Congress held in Lausanne on May 20–23, the PRC made a formal application to be the sole representative of China. The application was supported by many countries, including Albania, Algeria, Congo, Iran, Kuwait, North Korea, Pakistan, Romania, Senegal, and Tanzania.[63] On November 26, 1978, the IOC announced in Lausanne that a resolution had been approved by a vote of 62–17: the Chinese Olympic Committee (of the PRC) in Beijing would be the representative for China. The Chinese Olympic Committee (of Taiwan) in Taipei would no longer be the representative of China but could attend the Olympic Games under the name of "Chinese Taipei," with a new anthem, flag, and emblem.

Rejoining the IOC strengthened China's position in international sport and politics. One year later, in February 1980, the Chinese Olympic Committee sent a team of twenty-eight athletes to the Lake Placid Winter Olympics. Although they did not win any medals, their ice-breaking journey marked the PRC's reemergence in the Olympic movement. PRC athletes, who had been kept outside of the Olympic stadium by politics for twenty-eight years, were finally reembraced by the Olympic movement. However, it was not long before Chinese athletes' Olympic dreams were again interrupted by Cold War politics. Following the Soviet invasion of Afghanistan, the 1980 Moscow Olympics were boycotted by more than sixty countries, led by the United States. Guided by a foreign diplomatic policy that stressed the importance of a cooperative Sino-American relationship, China answered the call of the United States and joined the boycott.[64]

Four years later, in response to the Moscow boycott, the Soviet Union announced on May 8, 1984, that it would boycott the 1984 Los Angeles Olympics. Several countries, including Afghanistan, Angola, Bulgaria, Cuba, Ethiopia, Hungary, Iran, Mongolia, Poland, and Vietnam, soon joined the boycott. Fearing that the Games would become a repeat of the Moscow Olympics, the United States immediately sent envoys to countries all over the world to try to persuade world leaders and politicians to defy the Soviet-led boycott. China was the major US concern. A team led by federal prosecutor Charles Lee was sent to China to persuade Beijing to send a team to Los Angeles. China again chose to support the United States for political, diplomatic, economic, and strategic reasons, making the Los Angeles Olympics the first Summer Olympics that the PRC had attended since 1952. China's participation in the Games was praised by Peter Ueberroth, head of the Los Angeles organizing committee, as an important step that "changed the whole face of the Games."[65] Sport had again aided the implementation of China's foreign policy and contributed significantly to the improvement of Sino-American relations.

## Conclusion

The establishment of the PRC in 1949 was seen by the CCP leadership and most of the Chinese people as the starting point for a "New China"— politically independent and economically prosperous. From the very beginning, sport was used to serve the PRC's foreign policy, which focused on uniting the newly independent countries in Asia, Africa, and Latin America to compete against the two superpowers, the United States and the Soviet Union. In the 1950s and first half of the 1960s, the PRC's leadership allied itself with the NAM member states to use the Fourth Asian Games and GANEFO to win support from, and to reinforce its position in, the Third World. The games helped China to implement its foreign policy, which aimed to establish and consolidate friendly relations with many African, Asian, and Latin American countries. Consequently China successfully established its position as a leading power in the Third World and changed the political landscape of the world, which had mainly been shaped by the Western capitalist bloc, led by the United States, and the Eastern socialist bloc, led by the Soviet Union.

All these efforts to build China into a world power were put on hold during the Cultural Revolution in late 1960s. It was not until the early 1970s that the Chinese government's foreign policy shifted focus back and sought to reengage with the outside world. The PRC turned to the United States and tried to forge an alliance against the Soviet Union in order to ensure national security. At the same time, the PRC rebuilt China's image and influence in the Third World with a view to establishing China's leadership. Sport served both purposes. Indeed, the use of sport during these two decades should be considered to be one of the most successful diplomatic initiatives undertaken by the PRC during the Cold War.

## Notes

1. L. S. Stavrianos, *The World since 1500: A Global History* (New York: Prentice Hall, 1966).

2. Michael Leifer, *Dictionary of the Modern Politics of South-East Asia* (London: Routledge, 1996), 63.

3. Dewi Fortuna Anwar, "Indonesia and the Bandung Conference: Then and Now," in *Bandung Revisited: The Legacy of the 1955 Asian-African Conference for International Order,* ed. See Seng Tan and Amitav Acharya (Singapore: National University of Singapore Press, 2008), 180–97, 187.

4. Bo Ding, *The Battle against Imperialism and Colonialism* (Zhengzhou: Henan People's Press, 1957).

5. The founding fathers of the NAM were Sukarno of Indonesia, Jawaharlal Nehru of India, Josip Broz Tito of Yugoslavia, Gamal Abdul Nasser of Egypt, and Kwame Nkrumah of Ghana. They were known as "The Initiative of Five."

6. Fan Hong and Xiong Xiaozheng, "Communist China: Sport, Politics and Diplomacy," in *Sport in Asian Society,* ed. J.A. Mangan and Fan Hong (London: Frank Cass, 2003), 319–43, 327.

7. Ibid.

8. Lijuan Liang, *He Zhengliang and the Olympics* (Beijing: World Knowledge Press, 2004), 84.

9. Sports Ministry, ed., *Minutes of the 1st GANEFO* (Beijing: National Sports Bureau Archives, 1963), 135.

10. Fan Hong, "Communist China and the Asian Games 1951–1990: The Thirty-Nine Year Struggle to Victory," in *Sport, Nationalism and Orientalism: The Asian Games,* ed. Fan Hong (London: Routledge, 2006), 75–88, 78.

11. Lijuan, *He Zhengliang and the Olympics.*

12. Minxin Tang, *China at the Olympic Games* (Taipei: Chinese Taipei Olympic Committee Press, 2000), 199.

13. Alfred Senn, *Power, Politics and the Olympic Games* (Champaign, IL: Human Kinetics, 1999), 129.

14. Dan Ren, *The New Flag in International Sport* (Beijing: People's Sport Press, 1963), 16.

15. Yannong Fu, ed., *The History of Sport in China,* vol. 5, *1949–1979* (Beijing: People's Sport Press, 2007).

16. For example, see Pascal Charitas's chapter in this volume on Franco-African sport relations in the shadow of decolonization.

17. Ibid.

18. Editorial Team of the Yearbook of Chinese Sport, ed., *Yearbook of Chinese Sport 1949–1994* (Beijing: People's Sport Press, 1993), 39.

19. Yannong, ed., *History of Sport in China*.

20. Richard Espy, *The Politics of the Olympic Games* (Berkeley: University of California Press, 1979), 81.

21. Ibid.

22. Liang, *He Zhengliang and the Olympics*.

23. Ibid.

24. Yu Gu, "Huang Zhong's Memory: Premier Zhou and the GANEFO," *Sports Culture Guide* 1 (1986): 4–7.

25. Yannong, ed., *History of Sport in China*.

26. *Document of the First GANEFO Congress,* Jakarta, November 24–25, 1963, 45.

27. Ibid., 51.

28. Baoli Sun, "GANEFO," *Tiyu Weekly,* no. 5 (1999): 6.

29. Brundage to Exeter, November 28, 1964, Papers of Avery Brundage, box 55, Fryer box 2, microfilm reel 33, University of Queensland Library.

30. By winning sixty-six gold medals, fifty-six silver medals, and forty-six bronze medals and ranking first in the medal tally, the PRC established itself as a sporting superpower in the Third World.

31. Lijuan, *He Zhengliang and the Olympics*.

32. The conference was canceled due to the political unrest in Algeria.

33. Lijuan, *He Zhengliang and the Olympics*.

34. Afghanistan, British Hong Kong, Burma, Ceylon, India, Indonesia, Iran, Israel, Japan, Malaysia, Nepal, Pakistan, the Philippines, the Republic of China (Taiwan), Singapore, South Korea, South Vietnam, and Thailand.

35. Peter Dale Scott, "The United States and the Overthrow of Sukarno, 1965–1967," *Pacific Affairs* 58, no. 2 (1985): 239–64, and Robert Cribb, "Unresolved Problems in the Indonesian Killings of 1965–1966," *Asian Survey* 42, no. 4 (2002): 550–63.

36. John Lewis Gaddis, *The Cold War: A New History* (London: Penguin, 2005).

37. Kuisong Yang, "The Sino–Soviet Border Clash of 1969: From Zhenbao Island to Sino–American Rapprochement," *Cold War History* 1 (2000): 21–52, and Iktor M. Gobarev, "Soviet Policy toward China: Developing Nuclear Weapons 1949–1969," *Journal of Slavic Military Studies* 12, no. 4 (1999): 43–47.

38. Guangxiang Wu, "The Four Marshals Discussed the National Security Issue in 1969," *The 20th Century* 8 (2008): 18–23.

39. The Khmer Republic was established on October 9, 1970. It was under the governance of a pro-US military-led government. The establishment of the Khmer Republic was the outcome of the Cambodian Civil War (1967–1975), which was part of the larger Vietnam War (1959–1975).

40. Dinghua Wang, "The Ping-Pong Diplomacy," *Secretary Affaires* 7 (2008): 42–44.

41. Shaozu Wu, ed., *The History of Sport in the People's Republic of China* (Beijing: China Book Press, 1999), 238.

42. Ke Lin, Tao Xu, and Xujun Wu, *The True History* (Beijing: Central China Literature Press, 1998), 304.

43. "Six Countries in Asia and Africa Initiated the Asian-African Table Tennis Friendship Invitational Tournament," in *Yearbook of Chinese Sport 1966–1972,* ed. Editorial Team of the Yearbook of Chinese Sport (Beijing: People's Sport Press, 1983), 39.

44. Yuzhi Gong, "The Asian-African Table Tennis Friendship Invitational Tournament Was Held in Beijing between 2 and 14 November," in *China in the 20th Century 1961–1980,* ed. Yuzhi Gong (Beijing: Xianzhuang Press, 2002), 4778.

45. "Big Events in Sport," in *Yearbook of Chinese Sport 1966–1972,* 3–18.

46. "Minutes of the Asian-African Table Tennis Friendship Invitational Tournament," in *Yearbook of Chinese Sport 1966–1972,* 22–23.

47. "Big Events in Sport," 3–18.

48. Gong, "Asian-African Table Tennis Friendship Invitational Tournament," 4907–8.

49. "Press Release of the Asian-African–Latin American Table Tennis Friendship Invitational Tournament," in *Yearbook of Chinese Sport 1973–1974,* ed. Editorial Team of the Yearbook of Chinese Sport (Beijing: People's Sport Press, 1982), 37–38.

50. "Hua Guofeng Attended the Asian-African–Latin American Table Tennis Friendship Invitational Tournament," *People's Daily,* August 26, 1973.

51. Ibid.

52. "The Asian-African Table Tennis Friendship Invitational Tournament Was Held in Beijing," *Guangming Daily,* August 26, 1973.

53. "A Celebration of Unity and Friendship," *People's Daily,* September 3, 1973; "Promote Friendship, Improve the Level of Performance," *People's Daily,* September 5, 1973; and "Promote Friendship, Exchange Technique," *People's Daily,* September 6, 1973.

54. "Press Release of the Asian-African–Latin American Table Tennis Friendship Invitational Tournament," 37–38.

55. "The 2nd Asian-African–Latin American Table Tennis Friendship Invitational Tournament," in *Yearbook of Chinese Sport 1975,* ed. Editorial Team of the Yearbook of Chinese Sport (Beijing: People's Sport Press, 1982), 363–66.

56. "The 3rd Asian-African–Latin American Table Tennis Friendship Invitational Tournament," *PLA Daily,* October 14, 1976; "The 3rd Asian-African–Latin American Table Tennis Friendship Invitational Tournament Finished with Success," *PLA Daily,* July 18, 1975; and "Chinese Athletes Won Five Gold Medals," *PLA Daily,* September 8, 1980.

57. "The 3rd Asian-African–Latin American Table Tennis Friendship Invitational Tournament," in *Yearbook of Chinese Sport 1976,* ed. Editorial Team of the Yearbook of Chinese Sport (Beijing: People's Sport Press, 1981), 225–30.

58. "The 3rd Asian-African–Latin American Table Tennis Friendship Invitational Tournament," *PLA Daily,* October 14, 1976.

59. "The 4th Asian-African–Latin American Table Tennis Friendship Invitational Tournament," in *Yearbook of Chinese Sport 1980,* ed. Editorial Team of the Yearbook of Chinese Sport (Beijing: People's Sport Press, 1983), 373–78.

60. China withdrew from membership of the IOC in 1958 due to the "two Chinas" issue.

61. Yannong, ed., *History of Sport in China,* 361.

62. Ibid.

63. Dongguang Pei, "A Question of Names: The Solution to the 'Two Chinas' Issue in Modern Olympic History: The Final Phase, 1971–1984," in *Cultural Imperialism in Action: Critiques in the Global Olympic Trust*, ed. Nigel B. Crowther, Robert K. Barney, and Michael K. Heine (London, ON: Centre for Olympic Studies, 2006), 19–31,

64. Bin Zhang, "1984: China Saved the Olympics," *Success* 9 (2008): 20–22.

65. Lynn Zinser, "Phone Call from China Transformed '84 Games," *New York Times,* July 14, 2008.

13

# Reds, Revolutionaries, and Racists

Surfing, Travel, and Diplomacy in the Reagan Era

*Scott Laderman*

Paul Holmes had a dream. It was the early 1980s, and Ronald Reagan was president, the Soviet Union was the Evil Empire, and the American loss in Vietnam was less than a decade old. Holmes was a British-born surfer living in the United States. Like most surfers, he fantasized about a terra incognita of perfect, unridden waves. Unlike most surfers, he was uniquely positioned to find it. Holmes was, after all, the editor of California-based *Surfer* magazine. Occupying the most exalted perch in American surf journalism gave him resources unavailable to others. When Holmes perused a map to scout out untapped sections of the littoral world, most of what lay before him was well-trod territory. Much of Latin America and Africa had been covered, Europe was overridden, and the polar regions were much too cold. The possibility of a new discovery—at least for American surfers constrained by the geopolitics of the Cold War—seemed remote. But his eyes kept drifting to China. The People's Republic enjoyed thousands of miles of shoreline without, Holmes assumed, a single surfer to ride its countless waves. Could this communist heartland be the sport's next frontier?[1]

Just days after scrutinizing the map, Holmes received a phone call from Jon Damm. Damm was familiar to the magazine editor, as he was to many surfers, as a talented wave-rider on Oʻahu's North Shore. But even more significantly to Holmes, Damm was a flight attendant and surf adventurer who enjoyed a cosmopolitan past. Shortly after he was born in Chicago in 1957, his family decamped for precommunist Cuba. Led by his father, an executive with the Sherwin-Williams Company, the Damms then moved to El Salvador, Venezuela, and Ohio before finally settling in Puerto Rico. It was there, at the age of thirteen, that Damm first took to the waves. He quickly became the island's most successful competitor, with his obvious talent earning him victories in the Puerto Rican championships from 1973 to 1975. Then, in 1976, Damm enrolled at the University of Hawaiʻi. As the birthplace of modern surfing and home to its most celebrated stretch of coast, the Aloha State was a natural draw to wave-riding talent, and it was not long before Damm became a well-known presence on the world-famous North Shore.[2]

Yet when Damm called Holmes, it was not for a chat about the warm Hawaiian waves. He wanted to discuss a potential expedition to China. "Funny. I was just thinking the same thing," Holmes told the young surfer. And so they hatched their plans. It would be a few years before the trip unfolded. There were "months of planning, countless negotiations, setbacks, reams of telexes and letters," with the entire project almost shelved at the "eleventh hour."[3] But aided by Robert Roos and the Delta Institute, which worked to promote closer Sino-US ties, an invitation was ultimately secured for them to go to the island province of Hainan. It came from the most seemingly natural sponsor in a nation lacking a surf culture: the Chinese Yachting Association.[4] Financial assistance came from Quiksilver, O'Neill, and several other surf-related companies. With an invitation and funding in hand, it was time to assemble the cohort. The participants had to be carefully selected. "We wanted the team members to be not only skillful surfers but great representatives of the sport and of the nation," Holmes said. "We wanted them to be articulate in their appreciation of all the elements that make up the surfing experience. We wanted one of them to be female so it was understood that surfing was not just a men-only activity. We wanted to be sure that the sport could be proud of them." In the end Damm, Hawaiian Rell Sunn, and Californians Willy Morris and Matt George traveled with photographer Warren Bolster to the People's

Republic. This was, for surfing enthusiasts, a monumental development. It had been organized by surfers with the express purpose of fostering cross-cultural understanding. And it was bridging a Cold War divide between the capitalist West and the communist East. *Surfer* decreed it an updated version of "ping-pong diplomacy," the 1971 tour by the US table tennis team that helped to thaw Cold War tensions and set the stage for Richard Nixon's 1972 visit to Beijing. It was, the magazine proudly stated, a case of "surfing diplomacy."[5]

Surfing and cultural diplomacy are not typically spoken of in the same breath. That is a shame. For while surfing has not played a major role in *official* US cultural diplomacy, surfers have, through their exploits abroad, played a somewhat more substantial role in *unofficial* cultural diplomacy.[6] Whether serving as cultural ambassadors for the United States in China, denouncing the repression of the military regime in El Salvador, or joining the Australian government in trying to end apartheid in South Africa, surfers revealed themselves in the 1980s to be far more than mindless beach bums seeking carefree pleasure. To be sure, surfing is ultimately about fun; riding waves can provide incredible enjoyment. But surfers in the Reagan era demonstrated that they were not simply countercultural ignoramuses of the *Fast Times at Ridgemont High* (1982) sort. Americans and Australians alike drew on their heightened public profiles and broad international experience to assert themselves as global political actors. If surfing's leading professional association had tried, with support from influential elements of its membership, to envelop the sport in something of a protective bubble—studiously side-stepping, for instance, the international call for a sporting boycott of South Africa—many surfers would have none of it. Their journeys abroad had exposed them to a highly politicized world, and they attempted in the 1980s to further their growing sense of global citizenship.

Travel was at the heart of these developments. And international travel, as was made clear after World War II, was hardly apolitical. With the onset and polarization of the Cold War, American officials developed an appreciation that tourism provided both promise and peril in the struggle against the perceived communist menace. Tourists could, for instance, serve as helpful instruments in transferring dollars to nations such as France in desperate need of foreign exchange; in the wake of the Second

World War, the Americans would enjoy an enriching cultural experience, and the French would acquire the dollars needed to rebuild their war-torn country.[7] As Wanda Ellen Wakefield shows elsewhere in this volume, a similar process unfolded in Austria. But it was not just about economic development. Perhaps the most significant benefit was social. Tourists' friendly interactions abroad would create a positive impression of the United States. Of course, there was also fear of the opposite: that negative experiences could alienate host communities and do damage in America's global campaign. The key was to ensure that the positive experiences far outnumbered the negative.

With the growing accessibility of air travel and the postwar expansion of the middle class, government officials recognized that more Americans, just like Australians, would find themselves traveling overseas in the 1950s and 1960s. They were thus proactive. "You represent us all in bringing assurance to the people you meet that the United States is a friendly nation and one dedicated to the search for world peace and to the promotion of the well-being and security of the community of nations," President Dwight Eisenhower began telling American passport holders in 1957.[8] The American people, one of his special assistants insisted, must unreservedly be "ambassadors of good will."[9]

In the 1950s American surfers joined their white, middle-class compatriots in boarding planes and flying to various far-flung destinations. The most popular was Hawai'i, where some Californians liked what they found and decided to stay. But, for others, more distant shores began to beckon. By the 1960s the "surfaris" had gone global. At roughly the same time that Bruce Brown's celebrated surf-travel documentary *The Endless Summer* opened on the beach-city circuit in 1964 (it opened to enormous acclaim two years later in theaters nationwide), American and Australian surfers had started venturing to Europe, Africa, Asia, Latin America, and the various islands of the Pacific. The surf tourists who undertook these international journeys served as ambassadors for both their sport and their respective nations. Usually traveling independently and on a limited budget, they differed from most high-end tourists in their greater interaction with host communities. Wealthier travelers, and especially those on package tours, tended to stay in large hotels and to eat their meals surrounded by other foreigners. Traveling surfers, conversely, often stayed with locals or in small family-owned accommodations, consuming their meals in tiny eateries or restaurants. They were in fact much like the backpacker tourists who joined the "hippie trail" in the 1960s. There was, however, an important difference. The "hippies" appeared to wander aimlessly. Surfers, conversely, were looking for what Brown's film famously called "that perfect wave." And when they found it, their wave-riding enamored the locals. "Amazed spectators stared at us from the beach," Australian Rennie Ellis, feeling like a "surfing missionar[y]," reported from Salazar's Portugal in 1964. "Afterwards a local approached us and in halting English and raptured tones he told us that until then he had thought Christ was the only person who could walk on the water."[10]

Much of this surf travel occurred in the Third World. For white Americans and Australians, this was new. There was no meaningful tourism infrastructure in many of the nations they visited, and the political tensions of the Cold War and decolonization made such travel at times seem fraught. Surfers, in other words, were often tourism pioneers, scouting out and establishing beachheads in portions of the littoral world where most mass tourists dared not venture. Along the way the young wave-riders would meet and interact with the locals, impressing them with their aquatic feats. While they were still a part of the 1960s-era counterculture, their athleticism distinguished them from their more terrestrial counterparts. In Indonesia, for example, where both surfers and "hippies" poured into Bali in the 1970s, the authorities carefully drew a distinction between the two groups: the former were athletes, the latter a social nuisance.[11]

## Peacebuilding in China

Yet the unwitting diplomacy of surf tourism was only part of the story. By the 1980s surfers were starting to consciously envision themselves as roving diplomats. The case of Holmes's China is illustrative. As the *Surfer* editor envisioned the 1986 trip to America's Cold War adversary, it was "not just a mission in search of surf, but a real-life diplomatic and cultural expedition, a chance to spread the word about the joys of surfing and make a contribution to peace and understanding between peoples of the world."[12] The Americans spent three weeks in the country. They toured Beijing, toted their surfboards through fascinated crowds at the Great Wall, and gave surfing lessons on the beaches of Hainan. They were accompanied by two Chinese journalists, two translators, and three officials from the Chinese Yachting Association. "The Chinese are interested in learning about surfing, along with all popular foreign sports, to improve their competitive standing and to promote cultural understanding," Liu Haiming, a cultural official at the Chinese embassy in Washington, told the *Los Angeles Times*. Surfing, moreover, might "further China's plans to modernize and develop the tropical Hainan Island as a tourist area." It was possible that "the local people might also take up the sport," but, the diplomat added, that would take "a long, long time. They don't have the leisure as Californians [do] to develop it as a popular pastime."[13]

The Americans found only mediocre waves in Hainan. Still, they believed, the *Surfer*/China Exchange, as it had been officially dubbed, was a success. "We had been met at the airport with the fanfare of a rock group, hustled into a huge tour bus, and put up in the finest hotel in Beijing," one participant recalled. "We had received five-star treatment, six-course meals, and a major tour of every great sight and temple and holy ground that Beijing had to offer. Our hosts had been unendingly kind, and these sights *had* been impressive."[14] Their stay on the coast was less luxurious but equally warm. They made friends of the local titanium miners. They spent days teaching kids how to surf. They put on wave-riding displays to great applause. They drank and laughed long into the night with their sponsors, who dutifully provided daily reports to the All-China Sports Federation. They played Bruce Springsteen. It was everything a grassroots diplomatic exchange should be.[15]

Despite the limitations placed on their travel—the Americans were allowed to visit only a fraction of the Chinese coast—their hosts, Holmes later wrote, "received us graciously, treated our sport with interest and respect, and were genuinely anxious to hear our assessment of the surf potential we had seen."[16] When the group finally left China, they left behind what Matt George called a "completely isolated microcosm of surf spirit," one that "has never existed so exotically in all the world."[17] While later confessing that the "soul" of the sport seemed absent from their diplomatic performance, the Americans appeared generally gratified with their cross-cultural venture. "If sometime in the future there is a team of stoked Chinese surfers taking part in the [biannual International Surfing Association] World Contest, we will be able to say that we helped, in some small way, to bring it about," Holmes wrote. "That in itself is something to be proud of."[18]

Australian surfer Peter Drouyn had in fact tried, only months earlier, to create just such a Chinese team. Indeed, Holmes's group would meet some of the young people Drouyn had assembled; they were the same kids who received the Americans' instruction. It was a reminder that the US delegation was not in fact the first to take surfing to the People's Republic, as well as that surfing diplomacy was not an exclusively American affair. Surfing had been attempted in the then-British colony of Hong Kong in the early 1960s, but it was Drouyn's 1985 decision to move to Hainan that represented the first serious effort to spread surf culture to Chinese shores.[19] Drouyn was by then an Australian legend. A former world-title contender, by the time he reached his early thirties he had become disillusioned with professional surfing and increasingly captivated with the East. He entered an Asian studies program at Queensland's Griffith University, learned Mandarin, and proposed to the Chinese government that he introduce his beloved sport along the vast Chinese coast.[20] Surfing would assist with China's modernization, he argued, and the Chinese were undoubtedly aware of the chatter about its potentially becoming an Olympic sport.[21] Drouyn's efforts would also correct what he saw as surfing's corruption by its professionalization in the West. "By taking surfing to the other side," he asserted somewhat myopically, "the West, by virtue of détente, will come back to equality for all who surf and prefer peace. The only way now is to introduce the East to surfing in order to combat the West's offensive on free surfing."[22] The Chinese regime accepted Drouyn's proposal, and he made the move to Hainan, near the Vietnamese border, in September 1985.[23]

Drouyn immediately took to scouting the coast for surfing breaks while training a government-assembled group of roughly thirty young men and women, most of them gymnasts, in the practiced art of waveriding. He traveled to four provinces and, he reported, found "good waves." His days were spent meeting with officials, screening surf films for various Chinese, and instructing his students in the basics of the sport. There were long bus rides and, when there were no roads, exploratory trips aboard a navy frigate. Drouyn returned to Australia a short time later while the Chinese government evaluated whether to declare surfing a national sport. Interviewed in Australia, he was excited: "If surfing gains this national sport recognition it becomes probably the most highly respected symbol for surfing in history. Probably higher than in any country including America and Australia in terms of its status and application from the Government. I'm just waiting at the moment," he continued. "But hopefully I'll be back there to take on stage two of my programme which is the advance[d] stage. We'll have a national team and hopefully I'll be with them introducing them to international competition. Maybe not at the next world titles in Britain but possibly the ones after that."[24]

To Drouyn's disappointment, Beijing punted. Surfing would not yet be designated a national sport. But it was not a total defeat. He had, after all, met and interacted with countless ordinary Chinese, introducing them to one of the pleasures to be found in the ocean. Such grassroots encounters were the essence of people-to-people diplomacy.

## Negotiating Repression in El Salvador

The experiences of both Drouyn and the Americans point to the ways that surf tourists navigated some of the contested landscapes of the Cold War. If they saw opportunities for peacebuilding with international adversaries such as the Chinese, how might they respond to right-wing governments allied with the United States? Here the case of Central America may be instructive. In the 1980s, after years of repression by several of the region's US-backed regimes, the Reagan administration escalated the American war on leftism in, most obviously, Nicaragua, El Salvador, and Guatemala. The result was an orgy of blood and death. Guatemala was not noted for its surf, and the aggression of a CIA-backed army, the Contras, made surf exploration exceedingly difficult in Nicaragua. But El Salvador enjoyed excellent waves and had for years attracted visiting Brazilian and American surfers. When Hollywood director and screenwriter John Milius went looking for a Malibu stand-in while shooting *Big Wednesday* (1978), for instance, he sent his crew to La Libertad, a coastal town roughly twenty miles from the Salvadoran capital. The outbreak of civil war in 1980 put a serious damper on travel, however. "For those into tubes and bullets, now is the time to go to El Salvador," *Surfer* noted only half-jokingly that year. "All the local surfers are gone and the Americans are staying home."[25]

A small number did go. But many more watched in horror. Not all of them remained silent. After a stint working in Mexico City, Australian Rob Debelle had spent two months in El Salvador in 1977 with a group of Californians. Several years later, as the civil war escalated, he provided a scathing report for the popular Australian surfing magazine *Tracks* about the Salvadoran junta and US foreign policy. From La Libertad, he confessed in 1981, the country's violence was often hard to fathom: "The lovely tropical beach which was to become our home for two months seemed so removed from war, and the people were extremely warm and generous, despite their poverty." It was easy to "forget about the people's struggle" or the repression unfolding nearby. But Debelle was under no illusions. By the early 1980s, a "small force of U.S. Marines" propped up a corrupt regime, one that represented the interests of a tiny elite in a country of vast "inequalities and government atrocities," he wrote. American allegations to the contrary, there were "no Cubans or Russians down there, just bitter people fighting for social reforms that have been denied them for centuries." How tragically ironic, Debelle noted, that "the set for John Milius' *Big Wednesday* has become the real life Vietnam of Milius' and Coppola's *Apocalypse Now*."[26]

Debelle's anger proved infectious. "What does the American Govt. think they're playing at by backing up the fake bastards that've forgotten that they're human?" one outraged Australian responded after reading his article. "How could we let something like that happen? . . . Isn't there something we could do?"[27] It may have been a modest gesture, but the editors of *Tracks* pointed her to one possible action: answer the Australian Council of Churches advertisement in the same issue calling on surfers to fund "food, medicines, and clothes" needed by hundreds of thousands of Salvadorans uprooted by the "terror and repression" in their country.[28]

Across the Pacific, America's leading surfing publication could not have presented the violence in El Salvador more dissimilarly. In 1983 *Surfer* ran a lengthy piece on a trip to the country by the former martial arts editor of *Soldier of Fortune* magazine, a Cuban American surfer who had trained some of the paramilitary forces allied with the right-wing Central American regimes favored by the Reagan administration. The author, like Debelle, spent time at La Libertad. Rafael Lima, however, exalted the counterrevolutionary ideology that was central to Reagan-era US foreign policy; the leftist guerrillas resisting the regime were to him not revolutionaries but "hostile attackers." And whereas Debelle seemed to admire the courage and tenacity of the local people, Lima's characterization of them suggested utter contempt: a "drunk Indio in a beat-up straw hat," "a camouflaged [G]alil-toting Indian with one foot still in the cave," a "fifteen-year-old Salvadorean whore . . . all red lips and too much mascara" ("This revolution is prettier than you are," he told her), a "drunk Indian . . . passed out" with "drool trickl[ing] out of the corner of his mouth." Even those affiliated with the regime came in for scorn. One young soldier, allegedly unable to read, was said to have examined Lima's and his companion's passports upside-down. One of the few positive comments Lima could muster was that those he called "my Indians" would, during his stints training the paramilitaries, serve as his personal armed guards, enabling him to sneak out for an occasional surf.[29]

In a seeming reflection of the political environment in which the two publications operated, the Australian surfer tapped to write for *Tracks* conveyed to its thousands of readers his unequivocal condemnation of American support for the Salvadoran regime and his sympathy for the Salvadoran masses.[30] The American writer for *Surfer,* conversely, provided an account imbued with the ideological tenets of the Reagan administration's Cold War. The magazine's usually astute editor, Paul Holmes, seemed oblivious to the political undertones of Lima's surf exploration. The war in El Salvador was not a conflict begging for analysis, in his estimation, but a wake-up call that life can sometimes be a drag. "Traveling for surf can be an eye-opener," Holmes wrote in introducing the account, "and if you check out the El Salvador feature in this issue you'll discover how sometimes a surf trip can be anything but an escape from the worries of the world and more like a slap in the face by a shocking reality."[31] When a number of readers wrote outraged responses to Lima's travelogue—"please do not publish any more articles by soldiers of fortune who deal in death for the highest bidder and who happen to surf," begged one—Holmes was defensive.[32] "It was not our intention to moralize or politicize about this troubled tropical surf paradise," he claimed. It was "merely to emphasize the horrors being perpetrated in this region. Who better to write the story than one who has had direct experience?" he asked, distressingly unmindful of why an advisor to the regime's loathed paramilitary gunmen who were perpetrating most of those same horrors might not qualify as the most appropriate author.[33]

*Surfer* did report a less contentious visit a few years later. Bernie Baker was a well-known journalist and photographer with pleasant memories of the Salvadoran coast, which he had visited prior to the civil war. In the mid-1980s he returned to the country with Jon Damm, who, as mentioned, had briefly lived in El Salvador in his youth. Greeted at the airport by an army patrol and a tank, the two Americans traveled with an armed bodyguard and two Salvadoran expatriates who had flown over from Miami. The quartet surfed at La Libertad with a number of locals, and they made a couple of trips to the capital. At one point they encountered a "true test of our diplomacy" when stopped at a military checkpoint, though a small bribe by one of the expats managed to put an end to their ordeal.

If Baker's account is any indication, the Americans got no real sense of the nature of the Salvadoran strife or the concerns that drove the insurgency, however. Baker and Damm listened to the mother of one of their traveling companions "trying to explain the turmoil, fighting, and history of their country," but the insurgents remained simply a vague threat, Baker suggested, "killers" who a couple of months later "gunned down" six "Americans and Marines" at a restaurant the surfers visited during their stay. If Baker failed to demonstrate an appreciation for the politics of the Salvadoran conflict, there was at least an acknowledgment that wave-riding does not occur in a vacuum. "Even while surfing and having fun," he confessed, "the uneasy business of dealing with everyday life overshadows the allure and romance of the waves, the quiet beaches and great people who live here. I'd like to return soon—but so would many of their own people who've left through the years. If the situation there worsens, I'm afraid El Salvador will be lost—for everyone."[34]

## Challenging Apartheid in South Africa

Whether US foreign policy was in any way connected to the violence in El Salvador was, it seems, a mystery. But Baker's travels did at least hint at the developing recognition that surfing could not be divorced from the larger political world in which surfers went searching for waves. In many instances this might have simply been an appreciation that life was not always as rosy as it may have appeared from the water. In others this meant direct involvement in state affairs, such as Peter Drouyn's collaboration with the Chinese authorities in 1985. Drouyn's collaboration may, in fact, have come as a surprise to many surfers. With the pastime having experienced a countercultural turn a decade or two earlier in which the "freedom" that surfers associated with wave-riding seemed to naturally assume a hostility to state power, the developments of the mid-1980s represented a somewhat startling evolution of the sport. They speak to both surfing's professionalization—particularly the creation in 1976 of the International Professional Surfers (IPS) world tour—as well as its growing mainstream acceptance. In no case was this more pronounced than in the relationship that developed between Australian surfer Tom Carroll and Australian prime minister Bob Hawke. What brought them together midway through the 1980s was the global struggle against South African apartheid.[35]

Tom Carroll was, by 1985, an internationally renowned competitor. A short but powerful goofy-footer from New South Wales, he won his first ASP world championship in 1983. (The ASP was the Association of Surfing Professionals into which the IPS was subsumed in 1982.) In 1985, shortly after securing his second world championship, Carroll announced in the beachside town of Torquay, Victoria, that he would boycott the South African leg of the next world tour.[36] This came as a shock to countless surfers, who saw his position as an ill-advised politicization of their sport. But Carroll's announcement was in fact an unsurprising culmination of years of debate within the surf community about how to respond to the brutal South African system of racial separation. This had more significance for surfing than it did for many other sports, as South Africa was hardly a marginal consideration to the international community of wave-riders. Outside of the United States and Australia, it had probably the most vibrant surf culture on the planet. Indeed, its top surfers were a perennial presence in the elite ranks of the professional world tour, and South African Shaun Tomson was the 1977 men's world champion and one of the tour's most popular competitors. When Carroll won his second world championship in 1985, Tomson was the runner-up.

Carroll did not arrive at his decision lightly. He first competed in South Africa in 1981 and returned several times. Aware of apartheid before ever stepping foot in the country, he was nevertheless shocked by what he saw during his visits, both within the South African surf community and in South African society more broadly. There were, for example, the country's segregated beaches.[37] There could be no equality among surfers when their sport's venue was not open to all, he believed. There were also some South Africans' exterminationist fantasies: the "father of a couple of guys I surf with in South Africa" told him that "we were lucky in Australia—all our Aborigines had been killed."[38] Carroll, as an Australian, was "acutely aware" of the injustices faced by Aborigines in his own country, but the behavior he witnessed in South Africa was unlike anything he had ever seen at home. And then there was the experience of driving with a friend from Durban. Heading to the beach together in the early morning, the South African—a young man Carroll's age who had performed his national service by intermittently working as a police officer for four years rather than serving in the military for two—attempted to drive over some of the black housekeepers and other domestic employees making their way to the white homes in which they worked. Carroll was especially troubled that his friend, who one moment was "trying to kill people," was just moments later "really gracious and giving" and "a really nice guy." What could make even seemingly decent people do such things? The experience left the Australian sobered.[39]

By 1984, cognizant of the growing international debates over the relationship between sport and apartheid—proponents were insistent that there could "never be normal sport in an abnormal society"—Carroll was consciously considering the implications of his participation in the South African leg of the world tour.[40] He left the Gunston 500 contest in Durban that year, which he won, feeling "ashamed" that his presence might be contributing in some way to the maintenance of the apartheid regime. Although he "didn't understand all the deeper details" of the issue, he knew that it "just didn't feel right." The time had come, he believed, to move from thought to action. It would be his last trip to South Africa as a professional competitor.[41] In April 1985, just moments after securing his second world title, Carroll announced that he would boycott the South African contests scheduled for later that year.

He initially intended to organize other professional surfers to do the same, asking his manager, Peter Mansted, to draft an agreement with all the Australian, American, and Japanese competitors. In the end, however, Carroll decided to back away from that collective effort.[42] He was nevertheless almost immediately joined by two other future world champions: young California standout Tom Curren and Martin Potter, a British national raised in Durban and a highly regarded surfer. Collectively these three men would account for six world titles—Carroll won two, Curren won three, and Potter won one—serving as a dominant force in professional surfing from much of the early 1980s to early 1990s. The symbolic significance of their actions was thus great, inspiring other athletes—golfer Greg Norman, footballer Glen Ella, and several Australian cricketers, according to veteran surf journalist Phil Jarratt—to not compete in South Africa.[43]

Just as Tom Carroll was no slouch in the international surf community, Bob Hawke was no slouch in the global movement to end apartheid. A veteran trade unionist and self-described sports fanatic, Hawke was also a vocal opponent of the violent South African system. As the prime minister of a Commonwealth nation, he was aware of Australia's obligations under the 1977 Gleneagles Agreement that discouraged involvement in apartheid sport, and he was a leader of the effort by the Commonwealth states to diplomatically shun the apartheid regime. When Carroll announced his boycott and faced immediate legal difficulties, Hawke quickly responded. In the 1980s, when prize money in competitions was still relatively limited, surfers relied mostly on marketing deals with their corporate sponsors to make a living in the sport. One of Carroll's primary sponsors was Shaun Tomson's South Africa–based Instinct Clothing. After announcing his decision to forgo the South African events, Carroll "resigned his contract" with Instinct the next day. There was "no way he could stay with Instinct, a company based in South Africa and employing cheap black labour," he told *Tracks*—prompting the surfwear brand to threaten an injunction that would prevent him from accepting other sponsorships in Australia and the United States for twelve months.[44] (Quiksilver, which had earlier sponsored Carroll but had let him go in the early 1980s, was interested in re-signing the now two-time world champion, and the company subsequently did so.)

It was clear the business relationship between Instinct and Carroll was over, but the terms of its cessation were uncertain. With the possibility of a lawsuit by the South African firm, Hawke intervened. The prime minister met with Carroll at Parliament House in Canberra and offered his government's assistance in defending against Tomson's company. Carroll, Hawke told the surfer, had made a "courageous decision" and was "setting an inspiring example for millions of young Australians." Therefore, the prime minister promised, "the Government is prepared to provide legal assistance to you by meeting the costs of a legal opinion and advice from senior counsel."[45] Hawke's offer was not without controversy. It was quickly dismissed as "entirely unjustified" by the political opposition, but the issue became moot as Instinct—presumably reeling from a one-two punch of bad publicity and the resources proffered by the Australian government—opted not to seek the injunction.[46] The company quickly signed boycott opponent Barton Lynch.[47]

Hawke and Carroll maintained their unlikely relationship—one Australian newspaper referred to the twenty-something surfer and fifty-something politician as the "odd couple"—for years.[48] Carroll's support for Hawke gave the prime minister credibility among the youth demographic, while Hawke's endorsement of Carroll legitimized his stand and the sport of surfing more broadly. The surfer's boycott, moreover, lent support to Hawke's denunciation of those who failed to follow his example. He pointed in 1987, for instance, to Carroll's "admirable" sacrifice in jeopardizing his chances for another world title by forgoing the South African contests when criticizing the decision of tennis star Pat Cash, fresh off a victory at Wimbledon, to play in the apartheid state.[49] Carroll was again publicly thanked by the prime minister for his principled position in 1989.[50] And at a testimonial dinner in 1993, Hawke movingly said of Carroll that he could think of "no example in the history of Australian sport where a champion has been prepared to put principles so manifestly in front of his or her own interests." There was "no Australian sporting hero or legend," Hawke volunteered, for whom he felt a "greater surge of affection and admiration."[51] Even after the crumbling of apartheid in 1994, when Carroll finally ended his South African boycott, the "odd couple" remained friends. In 1997, for instance, Hawke introduced Carroll to Nelson Mandela in what the former world champion recalled as a "very, very touching moment."[52]

Surfing's entanglement with South African apartheid was bigger than Tom Carroll and Bob Hawke, however, and it involved nations other than Australia. Most obviously, in February 1989 the two top-seeded surfers in the ASP East, Americans Rich Rudolph and Charlie Kuhn, were prohibited from competing in the West Indies at the Natural Art / Carib Beer Pro-Am, the first Caribbean professional contest sanctioned by that organization.[53] Prompted by a letter to the editor from a visiting Briton, a local newspaper, the *Barbados Advocate,* had launched an investigation of who, among the more than 125 foreign surfers descending on the predominantly black island, had competed in any South African events.[54] When the paper disclosed just a day before the contest that Rudolph and

Kuhn had done so, official investigations were immediately opened by the Barbadian Immigration Department and the Ministry of Sports.[55] "I don't support apartheid or anything like that," Kuhn explained. "It is just that when you are a professional you are sometimes forced to do things you wouldn't do normally." Rudolph opted for a different tack, appearing to claim ignorance. "We are not politicians," he told the *Advocate*. "When we go to South Africa we are fairly isolated and not allowed to travel around and see what the country is really like. . . . We just simply surf."[56] The Barbadian authorities were apparently not impressed. The two Americans, the government decreed the next day, could not surf in the contest.[57] They quickly decided to leave.

This was an unprecedented development: surfers allowed into a country but then barred from competition. South Africans had for years faced problems in securing visas to compete abroad, from Shaun Tomson in Brazil to a host of professionals in Japan, New Zealand, Australia, and France.[58] But this was new. The two top seeds in the ASP East's inaugural Barbadian contest had been disqualified, the Barbados Surfing Association had at least temporarily taken a public drubbing, and a number of sponsors were so upset—not with the surfers, but with the *Advocate*—that they had withdrawn their advertisements from a special supplement generated by the newspaper for the three-day event.[59] Bitter contest officials, meanwhile, hindered the *Advocate*'s ability to cover the competition, inviting the condemnation of the Barbados Association of Journalists.[60]

In an effort to tamp down the outrage of the local media and authorities, the director of the ASP East, Mike Martin, hastily called a press conference as the contest got under way. His response to what *Surfer* magazine took to calling "The Incident" was, in typical ASP fashion, markedly wishy-washy. When the ruckus had first erupted several days earlier, Martin claimed that his "association does not take its competitions to South Africa and does not encourage sporting links with that country," an initial statement in which he apparently attempted to draw a distinction between the ASP as an umbrella organization and the regional circuit under his charge.[61] But several days later, following a late-night conversation with ASP executive director Graham Cassidy, Martin, while condemning apartheid as "repugnant and indefensible," defended the American surfers by noting that they were technically not in violation of the Gleneagles Agreement; they had competed in South Africa as individual athletes and not as representatives of a signatory nation.[62] Faced with questions about how many of the other surfers in Barbados had traveled to the apartheid state, Martin was skillfully evasive. His performance—a well-mixed combination of prevarication and calm reasoning—demonstrated the "aplomb of a natural diplomat," *Surfer* reckoned.[63]

Controversy would greet the Barbados contest again the following year. Wes Laine, a Virginia Beach local who had been ranked ninth on the world tour in 1983 and 1985 but retired from it in 1989 to concentrate on the East Coast professional circuit, professed to California-based *Surfing* magazine his absolute refusal to abide by the South Africa boycott. "I'm not going to jeopardize my livelihood or miss out on a good surf trip for anything," he declared. Frankly, Laine gushed, he "loved South Africa, [and] couldn't *not* go there, because the waves are just too good." The boycott, moreover, was a futile effort; it was not going to have "any impact on South Africa's politics, period," the Virginian insisted. None of this pleased Barbadian contest officials, who, upon learning of Laine's comments, promptly told the American that he would be prohibited from entering the country. An angry Laine responded by pledging to disrupt the 1990 contest by, of all things, organizing a boycott of Barbados.[64] It went nowhere.

When combined with the ongoing professional boycott of South Africa, international incidents such as those in the West Indies threatened the surfing world-tour's continuation in the apartheid state. "The Barbadian government had put the ASP on notice," *Surfer* observed. "Let your surfers know they have a choice. They can compete in South Africa or they can compete here. They can't do both."[65] The fiasco in Barbados culminated an unanticipated series of developments in the 1980s. If the Reagan era is often remembered as a time of heightened Cold War polarization, surfers contributed to growing efforts to ease some of the tensions between the capitalist bloc and its communist adversaries. When Australian Peter Drouyn and the American group organized by *Surfer* magazine ventured to China, for instance, they did so with the explicit purpose of building peace. And their efforts did generate goodwill.

Peace may not have been Rafael Lima's goal in El Salvador—the American was there, after all, to train the regime's despised paramilitaries—but the response by some of his compatriots to his story, as well as the lengthy denunciations of US foreign policy leveled by surfers such as Rob Debelle, indicated the extent to which even the surf media became entangled in the political contest over Central America. This was certainly the case with South Africa, as well. When two-time world champion Tom Carroll announced his boycott of the apartheid state and was immediately joined by fellow competitors Tom Curren and Martin Potter, the trio was honoring a call issued as early as 1971 by *Tracks*.[66] (Demonstrating the extent to which even sports media was construed as politically influential, the South African regime banned *Tracks* in the 1980s.)[67] Carroll's position was an assertion of sport's role in international affairs. Like many athletes, he did not see himself as "political." But in taking what he saw as a "humanitarian stand," Carroll most certainly did demonstrate the power of sport in shaping global politics, from Australia and South Africa to Barbados and the United States.

These were remarkable developments. Surfers had for years envisioned their pastime as an escape from the stresses and concerns of industrial society. Political and social realities—death squads in El Salvador, peacemaking in China, systemic racism in South Africa—were now intruding on the cloistered fantasy world that surfers had constructed for themselves. If surfing had once been a welcome respite from modern life, the sport was now proving itself an instrument of diplomacy and social change, a transformation that was welcomed by some but denounced by others. By the late 1980s, it was apparent to most surfers that they could no longer pretend to be simply a people apart. The ocean may have been a sanctuary, but one could not stay in the water forever. Surfers inevitably had to return to shore, and what happened there—state repression, international tensions, the Cold War—could not be easily ignored. The fact that surf culture had gone global made such provincialism impossible.

## Notes

1. Paul Holmes, "The China Exchange: A Surfari with a Difference," *Surfer* 28, no. 6 (June 1987): 54.

2. Matt Warshaw, *The Encyclopedia of Surfing* (Orlando, FL: Harcourt, 2003), 148.

3. Matt George, "Beyond the Great Wall: The First Surfers in China," *Surfer* 28, no. 6 (June 1987): 103.

4. Holmes, "The China Exchange," 54.

5. "*Surfer* Stages China Surf Expedition: Historic Journey in Sports' Diplomacy," *Surfer* 28, no. 4 (April 1987): 21.

6. For more on surfing and cultural diplomacy, see Scott Laderman, *Empire in Waves: A Political History of Surfing* (Berkeley: University of California Press, 2014), chap. 2.

7. Christopher Endy, *Cold War Holidays: American Tourism in France* (Chapel Hill: University of North Carolina Press, 2004).

8. "Letter of President to Be Included in U.S. Passports," *Department of State Bulletin* 37, no. 946 (August 12, 1957): 276.

9. Clarence B. Randall quoted in Scott Laderman, *Tours of Vietnam: War, Travel Guides, and Memory* (Durham, NC: Duke University Press, 2009), 17–18.

10. Rennie Ellis, "Odyssey of a Surfer," *Surfing World* 4, no. 1 (March–April 1964): 46, reprinted in Peter Troy, *To the Four Corners of the World: The Lost Journals of the Original Surf Explorer* (Jan Juc, Victoria: Flying Pineapple Media, 2010), 64.

11. Phil Abraham, "Indonesia Needs You!," *Tracks* 119 (August 1980): 5.

12. Holmes, "The China Exchange," 54.

13. Lynn Smith, "Surfers Test Chinese Waters in a Diplomatic Junket," *Los Angeles Times,* December 4, 1986. For more on China's embrace of sport as an instrument of international relations, see the chapter by Fan Hong and Lu Zhouxiang in this volume.

14. George, "Beyond the Great Wall," 103.

15. Ibid., 104–7, and Matt George, "Does the Dragon Have Soul?," *Surfer* 31, no. 7 (July 1990): 118.

16. Smith, "Surfers Test Chinese Waters in a Diplomatic Junket," and Holmes, "The China Exchange," 54.

17. George, "Beyond the Great Wall," 107.

18. Holmes, "The China Exchange," 54, and George, "Does the Dragon Have Soul?," 118, 120.

19. Terrence Ogden and Thomas Ling reported surfing in Hong Kong in 1963; see "Surf Spots," *Surfer Bi-Monthly* 4, no. 2 (April–May 1963): 36, and "Surf Spots," *Surfer Bi-Monthly* 4, no. 6 (December 1963–January 1964): 62. On Rod Payne's 1979 effort to surf at Hong Kong's Big Wave Bay—he was removed from the water by the police—see Warshaw, *The Encyclopedia of Surfing,* 120.

20. Mike Perry, "Drouyn's Foray," *Surfer* 28, no. 6 (June 1987): 108.

21. "Peter Drouyn Bails to China! More Than a Surf Trip," *Surfer* 27, no. 3 (March 1986): 21.

22. Perry, "Drouyn's Foray," 160.

23. "Peter Drouyn Bails to China!," 21.

24. "Peter Drouyn: Back From China," *Tracks* (January 1986): 11.

25. "Pipeline: The Hawaiian Grapevine," *Surfer* 21, no. 8 (August 1980): 88.

26. Rob Debelle, "El Salvador: Is Paradise Lost?," *Tracks* 128 (May 1981): 15.

27. "Zoe," "El Salvador," Letter, *Tracks* 129 (June 1981): 3.

28. Advertisement for the Australian Council of Churches, *Tracks* 129 (June 1981): 28.

29. Rafael Lima, "Combat Surf: The Last Expedition to El Salvador?," *Surfer* 24, no. 10 (October 1983): 72, 76, 80.

30. A later feature in *Tracks,* while commending El Salvador's "unreal waves," cautioned that traveling there was a "definite life risk," as the insurgents "may mistake you for an American (imperialist dogs) and kill you." "Travel Tips," *Tracks* (January 1986): 19.

31. Paul Holmes, "Behind the Lines," *Surfer* 24, no. 10 (October 1983): 23.

32. Guy McCullough, "El Salvador," Letter, *Surfer* 25, no. 1 (January 1984): 11.

33. Editorial comment following McCullough, "El Salvador," 11. A subsequent piece in the magazine featured a photograph of an American surfer serving in the US armed forces in El Salvador, where he was waiting for the "all clear" so that he could "get back to his aquatic attack of the 'rad waves around the area.'" "Another Lovely Day in El Salvador!," *Surfer* 26, no. 10 (October 1985): 21.

34. Bernie Baker, "Return to El Salvador," *Surfer* 28, no. 3 (March 1987): 88–89, 122.

35. For more on surfing and apartheid, see Laderman, *Empire in Waves,* chap. 4.

36. Carroll's victories in 1985 made him—in light of the world tour calendar—the 1984 world champion, meaning that he secured back-to-back world championships.

37. Interview of Tom Carroll, Newport, New South Wales, October 8, 2008.

38. Tom Carroll and Kirk Willcox, *The Wave Within* (Sydney: Ironbark, 1994), 84.

39. Carroll, for personal reasons, wished not to identify his friend. Interview of Tom Carroll, October 8, 2008. Peter Simons, an Australian surfer and photographer, experienced a similar episode of what his white South African acquaintances called "coon hunting" along a shantytown's disused airfield on which young local children played soccer. "My eyes and mind still remember," he wrote. E-mail correspondence with Peter Simons, May 21–22, 2013.

40. For a contemporaneous brochure arguing that "normal sports" were not possible in an "abnormal society," see *Apartheid Sport: Change but No Improvement* (N.p.: Continental Sports, 1984). The quote is attributed broadly to "the discriminated South African" by journalist Fekrou Kidane on page 5 of the brochure. On South African surfers of color embracing the sentiment, see Muhammad Shafique, "Black Surfing in South Africa: A Look at Wynberg Surf Club," *Tracks* (August 1986): 46.

41. Interview of Tom Carroll, October 8, 2008.

42. Carroll and Willcox, *The Wave Within,* 83.

43. Phil Jarratt, "Apartheid: The Cries Won't Die," Letter, *Surfer* 27, no. 4 (April 1986): 11. Jarratt cited the case of Glen Ella but may have meant his brother Mark. Glen Ella competed in South Africa in 1985; Mark Ella publicly stated that while he would be assured of significant financial rewards if he did so, he could not play in South Africa "until the apartheid system is disbanded." S. O'Connor (Queensland Newspapers), "Aussies High in SA Links," *Telegraph,* December 17, 1985.

44. Nick Carroll, "South Africa: To Be or Not to Be?," *Tracks* (June 1985): 12;

John Elliss, "Interview: Tom Carroll," *Tracks* (October 1985): 51; and Queensland Newspapers, "Legal Aid to Surfer 'Entirely Unjustified,'" *Courier-Mail* (Brisbane), May 23, 1985. It is unclear whether Carroll's comment about Instinct is a direct quote; the words do not appear in quotation marks, though the interviewer wrote that Carroll "state[d]" them.

45. Greg Kelton, "Hawke Strengthens Trade Policy against S. Africa," *Courier-Mail* (Brisbane), May 22, 1985.

46. Queensland Newspapers, "Legal Aid to Surfer 'Entirely Unjustified.'" *Tracks* attributed the decision to Shaun Tomson. "Buzzzzzzz," *Tracks* (July 1985): 7.

47. "Buzzzzzzz," *Tracks* (August 1985): 7. Instinct also signed Greg Anderson.

48. "Odd Couple Make a Splash in the Name of Mateship," *Advertiser* (Adelaide), April 16, 1993.

49. Queensland Newspapers, "I'm Disappointed in Cash: Hawke," *Courier-Mail* (Brisbane), November 18, 1987. See also Helen Pitt, "Cash's South Africa Trip Disappoints PM," *Sydney Morning Herald,* November 18, 1987.

50. Peter Brewer, "New Wave of Enthusiasm for South African Meet," *Sunday Tasmanian* (Hobart), June 24, 1990.

51. Carroll and Willcox, *The Wave Within,* 85–87.

52. Interview of Tom Carroll, October 8, 2008.

53. On the contest being the first Caribbean event sanctioned by the ASP East, see Paul Holmes, "Barbados Political Pepper Sauce: Apartheid Is Hot Issue on Caribbean TV Shoot," *Surfer* 30, no. 7 (July 1989): 56.

54. Roger Baxter, "Look at Surfing before It's Too Late," *Barbados Advocate,* February 11, 1989.

55. Hayden Coppin, "Surfers with S.A. Links," *Barbados Advocate,* February 16, 1989. On a cheery profile of Rudolph and Kuhn a day earlier, see "Surfers Get Set: Two Test Waves," *Barbados Advocate,* February 15, 1989.

56. Coppin, "Surfers with S.A. Links."

57. Hayden Coppin, "2 Surfers Banned," *Barbados Advocate,* February 18, 1989. For more on how the Commonwealth Caribbean responded at the level of sport to the international anti-apartheid campaign, see the chapter by Aviston Downes in this volume.

58. Moira Hodgson, "SA's Image Improving," *Zigzag* 11, no. 3 (May/June 1987): 7; "Interviews: Mike Burness," *Zigzag* 10, no. 5 (September/October 1986): 10; Craig Sims, "Backwash: ASP Update," *Zigzag* 11, no. 4 (July/August 1987): 54; Craig Sims, "Backwash: ASP Update," *Zigzag* 11, no. 6 (November/December 1987): 11; and Robert Archer and Antoine Bouillon, *The South African Game: Sport and Racism* (London: Zed Press, 1982), 295.

59. On the withdrawal of the advertisements, see Robert Best, "We Have to Laugh to Cry," *Barbados Advocate,* February 18, 1989, and "BSA Officials Shun Advocate Sports Team," *Barbados Advocate,* February 18, 1989.

60. "BSA Officials Shun Advocate Sports Team," and "BAJ Takes Up Surfing Issue," *Barbados Advocate,* February 24, 1989.

61. Coppin, "Surfers with S.A. Links."

62. "Immigration Dept. under Fire," *Barbados Advocate,* February 19, 1989, and Holmes, "Barbados Political Pepper Sauce," 61. For more on the Gleneagles Agreement and the nations of the Caribbean, see Aviston D. Downes, "Sport and International Diplomacy: The Case of the Commonwealth Caribbean and the Anti-Apartheid Campaign, 1959–1992," *Sports Historian* 22, no. 2 (November 2002): 23–45.

63. Holmes, "Barbados Political Pepper Sauce," 61.

64. Warshaw, *The Encyclopedia of Surfing,* 331, and Matt Warshaw, *The History of Surfing* (San Francisco: Chronicle Books, 2010), 398.

65. Holmes, "Barbados Political Pepper Sauce," 61.

66. "Black Africa," *Tracks* 12 (September 1971): 4.

67. John Elliss, "South Africa: Surfing in the Emergency Zone," *Tracks* (September 1985): 22.

# Conclusion

## Fields of Dreams and Diplomacy

### *Thomas W. Zeiler*

Scholars and almost all commentators, save for an unsophisticated crowd of sport addicts and die-hard fans, have long acknowledged that athletics are not just fun and games. As these essays show, sport is situated far from that realm of child's play and spectator interest. For a while now, studies in the wide-ranging field of professional and amateur, adult and youth, and team and individual athletics have revealed that the history of all sports is deeply embedded in politics, society, and culture. Sport is closely aligned to business and profits, organizations, culture, and media. They are fertile ground for study through archives, so hobbyists and sport lovers beware: the field of sport is serious and engages most major trends in the historiography through innovative methodologies. This collection has made the linkages beyond pure recreation and spectator entertainment even more clear by bonding sport to international politics. The essays move the analysis and discussion past the fact that sport is global to the converse: the idea that the global is closely related to playing arenas.[1]

Such a relationship is not often to our liking, for we tend to think of sports as pleasure activities or chock full of rivalries—either way, a distraction from the reality of world politics. But this reality is nonetheless prevalent and more often than not through negative manifestations. The "spirit of sport," as Heather Dichter writes in this volume, is violated when this happens. Leaving aside the instances when the injection of sport into politics has had salutary effects—such as calling attention to South African apartheid, as Aviston Downes writes, or in facilitating good relations, as in the case of the Chinese player losing purposely in badminton to an Indonesian in 1963 in order to encourage emerging nations, as recounted by Fan Hong and Lu Zhouxiang, or even to boost prestige, in the case of Perón in Argentina or the Soviets among their satellites—the relationship of sport to global politics is more frequently decried than celebrated. The relationship of the athletic field to national values and international machinations is often fraught with bad feelings and outcomes. The Olympics, that venue for world friendship, has nonetheless also been the scene of horrific violence (the 1972 Munich Summer Games, when Palestinian terrorists killed eleven Israeli team members), big power politics at the expense of athletes (the American boycott of the 1980 Summer Olympics in Moscow and the Soviets' return favor in 1984 when the events were held in Los Angeles), and political statements and symbolism. All run counter to the Athenian spirit of fair play, healthy competition, and displays of human athletic prowess and accomplishment that remain a staple of marketing ploys for the Games and that classicists have long questioned as accurate characteristics of the ancient Olympics. Think of Hitler's racially charged Berlin Games in 1936 or American sprinters raising the clenched fist of black power on the podium in Mexico City in 1968 (though I do not equate these two events, as the race issues and intentions were wholly different). The Israeli massacre remains the most infamous event of the Olympics. Thus, Dr. Eric Williams, the prime minister of Trinidad, spoke volumes when he announced that "I do not like political interference in sport."

The "negative" aspect of the Olympics as a sounding board for protesters is also prevalent. Less-remembered episodes that touch on the international and exemplify the Olympics as a stage for political dissent include the 1992 Barcelona Games, when Spanish Basque separatists threatened violence, and the 2000 Sydney Games, when Aborigines peacefully demonstrated against discrimination. But international politics is never far from the Olympics. The 2004 Athens Games witnessed protests at the US embassy against the American military conflict in Iraq, and the Beijing Olympics dealt with human rights complaints against bad working conditions in China, degradation of the environment, and treatment of political prisoners. When the torch was carried around the globe, activists campaigned against Chinese policies in Tibet and the arming of Sudanese government troops. Sadly, the specter of international terrorism will likely hover over security preparations for Olympics for years to come (and the topic deserves scholarly attention as well).[2]

Other instances beyond the Olympics of the mix of the real world and the sporting world include boycotts or threatened shutdowns of games, test matches, and the like, involvement of government agencies in events, and head-to-head competitions that draw national audiences and cause reflections of national greatness or weakness. "Keep politics out of sports" or the reverse, we hear, but as sociologist George Sage has noted, the "more realistic point of view" is to acknowledge that the "examples of the ties between sports and politics are plentiful."[3] Scholars no longer argue about state involvement in sports. The record of intervention, ideological trumpeting, nationalism, diplomatic intrigue and pressures, and individual leaders' self-promotion for political gain at the national or international levels bears out the intimate ties of sport to diplomacy and world politics.[4]

And so do the essays in this volume. Actually, several cover quite familiar ground—the promotion of, and tension within, the sport/political systems of the communist bloc; small powers' (though oftentimes not weak sport powers') submission and/or resistance to big powers; and the US influence in (or inability to influence) the Olympic movement. As Andrew Johns makes clear in opening the volume, sport has become integral to public diplomacy—in fact, it is a key tool in that large endeavor, although I wish there had been more expansion in this collection of the nature of sporting public diplomacy and its prominence (or not) in government decisions on a broad scale.

The exclusion of some issues and interests merely speaks to the possibilities of the research agenda in the future. For example, there is little here on gender (though there are related asides to manhood) and international politics, particularly historical work on organizational gender disputes and how women have affected the man's (and the politician's) world of sport.[5] What comes most strikingly to mind in this regard is the 2012 London Olympics, where five Muslim women competed, and Saudi Arabia, Qatar, and Brunei entered female athletes for the first time in history. Talk of headscarves injected political, social, and cultural norms into the Games and certainly had an impact on cultural relations between nations in the Middle East, not to mention reshaping perceptions in the West. And the arrival of these women was a change from just eight years before;

Figure 14.1. Woroud Sawalha, one of Palestine's first two female Olympians, running in the preliminary heats of the 800-meter race at the 2012 London Olympics. Sawalha finished her heat with a time of 2:29.16, the third slowest time among the forty women who finished the race. (Photo by Heather L. Dichter)

at the Athens Olympics, over twenty countries, of which about half were predominantly Muslim countries, sent no female athletes. So, do women's issues and the diversity in the treatment of women across cultures—as witnessed in many Olympics—have a bearing on international relations, the status of certain countries, and even on aid given to them? Does gender shape political discourse that is then reflected abroad? These and other questions await researchers.

This development in the Islamic world can be contextualized within the era of globalization (also an issue not explicitly addressed in this volume), as criticism about the lack of gender equity—and male domination / female subordination—has been, and remains, a rather ritualized dispute since the 1970s. While, on the whole, high politics are the focus of these essays, it should be noted that society matters in international relations. Thus a mere 25 percent of Olympic competitors in 1964 were women; forty years later, 41 percent of the participants were women at the Athens Games, although 170 of the 300 or so events were men-only.[6] Will such a discrepancy (though the gap is closing, and some nations, such as Canada in 1996, have more women than men on their team) reflect on global politics? Does international leadership for women depend on sport, among other institutions, to provide positions for females that will possibly ease discrimination, patriarchy, violence, and poverty worldwide? Does sport offer avenues for progress in this regard, much like microfinance has altered economies and societies in poor countries?

This volume does a good job on the large, controversial, and abundantly publicized issue of racial politics; several essays touch on the subject from the traditional angle of oppression, namely apartheid and the sporting worlds of the Olympics, soccer, and cricket. While well-worn topics, they are treated in these essays in refreshing ways that deal with a host of nations and inter-Commonwealth relations as well, rather than just focusing on the Olympics or US leadership. As Jenifer Parks explains, there are dimensions of race beyond apartheid, such as the Soviets trying but failing, due to Avery Brundage's bow to racism, to insert African nations into the International Olympic Committee (IOC) in the early 1960s. Black power is another theme that has been explored, but the black nationalist movements are also fodder for research.

While gender and race are not basic themes of this volume (contrary to many other studies on sport), the interchange between diplomacy and culture is certainly prominent. The anthology posits that cultural and social power is expressed through sport and that they transfer to international politics. This occurs whether within an alliance or between rivals and on a multilateral or bilateral basis. The wielding of sport as a cultural-power tool happened also within nations and within empires themselves, and not just between them (as Pascal Charitas amply shows in his chapter on French sport and decolonization in Africa). In other words, these essays demonstrate the surprising heft in expressions of soft power. Many elements go into such a projection, such as prestige, recognition of a lesser power's status, propaganda, national identity, and the like. Examples abound, such as the 1968 Olympics where the Soviets were deemed weak, so they decided to pursue solutions to their own status anxiety in sport at the expense of the German Democratic Republic (GDR) and other satellites. Likewise, note Moscow's intention to compete in America's game—basketball—which Kevin Witherspoon discusses, even though the sport was as foreign to it as baseball. Meanwhile, as Evelyn Mertin shows, sporting contacts mimicked actual formal relations, as the GDR played a role as deferential little brother to Moscow. Canadian hockey has a history of prestige as a major factor in, at least, shaping attitudes toward a foreign policy nemesis, whether the United States as the overweening neighbor or the USSR as a Cold War bully. The Czechoslovaks were feeble in comparison to Soviet power but could be independent when it came to hockey—and even be an unofficial carrier of grievances, as in 1968 after the Prague coup, when the crowds chanted the name of deposed leader Aleksandr Dubček at a game against the Soviets.

Ideology—grounded in capitalism, socialism, and national superiority—has ruled the sports world. The Peronist state cashed in on sport as a "social technology"—a most useful and illustrative term used by Cesar Torres in this volume—as a means of socializing Argentines and symbolizing to the world the leadership credentials of Juan Perón. Thus Perón boastfully sought to bring the 1956 Olympics to Buenos Aires, recognizing that he could project Argentina's image, through sport diplomacy, to its people and foreigners. The effort failed, but when his country beat the United States team in basketball, he could readily tell the team's captain that the victory had done more "than the work of one hundred ambassadors." I imagine the Soviet victory in Olympic basketball over the undefeated American team in 1972—beating the Cold War rival at its own sport—was trumpeted similarly throughout the USSR!

The flip side is that symbols can undermine diplomacy. When the Soviets accidentally played the West German national anthem at a meet between its divers and East Germany's, heads rolled as protest reached the heights of foreign ministries. No such negative fate awaited the comically inadvertent gaffe by the Atlanta Braves when they hoisted the Canadian flag upside down at the World Series in 1992, but cranky northern neighbors and journalists took note. Such sentiment spoke to Orwell's warning that nationalistic sport is the most serious of all sport because it addresses hatreds and rivalries, but it nonetheless vindicates the wielding of soft power. The cultural competition of sport, therefore, has taken on new and novel roles, as these historians have noted. And cultural comparisons address more than just dazzling displays of athleticism. They directly relate to international politics and the wielding of power on the world stage.

Another theme that arises from the collection is that structure matters. That is, how and who controlled the sport organizations were critical to the politics that was reflected in these institutions. Pascal Charitas unravels the intricacies of French postcolonial administration in sport, the efforts by France to erect a francophone sporting union out of desperation to retain its imperial glory through cultural ties (without formal bonds of empire), and the struggles by the IOC to maintain a modicum of control over black African sports. The superpowers, furthermore, dominated the politics of the Olympics and other venues. This could be accomplished by dominating decision-making bodies or exchanging delegations (as in the case of the Table Tennis Friendship Invitation Tournament in Beijing in 1973 that moved China and the United States toward détente) or appointing cronies (as Perón did in Argentina) to sport federations. Bureaucracies oftentimes ruled in sport (and in international politics as well, of course); they could be bloated and out of touch but all-powerful. This hegemony was demonstrated on numerous occasions, such as the banning of South Africa during the apartheid era, even though national governments thought differently, or when Cuba was permitted to enter world games when state leaders, especially in the United States, vehemently opposed. There are lessons in both the positive and negative influence of sport bureaucracies, but it cannot be denied that although they are inherently undemocratic (like, for instance, the World Trade Organization and the International Monetary Fund, whose personnel is unelected), they can resist the worst politicizing impulses of nations.

Somewhat related to structure in these essays is the important, mostly unstated, methodological theme of transnational, person-to-person or other unofficial exchanges inherent in sport. Transnationalism, of course, has been a fashionable and increasingly transformative trend in the field of diplomatic history, to the point that many scholars have veered from state-centered research to exploring people, movements, and organizations across borders. This same pattern holds for sport, at least in this volume. Simply, sport lends itself to analysis of nonstate exchanges because they are not often officially sanctioned, although this collection purposely makes the links between transnational "movement" of games, athletes, and organizations, and national governments. In fact, it is clear that sport often transcended national restrictions. For instance, US policy could ban travelers from the GDR from obtaining visas, but an Allied Travel Office could provide them instead. Surfers, as Scott Laderman notes, served as tourists who might prevail on nations (such as the People's Republic of China in the 1980s) to allow competitions, but they were also viewed as hippies carrying cultural influence as they rode the waves. From such grassroots diplomacy emerged the potential for changing diplomatic relations, or so was the case in some instances.

But where the state stops and private citizens emerge is not always evident, and this lack of clarity poses a challenge for historians. That task, to be sure, is daunting due to the complex interplay of state and society in international sports as well as politics. Stretching back to the immediate post–World War II period, even agents of the state—soldiers—became diplomats by using sport to make contact with average citizens under occupation. Such was the case for American soldiers (representatives of the state), who played baseball with beleaguered citizens in city streets in Japan, and in Austria during its occupation. Officially sanctioned Germans and British played soccer after the war. The Marshall Plan spurred youth in Austria to ski; American diplomacy midwifed the reemergence of the country's tourism industry. The state was instrumental in building cooperative relationships, while turning over the mechanisms and processes to private groups and individuals. Such observations are important to the historiography of political and diplomatic history, as noted by current trends in transnational research and the cultural turn that privileges individuals over impersonal structures, events, and the state.

On the other hand, however, there are instances when the opposite was true—that governments had the upper hand. For example, nations divided on whether to invite the People's Republic of China to the 1962 Asian Games or have Taiwan only attend, in a debate that was entrenched in official policies. Margaret Thatcher's endorsement of the 1980 American boycott of the Moscow Games, while permitting British teams to play in South Africa, was another example of state-dominated sport policies (not to mention rampant hypocrisy). And as Antonio Sotomayor notes, the Cold War permeated the Olympic Games when the subject of inviting communist Cubans arose and when a Cuban ship tried to bring a delegation of athletes into US waters off Puerto Rico in 1966, only to be greeted by both supporters and hostile exile groups. Again the politics of the games mirrored international politics.

But it is just as clear that sport operates at a different level, somewhat beyond the reach of governments. Note, for instance, that sport figures can actually attain a higher profile than world leaders. As Downes correctly, and ironically, writes, even prime ministers in the British Commonwealth were less recognizable to the public than sport heroes. While this also indicates a certain shallowness in public political discourse, it also reveals the utter significance of sport in everyday life at a gut emotional level, as well as at the highest reaches of diplomacy. Such transnational notables as tennis player Arthur Ashe, cricketeers from the West Indies, and even a surfer, Australian Tom Carroll, influenced the movement against apartheid. Leonid Brezhnev, Jimmy Carter, Eric Williams, Juan Perón, and other leaders might have held the podium, but Canadian hockey players, Cuban track stars, British soccer hooligans, and Soviet and American basketball players (and coaches) grabbed the headlines and attention of the masses in ways that compelled consideration by policymakers. Athletes rendered political movements—whether against apartheid or the Vietnam War (see Bill Walton or Muhammad Ali)—high-profile issues by speaking to nationalistic sentiments through the dramatic and visible means of sporting competitions. To be sure, international athletes could easily become pawns in the great game of power politics, and in the final analysis few became political champions like Ashe, Ali, and other stars. And all of them, essentially, wished simply to play their sports and compete; they were athletes first, and politics came second. But like Ali, they could—and still can—also forge out ahead of the crowd (and governments), making the links across borders that states try to obstruct. Thus, for instance, Ali called attention to Islam (as did the women from Saudi Arabia at the 2012 Summer Games), and the American sprinters in Mexico City spurred a dialogue about (and certainly much irritation and animosity toward) black nationalism.

Nonstate actors certainly have moved policymakers. Across the Caribbean, for instance, unions representing workers, teachers, and churches linked with the Southern Africa Liberation Committee to launch anti-apartheid campaigns. Nelson Mandela followed on an opposite track of engaging the National Party by seeking South Africa's readmittance to international cricket associations, using it as a tool to negotiate an end to the apartheid regime. Either way, transnationals played major roles—if not decisive ones—in international relations. As many of these essays posit, and Andrew Johns makes clear at the outset, sport competitions could be an extension of political relations between the two. They also indicated the ability of people—spectators, the masses—to build bridges by the sheer interest in sport, as well as nationalistic rooting for their countries' teams—to compel leaders to talk. Sport crossed these frontiers to make links on which officials then based diplomatic overtures. Such transnational exchanges did not necessarily end in happy outcomes. Restrictions on Muslims celebrating victories in India or British soccer fans' misbehavior can explode into international incidents (and even death). The infamous "soccer war" between Honduras and El Salvador in 1969 was the culmination of bilateral tensions resulting at least partially from transnational migration by workers seeking employment. Conflict over Kashmir was played out, in part, on cricket pitches. A resolution of international tensions through sport—and particularly by athletes—is a possibility but not always a happy or easy one.

Regardless of such tragedies, transnationalism matters. Ask the Soviets who greeted Bobby Hull in Moscow in 1976 during the era of détente. Or note that, as Nicholas Sarantakes explains, Jimmy Carter's plans for an alternative Olympic Games might have swayed some disappointed American athletes, but the public was apathetic or opposed to politicizing the event. Even in this highly charged atmosphere of superpower tensions, Olympic national committees, somewhat insulated from the state, rose above presidents and parliaments. The British decided to attend the Moscow Games regardless of the pressure from the House of Commons to boycott. The Games went on, an alternative did not materialize, and the Cold War did not entirely prevail over the people's desire to witness competition.

Come the era of modern-day globalization and the demise of the Cold War, the state's power became more tenuous. In an era of heightened fears of terrorism that required greater state involvement in securing sporting events such as the Olympics, the world economy and cultural ties nonetheless took precedence. The Olympics might still be public displays of national greatness, especially in the opening ceremonies, team competitions, and the silly country medal count, but even the oftentimes innocuous media coverage focuses on biographies of individual athletes. The athletes cross frontiers, and it is the state that gets in the way (note Mitt Romney's ill-timed appearance at the London Games in 2012), provoking such wonderment as to why nations cannot get along just as people do on the playing fields. The viewing publics clearly care much about play and hardly at all about disputes.

But there are the lamentations that speak to the importance of sport to societies and even to a country's global stature. When a nation or person does not win (and no country or athlete can hide behind a façade of being just good, because sport exposes a brutal reality: one triumphs or one loses, and there is no avoiding the ignominy of the latter), then there are often hand-wringing and recriminations. "We're never going to win as long as our youth is more interested in hot rods, television and fun," protested the head of the US Rowing Federation in 1960 when the Soviets had caught up in the Olympic medal count after years of American Cold War dominance. A softness had seemingly replaced a competitive streak, so much so that both Dwight Eisenhower and John Kennedy expanded physical fitness programs for all Americans but particularly children, to counter, as JFK warned, "the menace to our security" created by flaccidity and laziness. As historian Kathryn Jay argues, the United States needed to "prove on a world stage that a free society produced better athletes— stronger, more talented, more eager to win—than a communist society."[7] Did such muscle-flexing have international ramifications? Possibly, by bolstering morale or being a part of convincing the public to endorse a more masculine, aggressive foreign policy.[8]

One thought that arises regarding the focus on the Olympics is that today the real driver of sports (and, sadly, much of our politics) comes from profit-seeking, oftentimes predatory corporations and individuals. Thus, if I could expand this collection, I would include more work on professional sports. It is striking that there is little discussion of pay-for-play except in exhibitions. Of course, cricket, soccer, hockey, and other sports involve professionals, but in an era of globalization, the exchange of transnational athletes—and governance of them as well as their prominence—would seem to be a ripe field for historical and contemporary research.

For instance, how globalization merged with sport to affect international politics, economics, and cultural images demands attention. Much of the literature focuses only on the process of globalization itself, with little linkage to politics. Still, even in these studies, such issues as apartheid, the funneling of capital back into nations such as the Dominican Republic by baseball players, and the signing of top baseball players from

East Asia relate globalization to national identity (through branding, for example) and cultural diplomacy.[9]

The economics was clear as well. For instance, Florence Griffith-Joyner, or "Flo-Jo," a world-record-holding sprinter in the 1988 Olympics, appeared just as the Cold War was ending. She was so attractive, in her tight outfits and flashy long nails, that several sporting goods and other companies endorsed her, nicknaming her "Cash-Flo" for her ubiquitous marketing presence worldwide. Michael Jordan and then a host of skate-boarders, snowboarders, skaters, bikers, and other extreme-sports athletes, as well as basketball players from outside of the United States, joined the global feeding frenzy of sponsorships led by Nike and other companies. Professional soccer—the world game replete with high-priced, migratory stars—came to America (again) and this time stuck. Tennis marketed superstars such as the Williams sisters, just as Tiger Woods emerged as a worldwide golf phenom worth millions of dollars by the end of the 1990s. At the very least, sport was shown to be not so pure but a business propo-sition and a consumer item. At the most, professional sport, and even the Olympics, revealed the transformation in world politics wrought by the globalized economy that transcended international politics and made a memory of the Cold War era.[10]

There are marked absences from this anthology when it comes to indi-vidual sports, especially since such a minor pastime as surfing is included. To be sure, this is meant not as a criticism, for choices must be made, but to point out links to other sports that strengthen arguments made in these chapters and to direct readers to possible outlets for future re-search. Soccer does not receive its due, a surprising omission considering its worldwide following as the global game. The lack of attention to soccer is mystifying, particularly because the sport has been at the center of some diplomatic intrigues, national identities, business ties, and corporate glo-balization.[11] Perhaps because soccer has been so well researched, the edi-tors chose to focus on other sports and incidents. But another interesting exclusion from this volume, particularly for a sport that stretches across the amateur and professional ranks, includes transnational contacts, and has a long history of diplomatic ties, is baseball. Not explored in this col-lection (likely because it has been so heavily investigated elsewhere and did not have the global reach of the Olympics until recently), baseball nonetheless had close affiliations with international politics in many eras, including the Cold War, and reflected many of the themes of this volume. This is not to conclude, moreover, that it is the only (American) sport not studied in this collection; college football, for starters, was also steeped in Cold War politics, at least at home.[12] But with its long history that included outreach into Latin America and Asia, the (former) American national pastime connected intimately to diplomacy.

For instance, one author has implicated baseball for abetting imperialism since the late nineteenth century by promoting the American dream and way abroad, thus being a carrier of US economic, cultural, and, on occasion, military and national security interests. Baseball toed (and still does) the government line, like much of the American public, of jingoistic patriotism (as did American basketball fans, players, and coaches in almost every international appearance), get-tough foreign policies, the self-interested commodification of the sport, and the hegemonic lure of the best foreign players to American shores.[13] In addition, the local-international political nexus has been explored through the sport, such as in Taiwan and that nation's climb out of Japanese colonialism (which introduced the game).[14] Sophisticated treatments of borderlands history through baseball, likewise, have highlighted notions of imperialism, liberation movements, nationalism, Marxism, regionalism, economic integration, immigration, race, and consumerism—all relevant to diplomacy.[15] Just by itself, Japan has represented a cottage industry by showing the international reach of the game.[16] Archival research reveals how baseball reflected larger diplomatic concerns and issues of national identity with international culture and how the game's transpacific and bilateral networks disseminated, transnationally, values, business practices, politics, and peace and cooperation.[17] The results were profound, though not surprising. Americans grabbed Japanese stars, and Japan adopted US consumer values. The state was not always a determining factor, but baseball sometimes determined politics, especially by being a cultural agent of change.

Of course, although it is innovative in topics and scope, this collection cannot include every permutation of sport and diplomacy. The authors have, however, indicated an agenda for future research. Defections as a subject begs for a focused examination, as does religion, sport, and international politics, although a few essays here at least cursorily address both issues. Regarding religion, faith and sport, in global context, actually offer the basis for another collection by themselves.[18] Obviously the post–

World War II era provides the timeline for these essays, and although there are plenty of studies looking at particular issues (the Berlin Olympics and so forth) in the prewar period, an overview like this one covering, say, 1896 (the advent of the modern-day Olympics) to 1940, would be welcome.[19] Still, as Andrew Johns correctly notes in the introduction, the connections made by sport leaders to politics and foreign policy grew stronger and stronger in the post–World War II years. Of course, there needs to be more research to confirm this linkage and perhaps a means of prioritizing sports for leaders along with other factors they weigh and use in the diplomatic arena to make their points, such as national technological prowess and the like. Still, the point is well taken; the Cold War lends coherence to this volume but so would explorations of the Eurocentric world or technology and sport diplomacy in the earlier era. That said, the anthology provides much new information and analysis of sport and diplomacy, a roadmap for more research into untapped or understudied areas of the world when it comes to athletics, and a glimpse of how these fields, arenas, and waters of dreams translate into cultural agency and politics often at the highest reaches of the state.

## Notes

1. This is not a new assertion, as scholars in a variety of fields have already made the linkages of sport to diplomacy. This collection, however, focuses on the Cold War era and extends coverage beyond the European and American realms typically explored. See Jim Riordan and Arnd Kruger, *The International Politics of Sport in the 20th Century* (London: E & FN Spon, 1999). For an excellent companion to this volume (and one in which there is overlap of authors—Jenifer Parks and Evelyn Mertin), see Stephen Wagg and David L. Andrews, *East Plays West: Sport and the Cold War* (London: Routledge, 2007).

2. A forthcoming special issue of *Surveillance and Society* edited by David Murakami Wood and Nils Zurawski will address the topic of surveillance in sport.

3. George H. Sage, *Globalizing Sport: How Organizations, Corporations, Media, and Politics Are Changing Sports* (Boulder: Paradigm, 2010), 185, 213–14.

4. Indeed, studies have explored discrete periods, such as the interwar period, to tease out connections (and fill gaps) between societies, politics, and sports. In Pierre Arnaud and James Riordan, eds., *Sport and International Politics: The Impact of Fascism and Communism on Sport* (London: Taylor & Francis, 1998), for instance, the authors show how nations used sports as propaganda and psychological pressure instruments and how transnational entities such as the Catholic Church and worker

movements tried also to shape European and American responses to fascism and communism through sports.

5. But see several articles in the Wagg and Andrews collection, *East Plays West,* as well as Annette Muller, "Women in Sport and Society," and Arnd Kruger, "The Homosexual and Homoerotic in Sport," in Riordan and Kruger, eds., *The International Politics of Sport.*

6. Sage, *Globalizing Sport,* 203.

7. Kathryn Jay, *More Than Just a Game: Sports in American Life since 1945* (New York: Columbia University Press, 2004), 59, 60.

8. On Kennedy and a masculine foreign policy, see Robert D. Dean, *Imperial Brotherhood: Gender and the Making of Cold War Foreign Policy* (Amherst: University of Massachusetts Press, 2001), especially chap. 7.

9. See, for example, Alan M. Klein, *Growing the Game: The Globalization of Major League Baseball* (New Haven, CT: Yale University Press, 2006).

10. Jay, *More Than Just a Game,* 204, 219, 229–42.

11. See, for instance, Franklin Foer, *How Football Explains the World: An Unlikely Theory of Globalization* (New York: Harper Perennial, 2010).

12. See Kurt Edward Kemper, *College Football and American Culture in the Cold War Era* (Urbana: University of Illinois Press, 2009).

13. Robert Elias, *The Empire Strikes Out: How Baseball Sold U.S. Foreign Policy and Promoted the American Way Abroad* (New York: New Press, 2010).

14. Andrew Morris, "Taiwan: Baseball, Colonialism, and Nationalism," in *Baseball without Borders: The International Pastime,* ed. George Gmelch (Lincoln: University of Nebraska Press, 2006), 65–85. For similar experiences in Korea, see also Joseph A. Reaves, *Taking in a Game: A History of Baseball in Asia* (Lincoln: University of Nebraska Press, 2002), 117–20. In this case, missionaries were significant influences, as in other parts of Asia.

15. Alan M. Klein, *Baseball on the Border: A Tale of Two Laredos* (Princeton, NJ: Princeton University Press, 1997), especially 243–59.

16. The classic studies of Japan and baseball (and American influence on the rise of the sport in the country) are Robert Whiting's *The Chrysanthemum and the Bat: The Game Japanese Play* (Tokyo: Permanent Press, 1977) and *You Gotta Have Wa* (New York: Vintage, 1990). See also Robert Whiting, *The Meaning of Ichiro: The New Wave from Japan and the Transformation of Our National Pastime* (New York: Grand Central, 2004). The latter more directly addresses, but only touches on, diplomatic trends such as globalization.

17. Sayuri Guthrie-Shimizu, *Transpacific Field of Dreams: How Baseball Linked the United States and Japan in Peace and War* (Chapel Hill: University of North Carolina Press, 2012).

18. Although a good start is the brief essay by Swantje Scharenberg, "Religion and Sport," in Riordan and Kruger, eds., *The International Politics of Sport.*

19. See Peter J. Beck, *Scoring for Britain: International Football and International*

*Politics, 1900–1939* (London: Frank Cass, 1999), and Barbara Keys, *Globalizing Sport: National Rivalry and International Community in the 1930s* (Cambridge, MA: Harvard University Press, 2006), two of the earliest, and few, explorations of sport and diplomacy before World War II.

# Acknowledgments

This project began during a conversation at the book exhibit at the American Historical Association conference in San Diego in January 2010. We ran into each other unexpectedly for the first time in two years, and in the course of catching up and talking about college football, we had an epiphany and decided to collaborate on an edited volume that would bring together our research fields.

Over the past three years, we have been fortunate to work with a number of talented scholars as this anthology evolved. The contributors to the volume—Pascal Charitas, Aviston Downes, Fan Hong, Scott Laderman, Evelyn Mertin, Jenifer Parks, Nick Sarantakes, John Soares, Antonio Sotomayor, Cesar Torres, Wanda Wakefield, Kevin Witherspoon, Tom Zeiler, and Lu Zhouxiang—have been great to work with, and it is to them that we owe the success of this collection. The research exemplified in the essays demonstrates the best combination of international and multiarchival history from scholars representing Argentina, Australia, Barbados, China, France, Germany, Ireland, Puerto Rico, and the United States. We express our heartfelt gratitude to all of them for their exceptional work in helping to make this book a reality.

In addition, we appreciate the assistance, advice, and support—both tangible (with feedback on essays, assistance with sources, translations, and ideas) and intangible—we received along the way from friends, family, colleagues, and archivists, including Jessica Chapman, Brian Etheridge, Sayuri Guthrie-Shimizu, Andrew Johnstone, Debralyn Muscato, Guy Nasuti, Jason Parker, Kelsey Piel, Laura Sims, Andrew Skabelund, Kathryn Statler, Sarah Teetzel, Dustin Walcher, and Christopher Young.

Our sincere thanks also go out to Steve Wrinn, the outstanding director of the University Press of Kentucky who is an even better friend. Steve has been enthusiastic about this project literally since its inception—the original discussion about the project actually took place at the UPK book display—and he has been unfailingly supportive of our efforts ever since.

We could not ask for a better, more professional, and more collegial experience than we have had with UPK, and we want to express our gratitude to Allison Webster, David Cobb, Don McKeon, Mack McCormick, Amy Harris, and the rest of the production, editing, and publicity team at the press for all of their expertise and assistance in bringing the volume to publication in the Studies in Conflict, Diplomacy, and Peace series. Thanks as well to the general editors of the series, George Herring and Kathryn Statler, for their confidence in the project and for including it in what is really a terrific series.

We also thank the anonymous reviewers who worked with UPK for their careful reading of earlier versions of the manuscript. Their cogent comments and insightful suggestions improved the volume significantly, and we very much appreciate their contributions to the final manuscript.

Portions of the essay by Nicholas Sarantakes were derived from material that was published originally in his book *Dropping the Torch: Jimmy Carter, the Olympic Boycott, and the Cold War* (2009) and appear here with permission of the publisher. In addition, portions of the essay by Aviston Downes were derived from material that was published originally in "Sport and International Diplomacy: The Case of the Commonwealth Caribbean and the Anti-Apartheid Campaign, 1959–1992," *The Sports Historian* 22, no. 2 (November 2002): 23–45, and appear here with permission of the publisher. We are grateful to both Cambridge University Press and the British Society for Sports History for their generosity.

Finally, dedications from both of the editors:

**AJ**: This book is dedicated to my children, Mitch, Jenna, and Matthew. All three inherited my love of (and obsession with) sports, if not my interest in the history of US foreign relations. Mitch is a sports journalism major who is almost as fanatical about sports as I am—he has been playing and watching sports ever since he was six days old and experienced his first Super Bowl. Jenna excels at volleyball, and she and her Pleasant Grove Vikings teammates (including the rest of the class of 2014 with whom she has played for seven years: Phoebe, Meagan, Stacey, Rachel, Brisa, Ashli, and Madison) won the 2012 and 2013 Utah state high school 5A championships. Matthew loves ESPN, manages the PG high school baseball team, and is the world's biggest New York Yankees fan despite my best efforts to get him to like the Cincinnati Reds. They have grown up far too quickly, but every day they make me proud and humble to be their father.

**HD**: This book is dedicated to Rudi Lindner, who has been a wonderful mentor. Rudi guided my class through the history honors program at the University of Michigan—although I am sure at the time he did not realize how many years of guidance he would actually be providing me. Rudi encouraged me to continue to pursue my interest in sport history, regardless of the challenges I faced. I am incredibly grateful for his support and advice all these years.

# Selected Bibliography

Abelson, Donald E. "Politics on Ice: The United States, the Soviet Union, and a Hockey Game in Lake Placid." *Canadian Review of American Studies* 40, no. 1 (2010): 63–94.

Abrams, Lynn. *Oral History Theory.* New York and London: Routledge, 2010.

Ageron, Charles-Robert, and Marc Michel, eds. *L'ère des décolonisations.* Actes du Colloque d'Aix-en-Provence, CNRS. Paris: Karthala, 1995.

Alabarces, Pablo. *Fútbol y patria: El fútbol y las narrativas de la nación en Argentina.* Buenos Aires: Prometeo, 2002.

Alegi, Peter. *African Soccerscapes: How a Continent Changed the World's Game.* Athens: Ohio University Press, 2010.

———. *Laduma! Soccer, Politics and Society in South Africa.* Scottsville, SA: University of KwaZulu-Natal Press, 2004.

Allain, Jean-Claude, Pierre Guillen, Georges-Henri Soutou, Laurent Theis, and Maurice Vaïsse. *Histoire de la diplomatie française: Tome 2, de 1815 à nos jours.* Paris: Librairie Académique Perrin, 2007.

Allen, E. John B. *The Culture and Sport of Skiing: From Antiquity to World War II.* Amherst: University of Massachusetts Press, 2007.

Allen, Kevin. *USA Hockey: A Celebration of a Great Tradition.* Chicago: Triumph Books, 1997.

Allison, Lincoln. *The Changing Politics of Sport.* Manchester: Manchester University Press, 1993.

———, ed., *The Global Politics of Sport: The Role of Global Institutions in Sport.* London: Routledge, 2005.

Al-Tauqi, Mansour S. "Solidarité Olympique: Ordre global et diffusion du sport moderne entre 1961 et 1980." PhD diss., Loughborough University, 2003.

Andrews, David L., and Ben Carrington, eds. *A Companion to Sport.* Hoboken, NJ: Wiley-Blackwell, 2013.

Anwar, Dewi Fortuna. "Indonesia and the Bandung Conference: Then and Now." In *Bandung Revisited: The Legacy of the 1955 Asian-African Conference for International Order*, edited by See Seng Tan and Amitav Acharya, 180–97. Singapore: National University of Singapore Press, 2008.

Archer, Robert, and Antoine Bouillon. *The South African Game: Sport and Racism.* London: Zed Press, 1982.

Arnaud, Pierre, and James Riordan, eds. *Sport and International Politics: Impact of Fascism and Communism on Sport.* London and New York: E & FN Spon, 1998.

Arndt, Richard T. *The First Resort of Kings: American Cultural Diplomacy in the Twentieth Century.* Washington, DC: Potomac Books, 2005.

Aron, Raymond. *Paix et guerre entre les nations.* Paris: Calmann-Lévy, 1962.

Atiles Osoria, José M. "Pro-State Violence in Puerto Rico: Cuban and Puerto Rican Right-Wing Terrorism from the 1960s to the 1990s." *Socialism and Democracy* 26, no. 1 (March 2012): 127–42.

Augustin, Jean-Pierre, and Pascal Gillon. *L'Olympisme: Bilan et enjeux géopolitique.* Paris: Armand Colin, 2004.

Ayache, Georges. "Puissance et influence dans le cadre des relations internationales post–guerre froide: Le cas de la France." *Annuaire français de relations internationales* 7 (2006): 384–98.

Ayala, Cesar J., and Rafael Bernabe. *Puerto Rico in the American Century: A History since 1898.* Chapel Hill: University of North Carolina Press, 2007.

Balbier, Uta A. *Kalter Krieg auf der Aschenbahn: Der deutsch-deutsche Sport, 1950– 1972; Eine politische Geschichte.* Paderborn: F. Schöning, 2007.

Bale, John, and Mike Cronin. *Sport and Postcolonialism.* Oxford: Berg, 2003.

Bancel, Nicolas. *Entre acculturation et révolution: Mouvements de jeunesse et sports dans l'évolution politique et institutionnelle de l'AOF (1945–1962).* PhD diss., University of Paris I–Sorbonne, 1999.

Bancel, Nicolas, Pascal Blanchard, and Françoise Vergès. *La République coloniale.* Paris: Hachette Littératures, 2006.

Barghoorn, Frederick C. *The Soviet Cultural Offensive: The Role of Cultural Diplomacy in Soviet Foreign Policy.* Princeton, NJ: Princeton University Press, 1960.

Bark, Dennis L., and David R. Gress. *A History of West Germany: Vol. 1, From Shadow to Substance, 1945–1963.* Oxford: Basil Blackwell, 1989.

———. *A History of West Germany: Vol. 2, Democracy and Its Discontents, 1963– 1988.* Oxford: Basil Blackwell, 1989.

Barton, Susan. *Healthy Living in the Alps: The Origins of Winter Tourism in Switzerland, 1860–1914.* Manchester: Manchester University Press, 2008.

Baumann, Robert F. "The Central Army Sports Club (TsSKA): Forging a Military Tradition in Soviet Ice Hockey." *Journal of Sport History* 15 (1988): 151–66.

Bazenguissa-Ganga, Rémy. *Les voies du politique au Congo.* Paris: Karthala, 1997.

Beacom, Aaron. *International Diplomacy and the Olympic Movement: The New Mediators.* New York: Palgrave Macmillan, 2012.

Beamish, Rob, and Ian Ritchie. *Fastest, Highest, Strongest: A Critique of High-Performance Sport.* London: Routledge, 2006.

Beck, Peter. *Scoring for Britain: International Football and International Politics, 1900–1939.* London: Frank Cass, 1999.

Beckles, Hilary. *The Development of West Indies Cricket: Vol. 1, The Age of Nationalism.* Kingston: University of the West Indies Press, 1998.

Bélanger, Louis. "Redefining Cultural Diplomacy: Cultural Security and Foreign Policy in Canada." *Political Psychology* 20 (1999): 677–99.

Belmonte, Laura A. *Selling the American Way: U.S. Propaganda and the Cold War.* Philadelphia: University of Pennsylvania Press, 2008.

Bischof, Günter, Anton Pelinka, and Dieter Stiefel, eds., *The Marshall Plan in Austria.* New Brunswick, NJ: Transaction, 2000.

Blasius, Tobias. *Olympische Bewegung, Kalter Krieg und Deutschlandpolitik 1949–1972.* Frankfurt a.M.: Lang, 2001.

Bolland, Nigel. *On the March: Labour Relations in the British Caribbean, 1934–39.* Kingston: Ian Randle, 1995.

Bollsmann, Chris. "Mexico 1968 and South Africa 2010: Sombreros and Vuvuzelas and the Legitimisation of Global Sporting Events." *Bulletin of Latin American Research* 29 (2010): 93–106.

Booth, Douglas. "Accommodating Race to Play the Game: South Africa's Readmission to International Sport." *Sporting Traditions* 8, no. 2 (1992): 182–209.

———. "Hitting Apartheid for Six? The Politics of the South African Sports Boycott." *Journal of Contemporary History* 38, no. 3 (July 2003): 477–93.

———. *The Race Game: Sport and Politics in South Africa.* London: Frank Cass, 1998.

———. "United Sport: An Alternative Hegemony in South Africa." *International Journal of the History of Sport* 12, no. 3 (December 1995): 105–24.

Bose, Mihir. *A History of Indian Cricket.* London: Andre Deutsch, 1990.

———. *Sporting Colours: Sport and Politics in South Africa.* London: Robson Books, 1994.

Bouche, Denise. "L'ouverture de l'Afrique occidentale au monde extérieur: La fin de l'Empire et l'échec de l'Union française." *Relations internationales* 34 (Summer 1983): 173–85.

Braillard, Philippe. *Mythe et réalité du non alignement.* Paris: PUF, 1987.

Brennan, James. *Peronism and Argentina.* Wilmington, DE: Scholarly Resources, 1998.

Brewster, Mike, and Taps Gallagher. *Stolen Glory: The U.S., the Soviet Union, and the Olympic Basketball Game That Never Ended.* Los Angeles: G. M. Books, 2012.

Brokhin, Yuri. *The Big Red Machine: The Rise and Fall of Soviet Olympic Champions.* New York: Random House, 1978.

Brzezinski, Zbigniew. *Power and Principle: Memoirs of the National Security Advisor, 1977–1981.* New York: Farrar, Straus and Giroux, 1983.

Buckel, Bart. "Nationalism, Mass Politics, and Sport: Cold War Case Studies at Seven Degrees." Unpublished thesis. Naval Postgraduate School, Monterey, CA, 2008.

Buss, Wolfgang. "(Sport)politisch-historischer Handlungsrahmen." In *Der Sport in der SBZ und frühen DDR: Genese—Strukturen—Bedingungen*, edited by Wolfgang Buss and Christian Becker, 110–63. Schorndorf: Hofmann 2001.

Cane, James. *The Fourth Enemy: Journalism and Power in the Making of Peronist Argentina, 1930–1955.* University Park: Pennsylvania State University Press, 2011.

Cantelon, Hart, and Michael Letters. "The Making of the IOC Environmental Policy as the Third Dimension of the Olympic Movement." *International Review for the Sociology of Sport* 35 (2000): 294–308.

Caraccioli, Tom, and Jerry Caraccioli. *Boycott: Stolen Dreams of the 1980 Moscow Olympic Games.* Washington, DC: New Chapter Press, 2008.

———. *Striking Silver: The Untold Story of America's Forgotten Hockey Team.* Champaign, IL: Sports Publishing, 2006.

Carafano, James Jay. "The Occupation of Germany, Austria, Trieste, Japan, Okinawa and Korea." In *Companion to American Military History, Vol. II,* edited by James C. Bradford, 564–71. Malden, MA: Wiley-Blackwell, 2010.

———. *Waltzing into the Cold War: The Struggle for Occupied Austria.* College Station: Texas A&M University Press, 2002.

Carr, G. A. "The Involvement of Politics in the Sporting Relationships of East and West Germany, 1945–1972." *Journal of Sport History* 7, no. 1 (1980): 40–51.

Carroll, Tom, and Kirk Willcox. *The Wave Within.* Sydney: Ironbark, 1994.

Carter, Jimmy. *Keeping Faith: Memoirs of a President.* New York: Bantam, 1982.

———. *White House Diary.* New York: Farrar, Strauss and Giroux, 2010.

Caute, David. *The Dancer Defects: The Struggle for Cultural Supremacy during the Cold War.* Oxford: Oxford University Press, 2005.

Cha, Victor D. *Beyond the Final Score. The Politics of Sport in Asia.* New York: Columbia University Press, 2009.

Chaliand, Gérard. *L'enjeu africain: Stratégies des puissances.* Paris: Seuil, 1980.

Charitas, Pascal. "Anglophone Africa in the Olympic Movement: The Confirmation of a British Wager (1948–1962)." *African Research and Documentation* 116 (2011): 35–52.

———. "La Commission d'Aide Internationale Olympique (CAIO): Un instrument de propagande soviétique? (1951–1962)." *Sport History Review* 40 (2009): 143–66.

———. "L'Afrique au mouvement olympique: Enjeux, stratégies et influences de la France dans l'internationalisation du sport africain (1944–1966)." PhD diss., University of Paris–South, 2010.

———. "Les conditions d'émergence du développement sportif olympique: Comparaison entre la France et le Royaume-Uni (1944–1966)." Postgraduate fellowship report, OSC-IOC, Lausanne, 2009.

Charitas, Pascal, and Yann Drouet. "La Commission d'Aide Internationale Olympique (CAIO): Nécessité d'un nouveau médiateur entre la France et l'Afrique noire? (1960–1963)." *Stadion* 33, no. 2 (2008): 207–28.

Charitas, Pascal, and David-Claude Kemo-Keimbou. "The United States of America and the Francophone African Countries at the International Olympic Committee (IOC): Sports Aid, a Barometer of American Imperialism? (1952–1963)." *Journal of Sport History* 40 no. 1 (2013): 69–91.

Châtaignier, Jean-Marc. "Principes et réalités de la politique africaine de la France." *Afrique contemporaine* 220, no. 4 (2006): 247–61.

Chatterjee, Partha. *The Nation and Its Fragments: Colonial and Postcolonial Histories.* Princeton, NJ: Princeton University Press, 1993.

Chatziefstathiou, Dikaia. "The Changing Nature of the Ideology of Olympism in the Modern Olympic Era." PhD diss., University of Loughborough, 2005.

———. *The Diffusion of Olympic Sport through Regional Games: A Comparison of the Pre– and Post–Second War Contexts.* Lausanne: International Olympic Committee, 2008.

Chatziefstathiou, Dikaia, Ian Henry, Mansour Al-Tauqi, and Eleni Theodoraki. "Cultural Imperialism and the Diffusion of Olympic Sport in Africa: A Comparison of Pre– and Post–Second World War Contexts." In *Olympic Studies Reader*, edited by H. Ren and L. Dacosta, 111–28. Barcelona: Centre d'Estudis Olímpics, 2008.

Chehabi, H. E. "Sport Diplomacy between the United States and Iran." *Diplomacy & Statecraft* 12, no. 1 (2001): 89–106.

Childs, David. "The German Democratic Republic." In *Sport under Communism: The U.S.S.R., Czechoslovakia, the G.D.R., China, Cuba,* 2nd ed., rev., edited by James Riordan, 67–101. London: C. Hurst, 1981.

Cisneros, Andrés, and Carlos Escudé. *Historia general de las relaciones exteriores de la República Argentina*, 16 vols. Buenos Aires: Grupo Editor Latinoamericano, 1999.

Clapham, Christopher. *Africa and the International System: The Politics of State Survival.* New York: Cambridge University Press, 1996.

Cocanour, Spencer C. "Sports: A Tool for International Relations." Thesis, Air Command and Staff College, Air University, 2007.

Cohen, G. Daniel. "Between Relief and Politics: Refugee Humanitarianism in Occupied Germany, 1945–1946." *Journal of Contemporary History* 43, no. 3 (2008): 437–49.

Cohen, Gerald Leonard. *In War's Wake: Europe's Displaced Persons in the Postwar Order.* Oxford: Oxford University Press, 2012.

Colvin, Milton. "Principal Issues in the U.S. Occupation of Austria, 1945–1948." In *U.S. Occupation in Europe after World War II*, edited by Hans Schmitt, 103–25. Lawrence: University Press of Kansas, 1978.

Combeau-Mari, Evelyne. "Colonial Sport in Madagascar, 1896–1960." *International Journal of the History of Sport* 28, no. 12 (2011): 1557–729.

Comité Olímpico Argentino. *Olimpismo: Historia y Proyección.* Buenos Aires: Servicios Informativos Parlamentarios Argentinos, 1997.

Conacher, Brian. *Hockey in Canada: The Way It Is!* Toronto: Gateway, 1970.

Conil Paz, Alberto, and Gustavo Ferrari. *Argentina's Foreign Policy, 1930–1962.* Translated by John J. Kennedy. Notre Dame, IN: University of Notre Dame Press, 1966.

Cornelissen, Scarlett. "'It's Africa's Turn!': The Narratives and Legitimations Surrounding the Moroccan and South African Bids for the 2006 and 2010 FIFA Finals." *Third World Quarterly* 25, no. 7 (2000): 1293–309.

Corthon, Paul. "The Cold War and British Debates over the Boycott of the 1980 Moscow Olympics." *Cold War History* 13, no. 1 (2013): 43–66.

Cowan, Geoffrey, and Nicholas J. Cull. "Preface: Public Diplomacy in a Changing World." *The Annals of the American Academy of Political and Social Science* 616 (March 2008): 6–8.

Cozier, Tony. "West Indian Contretemps." In *Cricket in Isolation: The Politics of Race and Cricket in South Africa*, edited by André Odendaal. Cape Town: The Editor, 1977.

Crawford, Russ. *The Use of Sports to Promote the American Way of Life during the Cold War: Cultural Propaganda, 1945–1963.* Lewiston, NY: Edwin Mellen, 2008.

Cribb, Robert. "Unresolved Problems in the Indonesian Killings of 1965–1966." *Asian Survey* 42, no. 4 (2002): 550–63.

Critchlow, James. "Public Diplomacy during the Cold War: The Record and Its Implications." *Journal of Cold War Studies* 6, no. 1 (Winter 2004): 75–89.

Cull, Nicholas J. *The Cold War and the United States Information Agency: American Propaganda and Public Diplomacy, 1945–1989.* New York: Cambridge University Press, 2008.

———. "Public Diplomacy: Taxonomies and Histories." *The Annals of the American Academy of Political and Social Science* 616 (2008): 31–54.

Cunningham, Carson. *American Hoops: U.S. Men's Olympic Basketball from Berlin to Beijing.* Lincoln: University of Nebraska Press, 2009.

Dallek, Robert. *The American Style of Foreign Policy: Cultural Politics and Foreign Affairs.* New York: Oxford University Press, 1983.

Darby, Paul. "Africa and the 'World' Cup: FIFA Politics, Eurocentrism and Resistance." *International Journal of the History of Sport* 22, no. 5 (September 2005): 883–905.

Darwin, John. "Was There a Fourth British Empire?" In *The British Empire in the 1950s: Retreat or Revival?*, edited by Lynn Martin, 16–31. Basingstoke: Palgrave, 2006.

de Almedia Lico, Flavio, and Katia Rubio. "The Brazilian Position Considering the Boycott of the 1980 Moscow Olympic Games." In *Olympia als Bildungsidee: Beiträge zur Olympischen Geschichte und Pädogogik*, edited by Annette R. Hofmann and Michael Krüger, 113–31. Wiesbaden: Springer Fachmedian Wiesbaden, 2013.

Dean, Robert D. *Imperial Brotherhood: Gender and the Making of Cold War Foreign Policy.* Amherst: University of Massachusetts Press, 2001.

de Ípola, Emilio. "Ruptura y continuidad: Claves parciales para un balance de las interpretaciones del peronismo." *Desarrollo Económico* 29, no. 115 (1989): 331–59.

Del Pero, Mario. "On the Limits of Thomas Zeiler's Historiographical Triumphalism." *Journal of American History* 95, no. 4 (March 2009): 1079–82.

Denault, Todd. *The Greatest Game: The Montreal Canadiens, the Red Army and the Night That Saved Hockey.* Toronto: McClelland & Stewart, 2011.

Deville-Danthu, Bernadette. *Le Sport en noir et blanc: Du sport colonial au sport africain dans les anciens territoires français d'Afrique occidentale (1920–1965).* Paris: L'Harmattan, 1997.

Diamond, Dan, ed. *Total Hockey: The Official Encyclopedia of the National Hockey League,* 2nd ed. New York: Total Sports, 2000.

Dichter, Heather. "'Strict Measures Must Be Taken': Wartime Planning and the Allied Control of Sport in Occupied Germany." *Stadion* 34, no. 2 (2008): 193–217.

Dietz, James. *The Economic History of Puerto Rico: Institutional Change and Capitalist Development.* Princeton, NJ: Princeton University Press, 1986.

Di Giano, Roberto, and Marcelo Massarino. "El peronismo y los deportes profesionales." In *El pensamiento alternativo en la Argentina del siglo XX*, 2 vols., edited by Hugo E. Biagini and Arturo A. Roig, 457–63. Buenos Aires: Biblos, 2006.

Dimeo, Paul. *A History of Drug Use in Sport 1876–1976.* London: Routledge, 2007.

Ding, Bo. *The Battle against Imperialism and Colonialism.* Zhengzhou: Henan People's Press, 1957.

Dizard, Wilson P., Jr. *Inventing Public Diplomacy: The Story of the U.S. Information Agency.* Boulder, CO: Lynne Rienner, 2004.

*Do You Believe in Miracles? The Story of the 1980 U.S. Hockey Team.* Documentary produced by Brian Hyland. HBO Home Video, 2001.

D'Oliveira, Basil. *The D'Oliveira Affair.* London: Collins, 1969.

Dorn, Glenn J. "'Bradenism' and Beyond: Argentine Anti-Americanism, 1945–1953." In *Anti-Americanism in Latin America and the Caribbean*, edited by Alan McPherson, 61–83. New York: Berghahn Books, 2006.

Downes, Aviston. "Flannelled Fools? Cricket and the Political Economy of the British West Indies, c. 1985–1906." *International Journal of the History of Sport* 17, no. 4 (December 2000): 59–80.

———. "From Boys to Men: Colonial Education, Cricket and Masculinity in the Caribbean, 1870–c.1920." *International Journal of the History of Sport* 22, no. 1 (2005): 3–21.

———. "Sport and International Diplomacy: The Case of the Commonwealth Caribbean and the Anti-Apartheid Campaign, 1959–1992." *The Sports Historian* 22, no. 2 (November 2002): 23–45.

Dryden, Ken. *The Game: 20th Anniversary Edition.* Toronto: J. Wiley, 2005.

Dubček, Alexander. *Hope Dies Last: The Autobiography of Alexander Dubček.* Edited and translated by Jiri Hochman. New York: Kodansha International, 1993.

Dubois, Laurent. *Soccer Empire: The World Cup and the Future of France.* Berkeley: University of California Press, 2010.

Duignan, Peter, and L. H. Gann. *The United States and Africa: A History.* New York: Cambridge University Press, 1987.

Durand, Pierre-Michel. "Alliance objective, méfiances réciproques: Les Etats-Unis, la France et l'Afrique noire dans les années soixante." PhD diss., University of Paris III–Sorbonne Nouvelle, 2003.

Duroselle, Jean-Baptiste. "Opinion, attitude, mentalité, mythe, idéologie: Essai de clarification." *Relations internationales* 2 (November 1974): 3–23.

Durpaire, François. *Les États-Unis: Ont-ils décolonisé l'Afrique noire francophone?* Paris: L'Harmattan, Études Africaines, 2005.

Dyreson, Mark. *Making the American Team: Sport, Culture, and the Olympic Experience.* Urbana: University of Illinois Press, 1998.

———. "Mapping Sport History and the History of Sport in Europe." *Journal of Sport History* 38, no. 3 (Fall 2011): 397–405.

Eckert, Horst, and Ernst Martini. *90: IIHF 90th Anniversary, 1908–1998.* Zürich: IIHF, 1998.

Edelman, Robert. *Serious Fun: A History of Spectator Sports in the USSR.* New York: Oxford University Press, 1993.

———. "A Small Way of Saying 'No': Moscow Working Men, Spartak Soccer, and the Communist Party, 1900–1945." *American Historical Review* 107, no. 5 (2002): 1441–74.

———. *Spartak Moscow: A History of the People's Team in the Workers' State.* Ithaca, NY: Cornell University Press, 2009.

Edmonds, David, and John Eidinow. *Bobby Fischer Goes to War: How a Lone American Star Defeated the Soviet Chess Machine.* New York: HarperCollins, 2004.

Eichengreen, Barry. *The European Economy since 1945: Coordinated Capitalism and Beyond.* Princeton, NJ: Princeton University Press, 2006.

Eke, Viktor Kalu. "Soviet-African Relations: A Critique of the Moving Forces." In *The Soviet Union in World Politics: The Global Significance of the USSR and Issues in Soviet-African Relations,* edited by Viktor Kalu Eke, 89–110. Nigeria: Fourth Dimension, 1988.

Elias, Robert. *The Empire Strikes Out: How Baseball Sold U.S. Foreign Policy and Promoted the American Way Abroad.* New York: The New Press, 2010.

Elzey, Chris. "Cold War on the Court: The 1973 American-Soviet Basketball Series." North American Society for Sport History. http://library.la84.org/SportsLibrary/NASSH_Proceedings/NP2000/NP2000o.pdf. Accessed June 10, 2012.

Elzey, Christopher Clark. "Munich 1972: Sport, Politics, and Tragedy." Ph.D. diss., Purdue University, 2004.

Endy, Christopher. *Cold War Holidays: American Tourism in France.* Chapel Hill: University of North Carolina Press, 2004.

Escudé, Carlos. *Gran Bretaña, Estados Unidos y la declinación argentina, 1942–1949.* Buenos Aires: Editorial de Belgrano, 1983.

Espagne, Michel. *Les transferts culturels franco-allemands.* Paris: PUF, 1999.

Espy, Richard. *The Politics of the Olympic Games.* Berkeley: University of California Press, 1979.

Ewald, Manfred, and Reinhold Andert. *Manfred Ewald—Ich war der Sport: Wahrheiten und Legenden aus dem Wunderland der Sieger.* Berlin: Elefanten, 1994.

Fair, Laura. "Kickin' It: Leisure, Politics and Football in Colonial Zanzibar, 1900s–1950s." *Africa* 67, no. 2 (1997): 224–51.

Faria, Norman. *Sports and Apartheid: Caribbean Sports People and the Boycott of South Africa.* St. Michael, Barbados: South African Liberation Committee, 1983.

Fauriol, Georges A. *Foreign Policy Behaviour of Caribbean States: Guyana, Haiti, and Jamaica.* Lanham, MD: University Press of America, 1984.

Feinstein, Margarete Myers. *State Symbols: The Quest for Legitimacy in the Federal Republic of Germany and the German Democratic Republic, 1949–1959.* Boston: Brill, 2001.

Fernández Moores, Ezequiel. *Breve historia del deporte argentino.* Buenos Aires: Editorial El Ateneo, 2010.

Finney, Patrick, ed. *Palgrave Advances in International History.* Basingstoke: Palgrave Macmillan, 2005.

Fitts, Robert K. *Banzai Babe Ruth: Baseball, Espionage, and Assassination during the 1934 Tour of Japan.* Lincoln: University of Nebraska Press, 2012.

Foer, Franklin. *How Football Explains the World: An Unlikely Theory of Globalization.* New York: Harper Perennial, 2010.

Fontaine, André. *La guerre froide, 1917–1991.* Paris: La Martinière, 2006.

Forrest, Lisa. *Boycott: Australia's Controversial Road to the 1980 Moscow Olympics.* Sydney: ABC Books, 2008.

Frank, Robert. "Introduction." *Relations internationales* 115 (Autumn 2003): 325–48.

Frascara, Félix D. "Deportes." In *Argentina, 1930–1960*, edited by Jorge A. Paita, 374–82. Buenos Aires: Sur, 1961.

Frenkiel, Stanislas, and David-Claude Kémo-Keimbou. "La mission FFA/L'Auto: 'Pourquoi négliger nos noirs d'Afrique?' (December 3, 1937–January 15, 1938)." *Modern & Contemporary France* 18, no. 1 (2010): 33–50.

Fu, Yannong, ed. *The History of Sport in China*, vol. 5, *1949–1979.* Beijing: People's Sport Press, 2007.

Fulcher, Kara Stibora. "A Sustainable Position? The United States, the Federal Republic, and the Ossification of Allied Policy on Germany, 1958–1962." *Diplomatic History* 26, no. 2 (Spring 2002): 283–307.

Fumanti, Mattia. "Burying E.S.: Educated Elites, Subjectivity and Distinction in Rundu, Namibia." *Journal of Southern African Studies* 33 (2007): 469–83.

Fursenki, Aleksandr, and Timothy Naftali. *One Hell of a Gamble: Khrushchev, Castro, and Kennedy, 1958–1964: The Secret History of the Cuban Missile Crisis.* New York: Norton, 1998.

Gaddis, John Lewis. *The Cold War: A New History.* New York: Penguin, 2005.

———. *Strategies of Containment: A Critical Appraisal of American National Security Policy during the Cold War.* Revised and expanded edition. New York: Oxford University Press, 2005.

Galiani, Sebastián, and Pablo Gerchunoff. "The Labor Market." In *A New Economic History of Argentina*, edited by Gerardo della Paolera and Alan M. Taylor, 122–69. New York: Cambridge University Press, 2003.

Gallup, Stephen. *A History of the Salzburg Festival.* London: Weidenfield & Nicolson, 1987.

Galtung, Johan. "A Structural Theory of Imperialism?" In *Perspectives on World Politics*, edited by Richard Little and Michael Smith, 233–41. New York: Routledge, 1991.

Gems, Gerald R. *The Athletic Crusade: Sport and American Cultural Imperialism.* Lincoln: University of Nebraska Press, 2006.

Gené, Marcela. *Un mundo feliz: Imágenes de los trabajadores en el primer peronismo, 1946–1955.* Buenos Aires: Fondo de Cultura Economica, 2005.

Geyer, Martin H. "On the Road to a German 'Postnationalism'? Athletic Competition between the Two German States in the Era of Konrad Adenauer." *German Politics and Society* 25, no. 2 (2007): 140–67.

Gienow-Hecht, Jessica. *Transmission Impossible: American Journalism as Cultural Diplomacy in Postwar Germany.* Baton Rouge: Louisiana State University Press, 1999.

Gienow-Hecht, Jessica C. E. "What Bandwagon? Diplomatic History Today." *Journal of American History* 95, no. 4 (March 2009): 1083–86.

Gienow-Hecht, Jessica C. E., and Mark C. Donfried. *Searching for a Cultural Diplomacy.* New York: Berghahn Books, 2010.

Gilboa, Eytan. "Searching for a Theory of Public Diplomacy." *The Annals of the American Academy of Political and Social Science* 616 (2008): 55–77.

Gillingham, John. *Coal, Steel and the Rebirth of Europe, 1945–1955: The Germans and French from the Ruhr Conflict to the Economic Community.* New York: Cambridge University Press, 2005.

Gilpin, Robert. *War and Change in World Politics.* New York: Cambridge University Press, 1981.

Girard, René. *Le bouc-émissaire.* Paris: Le Livre de Poche, 1986.

Gmelch, George, ed. *Baseball without Borders: The International Pastime.* Lincoln: University of Nebraska Press, 2006.

Gobarev, Iktor M. "Soviet Policy toward China: Developing Nuclear Weapons 1949–1969." *Journal of Slavic Military Studies* 12, no. 4 (1999): 43–47.

Gold, John R., and Margaret M. Gold, eds. *Olympic Cities: City Agendas, Planning, and the World's Games, 1896–2016*, 2nd ed. London: Routledge, 2011.

Gouda, Souaïbou. "Etats, sports et politiques en Afrique noire francophone: Cas du Bénin, du Congo, du Niger, et du Sénégal." PhD diss., University of Grenoble 1, 1997.

Gray, William Glenn. *Germany's Cold War: The Global Campaign to Isolate East Germany, 1949–1969.* Chapel Hill: University of North Carolina Press, 2003.

Greenhorn, Donna, and David Black. *Sport and Canadian Diplomacy.* Montreal: McGill-Queen's University Press, 1994.

Grimshaw, Anna, and C. L. R. James. *Cricket.* London: Allison & Busby, 1986.

Gripentrog, John. "The Transnational Pastime: Baseball and American Perceptions of Japan in the 1930s." *Diplomatic History* 34, no. 2 (2010): 247–73.

Gu, Yu. "Huang Zhong's Memory: Premier Zhou and the GANEFO." *Sports Culture Guide* 1 (1986): 4–7.

Guelke, Adrian. "The Politicisation of South African Sport." In *The Politics of Sport*, edited by Lincoln Allison, 118–48. Manchester: Manchester University Press, 1986.

———. "Sport and the End of Apartheid." In Allison, *Changing Politics of Sport*, 151–70

Guoqi, Xu. *Olympic Dreams: China and Sports, 1895–2008*. Cambridge, MA: Harvard University Press, 2008.

Guthrie-Shimizu, Sayuri. "For Love of the Game: Baseball in Early U.S.-Japanese Encounters and the Rise of a Transnational Sporting Fraternity." *Diplomatic History* 28, no. 5 (2004): 637–62.

———. *Transpacific Field of Dreams: How Baseball Linked the United States and Japan in Peace and War*. Chapel Hill: University of North Carolina Press, 2012.

Guttmann, Allen. "The Cold War and the Olympics." *International Journal* 43 (1988): 554–68.

———. *Games and Empire: Sport and Cultural Imperialism*. New York: Columbia University Press, 1994.

———. *The Games Must Go On: Avery Brundage and the Olympic Movement*. New York: Columbia University Press, 1984.

———. "La diffusion des sports: Un impérialisme culturel." In *L'Empire des sports: Une histoire de la mondialisation culturelle*, edited by Pierre Singaravélou and Julien Sorez, 17–19. Paris: Belin, Collection Histoire & Société, 2010.

———. *The Olympics: A History of the Modern Games*, 2nd ed. Urbana: University of Illinois Press, 2002.

Hain, Peter. *Don't Play with Apartheid: The Background to the Stop the Seventy Tour Campaign*. London: Allen & Unwin, 1971.

Hall, K. O., A. Thomas, and J. Farier. "The Anti-Apartheid Campaign in the Caribbean: The Case of Sport." *Caribbean Journal of African Studies* 1, no. 1 (1978): 43–74.

Hampton, Janie. *The Austerity Olympics: When the Games Came to London in 1948*. London: Aurum Press, 2008.

Harrison, Hope. *Driving the Soviets up the Wall: Soviet-East German Relations, 1953–1961*. Princeton, NJ: Princeton University Press, 2003.

———. "The German Democratic Republic, the Soviet Union and the Berlin Wall Crisis." In *The Berlin Wall Crisis: Perspectives on Cold War Alliances*, edited by John P. S. Gearson and Kori Schake, 96–124. New York: Palgrave Macmillan, 2002.

Hart-Davis, Duff. *Hitler's Games: The 1936 Olympics*. New York: Harper & Row, 1986.

Hazan, Baruch A. *Olympic Sports and Propaganda Games: Moscow 1980*. New Brunswick, NJ: Transaction, 1982.

Heiss, Mary Ann, and S. Victor Papacosma, eds. *NATO and the Warsaw Pact: Intra-bloc Conflicts*. Kent, OH: Kent State University Press, 2008.

Heller, Francis H., and John R. Gillingham, eds. *NATO: The Founding of the Atlantic Alliance and the Integration of Europe*. New York: St. Martin's, 1992.

Hibbitts, Bernard J. "The CBC International Service as a Psychological Instrument of Canadian Foreign Policy in the Cold War, 1948–1963." MA thesis, Carleton University, 1981.

Hill, Christopher. *Olympic Politics*. New York: St. Martin's, 1992.

Hill, Jeffrey. "Introduction: Sport and Politics." *Journal of Contemporary History* 38, no. 3 (2003): 355–61.

Hills, Alice. *Britain and the Occupation of Austria, 1943–45*. New York: St. Martin's, 2000.

Hixson, Walter. *Parting the Curtain: Propaganda, Culture and the Cold War, 1945–1961*. New York: St. Martin's Griffin, 1998.

Hoberman, John. *The Olympic Crisis: Sport, Politics and the Moral Order*. New Rochelle, NY: A. D. Caratzas, 1986.

———. *Sport and Political Ideology*. Austin: University of Texas Press, 1984.

Hogan, Michael. *The Marshall Plan: America, Britain and the Reconstruction of Western Europe, 1947–1952*. New York: Cambridge University Press, 1987.

Hogan, Michael J., and Thomas G. Paterson, eds. *Explaining the History of American Foreign Relations*, 3rd ed. New York: Cambridge University Press, forthcoming.

Hoganson, Kristin. "Hop off the Bandwagon! It's a Mass Movement, Not a Parade." *Journal of American History* 95, no. 4 (March 2009): 1087–91.

Holian, Anna Marta. *Between National Socialism and Soviet Communism: Displaced Persons in Postwar Germany*. Ann Arbor: University of Michigan Press, 2011.

Holzweißig, Gunter. *Diplomatie im Trainingsanzug: Sport als politisches Instrument der DDR in den innerdeutschen und internationalen Beziehungen*. Munich/Vienna: Oldenbourg, 1981.

Hong, Fan. "Communist China and the Asian Games 1951–1990: The Thirty-Nine Years Struggle to Victory." In *Sport, Nationalism and Orientalism: The Asian Games,* edited by Fan Hong, 75–88. London: Routledge, 2006.

Hong, Fan, Duncan Mackay, and Karen Christensen. *China Gold: China's Quest for Global Power and Olympic Glory*. Great Barrington, MA: Berkshire Publishing Group, 2008.

Hong, Fan, and Xiong Xiaozheng. "Communist China: Sport, Politics and Diplomacy." In *Sport in Asian Society*, edited by J. A. Mangan and Fan Hong, 319–43. London: Frank Cass, 2003.

Houlihan, Barrie. *Sport and International Politics*. New York: Harvester Wheatsheaf, 1994.

Howell, Denis. *Made in Birmingham: The Memoirs of Denis Howell*. London: Queen Anne Press, 1990.

Huertas González, Félix R. *Deporte e identidad: Puerto Rico y su presencia deportiva internacional (1930–1950)*. San Juan: Terranova Editores, 2006.

Huish, Robert. "Punching above Its Weight: Cuba's Use of Sport for South-South Cooperation." *Third World Quarterly* 32, no. 3 (2011): 417–33.

Hulme, Derick L., Jr. *The Political Olympics: Moscow, Afghanistan, and the 1980 U.S. Boycott*. New York: Praeger, 1990.

Hunt, Thomas M. "American Sport Policy and the Cultural Cold War: The Lyndon B. Johnson Presidential Year." *Journal of Sport History* 33, no. 3 (2006): 273–97.

————. *Drug Games: The International Olympic Committee and the Politics of Doping, 1960–2008.* Austin: University of Texas Press, 2011.

Hutchinson, John. "Cultural Nationalism and Moral Regeneration." In *Nationalism*, edited by John Hutchinson and Anthony Smith, 122–31. Oxford: Oxford University Press. 1994.

Iandolo, Alessandro. "The Rise and Fall of the 'Soviet Model of Development' in West Africa, 1957–64." *Cold War History* 12, no. 4 (2012): 683–704.

James, C. L. R. *Beyond a Boundary.* London: Stanley Paul, 1963.

Jasper, William F. *Global Tyranny . . . Step by Step: The United Nations and the Emerging New World Order.* Appleton, WI: Western Islands, 1992.

Jay, Kathryn. *More than Just a Game: Sports in American Life since 1945.* New York: Columbia University Press, 2004.

Jefferys, Kevin. "Britain and the Boycott of the 1980 Moscow Olympics." *Sport in History* 32, no. 2 (September 2012): 279–301.

Johnson, Daniel. *White King and Red Queen: How the Cold War Was Fought on the Chessboard.* New York: Houghton Mifflin, 2008.

Kanet, Roger E. "The Superpower Quest for Empire: The Cold War and Soviet Support for Wars of National Liberation." *Cold War History* 6, no. 3 (2006): 331–52.

Kanin, David B. *A Political History of the Olympic Games.* Boulder, CO: Westview, 1981.

Karush, Matthew B., and Oscar Chamosa. *The New Cultural History of Peronism: Power and Identity in Mid-Twentieth-Century Argentina.* Durham, NC: Duke University Press, 2011.

Keech, Marc. "At the Centre of the Web: The Role of Sam Ramsamy in South Africa's Readmission to International Sport." *Culture, Sport, Society* 3, no. 3 (Autumn 2000): 41–62.

Keech, Marc, and Barrie Houlihan. "Sport and the End of Apartheid." *Round Table* 349 (1999): 109.

Kemper, Kurt Edward. *College Football and American Culture in the Cold War Era.* Urbana: University of Illinois Press, 2009.

Kent, John. *The Internationalization of Colonialism: Britain, France and Black Africa, 1939–1956.* Oxford: Clarendon, 1992.

Kereliuk, Sandra L. "The Canadian Boycott of the 1980 Moscow Olympic Games." In *Sport and Politics*, edited by Gerald Redmond, 153–59. Champaign, IL: Human Kinetics, 1986.

Keys, Barbara. "The Dictatorship of Sport: Nationalism, Internationalism, and Mass Culture in the 1930s." PhD diss., Harvard University, 2001.

————. "The Early Cold War Olympics, 1952–1960: Political, Economic and Human Rights Dimensions." In *The Palgrave Handbook of Olympic Studies*, edited by Helen Lenskyi and Stephen Wagg, 72–87. Houndsmills: Palgrave Macmillan, 2012.

————. *Globalizing Sport: National Rivalry and International Community in the 1930s.* Cambridge, MA: Harvard University Press, 2006.

———. "The Internationalization of Sport, 1890–1939." In *The Cultural Turn: Essays in the History of U.S. Foreign Relations*, edited by Frank A. Ninkovich and Liping Bu, 201–20. Chicago: Imprint Publications, 2001.

———. "Soviet Sport and Transnational Mass Culture in the 1930s." *Journal of Contemporary History* 38, no. 3 (2003): 413–34.

———. "Spreading Peace, Democracy, and Coca-Cola." *Diplomatic History* 28, no. 2 (2004): 165–96.

Kidd, Bruce. "The Campaign against Sport in South Africa." *International Journal* 43, no. 4 (Autumn 1988): 641–64.

———. "Canadian Opposition to the 1936 Olympics in Germany." *Canadian Journal of History of Sport and Physical Education* 9, no. 2 (1978): 20–40.

Kidd, Bruce, and John Macfarlane. *The Death of Hockey.* Toronto: New Press, 1972.

Killanin, Lord. *My Olympic Years.* London: Secker & Warburg, 1983.

Kipré, Pierre. "Le témoignage de Jacques Foccart." *Les cahiers du Centre de Recherches Historiques* 30 (2002). Accessed July 15, 2013. http://ccrh.revues.org/452;DOI: 10.4000/ccrh.452.

Kissoudi, P. "Sport, Politics and International Relations in the Twentieth Century." *International Journal of the History of Sport* 25, no. 13 (November 2008): 1689–1706.

Klein, Alan M. *Baseball on the Border: A Tale of Two Laredos.* Princeton, NJ: Princeton University Press, 1997.

———. *Growing the Game: The Globalization of Major League Baseball.* New Haven, CT: Yale University Press, 2006.

Knecht, Willi. "DDR-Leistungssport wird zum sowjetischen Trauma." *Deutschland Archiv* 9 (1976): 945–50.

———. *Der Boykott.* Cologne: Verlag Wissenschaft und Politik, 1980.

———. "Sportpolitische Bilanz 1972." *Deutschland Archiv* 5, no. 12 (1972): 1283–84.

Kourouma, Ahmadou. *Les soleils des indépendances.* Paris: Éditions du Seuil, 1995.

Krüger, Arnd, and William Murray, eds. *The Nazi Olympics: Sport, Politics, and Appeasement in the 1930s.* Urbana: University of Illinois Press, 2003.

Kunz, Josef L. "The Inter-American Treaty of Reciprocal Assistance." *The American Journal of International Law* 42, no. 1 (1948): 111–20.

Laderman, Scott. *Empire in Waves: A Political History of Surfing.* Berkeley: University of California Press, 2014.

———. *Tours of Vietnam: War, Travel Guides, and Memory.* Durham, NC: Duke University Press, 2009.

LaFeber, Walter. *Michael Jordan and the New Global Capitalism.* New York: Norton, 1999.

Lahey, Daniel James. "The Thatcher Government's Response to the Soviet Invasion of Afghanistan, 1979–1980." *Cold War History* 13, no. 1 (2013): 21–42.

Laïdi, Zaki. *L'URSS vue du Tiers-Monde.* Paris: Karthala, 1984.

Lapchick, Richard E. *Apartheid Sport and South Africa's Foreign Policy: 1976.* New

York: UN Centre against Apartheid, Department of Political and Security Council Affairs, 1976.

Laville, Helen, and Hugh Wilford, eds., *The U.S. Government, Citizen Groups and the Cold War: The State-Private Network.* New York: Routledge, 2006.

Lehmann, Norbert. *Internationale Sportbeziehungen und Sportpolitik der DDR.* Munster: Lit, 1986.

Leifer, Michael. *Dictionary of the Modern Politics of South-East Asia.* London: Routledge, 1996.

Lenskyj, Helen Jefferson. *Inside the Olympic Industry: Power, Politics, and Activism.* Albany: State University of New York Press, 2000.

Levermore, Roger, and Adrian Budd. *Sport and International Relations: An Emerging Relationship.* London: Routledge, 2004.

Lewin, André. "Les Africains à l'ONU." *Relations internationales* 128 (2006): 55–78.

Lijuan, Liang. *He Zhengliang and the Olympics.* Beijing: World Knowledge Press, 2004.

Lin, Ke, Tao Xu, and Xujun Wu. *The True History.* Beijing: Central China Literature Press, 1998.

Lipman, Jana K. "Between Guantánamo and Montego Bay: Cuba, Jamaica, Migration and the Cold War, 1959–1962." *Immigrants and Minorities* 21, no. 3 (November 2002): 25–51.

Logevall, Fredrik. "Politics and Foreign Relations." *Journal of American History* 95, no. 4 (March 2009): 1074–78.

Louis, William Roger. *Imperialism at Bay: The United States and the Decolonization of the British Empire, 1941–1945.* New York: Oxford University Press, 1977.

Lucas, John. "Ernest Lee Jahncke: The Expelling of an IOC Member." *Stadion* 17, no. 1 (1991): 53–78.

Lucas, Scott. *Freedom's War: The American Crusade against the Soviet Union.* New York: New York University Press, 1999.

Lumsden, Ian, ed. *Close the 49th Parallel, Etc.: The Americanization of Canada.* Toronto: University of Toronto Press, 1975.

Lunn, Arnold. *Memory to Memory.* London: Hollis & Carter, 1956.

Lupiano Cano, Joaquín. "Las políticas deportivas durante la primera presidencia de Juan Domingo Perón (1946–1952)." BA thesis, Universidad Nacional de Luján, 2003.

Lutan, Rusli, and Fan Hong. "The Politicization of Sport: GANEFO—A Case Study." *Sport in Society* 8, no. 3 (2005): 425–39.

Lyberg, Wolf. *Fabulous 100 Years of the IOC: Facts, Figures—and Much, Much More.* Lausanne: International Olympic Committee, 1996.

MacAloon, John. "La pitada Olímpica." In *Text, Play, and Story: The Construction and Reconstruction of Self and Society,* edited by Edward M. Bruner. Washington, DC: American Ethnological Society, 1984.

MacDonald, Gordon. "'A Colossal Embroglio': Control of Amateur Ice Hockey in the United States and the 1948 Winter Olympic Games." *Olympika: The International Journal of Olympic Studies* 7 (1998): 43–60.

Macfarlane, Neil, with Michael Herd. *Sport and Politics: A World Divided.* London: Willow Books, 1986.

Macintosh, Donald, and Donna Greenhorn. "Hockey Diplomacy and Canadian Foreign Policy." *Journal of Canadian Studies* 28 (1993): 101–5.

Macintosh, Donald, Donna Greenhorn, and David Black. "Canadian Diplomacy and the 1978 Edmonton Commonwealth Games." *Journal of Sport History* 19, no. 1 (Spring 1992): 26–55.

Macintosh, Donald, and Michael Hawes. *Sport and Canadian Diplomacy.* Montreal: McGill-Queen's University Press, 1994.

MacSkimming, Roy. *Cold War: The Amazing Canada-Soviet Hockey Series of 1972.* Vancouver: Greystone Books, 2012.

Maier, Charles S., and Günter Bischof, eds., *The Marshall Plan and Germany: West German Development within the Framework of the European Recovery Program.* New York: Berg, 1991.

Malone, Gifford D. *Political Advocacy and Cultural Communication: Organizing the Nation's Public Diplomacy.* Lanham, MD: University Press of America, 1988.

Maloney, Sean M. "Berlin Contingency Planning: Prelude to Flexible Response, 1958–63." *Journal of Strategic Studies* 25, no. 1 (March 2002): 99–134.

Mandell, Richard. "The Invention of the Sports Record." *Stadion* 2, no. 2 (1976): 250–64.

Mandell, Richard D. *The Nazi Olympics.* New York: Macmillan, 1971.

Mangan, J. A. *Athleticism in the Victorian and Edwardian Public School: The Emergence and Consolidation of an Educational Ideology.* London: Frank Cass, 1981.

Manheim, Jarol B. *Strategic Public Diplomacy and American Foreign Policy: The Evolution of Influence.* New York: Oxford University Press, 1994.

Manley, Michael. *History of West Indies Cricket.* London: André Deutsch, 1995.

Maraniss, David. *Rome 1960: The Olympics That Changed the World.* New York: Simon & Schuster, 2008.

Marshall, Trevor. "The Anti-Apartheid Campaign in the Caribbean." In *The African-Caribbean Connection: Historical and Cultural Perspectives,* edited by Alan Cobley and Alvin Thompson, 92–106. Bridgetown, Barbados: University of the West Indies, Department of History/National Cultural Foundation, 1990.

Martínez-Rousset, Joaquín. *50 años de Olimpismo.* San Juan, PR: Editorial Edil, 2003.

Mason, Tony, and Eliza Riedl. *Sport and the Military: The British Armed Forces, 1880–1960.* New York: Cambridge University Press, 2011.

Mayo Santana, Raúl. *El juguete sagrado: Germán Rieckehoff Sampayo.* San Juan, PR: Editorial Plaza Mayor, 2000.

McKenzie, Brian Angus. *Remaking France: Americanization, Public Diplomacy, and the Marshall Plan.* New York: Berghahn Books, 2005.

Mel, Frédéric Grah. *Félix Houphouët-Boigny: Biographie.* Paris: Cerap, Maisonneuve & Larose, 2003.

Merrett, Christopher. "'In Nothing Else Are the Deprivers So Deprived': South African Sport, Apartheid and Foreign Relations, 1945–71." *International Journal of the History of Sport* 13, no. 2 (August 1996): 146–65.

Mertin, Evelyn. *Sowjetisch-deutsche Sportbeziehungen im "Kalten Krieg."* Sankt Augustin, Germany: Academia Verlag, 2009.

Michel, Marc. *Décolonisations et émergence du tiers monde.* Paris: Hachette, 2005.

Milza, Pierre. *Les relations internationales de 1945 à 1973.* Paris: Hachette, 1996.

Milza, Pierre, Philippe Tétart, and François Jéquier, eds. *Le pouvoir des anneaux: Les jeux olympiques à la lumière de la politique 1896–2004.* Paris: Vuibert, 2004.

Mitrovich, Gregory. *Undermining the Kremlin: America's Strategy to Subvert the Soviet Bloc, 1947–1956.* Ithaca, NY: Cornell University Press, 2000.

Morgan, Michael Cotey. "The Seventies and the Rebirth of Human Rights." In *The Shock of the Global: The 1970s in Perspective*, edited by Niall Ferguson, Charles S. Maier, Erez Manela, and Daniel J. Sargent, 237–50. Cambridge, MA: Belknap, 2010.

Morton, Henry W. *Soviet Sport: Mirror of Soviet Society.* New York: Collier, 1963.

Mosamete, Sekola. *L'Afrique et la perestroïka: L'évolution de la pensée soviétique sous Gorbatchev.* Paris: L'Harmattan, 2007.

Mullner, Rudolph. "The Importance of Skiing in Austria." *International Journal of the History of Sport* 30, no. 6 (2013): 659–73.

Munton, Don, and David A. Welch. *The Cuban Missile Crisis: A Concise History.* New York: Oxford University Press, 2007.

Murray, Bruce K. "The Sports Boycott and Cricket: The Cancellation of the 1971/72 South African Tour of Australia." *South African Historical Journal* 49, no. 1 (2003): 162–71.

Mzov, Sergey. *A Distant Front in the Cold War: The USSR in West Africa and the Congo, 1956–64.* Stanford, CA: Stanford University Press, 2010.

Nandjui, Pierre. *Félix Houphouët-Boigny: L'homme de la France en Afrique.* Paris: L'Harmattan, 1995.

Nauright, John. *Sport, Cultures and Identities in South Africa.* London: Leicester University Press, 1997.

Ndee, Hamad S. "Sport as a Political Tool: Tanzania and the Liberation of Africa." *International Journal of the History of Sport* 22, no. 4 (2005): 671–88.

Newton, Ronald C. *The "Nazi Menace" in Argentina, 1931–1947.* Stanford, CA: Stanford University Press, 1992.

Norden, Deborah L., and Roberto Russell. *The United States and Argentina: Changing Relations in a Changing World.* New York and London: Routledge, 2002.

Novak, Andrew. "Rhodesia's 'Rebel and Racist' Olympic Team: Athletic Glory, National Legitimacy and the Clash of Politics and Sport." *International Journal of the History of Sport* 23, no. 8 (2006): 1369–88.

Numerato, Dino. "Between Small Everyday Practices and Glorious Symbolic Acts: Sport-Based Resistance against the Communist Regime in Czechoslovakia." *Sport in Society: Cultures, Commerce, Media, Politics* 13, no. 1 (2010): 107–20.

Nye, Joseph S., Jr. "Public Diplomacy and Soft Power." *The Annals of the American Academy of Political and Social Science* 616 (2008): 94–109.

———. "Soft Power and American Foreign Policy." *Political Science Quarterly* 119, no. 2 (Summer 2004): 255–70.

———. *Soft Power: The Means to Success in World Politics.* New York: PublicAffairs, 2004.

*The Official Report of the Organising Committee for the XIV Olympiad.* London: Organising Committee for the XIV Olympiad, 1948.

*The Official Report of the Organising Committee for the Games of the XV Olympiad: Helsinki 1952.* Porvoo and Helsinki: Organising Committee for the XV Olympiad, 1955.

Olderr, Steven. *The Pan American Games: A Statistical History, 1951–1999.* Jefferson, NC: McFarland, 2003.

O'Mahony, Mike. *Sport in the USSR: Physical Culture—Visual Culture.* London: Reaktion, 2006.

Osgood, Kenneth. *Total Cold War: Eisenhower's Secret Propaganda Battle at Home and Abroad.* Lawrence: University Press of Kansas, 2006.

Osgood, Kenneth A., and Brian C. Etheridge, eds. *The United States and Public Diplomacy: New Directions in Cultural and International History.* Leiden: Brill, 2010.

Park, Roberta J. "'Forget about That Pile of Papers': Second World War Sport, Recreation and the Military on the Island of Puerto Rico." *International Journal of the History of Sport* 20, 1 (2003): 50–64.

———. "From *La Bomba* to *Béisbol*: Sport and the Americanisation of Puerto Rico, 1898–1950." *International Journal of the History of Sport* 28, no. 17 (2011): 2575–93.

Parks, Jenifer. "'Nothing but Trouble': The Soviet Union's Push to 'Democratise' International Sports during the Cold War, 1959–1962." *International Journal of the History of Sport* 30, no. 13 (2013): 1554–67.

———. "Red Sport, Red Tape: The Olympic Games, the Soviet Sports Bureaucracy, and the Cold War, 1952–1980." PhD diss., University of North Carolina, 2009.

Payne, Anthony. "The International Politics of the Gleneagles Agreement." *The Round Table* 320 (1991): 418–19.

Pei, Dongguang. "A Question of Names: The Solution to the 'Two Chinas' Issue in Modern Olympic History; The Final Phase, 1971–1984." In *Cultural Imperialism in Action: Critiques in the Global Olympic Trust,* edited by Nigel B. Crowther, Robert K. Barney, and Michael K. Heine. London, ON: Centre for Olympic Studies, 2006.

Peppard, Victor, and James Riordan. *Playing Politics: Soviet Sport Diplomacy to 1992.* Greenwich, CT: JAI Press, 1992.

Pérez, Louis A., Jr. "Between Baseball and Bullfighting: The Quest for Nationality in Cuba, 1868–1898." *Journal of American History* 81, no. 2 (1994): 493–517.

Perks, Robert, and Alistair Thompson, eds. *The Oral History Reader.* London: Routledge, 2006.

Perón, Juan D. *Obras completas*, 24 vols. Buenos Aires: Proyecto Hernandarias, 1984.

Peterson, Harold F. *Argentina and the United States, 1810–1960.* Albany: State University of New York Press, 1964.

Philips, Bob. *The 1948 Olympics: How London Rescued the Games.* London: Sports Books, 2007.

Pigman, Geoffrey A. *Contemporary Diplomacy: Representation and Communication in a Globalized World.* Cambridge, MA: Polity, 2010.

Pinchuk, Anatoly. "From Helsinki to Munich." In *USSR-USA Sports Encounters*, edited by Victor Kuznetsov and Mikhail Lukashev, 101–20. Moscow: Progress Publishers, 1977.

Pipes, Richard. *U.S.-Soviet Relations in the Era of Détente.* Boulder, CO: Westview, 1981.

Plotkin, Mariano Ben. *Mañana es San Perón: A Cultural History of Perón's Argentina.* Translated by Keith Zahniser. Wilmington, DE: SR Books, 2003.

Polley, Martin. *Moving the Goalposts: A History of Sport and Society in Britain since 1945.* London: Routledge, 1998.

———. "'No Business of Ours': The Foreign Office and the Olympic Games, 1897–1914." *International Journal of the History of Sport* 13, no. 2 (February 1996): 96–113.

———. "Olympic Diplomacy: The British Government and the Projected 1940 Olympic Games." *International Journal of the History of Sport* 9, no. 2 (August 1993): 169–87.

Pope, M. R. G. "Public Diplomacy, International News Media and London 2012: Cosmopolitanism." *Sport in Society,* forthcoming 2014.

Proctor, Mike. *South Africa: The Years of Isolation and the Return to International Cricket.* Harpenden, UK: Queen Anne Press, 1994.

Prozumenshtshikov, Michail. *Bol'shoj sport i bol'shaja politika.* Moscow: Rosspen, 2004.

Ragaru, Nicolas, and Pierre Conesa. "Les stratégies d'influence en affaires étrangères: Notion insaisissable ou absence de volonté?" *Revue Internationale et Stratégique* 52 (2003): 83–88.

Ramsamy, Sam. *Apartheid: The Real Hurdle, Sport in South Africa and the International Boycott.* London: International Defence and Aid Fund for Southern Africa, 1982.

Rapoport, Mario. *Gran Bretaña, Estados Unidos y las clases dirigentes argentinas: 1940–1945.* Buenos Aires: Editorial de Belgrano, 1980.

Rapoport, Mario, and Claudio Spiguel. *Estados Unidos y el Peronismo: La política norteamericana en la Argentina, 1949–1955.* Buenos Aires: Grupo Editor Latinoamericano, 1994.

Reaves, Joseph A. *Taking in a Game: A History of Baseball in Asia.* Lincoln: University of Nebraska Press, 2002.

Rein, Raanan. "'*El Primer Deportista*': The Political Use and Abuse of Sport in Peronist Argentina." *International Journal of the History of Sport* 15, no. 2 (1998): 54–76.

Ren, Dan. *The New Flag in International Sport.* Beijing: People's Sport Press, 1963.

Renouvin, Pierre, and Jean-Baptiste Duroselle. *Introduction à l'histoire des relations internationales,* 4th ed. Paris: Armand Colin, 1991.

Richmond, Yale. *Cultural Exchange and the Cold War: Raising the Iron Curtain.* University Park: Pennsylvania State University Press, 2003.

Rider, Toby. "The Olympic Games and the Secret Cold War: The U.S. Government and the Propaganda Campaign against Communist Sport, 1950–1960." PhD diss., University of Western Ontario, 2011.

———. "Political Warfare in Helsinki: American Covert Strategy and the Union of Free Eastern European Sportsmen." *International Journal of the History of Sport* 30, no. 13 (2013): 1493–507.

Rinehart, Robert E. "'Fists Flew and Blood Flowed': Symbolic Resistance and the International Response in Hungarian Water Polo at the Melbourne Olympics, 1956." *Journal of Sport History* 23, no. 2 (1996): 120–39.

Riordan, James. "Great Britain and the 1980 Olympics: A Victory for Olympism." In *Sport and International Understanding*, edited by Maaret Ilmarinen, 138–44. New York: Springer-Verlag, 1984.

———. "Rewriting Soviet Sports History." *Journal of Sport History* 20, no. 3 (1993): 247–58.

———. *Soviet Sport: Background to the Olympics.* New York: New York University Press, 1980.

———. "Soviet Sport and Soviet Foreign Policy." *Soviet Studies* 26 (1974): 322–43.

———. *Sport and Soviet Society: Development of Sport and Physical Education in Russia and the USSR.* New York: Cambridge University Press, 1977.

———. *Sport, Politics, and Communism.* Manchester: Manchester University Press, 1991.

———. *Sport soviétique.* Paris: Vigot, 1980.

———, ed. *Sport under Communism. The U.S.S.R., Czechoslovakia, the G.D.R., China, Cuba.* Montreal: McGill-Queen's University Press, 1978.

Riordan, Jim. "Playing to New Rules: Soviet Sport and Perestroika." *Soviet Studies* 42 (1990): 133–45.

———. "The Rise and Fall of Soviet Olympic Champions." *Olympika: The International Journal of Olympic Studies* 2 (1993): 25–44.

———. "The Role of Sport in Soviet Foreign Policy." *International Journal* 43 (1988): 569–95.

Riordan, Jim, and Arnd Kruger. *The International Politics of Sport in the 20th Century.* London: E & FN Spon, 1999.

Risso, Linda. "'Don't Mention the Soviets!' An Overview of the Short Films Produced by the NATO Information Service between 1949 and 1969." *Cold War History* 9, no. 4 (2009): 501–12.

———. "'Enlightening Public Opinion': A Study of NATO's Information Policies between 1949 and 1959 Based on Recently Declassified Documents." *Cold War History* 7, no. 1 (February 2007): 45–51.

———. "Propaganda on Wheels: The NATO Travelling Exhibitions in the 1950s and 1960s." *Cold War History* 11, no. 1 (2011): 9–25.

Rivera Ramos, Efrén. *The Legal Construction of Identity: The Judicial and Social Legacy of American Colonialism in Puerto Rico.* Washington, DC: American Psychological Association, 2002.

Robin, Ron. "Requiem for Public Diplomacy?" *American Quarterly* 57, no. 2 (June 2005): 345–53.

Roche, Christian. *Léopold Sédar Senghor: Le président humaniste.* Toulouse: Privat, 2006.

Rock, David. *Argentina, 1516–1987: From Spanish Colonization to Alfonsín.* Berkeley: University of California Press, 1987.

Rodríguez, Ernesto. *Libro I de los juegos panamericanos, 1951 a 2011.* Buenos Aires: Alarco Ediciones, 2011.

Rodríguez, Rodolfo. *Carlos Vicente Aloé: Subordinacíon y valor.* La Plata: Asociación Amigos del Archivo Histórico, 2007.

Rofe, J. Simon. "'It Is a Squad Game': Manchester United as a Diplomatic Non-State Actor in International Affairs." *Sport in Society*, forthcoming 2014.

Romany Siaca, Celina. *La verdadera historia de Roberto Sánchez Vilella.* San Juan, PR: Ediciones Puerto, 2011.

Romero, Luis Alberto. *A History of Argentina in the Twentieth Century.* Translated by James P. Brennan. University Park: Pennsylvania State University Press, 2002.

Rosenau, James N. *Turbulence in World Politics: A Theory of Change and Continuity.* Princeton, NJ: Princeton University Press, 1990.

Ryan, David, and Victor Pungong, eds. *The United States and Decolonization: Power and Freedom.* Basingstoke: Macmillan, 2000.

Sage, George H. *Globalizing Sport: How Organizations, Corporations, Media, and Politics Are Changing Sports.* Boulder, CO: Paradigm, 2010.

Sanga, Ernest Guy. *Diplomatie et diplomate: L'Afrique et le système des relations internationales.* Paris: L'Harmattan, 2010.

Sarantakes, Nicholas Evan. *Dropping the Torch: Jimmy Carter, the Olympic Boycott and the Cold War.* New York: Cambridge University Press, 2011.

Saunders, Frances Stoner. *Who Paid the Piper? The CIA and the Cultural Cold War.* London: Granta Books, 1999.

Saura, André. *Philibert Tsiranana (T1): Premier président de la République de Madagascar (1910–1978).* Paris: L'Harmattan, 2006.

Scher, Ariel, Guillermo Blanco, and Jorge Búsico. *Deporte nacional: Dos siglos de historia.* Buenos Aires: Emecé, 2010.

Scherer, Karl Adolf. *100 Jahre Olympische Spiele: Idee, Analyse und Bilanz.* Dortmund: Harenberg, 1995.

Schiller, Kay, and Christopher Young. *The 1972 Munich Olympics and the Making of Modern Germany.* Berkeley: University of California Press, 2010.

Schmidt, Gustav, ed. *A History of NATO: The First Fifty Years*, 3 vols. New York: Palgrave, 2001.

Schulz, Walter. *Die Stellung der Kultur: Und Sportpolitik im System der Auswärtigen Politik der Deutschen Demokratischen Republik und ihre Bedeutung für das Staatsbewusstsein der DDR-Bevölkerung.* Inaugural-Dissertation Rheinische Friedrich-Wilhelms-Universität Bonn. Bonn, 1978.

Scott, Peter Dale. "The United States and the Overthrow of Sukarno, 1965–1967." *Pacific Affairs* 58, no. 2 (1985): 239–64.

Seijo Bruno, Miñi. *La insurrección nacionalista en Puerto Rico, 1950.* San Juan, PR: Editorial Edil, 1997.

Seipp, Adam R. "Refugee Town: Germans, Americans, and the Uprooted in Rural West Germany, 1945–52." *Journal of Contemporary History* 44, no. 4 (2009): 675–95.

Senén González, Santiago. "Perón y el deporte." *Todo es Historia* 345 (1996): 8–20.

Senn, Alfred E. *Power, Politics, and the Olympic Games.* Champaign, IL: Human Kinetics, 1999.

Senn, Alfred Erich. "American Lithuanians and the Politics of Basketball in Lithuania, 1935–1939." *Journal of Baltic Studies* 19, no. 2 (1988): 146–56.

———. "Perestroika and Lithuanian Basketball." *Journal of Sport History* 17, no. 1 (1990): 56–61.

Sharp, Tony. *The Wartime Alliance and the Zonal Division of Germany.* Oxford: Clarendon, 1975.

Shephard, Ben. *The Long Road Home: The Aftermath of the Second World War.* New York: Knopf, 2010.

Sindjoun, Luc. *Sociologie des relations internationales africaines.* Paris: Karthala, 2003.

Sirven, Pablo. *Perón y los medios de comunicación (1943–1955).* Buenos Aires: Centro Editor de América Latina, 1984.

Skoug, Kenneth N., Jr. *Czechoslovakia's Lost Fight for Freedom, 1967–1969: An American Embassy Perspective.* Westport, CT: Praeger, 1999.

Smith, Tony. "New Bottles for New Wine: A Pericentric Framework for the Study of the Cold War." *Diplomatic History* 24, no. 4 (Fall 2000): 567–91.

Snow, Nancy. *Propaganda, Inc.: Selling America's Culture to the World.* New York: Seven Stories, 1998.

Soares, John. "Cold War, Hot Ice: International Ice Hockey, 1947–1980." *Journal of Sport History* 34 (2007): 215–16.

———. "East Beats West: Ice Hockey and the Cold War." In *Sport and the Transformation of Modern Europe: States, Media and Markets, 1950–2010*, edited by Alan Tomlinson, Christopher Young, and Richard Holt, 35–49. London: Routledge, 2011.

———. "'Very Correct Adversaries': The Cold War on Ice from 1947 to the Squaw Valley Olympics." *International Journal of the History of Sport* 30, no. 13 (2013): 1536–53.

Sobers, Garfield, with Brian Scovell. *Sobers: Twenty Years at the Top.* London: Macmillan, 1988.

Sotomayor, Antonio. "Playing the Nation in a Colonial Island: Sport, Culture, and Politics in Puerto Rico." PhD diss., University of Chicago, 2012.

Spurr, David. *The Rhetoric of Empire.* Durham, NC: Duke University Press, 1993.

Stavrianos, L S. *The World since 1500: A Global History.* New York: Prentice-Hall, 1966.

Steinberg, Michael P. *The Meaning of the Salzburg Festival: Austria as Theater and Ideology, 1890–1938.* Ithaca, NY: Cornell University Press, 1990.

Stevenson, Richard. *The Rise and Fall of Détente.* Urbana: University of Illinois Press, 1985.

Stollmeyer, Jeff. *Everything under the Sun: My Life in West Indies Cricket.* London: Stanley Paul, 1983.

Strassler, Robert B., ed. *The Landmark Thucydides: A Comprehensive Guide to the Peloponnesian War.* New York: Simon & Schuster, 1996.

Suri, Jeremi. *Henry Kissinger and the American Century.* Cambridge, MA: Belknap Press, 2009.

Talton, Benjamin. "1960s Africa in Historical Perspective: An Introduction." *Journal of Black Studies* 43 (2012): 3–10.

Tang, Minxin. *China at the Olympic Games.* Taipei: Chinese Taipei Olympic Committee Press, 2000.

Tarasov, Anatoli. *Road to Olympus.* Toronto: Pocket Books, 1972.

Teichler, Hans Joachim. "Vom Lehrling zum Musterschüler und Konkurrenten: Die sportpolitischen Beziehungen der DDR zur UDSSR [sic]." In *Proceedings of the 6th Congress of the International Society for the History of Physical Education and Sport "Sport and Politics"* (July 14–19, 1999, Budapest), edited by Katalin Szikora, 296–303. Budapest: Semmelweis University, 2002.

Tenzer, Nicolas. "Constituer des réseaux d'influence: Acteurs et vecteurs de décision en affaires étrangères; Organiser l'influence, Une stratégie intellectuelle de la France." *Revue Internationale et Stratégique* 52 (2003): 89–96.

Tété-Adjalogo, Têtêvi G. *La question du Plan Marshall et l'Afrique.* Paris: L'Harmattan, 1989.

Thaler, Peter. *The Ambivalence of Identity: The Austrian Experience of Nation-Building in a Modern Society.* West Lafayette, IN: Purdue University Press, 2001.

Thatcher, Margaret. *The Downing Street Years.* London: HarperCollins, 1993.

Thomas, Brooke. "A Constitution Led by the Flag." In *Foreign in a Domestic Sense: Puerto Rico, American Expansion, and the Constitution,* edited by Christina Duffy Burnett and Burke Marshall, 82–103. Durham, NC: Duke University Press, 2001.

Thomas, Damion L. *Globetrotting: African American Athletes and Cold War Politics.* Urbana: University of Illinois Press, 2012.

Thomson, Oliver. *Easily Led: A History of Propaganda.* Stroud, Gloucestershire: Sutton, 1999.

Torres, Cesar R. "The Latin American 'Olympic Explosion' of the 1920s: Causes and Consequences." *International Journal of the History of Sport* 23, no. 7 (2006): 1088–111.

———. "The Limits of Pan-Americanism: The Case of the Failed 1942 Pan-American Games." *International Journal of the History of Sport* 28, no. 17 (2011): 2547–74.

———. "Stymied Expectations: Buenos Aires' Persistent Efforts to Host Olympic Games." *Olympika: The International Journal of Olympic Studies* 16 (2007): 43–75.

———. "Tribulations and Achievements: The Early History of Olympism in Argentina." *International Journal of the History of Sport* 18, no. 3 (2001): 59–92.

Torruella, Juan R. "One Hundred Years of Solitude: Puerto Rico's American Century." In *Foreign in a Domestic Sense: Puerto Rico, American Expansion, and the Constitution,* edited by Christina Duffy Burnett and Burke Marshall, 241–50. Durham, NC: Duke University Press, 2001.

Trías Monge, José. *Puerto Rico: The Trials of the Oldest Colony in the World.* New Haven, CT: Yale University Press, 1997.

Troy, Peter. *To the Four Corners of the World: The Lost Journals of the Original Surf Explorer.* Jan Juc, Victoria, Australia: Flying Pineapple Media, 2010.

Troyanovsky, Oleg. "The Making of Soviet Foreign Policy." In *Nikita Khrushchev,* edited by William Taubman, 209–41. New Haven, CT: Yale University Press, 2000.

Tuch, Hans N. *Communicating with the World: U.S. Public Diplomacy Overseas.* New York: St. Martin's, 1990.

Tulchin, Joseph. *Argentina and the United States: A Conflicted Relationship.* Boston: Twayne, 1990.

Turkel, Studs. *The Good War: An Oral History of World War II.* New York: The New Press, 1997.

Turrini, Joseph M. "'It Was Communism versus the Free World': The USA-USSR Dual Track Meet Series and the Development of Track and Field in the United States, 1958–1985." *Journal of Sport History* 28, no. 3 (2001): 427–71.

Twigge, Stephen, and Alan MacMillan. "Britain, the United States, and the Development of NATO Strategy, 1950–1964." *Journal of Strategic Studies* 19, no. 2 (June 1996): 260–81.

Ueberroth, Peter, with Richard Levin and Amy Quinn. *Made in America: His Own Story.* New York: Morrow, 1985.

Ungerleider, Steven. *Faust's Gold: Inside the East German Doping Machine.* New York: St. Martin's, 2001.

Urban, André. *Etats-Unis, Tiers-Monde et crises internationales (1953–1960).* Paris: L'Harmattan, 2005.

Uriarte González, Carlos. *80 años de acción y pasión: Puerto Rico en los Juegos Centroamericanos y del Caribe, 1930 al 2010.* San Juan, PR: Nomos Impresores, 2009.

Vinokur, Martin Barry. *More than a Game: Sports and Politics.* New York: Greenwood, 1988.

Von Eschen, Penny M. *Satchmo Blows Up the World: Jazz Ambassadors Play the Cold War.* Cambridge, MA: Harvard University Press, 2006.

Wagg, Stephen, and David L. Andrews, eds. *East Plays West: Sport and the Cold War.* London: Routledge, 2006.

Wagnleitner, Reinhold. *Coca-colonization and the Cold War: The Cultural Mission of the United States in Austria after the Second World War.* Translated by Diana M. Wolf. Chapel Hill: University of North Carolina Press, 1994.

Wakefield, Wanda Ellen. *Playing to Win: Sports and the American Military, 1989–1945.* Albany: State University of New York Press, 1997.

Walcott, Clyde, with Brian Scovell. *Sixty Years on the Back Foot: The Cricketing Life of Sir Clyde Walcott.* London: Victor Gollancz, 1988.

Wang, Dinghua. "The Ping-Pong Diplomacy." *Secretary Affaires* 7 (2008): 42–44.

Ward, Paul. "Last Man Picked: Do Mainstream Historians Need to Play with Sports Historians?" *International Journal of the History of Sport* 30, no. 1 (January 2013): 6–13.

Warshaw, Matt. *The Encyclopedia of Surfing.* Orlando, FL: Harcourt, 2003.

Wenn, Stephen R. "A House Divided: The U.S. Amateur Sport Establishment and the Issue of Participation in the 1936 Berlin Olympics." *Research Quarterly for Exercise and Sport* 67, no. 3 (1996): 161–71.

Wenn, Stephen R., and Jeffrey P. Wenn. "Muhammad Ali and the Convergence of Olympic Sport and U.S. Diplomacy in 1980: A Reassessment from behind the Scenes at the U.S. State Department." *Olympika: The International Journal of Olympic Studies* 2 (1993): 45–66.

Westad, Odd Arne. *The Global Cold War: Third World Interventions and the Making of Our Times.* New York: Cambridge University Press, 2007.

Whiting, Robert. *The Chrysanthemum and the Bat: The Game Japanese Play.* Tokyo: Permanent Press, 1977.

———. *The Meaning of Ichiro: The New Wave from Japan and the Transformation of Our National Pastime.* New York: Grand Central, 2004.

———. *You Gotta Have Wa.* New York: Vintage, 1990.

Whitnah, Donald R., and Floreintine E. Whitnah. *Salzburg under Siege: U.S. Occupation, 1945–1955.* New York: Greenwood, 1991.

Wiese, René. "Der Ursprung der Kinder—und Jugendsportschulen der DDR—eine sowjetische Geburt?" *Deutschland Archiv. Zeitschrift für das vereinigte Deutschland* 37 (2004): 422–30.

Wilson, Harold E., Jr. "The Golden Opportunity: Romania's Political Manipulation of the 1984 Los Angeles Olympic Games." *Olympika: The International Journal of Olympic Studies* 3 (1994): 83–97.

Winch, Jonty. "Unlocking the Cape Code: Establishing British Football in South Africa." *Sport in History* 30, no. 4 (2010): 501–22.

Witherspoon, Kevin B. *Before the Eyes of the World: Mexico and the 1968 Olympic Games.* Dekalb: Northern Illinois University Press, 2008.

———. "Going 'to the Fountainhead': Black American Athletes as Cultural Ambassadors in Africa, 1970–1971." *International Journal of the History of Sport* 30, no. 13 (2013): 1508–22.

Wolper, Gregg. "Wilsonian Public Diplomacy: The Committee on Public Information in Spain." *Diplomatic History* 17, no. 1 (Winter 1993): 17–34.

Wonneberger, Günther. *Körperkultur und Sport in der DDR: Gesellschaftswissenschaftliches Lehrmaterial.* Berlin: Sportverlag, 1982.

Wu, Guangxiang. "The Four Marshals Discussed the National Security Issue in 1969." *The 20th Century* 8 (2008): 18–23.

Wu, Shaozu, ed. *The History of Sport in the People's Republic of China.* Beijing: China Book Press, 1999.

Wyman, Mark. *DPs: Europe's Displaced Persons, 1945–1951.* Ithaca, NY: Cornell University Press, 1998.

Yamada, Shoko. "'Traditions' and Cultural Production: Character Training at the Achimota School in Colonial Ghana." *History of Education* 38, no. 1 (2009): 29–59.

Yang, Kuisong. "The Sino-Soviet Border Clash of 1969: From Zhenbao Island to Sino-American Rapprochement." *Cold War History* 1 (2000): 21–52.

Zeiler, Thomas W. *Ambassadors in Pinstripes: The Spalding World Baseball Tour and the Birth of the American Empire.* Lanham, MD: Rowman & Littlefield, 2006.

———. "The Diplomatic History Bandwagon: A State of the Field." *Journal of American History* 95, no. 4 (March 2009): 1053–73.

Zhang, Bin. "1984: China Saved the Olympics." *Success* 9 (2008): 20–22.

Zubkova, Elena. *Russia after the War: Hopes, Illusions, and Disappointments, 1945–1957.* Translated by Hugh Ragsdale. Armonk, NY: M. E. Sharpe, 1998.

Zubok, Vladislav M. *A Failed Empire: The Soviet Union in the Cold War from Stalin to Gorbachev.* Chapel Hill: University of North Carolina Press, 2007.

# Contributors

**Pascal Charitas** is lecturer at the Université de Nanterre, Paris-Ouest, La Défense. His research has appeared in the *Journal of Olympic History,* the *Journal of Sports History, Sport History Review,* and *Stadion.* He received his doctorate in 2010 at the Université de Paris–Sud and is a member of the North American Society of Sport History and the French Society of the History of Sport.

**Heather L. Dichter** is assistant professor of sport management and media at Ithaca College. Her work explores the intersection of sport and politics in postwar Germany and has been funded by the Society for Historians of American Foreign Relations, the George C. Marshall Foundation, and the International Society for Olympic Historians. She is the coeditor, with Bruce Kidd, of *Olympic Reform Ten Years Later* (2012), has published articles on the Allied use of sport in occupied Germany in *Stadion,* the *International Journal of the History of Sport,* and *History of Education*; and currently serves on the editorial board of the *International Journal of Sport Communication.* She received her doctorate in history from the University of Toronto in 2008.

**Aviston D. Downes** is senior lecturer in Caribbean social and cultural history and graduate studies coordinator in the Department of History and Philosophy at the University of the West Indies at Cave Hill, Barbados. He has published widely on Freemasonry, Caribbean masculinities, mutual cooperation and black economic enfranchisement in Barbados, and sport and recreation history, including articles in the *International Journal of the History of Sport* and *The Sports Historian.* He has served as deputy chairman of the UNESCO Memory of the World Committee, as director of the National Oral History Project, and was an elected member of the executive council of the International Oral History Association from 2004 to 2006.

**Fan Hong** is Winthrop Professor in Chinese Studies at the University of Western Australia. Her primary research interests are in the areas of culture, politics, gender, and sport. Her publications include *The History of World Sport: From Ancient to Modern Society* (1988); *Modern Sport, the Global Obsession: Politics, Class, Religion, Gender* (2005); and *China Gold: China's Quest for Global Power and Olympic Glory* (2008). She is an editor of the *International Journal of the History of Sport* and a member of the editorial boards of the *Sports Studies Journal* and the *International Encyclopedia of Women and Sport.*

**Andrew L. Johns** is associate professor of history at Brigham Young University and the David M. Kennedy Center for International Studies. He is the author of *Vietnam's Second Front: Domestic Politics, the Republican Party, and the War* (2010); coeditor, with Kathryn Statler, of *The Eisenhower Administration, the Third World, and the Globalization of the Cold War* (2006); and editor of *A Companion to Ronald Reagan* (forthcoming in 2014). In addition, he serves as editor of *Passport: The Society for Historians of American Foreign Relations Review* and is general editor of the Studies in Conflict, Diplomacy, and Peace book series, published by the University Press of Kentucky.

**Scott Laderman** is associate professor of history at the University of Minnesota, Duluth. He is the author of *Empire in Waves: A Political History of Surfing* (2014) and *Tours of Vietnam: War, Travel Guides, and Memory* (2009). He is also the coeditor, with Edwin Martini, of *Four Decades On: Vietnam, the United States, and the Legacies of the Second Indochina War* (2013).

**Evelyn Mertin** teaches English and physical education at the Kaiser-Karls-Gymnasium in Aachen, Germany, and taught previously at the Institute of Sport History at the German Sport University in Cologne, Germany. Her doctoral dissertation, "Soviet-German Sport Relations during the Cold War," received the ISHPES Junior Scholar Award in 2009 and the Award of the German Olympic Academy Willi Daume in 2010.

**Jenifer Parks** is assistant professor of history at Rocky Mountain College in Billings, Montana. Her primary research interests include sport and politics in the Soviet Union and Soviet participation in the Olympic Games during the Cold War. She received her doctorate in Russian and Soviet history in 2009 at the University of North Carolina at Chapel Hill.

**Nicholas Evan Sarantakes** is associate professor of strategy at the US Naval War College. A fellow of the Royal Historical Society, he is the author of four books and numerous articles, including *Keystone: The American Occupation of Okinawa and U.S.-Japanese Relations* (2000), and *Dropping the Torch: Jimmy Carter, the Olympic Boycott, and the Cold War* (2011). His current projects include a book examining the making of the film *Patton* and a book on Richard Nixon and sports. He also serves as the book review editor for *Presidential Studies Quarterly.*

**John Soares** is adjunct assistant professor of history at the University of Notre Dame. In 2010 he was Fulbright Visiting Research Chair in North American Studies at Carleton University in Ottawa, Canada. Among his recent publications are articles on US foreign relations in *Cold War History* and the *Journal of Cold War Studies* and articles on Cold War hockey in the *International Journal of the History of Sport,* the *Journal of Sport History,* the *Brown Journal of World Affairs,* and several anthologies.

**Antonio Sotomayor** is assistant professor and librarian for Latin American and Caribbean studies and adjunct professor in the Department of Recreation, Sport, and Tourism at the University of Illinois at Urbana-Champaign. He received his PhD in history from the University of Chicago and has taught at the University of Illinois, the University of Chicago, and Knox College. His most recent work is titled "*Un parque para cada pueblo:* Julio Enrique Monagas and the Politics of Sport and Recreation in Puerto Rico during the 1940s," and he is currently working on a book manuscript on Puerto Rican Olympism, national identity, and international politics.

**Cesar R. Torres** is professor in the Department of Kinesiology, Sport Studies, and Physical Education at The College at Brockport, State University of New York. He received his early professional training in Argentina and obtained his PhD from the Pennsylvania State University. A philosopher and historian of sport, he has published over forty pieces in peer-reviewed journals and edited collections. He has published *Jogos Olímpicos Latino-Americanos Rio de Janeiro 1922* (2012) and *Gol de media chancha: Conversacionecs para disfrutar el deporte plenamente* (2011); edited *Niñez, deporte y actividad física: Reflexiones filosóficas sobre una relación compleja* (2008); and coedited *¿La pelota no dobla? Ensayos filosóficas en torno al fútbol* (2006). He serves on several editorial boards and is the associate editor and book review editor of the *Journal of the Philosophy of Sport.* He is a former president of the International Association for the Philosophy of Sport (2009–2011) and a fellow in the National Academy of Kinesiology.

**Wanda Ellen Wakefield** is associate professor of history at The College at Brockport, State University of New York. She received her JD from the University of Illinois and her PhD from the University of Buffalo. She is the author of *Playing to Win: Sports and the American Military, 1898–1945* (1997) and is completing a new monograph on winter sports and the Cold War. She is an official with the International Luge Federation and was chief of control for the luge competition at the 2002 Olympic Winter Games in Salt Lake City, Utah.

**Kevin B. Witherspoon** is associate professor of history at Lander University. He received his PhD at Florida State University, where he taught from 1999 to 2006. His book *Before the Eyes of the World: Mexico and the 1968 Olympics* (2008) won the 2009 North American Society of Sports Historians (NASSH) Annual Book Award, and he has published several articles dealing with sports during the Cold War. In 2009 he was awarded the Young Faculty Scholar Award at Lander University. His current research is focused on the US-Soviet sports rivalry during the Cold War.

**Thomas W. Zeiler** is professor of history and international affairs at the University of Colorado at Boulder, where he directs the Global Studies Academic Program. He is the author and editor of several books on US foreign relations, international economy and globalization, sports and diplomacy, and military history, including *Ambassadors in Pinstripes: The Spalding World Baseball Tour and the Birth of the American Empire* (2006) and *Annihilation: A Global Military History of World War II* (2011). He served as president of the Society for Historians of American Foreign Relations in 2012 and as editor of *Diplomatic History,* the journal of record in the field of US foreign relations, from 2010 to 2014. He also serves on the Historical Advisory Committee on Documentation in the US Department of State.

**Lu Zhouxiang** is lecturer in Chinese studies in the School of Modern Languages, Literatures and Cultures at National University of Ireland, Maynooth. His research interests focus on sports management, comparative studies between the West and China in the field of sport, nationalism, and globalism. He is the coauthor, with Fan Hong, of *The Rights to Sport* (2008), and received his doctorate at the National University of Ireland, Cork.

# Index

STUDIES IN CONFLICT, DIPLOMACY, AND PEACE

SERIES EDITORS: George C. Herring, Andrew L. Johns, and Kathryn C. Statler

This series focuses on key moments of conflict, diplomacy, and peace from the eighteenth century to the present to explore their wider significance in the development of U.S. foreign relations. The series editors welcome new research in the form of original monographs, interpretive studies, biographies, and anthologies from historians, political scientists, journalists, and policymakers. A primary goal of the series is to examine the United States' engagement with the world, its evolving role in the international arena, and the ways in which the state, nonstate actors, individuals, and ideas have shaped and continue to influence history, both at home and abroad.

ADVISORY BOARD MEMBERS

David Anderson, California State University, Monterey Bay
Laura Belmonte, Oklahoma State University
Robert Brigham, Vassar College
Paul Chamberlin, University of Kentucky
Jessica Chapman, Williams College
Frank Costigliola, University of Connecticut
Michael C. Desch, University of Notre Dame
Kurk Dorsey, University of New Hampshire
John Ernst, Morehead State University
Joseph A. Fry, University of Nevada, Las Vegas
Ann Heiss, Kent State University
Sheyda Jahanbani, University of Kansas
Mark Lawrence, University of Texas
Mitchell Lerner, Ohio State University
Kyle Longley, Arizona State University
Robert McMahon, Ohio State University
Michaela Hoenicke Moore, University of Iowa
Lien-Hang T. Nguyen, University of Kentucky
Jason Parker, Texas A&M University
Andrew Preston, Cambridge University
Thomas Schwartz, Vanderbilt University
Salim Yaqub, University of California, Santa Barbara

BOOKS IN THE SERIES

*The Gulf: The Bush Presidencies and the Middle East*
Michael F. Cairo

*Diplomatic Games: Sport, Statecraft, and International Relations since 1945*
Edited by Heather L. Dichter and Andrew L. Johns

*Nothing Less Than War: A New History of America's Entry into World War I*
Justus D. Doenecke

*Grounded: The Case for Abolishing the United States Air Force*
Robert M. Farley

*The Currents of War: A New History of American-Japanese Relations, 1899–1941*
Sidney Pash

*So Much to Lose: John F. Kennedy and American Policy in Laos*
William J. Rust

www.ingramcontent.com/pod-product-compliance
Lightning Source LLC
Chambersburg PA
CBHW030855270326
41929CB00008B/424